BRITISH FOOD FINDS 1989

BRITISH FOOD FINDS 1989

A DIRECTORY OF FINE BRITISH FOODS

EDITED BY HENRIETTA GREEN

Rich & Green Ltd

MPI GROUP

First published 1987 by Rich & Green Ltd.

Second edition published jointly by Rich & Green Ltd and MPI Group.

ISBN 0 9513940 0 2

Advisory Committee to British Food Finds

The ANDRÉ SIMON MEMORIAL FUND Book Awards

In 1972, soon after the death of André Simon, the André Simon Memorial Fund was set up. It was started as a charitable trust by a group of people who felt that they would like to perpetuate the memory of André Simon.

One objective of the Fund is to benefit the public generally in the fields of food and drink, and one of the ways in which the Fund tries to meet this objective is through its book awards.

Originally two separate awards were given to Elizabeth David and Rosemary Hume for their outstanding contribution in the field of food and cooking which have done so much to improve present day standards in the home. More recently awards have been given for specific books. The first one went to Alan Davidson for his 'North Atlantic Seafood'. The fund then started to make annual awards and recently winners have been:

1981 Anne Willian for *'French Regional Cooking'*
John R. Hume and Michael S. Moss for *"The making of Scotch Whisky'*

1982 Jane Grigson for her *"Fruit Book'*
Barbara Maher for *'Cakes'*
David Peppercorn for *'Bordeux'*

1983 Roger Phillips for *'Wild Food'*
Hugh Johnson for his *'Wine Companion'*
1984

1984 Yan-Kit So for *'Classic Chinese Cookbook'*
Rosemary George for *'The Wines of Chablis'*

1985 Hannah Wright for *'Soups'*
Nicolas Belfrage for *'Life Beyond Lambrusco'*

1986 Harold McGee for *'On Food and Cooking'*
Jancis Robinson for *'Vines, Grapes and Wines'*

1987 **Henrietta Green for *'British Food Finds 1987'***
Stephen Brook for *'Liquid Gold: Dessert Wines of the World'*

CONTENTS

FOREWORD

by Sir Richard Body, Chairman of the Advisory Committee

The call for a second edition always comes as music to the ears of any author. For this new volume of **BRITISH FOOD FINDS,** the call seems to have been crescendo: a gratifying response for all who have taken part in preparing and launching **BRITISH FOOD FINDS,** and especially for Henrietta Green, who has masterminded the whole venture.

To Henrietta and her team, congratulations must go for receiving the Andre Simon Memorial Prize for the best book on food published in 1987. Gratitude is also due. For many years I have been campaigning for the small farmer and grower. They have been going out of business at a rate of thousands every year, although, as a general rule they may be just as efficient, as measured by any yardstick, as the large farmer. The difference between them is that the latter gets the lion's share of the grants, subsidies and any other benefits from the taxpayer, which enable him to stay in business while the small man goes under.

BRITISH FOOD FINDS is helping the small farmer and grower in an excellent way. Being small, he can provide the personal attention to detail which enables the highest standards to be reached. But how is he then to develop a market except locally? This Directory can do most of it for him.

So, on behalf of many small farmers and growers who are striving for excellence, I say a big Thank You to Henrietta for producing for them this link with the quality end of the retail market.

May this new edition continue the good work of bringing together everyone in the food business, from those who till the field to those who put the plate on the table, who are trying to raise standards to the highest level.

Richard Body

FOREWORD

by J D M Hearth, Chief Executive of
the Royal Agricultural Society of England

1989 sees the 150th anniversary of the Royal Show. The year also marks the centenary of the Ministry of Agriculture, Fisheries & Food. These anniversaries have been the catalyst for British Food & Farming Year in 1989 when the whole food and farming industry will be celebrating its history and achievements. The joint initiative is designed to bring home to the general public the importance of our agricultural and food producing industry, and the wide range and variety of top quality foods produced by British farms and processed by British companies.

As Chairman of the Policy and Co-ordinating Committee for the Year, I am pleased to be associated with **BRITISH FOOD FINDS** which - in only its second edition - has proved to be the authoritative source of information on where to go for the best of British home-produced food and drink products.

A quick glance through the pages of **BRITISH FOOD FINDS** shows a mouth-watering array of speciality foods to tempt every palate. No more comprehensive directory exists. Food trade buyers and consumers alike will find the book an invaluable aid.

Many of the producers listed here will be exhibiting their produce at one of the highlights of British Food & Farming Year, a three day Festival in London's Hyde Park from 5th - 7th May 1989 (trade preview day - 4th May). The Festival will provide the one thing British Food Finds lacks - a chance actually to taste these delicious delicacies!

THE ACADEMIE CULINAIRE

The Academie Culinaire de France was founded in Paris is 1883 by Joseph Favre, Master Chef. Past members include Careme, Ude Soyer, Landry, Escoffier and Cesar Ritz. Although an English connection existed, it was not until 1980 that it was officially formalised in London and known as the Academie Culinaire de France - Filiale de Grande Bretagne.

After beginning with fifteen active members, it has now reached its limit of thirty-five professional chefs, all aged over 35. Amongst them are Michel Bourdin (President), Raymond Blanc, John Huber, Pierre Koffmann, Peter Kromberg, Albert Roux, Michel Roux and Richard Shepherd, some of the best known chefs in Britain. As experts in the classical traditions of cooking, practised by great chefs for over two hundred years, they are recognised as leaders in the arts of cooking and eating: consequently, they are arbiters of opinion in matters of culinary taste. The Acadmie Culinaire is dedicated to the pursuit of the highest levels of culinary endeavour and its aims, therefore, are education and training through the encouragement of others to emulate and practice its high standards.

In 1987 a British-born chef was appointed Chairman of the Academie Culinaire: Richard Shepherd, a culinary personality of whom the profession is proud and who is respected for his efforts to bring together the traditions of France and Britain, for improving standards in the kitchen and for revitalising education.

"I am increasingly aware of the improvement, both in quality and variety, of foods grown and produced in Britain. Although we, as chefs, appear to be exacting perfectionists, we do take pride in impressing and pleasing our customers and producers are, at last, responding to our special needs.

I was very enthusiastic about the First Edition of **British Food Finds** and delighted by the response it received. It was a timely and valuable move to motivate suppliers and to bridge the gap between the garden and the kitchen. The Second Edition is even more encouraging, the new producers, growers and products.

As chefs, we believe that, wherever and whenever possible, our food and cooking should reflect the culinary traditions of our country, be it native or adopted, and **British Food Finds** is the key to achieving this. It is invaluable as a 'Source Directory' and has won the whole-hearted support of the Academie Culinaire. You are almost certain to find a dog-eared, stock-stained copy in each of our members' kitchens."

Richard A. Shepherd
Chairman

THE BRITISH CULINARY INSTITUTE

By Ian McAndrew, Chairman

The British Culinary Institute was founded four years ago by a group of young British chefs. Its aims are to improve the standards of catering, the training of chefs and the production and distribution of produce.

We are British Chefs catering for the British in Britain, therefore it is logical that we want to buy British produce. The smaller producer, as featured in this directory, is the key to our supplies as generally they are more flexible and their standards are in sympathy with ours.

The situation is quite simple - there are producers producing who don't know what we want and chefs wanting good produce who don't know the problems and difficulties involved in producing it. Communication is the key which is why **BRITISH FOOD FINDS** is such a help.

We launched in 1988 our Logo of Excellence given to any product which has first been recommended by two chefs and then gains the approval of the tasting panel. It is awarded for flavour and for quality and, because the products are used constantly in the kitchens, the chefs are able to see that the quality is maintained.

The British Culinary Institute believes that we must all work together, talk together and encourage and promote our producers. We're looking for a better eating future in Britain. And with the help of **BRITISH FOOD FINDS,** we may get there.

INTRODUCTION

by Henrietta Green, Editor of British Food Finds

When **BRITISH FOOD FINDS** was first published in 1987, I never dared hope that it would create so much interest. It even won a coveted award the André Simon Memorial Prize given to the book judged to have made an outstanding contribution to the world of food. You can imagine just how honoured and thrilled I was to receive it.

BRITISH FOOD FINDS is the source directory of speciality foods in this country. Few buyers - whether restaurateurs, chefs, hoteliers or retailers know how to find or order the produce; in some cases they are not even aware of its existence. Therefore it works both in telling the buyer what exists and how to get hold of it.

The actual compilation of the first edition was comparatively easy. I had already been researching and working with British producers for several years and had discovered a wealth of produce - both fresh and lightly processed. It was a question of assembling the information in a "user friendly" form, to forge the vital link in the chain of food supplies, from producer to buyer, to the ultimate benefit of the consumer.

This year the directory is even bigger. It contains detailed information of twelve hundred producers who offer an incredible range of over four thousand products. There are new sections on Prepared Salads, Vegetable Dishes and Soups and, as you see from the following pages, just about every kind of food is featured.

The interest in speciality food is certainly growing. Take British cheeses, ten years ago only a handful existed, now you will find in **BRITISH FOOD FINDS** detailed information of over two hundred and fifty with more and more buyers seeking them out. And this is only one of the areas where **BRITISH FOOD FINDS** is indispensible. It is unique - the only directory of its kind.

Its primary function is to dispense information. However if the speciality British producer is to survive and to carry on expanding, certain issues need closer examination. We need, for example, to define who are the producers, what is a speciality food and the standards to which they work.

Attempting this is no simple matter. When I questioned the producers about how they described speciality food, they mostly thought it covered a number of factors - whether it was organically grown, handmade, or came from a small unit, or from a farm, or if it was made from a traditional or regional recipe. I do not claim to know the answers but does small necessarily mean better? How in this mechanical age do you define handmade? And does a traditional recipe taste any better just because it has been made in exactly the same way for the last one hundred years - times and taste change - anyhow the recipe may have been wrong in the first place?

And how does the place where the food is made affect the end result? Some discerning buyers believe it does not matter how or where the food is made. They have a point. Methods of production are worthless if the food does not taste any good. If a product claims to be special, surely it is to the eating quality we should look?

Take sausages - many producers say that their sausages are made in natural skins, with a high meat content, no preservatives or artificial flavourings. What they are describing is exactly what you would expect and hope for in a sausage - meat, good flavours, fresh product and - providing they have got the balance right - a quality, tasty product. Taste is such a subjective matter that it is impossible to form an objective opinion. But it is what matters, the ultimate test of food is what it is like to eat.

Quality control and the consistency and continuity of a product are also important. It is all very well to make excellent sausage but it will only succeed if the standard can be maintained. This need not be absolute, just maintained at the level set. All too often I hear complaints from buyers that one week a product was splendid, the next indifferent, or worse, unavailable. This side of the industry leaves a lot to be desired.

The next contentious issue is labelling. **BRITISH FOOD FINDS** with the help of Dr Margaret Ashwell of The Good Housekeeping Institute and the voluntary MAFF guidelines, attempted to direct the producers in defining their product descriptions. We wanted to avoid negative claims, cut out misleading adjectives and energy, protein, fat, sugar, fibre and salt claims unless they could be substantiated. Regretfully we were not that successful and feel strongly that the government must take a lead over labelling controls.

Additive free is a very emotive term and everyone tries to use it in order to reassure the suspicious public. In **BRITISH FOOD FINDS** its use is avoided whenever possible. Occasionally it does appear but only to describe a single food to which nothing has been added and which has been subjected only to such processing as to render it suitable for human consumption, or to a compound food if all the individual ingredients meet the above criterion.

Everyone agrees that speciality foods should be special and of excellent quality. It is these foods I have tried to feature in the directory. In France this area of produce is highly valued with many of the products sold with a "label rouge" giving a guarantee of high standards and a commitment to quality. In Britain there are no such schemes and it is left to organizations such as **BRITISH FOOD FINDS,** The British Culinary Institute and The Soil Association to improve the food.

It is encouraging to see the interest in food and the renaissance that is taking place in this country. This area of speciality food is the one to which the directory is dedicated and from its pages come tasty exciting food and, as an extra bonus, some of the products of the nineties which in time will become household names.

BRITISH FOOD FINDS is the directory that no buyer of food can afford to be without.

THE ADVISORY COMMITTEE

The Advisory Committee welcome wholeheartedly **British Food Finds . . .**

British Food Finds fills a void. It will provide a most valuable service for the benefit of the farmer, grower, food processor and the food buying trade - the consumer deriving the ultimate benefit.'

Sir Richard Body, MP

'This consequential book is just what the food trade has been waiting for.'

Justin de Blank

'I welcome this book as I welcome anything that helps our small producers. We need more better quality food on the British Market.'

Jane Grigson

'As an oyster farmer in the highlands and as a smoker of local salmon we welcome the emergence of **British Food Finds** which we think will be a most helpful link between the producers of natural foods and those wishing to use this produce.'

John Noble

'There are a great deal of high quality foods - cheeses in particular - produced on many British farms little known to the public: I am delighted to see **British Food Finds,** an enterprise devoting itself to the marketing of the best of all British produce.'

Patrick Rance

"**British Food Finds** is a step in the right direction in making quality produce more easily available to all chefs.

Richard Shepherd

'For those producers now actually looking for new markets and new opportunities and for the chef or shopkeeper looking for exciting, interesting foods, this directory will be a major asset in bringing both ends of the chain together.'

Teresa Wickham

REGIONAL MAP

A TYPICAL ENTRY

1 ↔ **Freshwater Fish Farm**
Riverside House, Somertown, Devon EX3 25D
Tel: 012 3456
Contact: John Brown

Trout — Rainbow trout reared in natural ponds fed by local spring waters. Sold fresh or gutted and frozen from 1-7lb. Small quantities of oak smoked fillets also available.
[C] 10 ton p.mth
[W] B S W Fish 0232 1234
[D] By wholesaler
See also: Fish and Shellfish Products: Pates and Pastes

In left margin of column symbols and selected products are provided for ready reference.

SYMBOLS

[1] Map reference. The British Isles has been divided into the areas listed below, in order to facilitate the location of the producers and their nearest points of distribution.

1 **Highlands and Islands** – Western Isles, Highland Region, Orkney, Shetland.

2 **Grampian Region.**

3 **Central Lowlands** – Strathclyde, Central, Tayside, Fife and Lothian Regions.

4 **Northern Ireland.**

5 **Border Region** – Dumfries and Galloway, and Borders Regions.

6 **North England and the Isle of Man** – Cumbria, Northumberland, Tyne and Wear, Durham, Cleveland.

7 **North West England** – Merseyside, Lancashire, Greater Manchester, Cheshire.

8 **Yorkshire and Humberside** – South Yorkshire, West Yorkshire, North Yorkshire, Humberside.

9 **Wales** – Dyfed, Gwynedd, Clwyd, Powys, Gwent, South Glamorgan, Mid Glamorgan, West Glamorgan.

10 **West Midlands** – Hereford and Worcester, Shropshire, Staffordshire, West Midlands, Warwickshire.

11 **East Midlands** – Northamptonshire, Leicestershire, Derbyshire, Nottinghamshire, Lincolnshire.

12 **Oxford and the West Country** – Somerset, Avon, Gloucestershire, Oxfordshire, Wiltshire.

13 **Northern Home Counties** – Buckinghamshire, Bedfordshire, Hertfordshire.

14 **East Anglia and Essex** – Cambridgeshire, Norfolk, Suffolk, Essex.

15 **South West and the Channel Islands** – Cornwall, Devon.

16 **London and South East** – Hampshire, Berkshire, Greater London, Surrey, West Sussex, East Sussex, Kent.

● Organic symbol authenticated indicates producers who are licensed or authorised to use any of the three organic marks described below.

○ Organic symbol unauthenticated indicates producers who claim to be producing organic produce but who are not authorised users of any recognised mark.

Standards for Organic Production

Although there are no internationally agreed standards for organic production, in 1982, the International Federation of Organic Agriculture Movements (IFOAM) set standards for organic production which are regarded by most countries as a reasonable basis for national standards.

The principles of organic farming, as expressed by IFOAM, are:-

1 To work as far as possible within a closed system, and to draw upon local resources.

2 To maintain the long-term fertility of soils.

3 To avoid all forms of pollution that may result from agricultural techniques.

4 To produce foodstuffs of high nutritional value and sufficient quantity.

5 To reduce the use of fossil energy in agricultural practice to a minimum.

6 To give livestock conditions of life that conform to their physiological needs and to humanitarian principles.

7 To make it possible for agricultural producers to earn a living through their work and develop their potentialities as human beings.

The United States Department of Agriculture gave its own definition of organic farming in 1981:-

'Organic farming is a production system which avoids or largely excludes the use of synthetically compounded fertilisers, pesticides, growth regulators and livestock feed additives. To the maximum extent feasible, organic farming systems rely on crop rotations, crop residues, animal manures, legumes, green manures, off-farm organic wastes, mechanical cultivation, mineral-bearing rocks, and aspects of biological pest control to maintain soil productivity and tilth, to supply plant nutrients and to control insects, weeds and other pests.'

In Britain, there are two organisations which have their own organic standards, both of which are stated to follow IFOAM standards.

One – the Soil Association, who, after a minimum of a two year conversion period including visits by their inspectors, will licence individual farmers and growers to use their Symbol.

The other – Organic Farmers and Growers Ltd, is a co-operative with an organic standard OFG1. Their members are allowed to use this after a similar period of conversion and inspection.

Consumers seeing either the Soil Association Symbol or the OFG1 brand mark on produce will know that it has been grown to standards complying to British standards which are in line with those accepted for international trade.

Since much organically grown produce is imported into this country, it should be mentioned that another organic label may be seen from time to time. This is the Demeter symbol for Bio-Dynamic agriculture. There is relatively little bio-dynamic production in this country. Standards for such production are more exacting than those under IFOAM and there is universal acceptance of the Demeter Symbol.

★ Denotes that milk or milk content is unpasteurised.

↔ Contract symbol indicates whether the producer is willing to work to pre-arranged terms or has the potential to expand.

SYMBOLS WITHIN ENTRY

[C] Details of capacity and seasonality as provided.

[W] Wholesaler details as provided.

[D] Distribution and transport details as provided.

Entries highlighted in green indicate that the producer, once his entry has been accepted, has paid for the entry(ies) to be highlighted.

1

MEAT

FRESH MEAT

8

Albert Hirst Butchers
36 Queen's Road, Barnsley, Yorkshire S71 1AR
Tel: 0226 284851
Contact: Albert Hirst

Mutton

Beef, lamb, mutton and pork reared in Yorkshire and butchered on premises, available fresh in whole carcasses or to customers requirements. Offal on demand.
[C] Undisclosed
[D] By arrangement
See Also: Meat: Sausages and Puddings

16 ↔

A J Barkaway
20 Ospringe Street, Faversham, Kent
Tel: 0795 532040
Contact: Mr A J Barkaway

Veal

Fresh beef, veal, lamb and pork reared in traditional manner and butchered to requirements, in whole carcasses or smaller joints.
[C] 30 p.wk
[D] By own transport within area
See Also: Meat: Sausages and Puddings, Game Dealers

3 ↔

Benshie Cattle Company
Ballinshoe, Kirriemuir, Angus DD8 5QG
Tel: 0575 73466
Contact: Lord Mackie of Benshie

Pork

Free-range pork butchered on premises to customers requirements, available fresh in autumn, frozen all year.
[C] 50-100 p.mth
[D] By arrangement
See Also: Bacon and Hams, Meat: Sausages and Puddings

15 ○

Blackdown Farm & Loddiswell Cheese
Blackdown, Loddiswell, Kingsbridge, Devon TQ7 4EA
Tel: 054882 387
Contact: Mr and Mrs W L Martin

Goat

Organically produced goat meat, in whole carcasses or butchered to customers requirements.
[C] Undisclosed
[D] By arrangement
See Also: Meat: Sausages and Puddings, Cheese

16 ●

Boathouse Farm Organic Produce
Isfield, nr Uckfield, East Sussex TN22 5TY
Tel: 082575 302
Contact: Laurence Hill

Beef

Lamb, Simmental bullocks and single suckled beef, whole carcasses or butchered, fresh or frozen.
[C] Beef 60 p.a, lamb 180 p.a, Jun-Jul
[D] By arrangement
See Also: Fresh Vegetables, Eggs, Millers

16 ○

Bowyers Court Farm
Wisborough Green, West Sussex RH14 0EP
Tel: 0403 700494
Contact: Mr K Watson

Kid

Lean kid meat, organically reared, available fresh or frozen, in whole carcasses or butchered to customers requirements.
[C] 200 p.a mainly Jan-Feb, Jul-Aug
[D] By arrangement
See Also: Milk

6

Wm Brennand & Sons
18 Finkle Street, Kendal, Cumbria LA9 4AB
Tel: 0539 20323
Contact: Mr A W Brennand

Pork

Fresh pork from Large White Cross strain, in whole or butchered carcasses. Also available beef, lamb and offal.
[C] Undisclosed
[D] By arrangement
See Also: Meat: Pies and Prepared Dishes, Meat: Sausages and Puddings

12

Brentlands Cotswold Beef
Brookethorpe, Gloucester, Gloucestershire
Tel: 0452 813447
Contact: Michael Warner

Beef

Hereford cattle reared for eighteen months to two years and hung for a minimum of fourteen days. Butchered on the premises to customers requirements or supplied as fresh, whole carcasses or in 20, 25, 50lb frozen, gourmet, hot-pot or family packs.
[C] 40 p.a
[D] By arrangement

16 ↔

Bunker Farm Produce
Bunker Farm, Basingstoke Road, Greenham Common South, Newbury, Berkshire RG15 8HH
Tel: 0635 45535
Contact: Ken Neale

Goat

Full range of frozen goat meat from suckling kid, kid goat, to mature goat meat, weighing 20-30lb. Antibiotic free meat produced as required.
[C] Kid and goats 10 p.mth Jan-Aug
[D] By arrangement
See Also: Meat: Sausages and Puddings, Poultry Producers, Cheese, Purees and Sauces

6 ↔

Burbush's
Gilwilly Trading Estate, Penrith, Cumbria
Tel: 0768 63841
Contact: T W H Burbush

Pork

Lowthwaite pork, whole or half pig boned and rolled, cut and bagged or frozen and cut as joints, chops and sausages.
[C] Undisclosed
[D] By own transport within area
See Also: Meat: Sausages and Puddings, Game: Pies and Prepared Dishes

16

Burstye Soay Lamb
Burstye Farm, Lindfield, Haywards Heath, West Sussex RH16 2QY
Tel: 04447 3376
Contact: Ann Knowles

Soay Lamb

Soay lamb, a rare breed with a low fat cover and distinctive taste similar to venison. Supplied as whole carcasses or boned joints.
C 40 p.mth Oct-Jan
D By arrangement

15

Clarksons Wholesale Foods
Alansway, Ottery St Mary, Devon EX11 1NR
Tel: 040481 3581
Contact: Mr B Moran and Mr B Dean

Pork

Beef, lamb and pork produced in Devon, fresh, chilled or frozen, in whole carcasses or butchered to customers requirements. Offal also supplied.
C Undisclosed
D By own transport nationally
See Also: Bacon and Hams

12

Clutton Hill Farm Shop
Clutton, nr Bristol, Avon BS18 4QQ
Tel: 0761 52458
Contact: Mr A Appleyard

Mutton

Beef, lamb, mutton and pork, reared with no antibiotics, fresh, chilled or frozen, in whole carcasses or butchered to customers requirements. Pig chitterlings and tripe also supplied.
C Undisclosed, beef and pork all year
D By own transport within area
See Also: Bacon and Hams, Meat: Sausages and Puddings

4

Corrie's Meats
13 Crossnamuckley Road, Newtownards, Co Down BT22 2AA
Tel: 0247 812297/812817
Contact: Mrs M Patterson

Beef

Beef, lamb and pork hung 1-2 weeks, fresh, chilled or frozen, in whole carcasses or butchered into specific joints.
C Undisclosed
D By arrangement

12 ↔

Cotswold Stile
The Old Bakehouse, 17a Long Street, Wotton-Under-Edge, Gloucestershire GL12 7E3
Tel: 0453 844994
Contact: Henrietta White

Beef

Limited supply of beef, lamb and pork reared with no antibiotics.
C Undisclosed, mainly Christmas
D By own transport within area
See Also: Meat: Sausages and Puddings

6

Cranston
Sandhill, Kirkoswald, Penrith, Cumbria CA10 1EN
Tel: 0228 21345
Contact: Mr P J Cranston

Beef

Beef, lamb, mutton, pork, all locally reared. Beef and lamb hung for minimum one week. All meat butchered into specific joints or cuts. Liver also supplied.
C Cattle 18 p.wk, lamb 30-60 p.wk
D By arrangement
See Also: Meat: Pies and Prepared Dishes, Meat: Sausages and Puddings

4

David Burns
112 Abbey Street, Bangor, Co Down BT20 4JB
Tel: 0247 270073
Contact: Mr David Burns

Beef

Selected breeds of beef and lamb chosen from farms with naturally heavy salt deposit pastures, butchered to customers requirements.
C Cattle 5,500lb p.wk, lamb 500lb p.wk
D By own transport within area
See Also: Meat: Sausages and Puddings

15

Dorset Farms
Manor Farm, Little Windsor, Beaminster, Dorset DT8 3QU
Tel: 0308 68822
Contact: Mr H Birch

Lamb

Pork, maize and corn fed with no antibiotics, butchered on farm in whole carcasses or specific joints and cuts, fresh, chilled or frozen.
C 120-140 p.wk
D By own transport within area
See Also: Bacon and Hams, Meat: Sausages and Puddings, Game Dealers

15

K W Durrant Family Butchers
Main Street, Chillington, nr Kingsbridge, Devon TQ7 2JX
Tel: 0548 580217
Contact: Mr K Durrant

Veal

Beef, veal, lamb, mutton and pork all produced locally. Beef hung two weeks, lamb and free-range pork hung one week. All animals humanely killed at own abbatoir, supplied fresh and butchered.
C Undisclosed
D By own transport within area
See Also: Game Dealers

9

Edward Hamer Ltd
Plynlimon House, Llamidloes, Powys SY18 6EF
Tel: 05512 2114
Contact: Edward Hamer

Welsh lamb

Plynlimon lamb, a Welsh breed, fresh, chilled or frozen, in whole carcasses or butchered to customers requirements. Also available beef and pork.
C 12,000 p.mth mainly Jul-Dec
D By own transport within area
See Also: Meat: Pâtés and Pastes

NOTHING COMPETES
WITH MEAT
BRITISH
MEAT
LEAN BRITISH MEAT

15

Elsworth Farms
Yelland Cross Farm, Rattery, South Brent, Devon PQ10 9LH
Tel: 0364 43741
Contact: Mr R A Elsworth

Lamb

Jacob ewe and Suffolk ram cross lamb, antibiotic free lean meat, butchered to customers requirements. Beef also available.
[C] Undisclosed, summer only
[D] By arrangement

3 ↔

Ewing's
83 Main Street, Baillieston, Glasgow G69 6AD
Tel: 041 773 0274
Contact: Mr J Ewing

Pork

Beef, lamb and pork butchered from local animals, fresh only in specific cuts and joints. Also available liver, kidneys and tripe.
[C] Undisclosed
[D] By own transport within area
See Also: Meat: Pies and Prepared Dishes, Meat: Sausages and Puddings

7

Farmhouse Country Delicacies
The Homestead Farm, Pott Shrigley, Macclesfield, Cheshire SK10 5RU
Tel: 0625 72381
Contact: Joyce Dalton

Tamworth pork

Pork from Tamworth pigs, lamb, mutton and kid, reared on farm, in whole carcasses or butchered to customers requirements.
[C] Kid 25 p.a Oct-Feb, lamb 40-50 p.a Sep-Dec
[D] By arrangement
See Also: Bacon and Hams, Meat: Sausages and Puddings, Cheese

3

FMC(Meat)
Inveralmond Industrial Estate, Ruthvenfield Road, Perth PH1 3XB
Tel: 0738 24242 Telx: 76697 Fax: 0738 27047
Contact: Mr A J McNaughton

Lamb

Scotch beef, lamb and pork, slaughtered and butchered on premises, sold whole or butchered to customers requirements. Also available red and white offal.
[C] Cattle 2,400 p.mth, lamb 1,200 p.mth, pigs 1,600 p.mth
[D] By own transport

10 ● ↔

Fordhall Organic Farm
Fordhall Farm, Market Drayton, Shropshire TS9 3PS
Tel: 063 083 255
Contact: Mr Hollins

Suckling beef

Organically reared beef, lamb, veal and pork, suckling beef produced from Blonde Aquitaine herd, beef calves grass fed and slaughtered early autumn for veal. Lamb and pork free-range fed. All meat sold fresh or frozen, and butchered to requirements.
[C] Beef 63 p.a, veal 23 Sep-Nov, lamb 50 p.a Jul-Dec
[W] Ray Cornmell 0204 46844
[D] By wholesaler, by arrangement
See Also: Bacon and Hams

8

S C & J H Gibson
Hopetown House, Burneston, Bedale, North Yorkshire DL8 2JN
Tel: 0845 567252
Contact: Mr S C Gibson

Lamb

Beef, lamb and pork. Beef hung for two weeks, pigs reared on farm with no antibiotics in stress free farming system. All fresh, chilled or frozen, in whole carcasses or butchered.
[C] Pigs 10 p.wk, lamb 6-7 p.wk, cattle 2-3 p.wk
[D] By own transport within area
See Also: Meat: Sausages and Puddings

12

The Ginger Pig
Broadleaze, Boyton, Warminster, Wiltshire
Tel: 0985 50208
Contact: Mrs C Wheatley-Hubbard

Pork

Pork from non-intensively reared Tamworth pigs, supplied fresh or frozen as whole carcasses or butchered to customers requirements. Cured pork also available.
[C] 2 p.wk
[D] By arrangement

10 ● ↔

Gold Label Produce
Knightley Grange Cottage, Grange Road, Woodseaves, Staffordshire ST20 OJU
Tel: 0785 74495
Contact: Mr D Dale

Pork

Beef, lamb and pork fed with conservation grade grain and reared with no antibiotics. Chester White pigs range reared for lean meat with intra-muscular fat (marbling).
[C] Pigs 40 p.wk
[D] By own transport nationally
See Also: Bacon and Hams, Game Dealers

10 ● ↔

Green Acres Organic Growers
Green Acres, Dinmore, Hereford HR4 8ED
Tel: 056884 7045
Contact: David Jenkins

Beef

Organic fresh and frozen beef and lamb butchered to customers requirements.
[C] Undisclosed
[D] By arrangement
See Also: Fresh Vegetables

14 ○

Guist Gloucesters
Ferndale House, Wood Norton, Dereham, Norfolk NR20 5BA
Tel: 036 284530
Contact: John Wratten

Pork

Organically produced pork from traditional English rare breed pigs, fresh, chilled or frozen, butchered or in whole sides.
[C] 10-20 p.wk Apr-May and Nov-Dec
[D] By own transport within area
See Also: Bacon and Hams

12 ● ↔

Hardwick Estate
Path Hill Farm, Whitchurch, nr Reading, Oxfordshire RG8 7RE
Tel: 07357 2955
Contact: Sir Julian Rose Bt

Pork

Organic pork from free-range Canberra Blue and Gloucester Old Spot fed on barley, skimmed milk and oats. Also organic beef from free-range cattle suckled for six months and fed on hay, barley and oats, supplied fresh or frozen, whole carcasses or butchered to customers requirements. Pig kidneys and livers also supplied.
Ⓒ Pigs 130 p.a Sep-Jun, cattle 30 p.a
Ⓓ By arrangement
See Also: Meat: Sausages and Puddings, Cream

15 ↔

Heal Farm
Kings Nympton, Umberleigh, Devon EX37 9TB
Tel: 07695 2077
Contact: Anne Petch

St Kilda lamb

Ruby Red beef hung for three weeks, Dorset Cross, Suffolk and St Kilda lamb hung for two weeks, Middle White, Gloucester Old Spots, Tamworth and Berkshire pork. All reared with no antibiotics and supplied fresh, chilled or frozen and butchered to customers requirements. Caul fat, sausage skins, hard back, clarified and flare fat also available.
Ⓒ Pigs 100-150 p.wk
Ⓓ By own transport within area, by AM Express and British Rail
See Also: Bacon and Hams, Meat: Pâtés and Pastes, Meat: Pies and Prepared Dishes, Meat: Sausages and Puddings, Meat: Smoked, Game Dealers, Hampers

3 ↔

Highland Glen Producers
1 Crieff Road, Aberfeldy, Perthshire PH15 2BJ
Tel: 0887 20666
Contact: Mark Lumsden

Lamb

Lamb, pure or cross bred, grazed on heather and grass producing lean, fine grained meat, fresh, chilled or frozen, in whole carcasses. Mutton also available.
Ⓒ 3000 p.mth, mainly Dec-Feb
Ⓓ By arrangement

16 ↔

Hockeys - Naturally
Newtown Farm, South Gorley, Fordingbridge, Hampshire ST6 2PW
Tel: 0425 52542
Contact: Phillip Hockeys

Charolais beef

Charolais beef, with low fat content, lamb, veal and pork, supplied fresh, chilled or frozen in butchered joints and cuts. Offal, brain and tongue also available.
Ⓒ Undisclosed
Ⓓ By own transport nationally
See Also: Meat: Sausages and Puddings, Game Dealers

8 ○ ↔

R Holmes & Sons
West House Farm, Birstwith, Harrogate, North Yorkshire HG3 3AW
Tel: 0423 770200
Contact: Mr I Holmes

Beef

Beef and lamb reared with no antibiotics, butchered on farm, fresh, chilled or frozen, beef hung for fourteen days. Turkey, pork, offal and sweetbreads also available.
Ⓒ Undisclosed
Ⓓ By arrangement
See Also: Fresh Fruit

14 ○ ↔

A & K Hood
The Stables, Gresham, Norfolk NR11 8AD
Tel: 026377 468
Contact: Mr Hood

Beef

Beef and pork from organically reared animals, slaughtered and butchered on farm, fresh or frozen.
Ⓒ Undisclosed
Ⓓ By arrangement
See Also: Poultry Producers, Cheese, Fresh Vegetables, Jams and Preserves

16 ○ ↔

Island Country Farms
Asheybrook, Ashey, Ryde, Isle of Wight PO33 4AT
Tel: 0983 65686
Contact: Mr J H Fisher

Tamworth pork

Organically reared Tamworth pork, suckling pigs to order, supplied fresh, chilled or frozen or butchered to customers requirements. Also sausages, pâtés and hamburgers.
Ⓒ 2-4 p.wk
Ⓓ By arrangement
See Also: Poultry Producers, Milk, Fresh Fruit

3

James McIntyre
74 Montague Street, Rothesay, Isle of Bute PA20 OHL
Tel: 0700 3672
Contact: Mr J McIntyre

Bute beef

Beef hung for two weeks, pork and lamb hung for one week, all reared on the Isle of Bute and butchered traditionally in whole carcasses or specific joints and cuts, fresh, chilled or frozen.
Ⓒ Undisclosed
Ⓓ By own transport within area
See Also: Bacon and Hams, Meat: Sausages and Puddings, Game Dealers

1

John M Munro Ltd
12 High Street, Conon Bridge, Dingwall, Ross & Cromarty
Tel: 0349 61398
Contact: R M Munro

Scotch beef

Prime Scotch beef, lamb and pork, locally produced, as whole carcasses or vacuum packed. Also salmon and smoked salmon.
Ⓒ 1000lb p.wk
Ⓓ By arrangement
See Also: Meat: Sausages and Puddings

[3]

John Scott Meat (Paisley) Ltd
Abattoir, Sandyford Road, Paisley, Renfrewshire PA3 4HP
Tel: 041 889 3205
Contact: John Scott

Scotch beef

Scotch beef, lamb, mutton and pork supplied fresh as whole carcasses or butchered to customers requirements. Also available liver, tripe and suet.
[C] Undisclosed
[D] By arrangement

[11]

F A & J Jones & Sons
Red House Farm, North Scarle, Lincoln LN6 9HB
Tel: 052 277224
Contact: Mrs Jean Jones

Beef

Beef hung for two weeks, butchered to customers requirements, fresh, chilled or frozen.
[C] Undisclosed
[D] By arrangement
See Also: Meat: Pies and Prepared Dishes, Meat: Sausages and Puddings, Poultry Producers

[5] ↔

J Kerr Little, Master Butcher
58-60 High Street, Dumfriesshire DG1 2BS
Tel: 0387 53818
Contact: Mr J Kerr Little

Beef
Veal

Beef, veal, lamb and pork, produced by prize winning butchers. Beef hung for minimum ten days, supplied fresh, chilled or frozen, in whole carcasses or butchered to customers requirements. All by-products supplied.
[C] Undisclosed
[D] By own transport within area
See Also: Bacon and Hams, Meat: Sausages and Puddings

[16]

Langrish & Sons (Farmers)
Ludley Farm, Beckley, nr Rye, East Sussex
Tel: 0424 882250
Contact: Frank Langrish

Romney Marsh lamb

Lamb and mutton grazed on naturally salty pastures of Romney Marsh.
[C] Lamb 2500 mainly Jul-Feb
[D] By arrangement

[16] ↔

C Lidgate Ltd
110 Holland Park Avenue, London W11 4VA
Tel: 01 727 8243
Contact: Mr Lidgate

Scotch beef

Best Scotch beef, veal, English lamb, mutton, range reared pork, fresh or chilled, in whole carcasses or butchered to continental cuts, trimming a speciality. Also available fresh offal.
[C] Undisclosed
[D] By own transport within area
See Also: Meat: Sausages and Puddings

[12]

J Lindsey & Son
47 The Covered Market, Oxford, Oxfordshire OX1 3DX
Tel: 0865 242933
Contact: Mr M Feller

Beef

Beef, mainly Angus cross bred from Scotland, reared with no antibiotics, well-hung and butchered to customers requirements. Also lamb, mutton and pork.
[C] Cattle 10-20 p.wk
[D] By own transport within area
See Also: Meat: Sausages and Puddings, Game Dealers

[16] ● ↔

Malthouse Cottage Farm
Malthouse Lane, Ashington, Pulborough, West Sussex RH20 3BU
Tel: 0903 892456
Contact: Mrs J Ferris

Lamb

Small quantities of organic lamb.
[C] Undisclosed
[D] By own transport within area
See Also: Poultry Producers, Cheese

[15] ● ↔

J Morrish Farm Shop
East Acland, Landkey, Barnstaple, Devon EX32 OLD
Tel: 0271 830216
Contact: Mrs J Morrish

Beef

Beef and lamb produced organically, frozen, butchered and supplied in packs, lamb packs containing one whole lamb with joints separately wrapped or chops in packs of four, beef packs containing hind quarter or forequarter joints.
[C] Undisclosed
[D] By arrangement
See Also: Fresh Vegetables

[15] ● ↔

Murray's Meat
West Rock, Broadhempston, nr Totnes, Devon TQ9 6BH
Tel: 0803 813172
Contact: Christopher Murray

Beef

Beef, lamb, mutton, pork and kid goat reared on pastures of grass, clover and herbs. Beef sold as half hind 57lb, forequarter 59lb, special steak packs 9, 17lb, lamb, whole 40lb, half 20lb, pork, whole 105lb, half 52lb, pork pack 24½lb. All chilled or frozen.
[C] Undisclosed
[D] By arrangement
See Also: Game: Smoked

[11] ●

T D Organ
East Farm, Normanby-by-Stow, Gainsborough, Lincolnshire DN21 5LQ
Tel: 0427 788629
Contact: Dr T D Organ

Beef

Organically reared beef, butchered locally, sold in quarters, fresh or frozen.
[C] 4 p.a
[D] By arrangement
See Also: Fresh Vegetables

[3] ●

Organic Meat and Products (Scotland)
Endrigg, Jamesfield, Newburgh, Fife KY14 6EW
Tel: 073 88598
Contact: Ian Miller

Lamb

Aberdeen Angus beef, lamb and pork

organically reared in the Highlands, supplied fresh or frozen, whole carcasses or butchered to customers requirements. By-products and venison also available.
C Cattle 30 p.mth, lamb 100 p.mth
D By arrangement

9 ○ **Oriel Jones & Son**
Teify Park Abattoir, Llanybydder, Dyfed SA40 9QE
Tel: 0570 480284
Contact: Mr O Jones

Welsh lamb — Lamb produced organically from pure bred Welsh lamb reared on mountainside, fresh or chilled. Also available beef, pork and goat.
C 20,000 p.mth Jun-Nov
D By own transport nationally

1 **Orkney Meat Ltd**
The Abattoir, Hatston Industrial Estate, Kirkwall, Orkney KW15 1RE
Tel: 0856 4326
Contact: Mr E Balfour

Beef — Beef reared in the Orkney Isles, boned, vacuum packed and hung for two weeks.
C 100 p.wk
D By own transport nationally

14 **Peartree Pork and Poultry**
High Birch Farm, Weeley Heath, nr Clacton-on-Sea, Essex CO16 9BU
Tel: 0255 830291
Contact: Mr P Ernst

Pork — Fresh, frozen or chilled lean pork, in whole carcasses or butchered to customers requirements.
C 200 p.mth
D By arrangement
See Also: Bacon and Hams, Meat: Pies and Prepared Dishes, Game Dealers

10 ○ ↔ **Pimhill**
Lea Hall, Harmer Hill, Shrewsbury, Shropshire SY4 3DY
Tel: 0939 290342
Contact: Ginny Mayall

Pork — Free-range organic pigs available in small quantities.
C Undisclosed
D By arrangement
See Also: Fresh Vegetables, Millers

15 **The Pure Meat Company**
1 The Square, Moretonhampstead, Devon
Tel: 0647 40944
Contact: Mr J Blackburn

Pork — Range of beef, lamb and pork available in specific joints and cuts.
C Undisclosed
D By arrangement
See Also: Game: Sausages and Puddings

15 **Quantock Foods**
Bellinger House, Poundbury Road, Dorchester, Dorset DT1 2PJ
Tel: 0305 251100
Contact: Janet Sands

Veal — Loose housed veal slaughtered and butchered on farm to customers requirements.
C 3000 ton p.a
D By own transport nationally

3 **Ramsay of Carluke**
Wellriggs Factory, 22 Mount Stewart, Lanarkshire ML8 5ED
Tel: 0555 72277
Contact: Mr J Ramsay

Pork — Fresh pork, whole carcasses. Also available bones and offal.
C 125 p.wk
D By own transport within area, by carrier to London
See Also: Bacon and Hams

12 **Real Meat Company**
East Hill Farm, Heytesbury, Warminster, Wiltshire BA12 0HR
Tel: 0985 40436/40060
Contact: Mr Richard Guy

Beef — Beef, lamb and pork, reared with no antibiotics, fresh or frozen in whole carcasses or butchered to customers requirements.
C Cattle 40 p.wk, pigs 100 p.wk, lamb 50 p.wk
D By arrangement
See Also: Bacon and Hams, Meat: Pies and Prepared Dishes, Meat: Sausages and Puddings, Poultry Producers

15 ↔ **Riverford Farm Foods**
Riverford farm, Staverton, Totnes, Devon TQ9 6AF
Tel: 080 426423
Contact: Ben Watson

Pork — Antibiotic free pork, supplied fresh or chilled in whole carcasses or butchered to customers requirements.
C 100 p.wk
D By arrangement
See Also: Bacon and Hams, Meat: Sausages and Puddings, Meat: Smoked

12 ↔ **Rose Cottage Produce**
Rose Cottage, Nottwood Lane, Stoke Row, Oxfordshire
Tel: 0491 681729
Contact: Mrs K Fotherby

Beef
Pork — Beef and lamb reared on grass, milled cereals, skimmed milk and apples. Supplied hung in whole carcasses, butchered or specific joints, fresh and chilled. Also pork, whole and butchered supplied with pork sausages in place of head, belly and trotters.
C Undisclosed
D By arrangement
See Also: Meat: Sausages and Puddings, Fresh Vegetables

12 ↔ **Rusland Farm**
Rusland Farm, Butcombe, Bristol, Avon BS18 6LQ
Tel: 027587 2209
Contact: Mr R Wear

Lamb — Lamb from Ryeland, Shropshire, Shetland,

St Kilda, Portland, Wiltshire Horn and White Face Woodland sheep, some cross bred. All fattened and supplied fresh in whole carcasses. Beef and mutton also available.
Ⓒ Lamb 100 p.a mainly Apr-May
Ⓓ By arrangement

3 ↔
Scottish Goat Products
Station Road, Newtonmore, Invernesshire PH2 D1AR
Tel: 05403 692
Contact: The Manager

Goat
Goat and kid meat, whole carcasses or butchered in specific cuts, chilled and frozen.
Ⓒ Undisclosed
Ⓓ By arrangement
See Also: Ice Creams and Sorbets

14 ● ↔
Select Livestock Producers
Church Farm, Northborough, Peterborough, Cambridgeshire P6 9BN
Tel: 0733 252224
Contact: Mr J Hall

Beef
Lamb
Pork
Beef, lamb and pork organically reared, available fresh or frozen, butchered and packed to specific requirements.
Ⓒ Lamb 60-70 p.wk, cattle 30 p.wk
Ⓓ By arrangement

12
Spring Farm Vineyard
Moorlinch, Bridgwater, Somerset
Tel: 0458 210 393
Contact: Mrs J Rees

Berkshire pork
Berkshire pigs reared with no antibiotics, fresh or frozen, whole or butchered.
Ⓒ Undisclosed
Ⓓ By arrangement

10 ●
Stoke Court Organic Farm Enterprise
Stoke Court, Greete, Ludlow Shropshire SY8 3BX
Tel: 0584 810655
Contact: Mr K E Kolind

Beef
Organically reared Highland and Red Devon beef, available fresh, chilled or frozen and butchered locally to customers requirements.
Ⓒ 2 p.mth
Ⓓ By arrangement
See Also: Poultry Producers

3
Strathmore Meat Ltd
Carseview Road, Forfar, Angus DD8 3NG
Tel: 0307 62333
Contact: Colin Muir

Sweetbreads
Beef, pork and lamb supplied in whole carcasses. Also availale sweetbreads and caul fat.
Ⓒ Cattle 100 p.mth, pigs 70-80 p.mth, lamb 150 p.mth
Ⓓ By arrangement
See Also: Meat: Pies and Prepared Dishes

14
Susan Moore - Dairy Products
Cranes Watering Farm, Starston, Harleston, Norfolk IP20 9NE
Tel: 0379 852387
Contact: Susan Moore

Pork
Dairy fed pork, available fresh or frozen, in whole carcasses and butchered to customers requirements.
Ⓒ 20 p.mth May-Jun
Ⓓ By arrangement
See Also: Meat: Sausages and Puddings, Cheese, Ice Creams and Sorbets

12 ○
Swaddles Green Farm
Swaddles Green Farm, Hare Lane, Buckland St Mary, Chard, Somerset TA20 3JR
Tel: 046034 387
Contact: Charlotte Reynolds

Pork
Organic free-range pork from rare breeds, butchered on site. Also organically reared Red Poll beef, suckler raised, available fresh and butchered to customers requirements.
Ⓒ Pigs 20 p.mth, cattle 1 p.mth
Ⓓ By own transport within area
See Also: Bacon & Hams, Meat: Pies and Prepared Dishes, Meat: Sausages and Puddings, Poultry Producers

7
Thornley & Son Ltd
Ridgewood Farm, Flag Lane, Heath Charnock, Chorley, Lancashire PR6 9ED
Tel: 02572 71251
Contact: C.D Hewitt

Pork
Pork slaughtered and butchered on farm, supplied fresh or frozen, as whole carcasses or to customers requirements.
Ⓒ 8000 p.mth
Ⓓ By arrangement
See Also: Meat: Sausages amd Puddings

1
Walter McDonald
Great North Road, Muir of Ord, Ross-shire IV6 7TP
Tel: 0463 870238
Contact: Mr W L Barras

Beef
Scotch beef, slaughtered and butchered, whole carcasses or boned and boxed.
Ⓒ Undisclosed
Ⓓ By arrangement
See Also: Meat: Sausages and Puddings

9 ↔
Welsh Bros
Rhymney River Bridge Road, Cardiff, Glamorgan CF3 7AF
Tel: 0222 482226/489221
Contact: George Welsh

Welsh Lamb
Beef, Welsh lamb, mutton, pork and veal, supplied butchered in specific joints and cuts, chilled or frozen. A small quantity of fresh sweetbreads also available.
Ⓒ Autumn-Christmas peak season
Ⓓ By own transport within area
See Also: Bacon and Hams, Meat: Pies and Prepared Dishes

9

Welsh Lamb Products
Unit 1, Felin Fach, Lampeter, Dyfed SA44 4RG
Tel: 0570 470729
Contact: Mrs Mary Davies

Lamb — Beef, lamb, mutton and pork available fresh, chilled or frozen and butchered to customers requirements, usually on site. Sweetbreads also available.
[C] Undisclosed
[D] By own transport within area
See Also: Meat: Pies and Prepared Dishes, Meat: Sausages and Puddings

15 ↔

West Country Trout
Trafalgar Farm, Boscastle, North Cornwall PL35 0BW
Tel: 08405 224
Contact: E R and D F L Ruscombe-King

Jacob lamb — Jacob lamb, grass fed for a lean, sweet and gamey taste, in whole carcasses weighing 30lb, also cross breed available producing 45lb carcasses. All frozen.
[C] Jacob lamb 10 p.a Nov-Jan, cross bred 50 p.a Nov-Jan
[D] By arrangement
See Also: Fish Farmers

14

J D Williams
Manor Farm, Glatton, Huntingdon, Cambridgeshire PE17 5RR
Tel: 0487 830247
Contact: Mr J D Williams

Pork — Pork from Large Welsh cross pigs butchered on farm. Liver and lights also available.
[C] 50 p.wk
[D] By own transport within area
See Also: Bacon and Hams

4 ●

H A Young & Family
Kite's Nest Farm, Broadway, Hereford & Worcester WR12 7JT
Tel: 0386 853320
Contact: Richard Young

Beef — Lincoln Red and Welsh Black, reared for beef, butchered on farm, hung for two weeks. Pure beef dripping and offal also available on request.
[C] 70 p.a Jun-Dec
[D] By arrangement
See Also: Meat: Sausages and Puddings

BACON AND HAMS

11 ↔

Belvoir Bacon Company Ltd
Mantle Lane, Coalville, Leicester LE6 4DR
Tel: 0530 3650/1/2/3 Fax: 0530 510708
Contact: Dinah Simmonds

Ham — Range of traditionally produced hams, gammon and bacon including 5lb honey roasted ham and 17-19lb boned or boneless hams.
[C] Undisclosed
[D] By own transport nationally
See Also: Meat: Pies and Prepared Dishes, Meat: Sausages and Puddings

3 ↔

Benshie Cattle Company
Ballinshoe, Kirriemuir, Angus DD8 5QG
Tel: 0575 73466
Contact: Lord Mackie of Benshie

Ham — Traditionally cured and smoked hams from free-range pigs.
[C] Undisclosed
[D] By arrangement
See Also: Fresh Meat, Meat: Sausages and Puddings

11

E A Bird & Sons Ltd
Wolsey Drive, Low Moor Road, Kirby-In-Ashfield, Nottinghamshire NG17 7JR
Tel: 0623 753834
Contact: Mrs K Attenborough

Wiltshire ham — Traditionally home cured ham to an eighty five year old recipe for Wiltshire style hams from Lincolnshire pigs.
[C] Undisclosed
[D] By own transport within area

7

Bodfari Creamery
Rough Hill Farm, Marlston Cwm Lache, nr Chester, Cheshire CH4 9JS
Tel: 0244 671111
Contact: Cavan Molloy

Honey roast ham

Additive free hams, plain or honey roast with demerara sugar and treacle, baked in steam oven. Supplied whole, in halves and sliced to customers requirements.
C 500 p.wk
D By arrangement
See Also: Milk

7 ◯ ↔

Bowling Alley Herb Farm
Commonside, Alvanley, nr Warrington, Cheshire
Tel: 09289 285
Contact: Mrs Felicity Elphick

Cumberland ham

Range of ham and bacon including Cumberland and honey roast. Also sausages and pâtés.
C Undisclosed
D By arrangement
See Also: Cheese, Fresh Herbs, Purees and Sauces

6

Cavaghan & Grey Ltd
Harraby, Carlisle, Cumbria CA1 3EU
Tel: 0228 24451 Telx: 64420
Contact: Mr E Lowe

Bacon

Mild cure, salt free bacon produced on a large scale. Trimmed to 10% fat, vacuum packed in clear box to separate rashers. Also flans, pies, sausages, puddings and haggis.
C 160 ton p.wk
D By own transport nationally

15

Clarksons Wholesale Foods
Alansway, Ottery St Mary, Devon EX11 1NR
Tel: 040481 3581
Contact: Mr B Moran and B Dean

Wiltshire cure bacon

Traditionally produced, additive free ham. Also available Wiltshire cure bacon, cooked and smoked meats.
C Undisclosed
D By Datapost, by own transport nationally
See Also: Fresh Meat

12

Clutton Hill Farm Shop
Clutton, nr Bristol, Avon BS18 4QQ
Tel: 0761 52458
Contact: Mr A Appleyard

Ham

Cooked hams produced with no added water.
C Undisclosed
D By own transport within area
See Also: Fresh Meat, Meat: Sausages and Puddings

12

H H Collins (Broadway) Ltd
28 North Street, Broadway, Worcester WR12 7DT
Tel: 0386 852374
Contact: Mr B Knight

Bacon

Bacon, smoked over oak or elm sawdust, in whole sides, selected cuts or sliced in 3lb packs.
C Undisclosed
D By own transport nationally
See Also Meat: Pies and Prepared Dishes, Meat: Sausages and Puddings

16

Dixies Fine Foods
Unit 14, The Business Park, Avenue One, Letchworth Garden City, Hertfordshire
Tel: 0462 675540
Contact: Mr N Tracey-Williams

Norfolk ham

Traditionally oak smoked Norfolk, cider, honey and plain hams. Also oak smoked sweetcure back bacon from Norfolk pigs. Half and whole hams weighing 5, 10lb. Bacon cryovacked in slices or sides of 3lb.
C Oak smoked ham 500x10lb p.wk, bacon undisclosed
D By arrangement

15

Dorset Farms
Manor Farm, Little Windsor, Beaminster, Dorset DT8 3QU
Tel: 0308 68822
Contact: Mr H Birch

Cider ham

Honey and cider hams and bacon traditionally farm cured with no additives.
C 200-300 p.wk
D By own transport within area
See Also: Fresh Meat, Meat: Sausages and Puddings, Game Dealers

11

E W Edgson (Products) Ltd
Pullman Road, Wigston, Leicester LE8 2DB
Tel: 0533 886461
Contact: D Davis

Ham

Traditionally cured hams, additive free, weighing approximately 10lb.
C Undisclosed
D By arrangement
See Also: Meat: Pies and Prepared Dishes

14 ↔

Emmett's
Peasenhall, Suffolk IP17 2HJ
Tel: 072879 250
Contact: Mr F G Jerrey

Suffolk ham

Smoked ham including Suffolk sweet pickled ham made with home brewed stout and black treacle, Suffolk cider pickled ham, mild cured oak smoked ham. Also Suffolk sweet pickled back and streaky bacon and Suffolk mild cured oak smoked bacon. Fresh and smoked sausages and freshly baked pies also available.
C Undisclosed
D By arrangement

7

Farmhouse Country Delicacies
The Homestead Farm, Pott Shrigley, Macclesfield, Cheshire SK10 5RU
Tel: 0625 72381
Contact: Joyce Dalton

Bacon

Bacon and hams sweet cured with honey

Ham

and molasses and smoked over applewood.
Ⓒ Undisclosed
Ⓓ By arrangement
See Also: Fresh Meat, Meat: Sausages and Puddings, Cheese

10 ● ↔

Fordhall Organic Farm
Fordhall Farm, Market Drayton, Shropshire TS9 3PS
Tel: 063 083 255
Contact: Mr Hollins

Applewood smoked ham

Range of hams and bacon smoked over applewood including honey and dry salt cures.
Ⓒ Undisclosed
Ⓓ By arrangement
See Also: Fresh Meat

11

Geo Adams & Sons Ltd
25-26 The Crescent, Spalding, Lincolnshire PE11 1AG
Tel: 0775 66161 Telx: 32858 Fax: 0775 710717
Contact: Mr N Broadhead

Dry salted ham

Range of dry salted hams.
Ⓒ Undisclosed
Ⓓ By arrangement
See Also: Meat: Pies & Prepared Dishes, Meat: Sausages and Puddings

10 ⦿ ↔

Gold Label Produce Ltd
Knightley Grange Cottage, Grange Road, Woodseaves, Staffordshire ST20 OJU
Tel: 0785 74495
Contact: Mr D Dale

Applewood smoked bacon

Sweet cure bacon from Chester White pigs, smoked over applewood.
Ⓒ Undisclosed
Ⓓ By own transport nationally
See Also: Fresh Meat, Game Dealers

9

Gorno's Charcuterie
30 Tudor Street, Riverside, Cardiff, South Glamorgan
Tel: 0222 372782
Contact: Mr Franco Gorno

Coppa di Palma

Range of additive free Italian style hams including Proscuitto Crudo and Coppa di Palma made from fresh meat and vacuum packed on site.
Ⓒ Undisclosed
Ⓓ By arrangement
See Also: Meat: Sausages and Puddings

14 ⦿

Guist Gloucesters
Ferndale House, Wood Norton, Dereham, Norfolk NR20 5BA
Tel: 036 284530
Contact: John Wratten

Ham

Home cured and smoked ham from Gloucester Old Spot pigs.
Ⓒ Undisclosed
Ⓓ By own transport within area
See Also: Fresh Meat

8 ↔

Harris-Leeming Bar
20 Leases Road, Leeming Bar, Northallerton, North Yorkshire DL7 9AW
Tel: 0677 22661
Contact: Steve Smith

Bradenham ham

Range of hams including Bradenham, dry salt cured, then immersed in wet cure marinade of crushed juniper berries, molasses and spices and finally lightly smòked. York, salt cured, scrubbed and re-salted, then dried and matured for four months. Wiltshire rolled and cooked. All available whole 12-14lb, halves 6-7lb, boneless 7-8lb.
Ⓒ Undisclosed
Ⓓ By arrangement

15

Heal Farm
Kings Nympton, Umberleigh, Devon EX37 9TB
Tel: 07695 2077
Contact: Anne Petch

Ham

Hams and bacon brine cured in the traditional way and cold smoked for several days over oak. Cooked hams skinned and covered with wholemeal breadcrumbs, uncooked hams supplied in boil-in-the-bag for easy boiling. Whole hams 8-12lb. Also bacon in 5lb packs.
Ⓒ Hams 60 p.wk, bacon 900lb p.wk.
Ⓓ By own transport within area, British Rail and TNT
See Also: Fresh Meat, Meat: Pâtés and Pastes, Meat: Pies and Prepared Dishes, Meat: Sausages and Puddings, Meat: Smoked, Game Dealers, Hampers

12 ↔

Hilliers Cotswold
Newmarket, Nailsworth, Stroud, Gloucestershire GL6 0RG
Tel: 045383 2691
Contact: Mr D C Hedges

Cotswold Ham

Cotswold ham made to traditional recipe.
Ⓒ Undisclosed
Ⓓ By arrangment
See Also: Meat: Pies and Prepared Dishes, Meat: Sausages and Puddings

3

James McIntyre
74 Montague Street, Rothesay, Isle of Bute PA20 OHL
Tel: 0700 3672
Contact: Mr J McIntyre

Beef ham

Beef ham produced from topside, cured and sliced in the same way as bacon.
Ⓒ ½ cwt p.wk
Ⓓ By own transport within area
See Also: Fresh Meat, Meat: Sausages and Puddings, Game Dealers

5

J Kerr Little, Master Butcher
58-60 High Street, Dumfriesshire DG1 2BS
Tel: 0387 53818
Contact: Mr J Kerr Little

Apple roast ham

Range of twelve hams including apple roast, charcoal, sandwich and peppered, all

weighing on average 6-7lb.
[C] Undisclosed
[D] By arrangement
See Also: Fresh Meat, Meat: Sausages and Puddings

[11] ⦿ ↔ **Maynards Farm Bacon**
Hough Farm, Weston-under-Redcastle, Shrewsbury, Shropshire SY4 5LR
Tel: 0984 840252
Contact: Mr M Davies

Sweet cure ham — Organically produced additive free hams and bacon cured traditionally for three months. Range includes sweet ham with molasses, sweet ham with demerara, applewood smoked ham, plain dry salted ham or with honey. Bacon comes in same flavours.
[C] Bacon and ham 1 ton p.mth
[D] By arrangement

[9] **R K Palfrey & Sons**
36a Church Road, Newport, Gwent NP9 7EL
Tel: 0633 59385
Contact: Mr G Palfrey

Ham — Hams, traditionally cured and boiled or roasted.
[C] Cooked ham 12 p.wk
[D] By arrangement
See Also: Meat: Sausages and Puddings, Poultry Producers

[14] **Peartree Pork and Poultry**
High Birch Farm, Weeley Heath, nr Clacton-on-Sea, Essex CO16 9BU
Tel: 0255 830291
Contact: Mr P Ernst

Black treacle ham — Bacon and ham traditionally cured and smoked over oak including mild cure and sweet cure, pickled with black treacle, sugar and herbs.
[C] Undisclosed
[D] By arrangement
See Also: Fresh Meat, Meat: Pies and Prepared Dishes, Game Dealers

[11] **Pickerings**
30 The Street, Old Costessey, Norwich Norfolk
Tel: 0603 742002
Contact: Mr Bryan Pickering

Weasenham ham — Range of hams and bacons including Swiss style peppered Black Forest, Virginia Roast and Weasenham hams with an average weight of 13lb.
[C] Undisclosed
[D] By own transport nationally
See Also: Meat: Sausages and Puddings

[14] **Poachers Pies Ltd**
5 Marston Road, St Neots, Cambridgeshire PE19 2HB
Tel: 0480 407777 Fax: 0480 407788
Contact: Richard West

Honey roast ham — Large range of oak smoked hams and gammons including honey roast, on or off the bone.
[C] Undisclosed
[D] By own transport within area
See Also: Meat: Pies and Prepared Dishes, Meat: Smoked, Game: Pâtés and Pastes

[3] **Ramsay of Carluke**
Wellriggs Factory, 22 Mount Stewart, Lanarkshire ML8 5ED
Tel: 0555 72277
Contact: Mr J Ramsay

Ayrshire bacon — Ayrshire bacon, from Great White premier grade pigs, produced to traditional Ayrshire cure with no added water and smoked over hardwood sawdust. Also available hamburgers, pâtés and pies.
[C] Undisclosed
[D] By arrangement
See Also: Fresh Meat

[12] **Real Meat Company Ltd**
East Hill Farm, Heytesbury, Warminster, Wiltshire BA12 0HR
Tel: 0985 40436/40060
Contact: Mr Richard Guy

Bacon — Bacon and ham cured with brine and salt-petre, smoked or unsmoked, in ½lb packs upwards.
[C] Undisclosed
[D] By arrangement
See Also: Fresh Meat, Meat: Pies and Prepared Dishes, Meat: Sausages and Puddings, Poultry Producers

11 ↔

Red Griffin Ltd/The Country Victuallers
Winkburn Hall, Newark, Nottinghamshire NG22 8PQ
Tel: 0636 86465
Contact: Richard Craven-Smith-Milnes

Alderton ham

Alderton ham, baked on the bone with marmalade glaze weighing 11-15lb. Also Rectory easy-to-carve ham, supplied vacuum packed.
[C] 250 p.wk
[D] By arrangement
See Also: Meat: Pâtés and Pastes, Game: Pies and Prepared Dishes, Game: Pies and Puddings

16

Regale Foods Ltd
33 Hythe Road, London NW10 6RS
Tel: 01 969 8320
Contact: Mr T D Fenner

Virginia ham

Hams cured traditionally, including honey roast and Virginia, supplied netted with knuckle bone or on or off the bone.
[C] 1½ ton p.wk
[D] By own transport within area
See Also: Meat: Sausages and Puddings, Meat: Smoked, Game: Pâtés and Pastes

6 ↔

Richard Woodall
Lane End, Waberthwaite, nr Millom, Cumbria LA19 5YJ
Tel: 06577 237/386
Contact: Mr Richard Woodall

Cumbria air-dried ham

Cumbria air-dried ham, similar in style to Parma ham, cured in farmhouse manner with brown sugar and salt and hung for eight months. Supplied boned, finely sliced and vacuum packed if required. Also a range of traditionally cured Cumbrian hams and bacon.
[C] Undisclosed Mar-Oct
[D] By arrangement
See Also: Meat: Sausages and Puddings

15 ↔

Riverford Farm Foods
Riverford farm, Staverton, Totnes, Devon TQ9 6AF
Tel: 080 426423
Contact: Ben Watson

Devon cider ham

Bacon and ham from own pigs. Bacon cured traditionally with sea-salt and brown sugar for good flavour and smoked over oak or left unsmoked. Hams cured as bacon, baked in Devon cider and apple juice, glazed with apple juice, brown sugar and mustard. Supplied on or off the bone.
[C] Bacon 30 sides p.wk, ham 30 p.wk
[D] By arrangement
See Also: Fresh Meat, Meat: Sausages and Puddings, Meat: Smoked

9

Roberts of Port Dinorwic
Griffiths Crossing Industrial Estate, Caernarfon, Gwynedd LL55 1TS
Tel: 0286 76111
Contact: Mr Roberts

Welsh cure ham

Range of Welsh and sweet cure hams weighing 10-16lb on the bone. Also gammon.
[C] Undisclosed
[D] By arrangement
See Also: Meat: Pies and Prepared Dishes, Meat: Sausages and Puddings, Hampers

9 ↔

Roys Cooked Meats Ltd
Viking Way, Winch Wen Industrial Estate, Swansea, West Glamorgan SA1 7DE
Tel: 0792 796519 Telx: 48232
Contact: Mr John F Archer

Jubilee ham

Jubilee hams supplied as whole or half.
[C] Undisclosed
[D] By arrangement
See Also: Meat: Pies and Prepared Dishes, Game: Pies and Prepared Dishes

8

G Scott of York
81 Low Petergate, York, Yorkshire
Tel: 0904 622972
Contact: Mr W Bailey

York ham

York ham prepared in traditional manner, dry cured in sugar, salt and salt-petre.
[C] Undisclosed Jul-Dec
[D] By arrangement
See Also: Meat: Pies and Prepared Dishes, Meat: Sausages and Puddings

6 ↔

M F & D J Slack
Newlands Farm, Raisbeck, Orton, Penrith, Cumbria CA10 3SG
Tel: 05874 446/667
Contact: Michael Slack

Air-dried ham

Traditionally home cured air-dried ham and bacon with good keeping qualities. Sliced bacon in vacuum packs 1lb upwards, bacon joints 2-6lb, middles 14-18lb and slicing shoulders 5-6lb.
[C] Full sides of bacon 60 p.wk
[D] By own transport nationally
See Also: Meat: Sausages and Puddings

12

Somerset Farm Foods Ltd
32-34 Long Street, Williton, Somerset
Tel: 0984 32307
Contact: Mr K Stunt

Apple roast ham

Gammon hams including plain, breadcrumbs, honey roast, apple roast and D-shaped pressed shoulder with fresh honey and apples.
[C] 400 p.wk
[D] By arrangement

14

Suffolk Larder Foods
9a Charles Industrial Estate, Stowmarket, Suffolk
Tel: 0449 676162
Contact: Tony Constantine Smith

Suffolk ham

Suffolk cured ham, trimmed and roasted, in packs 12-16lb.
[C] 50 p.wk
[D] By arrangement
See Also: Meat: Smoked, Game Dealers

12 ○

Swaddles Green Farm
Swaddles Green Farm, Hare Lane, Buckland St Mary, Chard, Somerset TA20 3JR
Tel 046034 387

Contact: Charlotte Reynolds

Sweet cure ham — Traditionally spiced sweet cure hams from organically raised pigs, available as whole or half weighing 7-14lb.
[C] Undisclosed
[D] By arrangement
See Also: Fresh Meat, Meat: Pies and Prepared Dishes, Meat: Sausages and Puddings, Poultry Producers

11

Walker & Son (Leicester) Ltd
4 Cheapside, Leicester, Leicestershire LE1 2LB
Tel: 0533 24743
Contact: Mr J H Cox

Ham — Hams made in traditional manner and cured for three weeks.
[C] Undisclosed
[D] By arrangement
See Also: Meat: Pies and Prepared Dishes

14

A Waller & Son
15 Victoria Avenue, Cambridge, Cambridgeshire CB4 1EG
Tel: 0223 515533
Contact: Mr P Welton

Ham — Ham, on or off the bone, boiled in old fashioned way.
[C] Undisclosed
[D] By own transport within area
See Also: Meat: Sausages and Puddings, Game Dealers

9 ↔

Welsh Bros
Rhymney River Bridge Road, Cardiff, Glamorgan CF3 7AF
Tel: 0222 482226/489221
Contact: George Welsh

Ham — Range of roasted meats available including ham, pork, beef. Also boned fresh turkey.
[C] Undisclosed
[D] By own transport within area
See Also: Fresh Meat

4

William Pinkerton & Son Ltd
21-25a Scotch Street, Armagh
Tel: 0861 522434
Contact: Mr M Best

Belfast ham — Belfast ham, traditional dry cure, available smoked or unsmoked.
[C] 100 hams p.wk
[D] By arrangement

14

J D Williams
Manor Farm, Glatton, Huntingdon, Cambridgeshire PE17 5RR
Tel: 0487 830247
Contact: Mr J D Williams

Bacon — Bacon, cured in Cheshire salt and salt-petre salt brine. Ham smoked traditionally on farm over oak chippings. Also additive free pork sausages.
[C] Undisclosed
[D] By own transport within area
See Also: Fresh Meat

PATES AND PASTES

3

Castle MacLellan Foods Ltd
Riverside, Dee Walk, Kirkcudbright DG6 4DR
Tel: 0557 30905
Contact: Mr C Warden

Galloway pâté — Range of pâtés including wild Scottish garlic and brandy, Galloway with a fat content of 7.7%, Scottish venison with burgundy (coarse textured), Balmoral Highland Game. All with an average meat content of 83.9% and lean meat content of 76.2%, in 250g packs and 3, 4lb dishes for microwave. Also smoked fish and turkey pâtés.
[C] 5 ton p.wk
[D] By own transport nationally

15

Devon Pâté Co Ltd/Hazlewood Food Group
Unit 91, Heathpark Estate, Honiton, Devon EX14 8BB
Tel: 0404 41528
Contact: Mr Smith

Normandy pâté — Varieties of pâtés including low fat, Brussels and Normandy. All supplied in 4, 6oz, 4lb packs, pre-packed for delicatessens. Also fish and speciality vegetable pâtés.

[C] Undisclosed
[D] By arrangement
See Also: Meat: Pies and Prepared Dishes

9

Edward Hamer Ltd
Plynlimon House, Llamidloes, Powys SY18 6EF
Tel: 05512 2114
Contact: Edward Hamer

Liver and sweetbread pâté

Range of pâtés available, including lambs liver and sweetbread, lambs liver and mint in 4lb loaves.
[C] 1000lb p.wk
[D] By own transport within area
See Also: Fresh Meat

15

Heal Farm
Kings Nympton, Umberleigh, Devon EX37 9TB
Tel: 07695 2077
Contact: Anne Petch

Coarse pâté

Coarse slicing pâté made with pork, bacon, liver, local cider, garlic, herbs and streaky bacon, in various sizes.
[C] Undisclosed
[D] By own transport nationally
See Also: Fresh Meat, Bacon and Hams, Meat: Pies and Prepared Dishes, Meat: Sausages and Puddings, Meat: Smoked, Game Farmers, Hampers

6

Henry Newbould Ltd
2 Startforth Road, Riverside Park, Middlesbrough, Cleveland TS2 1PT
Tel: 0642 225411
Contact: Mr M H Newbould

Cleveland cream pâté

Smooth and coarse pâtés from original recipes, vacuum packed in 2kg containers.
[C] 1000lb p.dy
[W] Freshfayre 0642 52739
[D] By own transport within area
See Also: Meat: Pies and Prepared Dishes, Meat: Sausages and Puddings, Meat: Smoked

15 ↔

La Charcuterie of Dorset
Railway Triangle Estate, Poundbury Road, Dorchester, Dorset DT1 2PJ
Tel: 0903 66900
Contact: H J Cocklin

Dorset pâté

Range of additive free roasted pâtés containing more than 70% meat including Dorset with pork and pork liver, Gascogne with pork and poultry liver and Dorset Farmhouse, a country style pork and liver pâté with real ale. All in 1kg, 1300g packs and 375, 750g roulades.
[C] Undisclosed
[W] Quantock Foods Ltd 0903 251100
[D] By wholesaler
See Also: Meat: Sausages and Puddings, Game: Pâtés and Pastes, Fish: Pâtés and Pastes

14 ↔

Norfolk Smokehouses Ltd
Poplar Farm, Worlingworth, Woodbridge, Suffolk IP13 7LR
Tel: 072 876212
Contact: J D Hildreth

Country pâté

Range of additive free farmhouse pâtés, including Country with pork, liver and tongue, Norfolk with pork and liver, and farmhouse liver terrine. All in 1.81kg containers.
[C] Undisclosed
[D] By arrangement
See Also: Game: Pâtés and Pastes, Fish: Pâtés and Pastes, Vegetable Dishes

1 ↔

Orkney Foods
Little Stonehall, Deerness, Orkney KW17 2QQ
Tel: 085674 333
Contact: Mrs Floris Couperwhite

Orkney Island pâté

Variety of additive free, deep frozen meat pâtés using traditional recipes, including farmhouse, country and Orkney Island. All in 227, 454, 910g packs.
[C] 50kg p.wk
[D] By arrangement
See Also: Fish: Pâtés and Pastes, Pies and Puddings

11 ↔

Red Griffin Ltd/The Country Victuallers
Winkburn Hall, Newark, Nottinghamshire NG22 8PQ
Tel: 0636 86465
Contact: Richard Craven-Smith-Milnes

Chicken liver pâté

Range of pâtés including terrine de campagne, a coarse pâté from pork and pork liver, and chicken liver with brandy. Also smoked salmon pâté.
[C] 1200lb p.wk
[D] By arrangement
See Also: Bacon and Hams, Game: Pâtés and Pastes, Pies and Puddings

8 ↔

E T Sutherland & Son Ltd
Waleswood Food Factory, Kiveton, Sheffield, South Yorkshire SR1 8PF
Tel: 0909 770861 Telx: 54130 Fax: 0909 772797
Contact: Mr P Evans

Potted beef

Range of five spreads including Yorkshire potted beef made to traditional recipes. All in 4oz cartons, 1lb packs. Also available range of fifty cooked meats including beef, pork, ham and gammon, in various weights 5-12lb.
[C] Undisclosed
[D] By own transport nationally

PIES AND PREPARED DISHES

15 ↔

Bangers/Food Naturally
1 Eppleton Farm, Copplestone, Crediton, Devon EX17 5LE
Tel: 03635 794
Contact: Nigel Schofield

Ham and chicken

Handmade pies, including ham and chicken, turkey and chestnut, duck and orange and game, in 2½, 5½, 7lb vacuum packed whole pies or portions. Also a range of small pies and prepared meals in earthenware dishes including lasagne, chilli con carne, chicken curry and fishermans pie.
C 40,000 p.a
D By own transport within area
See Also: Meat: Sausages and Puddings

11 ↔

Belvoir Bacon Company Ltd
Mantle Lane, Coalville, Leicester LE6 4DR
Tel: 0530 3650/1/2/3 Fax: 0530 510708
Contact: Dinah Simmonds

Pork pie

Range of traditionally produced pork pies, 2oz-6lb, sausage rolls, pastries and Cornish pasties fresh baked to order.
C Undisclosed
D By own transport nationally
See Also: Bacon and Hams, Meat: Sausages and Puddings

6

Wm Brennand & Sons Ltd
18 Finkle Street, Kendal, Cumbria LA9 4AB
Tel: 0539 20323
Contact: Mr A W Brennand

Pork pie

Handmade, raised pork pies made to sixty year old recipe. Also available cooked meats.
C Undisclosed
D By arrangement
See Also: Fresh Meat, Meat: Sausages and Puddings

11 ↔

Catlin Bros Ltd
11 High Street, Grantham, Lincolnshire
Tel: 0476 65428
Contact: S P Hallam

Stuffed chine

Lincolnshire stuffed chine, prepared from cured pork shoulder, stuffed with fresh parsley.
C Undisclosed
D By own transport within area
See Also: Meat: Sausages and Puddings, Game: Pies and Prepared Dishes, Breads

11 ●

A E Chambers Ltd
31 Front Street, Arnold, Nottinghamshire NG5 7EA
Tel: 0602 267034
Contact: Mr Philip Chambers

Pork pie

Range of handmade traditional pies including beef, ham, pork, 4½-5lb. Also cooked and prepared meats.
C Undisclosed
W Lever Bros, Nottingham, Centre Parks, Nottingham
D By wholesaler

12

H H Collins (Broadway) Ltd
28 North Street, Broadway, Worcester WR12 7DT
Tel: 0386 852374
Contact: Mr B Knight

Stow pie

Range of pies made to traditional recipes including Stow with diced beef and venison in a Burgundy wine sauce, steak and kidney, pork, pork, ham and egg, game, chicken and ham, turkey and ham, turkey, ham and cranberry, chicken and mushroom. Additive free Cornish pasties also available.
C Undisclosed
D By own transport within area
See Also: Bacon and Hams, Meat: Sausages and Puddings

10 ↔

Country Cooks Ltd
Unit 1, Great Western Court, Ashburton Industrial Estate, Ross-on-Wye, Herefordshire HR9 7BW
Tel: 0989 66868
Contact: Jenny Allday

Navarin of lamb

Main course additive free dishes including boeuf bourguignonne, chilli con carne, navarin of lamb, pork with peppers, moussaka and lasagne.
C 3000kg p.mth
D By arrangement
See Also: Vegetable Dishes, Ice Creams and Sorbets

6

Cranston
Sandhill, Kirkoswald, Penrith, Cumbria CA10 1EN
Tel: 0228 21345
Contact: Mr P J Cranston

Pork pie

Raised pork pies, baked daily, in 5oz, 1lb sizes. Also available boiled ox tongue, roast ham, roast beef and roast pork.
C Undisclosed
D By arrangement
See Also: Fresh Meat, Meat: Sausages and Puddings

11

A W Curtiss & Son Ltd
164 High Street, Lincoln, Lincolnshire LN5 7AF
Tel: 0522 30802
Contact: Mr L C Dickens

Stuffed chine

Traditional stuffed Lincolnshire chine, split in half and hand sliced, the chine and neck salted and stuffed with herbs, weighing 14lb. Also supplied pork pies in 1lb or hand raised 4-5lb sizes.
C Stuffed chine 50 p.wk May-Dec
D By own transport nationally
See Also: Meat: Sausages and Puddings, Breads

16

Dawson & Daughters Ltd
28/31 Hythe Road, Shepherds Bush, London W10 6RX
Tel: 01 969 9968 Fax: 01 960 6057
Contact: Mr G Gutteridge

Ham and turkey pie

Range of hand raised pies including ham and turkey with cranberries and walnuts weighing 6lb.
[C] 1000 p.mth
[W] Laurel Farm, Hull
[D] By wholesaler, by own transport within area
See Also: Meat: Sausages and Puddings

15

Devon Pate Co Ltd/Hazlewood Food Group
Unit 91, Heathpark Estate, Honiton, Devon EX14 8BB
Tel: 0404 41528
Contact: Mr Smith

Spare ribs

Pork spare ribs including ribs prepared in barbecue or sweet and sour sauce. Also liver and bacon ready meals.
[C] Undisclosed
[D] By arrangement
See Also: Meat: Pâtés and Pastes

6 ↔

The Dutch Butcher
4 Park Avenue, Whitley Bay, Tyne & Wear
Tel: 091 252 2047
Contact: Peter and Shirley Van Der Laan

Beef olives

Range of oven-ready dishes including minced steak and pork pies, beef stroganoff, sausage casserole with own sausages, veal, bacon and beef olives, steak tartare, chicken Kiev, marinaded steaks and ribs, weiner schnitzels and low fat burgers. Also available pâtés and cooked meats.
[C] Undisclosed
[D] By own transport within area
See Also: Meat: Sausages and Puddings

11

E W Edgson (Products) Ltd
Pullman Road, Wigston, Leicester LE8 2DB
Tel: 0533 886461
Contact: D Davis

Pork pie

Range of traditional pork pies weighing 4oz-7lb. Also available prepared meats.
[C] Undisclosed
[D] By arrangement
See Also: Bacon and Hams

14 ↔

Essex Larders
Pyes Farm, Barnston, Dunmow, Essex CM6 3PR
Tel: 0371 820272
Contact: Zinnia Campling

Pork and apricot

Raised meat and poultry pies with jelly including pork and apricot, turkey and walnut, game with brandy jelly, in long 6-6½lb, or round 1, 4, 5lb sizes. Also deep quiches with wholemeal pastry and meat and vegetarian fillings in 6, 11″ rounds.
[C] 1500-2000lb p.wk
[D] By arrangement
See Also: Meat: Pies and Puddings

3 ↔

Ewing's
83 Main Street, Baillieston, Glasgow G69 6AD
Tel: 041 773 0274
Contact: Mr J Ewing

Steak pie

Range of Scotch pies, sausage rolls, mince rounds and rump steak pies in various sizes made to customers requirements.
[C] Undisclosed
[D] By own transport within area
See Also: Fresh Meat, Meat: Sausages and Puddings

12

A Ford & Son
102 Devon Road, Easton, Bristol, Avon BS5 6ED
Tel: 0272 511515
Contact: Mr A R Ford

Chitterlings

Tripe, and pig chitterlings, well cleaned and cured in home prepared brine. Other offal products available.
[C] Undisclosed
[D] By own transport within area

11

Geo Adams & Sons Ltd
25-26 The Crescent, Spalding, Lincolnshire PE11 1AG
Tel: 0775 66161 Telx: 32858 Fax: 710717
Contact: Mr N Broadhead

Lincolnshire manor pie

Range of pies including hand-raised pork, steak and kidney, beef and onion and Lincolnshire manor pies.
[C] Undisclosed
[D] By arrangement
See Also: Bacon and Hams, Meat: Sausages and Puddings

6

E Hall (Tripe & Poultry) Ltd
The Parade, Hendon, Sunderland, Tyne & Wear SR2 8NT
Tel: 091565 6370
Contact: Mr T Knight

Tripe

Range of tripe from stomachs of different animals including Corduroy (cow gut only), Reed, Weasand, Honeycomb, Thick and Bible. Handled fresh rather than frozen before cooking.
[C] 4½ ton p.wk
[D] By own transport within area

15

Heal Farm
Kings Nympton, Umberleigh, Devon EX37 9TB
Tel: 07695 2077
Contact: Anne Petch

Brawn

Additive free brawn made from cooked pig cheek with parsley, stock and local cider in small tubs. Also available salt beef, air-dried beef and hog pudding.
[C] Undisclosed
[D] By own transport within area
See Also: Fresh Meat, Bacon and Hams, Meat: Pâtés and Pastes, Meat: Sausages and Puddings, Meat: Smoked, Game Farmers, Hampers

6 **Henry Newbould Ltd**
2 Startforth Road, Riverside Park, Middlesbrough, Cleveland TS2 1PT
Tel: 0642 225411
Contact: Mr M H Newbould

Pork pie
Additive free meat pies, freshly made six days a week, some made to one hundred and thirty year old recipes, including steak and kidney, mince and onion, pork. Also available pasties, fruit pies, quiches and a range of prepared dishes.
[C] 10,000 p.dy
[D] By own transport within area
See Also: Meat: Pâtés and Pastes, Meat: Sausages and Puddings, Meat: Smoked

12 ↔ **Hilliers Cotswold**
Newmarket, Nailsworth, Stroud, Gloucestershire GL6 0RG
Tel: 045383 2691
Contact: Mr D C Hedges

Pork pie
Pork pies, all made with 85% meat. Also available range of pasties made with fresh vegetables and roast beef.
[C] ½ million pies p.wk
[D] By arrangement
See Also: Bacon and Hams, Meat: Sausages and Puddings

11 **F A & J Jones & Sons**
Red House Farm, North Scarle, Lincoln LN6 9HB
Tel: 052 277224
Contact: Mrs Jean Jones

Pork pie
Pork pies, hand-raised using hot crust pastry with natural jelly, in 1lb size or larger at Christmas.
[C] Undisclosed
[D] By arrangement
See Also: Fresh Meat, Meat: Sausages and Puddings, Poultry Producers

5 **Meikle Knox Farm Shop**
Meikle Knox, Castle Douglas, Dumfries & Galloway DG7Y 1NS
Tel: 0556 2736
Contact: Mr C Irving

Haslet
Haslet prepared with natural ingredients and spices. Also available half beef and half pork meat loaf made to traditional German recipe.
[C] Undisclosed
[D] By own transport within area
See Also: Meat: Sausages and Puddings

16 **Middle Farm Shop/English Farm Cider Centre**
Middle Farm, Firle, nr Lewes, East Sussex BN8 6LJ
Tel: 032183 411/303
Contact: Mr John Pile

Cornish pasties
Cornish pasties, sausage rolls, pizzas and steak and kidney pies, all handmade with organic wholemeal flour.
[C] Undisclosed
[D] By arrangement
See Also: Milk, Cakes, Biscuits and Pastries

14 **The Musk's Delicatessen (Greenstage) Ltd**
The Rookery, Newmarket, Cambridgeshire CB8 8EQ
Tel: 0638 661824
Contact: Mrs H J Waddilove

Sausage roll
Additive free sausage rolls made with homemade sausage meat.
[C] Undisclosed
[D] By arrangement
See Also: Meat: Sausages and Puddings

9 **Nannyma Foods Ltd**
114-116 Springvale Estate, Cwmbran, Gwent NP44 5BG
Tel: 06333 69949
Contact: Talfryn Jenkins

Beef curry
Range of handmade, additive free prepared Indian dishes, including beef and lamb curries, lamb samosas and beef kofte kebabs.
[C] Undisclosed
[W] King Frost, 0472 359261, Capper & Co Ltd 0443 225500, Cardigan Frozen Foods 0239 613691
[D] By wholesaler
See Also: Game: Pies and Prepared Dishes, Fish: Pies and Prepared Dishes

11 **Parrs**
Lilac Grove, Beeston, Nottingham, Nottinghamshire NG9 1PJ
Tel: 0602 258261
Contact: Mr D Stevenson

Pork pie
Cured meat pork pies, ranging from picnic individual to 10oz, 1, 2, 4¾, 6lb.
[C] ½ million pork pies p.wk
[D] By own transport nationally
See Also: Meat: Sausages and Puddings

14 ↔ **Peartree Pork and Poultry**
High Birch Farm, Weeley Heath, nr Clacton-on-Sea, Essex CO16 9BU
Tel: 0255 830291
Contact: Mr P Ernst

Meat pie
Additive free pies handmade to a traditional recipe, with high meat content. Also available boiled ham, roast pork with herbs and spices, sausages and hamburgers.
[C] Undisclosed
[D] By arrangement
See Also: Fresh Meat, Bacon and Hams, Game Dealers

10 **Peter Hollingsworth Ltd**
Horseley Fields, Wolverhampton, West Midlands WV1 3DG
Tel: 0902 52452
Contact: Mr P Guest

Beef stew and dumplings
Pork pies with 80% meat made to an old family recipe. Also a range of prepared meals including beef stew and dumplings, liver and bacon, chicken and vegetable casserole.
[C] Undisclosed
[D] By arrangement

14
Poachers Pies Ltd
5 Marston Road, St Neots, Cambridgeshire PE19 2HB
Tel: 0480 407777 Fax: 0480 407788
Contact: Richard West

Huntingdonshire pie

Range of additive free pies including ham and leek, poacher's, Huntingdonshire, Fidgit pie, pork and apricot, ham and chicken with mushroom, duck and orange with walnut, Abbot's, Gamekeeper's. Also prepared dishes in 5lb foil containers, including Lancashire hot pot, pork in cider, boeuf bourguignonne, chicken veronique, chilli con carne, venison in port, coq au vin, turkey marengo and lasagne.
C Undisclosed
D By own transport within area
See Also: Bacon and Hams, Meat: Smoked, Game: Pâtés and Pastes

15
Puddings Food Company
Welgoer Farm House, Poyntington, nr Sherborne, Dorset
Tel: 096322 293
Contact: Mrs Wendy Horne

Steak and kidney pie

Range of traditional handmade meat pies, with a minimum meat content of 40%, including steak and kidney, chicken, bacon and mushroom and cottage pie, in individual and family sizes. Larger pies on request.
C Undisclosed
D By arrangement
See Also: Meat: Pies and Puddings

12
Real Meat Company Ltd
East Hill Farm, Heytesbury, Warminster, Wiltshire BA12 0HR
Tel: 0985 40436/40060
Contact: Mr Richard Guy

Beef pie

Additive free meat pies including pork, beef, steak or chicken.
C Undisclosed
D By arrangement
See Also: Fresh Meat, Bacon and Hams, Meat: Sausages and Puddings, Poultry Producers

9
Roberts of Port Dinorwic Ltd
Griffiths Crossing Industrial Estate, Caernarfon, Gwynedd LL55 1TS
Tel: 0286 76111
Contact: Mr Roberts

Gala pie

Range of pies including pork and turkey with layered turkey breast meat in 5lb rounds, pork, turkey and cranberry in 5½lb rounds, Gala pie with seasoned pork meat filling and boiled eggs in 1, 4, 5, 6lb longs. All available chilled, vacuum packed or frozen.
C Undisclosed
D By arrangement
See Also: Bacon and Hams, Meat: Sausages and Puddings, Hampers

9 ↔
Roys Cooked Meats Ltd
Viking Way, Winch Wen Industrial Estate, Swansea, West Glamorgan SA1 7DE
Tel: 0792 796519 Telx: 48232
Contact: Mr John F Archer

Pork and potato pie

Range of pies made with beef, pork and fresh potatoes, with a minimum of 40% meat content, in 284, 370 and 567g sizes. Also prepared dishes.
C Undisclosed
D By arrangement
See Also: Bacon and Hams, Game: Pies and Prepared Dishes

8
H E Schofield
128 Ings Lane, Castleford, West Yorkshire WF10 2SA
Tel: 0977 552024
Contact: Mr R Schofield

Tripe

Tripe, boned cow heel and full cow heel, prepared by thorough cleaning and boiling, ready to eat, in 1, 5, 10, 20lb packs.
C Undisclosed
D By own transport within area

8
G Scott of York
81 Low Petergate, York, Yorkshire
Tel: 0904 622972
Contact: Mr W Bailey

Steak and kidney pie

Pies made to traditional recipes including pork, steak and kidney, minced beef and onion, bacon and egg and turkey. Also Cornish pasties, cheese and onion pasties and sausage rolls.
C 10,000 p.wk
D By own transport within area
See Also: Bacon and Hams, Meat: Sausages and Puddings

3
Strathmore Meat Ltd
Carseview Road, Forfar, Angus DD8 3NG
Tel: 0307 62333
Contact: Colin Muir

Beef and onion pie

Range of handmade chilled or frozen puddings and pies, including traditional Scotch pie, beef and onion and black puddings weighing 4oz-10lb or to customers requirements.
C Undisclosed
D By arrangement
See Also: Fresh Meat

12 ◯
Swaddles Green Farm
Swaddles Green Farm, Hare Lane, Buckland St Mary, Chard, Somerset TA20 3JR
Tel: 046034 387
Contact: Charlotte Reynolds

Cider pork pie

Handmade pork pies with apple and cider. Also Hindle Wake pies with chicken, prunes, lemon, cider and cream. Also game pies and a range of pork pâtés.
C Undisclosed
D By arrangement
See Also: Fresh Meat, Bacon and Hams, Meat: Sausages and Puddings, Poultry Producers

11
E J Swepstone & Son
Saracen's Head, Holbeach, Spalding, Lincolnshire PE12 8AY
Tel: 0406 23128/25465
Contact: Mr J Swepstone

Pork pie

Pork pies with high meat content.
C Undisclosed
D By own transport within area
See Also: Meat: Sausages and Puddings

15 ↔

Texas Bar-B-Que Ltd
Sheldon Grange, Dunkeswell, Honiton, Devon EX14 0RW
Tel: 0823 680565
Contact: Mrs Julia Burrough

Barbecued beef

Lean British beef barbecued over oak, packed in 125g single portions with sauce. Smoked pork spare ribs also available in vacuum packs for boil-in-the-bag or microwave heating.
C 700 packs p.dy
W Taylor Catering Foods 040481 4312
D By own transport within area

10

Tilbec Pies
11-15 Church Street, Bromyard, Hereford HR7 4DU
Tel: 0885 82429
Contact: Mr Bancroft

Pork and brandy pie

Range of handmade additive free pies including pork and brandy with gammon, beef nuts, brandy and pork liver, pork and sherry, and chicken fruity. All in 5lb, 8″ rounds and 4, 9lb oval pies.
C Undisclosed
D By arrangement

7 ↔

Tovah Meat Products Ltd
53-59 Collingham Street, Manchester M8 8RQ
Tel: 061 832 6354
Contact: Mr Entwistle

Kosher pressed beef

Range of kosher products including cottage pies, sausage rolls, sliced rolled beef in ¼lb packs and 10lb blocks of cooked pressed beef. Also available a range of continental sausages including wurst, salami, Vienna and cocktail sausages.
C Pressed beef 100x10lb blocks p.wk
D By arrangement
See Also: Fresh Meat

11

Walker & Son (Leicester) Ltd
4 Cheapside, Leicester, Leicestershire LE1 2LB
Tel: 0533 24743
Contact: Mr J H Cox

Pork and chicken pie

Additive free handmade, 100% meat filled pork pies, made to traditional recipe from 1820 in 2½, 5½, 11oz sizes. Also range of 6lb handmade, speciality pies including pork and egg, pork and chicken, pork, chicken and ham, veal, ham and egg. Also hot eating pies, pastes, spreads and hamburgers.
C 6lb pies 2000 p.wk, 1, 1½, 2lb pies 12,000 p.wk
D By arrangement
See Also: Bacon and Hams

9

Welsh Lamb Products
Unit 1, Felin Fach, Lampeter, Dyfed SA44 4RG
Tel: 0570 470729
Contact: Mrs Mary Davies

Lamb kidneys in red wine

Range of frozen individual portion boil-in-the-bag meals, including lamb kidneys in red wine and rice, beef and vegetable stew, Hungarian goulash. Also range of shortcrust pies in 9″ rounds, packed in cases of four, including steak, kidney and ale, minced beef, onions and herbs.
C Undisclosed
D By own transport within area
See Also: Fresh Meat, Meat: Sausages and Puddings

SAUSAGES AND PUDDINGS

8

Albert Hirst Butchers
36 Queen's Road, Barnsley, Yorkshire S71 1AR
Tel: 0226 284851
Contact: Albert Hirst

Black pudding

Range of traditional pies and pasties. Also award winning black pudding, made from intestines, diced fat, pearl barley and onions, in 4oz links or 18″ long 2lb sticks, garlic flavour available on request.
C Undisclosed
D By arrangement
See Also: Fresh Meat

8

T Appleton & Sons
6 Market Place, Ripon, North Yorkshire HG4 1BP
Tel: 0765 3198
Contact: Mr R Gaunt

Cumberland sausage

Sausages made to eighty year old family recipe, with 70-75% pork, herbs and spices, and Cumberland sausage, with 90% pork. Also available pies, cured and cooked meats and black puddings.
C 60lb p.dy
D By arrangement

15 ↔

Bangers/Food Naturally
1 Eppleton Farm, Copplestone, Crediton, Devon EX17 5LE
Tel: 03635 794
Contact: Nigel Schofield

Boerwors

Additive free range of sausages in natural casings, with 80% meat including South African boerwors, German bratwurst, Algerian spicy merguez, oriental peri peri with pork, chilli and lemon juice.
C 65,000lb p.a
D By arrangement
See Also: Meat: Pies and Prepared Dishes

16 ↔

A J Barkaway
20 Ospringe Street, Faversham, Kent
Tel: 0795 532040
Contact: Mr A J Barkaway

Pork sausage

Pork sausages in natural casings made to a one hundred year old recipe with 85% meat and traditional seasonings. Also available pies, pâtés, cooked and cured meats.
Ⓒ Sausages 1 ton p.wk
Ⓓ By own transport within area
See Also: Fresh Meat, Game Dealers

11 ↔

Belvoir Bacon Company Ltd
Mantle Lane, Coalville, Leicester LE6 4DR
Tel: 0530 3650/1/2/3 Fax: 0530 510708
Contact: Dinah Simmonds

Lincoln sausage

Range of sausages including low fat, high fibre with 70% meat, Cumberland with 75% meat, Lincoln and tomato flavoured.
Ⓒ Undisclosed
Ⓓ By own transport nationally
See Also: Bacon and Hams, Meat: Pies and Prepared Dishes

3 ↔

Benshie Cattle Company
Ballinshoe, Kirriemuir, Angus DD8 5QG
Tel: 0575 73466
Contact: Lord Mackie of Benshie

Herb sausage

Range of sausages with 80% meat including plain, herb, gluten free in 1lb or bulk packs.
Ⓒ Undisclosed
Ⓓ By arrangement
See Also: Fresh Meat, Bacon and Hams

15 ○ ★

Blackdown Farm & Loddiswell Cheese
Blackdown, Loddiswell, Kingsbridge, Devon TQ7 4EA
Tel: 054882 387
Contact: Mr and Mrs W L Martin

Goat sausage

Additive free goat meat sausages. Pork and smoked kid sausages also available.
Ⓒ Undisclosed
Ⓓ By arrangement
See Also: Fresh Meat, Cheese

6

Wm Brennand & Sons Ltd
18 Finkle Street, Kendal, Cumbria LA9 4AB
Tel: 0539 20323
Contact: Mr A W Brennand

Cumberland sausage

Cumberland sausage with 95% meat, supplied singly or in a roll. Also brawn and hamburgers.
Ⓒ Undisclosed
Ⓓ By arrangement
See Also: Fresh Meat, Meat: Pies and Prepared Dishes

16 ↔

Bunker Farm Produce
Bunker Farm, Basingstoke Rd, Greenham Common South, Newbury, Berkshire RG15 8HH
Tel: 0635 45535
Contact: Ken Neale

Goat sausage

Goat meat sausages with 85% meat in 1lb packs. Also Scotch eggs (pork, goat or vegetarian) made with free-range eggs.
Ⓒ Undisclosed
Ⓓ By arrangement
See Also: Fresh Meat, Poultry Producers, Cheese, Purees and Sauces

6 ↔

Burbush's
Gilwilly Trading Estate, Penrith, Cumbria
Tel: 0768 63841
Contact: T W H Burbush

Pork and apple

Sausages in natural skins including pork and apple, pork, sage and onion, Cumberland and venison.
Ⓒ Undisclosed
Ⓓ By own transport within area
See Also: Fresh Meat, Game: Pies and Prepared Dishes

11 ↔

Catlin Bros Ltd
11 High Street, Grantham, Lincolnshire
Tel: 0476 65428
Contact: S P Hallam

Lincolnshire sage sausage

Lincolnshire sage sausage made with home grown rubbed English sage and high percentage of pork filled into natural casings. Also sausage rolls.
Ⓒ Undisclosed
Ⓓ By own transport within area
See Also: Meat: Pies and Prepared Dishes, Game: Pies and Prepared Dishes, Breads

15

W F Chinn
Marsh Lane, Crediton, Devon EX17 1ES
Tel: 03632 2639
Contact: Tony and Rose Palmer

Pork chipolatas

Sausages prepared to one hundred year old recipes including Cumberland, traditional pork with 65% meat, pork chipolatas.
Ⓒ 1500lb p.wk
Ⓓ By own transport within area

14 ↔

Church's Pork Butchers
224 High Street, Epping, Essex
Tel: 0378 73231
Contact: Mr P N Barker

Old Epping sausage

Sausages including Old Epping coarse cut with rubbed sage, made to one hundred year old recipe, pork sausage, additive free with 68% meat, low fat pork with 90% lean meat, gluten free, garlic flavoured pork with 68% meat. All loose, or in ½, 1lb packs, with customers own label if required.
Ⓒ 8000-10,000lb p.wk
Ⓓ By own transport within area

12

Clutton Hill Farm Shop
Clutton, nr Bristol, Avon BS18 4QQ
Tel: 0761 52458
Contact: Mr A Appleyard

Garlic sausage

Additive free sausages made to order, with high meat content. Spices and garlic added to customers requirements.
[C] Undisclosed
[D] By own transport within area
See Also: Fresh Meat, Bacon and Hams

12 ↔

H H Collins (Broadway) Ltd
28 North Street, Broadway, Worcester WR12 7DT
Tel: 0386 852374
Contact: Mr B Knight

Gloucester sausage

Gloucester sausages with 90% meat in natural casings.
[C] Undisclosed
[D] By own transport nationally
See Also: Bacon and Hams, Meat: Pies and Prepared Dishes

12

Cooked Meat Shop
8a The Guildhall Market, Bath, Avon
Tel: 0225 25640
Contact: Mr Biss

Bath chaps

Range of products including sausages, black pudding, haggis and Bath chaps made with brined, boiled, boned, trimmed and breaded pork cheek.
[C] Bath chaps 12 p.dy
[D] By arrangement

12 ↔

Cotswold Stile
The Old Bakehouse, 17a Long Street, Wotton-under-Edge, Gloucestershire GL12 7ES
Tel: 0453 844994
Contact: Henrietta White

Hamburger

Sausages made with no mechanically recovered meat or added fat, rind or gristle, in 5, 10lb packs, individually packed. Also available hamburgers in 5, 10lb bags and pizzas individually packed 4 per box.
[C] 500lb p.wk
[D] By arrangement
See Also: Fresh Meat

6

Cranston
Sandhill, Kirkoswald, Penrith, Cumbria CA10 1EN
Tel: 0228 21345
Contact: Mr P J Cranston

Cumberland sausage

Cumberland sausage coarse cut with spices and 85% meat. Also hamburgers.
[C] Sausages 3 ton p.wk
[D] By arrangement
See Also: Fresh Meat, Meat: Pies and Prepared Dishes

3 ↔

Crombie's Quality Meats
97-101 Broughton Street, Edinburgh EH1 3RZ
Tel: 031 556 7643
Contact: Sandy Crombie

Haggis

Range of sausages including low fat beef and low fat pork with 70% meat, Bratwurst with 85% meat, and Cumberland with 60% meat. Also additive free and gluten free sausages made to order. Also available pork brisket with 80% meat, and haggis made to traditional recipe with natural casings.
[C] 700-1000lb p.wk
[D] By arrangement

11

A W Curtiss & Son Ltd
164 High Street, Lincoln, Lincolnshire LN5 7AF
Tel: 0522 30802
Contact: Mr L C Dickens

Lincolnshire sausage

Lincolnshire sausages with a blend of spices to give a gamey flavour, additive free, rough cut farmhouse sausages in natural casings, both in 1, 5lb packs.
[C] 3000lb p.wk
[D] By own transport nationally
See Also: Meat: Pies and Prepared Dishes, Breads

4

David Burns
112 Abbey Street, Bangor, Co Down BT20 4JB
Tel: 0247 270073
Contact: Mr David Burns

Beef sausage

Range of sausages including pork with 83% meat made with pork shoulder, small percentage of back fat, rusk, herbs, spices in natural casings, beef with 83% meat made with briskets and shanks, herbs, spices, rusk, in natural casings, gluten free, and vegetable sausage, a local speciality made with meat and fresh vegetables. Also home pickled ox tongues, roast beef and gammon.
[C] 5000lb p.wk
[D] By arrangement
See Also: Fresh Meat

16

Dawson & Daughters Ltd
28/31 Hythe Road, Shepherds Bush, London W10 6RX
Tel: 01 969 9968 Fax: 01 960 6057
Contact: Mr G Gutteridge

Smoked Cumberland sausage

Cumberland sausage made with pork and smoked over oak, in 3lb packs of twelve.
[C] Undisclosed
[W] Laurel Farm, Hull
[D] By wholesaler, by own transport within area
See Also: Meat: Pies and Prepared Dishes

15

Dorset Farms
Manor Farm, Little Windsor, Beaminster, Dorset DT8 3QU
Tel: 0308 68822
Contact: Mr H Birch

Cumberland sausage

Additive free sausages in natural casings including, low fat, gluten free pork, coarse cut, in various sizes, loose, or in ½, 1lb packs.
[C] 40-50 ton p.a
[D] By own transport within area
See Also: Fresh Meat, Bacon and Hams, Game Dealers

6 ↔

The Dutch Butcher
4 Park Avenue, Whitley Bay, Tyne & Wear
Tel: 091 252 2047
Contact: Peter and Shirley Van Der Laan

Northumberland leek sausage

Range of twelve sausages including Northumberland leek.
[C] Undisclosed
[D] By own transport within area
See Also: Meat: Pies and Prepared Dishes

3 ↔

Ewing's
83 Main Street, Baillieston, Glasgow G69 6AD
Tel: 041 773 0274
Contact: Mr J Ewing

Lorne sausage

A range of sausages and puddings including Lorne sausage, square slicing sausage with either 70 or 75% beef, rusk, water and seasonings, Scottish black pudding, haggis made with fresh meat, onions, oatmeal and seasonings in 1lb sizes or to order. Also fruit puddings.
[C] Undisclosed
[D] By own transport within area
See Also: Fresh Meat, Meat: Pies and Prepared Dishes

7

Farmhouse Country Delicacies
The Homestead Farm, Pott Shrigley, Macclesfield, Cheshire SK10 5RU
Tel: 0625 72381
Contact: Joyce Dalton

Manchester sausage

Range of additive free sausages, including tomato, Cumberland ring, Gloucestershire herb, Manchester seasoned with clove, pepper, mace, nutmeg, ginger, sage and coriander, pork and onion, pork and apple, oriental barbecue and tandoori.
[C] Undisclosed
[D] By arrangement
See Also: Fresh Meat, Bacon and Hams, Cheese

6

Fellside Foods Ltd
Shap, Penrith, Cumbria CA10 3PW
Tel: 09316 561
Contact: Mr A M Barraclough

Low fat pork sausage

Sausages produced on large scale including pork, pork and beef, low fat pork with high fibre bran content. All in synthetic casings. deep frozen in 1kg packs.
[C] Undisclosed
[D] By arrangement

11

Geo Adams & Sons Ltd
25-26 The Crescent, Spalding, Lincolnshire PE11 1AG
Tel: 0775 66161 Telx: 32858 Fax: 0775 710717
Contact: Mr N Broadhead

Lincolnshire sausage

Lincolnshire pork sausage made to original recipe, coarsely cut, seasoned with fresh sage and filled in natural casings. Also pork, beef, lean pork in 400g packs.
[C] Undisclosed
[D] By arrangement
See Also: Bacon and Hams, Meat: Pies and Prepared Dishes

8

S C & J H Gibson
Hopetown House, Burneston, Bedale, North Yorkshire DL8 2JN
Tel: 0845 567252
Contact: Mr S C Gibson

Lincolnshire sausage

Rough textured Lincolnshire sausage made to old family recipe with minimum 70% lean meat, filled in natural casings. Also available hamburger and black pudding.
[C] ½ ton p.wk
[D] By own transport within area
See Also: Fresh Meat

16

Gilberts Kosher Meat Technology Ltd
880 High Road, North Finchley, London N12
Tel: 01 445 2224
Contact: David Gilbert

Kosher beefburger

Kosher sausages and beefburgers.
[C] Undisclosed
[D] By own transport nationally
See Also: Meat: Smoked

1 ↔

J M Gordon
Mayfield Development, High Street, Dingwall, Ross & Cromarty
Tel: 0349 63105
Contact: David Gordon

Black pudding

Pork and beef sausages made to traditional recipes. Also black and white puddings and steak pies.
[C] Undisclosed
[D] By arrangement

9

Gorno's Charcuterie
30 Tudor Street, Riverside, Cardiff, South Glamorgan
Tel: 0222 372782
Contact: Mr Franco Gorno

Cotechino di Bologna

Range of additive free sausages and salamis including chorizos, Lombardy rosette, Mexican chilli, merguez, pepperoni, cotechino di Bologna. Also rillette de canard available.
[C] Undisclosed
[D] By arrangement
See Also: Meat: Bacon and Hams

7 ↔

Grant's Butchers
Cumberland Avenue, Clevelys, Blackpool FY5 2DU
Tel: 0253 853578
Contact: Mr D Abrahams

High fibre sausage

Range of sausages including pork, Cumberland, garlic, all with 80% meat, high fibre with 95% meat. All filled in natural casings.
[C] 400lb p.wk
[D] By arrangement

11

Gregory's
1a Granville Street, Market Harborough, Leicestershire LE16 9PB
Tel: 0858 62420
Contact: Mr A Bott

Continental sausage

Range of low fat sausages filled in natural casings including traditional beef, pork, pork and beef, continental with red and green peppers, fresh garlic, Lincolnshire with 85% meat, venison in season.
[C] 1000lb p.wk
[D] By own transport within area

12 ● ↔

Hardwick Estate
Path Hill Farm, Whitchurch, nr Reading, Oxfordshire RG8 7RE
Tel: 07357 2955
Contact: Sir Julian Rose Bt

Organic sausage

Organic meat sausages, pork, pork and beef flavoured with spices and sea-salt, vacuum packed in 1lb packs.
[C] Undisclosed
[D] By arrangement
See Also: Fresh Meat, Cream

6

R J Harrison
82 Main Street, Cockermouth, Cumbria CA13 OYR
Tel: 0900 823164
Contact: Tony Harrison

Cumberland sausage

Additive free Cumberland sausage made from old fashioned recipe, thick, coarse cut, with 98% meat, with thick or thin natural casing. Also brawn and hamburgers.
[C] 1 ton p.wk
[D] By Datapost, by own transport within area

15

Heal Farm
Kings Nympton, Umberleigh, Devon EX37 9TB
Tel: 07695 2077
Contact: Anne Petch

Tomato and chilli sausage

Range of sausages, with or without rusk, including tomato and chilli, pork with garlic, venison with bacon and garlic, Milano salami, chorizo, Landjaegar and cervelat continental sausages. Also available flavoured beefburgers.
[C] 1350lb p.wk
[D] By own transport within area, British Rail
See Also: Fresh Meat, Bacon and Hams, Meat: Pâtés and Pastes, Meat: Pies and Prepared Dishes, Meat: Smoked, Game Farmers, Hampers

15

F Heard Quality Meats
33 Nelson Road, Westward Ho, Bideford, Devon EX39 1LQ
Tel: 02372 74039
Contact: F Heard

Cider sausage

Additive free pork sausages, made from 70% meat, filled in natural casings including Lincolnshire, Cumberland, savoury cider made with sage, pork and Inch's cider, tomato made with tomato purée, and garlic. Also sausage rolls.
[C] ½ ton p.wk
[D] By arrangement

6

Henry Newbould Ltd
2 Startforth Road, Riverside Park, Middlesbrough, Cleveland TS2 1PT
Tel: 0642 225411
Contact: Mr M H Newbould

Bratwurst

Range of sausages made to own traditional recipes including continental, either raw, cooked or smoked, pork, beef, pork and beef and Bratwurst.
[C] 3000lb p.dy
[D] By own transport within area
See Also: Meat: Pâtés and Pastes, Meat: Pies and Prepared Dishes, Meat: Smoked

12 ↔

Hilliers Cotswold
Newmarket, Nailsworth, Stroud, Gloucestershire GL6 0RG
Tel: 045383 2691
Contact: Mr D C Hedges

Cotswold sausage

Range of sausages in natural casings including low fat pork, gluten free, Cotswold with 85% meat, and beef with 55% meat.
[C] 100 ton p.wk
[D] By arrangement
See Also: Bacon and Hams, Meat: Pies and Prepared Dishes

16 ↔

Hockeys - Naturally
Newtown Farm, South Gorley, Fordingbridge, Hampshire ST6 2PW
Tel: 0425 52542
Contact: Phillip Hockeys

Lamb and mint sausage

Additive free sausages with 100% meat and collagen casings for allergy sufferers, including lamb with mint, pork with herbs, beef, venison, and veal with herbs. All in 1lb packs.
[C] Undisclosed
[D] By own transport nationally
See Also: Fresh Meat, Game Dealers

9

K W Hutchings
124 Crwys Road, Cathays, Cardiff CF2 4NR
Tel: 0222 228383
Contact: Mr K Hutchings

Pork and hickory sausage

Range of sausages in natural casings with 75-80% meat including gluten free, additive free, Welsh pork and leek, barbecue, pork and hickory, lamb and mint, low fat beef. Also available smoked or pickled lamb, polony and stir fry prepared dishes.
[C] 500lb p.wk
[D] By own transport within area

3

James McIntyre
74 Montague Street, Rothesay, Isle of Bute PA20 OHL
Tel: 0700 3672
Contact: Mr J McIntyre

Haggis

Haggis made to traditional recipe, with oatmeal and seasoned with white pepper and nutmeg, filled in natural casings. Also available range of beef and pork sausages including Scottish slicing sausage.

Ⓒ Haggis 5 cwt p.wk, sausages 10 cwt p.wk
Ⓓ Haggis by Red Star, by own transport within area
See Also: Fresh Meat, Bacon and Hams, Game Dealers

3

James Reid (Birkhill) Ltd
Rowanbank, 140 Coupar Angus Road, Birkhill, Dundee DD2 5PG
Tel: 0382 580251
Contact: James C C Reid

Haggis

Sausages, black and white pudding and haggis in natural or plastic casings made to traditional recipes. All packed to customers requirements.
Ⓒ Undisclosed
Ⓓ By own transport, by arrangement

1

John M Munro Ltd
12 High Street, Conon Bridge, Dingwall, Ross & Cromarty
Tel: 0349 61398
Contact: R M Munro

Haggis

Prime local Scotch beef, lamb and pork prepared as traditional sausages, puddings and haggis. All packed to customers requirements.
Ⓒ 1000lb of each p.wk
Ⓓ By arrangement
See Also: Fresh Meat

11

F A & J Jones & Sons
Red House Farm, North Scarle, Lincoln LN6 9HB
Tel: 052 277224
Contact: Mrs Jean Jones

Lincolnshire sausage

Additive free traditional Lincolnshire pork sausage with sage, filled in natural casings, in 10lb packs. Also sausage rolls and pâtés.
Ⓒ Undisclosed
Ⓓ By arrangement
See Also: Fresh Meat, Meat: Pies and Prepared Dishes, Poultry Producers

5 ↔

J Kerr Little, Master Butcher
58-60 High Street, Dumfriesshire DG1 2BS
Tel: 0387 53818
Contact: Mr J Kerr Little

Cabanos

Range of nine continental sausages including chorizos, cabanos and bratwurst.
Ⓒ Undisclosed
Ⓓ By arrangement
See Also: Fresh Meat, Bacon and Hams

6

Kitty House Farm
Troutbeck, Cumbria
Tel: 08533 599
Contact: Mr Geisselmann

Cumberland black pudding

Additive free traditional Cumberland sausage with 95% meat and fresh herbs. Also traditional Cumberland black pudding made with fat, barley and fresh pig's blood and with no skin, baked in trays in the oven. Also available white pudding and haggis.
Ⓒ Sausages 200-300lb p.wk, puddings 20-25lb p.wk
Ⓓ By own transport within area

15 ↔

La Charcuterie of Dorset
Railway Triangle Estate, Poundbury Road, Dorchester, Dorset DT1 2PJ
Tel: 0903 66900
Contact: H J Cocklin

Veal sausage

Range of additive free sausages including veal, lamb and venison. Also pastrami in 1kg packs.
Ⓒ Undisclosed
Ⓦ Quantock Foods Ltd 0903 251100
Ⓓ By wholesaler
See Also: Meat: Pâtés and Pastes, Game: Pâtés and Pastes, Fish: Pâtés and Pastes

10

A W Lashford & Son
18 St John's Way, Knowle, Solihull, West Midlands
Tel: 05645 5808
Contact: Mr J Lashford

Beef and horseradish sausage

Range of sausages filled in natural casings, including Gloucester, Cumberland, tomato, beef, beef with horseradish, gluten free, Hereford with cider, and special traditional smoked bacon with 30% bacon content. Also beefburgers, black puddings, ham and pies.
Ⓒ 4500-5500lb p.wk
Ⓓ By own transport within area

16 ↔

C Lidgate Ltd
110 Holland Park Avenue, London W11 4VA
Tel: 01 727 8243
Contact: Mr Lidgate

Sausage
Haggis

Range of sausages, some based on one hundred and thirty year old recipes, supplied loose or packed to customers order. Also haggis made from ancient ancestral Scottish recipe, pâtés, pastes, pies, cured and cooked meats.
Ⓒ Undisclosed
Ⓓ By own transport within area
See Also: Fresh Meat

12

J Lindsey & Son
47 The Covered Market, Oxford, Oxfordshire OX1 3DX
Tel: 0865 242933
Contact: Mr M Feller

Sage sausage

Additive free traditional sausage made to 1860 recipe, with 80% pork and a high proportion of sage, filled in natural casings.
Ⓒ Undisclosed
Ⓓ By arrangement
See Also: Fresh Meat, Game Dealers

3 ↔

Macsweens of Edinburgh
130 Bruntsfield Place, Edinburgh EH10 4ES
Tel: 031 229 1216
Contact: Mr John A Macsween

Vegetarian haggis

Additive free haggis in natural skins, seasoned to own recipe with locally milled oatmeal, in 1-18lb sizes. Also traditional black pudding in natural casing supplied as

13oz rings, 3-3½lb sticks and vegetarian haggis in 1, 1½lb sizes.
Ⓒ Undisclosed
Ⓓ By arrangement

5
Meikle Knox Farm Shop
Meikle Knox, Castle Douglas, Dumfries & Galloway DG7Y 1NS
Tel: 0556 2736
Contact: Mr C Irving

Cumberland sausage
Cumberland sausage made with 70% meat and German spices.
Ⓒ Undisclosed
Ⓓ By own transport within area
See Also: Meat: Pies and Prepared Dishes

7
Morris's Gold Medal Black Pudding
120 Market Street, Farnworth, Bolton, Lancashire
Tel: 0204 71763
Contact: Mr J Morris

Black pudding
Additive free black pudding made to old family recipe with herbs and seasoning, filled in natural casings, in individual horseshoe shape 5-6oz puddings.
Ⓒ 2 ton p.wk
Ⓓ By arrangement

14
The Musk's Delicatessen (Greenstage) Ltd
The Rookery, Newmarket, Cambridgeshire CB8 8EQ
Tel: 0638 661824
Contact: Mrs H J Waddilove

Newmarket sausage
Musk's Newmarket Sausages made for over one hundred years from the entire pig with 80-85% pork, bread and spices and filled in natural casings. Also available chipolatas and sausage meat.
Ⓒ 1 ton p.wk
Ⓓ By arrangement
See Also: Meat: Pies and Prepared Dishes

9
R K Palfrey & Sons
36a Church Road, Newport, Gwent NP9 7EL
Tel: 0633 59385
Contact: Mr G Palfrey

Pork and beef
Range of sausages including traditional pork with 65-70% meat, pork and beef, pork and herbs, additive free low fat sausage, pork chipolatas, Cumberland, smoked and plain bratwurst.
Ⓒ Sausages 1000lb p.wk
Ⓓ By arrangement
See Also: Bacon and Hams, Poultry Producers

11
Parrs
Lilac Grove, Beeston, Nottingham, Nottinghamshire NG9 1PJ
Tel: 0602 258261
Contact: Mr D Stevenson

Tomato sausage
Pork, pork and beef, and tomato sausages made to traditional recipes.
Ⓒ 150 ton p.wk
Ⓓ By own transport nationally
See Also: Meat: Pies and Prepared Dishes

11
Pickerings
30 The Street, Old Costessey, Norwich, Norfolk
Tel: 0603 742002
Contact: Mr Bryan Pickering

Cervelat
Range of twenty sausages including Norfolk, pork with apple, pork with brandy, bratwurst, West Highland beef, Northumberland game and cervelat. Also range of pâteś including pork with walnut.
Ⓒ Undisclosed
Ⓓ By arrangement
See Also: Bacon and Hams

15
The Pure Meat Company
1 The Square, Moretonhampstead, Devon
Tel: 0647 40944
Contact: Mr J Blackburn

Beef sausage
Range of sausages including spiced beef, bacon and pork.
Ⓒ Undisclosed
Ⓓ By arrangement
See Also: Fresh Meat

12
Real Meat Company Ltd
East Hill Farm, Heytesbury, Warminster, Wiltshire BA12 0HR
Tel: 0985 40436/40060
Contact: Mr Richard Guy

Sausage
Range of additive free sausages filled in natural casings.
Ⓒ 500lb p.wk
Ⓓ By arrangement
See Also: Fresh Meat, Bacon and Hams, Meat: Pies and Prepared Dishes, Poultry Producers

16
Regale Foods Ltd
33 Hythe Road, London W10 6RS
Tel: 01 969 8320
Contact: Mr T D Fenner

Cumberland sausage
Cumberland type sausage with 80% meat in several sizes.
Ⓒ ¾ ton p.wk
Ⓓ By own transport within area
See Also: Bacon and Hams, Meat: Smoked, Game: Pâtés and Pastes, Juices

6 ↔
Richard Woodall
Lane End, Waberthwaite, nr Millom, Cumbria LA19 5YJ
Tel: 06577 237/386
Contact: Mr Richard Woodall

Cumberland sausage
Additive free Cumberland sausage made from 100% meat, herbs and spices.
Ⓒ Undisclosed
Ⓓ By arrangement
See Also: Bacon and Hams

16

Richardson Butchers
88 Northfield Avenue, London W13 9RR
Tel: 01 567 1064
Contact: Mr M Richardson

Chipolatas

Range of traditional English sausages filled in natural casings including Cumberland, pork with 75% meat, pork chipolata, beef, beef chipolata, pork and beef, turkey. Also available additive free English and German slicing sausages, cured brisket, liver sausage.
C Sausages ¾ ton p.wk
D By own transport within area

15 ↔

Riverford Farm Foods
Riverford farm, Staverton, Totnes, Devon TQ9 6AF
Tel: 080 426423
Contact: Ben Watson

French country sausage

Range of sausages including traditional pork made with 85% meat, rusk and seasoning, low fat chipolata, herb and pepper, sage, parsley and black pepper, lamb, bacon and garlic, French country with 100% meat, smoked Spanish style sausage with paprika, and Toulouse style sausage with garlic and wine. All in 1lb or catering packs.
C 1000lb p.wk
D By arrangement
See Also: Fresh Meat, Bacon and Hams, Meat: Smoked

9

Roberts of Port Dinorwic
Griffiths Crossing Industrial Estate, Caernarfon, Gwynedd LL55 1TS
Tel: 0286 76111
Contact: Mr Roberts

Pork and Herb

Range of sausages with minimum meat content of 65% including pork, pork and herb, pork and beef in 6lb catering packs.
C Undisclosed
D By arrangement
See Also: Bacon and Hams, Meat: Pies and Prepared Dishes, Hampers

12 ↔

Rose Cottage Produce
Rose Cottage, Nottwood Lane, Stoke Row, Oxfordshire
Tel: 0491 681729
Contact: Mrs K Fotherby

Herb sausage

Sausages made with fresh herbs and breadcrumbs supplied frozen in 1lb packs or loose.
C Undisclosed
D By arrangement
See Also: Fresh Meat, Fresh Vegetables

4

Schimmel Salami Co. (Ireland) Ltd
Unit 1, Gortrush Industrial Estate, Derry Road, Omagh, Co Tyrone
Tel: 0662 49333
Contact: Lawrence Schimmel

Salami

Salamis, German style cooked meats, continental style sausages and pâtés available.
C Undisclosed
D .By arrangement

8

G Scott of York
81 Low Petergate, York, Yorkshire
Tel: 0904 622972
Contact: Mr W Bailey

Cumberland sausage

Range of sausages filled in natural casings including pork with sage, Cumberland with 95% meat and a sausage with 5% eggs and seasoning. Puddings also available.
C 1 ton p.wk
D By own transport within area, Red Star rail
See Also: Bacon and Hams, Meat: Pies and Prepared Dishes

6 ↔

M F & D J Slack
Newlands Farm, Raisbeck, Orton, Penrith, Cumbria CA10 3SG
Tel: 05874 446/667
Contact: Michael Slack

Honey roast sausage

Cumberland sausage with 80% meat and herbs, made from one hundred and fifty year old recipe. Also available thin linked Cumberland and honey roast sausages.
C 600-700lb p.wk
D By arrangement
See Also: Bacon and Hams

16

Slater & Cooke
65-69 Brewer Street, London W1R 3FB
Tel: 01 437 2026/7
Contact: Mr M Contini

Britannia sausage

Range of handmade, additive free, own recipe sausages, filled in natural casings including pork with herbs, Toulouse with garlic and spices, Britannia with pork, veal, beef and spices, Algerian merguez with lamb, paprika, chilli, Park Lane with pork and spices, barbecue pork with tomatoes. Also available haggis and hamburgers.
C 800lb p.wk
D By own transport within area
See Also: Game Dealers

14

Susan Moore - Dairy Products
Cranes Watering Farm, Starston, Harleston, Norfolk IP20 9NE
Tel: 0379 852387
Contact: Susan Moore

Sausage

Additive free sausages made to traditional recipe, frozen in 1lb packs or to customers requirements.
C Undisclosed
D By arrangement
See Also: Fresh Meat, Cheese, Ice Creams and Sorbets

12 ◯

Swaddles Green Farm
Swaddles Green Farm, Hare Lane, Buckland St Mary, Chard, Somerset TA20 3JR
Tel: 046034 387
Contact: Charlotte Reynolds

Garlic sausage

Handmade, low fat sausages in a variety of flavours including garlic, herb, tomato and chilli, and red wine in 1lb packs.
C Undisclosed
D By arrangement
See Also: Fresh Meat, Bacon and Hams, Meat: Pies and Puddings, Poultry Producers

[11]

E J Swepstone & Son
Saracen's Head, Holbeach, Spalding, Lincolnshire PE12 8AY
Tel: 0406 23128/25465
Contact: Mr J Swepstone

Harrogate sausage

Range of sausages including Harrogate, Lincolnshire with sage and 72% meat, beef made to old traditional recipe. All loose or packed to customers requirements. Hamburgers also available.
[C] 1½ ton p.wk
[D] By own transport within area
See Also: Meat: Pies and Prepared Dishes

[7]

Thornley & Son Ltd
Ridgewood Farm, Flag Lane, Heath Charnock, Chorley, Lancashire PR6 9ED
Tel: 02572 71251
Contact: C.D Hewitt

Black pudding

Additive free black pudding. Also low fat sausages with 100% meat, packed loose or to customers requirements.
[C] Undisclosed
[D] By arrangement
See Also: Fresh Meat

[1]

A Urquhart & Sons
Main Street, Lairg, Sutherland
Tel: 0549 2475
Contact: Mr I E MacDonald

Black pudding

Additive free black pudding prepared with all fresh ingredients in ¾lb links and 3lb rolls. Also available haggis in 1lb packs.
[C] Black pudding 30-40lb p.wk, haggis 4 doz p.wk
[D] By arrangement

[14]

A Waller & Son
15 Victoria Avenue, Cambridge, Cambridgeshire CB4 1EG
Tel: 0223 350972
Contact: Mr P Welton

Royale Cambridge

Range of sausages filled in natural casings, including Royale Cambridge made to an old recipe with 75% pork and herbs, Cumberland with egg. Haggis made with fresh ingredients also available.
[C] 500lb p.wk, haggis mainly Jan
[D] By own transport within area
See Also: Bacon and Hams, Game Dealers

[1]

Walter McDonald Ltd
Great North Road, Muir of Ord, Ross-shire IV6 7TP
Tel: 0463 870238
Contact: Mr W L Barras

Red puddings

Haggis made to a fifty year old recipe. Also available black, white and red puddings made with fresh blood and onions. Also sausages and pies.
[C] Haggis ½ ton p.wk, sausages 1 ton p.wk, pies 800 p.wk
[D] By arrangement
See Also: Fresh Meat

[9]

Welsh Lamb Products
Unit 1, Felin Fach, Lampeter, Dyfed SA44 4RG
Tel: 0570 470729
Contact: Mrs Mary Davies

Lamburger

Lamburgers made to original recipe from quality Welsh lamb weighing 4oz each. Supplied frozen in boxes of twenty four.
[C] 7000 p.wk
[D] By arrangement
See Also: Fresh Meat, Meat: Pies and Prepared Dishes

[4] ◯

H A Young & Family
Kite's Nest Farm, Broadway, Hereford & Worcester WR12 7JT
Tel: 0386 853320
Contact: Richard Young

Organic sausage

Organic sausages made with lean, home raised beef, wholemeal bread, cut lump salt, pepper and mixed herbs, fresh or frozen. Also frozen hamburgers with 100% pure mixed beef and a fat content of less than 20%.
[C] Sausages 200lb p.wk, hamburgers 450lb p.wk
[D] By arrangement
See Also: Fresh Meat

SMOKED

6 ↔

Ashdown Smokers
Skellerah Farm, Corney, nr Nootle, Cumberland LA19 5TW
Tel: 06578 324
Contact: E H Fellows

Herdwick Macon

Range of smoked meats including Herdwick Macon ham from local hill sheep, dry cured with aromatics and slowly smoked over oak and juniper. Also available smoked Aberdeen Angus fillet, sirloin of beef and loin of pork whole, boned out or sliced.
[C] Undisclosed
[D] By arrangement
See Also: Game Dealers, Fish Dealers, Cheese

9 ↔

Cenarth Smokery
Cernarth Smokeries, Newcastle Emlyn, Dyfed
Tel: 023987 579
Contact: Jane Kelsey

Pork fillet

Range of meats smoked in a traditional chimney over oak chippings including beef topside in 2lb pieces and whole pork fillets weighing 7lb.
[C] Undisclosed
[D] By arrangement
See Also: Fish: Smoked

15 ↔

Devon Oak Smoked Foods Ltd
Unit 5, Townstal Trading Estate, Nelson Road, Dartmouth, Devon TQ6 9LA
Tel: 08043 4410
Contact: Mr A Watts

Smoked sausages

Range of smoked meats including ham, English pork sausages, chicken and turkey breasts and poussin. Any other meat smoked to customers orders.
[C] Undisclosed
[D] By arrangement
See Also: Fish: Smoked, Cheese

16

Fjordling Smokehouses
Heathlands Country Market, Honey Hill, Wokingham, Berkshire RG11 3PG
Tel: 0734 776688
Contact: Andrew Espir

Kasseler

Range of oak smoked meats including smoked beef fillet, kasseler, a boned smoked loin of pork and lightly spiced pork sausages. Beef in 1lb, kasseler in 1½lb packs and sausages in packs of eight.
[C] Undisclosed
[D] By arrangement
See Also: Game: Smoked, Fish: Smoked

16

Gilberts Kosher Meat Technology Ltd
880 High Road, North Finchley, London N12
Tel: 01 445 2224
Contact: David Gilbert

Kosher

Smoked meats prepared under kosher supervision, in 7-10lb blocks.
[C] Undisclosed
[D] By arrangement
See Also: Meat: Sausages and Puddings

15

Heal Farm
Kings Nympton, Umberleigh, Devon EX37 9TB
Tel: 07695 2077
Contact: Anne Petch

Smoked tenderloin

Smoked pork tenderloins. Also available smoked lamb
[C] Undisclosed
[D] By own transport within area, by British Rail
See Also: Fresh Meat, Bacon and Hams, Meat: Pâtés and Pastes, Meat: Pies and Prepared Dishes, Meat: Sausages and Puddings, Game Farmers, Hampers

6

Henry Newbould Ltd
2 Startforth Road, Riverside Park, Middlesbrough, Cleveland TS2 1PT
Tel: 0642 225411
Contact: Mr M H Newbould

Smoked pork rings

Range of sausages and cooked meats smoked over beech or oak chips including saveloys and pork rings.
[C] Undisclosed
[W] Freshfayre 0642 52739
[D] By wholesaler, by own transport within area
See Also: Meat: Pâtés and Pastes, Meat: Pies and Prepared Dishes, Meat: Sausages and Puddings

6

Johnny Cooke-Hurle
Startforth Hall, Barnard Castle, Co Durham D12 9RA
Tel: 0833 38370
Contact: Johnny Cooke-Hurle

Smoked leg of lamb

Smoked leg of lamb supplied as whole joints.
[C] Undisclosed
[D] By arrangement
See Also: Game Dealers

16 ↔

Kelmans Kosher Cooked Meat Products
85 Monier Road, Hackney, London E3 2PS
Tel: 01 904 7625 Telx: 8956552 KWISSA G
Contact: Lionel Kelman

Pastrami

Kosher smoked beef and pastrami, in 6oz vacuum packs and 5-6lb blocks. Also available hamburgers, sausages and haggis.
[C] Undisclosed
[D] By own transport within area

16 ↔

Kingsgate Farm Delicatessen
Kingsgate Farm, Wittersham, Kent TN30 7NS
Tel: 07977 626
Contact: Mr Luethi

Sirloin of beef

Range of meats including cold smoked sirloin of beef, cured in salt and spices and air-dried for fourteen days, in 4-5lb pieces or sliced to customers requirements. Also

available cold smoked pork tenderloin, cured in salt, herbs and paprika, in 4lb pieces or in 2½oz slices, rolled smoked ham as whole legs weighing 11-12lb, 2½lb cuts or sliced and smoked sausages.
C Undisclosed
D By Datapost

12 ↔ **Minola Smoked Products**
Kencot Hill Farmhouse, Filkins, Lechlade, Gloucestershire GL7 3QY
Tel: 036 786 391/556 Fax: 036 786 544
Contact: Hugh Forestier-Walker

Bacon

Grass fed Lambourne pigs smoked over whole oak logs as ham, bacon or gammon. Also smoked lamb, marinaded in strong ale, raw sugar and herbs, sliced in 8oz-1lb vacuum packs.
C Bacon 20 sides p.wk, gammon 30 sides p.wk, lamb 20-30 sides p.wk
D By arrangement
See Also: Game: Smoked, Fish Dealers, Cheese

14 **Poachers Pies Ltd**
5 Marston Road, St Neots, Cambridgeshire PE19 2HB
Tel: 0480 407777 Fax: 0480 407788
Contact: Martin Phillips

Loin of pork

Variety of smoked meats including loin of pork, spiced pork sausages. Also available breast of turkey and English chicken.
C Undisclosed
D By own transport within area
See Also: Bacon and Hams, Meat: Pies and Prepared Dishes, Game: Pâtés and Pastes

16 **Regale Foods Ltd**
33 Hythe Road, London W10 6RS
Tel: 01 969 8320
Contact: Mr T D Fenner

Peppered ham

Range of smoked meats including peppered or plain hams, duck, goose, breast or whole turkey, quail, and chicken drumsticks.
C Undisclosed
D By own transport within area
See Also: Bacon and Hams, Meat: Sausages and Puddings, Game: Pâtés and Pastes

14 **River Farm Smokery**
Great Wilbraham Road, Bottisham, nr Newmarket, Cambridgeshire CB1 5J
Tel: 0223 811382
Contact: R F Enoch

Smoked tongue

Easy to slice smoked ham with hock, pastrami and smoked tongue.
C Undisclosed
D By arrangement
See Also: Game: Smoked, Fish Dealers, Snacks and Savouries

15 ↔ **Riverford Farm Foods**
Riverford farm, Staverton, Totnes, Devon TQ9 6AF
Tel: 080 426423
Contact: Ben Watson

Lamb

Smoked lamb prepared to a traditional recipe, rubbed with salt and sugar for two days, cured in aromatic brine with bay leaves and juniper berries for ten days, hung for two days and finally smoked for ten days. Supplied in ¼lb vacuum packed slices.
C 10 legs p.wk
D By arrangement
See Also: Fresh Meat, Bacon and Hams, Meat: Sausages and Puddings

1· ↔ **The Shetland Smokehouse**
Skeld Industrial Estate, Skeld, Shetland ZE2 9NL
Tel: 0595 86 251 Telx: 937400 Onecom G
Fax: 0595 86 203
Contact: Mr David Hammond

Lamb

Shetland lamb and mutton smoked with herbs and spices to old Scottish recipe, in rolled boned fillets.
C 300kg p.wk
D By arrangement
See Also: Fish: Smoked

14 **Suffolk Larder Foods**
9a Charles Industrial Estate, Stowmarket, Suffolk
Tel: 0449 676162
Contact: Tony Constantine Smith

Spiced lamb

Hot smoked boned loin of pork, stuffed with gherkins, supplied in 2-4lb packs. Also hot smoked Suffolk spiced lamb, cured in brine with herbs, rubbed with paprika and treacle and boned.
C Lamb 100 p.wk, pork 30 p.wk
D By arrangement
See Also: Bacon and Hams, Game Dealers

GAME AND POULTRY

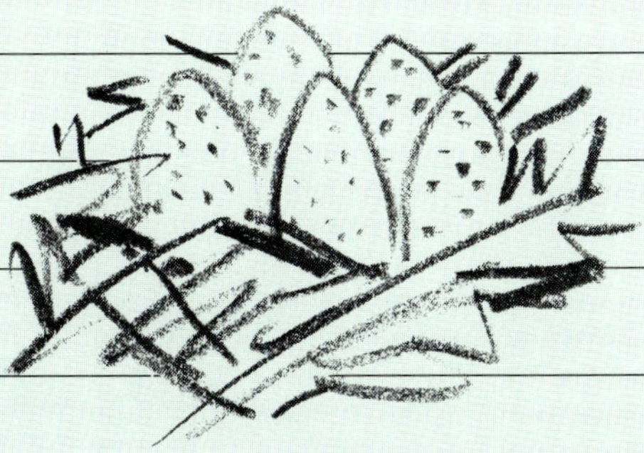

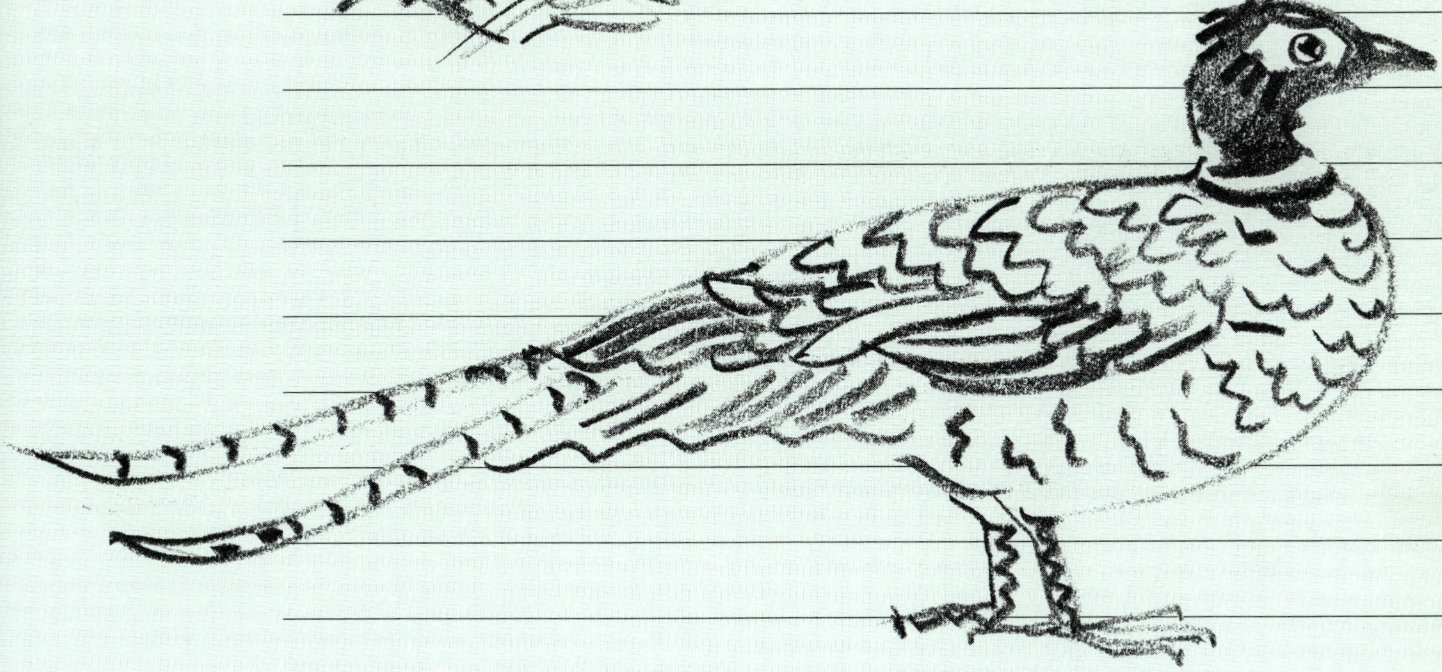

GAME DEALERS

14

Pigeon

Ark Foods Ltd
Hemingford House, Walcot Road, Diss, Norfolk
Tel: 0379 870717
Contact: Mr D A Cairns

Pheasant, pigeon, guinea-fowl and Mallard duck
D By arrangement
See Also: Game Farmers

6 ↔

Hare

Ashdown Smokers
Skellerah Farm, Corney, nr Nootle, Cumberland LA19 5TW
Tel: 06578 324
Contact: E H Fellows

Grouse, hare, partridge, quail, venison, wild duck, fresh and frozen.
D By arrangement
See Also: Meat: Smoked, Game: Smoked, Fish Dealers, Cheese

3

Partridge

Band's of Perth
135 Glover Street, Perth, Perthshire PH2 0JB
Tel: 0738 24222 Telx: 76279 Fax: 0738 21892
Contact: Mr R H Critchell

Fresh, chilled and frozen pheasant, partridge, grouse, venison, rabbit and wild duck.
D By own transport within area
See Also: Fish Dealers

16 ↔

Partridge

A J Barkaway
20 Ospringe Street, Faversham, Kent
Tel: 0795 532040
Contact: Mr A J Barkaway

Hare, partridge, pheasant and rabbit.
D By arrangement
See Also: Fresh Meat, Poultry Producers

16

Quail

E H Broome and Company
208 Central Markets, London EC1
Tel: 01 236 9725
Contact: D May

Guinea-fowl, grouse, partridge, pheasant, wild duck, venison and quail supplied fresh or frozen. Quail eggs also available.
D By arrangement

12 ↔

Venison

Coln Valley Fish & Game Co Ltd
Winson, Cirencester, Gloucestershire GL7 5ER
Tel: 028572 400/593/614 Telx: 437269
Contact: M Henriques

Grouse, guinea-fowl, hare, partridge, pheasant, pigeon, quail, rabbit, venison and wild duck, fresh, chilled or frozen.
D By arrangement
See Also: Game: Smoked, Fish Dealers

12

Venison

Combe Sydenham Fisheries
Combe Sydenham Country Park, Monksilver, Taunton, Somerset TA4 4JG
Tel: 0984 56284
Contact: Mr K C Y Jones

Park reared wild Fallow deer, whole or butchered, fresh or frozen.
D By arrangement
See Also: Fish Farmers

6

Teal

Cornvale Foods Ltd
Boxtree Farm, Barbon, Kirkby Lonsdale, Cumbria LA6 2LE
Tel: 0468 36386
Contact: Peter Dodd

Wild duck, hare, grouse, partridge, teal, pheasant, venison, wild rabbit, all supplied freshly prepared.
D By arrangement
See Also: Poultry Producers

1

Venison

Crawford Farm Enterprises Ltd
Cluanie, By Beauly, Inverness IV4 7AE
Tel: 0463 782534
Contact: Archie Crawford

Scottish venison. Also lamb and beef.
D By arrangement
See Also: Game: Sausages and Puddings

7

Hare

Danebridge Fisheries
Pingle Cottage, Wincle, nr Macclesfield, Cheshire SK11 0QE
Tel: 02607 293
Contact: D Chadwick

Grouse, hare, partridge, pheasant, rabbit and venison.
D By arrangement
See Also: Fish Farmers

11

Hare

Daniel Garrett (Gamedealer)
14 Sutton Street, Flore, Northamptonshire NN7 4LE
Tel: 0327 40672
Contact: Daniel Garrett

Grouse, hare, partridge, pheasant, venison and wild duck.
D By arrangement

8

Grouse

Derek Fox
25 Market Place, Malton, North Yorkshire
Tel: 0653 2528
Contact: Mr D Fox

Grouse, hare, partridge, pheasant, venison and wild duck. Also available quail, woodcock, rabbit and guinea-fowl. Also available free-range farmed quail and guinea-fowl eggs.
D By arrangement
See Also: Game Farmers, Game: Pies and Prepared Dishes

15 **Dorset Farms Ltd**
Manor Farm, Little Windsor, Beaminster, Dorset DT8 3QU
Tel: 0308 68822
Contact: Mr H Birch

Woodcock — Hare, partridge, pheasant, venison (Roe deer), snipe, wild duck (Mallard and Teal) and woodcock.
D By own transport within area
See Also: Fresh Meat, Poultry Producers

1 **Duncan Fraser (Game Dealer) Ltd**
17 Queensgate, Inverness IVI 1DF
Tel: 0463 232744
Contact: Mr Duncan Fraser

Grouse — Grouse, hare, partridge, pheasant, venison and wild duck.
D By arrangement
See Also: Fish: Smoked

15 **K W Durrant Family Butchers**
Main Street, Chillington, nr Kingsbridge, Devon TQ7 2JX
Tel: 0548 580217
Contact: Mr K Durrant

Hare — Grouse, hare, partridge and pheasant.
D By arrangement
See Also: Fresh Meat, Eggs

7 **Fayre Game Ltd**
Lodge Lane Nurseries, Lodge Lane, Lytham, Lancashire FY8 5RP
Tel: 0253 738640 Telx: 677125 FAYRE G
Contact: Jonathan Pusey

Venison — Grouse, hare, partridge, pheasant, venison and wild duck.
D By arrangement
See Also: Game Farmers, Eggs

3 **George Campbell & Sons**
The Smokehouse, West Harbour Road, Granton, Edinburgh
Tel: 031 552 0376
Contact: Iain Campbell

Pheasant — Grouse, hare, partridge, pheasant, rabbit, snipe, wild duck (Mallard and Teal) widgeon and woodcock.
D By arrangement
See Also: Poultry Producers, Game: Smoked, Eggs, Fish Dealers

5 **Glen Game (Scotland) Ltd**
Botany Mills, Roxburgh Street, Galashiels, Selkirkshire
Tel: 0896 2242
Contact: Mr Martin Rogers

Snipe — Grouse, hare, partridge, pheasant, pigeon, quail, rabbit, snipe, venison, wild duck and woodcock.
D By arrangement
See Also: Eggs

10 ● ↔ **Gold Label Produce Ltd**
Knightley Grange Cottage, Grange Road, Woodseaves, Staffordshire ST20 OJU
Tel: 0785 74495
Contact: Mr D Dale

Rabbit — Venison and rabbit.
D By arrangement
See Also: Fresh Meat, Game Farmers, Poultry Producers

12 **Hardwick Farms**
Horsecroft, Bury St Edmunds, Suffolk IP29 5NY
Tel: 0284 754611
Contact: Mr A J Brown

Venison — Hare, partridge, pheasant, rabbit, venison (Fallow and Roe deer) and Mallard duck.
D By Datapost
See Also: Game Farmers, Poultry Producers, Game: Smoked

14 ↔ **R T Harvey Ltd**
63 Grove Road, Norwich NR1 3RL
Tel: 0603 621908
Contact: Nigel R Harvey

Grouse — Grouse, quail, rabbit, woodcock, pigeon, hare, partridge, pheasant.
D By arrangement
See Also: Poultry Producers, Game: Sausages and Puddings

16 ↔ **Hazelbrow Turkeys**
Hazelbrow Farm, Rad Lane, Peaslake, nr Guildford, Surrey GU5 9PB
Tel: 0306 730313
Contact: John Richardson

Partridge — Hare, partridge, pheasant, pigeon, rabbit and venison.
D By own transport within area
See Also: Game Farmers, Poultry Producers, Game: Smoked, Eggs

16 ↔ **Hockeys - Naturally**
Newtown Farm, South Gorley, Fordingbridge, Hampshire ST6 2PW
Tel: 0425 52542
Contact: Phillip Hockeys

Pheasant — Hare, partridge, pheasant, rabbit, venison and Mallard duck.
D By arrangement
See Also: Fresh Meat, Game: Pies and Prepared Dishes

3 **James McIntyre**
74 Montague Street, Rothesay, Isle of Bute PA20 OHL
Tel: 0700 3672
Contact: Mr J McIntyre

Venison — Grouse, hare, partridge, pheasant, rabbit, wild duck and haunches and saddles of venison. Also occasionally boar, pigeon and woodcock.
D By arrangement
See Also: Fresh Meat

6 **John Curtis**
10 Woodbourne Road, Douglas, Isle of Man
Tel: 0624 73875
Contact: John Curtis

Pheasant — Grouse, hare, partridge, pheasant and rabbit.
D By arrangement
See Also: Poultry Producers

6 **Johnny Cooke-Hurle**
Startforth Hall, Barnard Castle, Co Durham D12 9RA
Tel: 0833 38370
Contact: Johnny Cooke-Hurle

Grouse
Duck — Grouse, pheasant, partridge, wild duck, venison and hare supplied oven-ready.
D By arrangement
See Also: Meat: Smoked, Game: Smoked

16 ↔ **Kennet Valley Fisheries**
Lower Way Farm, Lower Way, Thatcham, Berkshire RG13 4TL
Tel: 0635 66699 Telx: 847860 ICELT
Contact: Martin Duggan

Partridge — Pheasant, venison, partridge, guinea-fowl, quail, hare and rabbit.
D By arrangement
See Also: Fish Farmers

12 **J Lindsey & Son**
47 The Covered Market, Oxford, Oxfordshire OX1 3DX
Tel: 0865 242933
Contact: Mr M Feller

Mallard duck — Grouse, Mallard duck, partridge, pheasant, pigeon, rabbit and woodcock.
D By arrangement
See Also: Fresh Meat, Poultry Producers, Eggs

16 **D J & M Paul**
Ivory Farmhouse, Burghclere, Newbury, Berkshire RG15 9LP
Tel: 0635 27362/27375 Telx: 849141
Contact: D J Paul

Hare — Grouse, guinea-fowl, hare, partridge, pheasant, pigeon, quail, rabbit, venison and wild duck.
D By arrangement
See Also: Eggs

14 **Peartree Pork and Poultry**
High Birch Farm, Weeley Heath, nr Clacton-on-Sea, Essex CO16 9BU
Tel: 0255 830291
Contact: Mr P Ernst

Pheasant — Grouse, hare, partridge, pheasant and venison.
D By arrangement
See Also: Fresh Meat, Poultry Producers, Game: Pies and Prepared Dishes

8 **Pepper Arden Game & Game Pies**
Pepper Arden, Northallerton, North Yorkshire
Tel: 032578 548
Contact: Mrs Cherry Gatty

Hare — Pheasant, venison, hare, rabbit and wild duck supplied fresh, frozen and oven-ready.
D By arrangement
See Also: Game: Pies and Prepared Dishes

3 ↔ **Rannoch Smokery**
Kinloch Rannoch, by Pitlochry, Perthshire PH16 5QD
Tel: 08822 344
Contact: Mr Barclay

Venison — Scottish venison.
D By arrangement
See Also: Game: Pâtés and Pastes, Game: Smoked

16 **Slater & Cooke**
65-69 Brewer Street, London W1R 3FB
Tel: 01 437 2026/7
Contact: Mr M Contini

Snipe — Grouse, hare, partridge, pheasant, pigeon, quail, snipe, venison, Mallard duck and woodcock.
D By own transport within area
See Also: Meat: Sausages and Puddings, Poultry Producers, Eggs

11 **H M Stockdale**
Hill Farm, Mears Ashby, Northampton NN6 0DX
Tel: 0604 810206
Contact: Mr and Mrs Stockdale

Hare — Hare, partridge, pheasant, pigeon, quail, rabbit, venison and wild duck.
D By arrangement
See Also: Game: Sausages and Puddings

14

Suffolk Larder Foods
9a Charles Industrial Estate, Stowmarket, Suffolk
Tel: 0449 676162
Contact: Tony Constantine Smith

Woodcock

Hare, partridge, pheasant, rabbit, venison, wild duck and woodcock.
D By arrangement
See Also: Game: Pies and Prepared Dishes, Game: Smoked

3

Taygame/Carnbo
Units 5-6, Whitefriars Street, Perth PH1 5PP
Tel: 0738 36357 Fax: 0738 29893
Contact: Ian Thomson

Pigeon

Grouse, guinea-fowl, hare, partridge, pheasant, pigeon, quail, rabbit, venison and wild duck.
D By arrangement

16

Test Valley Game Produce Ltd
North Houghton, Stockbridge, Hampshire SO20 6LF
Tel: 0264 810526
Contact: D Dent

Grouse

Grouse, guinea-fowl, hare, partridge, pheasant, pigeon, quail, venison and wild duck. Available oven-ready and prepared.
D By arrangement
See Also: Fish Farmers

14

A Waller & Son
15 Victoria Avenue, Cambridge, Cambridgeshire CB4 1EG
Tel: 0223 350972
Contact: Mr P Welton

Widgeon

Grouse, hare, partridge, pheasant, pigeon, rabbit, venison, Mallard duck and widgeon.
D By arrangement
See Also: Bacon and Hams

GAME·FARMERS

10 ↔

Abberley Home Farm Deer
West Lodge, Stanford Road, Great Wittey, Hereford & Worcester
Tel: 0299 896704
Contact: Ian and Tracy Ballard

Venison

Farm slaughtered venison, guaranteed under two years old. Available as whole and half carcasses or joints, fresh or frozen.
C 70-100 carcasses p.a Jul-May
D By arrangement

14

Ark Foods Ltd
Hemingford House, Walcot Road, Diss, Norfolk
Tel: 0379 870717
Contact: Mr D A Cairns

Guinea fowl

Norfolk reared guinea-fowl hung for two to seven days, long legged New York dressed oven-ready weighing 2¼-2½lb, supplied chilled or frozen. Also available supremes and thighs packed two per tray.
C Undisclosed
D By arrangement
See Also: Game Dealers, Poultry Producers

12 ↔

Ashford Mill Farm Shop
East End, North Leigh, Witney, Oxfordshire
Tel: 099386 8121 Telx: 265871
Contact: P Edwards-Moss

Red deer

Red deer supplied at sixteen months, fresh or frozen, whole carcasses or butchered to customers requirements.
C 100 carcasses p.a Aug-Mar
D By arrangement
See Also: Poultry Producers, Game: Pâtés and Pastes, Game: Sausages and Puddings, Eggs

3

Beecraigs Deer Farm
Beecraigs Country Park, Whitebaulks Centre, Linlithgow, Fife
Tel: 0506 844516/7/8
Contact: Mr P Sutherland

Venison

Venison from deer reared on Scottish Lowland pastures, culled at fourteen months, whole or butchered, fresh or frozen. Also available smoked venison, venison pâté and venison sausages in 1lb packs.
C Carcasses 42-52 p.a, venison sausages 400-600lb p.a Sep onwards
D By arrangement

7

British Deer Producers Society Ltd
Sandlow Green, Holmes Chapel, Cheshire
Tel: 0477 32329 Telx: 367328 AMSG Fax: 0477 37598
Contact: Mr G Lawrence

Venison

Farmed venison, guaranteed under stipulated age and dressed to standards complying with the rules of the Society.
C Available Sep-Feb
D By arrangement

15 ↔

B & D Carver
Black Ness, East Cornworthy, Totnes, Devon TQ12 2EB
Tel: 080 422363
Contact: Basil Carver

Squab

Squab, young reared pigeon supplied clean plucked in graded sizes.
C Undisclosed
D By arrangement

15 ↔

Chilton Deer Farm
Deer Cottage, Cadeleigh, Tiverton, Devon
Tel: 08845 519
Contact: Anthony Bennett

Venison

Devon venison farmed in stress free environment, culled at between fourteen to eighteen months, supplied chilled and butchered.
C Undisclosed Aug-Jan
D By Datapost

[7]

Coney Europa Ltd
Statham, Lymm, Cheshire
Tel: 092575 6737 Telx: 628749
Contact: E Sutton

Rabbit

Farm bred rabbit packed sixteen per case, fresh or frozen. Also smoked rabbit.
[C] Undisclosed
[D] By arrangement

[9]

Crymych Venison
Cefn Canol Deer Farm, Crymych, nr Cardigan, Dyfed
Tel: 023973 526
Contact: Donald Clark

Venison

Farmed prime venison, culled at under twenty months, supplied whole, jointed or butchered to customers requirements, fresh or frozen.
[C] Undisclosed
[D] By own transport within area
See Also: Game: Pies and Prepared Dishes, Game: Sausages and Puddings

[8]

Derek Fox
25 Market Place, Malton, North Yorkshire
Tel: 0653 2528
Contact: Mr D Fox

Quail

Farm reared quail and pheasant, dressed on premises, available whole or butchered, fresh, frozen or oven-ready. Chicken and pheasant liver also supplied.
[C] Undisclosed
[D] By arrangement
See Also: Game Dealers, Game: Pies and Prepared Dishes

[15]

Devon Quail
Poole Farmhouse, Thorverton, Exeter, Devon EX5 5PN
Tel: 0392 860946
Contact: Tim Brooks

Quail

Quail and rabbit available, fresh, chilled, frozen, oven-ready, butchered and dressed to customers requirements.
[C] Undisclosed
[D] By arrangement
See Also: Poultry Producers, Game: Smoked, Eggs, Hampers

[8] [↔]

Elmhirst Fletcher Deer Farmers
Heatherdale, Bark Lane, Addingham, Ilkley, West Yorkshire LS29 0RB
Tel: 0943 830414
Contact: C P Fletcher

Venison

Red deer from Yorkshire Dales, culled just under three years, whole and butchered in variety of cuts, fresh or frozen.
[C] 6 p.wk
[D] By arrangement

[7]

Fayre Game Ltd
Lodge Lane Nurseries, Lodge Lane, Lytham, Lancashire FY8 5RP
Tel: 0253 738640 Telx: 677125 FAYRE G
Contact: Jonathan Pusey

Quail

Quail, whole or boned, supplied fresh, chilled or frozen. Also smoked quail.
[C] 12kg p.w
[D] By arrangement
See Also: Game Dealers, Eggs

[15]

Furzeland Deer Developments Ltd
Furzeland Deer Park, Cadbury, Devon EX5 5LA
Tel: 08845 556
Contact: Dr John Henshaw

Venison

Free-range venison reared on parkland dressed only with natural minerals such as calcified seaweed. Carcasses supplied whole or butchered, fresh or chilled.
[C] Undisclosed Jul-Dec
[D] By arrangement

[10] [○] [↔]

Gold Label Produce Ltd
Knightley Grange Cottage, Grange Road, Woodscaves, Staffordshire ST20 0JU
Tel: 0785 74495
Contact: Mr D Dale

Venison — Red deer, grazed on herbal leys, supplied under thirty months, fresh, whole or half carcasses.
[C] Undisclosed
[D] By arrangement
See Also: Fresh Meat, Game Dealers, Poultry Producers

[12]
Hardwick Farms
Horsecroft, Bury St Edmunds, Suffolk IP29 5NY
Tel: 0284 754611
Contact: Mr A J Brown

Partridge — Pheasant and partridge reared primarily for sport, sold as chicks, bought back in, plucked, drawn and re-sold. Also supplied, cuts of venison and rabbit carcasses.
[C] Oct-Feb
[D] By Datapost
See Also: Game Dealers, Poultry Producers, Game: Smoked

[16] [↔]
Hazelbrow Turkeys
Hazelbrow Farm, Rad Lane, Peaslake, nr Guildford, Surrey GU5 9PB
Tel: 0306 730313
Contact: John Richardson

Partridge — Red-leg partridge.
[C] Undisclosed Nov-Jan
[D] By own transport within area
See Also: Game Dealers, Poultry Producers, Game: Smoked, Eggs

[15]
Heal Farm
Kings Nympton, Umberleigh, Devon EX37 9TB
Tel: 07695 2077
Contact: Anne Petch

Venison — Park reared venison (Fallow and Roe deer) supplied butchered, chilled or frozen.
[D] By own transport within area, British Rail
See Also: Fresh Meat, Game: Sausages and Puddings, Game: Smoked, Hampers

[12]
Manor Farm Deer Farm,
The Manor Farm, Brockley, Backwell, nr Bristol, Avon BS19 3A4
Tel: 027583 2313
Contact: Dr Julian Ridge

Venison — Farmed venison, slaughtered at under twenty seven months and hung for ten days. Supplied fresh or frozen, in whole carcasses or butchered to requirements. Also sausages and burgers.
[C] 40 carcasses p.a
[D] By arrangement

[11]
Marasand
Westen Farm, Plantation Road, Aslacton, Norwich NR15 2ER
Tel: 0379 77358
Contact: Clayton Vernon

Squab — Fresh farmed squab slaughtered at twenty one days supplied unplucked or plucked with trail, weighing on average 1lb 2oz.
[C] 600 p.wk
[W] Snipe & Grouse 01 627 2327
[D] By wholesaler

[10]
Midland Counties Rabbit Co Ltd
Willersey Road, Badsey, Evesham, Hereford & Worcester WR11 5HB
Tel: 0386 830938 Telx: 337588 RABBIT G
Contact: Nick Jones

Rabbit — New Zealand White and California Giant rabbit fed on vegetable pellets. Supplied whole, boned or butchered, fresh or frozen.
[C] Undisclosed
[W] Sumeray & Rodgers of Smithfield Market
[D] By wholesaler

[3] [↔]
Monarch Deer Farm
Naemoor Road, Crook of Devon, Kinross KY13 7UH
Tel: 05774 310
Contact: Charles White

Venison — Farmed Scottish Red deer whole or butchered, fresh or frozen.
[C] Red deer 100 p.a
[D] By arrangement

15

Monument Venison Ltd
Hill Farm, Hemyock, Devon EX15 3UZ
Tel: 0823 680307
Contact: Graeme Wallace

Venison

Devon venison farmed in stress free environment, culled at under thirty months and hung for at least one week. Available whole or butchered, fresh or frozen in vacuum packs.
[C] 3 carcasses p.wk
[D] By own transport within area
See Also: Game: Sausages and Puddings

13 ↔

Nether Winchendon Farms
Estate Office, Nether Winchendon, Aylesbury, Buckinghamshire HP18 ODY
Tel: 0844 290101
Contact: Robert Spencer Bernard

Wild boar

Wild boar slowly reared in Buckinghamshire woodlands. Available whole, half carcasses, or jointed.
[C] Undisclosed Oct-Mar
[D] By arrangement

16 ○ ↔

Park Hill Produce & Appledore Salads
Park Hill, Appledore, Ashford, Kent TN26 2BJ
Tel: 023 383201
Contact: Mr Smith

Quail

Aviary housed, dry plucked quail. Also available farmed guinea-fowl.
[C] Undisclosed
[D] By arrangement
See Also: Eggs, Fresh Herbs

13

The Pelham Venison Company Ltd
Estate Office, Furnham Pelham Hall, Buntingford, Hertfordshire SG9 OJP
Tel: 0279 78348 Fax: 0279 507071
Contact: Christopher Hughes

Venison

Red deer stags slaughtered at under twenty four months and butchered to specific cuts and joints in consumer and catering vacuum packs.
[C] Undisclosed
[D] By arrangement
See Also: Game: Sausages and Puddings, Game: Smoked

12

Quality Quail
Hazelhurst, Weare, Axbridge, Somerset BS26 2ND
Tel: 0934 712619
Contact: A J Ham

Quail

Quail reared in Somerset, oven-ready, fresh or frozen. Also available smoked quail in packs of four.
[C] 300-400 p.wk
[D] By arrangement
See Also: Eggs

3

Reediehill Deer Farm
Reediehill Farm, Auchtermuchty, Cupar, Fife KY14 7HS
Tel: 0337 28369 Telx: 972165
Contact: Nichola Fletcher

Venison

Grass fed Scottish deer culled up to three years, hung between ten and fourteen days. Supplied whole or jointed, fresh or frozen.
[C] 15 carcasses p.wk, fresh to order Jul-Jan, frozen Jul-May
[D] By arrangement
See Also: Game: Pâtés and Pastes, Game: Sausages and Puddings

4

Robert Cousin
Hanold House, Annalong, Co Down BT34 4TT
Tel: 03967 68643 Telex:748176 COSMO G
Contact: W Robert McBride

Pheasant

Fresh, frozen and oven-ready pheasant. Also partridge and quail.
[C] 2000 p.wk
[D] By arrangement
See Also: Poultry Producers, Game; Smoked, Eggs

12 ↔

Sherston Quail
St Catherines, Sherston, Malmesbury, Wiltshire SN16 0NN
Tel: 0666 840387
Contact: Mrs Ann Maslen

Quail

Large wax finished quail reared from French stock, fresh or frozen.
[C] Undisclosed
[D] By arrangement
See Also: Poultry Producers, Eggs

9 ↔

Teifi Boar Company
Glynhynod, Ffostrasol, Llandysul, Dyfed
SA44 5JY
Tel: 023975 528
Contact: J Savage

Wild boar — Wild boar reared in West Wales, fresh or frozen.
[C] 10 p.mth Oct-May
[D] By arrangement

12

A B & F E Wood
Redlynch Farm, Redlynch, Bruton,
Somerset BA10 0NW
Tel: 0749 8221
Contact: The Proprietor

Quail — Quail farmed in Somerset, dressed and packed, fresh or frozen.
[C] 1000 p.wk
[D] By arrangement
See Also: Poultry Producers, Eggs

POULTRY PRODUCERS

14 ↔

Ann Harris Geese
Washingford House, Bergh Apton,
Norwich NR15 1AA
Tel: 0508 50469
Contact: Ann Harris

Goose — Free-range Embden-Toulouse goose weighing 12-22lb. Contract Christmas orders accepted if placed by April.
[C] 200 p.a, 150 Christmas
[D] By arrangement

12 ↔

Ashford Mill Farm Shop
East End, North Leigh, Witney,
Oxfordshire
Tel: 099386 8121 Telx: 265871
Contact: P Edwards-Moss

Turkey — Free-range turkey, supplied whole, fresh or frozen.
[C] 200 p.a Dec
[D] By arrangement
See Also: Game Farmers, Game: Pâtés and Pastes, Game: Sausages and Puddings, Eggs

16 ↔

A J Barkaway
20 Ospringe Street, Faversham, Kent
Tel: 0795 532040
Contact: Mr A J Barkaway

Cockerel — Free-range turkey and cockerel. Also frozen chicken liver.
[C] Undisclosed
[D] By arrangement
See Also: Fresh Meat, Game Dealers

16

Bunker Farm Produce
Bunker Farm, Basingstoke Road,
Greenham Common South, Newbury,
Berkshire RG15 8HH
Tel: 0635 45535
Contact: Ken Neale

Boiling fowl — Free-range boiling fowl.
[C] Jan-Feb, Sep-Oct
[D] By arrangement
See Also: Fresh Meat, Eggs, Cheese, Purees and Sauces

15

Mrs Clark's Delicious Ducks
Shortridge Hill, Seven Crosses, Tiverton,
Devon EX16 8HH
Tel: 0884 252632
Contact: Mrs Moira Clark

Duck — Ducks reared in Devon oven-ready. Duck liver also supplied.
[C] 100 p.wk
[D] By arrangement
See Also: Game: Pâtés and Pastes, Game: Pies and Prepared Dishes, Game: Smoked

16

Copas Bros
Lower Mount Farm, Cookham, nr
Maidenhead, Berkshire SL6 9EE
Tel: 06285 29595
Contact: Tom Copas

Turkey — Hand plucked turkey hung for a minimum of seven days before evisceration for greater flavour and tenderness. Goose and large chicken also available.
Ⓒ Turkey 11,000 p.a, goose 300 p.a, large chicken 1,500 Christmas season
Ⓓ By arrangement

6
Cornvale Foods Ltd
Boxtree Farm, Barbon, Kirkby Lonsdale, Cumbria LA6 2LE
Tel: 0468 36386
Contact: Peter Dodd

Gressingham duck — British hybrid Gressingham duckling with a high proportion of lean meat, available whole, fresh, New York dressed or whole fresh oven-ready. Five sizes available packed in cases of 12-14 according to grade.
Ⓒ Undisclosed
Ⓓ By arrangement
See Also: Game Dealers

16 ↔
Cottage Farms (Horsmonden) Ltd
Crundalls, Matfield, Tonbridge, Kent TN12 7EA
Tel: 0892 72 2887
Contact: D C Browning

Capon — Fresh, oven-ready, hand plucked, hung turkey weighing 12-30lb. Also capons weighing 8-12lbs available.
Ⓒ Turkey 2000-2,500 Dec, capons 1000-1,500 Dec
Ⓓ By own transport within area

14
A V R Cracknell & Son
Huish Episcopi, Langport, Somerset TA10 9EY
Tel: 0458 250731
Contact: The Proprietor

Duckling — Free-range, oven-ready chicken, duckling and goose. Also lamb.
Ⓒ Chicken 350 p.wk, duckling 100 p.mth May-Oct, goose 300 Oct-Dec
Ⓓ By arrangement

9
Cwmni'r Cardi
Tyn Parc, Llanddre, Bow Street, Dyfed SY24 5BU
Tel: 0970 828375
Contact: Dafydd Raw-Rees

Turkey — Turkey reared in West Wales, weighing 10-40lb, fresh or dry frozen.
Ⓒ Undisclosed
Ⓓ By arrangement
See Also: Game: Smoked

15
Devon Quail
Poole Farmhouse, Thorverton, Exeter, Devon EX5 5PN
Tel: 0392 860946
Contact: Tim Brooks

Cornfed chicken — Cornfed chicken, turkey, duck, and goose, fresh, chilled or frozen, dressed to customers requirements.
Ⓒ Undisclosed
Ⓓ By arrangement
See Also: Game Farmers, Game: Smoked, Eggs, Hampers

15
Dorset Farms
Manor Farm, Little Windsor, Beaminster, Dorset DT8 3QU
Tel: 0308 68822
Contact: Mr H Birch

Chicken — Free-range chicken and turkey, fresh or frozen.
Ⓒ Undisclosed
Ⓓ By own transport within area
See Also: Fresh Meat, Game Dealers

3
Fenton Barns (Scotland) Ltd
Fenton Barns, North Berwick, East Lothian EH39 5AQ
Tel: 062 085 202
Contact: Wilma Gourdie

Turkey — Air-dried oven-ready turkey, weighing 8-25lb, sold whole, jointed, chilled or frozen.
Ⓒ 12,000, Christmas only
Ⓓ By arrangement
See Also: Game: Pies and Prepared Dishes

14 ↔
Flaxmoor House Poultry
Flaxmoor House, Caston, nr Attleborough, Norfolk NR17 1DD
Tel: 095 383555
Contact: Jenny Richards

Black Norfolk turkey — Free-range chicken, duck, goose and Black Norfolk turkey, supplied whole. Goose fat to order.
Ⓒ Chicken 60 p.wk, turkey 100 p.wk Christmas only, duck 200 p.wk, goose 200 p.wk, capon 200 p.wk Christmas only
Ⓓ By arrangement
See Also: Eggs

15 ↔
J T & J M George
Higher Ringworthy Farm, Sandplace, Morval, nr Looe, Cornwall PL13 1PR
Tel: 05034 691
Contact: Mr George

Aylesbury Duck — Free-range Aylesbury duck.
Ⓒ Undisclosed Mar-Oct
Ⓓ By arrangement

3
George Campbell & Sons
The Smokehouse, West Harbour Road, Granton, Edinburgh
Tel: 031 552 0376
Contact: Iain Campbell

Duck — Barbary duck, maize fed chicken, goose, and turkey, whole or jointed.
Ⓒ Undisclosed
Ⓓ By arrangement
See Also: Game Dealers, Game: Smoked, Eggs, Fish Dealers

14

Godfreys Turkey Farm
Cherry Green, Broxted, Dunmow, Essex CM6 2DD
Tel: 0279 850293
Contact: Mr P L Mascaux

Turkey — British Union Turkey. Also small quantities of goose at Christmas.
[C] 4000 Christmas
[D] By arrangement
See Also: Game: Smoked

10 ● ↔

Gold Label Produce Ltd
Knightley Grange Cottage, Grange Road, Woodseaves, Staffordshire ST20 OJU
Tel: 0785 74495
Contact: Mr D Dale

Chicken — Range reared oven-ready chicken.
[C] 600 p.wk
[D] By arrangement
See Also: Fresh Meat, Game Dealers, Game Farmers

10

Goodman's Geese
Walsgrove Farm, Great Witley, Hereford & Worcester WR6 6JJ
Tel: 0299 896272
Contact: Mrs J Goodman

Embden Cross goose — Free-range large Embden Cross goose fed on diet of corn, grass and root crops, hung ten days, supplied oven-ready or long legged.
[C] Goose 600 Sep-Dec
[D] By arrangement

13

The Great British Goose
Battlers Green Farm, Radlett, Hertfordshire WD7 8PH
Tel: 09276 3978
Contact: Geraldine Haworth

Goose — Goose slaughtered at twelve weeks, supplied fresh, frozen and oven-ready. Also available goose fat and liver.
[C] 500 p.wk
[W] London Larder 01 403 6177, Giffords 0727 54503, Cornvale Foods 0468 21393
[D] By wholesaler
See Also: Game: Pâtés and Pastes, Game: Smoked

12

Hardwick Farms
Horsecroft, Bury St Edmunds, Suffolk IP29 5NY
Tel: 0284 754611
Contact: Mr A J Brown

Quail — Japanese quail supplied.
[C] Undisclosed
[D] By Datapost
See Also: Game Dealers, Game Farmers, Game: Smoked

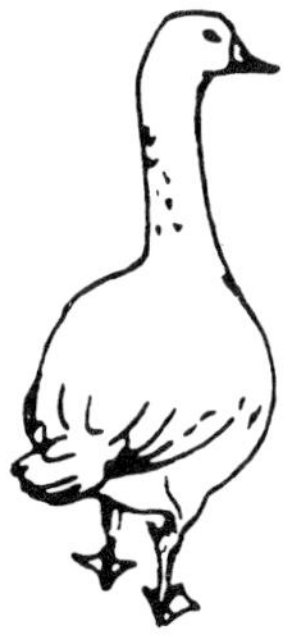

14

Harry Wright
Metton Rd, Felbrigg, Norfolk
Tel: 0263 512388
Contact: Harry Wright

Goose — Free-range White Embden goose fed on barley and sent to grass for seven weeks for fattening before slaughter. Supplied hung and clean plucked weighing 17-23lb.
[C] 80-100 Michaelmas, 200-300 Christmas
[D] By arrangement

14 ↔

R T Harvey Ltd
63 Grove Road, Norwich NR1 3RL
Tel: 0603 621908
Contact: Nigel R Harvey

Poussin — Range of oven-ready Norfolk poultry including chicken 3½-5lb, capon 6lb, poussin 14-16oz, dry plucked frozen turkey 8-30lb, frozen whole goose and breast fillets. Also available fresh Aylesbury duck 3½-5lb.
[C] Undisclosed
[D] By arrangement
See Also: Game Dealers, Game: Sausages and Puddings

16 ↔

Hazelbrow Turkeys
Hazelbrow Farm, Rad Lane, Peaslake, nr Guildford, Surrey GU5 9PB
Tel: 0306 730313
Contact: John Richardson

Turkey

British United Turkey (six strains) weighing 10-40lb, to order. Also small quantity of free-range goose in autumn.
C Undisclosed
D By own transport within area
See Also: Game Dealers, Game Farmers, Game: Smoked, Eggs

14 ○ ↔

A & K Hood
The Stables, Gresham, Norfolk NR11 8AD
Tel: 026377 468
Contact: Mr Hood

Chicken

Free-range, organically reared chicken and goose. Also available small quantities of eggs.
C Undisclosed
D By arrangement
See Also: Fresh Meat, Cheese, Fresh Vegetables, Jams and Preserves

13

M D How & Son
Woodlands Farm, The Vale, Chesham, Buckinghamshire HP5 3NS
Tel: 0494 783737
Contact: Mr Henry Slator

Turkey

Oven-ready turkey, supplied hung, fresh or frozen, whole or jointed in assorted packs including spare ribs and breast steaks.
C Undisclosed
D By arrangement
See Also: Game: Sausages and Puddings

16 ○ ↔

Island Country Farms
Asheybrook, Ashey, Ryde, Isle of Wight PO33 4AT
Tel: 0983 65686
Contact: Mr J H Fisher

Chicken

Free-range chicken and duck reared on the Isle of Wight. Also supplied frozen chicken liver
C Undisclosed Christmas and Easter
D By arrangement
See Also: Fresh Meat, Eggs, Milk, Fresh Fruit

6

John Curtis
10 Woodbourne Road, Douglas, Isle of Man
Tel: 0624 73875
Contact: John Curtis

Duck

Chicken, turkey, duck, goose and guinea-fowl supplied frozen, as whole or specific joints.
C Undisclosed
D By arrangement
See Also: Game Dealers

11

F A & J Jones & Sons
Red House Farm, North Scarle, Lincolnshire LN6 9HB
Tel: 052 277224
Contact: Mrs Jean Jones

Cockerel

Cockerel fed on breeders own special ration, weighing 8lb-12lb, chilled or frozen.
C Undisclosed
D By arrangement
See Also: Fresh Meat

16

Kortlang & Kortlang Ltd
The Duck Farm, Sandyhurst Lane, Ashford, Kent CM25 4PD
Tel: 0233 23431 Telx: 965451 DENNE G
Contact: Christian Kortlang

Duck

Aylesbury Cross White table duck, available freshly killed and hung for a minimum of forty eight hours, or New York dressed, weighing 7-8lb or 4-6lb eviscerated. Also supplied trays of half breast and leg portions.
C Undisclosed
D By own transport within area
See Also: Eggs

12

J Lindsey & Son
47 The Covered Market, Oxford, Oxfordshire OX1 3DX
Tel: 0865 242933
Contact: Mr M Feller

Corn fed chicken

Corn fed chicken, duck, goose, quail and turkey.
C Goose 50 p.wk, Michaelmas
D By arrangement
See Also: Fresh Meat, Game Dealers, Eggs

16 ● ↔

Malthouse Cottage Farm
Malthouse Lane, Ashington, Pulborough, West Sussex RH20 3BU
Tel: 0903 892456
Contact: Mrs J Ferris

Bronze turkey

Small quantities of broad breasted Bronze turkey.
C 36 at Christmas
D By arrangement
See Also: Fresh Meat, Cheese,

7

Moy Park Ltd
Royal Oak Building, High Street, Crewe, Cheshire CW2 7BJ
Tel: 0270 257722 Telx: 367248
Contact: Mr Richard Longworth

Chicken

Range of chicken including corn fed and free-range, fresh or frozen.
C 500,000-600,000 p.wk
D By arrangement
See Also: Game: Pies and Prepared Dishes

14

Norfolk Geese
Chestnut Farm, Pulham Market, Diss, Norfolk IP21 4TG
Tel: 037976 391
Contact: Mr John Adlard

Goose

Free-range goose reared in Norfolk.
C 2000 p.a Sep-Dec
D By arrangement

14 ↔

Norfolk Goose Breeders
Priory Farm, Tibenham, Norwich, Norfolk NR16 1NY
Tel: 0379 77334
Contact: Mr R W Sage

Goose

Free-range Danish goose, clean plucked and oven-ready weighing 17lb. Also supplied, frozen goose meat with red liver in 15lb portions suitable for pâté.
[C] Fresh goose 1,500lb p.a frozen goose meat 5,000lb p.a Aug-Oct
[D] By arrangement

9

R K Palfrey & Sons
36A Church Road, Newport, Gwent NP9 7EL
Tel: 0633 59385
Contact: Mr G Palfrey

Goose

Free-range goose. Also available chicken and turkey.
[C] Undisclosed, goose Christmas season
[D] By arrangement
See Also: Bacon and Hams

14

Peartree Pork and Poultry
High Birch Farm, Weeley Heath, nr Clacton-on-Sea, Essex CO16 9BU
Tel: 0255 830291
Contact: Mr P Ernst

Chicken

Home reared chicken hung for extra flavour, whole, jointed, chilled or frozen.
[C] 2000 p.wk
[D] By arrangement
See Also: Fresh Meat, Game Dealers, Game: Pies and Prepared Dishes

9 ↔

Pembroke Poultry
Eastwood, Boulston, Haverfordwest, Dyfed
Tel: 0437 66372
Contact: Richard Llewellyn

Goose

Free-range goose, guinea-fowl, and duck, wax finished, fresh or chilled.
[C] Goose and guinea-fowl 1000 Michaelmas-Christmas, duck 50 p.wk
[D] By arrangement
See Also: Cheese

12

Real Meat Company Ltd
East Hill Farm, Heytesbury, Warminster, Wiltshire BA12 0HR
Tel: 0985 40436/40060
Contact: Mr Richard Guy

Duck

Free-range chicken, duck, goose and guinea-fowl supplied to order. Also available chicken pies and free-range chicken eggs.
[C] 600 p.mth, goose in season
[D] By arrangement
See Also: Fresh Meat, Eggs

12 ↔

W A Reddington
East Close, Lippiatt Lane, Shipham, nr Winscombe, Avon BS25 1QZ
Tel: 093 484 3716
Contact: Mr W A Reddington

Quail

Quail reared to specific dietary requirements. For example large all male live birds as requested by Moslem buyers.
[C] Undisclosed
[D] By Red Star

4

Robert Cousin Ltd
Hanolde House, Annalong, Co Down BT34 4TT
Tel: 03967 68643 Telx: 748176 COSMO G
Contact: Mr W R McBride

Goose

Fresh or frozen chicken, turkey, duck, goose and guinea-fowl available.
[C] Undisclosed
[D] By arrangement
See Also: Game Farmers, Game: Smoked, Eggs

13 ●

Rosehaven
110 Cinques Road, Gamlingay, Sandy, Bedfordshire SG19 3NR
Tel: 0767 50142
Contact: Eleanor Hodges

Chicken

Free-range goose and chicken supplied whole, fresh, frozen or oven-ready.
[C] Goose 6 Dec, chicken 12-30 Nov-Feb
[D] By arrangement
See Also: Eggs, Fresh Salads

12 ↔

Sherston Quail
St Catherines, Sherston, Malmesbury, Wiltshire SN16 0NN
Tel: 0666 840387
Contact: Mrs Ann Maslen

Cockerel

Traditionally reared heavy cockerel, whole, fresh or frozen.
[C] Undisclosed
[D] By arrangement
See Also: Game Farmers, Eggs

16

Slater & Cooke
65-69 Brewer Street, London W1R 3FB
Tel: 01 437 2026/7
Contact: Mr M Contini

Duck

Maize fed chicken, free-range duck, goose, guinea-fowl and turkey, whole or jointed.
[C] Undisclosed
[D] By own transport within area
See Also: Meat: Sausages and Puddings, Game Dealers, Eggs

12

Somerset Ducks
Greenway Farm, North Newton, Bridgwater, Somerset TA7 0DS
Tel: 0278 662656
Contact: Mrs G Durman

Duck

Duck supplied oven-ready whole, in halves or portions. Duck fat also available.
[C] 300 p.wk, 2000 Christmas
[D] By Datapost
See Also: Game: Pies and Prepared Dishes

10 ○

Stoke Court Organic Farm Enterprise
Stoke Court, Greete, Ludlow, Shropshire SY8 3BX
Tel: 0584 810655
Contact: Mr K E Kolind

Chicken

Free-range chicken and guinea-fowl. Also goose reared to Soil Association standards.
[C] 100 chicken p.mth, 200 guinea-fowl p.mth
[D] By arrangement
See Also: Fresh Meat

12 ◯ **Swaddles Green Farm**
Swaddles Green Farm, Hare Lane, Buckland St Mary, Chard, Somerset TA20 3JR
Tel: 046034 387
Contact: Charlotte Reynolds

Chicken — Free-range organic chicken, duck, goose and guinea-fowl available. Also Bronze turkey.
Ⓒ Chicken 100 p.mth, duck Jul-Mar, goose 50 Dec, turkey 50 Dec
Ⓓ By arrangement
See Also: Fresh Meat

15 **Tiverton Poultry Group Ltd**
Blundells Road, Tiverton, Devon
Tel: 0884 254211
Contact: R J Parsons

Chicken — Devon Crest chicken.
Ⓒ Undisclosed
Ⓓ By arrangement
See Also: Game: Pies and Prepared Dishes

12 **A B & F E Wood**
Redlynch Farm, Redlynch, Bruton, Somerset BA10 0NW
Tel: 0749 8221
Contact: The Proprietor

Poussin — Poussin, turkey and large roasting chicken. Some birds supplied frozen.
Ⓒ Chicken 100 p.wk, turkey 300 p.wk
Ⓓ By arrangement
See Also: Game Farmers, Eggs

PATES AND PASTES

12 ↔ **Ashford Mill Farm Shop**
East End, North Leigh, Witney, Oxfordshire
Tel: 0993 868121 Telx: 265871 MMU003
Contact: P Edwards-Moss

Venison — Venison pâté in 4oz pot or larger container.
Ⓒ 10-20lb p.mth
Ⓓ By arrangement
See Also; Game Farmers, Poultry Producers, Game: Sausages and Puddings, Eggs

15 **Budleigh Salterton Pate & Otter Vale Products**
Perriams Place, Budleigh Salterton, Devon EX9 6LY
Tel: 03954 3487
Contact: Mr and Mrs Worrall

Devon country — Range of pâtés including chicken liver, coarse cut pork with red wine and Devon country, a rough pâté for slicing. All traditionally made in a variety of sizes.
Ⓒ Undisclosed
Ⓓ By own transport within area
See Also: Shellfish Dealers, Pies and Puddings, Chutneys and Pickles

15 **Mrs Clark's Delicious Ducks**
Shortridge Hill, Seven Crosses, Tiverton, Devon EX16 8HH
Tel: 0884 252632
Contact: Mrs Moira Clark

Duck — Duck liver and orange pâté.
Ⓒ Undisclosed
Ⓓ By arrangement
See Also: Poultry Producers, Game: Pies and Prepared Dishes, Game: Smoked

13 **The Great British Goose**
Battlers Green Farm, Radlett, Hertfordshire WD7 8PH
Tel: 09276 3978
Contact: Geraldine Haworth

Goose — Homemade additive free pâtés and pastes from own reared goose and pigs with smoked bacon, red wine and herbs. All packed in 4oz tubs, 7oz ceramic pots.
Ⓒ Undisclosed
Ⓓ By arrangement
See Also: Poultry Producers, Game: Smoked

15 ↔ **La Charcuterie of Dorset**
Railway Triangle Estate, Poundbury Road, Dorchester, Dorset DT1 2PJ
Tel: 0903 66900
Contact: H J Cocklin

New Forest — Range of additive free pâtés containing more than 70% game and poultry, including New Forest, with venison meat, liver, duck and soft pork, smooth Dorset Farmhouse, with chicken, chicken liver, mushrooms, and duck. All in 1kg, 1300g packs and 375, 750g roulades.
Ⓒ Undisclosed
Ⓦ Quantock Foods Ltd, Dorchester 0903 251100
Ⓓ By wholesaler, by arrangement
See Also: Meat: Pâtés and Pastes, Fish: Pâtés and Pastes

15 **Moorland Venison**
Shortacombe Deer Farm, East Down, Barnstaple, Devon
Tel: 0271 82585
Contact: Mrs J Redfern

Venison — Range of North Devon venison and poultry products including pâtés, pies, sausages and burgers. All available fresh or frozen.
Ⓒ Undisclosed
Ⓓ By arrangement

14 ↔ **Norfolk Smokehouses Ltd**
Poplar Farm, Worlingworth, Woodbridge, Suffolk IP13 7LR
Tel: 072 876212
Contact: J D Hildreth

Pheasant liver — Range of farmhouse, additive free pâtés including chicken liver with red wine, duck liver with cognac, pheasant liver with armagnac, and duck with orange. All in 1.8kg containers.

Ⓒ 2-3 ton p.wk
Ⓓ By arrangement
See Also: Meat: Pâtés and Pastes, Game: Smoked, Fish: Pâtés and Pastes, Vegetable Dishes

9

Patchwork
Faraway, Llandegla, Clwyd LL11 3BG
Tel: 097 888238
Contact: Margaret Carter

Chicken liver

Range of five homemade pâtés including chicken with white wine and peppers, chicken with brandy and herbs, chicken with cointreau and orange, and pheasant liver. Also chicken and ham pie.
Ⓒ Undisclosed
Ⓓ By arrangement
See Also: Cheese, Vegetable Dishes, Cakes, Biscuits and Pastries

3 ↔

Rannoch Smokery
Kinloch Rannoch, by Pitlochry, Perthshire PH16 5QD
Tel: 08822 344
Contact: Mr Barclay

Smoked venison and whisky

Smoked venison pâté with whisky or drambuie.
Ⓒ Undisclosed
Ⓓ By arrangement
See Also: Game Dealers, Game: Smoked

3

Reediehill Deer Farm
Reediehill Farm, Auchtermuchty, Cupar, Fife KY14 7HS
Tel: 0337 28369 Telx: 972165
Contact: Nichola Fletcher

Venison

Venison pâté with 70% game made with venison liver, butter, eggs, breadcrumbs, garlic and wine vinegar in 5, 10oz, 1lb packs or to customers requirements.
Ⓒ Undisclosed
Ⓓ By arrangement
See Also: Game Farmers, Game: Sausages and Puddings

16

Regale Foods Ltd
33 Hythe Road, London NW10 6RS
Tel: 01 969 8320
Contact: Mr T D Fenner

Venison roulade

Pâtés en croute including marinaded venison with ham, turkey with pistachios and truffles, chicken layered with spinach and carrot. Also duck galantine with truffles and pistachios, tongue wrapped in bacon, and venison roulade. All pâtés en croute weighing 7lb or to customers requirements.
Ⓒ 200 p.wk
Ⓓ By own transport within area
See Also: Bacon and Hams

PIES AND PREPARED DISHES

6 ↔

Burbush's
Gilwilly Trading Estate, Penrith, Cumbria
Tel: 0768 63841
Contact: T W H Burbush

Chicken and chestnut pie

Range of handmade pies with a variety of fillings including venison, pheasant, wild duckling, chicken and pork, all in 4-12″ rounds. Also chicken and chestnut pie topped with whole chestnuts, venison, turkey and madeira, both in 9″ rounds.
Ⓒ Undisclosed
Ⓓ By own transport within area
See Also: Fresh Meat

11 ↔

Catlin Bros Ltd
11 High Street, Grantham, Lincolnshire
Tel: 0476 65428
Contact: S P Hallam

Quail pie

Hand raised, additive free quail pie made with quail, hard-boiled quails eggs and sherry in 5¾lb sizes.
Ⓒ Undisclosed
Ⓓ By arrangement
See Also: Meat: Pies and Prepared Dishes, Bread

15

Mrs Clark's Delicious Ducks
Shortridge Hill, Seven Crosses, Tiverton, Devon EX16 8HH
Tel: 0884 252632
Contact: Mrs Moira Clark

Rolled stuffed duck

Boned, stuffed and rolled duck with a range of stuffings including apricot, cider, and rosemary.
Ⓒ Undisclosed
Ⓓ By arrangement
See Also: Poultry Producers, Game: Pâtés and Pastes, Game: Smoked

9

Crymych Venison
Cefn Canol Deer Farm, Crymych, nr Cardigan, Dyfed
Tel: 023973 526
Contact: Donald Clark

Venison pie

Venison pies made from haunch meat with red wine and mushrooms, in 1, 4, 8 portion sizes. Also Welsh chicken and leek pie, turkey and vegetable pie and venison Scotch eggs.
Ⓒ 150 p.wk
Ⓓ By own transport within area
See Also: Game Farmers, Game: Sausages and Puddings

8

Derek Fox
25 Market Place, Malton, North Yorkshire
Tel: 0653 2528
Contact: Mr D Fox

Yorkshire pot

Range of homemade game and poultry pâtés, pastes, pies and prepared dishes including Yorkshire pot with duck, chicken, pheasant, partridge and woodcock.
Ⓒ Undisclosed
Ⓓ By arrangement
See Also: Game Dealers, Game Farmers

13 **Farmer Giles Foods Ltd**
Broadfields, Bicester Road, Aylesbury, Buckinghamshire HP19 3AE
Tel: 0296 395262 Fax: 0296 395282
Contact: Ian Brough

Chicken quiche

Range of handmade, additive free pies including chicken with pepper and oatmeal in 4lb squares and 5lb rounds. Also available range of quiches including chicken and courgette with wine, and broccoli with Swiss cheese.
C Undisclosed
D By arrangement

15 **The Farmer's Oven**
Tuckmill Farm, Payhembury, Honiton, Devon EX14 OHF
Tel: 040484 313
Contact: Mrs Sylvia Evans

Game pie

Handmade savoury pies made to traditional recipes including turkey, chicken, duck, game, in 5-6oz, 1, 3, 5, 6, 6½lb pies. Fruit pies also available.
C Undisclosed
D By arrangement

3 **Fenton Barns (Scotland) Ltd**
Fenton Barns, North Berwick, East Lothian EH39 5AQ
Tel: 062 085 202
Contact: Wilma Gourdie

Turkey galantine

Selection of prepared cooked turkey breasts including luxury turkey breast 6, 8lb, standard turkey breast 7lb, Lothian turkey breast 7lb, all packed four per case. Also available honey roast turkey hams, peppered turkey hams and turkey galantines.
C Undisclosed
D By arrangement
See Also: Poultry Producers

11 ↔ **Goodman's Country Foods Ltd**
36 Chapel Street, Haconby, nr Bourne, Lincolnshire PE10 0UL
Tel: 077837 230
Contact: Geoff Goodman

Quail pie

Quail pie made with quail meat marinaded in red wine, whole quails eggs, port, herbs and spices, in a sherry flavoured jelly and encased in a hot water crust pastry, weighing 5¾lb. Also Lincolnshire Quaislet, a slicing meat based on haslett, but made with quail. Also cooked stuffed quail.
C Undisclosed
D By arrangement

16 ↔ **Hockeys - Naturally**
Newtown Farm, South Gorley, Fordingbridge, Hampshire ST6 2PW
Tel: 0425 52542
Contact: Phillip Hockeys

Game pie

Venison pâtés and game pies. Venison sausages also available.
C Undisclosed
D By arrangement
See Also: Fresh Meat, Game Dealers

7 **Moy Park Ltd**
Royal Oak Building, High Street, Crewe, Cheshire CW2 7BJ
Tel: 0270 257722 Telx: 367248
Contact: Mr Richard Longworth

Stuffed boned chicken

Lemon or garlic basted chicken, seasoned and stuffed, oven-ready weighing 3½lb or boned weighing 2½lb. Also wholemeal breaded turkey scallops.
C Whole 14,000 p.wk, boned 7000 p.wk
D By arrangement
See Also: Poultry Producers

9 **Nannyma Foods Ltd**
114-116 Springvale Estate, Cwmbran, Gwent NP44 5BG
Tel: 06333 69949
Contact: Talfryn Jenkins

Chicken curry

Range of handmade, additive free prepared Indian dishes including chicken curry, chicken tikka, chicken massala and chicken samosas.
C Undisclosed
W King Frost 0472 359261, Capper & Co Ltd 0443 225500, Cardigan Frozen Foods 0239 613691
D By wholesaler, by arrangement
See Also: Meat: Pies and Prepared Dishes, Fish: Pies and Prepared Dishes

16 ↔ **Oded Schwartz**
24 Claverley Grove, London N3 2DH
Tel: 01 349 2242
Contact: Oded Schwartz

Quail and pheasant pie

Range of raised game pies including quail and pheasant made with herb stuffed, boned quail surrounded by pheasant and pork forcemeat, rabbit made with rabbit fillet wrapped in vine leaves surrounded by rabbit and pork forcemeat flavoured with gin and venison. All weighing 3-7lb.
C 20-30 pies p.wk
D By arrangement
See Also: Chutneys and Pickles

14 **Peartree Pork and Poultry**
High Birch Farm, Weeley Heath, nr Clacton-on-Sea, Essex CO16 9BU
Tel: 0255 830291
Contact: Mr P Ernst

Smoked chicken pie

Hand raised buffet pies including savoury chicken pie with layers of smoked chicken. Also range of poultry pâtés, prepared dishes, pies and smoked poultry.
C Undisclosed
D By arrangement
See Also: Fresh Meat, Game Dealers, Poultry Producers

8 **Pepper Arden Game & Game Pies**
Pepper Arden, Northallerton, North Yorkshire
Tel: 032578 548
Contact: Mrs Cherry Gatty

Game pie

Range of handmade seasonal game pies prepared to traditional family recipes in 7oz, 1¼, 2½, 5, 8lb sizes. Also available game sausages and burgers.
C Undisclosed
D By arrangement
See Also: Game Dealers

14

Poachers Pies Ltd
5 Marston Road, St Neots, Cambridgeshire PE19 2HB
Tel: 0480 407777 Fax: 0480 407788
Contact: Martin Phillips

Turkey and tarragon pie

Range of pies including turkey and tarragon, turkey and cranberry and Gamekeepers. All in 8, 16 portion sizes or to customers requirements.
C Undisclosed
D By arrangement
See Also: Bacon and Hams, Game: Smoked

11 ↔

Red Griffin Ltd/The Country Victuallers
Winkburn Hall, Newark, Nottinghamshire NG22 8PQ
Tel: 0636 86465
Contact: Richard Craven-Smith-Milnes

Game pie

Game pie made with hare, pork and veal weighing 4½-5lb.
C 60-100lb p.wk
D By arrangement
See Also: Bacon and Hams, Game: Smoked, Pies and Puddings

9 ↔

Roys Cooked Meats Ltd
Viking Way, Winch Wen Industrial Estate, Swansea, West Glamorgan SA1 7DE
Tel: 0792 796519 Telx: 48232
Contact: Mr John F Archer

Chicken and potato pie

Range of chicken pies and prepared dishes including roast chicken and potato pie, 10″ hot or cold slicing pie with 40% meat content.
C Undisclosed
D By arrangement
See Also: Bacon and Hams

12

Somerset Ducks
Greenway Farm, North Newton, Bridgwater, Somerset TA7 0DS
Tel: 0278 662656
Contact: Mrs G Durman

Duck and orange pie

Boned, stuffed and cooked duck with a variety of stuffings including apple and cider with honey glaze, apricot with nuts and celery, sage and onion. Also available duck and orange pie in large and individual sizes, and duck pâté.
C Undisclosed
D By Datapost
See Also: Poultry Producers

14

Suffolk Larder Foods
9a Charles Industrial Estate, Stowmarket, Suffolk
Tel: 0449 676162
Contact: Tony Constantine Smith

Coriander stuffed chicken

Prepared chickens, stuffed with chicken meat and coriander weighing 2-3lb. Also range of pies including turkey and bacon with parsley and rosemary in 3½, 4½, 8½lb sizes.
C Stuffed chickens 40-50 p.wk
D By arrangement
See Also: Bacon and Hams, Game Dealers, Game: Smoked

15

Tiverton Poultry Group Ltd
Blundells Road, Tiverton, Devon
Tel: 0884 254211
Contact: R J Parsons

Roast chicken

Prepared chicken dishes including chicken kebabs in packs of three, chicken Kiev, roast chicken. Also chicken joints, breasts, thighs and drumsticks packed in single or double portions.
C Undisclosed
D By arrangement
See Also: Poultry Producers

SAUSAGES AND PUDDINGS

12 ↔

Ashford Mill Farm Shop
East End, North Leigh, Witney, Oxfordshire
Tel: 099386 8121 Telx: 265871
Contact: P Edwards-Moss

Venison sausage

Additive free venison sausages in 1, 2lb packs made to traditional recipes. Also 4oz burgers.
C Sausages 20-50lb p.wk
D By arrangement
See Also: Game Farmers, Poultry Producers, Game: Pies and Prepared Dishes, Eggs

1 ↔

Crawford Farm Enterprises Ltd
Cluanie, by Beauly, Inverness-shire IV4 7AE
Tel: 0463 782534
Contact: Archie Crawford

Venison burgers

Scottish farmed venison sausages in 1lb packs. Also available venison burgers and venison pâté with brandy and bacon in 5oz pots or to customers requirements.
C Sausages 50lb p.wk
D By arrangement
See Also: Game Dealers

9

Crymych Venison
Cefn Canol Deer Farm, Crymych, nr Cardigan, Dyfed
Tel: 023973 526
Contact: Donald Clark

Venison sausage

Venison sausages in three flavours, plain, juniper berry, and mixed herbs. All in 1-5lb packs.
C 300lb p.wk
D By own transport within area
See Also: Game Farmers, Game: Pies and Prepared Dishes

14 ↔ **R T Harvey Ltd**
63 Grove Road, Norwich NR1 3RL
Tel: 0603 621908
Contact: Nigel R Harvey

Venison sausage — Venison sausages prepared to traditional sixty five year old recipe. Also available game pâté.
C Undisclosed
D By arrangement
See Also: Game Dealers, Poultry Producers

15 **Heal Farm**
Kings Nympton, Umberleigh, Devon EX37 9TB
Tel: 07695 2077
Contact: Anne Petch

Venison and bacon sausage — Venison and bacon sausages made to own recipe in 1lb packs of four sausages.
C 350lb p.mth
D By arrangement
See Also: Fresh Meat, Game Farmers, Game: Smoked, Hampers

13 **M D How & Son**
Woodlands Farm, The Vale, Chesham, Buckinghamshire
Tel: 0494 783737
Contact: Henry Slator

Turkey burger — Range of prepared turkey joints including breast steaks, breast joints weighing 1½-8lb, soup packs with giblets minus the liver, pie pieces in 6lb bags. Also turkey burgers in packs of six, jumbo burgers in packs of four or eight, turkey olives, stir-fries, and sausages.
C Undisclosed
D By arrangement
See Also: Poultry Producers

15 **Monument Venison Ltd**
Hill Farm, Hemyock, Devon EX15 3UZ
Tel: 0823 680307
Contact: Graeme Wallace

Venison sausage — Range of venison sausages containing 90% venison meat and burgers supplied in 10lb boxes. Also available venison pâtés and pies.
C Undisclosed
D By arrangement
See Also: Game Farmers

13 **The Pelham Venison Company Ltd**
Estate Office, Furnham Pelham Hall, Buntingford, Hertfordshire SG9 OJP
Tel: 0279 78348 Fax: 0279 507071
Contact: Christopher Hughes

Venison burgers — Venison burgers in packs of four weighing 2, 4oz and catering packs. Also pre-cooked venison casserole packed in 16oz oven tray.
C Undisclosed
D By arrangement
See Also: Game Farmers, Game: Smoked

3 **Reediehill Deer Farm**
Reediehill Farm, Auchtermuchty, Cupar, Fife KY14 7HS
Tel: 0337 28369 Telx: 972165
Contact: Nichola Fletcher

Veniburgers — Range of Veniburgers including 4oz burger in 5lb packs, 3oz burgers in 10lb packs. Also supplied venison sausages in 1lb packs, and haggis.
C Veniburger 4000lb p.a, sausages 1000lb p.a
D By arrangement
See Also: Game Farmers, Game: Pâtés and Pastes

11 **H M Stockdale**
Hill Farm, Mears Ashby, Northampton NN6 0DX
Tel: 0604 810206
Contact: Mr Stockdale

Venison sausages — Range of prepared venison joints. Also venison burgers, venison sausages in packs of eight weighing 1lb.
C Undisclosed
D By arrangement
See Also: Game Farmers

SMOKED

6 ↔ **Ashdown Smokers**
Skellerah Farm, Corney, nr Nootle, Cumberland LA19 5TW
Tel: 06578 324
Contact: E H Fellows

Duck breast — Range of game smoked over oak or juniper including duck breasts packed seperately or in pairs. Also shoulder, loin, haunch and sliced venison.
C Undisclosed in season
D By arrangement
See Also: Meat: Smoked, Game Dealers, Fish Dealers, Cheese

16 ↔ **Atkinson Smoked Foods**
Beacon Hill Farm, Exton, nr Corhampton, Southampton, Hampshire SO3 1NW
Tel: 0489 877899
Contact: Mr Atkinson

Pheasant — Range of smoked game and poultry including pheasant, chicken and turkey in 4oz vacuum packs or to customers requirements.
C Undisclosed
D By own transport within area
See Also: Fish: Smoked

11 ↔ **Beechwood Foods**
Unit 2, North Kelsey Road, Caistor, Lincolnshire LN7 6SF
Tel: 0472 852432
Contact: S F Shaw

Turkey

Traditionally smoked turkey cured in salt, weighing 7-10lb or boned weighing 3- 6lb. Also hams weighing 10-14lb and hot smoked trout. All available in mixed cases.
C Undisclosed
D By own transport nationally

10 ↔

Blackhurst of Shropshire
Drawwell, Clive, Shrewsbury, Shropshire SY4 3JN
Tel: 093928 329
Contact: Frances Blackhurst

Guinea-fowl

Hot smoked, mildly cured chicken flavoured with tarragon weighing 2½-3½lb. Also hot smoked guinea-fowl weighing 2lb, quail weighing 4oz packed four to the tray, and pheasant lightly smoked over oak and applewood weighing 2lb.
C Undisclosed
D By arrangement
See Also: Fish: Smoked

15

Mrs Clark's Delicious Ducks
Shortridge Hill, Seven Crosses, Tiverton, Devon EX16 8HH
Tel: 0884 252632
Contact: Mrs Moira Clark

Breast of duck

Smoked breast of duck.
C : Undisclosed
D : By arrangement
See Also: Poultry Producers, Game: Pies and Prepared Dishes, Game: Pâtés and Pastes

12 ↔

Coln Valley Fish & Game Co Ltd
Winson, Cirencester, Gloucestershire GL7 5ER
Tel: 028572 400/593/614 Telx: 437269
Contact: M Henriques

Chicken

Range of game and poultry including chicken smoked in a modern version of the old London Smokeholes in 2½lb packs.
C 500-600 units p.wk
D By own transport nationally
See Also: Game Dealers, Fish Dealers

9

Cwmni'r Cardi
Tyn Parc, Llanddre, Bow Street, Dyfed SY24 5BU
Tel: 0970 828375
Contact: Dafydd Raw-Rees

Turkey

Crowns of smoked turkey weighing 14lb. Also smoked, boned and rolled turkey, and cooked or uncooked boned and rolled turkey.
C 1000 p.mth
D By arrangement
See Also: Poultry Producers

15

Devon Quail
Poole Farmhouse, Thorverton, Exeter, Devon EX5 5PN
Tel: 0392 860946
Contact: Tim Brooks

Quail

Quail cured to traditional recipe and smoked over local hardwoods. Also smoked guinea-fowl weighing 2lb, smoked quail eggs in 6x6 packs and smoked saddle of rabbit.
C Undisclosed
D By arrangement
See Also: Game Farmers, Poultry Producers, Eggs, Hampers

16

Fjordling Smokehouses
Heathlands Country Market, Honey Hill, Wokingham, Berkshire RG11 3PG
Tel: 0734 776688
Contact: Andrew Espir

Chicken

Range of game and poultry smoked over oak including whole chicken weighing 3½-4lb, whole turkey and turkey breast cut to customers requirements.
C Undisclosed
D By own transport, by arrangement
See Also: Meat: Smoked, Fish: Smoked

3

Fyne Craft Seafoods
Otterferry, Argyll PA21 2DH
Tel: 070 082237
Contact: Michael Buchanan

Venison

Traditionally smoked venison and chicken. Also cider cured ham weighing 14-16lb.
C Undisclosed
D By arrangment
See Also: Fish: Smoked

3

George Campbell & Sons
The Smokehouse, West Harbour Road, Granton, Edinburgh
Tel: 031 552 0376
Contact: Iain Campbell

Duck breast

Smoked chicken, turkey, duck breast and quail.
C Undisclosed
D By arrangement
See Also: Game Dealers, Eggs, Fish Dealers

14

Godfreys Turkey Farm
Cherry Green, Broxted, Dunmow, Essex CM6 2DD
Tel: 0279 850293
Contact: Mr P L Mascaux

Turkey

Whole oak smoked turkey weighing 12lb.
C Undisclosed
D By arrangement
See Also: Poultry Producers

13

The Great British Goose
Battlers Green Farm, Radlett, Hertfordshire WD7 8PH
Tel: 09276 3978
Contact: Geraldine Haworth

Goose

Own reared smoked goose in 4oz, 1lb packs or to order.
[C] Undisclosed
[W] London Larder 01 403 6177, Giffords 0727 543503, Cornvale Foods 0468 21393
[D] By wholesaler, by arrangement
See Also: Poultry Producers, Game: Pâtés and Pastes

12

Hardwick Farms
Horsecroft, Bury St Edmunds, Suffolk IP29 5NY
Tel: 0284 754611
Contact: Mr A J Brown

Partridge

Smoked pheasant and partridge in 1½lb single bird packs.
[C] Undisclosed
[D] By Datapost
See Also: Game Dealers, Game Farmers, Poultry Producers

16 ↔

Hazelbrow Turkeys
Hazelbrow Farm, Rad Lane, Peaslake, nr Guildford, Surrey GU5 9PB
Tel: 0306 730313
Contact: John Richardson

Turkey crowns

Range of smoked turkey joints including crown of turkey weighing 8-18lb, dark or white turkey roll weighing 3-6lb. Also available unsmoked.
[C] Undisclosed
[D] By own transport within area
See Also: Game Dealers, Game Farmers, Poultry Producers, Eggs

15

Heal Farm
Kings Nympton, Umberleigh, Devon EX37 9TB
Tel: 07695 2077
Contact: Anne Petch

Venison

Smoked haunch of venison from park reared Fallow and Roe deer hung and cured in light brine with juniper berries.
[C] Undisclosed
[D] By arrangement
See Also: Fresh Meat, Game Farmers, Game: Sausages and Puddings, Hampers

6

Johnny Cooke-Hurle
Startforth Hall, Barnard Castle, Co Durham D12 9RA
Tel: 0833 38370
Contact: Johnny Cooke-Hurle

Pigeon

Smoked pheasant, Mallard duck, pigeon and chicken.
[C] Undisclosed
[D] By arrangement
See Also: Meat: Smoked, Game Dealers

7 ↔

Lune Smoked Foods Ltd
Duke Street, St George's Quay, Lancaster LA1 1RB
Tel: 0524 69563
Contact: P A Flude

Pheasant

Range of smoked game and poultry including pheasant by the brace, haunch of venison weighing 5-8lb, quail in trays of four, poussin, Cornvale duckling coronets, chicken, and breast of turkey. Also silverside of beef and St George ham sliced and vacuum packed.
[C] Undisclosed
[D] By arrangement
See Also: Fish: Smoked

15

Marine Cuisine
Germoe, Penzance, Cornwall TR20 9QU
Tel: 0736 762816 Telx: 934999 TXLINK G MBX 736722816
Contact: Mr David Bruce

Poussin

Traditionally cured and oak smoked poussin.
[C] Undisclosed
[D] By own transport
See Also: Fish: Smoked

12 ↔

Minola Smoked Products
Kencot Hill Farmhouse, Filkins, Lechlade, Gloucestershire GL7 3QY
Tel: 036 786 391/556 Fax: 036 786 544
Contact: Hugh Forestier-Walker

Duck breast

Range of smoked game and poultry including corn fed chicken weighing 3-4½lb, hot or cold smoked Aylesbury and Barbary duck breasts weighing 6oz-1lb and supremes and fillets of pheasant.
[C] Chicken 100 p.wk, duck breasts 500 p.wk, pheasant 50 p.wk
[D] By arrangement
See Also: Meat: Smoked, Fish Dealers, Cheese

12

Mote Farm Turkeys Ltd
Mote Farm, Taynton, nr Gloucester Gloucestershire GL19 3AW
Tel: 0452 79666
Contact: Eric House

Turkey breast

Turkey hung, brined and smoked over beechwood and juniper berries. Available as boned breast 7-10lb or breast on the bone 8-12lb, 5kg packs.
[C] Undisclosed
[D] By arrangement

14 ↔

Norfolk Smokehouses Ltd
Poplar Farm, Worlingworth, Woodbridge, Suffolk IP13 7LR
Tel: 072 876212
Contact: J D Hildreth

Poussin

Range of cured, oak smoked poultry including turkey, chicken, duck, poussin. All in 2-2½lb vacuum packs.
[C] 2-3 ton p.wk
[D] By arrangement
See Also: Meat: Pâtés and Pastes, Game: Pâtés and Pastes, Fish: Pâtés and Pastes, Vegetable Dishes

13

The Pelham Venison Company Ltd
Estate Office, Furnham Pelham Hall, Buntingford, Hertfordshire SG9 OJP
Tel: 0279 78348 Fax: 0279 507071
Contact: Christopher Hughes

Venison — Smoked venison in 4-16oz packs.
C Undisclosed
D By arrangement
See Also: Game Farmers, Game: Sausages and Puddings

3 ↔ **Rannoch Smokery**
Kinloch Rannoch, by Pitlochry, Perthshire PH16 5QD
Tel: 08822 344
Contact: Mr Barclay

Venison — Wild Red deer brined, smoked and vacuum packed. Also available three varieties of smoked venison pâté.
C 150kg p.wk
D By arrangement
See Also: Game Dealers, Game: Pâtés and Pastes

11 ↔ **Red Griffin Ltd/The Country Victuallers**
Winkburn Hall, Newark, Nottinghamshire NG22 8PQ
Tel: 0636 86465
Contact: Richard Craven-Smith-Milnes

Turkey crowns — Range of smoked turkey including whole birds, crowns (breastbone and wings) and boned rolled breast. Also smoked chicken.
C Chicken 30 p.wk
D By arrangement
See Also: Bacon and Hams, Game: Pies and Prepared Dishes, Pies and Puddings

14 **River Farm Smokery**
Great Wilbraham Road, Bottisham, nr Newmarket, Cambridgeshire CB1 5J
Tel: 0223 811382
Contact: R F Enoch

Turkey supremes — Range of poultry smoked over oak and hardwood including poussin, chicken, duck, turkey crowns and supremes. Also available smoked pheasant and venison.
C Undisclosed
D By arrangement
See Also: Meat: Smoked, Fish Dealers, Snacks and Savouries

4 **Robert Cousin Ltd**
Hanolde House, Annalong, Co Down BT34 4TT
Tel: 03967 68643 Telx: 748176 COSMO G
Contact: Mr W R McBride

Game — Range of game and poultry cured in salt, sugar, vinegar, herbs and spices and smoked in either a modern smokehouse or a nineteenth century chimney kiln. All available vacuum packed in a range of sizes.
C Undisclosed
D By arrangement
See Also: Game Farmers, Poultry Producers, Eggs

11 **Shellfish Seafoods Ltd**
Watling Street, Hinckley, Leicestershire
Tel: 0455 619009 Telx: 34468 SHELFR G
Contact: Mr S West

Pheasant — Oak smoked chicken and pheasant.
C Undisclosed
D By arrangement
See Also: Fish Dealers

2 ↔ **Spey Valley Smokehouse**
Cromdale, Grantown-on-Spey, Morayshire PH26 3LN
Tel: 0479 3078
Contact: Mr Coulson

Quail — Range of smoked game and poultry including duck, goose, pheasant, quail and venison.
C Venison 2-3 ton p.a
D By arrangement
See Also: Fish: Smoked

14 ↔ **Suffolk Smoked Foods**
Unit 2, Jubilee End, Dale Hall Industrial Estate, Lawford, Manningtree Essex CO11 1UR
Tel: 0206 391212
Contact: Mr Roy Alborough

Chicken — Chicken and turkey cured in salt, sugar, herbs and spices, smoked over oak and beechwood. Available as whole chicken, packs of ten chicken drumsticks or turkey breasts.
C Undisclosed
D By arrangement

14

Suffolk Larder Foods
9a Charles Industrial Estate, Stowmarket, Suffolk
Tel: 0449 676162
Contact: Tony Constantine Smith

Venison

Smoked boned leg of venison. Also smoked venison sausages prepared with wine and herbs in 1lb packs.
[C] Undisclosed
[D] By arrangement
See Also: Bacon and Hams, Game Dealers, Game: Pies and Prepared Dishes

16

The Weald Smokery
Mount Farm, Hawkhurst Road, Flimwell, East Sussex TN5 7QL
Tel: 058087 601
Contact: B P Nicholas

Chicken breast

Chicken breasts smoked German-style over hardwood logs supplied two per vacuum pack. Also smoked Toulouse sausages made with pork, garlic and seasonings filled in natural skins in 12-14oz vacuum packs.
[C] Undisclosed
[D] By own transport locally
See Also: Fish: Smoked

EGGS

12 ↔

Ashford Mill Farm Shop
East End, North Leigh, Witney, Oxfordshire
Tel: 099386 8121 Telx: 265871
Contact: P Edwards-Moss

Chicken

Free-range chicken eggs.
[C] 400 doz p.wk
[D] By arrangement
See Also: Game Farmers, Poultry Producers, Game: Pâtes and Puddings, Game: Sausages and Puddings

11

Bitteswell Farm Eggs
Bitteswell Farm, Bitteswell, Lutterworth, Leicestershire
Tel: 04555 2354
Contact: A G Higgins

Free-range

Free-range eggs from chickens fed on home milled feed.
[C] Undisclosed
[D] By arrangement

16 ●

Boathouse Farm Organic Produce
Isfield, nr Uckfield, East Sussex TN22 5TY
Tel: 082575 302
Contact: Laurence Hill

Organic

Free-range, organic chicken eggs.
[C] 6000-10,000 doz p.yr
[D] By arrangement
See Also: Fresh Meat, Fresh Vegetables, Millers

16 ↔

Bunker Farm Produce
Bunker Farm, Basingstoke Road, Greenham Common South, Newbury, Berkshire RG15 8HH
Tel: 0635 45535
Contact: Ken Neale

Chicken

Free-range chicken eggs and some duck eggs brought in from various free-range farms.
[C] Undisclosed
[D] By arrangement
See Also: Fresh Meat, Poultry Producers, Cheese, Purees and Sauces

14 ● ↔

Calluna Farm Products
Lodge Road, Hollesley, Woodbridge, Suffolk
Tel: 0394 411927
Contact: Mrs Helen Douglas

Chicken

Free-range chicken eggs.
[C] 100 doz p.wk
[D] By own transport within area and London
See Also: Cheese, Fresh Salads

16 ↔

Clements Farm
c/o The Old Thatch, Crawley, Winchester, Hampshire SO21 2PR
Tel: 0962 72327
Contact: Mr A R Wyatt

Quail

Battery hen and quail eggs.
[C] Chicken eggs 12,000 doz p.wk, quail eggs 2000 doz p.wk
[D] By arrangement

15

Devon Quail
Poole Farmhouse, Thorverton, Exeter, Devon EX5 5PN
Tel: 0392 860946
Contact: Tim Brooks

Pickled quail eggs

Hen, turkey, duck, goose and guinea-fowl eggs. Also pickled, smoked and Scotch quail eggs available in a variety of pack sizes.
[C] Undisclosed
[D] By arrangement
See Also: Game Farmers, Poultry Producers, Game: Smoked, Hampers

15

K W Durrant Family Butchers
Main Street, Chillington, nr Kingsbridge, Devon TQ7 2JX
Tel: 0548 580217
Contact: Mr K Durrant

Chicken

Free-range chicken eggs.
[C] Undisclosed
[D] By arrangement
See Also: Fresh Meat, Game Dealers

7

Fayre Game Ltd
Lodge Lane Nurseries, Lodge Lane, Lytham, Lancashire FY8 5RP
Tel: 0253 738640 Telx: 677125 FAYRE G
Contact: Jonathan Pusey

Quail

Quail eggs.
[C] 3,500 doz p.wk
[D] By arrangement
See Also: Game Dealers, Game Farmers

14 ↔

Flaxmoor House Poultry
Flaxmoor House, Caston, nr Attleborough, Norfolk NR17 1DD
Tel: 095 383555
Contact: Jenny Richards

Maran
Bantam

Free-range chicken, duck, Maran and Bantam eggs.
[C] Chicken eggs 200 doz p.wk, Bantam eggs 10 doz p.wk Feb-Jul
[D] By arrangement
See Also: Poultry Producers

3

George Campbell & Sons
The Smokehouse, West Harbour Road, Granton, Edinburgh
Tel: 031 552 0376
Contact: Iain Campbell

Black headed-gull

Quail and Black-headed gull eggs.
[C] Undisclosed
[D] By arrangement
See Also: Game Dealers, Poultry Producers, Game: Smoked, Fish Dealers

5

Glen Game (Scotland) Ltd
Botany Mills, Roxburgh Street, Galashiels, Selkirkshire
Tel: 0896 2242
Contact: Mr Martin Rogers

Black-heade-d gull

Quail and Black-headed gull eggs.
[C] Undisclosed
[D] By arrangement
See Also: Game Dealers

5 ↔

Glenrath Pullets Ltd
Glenrath Farm, Kirkton Manor, Peebles, Tweedale EH45 9JW
Tel: 07214 221
Contact: Mr Campbell

Duck

Free-range duck eggs and some free-range chicken eggs, delivered within 24 hours of laying.
[C] Duck eggs 750 doz p.wk
[D] By arrangement

16 ↔

Hazelbrow Turkeys
Hazelbrow Farm, Rad Lane, Peaslake, nr Guildford, Surrey GU5 9PB
Tel: 0306 730313
Contact: John Richardson

Red-leg partridge

Red-leg partridge eggs.
[C] Mar-Apr
[D] By own transport within area
See Also: Game Dealers, Game Farmers, Poultry Producers, Game: Smoked

12 ↔

Isis Fish Farm
Eynsham Mill, Oxford, Oxfordshire OX8 1EJ
Tel: 0865 881751
Contact: Derek Chapman

Quail

Quail eggs.
[C] Undisclosed
[D] By arrangement
See Also: Fish Dealers

16 ○ ↔

Island Country Farms
Asheybrook, Ashey, Ryde, Isle of Wight PO33 4AT
Tel: 0983 65686
Contact: Mr J H Fisher

Duck

Free-range chicken and duck eggs.
[C] 100 doz p.wk
[D] By arrangement
See Also: Fresh Meat, Poultry Producers, Milk, Fresh Fruit

16

Kortlang & Kortlang Ltd
The Duck Farm, Sandyhurst Lane, Ashford, Kent CM25 4PD
Tel: 0233 23431 Telx: 965451 DENNE G
Contact: Christian Kortlang

Duck

Duck eggs.
[C] Undisclosed
[D] By own transport in South East England
See Also: Poultry Producers

12

J Lindsey & Son
47 The Covered Market, Oxford, Oxfordshire OX1 3DX
Tel: 0865 242933
Contact: Mr M Feller

Pheasant

Free-range chicken, quail and pheasant eggs.
[C] Undisclosed
[D] By arrangement
See Also: Fresh Meat, Game Dealers, Poultry Producers

16

Lympne Market Garden
Lympne Place, Lympne, Kent CT21 4PA
Tel: 0303 66183
Contact: C F O Bull

Khaki Campbell Duck

Chicken, Khaki Campbell duck and goose eggs.
[C] Chicken eggs 50 p.dy
[D] By arrangement

12

Martin Pitt
Levetts Farm, Marlborough, Wiltshire SN8 4DS
Tel: 0672 52035
Contact: Martin Pitt

Chicken

Free-range eggs from chickens fed on organic grain. Also goose eggs.
[C] Chicken eggs 20,000 doz p.mth
[D] By own transport
See Also: Cheese, Purees and Sauces

16

Midway Eggs
35 Standard Way, Fareham Industrial Park, Fareham, Hampshire PO16 8XG
Tel: 0329 822302
Contact: Mr R Johnson

Quail

Goldesborough quail and battery chicken eggs.
[C] Quail eggs 2,500 doz p.wk, chicken eggs 34,000 doz p.wk
[D] By own transport

16

Mierscourt Farm Shop
Mierscourt Road, Rainham, Kent ME8 8PJ
Tel: 0634 31743
Contact: Mr Ian Clark

Chicken — Free-range chicken eggs.
[C] 200 doz p.a
[D] By arrangement

10

Oaken Lawn Farm
Oaken Manor,
Wolverhampton, West Midlands WV8 2BD
Tel: 090 74 2028
Contact: Mr R M Iliff

Chicken — Free-range chicken eggs.
[C] 40-45 doz p.dy
[D] By own transport within area

16 ○ ↔

Park Hill Produce & Appledore Salads
Park Hill, Appledore, Ashford, Kent TN26 2BJ
Tel: 023 383201
Contact: Mr Smith

Quail — Free-range chicken and quail eggs.
[C] Undisclosed
[D] By arrangement
See Also: Game Farmers, Fresh Herbs

16

D J & M Paul
Ivory Farmhouse, Burghclere, Newbury, Berkshire RG15 9LP
Tel: 0635 27362/27375 Telx: 849141
Contact: D J Paul

Goose — Free-range chicken, duck, goose and quail eggs.
[C] Undisclosed
[D] By arrangement
See Also: Game Dealers, Game: Pies and Prepared Dishes

12

Quality Quail
Hazelhurst, Weare, Axbridge, Somerset BS26 2ND
Tel: 0934 712619
Contact: A J Ham

Quail — Hard-boiled quail eggs by the dozen.
[C] 100-200 doz p.wk
[D] By arrangement
See Also: Game Farmers

12

Real Meat Company Ltd
East Hill Farm, Heytesbury, Warminster, Wiltshire BA12 0HR
Tel: 0985 40436/40060
Contact: Mr Richard Guy

Chicken — Free-range chicken eggs.
[C] Undisclosed
[D] By arrangement
See Also: Fresh Meat, Poultry Producers

4

Robert Cousin Ltd
Hanoloe House, Annalong, Co Down BT34 4TT
Tel: 03967 68643 Telx: 748176 COSMO G
Contact: Mr W R McBride

Duck — Free-range chicken, duck and quail eggs.
[C] Undisclosed
[D] By arrangement
See Also: Game Farmers, Poultry Producers, Game: Smoked

13 ○

Rosehaven
110 Cinques Road, Gamlingay, Sandy, Bedfordshire SG19 3NR
Tel: 0767 50142
Contact: Eleanor Hodges

Chicken — Free-range chicken and organically produced goose eggs.
[C] Chicken eggs 15 doz p.wk
[D] By arrangement
See Also: Poultry Producers, Fresh Salads

12 ↔

Sherston Quail
St Catherines, Sherston, Malmesbury, Wiltshire SN16 0NN
Tel: 0666 840387
Contact: Mrs Ann Maslen

Quail — Quail eggs pickled to an old recipe, in malt vinegar, water and spices, packed twelve in a jar. Also fresh quail eggs.
[C] Undisclosed
[D] By arrangement
See Also: Game Farmers, Poultry Producers

16

Slater & Cooke
65-69 Brewer Street, London W1R 3FB
Tel: 01 437 2026/7
Contact: Mr M Contini

Gull — Quail and gull eggs.
C Undisclosed
D By own transport within area
See Also: Meat: Sausages and Puddings, Game Dealers, Poultry Producers

12 **A B & F E Wood**
Redlynch Farm, Redlynch, Bruton, Somerset BA10 0NW
Tel: 0749 88221
Contact: The Proprietor

Quail — Quail and barn reared chicken eggs.
C Undisclosed
D By arrangement
See Also: Game Farmers, Poultry Producers

Any Problems?

If any suppliers listed in **British Food Finds 1989** let you down, do not deliver their goods, supply you with inferior produce, please let us know and we can follow it up for the next edition. Contact **Henrietta Green on 01-927-9808.**

British Food Finds is here to help-

If you know of a producer of speciality food not listed in **British Food Finds 1989,** please let us know so that we can include them in our next edition.

For editorial entries contact **Henrietta Green on 01 727 9808.**

3

FISH AND SHELLFISH

FISH DEALERS

6 ↔

Ashdown Smokers
Skellerah Farm, Corney, nr Nootle, Cumberland LA19 5TW
Tel: 06578 324
Contact: E H Fellows

Sea trout
Bass

Range of fresh fish including salmon, wild sea trout and bass.
C Undisclosed
D By arrangement
See Also: Meat: Smoked, Game Dealers, Shellfish Dealers, Fish: Smoked, Cheese

3

Band's of Perth
135 Glover Street, Perth, Perthshire PH2 0JB
Tel: 0738 24222 Telx: 76279 Fax: 0738 21892
Contact: Mr R H Critchell

Wild salmon

Wild and farmed salmon and trout available fresh or frozen.
C Undisclosed
D By own transport within area
See Also: Game Dealers, Fish: Smoked

16

Botterell Seatrades Ltd
Harbour Road, Rye Harbour, Rye, East Sussex TN31 7TT
Tel: 0797 222875
Contact: Mr John Botterell

Garfish

Bass, turbot, red and grey mullet, monkfish, pollock, garfish, scads and gurnards, all in season.
C 2-5 ton p.wk Spring-Autumn
D By own transport within area
See Also: Shellfish Dealers, Sea Vegetables

12

Bristol Channel Fisheries
123 Hempsted Lane, Gloucester, Gloucestershire GL2 6JY
Tel: 0452 23534
Contact: Chris Lee

Elvers
Silver eel

Elvers from elver stations on the River Severn, available fresh or frozen with approximately 3000 p.kg. Also live locally caught silver eels 2'6" long and "as thick as your arm" with a high fat content.
C Elvers 20 ton p.a Mar-Apr, silver eels 5-6 ton p.a Oct-Dec depending on floods
D By arrangement

12 ↔

Brown & Forrest
Thorney, Langport, Somerset TA10 0DR
Tel: 0458 251520
Contact: Michael Brown

Elvers

Elvers caught from the Rivers Severn and Parrett. Supplied live transported in oxygenised containers, or frozen packed in 1kg tubs.
C 400kg Mar-May
D By arrangement
See Also: Fish: Pâtés and Pastes, Fish: Smoked

5

Burgon (Eyemouth) Ltd
Harbour Road, Eyemouth, Berwickshire TD14 5HZ
Tel: 08907 50272 Telx: 72365 Fax: 08907 51259
Contact: Grahame Sinclair

Herring

Range of fresh fish. Also marinaded herring.
C Undisclosed
D By arrangement
See Also: Shellfish Dealers

15

Channel Fisheries
13 Penpethy Road, Brixham, Devon TQ5 8NN
Tel: 08045 51210
Contact: Mr Purnell

Shark

Shark, shark steaks, squid, sea bass, red mullet, John Dory and turbot, in season.
C 14 ton p.mth
D By own transport within area
See Also: Shellfish Dealers, Fish: Smoked

12 ↔

Coln Valley Fish & Game Co Ltd
Winson, Cirencester, Gloucestershire GL7 5ER
Tel: 028572 400/593/614 Telx: 437269
Contact: M Henriques

Wild salmon

Wild salmon from own netting stations in Sutherland with catches of grilse Jun- Jul. Farmed salmon also stocked.
C Undisclosed Mar-Aug
D By arrangement
See Also: Game Dealers, Fish: Smoked

3

Fascadale Fisheries
Fascadale, Achateny, Acharacle, Argyll PH36 4LG
Tel: 097 23243
Contact: Mark James

Wild salmon

Wild Atlantic salmon caught in the waters around Ardnamurchan Point during the season.
C Undisclosed
D By arrangement

3

George Campbell & Sons
The Smokehouse, West Harbour Road, Granton, Edinburgh
Tel: 031 552 0376
Contact: Iain Campbell

Catfish

Range of fresh fish including carp, catfish, halibut, mackerel, pike, skate, sea trout and perch.
C Undisclosed
D By arrangement
See Also: Game Dealers, Fish: Smoked

7

Heaningbrook Trout Farm
The Heaning, Newton-in-Bowland, Clitheroe, Lancashire BB7 3ED
Tel: 02008 274/617 Fax: 02008 667
Contact: John Blanc

Rainbow trout

Fresh rainbow trout and a range of frozen seafish.
C Trout 10-12 tons p.a
D By arrangement
See Also: Fish Farmers, Shellfish Dealers

12 ↔

Isis Fish Farm
Eynsham Mill, Oxford, Oxfordshire OX8 1EJ
Tel: 0865 881751
Contact: Derek Chapman

Fresh fish

Any species supplied in season. Also available scallops and mussels.
C Undisclosed
D By arrangement
See Also: Eggs, Fish Farmers, Fish: Smoked

3 ↔

Loch Fyne Oysters Ltd
Ardkinglas, Cairndow, Argyll PA36 8BH
Tel: 04996 264/217
Contact: Mr Andrew Lane

Salmon

Wild salmon in season netted from Loch Fyne and farmed salmon from local fish farms.
C Salmon 75-100 ton p.a, wild salmon Jul-Aug
D By arrangement
See Also: Shellfish Dealers, Shellfish Farmers, Fish: Smoked

12 ↔

Minola Smoked Products
Kencot Hill Farmhouse, Filkins, Lechlade, Gloucestershire GL7 3QY
Tel: 036 786 391/556 Fax: 036 786 544
Contact: Hugh Forestier-Walker

Wild salmon

Wild salmon in season. Also farmed salmon bled and chilled.
C Wild salmon 500kg p.wk Jul-Sep
D By arrangement
See Also: Meat: Smoked, Game: Smoked, Fish: Smoked, Cheese

9

Mona Seafoods Ltd
The Oyster Hatchery, Brynsiencyn, Anglesey LL61 6TQ
Tel: 024873 411/412
Contact: D Lea-Wilson

Sea bass

Sea bass caught off the coast of Anglesey.
C 1000lb p.wk Aug-Oct
D By arrangement
See Also: Shellfish Farmers, Sea Vegetables

16 ↔

Moore & Moore
Parkview, Swallowfield Street, Swallowfield, Reading, Berkshire RG7 1QX
Tel: 0734 882844
Contact: Martin Moore

Pike

A selection of freshwater fish including pike weighing ½-7kg with an average weight of 2kg, grayling weighing ¼-1kg, and bream 1-2kg. All fish held in fresh running water and starved prior to sale for a clean fresh taste.
C Pike 200-300kg Sep-Mar, grayling 200-300kg Sep-Mar, bream 50kg Sep-Mar
D By arrangement
See also: Fish Farmers

16

C J Newnes & Partners
73 Billingsgate Market, London E14 8ST
Tel: 01 515 0793
Contact: C J Newnes

Zander

Range of fish including zander, carp, pike, wild and farmed Scottish salmon, sea bass, sea bream and John Dory according to season, in wholesale quantities. Range of shellfish also available.
C Undisclosed.
D By arrangement
See Also: Sea Vegetables

9

Raymond Rees & Son
11 Market Precinct, Carmarthen, Dyfed
Tel: 0267 234144
Contact: Mr Raymond Rees

Sewin

Sewin (sea trout) and salmon caught from the Rivers Towy, Tiefi and Taf. Range of locally caught shellfish also available.
C Undisclosed
D By arrangement
See Also: Sea Vegetables

14

River Farm Smokery
Great Wilbraham Road, Bottisham, nr Newmarket, Cambridgeshire CB1 5J
Tel: 0223 811382
Contact: R F Enoch

Salmon

Range of wet fish including turbot, halibut, Dover and lemon sole. Also wild and farmed Scotch salmon and rainbow trout.
C Undisclosed
D By arrangement
See Also: Meat: Smoked, Game: Smoked, Shellfish Dealers, Fish: Pâtés and Pastes, Fish: Pies and Prepared Dishes, Fish: Smoked, Sea Vegetables, Snacks and Savouries

11

Shellfish Seafoods Ltd
Watling Street, Hinckley, Leicestershire
Tel: 0455 619009 Telx: 34468 SHELFR G
Contact: Mr S West

Eel

Live trout and eel kept in holding tanks.
C Undisclosed
D By own transport nationally
See Also: Game: Smoked, Shellfish Dealers, Fish: Smoked

14

Stambridge Trout Fisheries
138a Flemming Avenue, Leigh-on-Sea, Essex SS9 3AX
Tel: 0702 26274
Contact: J G B Powling

Carp

Rainbow trout, carp and limited supplies of pike and eel.
C Trout 300kg p.mth, carp 150kg p.mth, eel Apr-Oct
D By arrangement

15

Salmon

Sylvesters Seafoods
Holt House, Richmond Road, Appledore, North Devon EX39 4LD
Tel: 02372 79101
Contact: Mrs Felicity Sylvester
Salmon, salmon trout and local seafish supplied fresh.
C Undisclosed
D By arrangement
See Also: Shellfish Dealers, Fish: Smoked

9

Fresh fish

Vin Sullivan of Abergavenny Ltd
Triley Mill, Abergavenny, Gwent NP7 8DE
Tel: 0873 2331
Contact: Mr John Sullivan
Sixty to seventy varieties of fresh fish supplied cleaned, gutted, filleted, boned and skinned to customers requirements.
C Undisclosed
D By own transport nationally, overnight deliveries
See Also: Shellfish Dealers, Sea Vegetables, Fresh Fruit

4

Trout

West Ulster Farmers Ltd
Dromore Road, Irvinestown, Co Fermanagh, Northern Ireland
Tel: 03656 21219 Telx: 74611 WSTULS G
Fax: 03656 28222
Contact: Mr John Kennedy
Trout available fresh, frozen and filleted. Also smoked trout.
C Undisclosed
D By arrangement
See Also: Cheese, Fungi

1

Salmon

William Jolly
Hatston Industrial Estate, Scott's Road, Kirkwall, Orkney
Tel: 0856 2417
Contact: Billy Jolly
Fresh and frozen salmon.
C 1 ton p.wk
D By arrangement
See Also: Shellfish Dealers, Fish: Smoked

FISH FARMERS

9

Trout

Abbey Fishery
Llangollen, Clwyd
Tel: 0978 860266
Contact: Mr D Penman
Trout reared in North Wales in earth ponds fed by fast flowing waters. Also fish or shellfish supplied to order.
C Trout 40 ton p.a
D By arrangement

6

Eels

Akebank Fish Farm and Smokery
Mosser, Cockermouth, Cumbria CA13 ORB
Tel: 0900 826517
Contact: P Carruthers
Trout farmed in the Lake District supplied fresh or frozen. Also local eels netted and held in holding tanks until required.
C Undisclosed
D By arrangement
See Also: Fish: Pâtés and Pastes

12 ↔

Trout

Alderley Trout Ltd
Alderley, Wotton-Under-Edge, Gloucestershire GL12 7QT
Tel: 0453 842540
Contact: J Costello
Trout reared in water from the Cotswold limestone hills available fresh or frozen.
C Undisclosed
D By own transport
See Also: Fish: Smoked

9

Trout

Alyn Fish Farm
Mold Road, Cefn-y-Bedd, nr Wrexham, Clwyd
Tel: 0978 761777
Contact: Mr T Morgan
Rainbow trout from lakes fed by local spring waters. Also oak smoked trout and small quantities of smoked trout pâté in ¼lb tubs available.
C Trout 10 ton p.a, smoked trout 500 ton p.a
D By arrangement

16

Trout

Andwell Mill Farms
Andwell Lane, Andwell, Basingstoke, Hampshire RG27 9PA
Tel: 025 672 4551 Telx: 858599
Contact: R E N Barder
Rainbow trout reared in concrete raceways in the spring waters of the river Lyde.
C 80-100 ton p.a
D By arrangement
See Also: Fish: Pâtés and Pastes, Fish: Smoked

16

Trout

Anna Valley Trout Farm
Salisbury Road, Abbott's Ann, Andover, Hampshire
Tel: 0264 710382
Contact: Mr E C Webb
Fresh trout farmed in Hampshire spring waters. Also available small quantities of smoked pâté in 100, 200gm containers.
C Pâté 60lb p.wk
D By arrangement

9

Salmon

Aqua Norse Ltd
Brunel Quay, Neyland, Dyfed SA73 1PY
Tel: 0646 601821
Contact: P Myrland
Farmed salmon supplied fresh and frozen. Also smoked salmon and salmon pâté in tubs.
C 500-600 ton p.a
D By arrangement

7

Bentham Trout Farm
Low Mill, Bentham, Lancaster LA2 7DA
Tel: 0468 61305
Contact: Mr R Currie

Trout — Rainbow trout farmed in a tributary of the River Lunt, supplied fresh and frozen, gutted or whole. Smoked trout in 5lb catering boxes also available.
[C] Fresh trout 50 ton p.a, frozen 10 ton p.a, smoked 8st p.wk
[D] By arrangement

12 ↔

Bibury Trout Farm
Bibury, Cirencester, Gloucestershire GL7 5NL
Tel: 028574 215
Contact: The Manager

Trout — Pink fleshed fresh rainbow trout. Also smoked whole and filleted trout and smoked trout pâté.
[C] 30 ton p.a
[D] By arrangement

12

Blaisdon Trout Farms & Isle Instant Ltd
Woodgreen, Blaisdon, Gloucestershire GL17 ORE
Tel: 0452 830936
Contact: R Wiggins

Trout — Trout farmed in hill streams weighing 8oz-1½lb, fresh or frozen, whole or filleted.
[C] 10 ton p.a
[D] By own transport within area
See Also: Fish: Smoked

15

Blakewell Fisheries
Muddiford, Barnstaple, Devon EX31 4ET
Tel: 0271 44533
Contact: Mr Ritchard Nickell

Trout — Fresh trout reared in stream fed tanks weighing 12oz-2lb, some available up to 5lb.
[C] 45 ton p.a
[D] By arrangement

1

Bratan Baghasdal Ltd/Lochboisdale Salmon
21 Kenneth Drive, Lochboisdale, South Uist, Western Isles PA81 5TJ
Tel: 08784 549/288
Contact: Ian Binnie

Salmon — Atlantic salmon farmed in the clear waters of the Western Isles, graded, packed on ice in polystyrene boxes.
[C] ½-1 ton p.wk
[D] By arrangement
See Also: Shellfish Farmers

12 ↔

Britford Trout Farm
Betts Lane, Britford, Salisbury, Wiltshire SP5 4DR
Tel: 0722 330055
Contact: Mr J Berkeley Matthew

Trout — Rainbow trout farmed in waters of the River Avon. Also small quantities of fresh trout pâté packed in 4oz-5kg containers.
[C] Trout 100 ton p.a
[D] By arrangement

14

Brown & May Ltd
Whitehouse Farm Office, Eye, Suffolk IP23 7HN
Tel: 0379 870181 Telx: 946240
Contact: S Appleby

Salmon — Atlantic salmon hatched and farmed in Loch Eisort Scotland, available fresh or frozen, whole, filleted or in steaks. Also smoked salmon and gravadlax available as whole sides or sliced. Also turbot and Dover sole.
[C] Salmon 250 ton p.a, other fish 200 ton p.a
[D] By arrangement

15 ↔

Burn Valley Trout Ponds
Burnhayes, Silverton, Exeter, Devon EX5 4BU
Tel: 08845 282
Contact: Chris Prentis

Trout — Free-range Rainbow trout extensively reared in ponds fed by springs and the waters of the River Burn, supplied live, chilled, whole, gutted or filleted 8oz-8lb.
[C] 1½ ton p.mth
[D] By own transport within area
See Also: Fish: Smoked

4

Bush Valley Fish Farm
35 Main Street, Stranocum, Ballymoney, Co Antrim
Tel: 02657 41354
Contact: James Chestnut

Trout

River Bush trout available fresh or chilled.
Ⓒ 1 ton p.wk
Ⓓ By arrangement

3

Castle Fisheries Ltd
Inverary, Argyll PA32 8XJ
Tel: 0499 2233
Contact: J McPherson

Trout

Trout farmed in Scotland, fresh or frozen. Own smoked trout also available, whole or in fillets.
Ⓒ Undisclosed
Ⓓ By arrangement

15

Cerne Valley Fisheries Ltd
Huish Trout Farm, Sydling St Nicholas, Dorchester, Dorset DT2 9NS
Tel: 03003 509
Contact: Mr G W Tottle

Trout

Rainbow trout reared in chalk water. Also available a very small quantity of carp.
Ⓒ 150-200 ton p.a
Ⓓ By arrangement

12

Clearwater Fish Farm
Ludbridge Mill, East Hendred, Wantage, Oxfordshire OX12 8LN
Tel: 0235 833732
Contact: Mr P R Austin

Trout

Fresh rainbow trout reared in clear water tanks weighing 6oz-4lb, filleted and gutted on request. 10lb freezer packs supplied. Smoked trout pâté also available.
Ⓒ 15 ton p.a
Ⓓ By arrangement

12

Combe Sydenham Fisheries
Combe Sydenham Country Park, Monksilver, Taunton, Somerset TA4 4JG
Tel: 0984 56284
Contact: Mr K C Y Jones

Trout

Rainbow trout reared in pure spring water weighing 8oz-5lb, fresh, whole, gutted and filleted.
Ⓒ Undisclosed
Ⓓ By arrangement
See Also: Game Dealers, Fish: Smoked

1

M Cowie & Son
6-7 Bank Row, Wick, Caithness KW1 5EY
Tel: 0955 2241
Contact: Jim Cowie

Salmon

Farmed Scottish salmon. Also smoked salmon, scallops, crab, lobster and a range of white fish available in season. All products supplied fresh or frozen, whole or filleted and vacuum packed.
Ⓒ Fresh salmon 15,000 p.a May-Sep, shellfish 2 ton p.a
Ⓓ By arrangement

1

Cromarty Salmon Co
George Street, Cromarty, Ross & Cromarty
Tel: 03817 448
Contact: Robert Davie

Salmon

Large salmon and pink fleshed trout, weighing a minimum 3 and 2½kg respectively, farmed in the cold waters of the North Sea. Also available smoked in sides or slices with a minimum weight of 1lb, vacuum packed to order.
Ⓒ ½ ton p.wk
Ⓓ By arrangement

9

Cwm Trout Farm
Maes-y-Gwenith, Llanvair Discoed, Chepstow, Gwent NP6 6LN
Tel: 02917 719
Contact: Mr J B Margesson

Trout

Pink fleshed trout available fresh or to customers requirements.
Ⓒ 80 ton p.a mid-late summer
Ⓓ By own transport within area
See Also: Fish: Pâtés and Pastes, Fish: Smoked

7

Danebridge Fisheries
Pingle Cottage, Wincle, nr Macclesfield, Cheshire SK11 0QE
Tel: 02607 293
Contact: D Chadwick

Trout

Fresh rainbow trout packed in 10lb boxes or to customers requirements.
Ⓒ Undisclosed
Ⓓ By arrangement
See Also: Game Dealers

12

Donnington Fish Farm
Condicote Lane, nr Upper Swell, Stow-on-the-Wold, Gloucestershire GL54 1EP
Tel: 0451 30873
Contact: Mr P Murray

Trout

Rainbow trout reared in the Cotswolds weighing 5oz-5lb.
Ⓒ Fresh trout 30 ton p.a
Ⓓ By arrangement
See Also: Fish: Smoked

4

Errington Trout Farm
Ballinamallard, Co Fermanagh
Tel: 036581 535
Contact: Mr Malcom Dickson

Trout

Fresh trout available whole, or split and frozen. Also smoked trout and smoked eel vacuum packed, weighing up to 1lb per pack.
Ⓒ Trout 25 ton p.a, smoked trout 10st p.wk, smoked eel 5st p.a
Ⓓ By arrangement

15

Exmoor Trout
North Molton, North Devon EX36 3JJ
Tel: 05984 321
Contact: Colin Folds

Trout

Fresh rainbow trout farmed in the waters of the River Mole. Also available hot smoked whole trout, cold smoked sides and smoked trout pâté.
C Fresh trout 10 ton p.a, smoked trout 3-4 ton p.a
D By arrangement

12 ↔

Fish Farm Services Ltd
The Old Manse, Tisbury, Wiltshire SP3 6LG
Tel: 0747 870791
Contact: Mr Berkley-Matthew

Trout

Rainbow trout reared in free flowing waters of chalk stream tributary of the River Avon, 8-12oz, fresh or frozen.
C 150 ton p.a
D By arrangement
See Also: Fish: Pâtés and Pastes

4

Flowing Rivers Farms
Tullylish, Gilford, Craigavon, Co Down BT63 9XX
Tel: 0762 831941
Contact: R M Dunlop

Trout

Rainbow trout reared in waters from the Mountains of Mourne, fresh or frozen.
C 25 ton p.a
D By arrangement

10 ↔

Fosseway Fisheries Ltd
Kineton, Warwickshire CV35 OJL
Tel: 0926 641611 Fax: 0789 414093
Contact: Richard Morgan

Pike
Grayling

Range of freshwater fish including pike weighing 12oz-7lb, grayling 10-16oz, eel 12oz-1lb, mirror or common carp 1-2lb. Larger fish available on request. All fish kept in clear water holding tanks and delivered as required.
C Undisclosed
D By arrangement

10

Freshwater Trout Farm
Macclesfield Road, Leek, Staffordshire
Tel: 053833 684
Contact: Mr R J Kimberley

Brown trout

Rainbow and a small amount of brown trout farmed.
Ⓒ Rainbow trout 23 ton p.a, brown trout 2 ton p.a
Ⓓ By arrangement
See Also: Fish: Smoked

16 ↔

Frog Island Fish Farm
Abinger Hammer, Dorking, Surrey RH5 6SA
Tel: 0306 730449 Fax: 0306 477019
Contact: Heidi Macnair

Trout

Fresh rainbow trout. Also available oak smoked trout and smoked trout pâté.
Ⓒ 30-50 ton p.a, mostly summer
Ⓓ By arrangement

15

Gears Mill Fisheries
Gears Mill, Cann, Shaftesbury, Dorset SP7 OLT
Tel: 0747 2825
Contact: Cdr R A Y Bridges RN

Carp

Live carp fed on the rich pond life of the waters of the Stirkel stream, weighing 1½-1¾lb, larger sizes on request.
Ⓒ 2 ton p.a
Ⓓ By own transport within area

3

Glen App Fisheries Ltd/Finnarts Bay Smokers Ltd
Glen App, Ballantrae, Ayrshire KA26 OPG
Tel: 05812 271
Contact: Mr Worsfold

Salmon

Salmon and trout farmed in Scotland.
Ⓒ Salmon 50 ton p.a
Ⓓ By arrangement
See Also: Fish: Smoked

4

Glen Oak Fisheries
Glen Oak House, 1 Nutts Corner Road, Crumlin, Co Antrim BT29 4BW
Tel: 08494 52975
Contact: Mr R J Mairs

Trout

Rainbow trout farmed in Northern Ireland, fresh or frozen. Smoked trout also available.
Ⓒ Trout 200 ton p.a, smoked trout 25 ton p.a
Ⓓ By own transport within area

6

Hawkshead Trout Farm
The Boathouse, Hawkshead, Ambleside, Cumbria LA22 0QF
Tel: 09666 541
Contact: Mr N Woodhouse

Trout

Rainbow trout reared in the Lake District, fresh or frozen in boxes weighing 1st. Also trout smoked four times a week, sold sleeved in packs of ten or to customers requirements.
Ⓒ Smoked trout 80 ton p.a
Ⓓ By own transport within area

15

Head Mill Trout Farm
Head Mill, Umberleigh, North Devon EX37 9HA
Tel: 07698 80862
Contact: Mr R Boa

Trout

Pink fleshed rainbow trout, fresh or chilled.
Ⓒ 60 ton p.a
Ⓓ By own transport within area
See Also: Fish: Smoked

7

Heaningbrook Trout Farm
The Heaning, Newton-in-Bowland, Clitheroe, Lancashire BB7 3ED
Tel: 02008 274/617 Fax: 02008 667
Contact: John Blanc

Trout

Small quantities of carp and rainbow trout available.
Ⓒ Trout 10-12 ton p.a
Ⓓ By arrangement
See Also: Fish Dealers, Shellfish Dealers

1 ↔

Hebrides Harvest Harris Ltd
Isle of Harris, Western Isles PA85 3BQ
Tel: 0859 2323 Fax: 2373
Contact: J S Luty

Salmon

Fresh salmon farmed in the Outer Hebrides.
Ⓒ 500 ton p.a
Ⓓ By arrangement

12 ↔

Isis Fish Farm
Eynsham Mill, Oxford, Oxfordshire OX8 1EJ
Tel: 0865 881751
Contact: Derek Chapman

Trout

Rainbow trout, 6oz-5lb, starved two days before being killed to improve flavour.
Ⓒ Undisclosed
Ⓓ By arrangement
See Also: Eggs, Fish Dealers, Fish: Smoked

3

Joseph Johnston & Sons Ltd
3 America Street, Montrose, Angus DD10 8DR
Tel: 0674 72666 Telx: 76332
Contact: Dr M Marshall

Salmon

Farmed Scottish salmon, fresh or frozen. Wild Atlantic salmon also available during Feb-Aug.
Ⓒ Farmed salmon 800 ton p.a
Ⓓ By arrangement

16 ↔ **Kennet Valley Fisheries**
Lower Way Farm, Lower Way, Thatcham, Berkshire RG13 4TL
Tel: 0635 66699 Telx: 847860 ICELT
Contact: Martin Duggan

Trout — Farmed rainbow trout available fresh, chilled, whole and filleted weighing 6oz-6lb. Also live eels and pike supplied in tanks.
[C] Trout 15 ton p.a
[D] By arrangement
See Also: Game Dealers, Shellfish Dealers, Fish: Smoked

16 **Kimbridge Trout Farm**
Kimbridge Farm House, Kimbridge, Romsey, Hampshire SO51 OLE
Tel: 0794 40269
Contact: Arthur Humbert

Trout — Trout reared in waters from the River Test, where it is claimed a continuous flow of the pure water produces a well fleshed fish, in 12-14oz, 3-3½lb sizes.
[C] Undisclosed
[D] By arrangement

7 **Kyles of Bute Salmon**
Tighnabruaich, Argyll PA21 2EH
Tel: 0700 811224
Contact: Captain R G Proes

Salmon — Scottish salmon reared in the strong sea currents of Argyll, which it is claimed produce quality fish, weighing 1-5kg.
[C] 80 ton p.a
[D] By arrangement

3 **Landcatch Ltd**
PO Box 7, Lochgilphead, Argyll PA31 8JH
Tel: 08803 244 Telx: 778832
Contact: Jim Foster

Salmon — Scottish Atlantic salmon 1-10kg with a guaranteed delivery within thirty six hours of harvesting.
[C] 650 tons p.a
[D] By arrangement

7 **Lea Forge Trout Farm**
Walgherton, Nantwich, Cheshire CW5 7LS
Tel: 0270 841108
Contact: Roy Wiggins

Trout — Brown and rainbow trout reared in Cheshire ½-1½lb, available gutted. Also smoked trout and general fish range supplied.
[C] Fresh trout 50 tons p.a
[D] By arrangement

1 **Loch Eiseort Ltd**
Heaste, Broadford, Isle of Skye, IV42 8QF
Tel: 04712 468 Telx: 75252 Iarman G Fax: 04712 468
Contact: Peter Williams

Salmon — Salmon reared in the unpolluted waters of the Isle of Skye, with an antibiotic free feed, in 1-5kg sizes.
[C] 150 tonne p.a
[D] By arrangement

15 **Lower Cowley Trout Farm**
nr Blackmoor Gate, Parracombe, Devon EX31 4PQ
Tel: 05983 365
Contact: Margaret Golden

Trout — Trout reared in spring fed water in North Devon, weighing 10oz-1½lb, whole or gutted. Some smoked trout available.
[C] 5000 p.a
[D] By own transport within area

15 **Ludbrook Trout Farm**
Meadfoot Meadow, Ermington, Ivybridge, Devon PL21 0LQ
Tel: 0548 830168
Contact: Mr D I Kerr

Trout — Rainbow trout farmed in waters from a moorland spring, 8oz-2lb. Some smoked trout available.
[C] 25 ton p.a
[D] By own transport within area

1 ↔

Mainland Salmon Farm/North Isles Salmon
Rousay, Orkney
Tel: 085682 384
Contact: Bruce Mainland

Salmon — Scottish salmon reared in tanks with pumped water currents for a firm muscle texture, fresh or frozen in fillets, steaks or as whole fish.
Ⓒ Fresh salmon 20,000 p.a
Ⓓ By arrangement

6

Marron Fish Farm
Mill House, Branthwaite, Workington, Cumbria CA14 4SZ
Tel: 0900 5089
Contact: Mr G Talbot

Trout — Rainbow trout farmed in water from the Lake District, fresh 8oz-2lb. Also whole hot smoked trout packed in sleeves.
Ⓒ Fresh trout 20 ton p.a
Ⓓ By own transport within area

3

McConnell Salmon Ltd
Clyde House, 170 Kilbowie Road, Clydebank, Dunbartonshire
Tel: 041941 3696
Contact: Anna Parkinson

Salmon — Farmed salmon available fresh, whole and gutted weighing 2-5kg between Oct-Apr, 1-3½kg May-Sep.
Ⓒ 15,000-20,000 tons p.a
Ⓓ By arrangement

16 ↔

Moore & Moore
Parkview, Swallowfield Street, Swallowfield, Reading, Berkshire RG7 1QX
Tel: 0734 882844
Contact: Martin Moore

Carp — Mirror and leather carp bred for the table, ½-1kg, larger fish available on request. All delivered in aerated fish transport.
Ⓒ 1-2 ton p.a Sep-Dec
Ⓓ By arrangement
See Also: Fish Dealers

6

New Mills Trout Farm
New Mills Trout Farm, Brampton, Cumbria CA8 2QS
Tel: 06977 2384
Contact: Mrs Jay Gray

Trout — Pink fleshed rainbow trout reared in spring fed Cumbria lake, 8oz-5lb, supplied fresh or frozen, whole or filleted.
Ⓒ 25 ton p.a
Ⓓ By arrangement
See Also: Fish: Smoked

1

North Atlantic Salmon Ltd
Mowbray, Walls, Shetland ZE2 9PF
Tel: 0595 71348
Contact: J B Tait

Salmon — Atlantic salmon reared in the Shetland Isles where growth rates are reportedly 10-15% greater than elsewhere in the UK, fresh or frozen, weighing 2-6kg.
Ⓒ 25,000 p.a
Ⓓ By arrangement

10 ↔

The Old Mill Fisheries
Clifford Chambers, Stratford upon Avon, Warwickshire CV37 8HU
Tel: 0789 295389
Contact: Barrie Spratt

Trout — Pink fleshed rainbow trout, 6oz-1lb and rainbow salmon trout, 6lb, raised in natural ponds fed by River Stour, whole, gutted, fresh or frozen.
Ⓒ 80,000 p.a
Ⓓ By arrangement
See Also: Fish: Smoked

1

Orkney Fish Farms
Cairston Road, Stromness, Orkney KW16 3JS
Tel: 0856 850514 Fax: 0856 850568
Contact: Kenneth Sutherland

Salmon — Orkney salmon, 2-4½kg, reared in the pure clear waters of Scapa Flow.
Ⓒ 50 ton p.a
Ⓓ By arrangement
See Also: Fish: Smoked

9

Pembrokeshire Fish Farms
Orielton Mills, Hundleton, Pembroke, Dyfed
Tel: 064681 393
Contact: Margot Bateman

Trout — Trout weighing 1½lb, salmon 6lb average weight. Both supplied fresh or frozen, whole or filleted. Also available 2-3lb sea reared rainbow trout.
Ⓒ 200 ton p.a
Ⓓ By arrangement
See Also: Fish: Smoked

12

Redlake Trout Farm
Littleton, nr Somerton, Somerset TA11 6NS
Tel: 0458 72296
Contact: Mrs R A Booth

Salmon — Spring water reared salmon and trout, weighing 9-16oz (some up to 24oz), fresh or frozen.
Ⓒ 10,000 p.a Mar-Sep
Ⓓ By arrangement

16 ↔

Richard Melhuish
Powdermill Fishery, Blacksmith Lane, Chilworth, nr Guildford, Surrey GU4 8NL
Tel: 0483 570419
Contact: Richard Melhuish

Trout

Brown and rainbow trout sold whole, 1-10lb.
C Undisclosed.
D By arrangement

3

Rothesay Seafoods Ltd
Ardmaleish, Kames Bay, Port Bannatyne, Isle of Bute
Tel: 0700 2451/2878 Telx: 776161
Contact: Mr T S Rae

Trout

Rainbow trout reared in fresh and salt water on the Isle of Bute weighing 140g-2kg.
C 1.5m p.a
D By arrangement

1

M J M Salmon Ltd
Stone Couple, Hillswick, Shetland ZE2 9RW
Tel: 080623 338
Contact: L A Mowat

Salmon

Salmon reared in the unpolluted waters of the Shetland Isles, weighing 1-5kg.
C 50 ton p.a Aug-Dec
D By own transport within area

7

Scot Trout Ltd
The Motherwell Food Park, Bellshill Industrial Estate, Bellshill, Lanarkshire ML4 3JA
Tel: 0698 747272
Contact: Mr Philip A Marshall

Trout

Scottish salmon and trout reared in fresh and salt water lochs. Fresh trout supplied whole and gutted 6-16oz, filleted 3-5oz, or as large trout 1- 2kg, fresh salmon whole and gutted 1-8kg, or in steaks. All products supplied in controlled atmosphere packs.
C Fresh and smoked trout 1500 p.a, fresh and smoked salmon 300-400 ton p.a
D By arrangement
See Also: Fish: Smoked

16 ↔

Scotnish Salmon/Craignish Salmon Ltd
31 Old Burlington Street, London W1X 1LB
Tel: 01 437 2066 Telx: 895 4748
Contact: Mr B Mohammadi

Salmon

Atlantic salmon farmed on the West Coast of Scotland, 1-4kg.
C 10-12 ton p.wk Jun-Aug, 10-12 ton p.wk Oct-Mar
D By arrangement

1

Shetland Marine Salmon Fisheries Ltd
Raga, Brae, Shetland
Tel: 080622 539
Contact: David MacDonald

Salmon

Scottish salmon, farmed in natural currents around the Shetland Isles, 2-7kg.
C 14,000 p.a
D By arrangement

4

Silver Stream Fisheries Ltd
Old Corby Mill, Clogh, Ballymena, Co Antrim
Tel: 026673 655
Contact: Mr T D Wadsworth

Trout

Fresh trout reared in natural streams, available whole weighing 10-16lb.
C 60-70 ton p.a
D By arrangement

9

R G Soden
Home Farm, Llanllawdog, Carmarthen, Dyfed SA32 7JE
Tel: 026784 436
Contact: R G Soden

Trout

Rainbow trout farmed in Carmarthenshire.
C 5 ton p.a
D By own transport within area

1 ↔

South Harris Seafoods
Geocrab Mill, Geocrab, Isle of Harris, Western Isles
Tel: 085983 220
Contact: Gordon Mackay

Salmon

Scottish salmon reared in loch water and matured in the clean seas around the Isle of Harris, in 1½, 2½, 3½kg sizes, delivered locally on ice four hours after harvesting.
C 15,000 p.a
D By own transport within area

16

Test Valley Game Produce Ltd
North Houghton, Stockbridge, Hampshire SO20 6LF
Tel: 0264 810526
Contact: D Dent

Salmon

Fresh Scottish farmed salmon.
C Undisclosed
D By arrangement
See Also: Game Dealers, Fish: Smoked

3

Tobermory Fish Farm Ltd
Main Street, Tobermory, Isle of Mull PA75 6PX
Tel: 0688 2120 Fax: 0688 2140
Contact: Mrs Susie Carmichael

Trout

Salmon and trout farmed in the clear waters of the west coast of Scotland, supplied fresh or frozen, whole or filleted.
C Undisclosed
D By arrangement
See Also: Fish: Smoked

6

Ullswater Trout
Sockbridge Mill Trout Farm, Sockbridge, nr Penrith, Cumbria CA10 2JT
Tel: 0768 65338
Contact: Gillian Claridge

Trout

Whole pink fleshed trout reared in natural streams supplied fresh, chilled or frozen, weighing on average 10oz-1lb.
C 100,000 p.a
D By own transport within area
See Also: Fish: Pâtés and Pastes

9

Upper Mills Trout Farm
Glyn Ceiriog, nr Llangollen, Clwyd LL20 7BY
Tel: 0691 72225
Contact: R I R I Cornes

Trout

Trout farmed in unpolluted river water, 8-12oz, whole or gutted. Smoked trout also available.
C 40 ton p.a
D By own transport within area

13

Weir House Trout Farms Ltd
Latimer Road, Chesham, Buckinghamshire HP5 1QQ
Tel: 0494 775954
Contact: S R Williams

Trout

Trout farmed in artesian spring water in Buckinghamshire from an all female stock, fresh or frozen, whole or filleted. Smoked trout and salmon also supplied.
C Trout undisclosed, smoked trout 50-60 ton p.a, smoked salmon 15-16 ton p.a
D By arrangement

15 ↔

West Country Trout
Trafalgar Farm, Boscastle, North Cornwall PL35 0BW
Tel: 08405 224
Contact: E R and D F L Ruscombe-King

Trout

Pink fleshed trout farmed in North Cornwall weighing 1-2lb, supplied live or boxed on ice.
C 24,000 p.a, 12,000 2lb fish Mar-Jun
D By arrangement
See Also: Fresh Meat

1

Wester Ross Salmon Ltd
Ardmair, Ullapool, Ross & Cromarty IV26 2TN
Tel: 0854 2121 Telx: 75570 ROSSAL G
Contact: Mrs Anne Richards

Salmon

Salmon bred in Highland spring water and matured in the clear waters of the west coast of Scotland, weighing 2-3kg in April, 3-4kg in September and 4-5kg in December.
C 600 ton p.a
D By arrangement

SHELLFISH DEALERS

6 ↔

Ashdown Smokers
Skellerah Farm, Corney, nr Nootle, Cumberland LA19 5TW
Tel: 06578 324
Contact: E H Fellows

Lobster
Crab

Fresh lobster and crab delivered live within Cumbria and possibly other nearby areas.
C Undisclosed
D By arrangement
See Also: Meat: Smoked, Game Dealers, Fish Dealers, Fish: Smoked, Cheese

1

Benesther Shellfish
Old Schoolhouse, Deerness, Orkney KW17 2QH
Tel: 0856 74267
Contact: Dennis Gowland

Scallops

Pacific oysters, queen scallops and mussels available to order.
C Undisclosed
D By arrangement
See Also: Shellfish Farmers, Fish: Smoked

16

Botterell Seatrades Ltd
Harbour Road, Rye Harbour, Rye, East Sussex TN31 7TT
Tel: 0797 222875
Contact: Mr John Botterell

Velvet crab

Live and cooked lobster, crab, spider crab, scallops, velvet crab and shrimps.
C 50-200kg p.wk mainly Apr-Oct
D By own transport
See Also: Fish Dealers, Sea Vegetables

15

Browse Bros
The Harbour, Paignton, Devon TQ4 6DT
Tel: 0803 559267
Contact: K Browse

Lobster

Devon crab and lobster, live, freshly boiled or frozen in individual vacuum packs.
C Undisclosed
D By own transport within area

5

Burgon (Eyemouth) Ltd
Harbour Road, Eyemouth, Berwickshire TD14 5HZ
Tel: 08907 50272 Telx: 72365 Fax: 08907 51259
Contact: Grahame Sinclair

Winkles

Live winkles and lobster. Also available crab meat in mixed dark and white 300g, 1lb catering packs, cooked and peeled prawns.
C Winkles 5-10 ton p.wk, crab 1000 ton Apr-Dec
D By arrangement
See Also: Fish Dealers

15

Channel Fisheries
13 Penpethy Road, Brixham, Devon TQ5 8NN
Tel: 08045 51210
Contact: Mr Purnell

Crayfish

Live crab, crayfish, lobster, scallops in or off the shell, mussels and Pacific oysters.
Ⓒ Scallops 100lb p.wk Sep-Apr
Ⓓ By own transport within area
See Also: Fish Dealers, Fish: Smoked

15

Copine Fish Ltd
The Stone Quay, Castletown Harbour, Portland, Dorset DT5 1DB
Tel: 0305 821185
Contact: Mr Newton

Crawfish

Spider crab, edible crab, crawfish (spiny lobster), lobster, winkles, and mussels caught off the Dorset coast and transported live packed on ice or in vivier tanks.
Ⓒ Spider crab 500-600 ton May-Aug, edible crab 600-700 ton p.a, crawfish 16-18 ton Jun-Sep, lobster 30-40 ton
Ⓓ By arrangement

4

R H Ennis & Son
5 New Road, Portavogie, Co Down BT22 1EN
Tel: 02477 71235
Contact: Rodney Ennis

Prawns

Winkles and head-on prawns. Also whiting, cod and herring.
Ⓒ Undisclosed Apr-Sep
Ⓓ By arrangement

15

Guernsey Fisherman's Trading Co Ltd
Castle Emplacement, St Peter Port, Guernsey
Tel: 0481 24420 Telx: GFTC 4191489
Contact: Mr Warren Brett

Lobster

Lobster and a wide range of shellfish including scallops fished from Guernsey waters and supplied fresh. Also a selection of wet fish including brill, bass, turbot and blond ray.
Ⓒ Undisclosed
Ⓓ By arrangement

15 ↔

W Harvey & Sons
The Coombe, Newlyn, Penzance, Cornwall TR18 5HF
Tel: 0736 62734/62983
Contact: Mr Matt Harvey

Winkles

Lobster, brown crab, crawfish and winkles. Also crab meat in 1lb bags.
Ⓒ Undisclosed
Ⓓ By arrangement

7

Heaningbrook Trout Farm
The Heaning, Newton-in-Bowland, Clitheroe, Lancashire BB7 3ED
Tel: 02008 274/617 Fax: 02008 667
Contact: John Blanc

Shellfish

Range of frozen shellfish.
Ⓒ Undisclosed
Ⓓ By arrangement
See Also: Fish Dealers, Fish Farmers

3 ↔

Inlaks Seafoods Ltd
Unit 14, Prospect Business Centre, Dundee DD2 1TY
Tel: 0382 561549
Contact: Mr Foster Gault

Scampi

Peeled scampi in 1lb packs or larger to order. Also whole cooked crab.
Ⓒ Scampi 50 ton p.a Oct-May, crab Apr-Oct
Ⓓ By arrangement
See Also: Fish: Smoked

16 ↔

Kennet Valley Fisheries
Lower Way Farm, Lower Way, Thatcham, Berkshire RG13 4TL
Tel: 0635 66699 Telx: 847860 ICELT
Contact: Martin Duggan

Crayfish

Live native crayfish, crab, lobster, oysters, mussels, langoustine and crawfish.
Ⓒ Undisclosed
Ⓓ By arrangement
See Also: Game Dealers, Fish Farmers, Fish: Smoked

3 ↔

Loch Fyne Oysters Ltd
Ardkinglas, Cairndow, Argyll PA36 8BH
Tel: 04996 264/217
Contact: Mr Andrew Lane

Langoustine

Langoustine fished in the Jura sound and landed at Crinan. Fresh mussels wild from Loch Etive also available.
Ⓒ Langoustine 1 ton p.wk, mussels 75-100 ton p.a
Ⓓ By arrangement
See Also: Fish Dealers, Shellfish Farmers, Fish: Smoked

1

Morayfish (Portree) Ltd
The Pier, Portree, Isle of Skye IV51 9DE
Tel: 0478 2414
Contact: Catriona Matheson

Dublin Bay prawns

Lobster, scallops and Dublin Bay prawns supplied in 10kg packs. Also available fresh wild salmon.
Ⓒ Undisclosed salmon Jun-Aug
Ⓓ By arrangement

14

River Farm Smokery
Great Wilbraham Road, Bottisham, nr Newmarket, Cambridgeshire CB1 5J
Tel: 0223 811382
Contact: R F Enoch

Cockles
Crayfish

Live brown clams, native oysters, mussels, crayfish, lobster, crab, king prawns, uncooked prawn tails, king and queen scallops.
Ⓒ Undisclosed
Ⓓ By arrangement
See Also: Meat: Smoked, Game: Smoked, Fish Dealers, Fish: Pâtés and Pastes, Fish: Pies and Prepared Dishes, Fish: Smoked, Sea Vegetables, Snacks and Savouries

1

Rousay Processors Ltd
Trumland Pier, Rousay, Orkney KW17 2PU
Tel: 085682 216 Telx: 75192
Contact: Pier Lees

Velvet crab

Velvet crab live or frozen, lobster and frozen whelks.
Ⓒ Lobster 10-12 tonne p.a Jun-Jan, velvet crab 50 tonne p.a Oct-May, whelks 20 tonne p.a Oct-May
Ⓓ By arrangement
See Also: Fish: Pies and Prepared Dishes

16

Shaw Shellfish
Dell Quay Boatyard, Dell Quay, Chichester, West Sussex
Tel: 0243 775626
Contact: Adam Shaw

Crab

Oysters, clams, crab and lobster supplied live or cooked. Also live eel.
Ⓒ Oysters Nov-Mar, eel spring and summer
Ⓓ By own transport within area
See Also: Fish: Smoked

14

J & J Shellfish Ltd
Alexandra Dock, King's Lynn, Norfolk
Tel: 0553 772520 Fax: 0553 691086
Contact: John Williamson

Cockles

Shrimps, cockles and mussels netted in own boats and supplied fresh. Also available frozen local whelks, small quantities of potted shrimps in 2oz pots and a full range of wet fish in season.
Ⓒ Undisclosed
Ⓓ By arrangement
See Also: Shellfish Farmers, Sea Vegetables

15

Shellfish Channel Islands Ltd
Patrommerie Road, St Peter Port, Guernsey
Tel: 0481 710089
Contact: Lloyd Savident

Spider crab

Spider crab, crab and lobster live from Guernsey. Also crab meat in 1, 2lb packs, fresh or frozen, pasteurised cocktail claws in ½lb packs and dressed crab.
Ⓒ 1 ton p.wk Apr-Jul, Dec-Mar
Ⓓ By arrangement

11

Shellfish Seafoods Ltd
Watling Street, Hinckley, Leicestershire
Tel: 0455 619009 Telx: 34468 SHELFR G
Contact: Mr S West

Crayfish

Live crab, crayfish and lobster kept in sea water tanks for freshness.
Ⓒ Undisclosed
Ⓓ By own transport nationally
See Also: Game: Smoked, Fish Dealers, Fish: Smoked

1

J Steer
The Lobster Pond, Ferry Road, Stromness, Orkney KW16 3AE
Tel: 0856 850465
Contact: J Steer

Scallops

Range of shellfish caught in the waters around the Orkney Isles, including crab, crab claws in 40lb cartons, lobster and scallops in 1lb cartons. Also available, crab meat for makers of pâté.
Ⓒ Undisclosed
Ⓓ By arrangement

15

Sylvesters Seafoods
Holt House, Richmond Road, Appledore, North Devon EX39 4LD
Tel: 02372 79101
Contact: Mrs Felicity Sylvester

Crab

Live crab, fresh crab claws, lobster, mussels and Dublin Bay prawns, in season.
Ⓒ Undisclosed, crab and prawns Apr-Oct
Ⓓ By arrangement
See Also: Fish Dealers, Fish: Smoked

9

Vin Sullivan of Abergavenny Ltd
Triley Mill, Abergavenny, Gwent NP7 8DE
Tel: 0873 2331
Contact: Mr John Sullivan

Lobster
Clam

Lobster, crawfish, Dublin Bay prawns, crayfish, crab, crab meat, abalones, clams, oysters, winkles, whelks, shrimps, cockles, and native mussels, live or cooked and split cleaned.
Ⓒ Undisclosed
Ⓓ By own transport nationally
See Also: Fish Dealers, Sea Vegetables, Fresh Fruit

1

William Jolly
Hatston Industrial Estate, Scott's Road, Kirkwall, Orkney
Tel: 0856 2417
Contact: Billy Jolly

Whelks

Frozen crab, scallops and whelks.
Ⓒ Crab shell on claws and brown meat 10-20 ton p.a Apr-Oct
Ⓓ By arrangement
See Also: Fish Dealers, Fish: Smoked

SHELLFISH FARMERS

3 ↔

A Abrahams
The Strand, Colonsay, Argyll PA61 7TR
Tel: 09512 365
Contact: A Abrahams

Oyster

Pacific oysters cultivated in the open sea for sweeter flavour and ground cultured mussels. Also available smoked oysters and smoked mussels.
[C] Oysters 50,000 p.a, mussels 2 ton p.a, smoked oysters 100 p.wk
[D] By own transport within area
See Also: Sea Vegetables, Honey

14

Andrew Athill
Scaldbeck Barn, Morston, Holt, Norfolk NR25 7BJ
Tel: 0263 740306
Contact: Andrew Athill

Oyster

Pacific oysters cultivated in Blakeney Harbours clean waters, graded as No.1 weighing over 100g or No.2 weighing 75-100g.
[C] 20,000 p.a
[D] By arrangement

1 ↔

Aquamarine Farm (Mussels) Ltd
12 St Brendan Road, Castleby, Isle of Barra, Outer Hebrides
Tel: 087 14467
Contact: William Blacker

Mussels

High meat yielding and grit free mussels cultivated by rope culture method in the clean waters of the Outer Hebrides.
[C] 20 ton p.a
[D] By arrangement

1 ↔

Benesther Shellfish
Old Schoolhouse, Deerness, Orkney KW17 2QH
Tel: 0856 74 267
Contact: Dennis Gowland

Oysters

Pacific oysters (Crasostrea Gigas) cultivated in the clean waters of Orkney, with a delivery service offered for orders over ten dozen.
[C] 300,000 p.a
[D] By arrangement
See Also: Shellfish Dealers, Fish: Smoked

1

Bratan Baghasdal Ltd/Lochboisdale Salmon
21 Kenneth Drive, Lochboisdale, South Uist, Western Isles PA81 5TJ
Tel: 08784 549/288
Contact: Ian Binnie

Mussels

Grit free mussels in a clean shell supplied in 30lb bags.
C 1 ton p.wk
D By arrangement
See Also: Fish Farmers

15 ↔

British Crayfish Marketing Association Ltd
Riversdale Farm, Stour Provost, nr Gillingham, Dorset SP8 5RZ
Tel: 074785 495
Contact: Mo Richards

Crayfish

Freshwater signal crayfish sold with two good claws, clean intestine, guaranteed live delivery and a maximum of eight per lb packed in 5kg boxes.
C Undisclosed Jul-Oct
D Interlink Road Service

14

Colchester Oyster Fisheries
North Farm, East Road, East Mersea, Essex
Tel: 0206 384141 Telx: Group tlx 987 562
Contact: Mr Kerrison

Oysters

Live Pacific oysters available all year round and native oysters during the season. Also available fresh crab meat.
C Undisclosed
D By arrangement
See Also: Fish: Pies and Prepared Dishes

1

Cromarty Mussels
George Street, Cromarty, Ross & Cromarty
Tel: 03817 314
Contact: Robert Davie

Mussels

Live mussels cultivated in the cold waters of the North Sea, reportedly succulent and meaty, packed in 30lb bags.
C 10 ton p.a Sep-Apr
D By arrangement

4

Cuan Sea Fisheries
Strangford Lough, Sketrick Island, Killinchy, Newtownards, Co Down BT23 6QH
Tel: 0238 541461 Telx: 747437
Contact: The Proprietor

Oysters

Pacific oysters cultivated in County Down. Also small quantities of smoked salmon supplied to order.
C Oysters 300 ton p.a
D By arrangement
See Also: Fish: Pies and Prepared Dishes

15

Devon Oysters Ltd
1 Webbers Way, Dartington, Totnes, Devon TQ9 6JD
Tel: 0803 866226
Contact: R Farrer

Pacific oysters

Pacific oysters cultivated in South Devon. Also available ground cultured mussels.
C Oysters 200,000 p.a, mussels 4 ton p.mth Oct-Mar
D By arrangement

15

Duchy of Cornwall Oyster Farm
Port Navas, Falmouth, Cornwall TR11 5RJ
Tel: 0326 40210
Contact: Len Hodges

Native oysters

Native oysters, local mussels and clams cultivated in the waters of the Rivers Halford and Percuil, leased from the Duchy of Cornwall.
C Oysters 250,000 p.a
D By arrangement

4

Exe River Shellfish
5 Vaughan Road, Heavitree, Exeter, Devon EX1 3DH
Tel: 0626 890133
Contact: Mr May

Oysters

Pacific oysters and mussels packed in wet seaweed and delivered throughout the UK within twenty four hours of harvesting. Also small quantities of Manila clams (palourdes) available.
C Oysters 3000 p.wk, mussels 2-3 ton p.wk Jul-Mar
D By arrangement

9

A J Folder
Tything Barn, West Williamston, Kilgetty, Dyfed SA68 OTN
Tel: 0646 651452
Contact: A J Folder

Manila clams

Manila clams (palourdes) and Pacific oysters cultivated in fattening ponds.
C Oysters 50 ton p.a Sep-Apr
W Garon Foods of Lawrenny 06467 692
D By wholesaler

1 ↔

Hebridean Shellfish Growers Ltd
Sandwick Road, Stornoway, Isle of Lewis, Western Isles
Tel: 085 983311
Contact: J S Luty

Mussels

Live mussels cultivated in sea lochs in the Outer Hebrides by rope culture method, resulting in a clean shell, grit and silt free with a high meat yield. Available 2″ long in 2st bags.
C 350 ton p.a
W Hebridean Shellfish
D By wholesaler

Colchester Oyster Fishery Limited

North Farm, East Mersea, Colchester, Essex
Telephone: (0206) 384141

At Pyefleet Creek, near Colchester, lies the famous fattening grounds for the Succulent Shellfish of Colchester Oysters.

From 1st May 1989 individuals may visit the fishery during working hours for a talk, a guided tour of the premises and an opportunity to sample some of the produce. Groups are also very welcome at anytime by appointment. A visit can be arranged to suit a group's particular interests and requirements and can include anything from a cornucopia of shellfish straight from the sea, to a gourmet's banquet prepared by a Cordon Bleu cook. Among the wares are Oysters - of course - live Lobster, Crabs, Mussels and Clams. Fresh fish landed by local boats is available and also Smoked Salmon and Eel which is distributed to wholesale customers at home and abroad and to better known seafood restaurants.

You can even go for a voyage on an oyster dredger or an Essex Shrimping Boat under sail and help catch the Oysters and Shrimps yourselves!

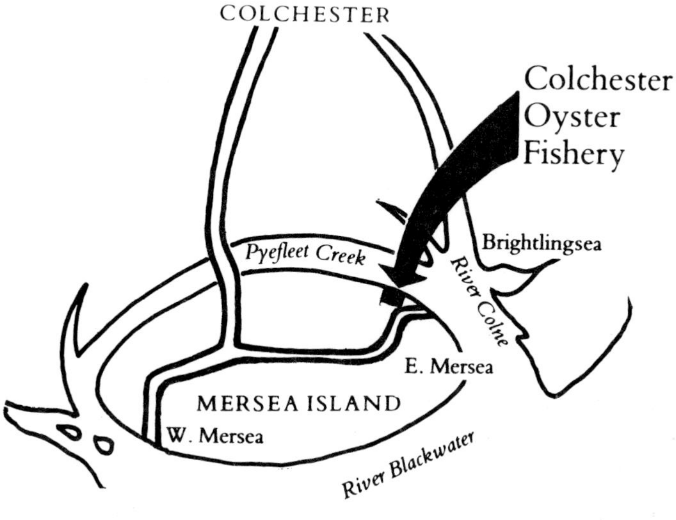

15 ↔

Isles of Scilly Shellfish Co Ltd
1 Buzza Street, St Marys, Isles of Scilly, Cornwall
Tel: 0720 22002/22180
Contact: Richard Chiverton

Oysters — Pacific oysters (Crasostrea Gigas) cultivated in the Scilly Isles.
[C] 15,000 p.a
[D] By arrangement

15

Jersey Sea Farms
Le Clos des Rues, La Longue Rue, St Lawrence, Jersey
Tel: 0534 63110
Contact: Tony Legg

Manila clam — Manila clams (palourdes) weighing 15-50g.
[C] 110 ton p.a
[D] By arrangement

15 ↔

Kingcombe Crayfish
St Francis Farm, Hooke, nr Beaminster, Dorset DT8 3NX
Tel: 0308 862711
Contact: Mr Colton

Crayfish — Live signal crayfish cultivated in fresh water ponds weighing 2oz each.
[C] 4 ton Jul-Oct
[W] British Crayfish Marketing Association Ltd, 0264 52474
[D] By wholesaler

3 ↔

Knapdale Sea Farms
PO Box 1, Lochgilphead, Argyll
Tel: 054685 288
Contact: P Williams

Manila clam — Variety of shellfish cultivated on beds in Loch Sween including Manila clams (palourdes), native and Pacific oysters.
[C] Undisclosed
[D] By own transport within area

1

Lang-Geo Oysters
Lang-Geo, Finstown, Orkney KW17 2EL
Tel: 0856 76544
Contact: Dave Bichan

Oysters — Live Pacific oysters (Crasostrea Gigas) cultivated in the clean, cold water of Orkney. Also available princess scallops, king scallops and velvet crab.
[C] 200,000 p.a
[D] By arrangement

3

Loch Etive Mussels
Tigh Na Speir, Connel, Argyll PA37 1PH
Tel: 063171 505
Contact: Janet Church

Mussels — Clean shell, rope cultivated mussels and one year old princess scallops available live from Loch Etive.
[C] ½ ton p.wk
[D] By own transport within area

3 ↔

Loch Fyne Oysters Ltd
Ardkinglas, Cairndow, Argyll PA36 8BH
Tel: 04996 264/217
Contact: Mr Andrew Lane

Gigas oysters — Crasostrea Gigas oysters, referred to as cupped oysters because of the cupped and slightly crinkly shell, cultivated at fishery on Loch Fyne. Supplied as Loch Fyne 1-medium, Loch Fyne 2-large, supplied packed in seaweed.
[C] 400-500 ton p.a
[D] By arrangement
See Also: Fish Dealers, Shellfish Dealers, Fish: Smoked

14

Mervyn Nudds
The Smithy, Brancaster, Kings Lynn, Norfolk
Tel: 0485 210638
Contact: Mervyn Nudds

Mussels — Mussels collected from the sandbanks in the Wash and laid out to fatten on plankton in the only EEC recognised pollution free harbour in Britain. Riddled by hand and sold fresh, minimum size 2″ long.
[C] 2 ton p.wk Oct-Apr
[D] By arrangement

9

Mona Seafoods Ltd
The Oyster Hatchery, Brynsiencyn, Anglesey LL61 6TQ
Tel: 024873 411/412
Contact: D Lea-Wilson

Oysters — Anglesey farmed oysters purified by ultra violet light and certified bacteria free. Fresh lobster also available.
[C] Oysters 1000 p.wk Jun-Sep, lobster 5-10,000 p.a
[D] By arrangement
See Also: Fish Dealers, Sea Vegetables

3 ↔

Mull Shellfish Ltd
Dunan, Ardtun, Bunessan, Isle of Mull, Argyll PA67 6DH
Tel: 06817 295
Contact: Ms Alice McKay

Mussels — Live mussels cultivated in the clean waters of the Isle of Mull.
[C] 50 ton p.a Sep-Mar
[D] By arrangement
See Also: Fish: Smoked

16 ↔

Newtown Oyster Fishery Co Ltd
Dodpits House, nr Yarmouth, Isle of Wight PO41 0TW
Tel: 0983 78303
Contact: Mr Lucas

Venus clams — Live cultivated mussels, re-laid for fattening, small quantities of native oysters and Venus Mercenaria clams.
[C] Mussels 25 ton p.a
[D] By arrangement

15 ↔

Rocquaine Shellfish Ponds
Guernsey
Tel: 0481 64633
Contact: R E Tostevin

Ormers — Ormers (flat abalone) recently introduced and now farmed commercially in the Channel Islands, with a taste similar to a whelk and a mussel. Also cultivated Portuguese oysters (Gigas).
[C] Ormers 3000-5000 p.a, oysters 1000-2000 p.wk
[D] By arrangement

1

Salen Shellfish Scotland Ltd
Unit 3, Blamhor Industrial Estate, Fort William, Inverness PH33 7PT
Tel: 096785 699/0397 4030
Contact: Mr K Cope

Scallops — Princess, queen and king scallops, oysters and mussels cultivated in the pure waters of a Scottish loch, live, chilled or frozen. Also small quantities of smoked princess scallops supplied.
[C] Princess scallops 200 ton p.a
[D] By arrangement

3 ↔

Seacroft Oysters (Shellfish Farms)
Baravalla, Tarbert, Argyll PA29 6YD
Tel: 08802 583
Contact: Dr Neil Duncan

Oysters — Velvet and shore crab available live. Also cultivated Pacific (cupped) oysters. All shellfish delivered within twenty four hours of harvesting.
[C] Crab 40 ton p.a, oysters 100 ton p.a
[D] By arrangement

1

Seafish Industry Authority
Marine Farming Unit, Ardtoe, Acharacle, Argyll PH36 4LD
Tel: 096 785666
Contact: Jeremy Paul

Princess scallops — Princess scallops measuring 4-5cm in the shell, recently developed as a smaller version of the queen scallop and regarded as an alternative to mussels, supplied packed on ice.
[C] 30,000-40,000 p.a Sep-Mar
[D] By arrangement

16

Seasalter Shellfish (Whitstable) Ltd
The Harbour, Whitstable, Kent CT5 1AB
Tel: 0227 262003/272003 Telx: 966293 OYSTER G
Contact: Dr C G Askew

Oysters

Pacific oysters raised on the ancient freehold oyster beds of Whitstable. Delivery within twenty four hours of oysters leaving holding tanks.
C 750,000 p.a
D By Datapost

14

J & J Shellfish Ltd
Alexandra Dock, King's Lynn, Norfolk
Tel: 0553 772520 Fax: 0553 691086
Contact: John Williamson

Mussels

Farmed oysters and mussels available fresh, chilled and frozen.
C Mussels 40 ton p.wk Sep-Mar
D By arrangement
See Also: Shellfish Dealers, Sea Vegetables

3

Shona Oysters
Eilean Shona, Acharacle, Argyll PH36 4LR
Tel: 096785 249
Contact: Mr Stead

Oysters

Pacific oysters cultivated in Scotland.
C 30,000-40,000 p.a
D By arrangement

15 ↔

Surfside Oysters
Unit 11, South Quay, The Harbour, Paignton, Devon TQ4 6DT
Tel: 0803 525194
Contact: Robert O'Kelly

Mussels

Barnacle free Devon mussels with a high meat content. Pacific oysters delivered daily throughout England. Also available lobster, crab and crayfish during summer months.
C Mussels 5 ton p.wk Aug-Apr, oysters 4000 p.wk
D By arrangement

1 ↔

Westend Shellfish
Glenborrowdale, Acharacle, Argyll PH36 4JP
Tel: 0972 4235
Contact: A C Bowker

Scallops

Princess scallops farmed in the clear waters of a Scottish loch and supplied packed on ice.
C Undisclosed Apr-Dec
D By arrangement

PATES AND PASTES

6

Akebank Fish Farm and Smokery
Mosser, Cockermouth, Cumbria CA13 ORB
Tel: 0900 826517
Contact: P Carruthers

Pike

Range of smoked pâtés including pike, salmon, trout and kipper, in 4oz pots or catering packs on request.
C Undisclosed
D By arrangement
See Also: Fish Farmers

16

Andwell Mill Farms
Andwell Lane, Andwell, Basingstoke, Hampshire RG27 9PA
Tel: 025 672 4551 Telx: 858599
Contact: R E N Barder

Trout

Additive free smoked trout pâté in 4oz, 2lb packs.
C 1 ton p.wk
D By arrangement
See Also: Fish Farmers, Fish: Smoked

12 ↔

Brown & Forrest
Thorney, Langport, Somerset TA10 0DR
Tel: 0458 251520
Contact: Michael Brown

Eel

Smoked eel pâté made with double cream, horseradish, lemon juice and black pepper, in 8oz packs or catering packs to order.
C Undisclosed
D By arrangement
See Also: Fish Dealers, Fish: Smoked

15

Cornish Smoked Fish Co Ltd
Charlestown, St Austell, Cornwall PL25 5NY
Tel: 0726 72356
Contact: Martin Pumphrey

Mackerel

Range of smoked pâtés including salmon and mackerel in 500g tubs.
C Undisclosed
D By arrangement
See Also: Fish: Smoked

9

Cwm Trout Farm
Maes-y-Gwenith, Llanvair Discoed, Chepstow, Gwent NP6 6LN
Tel: 02917 719
Contact: Mr J B Margesson

Trout

Smoked trout pâté made with own trout in 8, 12oz tubs.
C Undisclosed
D By own transport within area
See Also: Fish Farmers, Fish: Smoked

12 ↔

Fish Farm Services Ltd
The Old Manse, Tisbury, Wiltshire SP3 6LG
Tel: 0747 870791
Contact: Mr Berkley-Matthew

Trout

Fish Fare, fresh trout pâté in 4oz tubs packed in boxes of 1, 2 dozen, or in 3lb containers.
C 200-300lb p.wk
D By arrangement
See Also: Fish Farmers

15 ↔

La Charcuterie of Dorset
Railway Triangle Estate, Poundbury Road, Dorchester, Dorset DT1 2PJ
Tel: 0903 66900
Contact: H J Cocklin

Cornish crab

Range of additive free pâtés including Cornish crab with butter and cream, and smoked trout with butter, cream and lemon.
C Undisclosed
D By arrangement
See Also: Meat: Pâtés and Pastes, Game: Pâtés and Pastes

16

Mermaid Foods Of Bosham Ltd
18 Penwarden Way, Bosham, Chichester, West Sussex PO18 8LF
Tel: 0243 572950
Contact: Miss E Parish

Crab mousse

Homemade additive free crab mousse and smoked salmon pâté with own grown herbs, in 71g portion packs, 8, 16oz tubs. Also chicken liver pâté.
C 5000 tubs p.wk
D By arrangement

14 ↔

Norfolk Smokehouses Ltd
Poplar Farm, Worlingworth, Woodbridge, Suffolk IP13 7LR
Tel: 072 876212
Contact: J D Hildreth

Kipper

Range of pâtés including smoked mackerel and kipper in 1.81kg containers.
C 2-3 ton p.wk
D By arrangement
See Also: Meat: Pâtés and Pastes, Game: Pâtés and Pastes, Vegetable Dishes

1 ↔

Orkney Foods
Little Stonehall, Deerness, Orkney KW17 2QQ
Tel: 085674 333
Contact: Mrs Floris Couperwhite

Crab

Range of additive free frozen fish and shellfish pâtés including partan (crab) and smoked mackerel in 227, 454, 910g packs.
C 50kg p.wk
D By own transport within area
See Also: Meat: Pâtés and Pastes, Fish: Pies and Prepared Dishes, Pies and Puddings

16

Phillips of Wight Farm
Wight Farm, Binstead, Isle of Wight PO33 4EH
Tel: 0983 65100 Telx: 86415 SALMON G
Contact: R V D Phillips

Trout

Smoked trout pâté and smoked trout pâté with brandy and cream in 4, 8oz, 1kg packs.
C Undisclosed
D By arrangement
See Also: Fish: Smoked

14

River Farm Smokery
Great Wilbraham Road, Bottisham, nr Newmarket, Cambridgeshire CB1 5J
Tel: 0223 811382
Contact: R F Enoch

Mackerel

Homemade taramosalata, smoked trout, mackerel, and salmon pâtés.
C Undisclosed
D By arrangement
See Also: Meat: Smoked, Game: Smoked, Fish Dealers, Shellfish Dealers, Fish: Pies and Prepared Dishes, Fish: Smoked, Sea Vegetables, Snacks and Savouries

12

Sea Farm (Shearwater) Ltd
Robinson House, Nuffield Way, Abingdon, Oxon OX14 1RL Oxfordshire OX14 1RL
Tel: 0235 32030 Telx: 837822
Contact: Mr P W Stockdale

Tuna

Range of fish and shellfish mousses and pâtés including salmon, tuna, smoked mackerel, and crab, all with a seven day refrigerated life.
C Undisclosed
D By arrangement
See Also: Fish: Pies and Prepared Dishes

3

Tarbert Fyne Foods Ltd
10 Scottish Food Centre, Motherwell Food Park, Bellshill, Strathclyde ML4 3JA
Tel: 0698 844654 Telx: 779899
Contact: Calum J Ross

Salmon mousse

Additive free Scottish salmon mousse, in 58g pots in packs of ten. Also salmon en croute.
C Undisclosed
D By arrangement
See Also: Fish: Smoked

16

Three oh Four
The Old Hall, Iden, Rye, East Sussex TN31 7XD
Tel: 07978 304
Contact: The Proprietor

Crab

Range of six pâtés including smoked salmon, crab, and taramosalata, frozen in individual plastic pots.
C Undisclosed
D By arrangement
See Also: Fish: Smoked, Snacks and Savouries

6

Ullswater Trout
Sockbridge Mill Trout Farm, Sockbridge, nr Penrith, Cumbria CA10 2JT
Tel: 0768 65338
Contact: Gillian Claridge

Smoked trout cheesecake

Handmade smoked trout pâté weighing 4oz, 1, 2lb. Also smoked trout cheesecake in 7, 10″ diameters and rainbow trout terrine weighing 1, 2lb.
Ⓒ Smoked trout pâté 50lb p.wk, smoked trout cheesecake 20 p.wk, rainbow trout terrine 20 p.wk
Ⓓ By own transport within area
See Also: Fish Farmers

PIES AND PREPARED DISHES

16

Ark Fisheries
51-52 Cliffe High Street, Lewes, East Sussex BN7 2AN
Tel: 0273 476912
Contact: Mr B Wright

Fishcakes

Poached dressed salmon, seafood platter and a range of homemade fishcakes and pies.
Ⓒ Undisclosed
Ⓓ By arrangement
See Also: Sea Vegetables

16

Arrow Foods (1986) Ltd
71 Hillfield Road, Selsey, West Sussex PO20 OJA
Tel: 0243 603393 Telx:86647
Contact: Mr Arrow

Seafood coquille

Range of frozen shellfish dishes including seafood coquille, mixed shellfish in brandy sauce, crab au gratin, crabmeat in herb sauce, dressed crab, and cooked crabmeat surrounded by piped potato. All prepared on 12cm scallop shells in packs of 2, 12 suitable for the catering trade.
Ⓒ Undisclosed
Ⓓ By own transport nationally

1

Bannerman Seafood Ltd
The Burgage, Tain, Ross & Cromarty
Tel: 0862 2322 Telx: 75620 Fax: 0862 2812
Contact: R R Bannerman

Scampi

Frozen scampi and Dublin Bay prawns fished from Loch Inver on the west coast of Scotland, shelled and coated with butter and breadcrumbs.
Ⓒ 2 ton p.wk
Ⓓ By arrangement
See Also: Fish: Smoked

14

Colchester Oyster Fisheries
North Farm, East Road, East Mersea, Essex
Tel: 0206 384141 Telx: Group tlx 987 562
Contact: Mr Kerrison

Oyster

Range of frozen oyster dishes with sauces, supplied in dozen portion size pots.
Ⓒ Undisclosed
Ⓓ By arrangement
See Also: Shellfish Farmers

14

Cromer Crab Company
Old Station Yard, Norwich Road, Cromer, Norwich NR27 0HF
Tel: 0263 511158
Contact: John Williams

Cromer crab

Cromer crab cooked and dressed in own shell, fresh or frozen in 4, 7oz sizes.
Ⓒ Undisclosed Apr-Nov
Ⓓ By own transport nationally

4

Cuan Sea Fisheries
Strangford Lough, Sketrick Island, Killinchy, Newtownards, Co Down BT23 6QH
Tel: 0238 541461 Telx: 747437
Contact: The Proprietor

Oyster mornay

Range of frozen prepared dishes including oysters mornay, and oysters au gratin, supplied in shell in packs of six. Also angels on horseback, breaded oysters, and oysters in Guinness, supplied in packs of one dozen.
Ⓒ Undisclosed
Ⓦ Starfish Ltd of Ipswich
Ⓓ By wholesaler, by arrangement
See Also: Shellfish Farmers

1

Daniels Sweet Herring Ltd
Dell of Inshes, Inverness IV1 2BG
Tel: 0463 225349
Contact: Rosemary Griffin

Rollmops

Scottish herring prepared in a range of marinades including rollmops, sweet diced herring with onion and peppers, and skinned fillets in sherry or tomato sauce. All in 2½lt catering buckets, 250g packs.
Ⓒ 100 ton p.a
Ⓓ By arrangement

14

Dawnfresh Seafoods Ltd
17 Betts Avenue, Martlesham, Suffolk IP5 7RH
Tel: 0473 610060 Telx: 988821 Fax: 0473 625991
Contact: John V Catherall

Scampi

Scottish scampi fished from around Mallaig and Ullapool, peeled and breaded in a double coating of golden crumbs, in 1lb packs. Also a range of seafood platters including whole scampi tails, scallops, goujons of plaice, haddock fillets and Scottish white fish.
Ⓒ Undisclosed
Ⓓ By arrangement
See Also: Shellfish Dealers

9

Leslie A Parsons and Sons (Burry Port) Ltd
Ashburnham Works, Burry Port, Dyfed SA16 0ET
Tel: 05546 3351/2 Telx: 48297 JOYTEL G Ref E230
Contact: Rory Parsons

Cockles

Bottled cockles and mussels, in 150ml jars in outers of twelve and catering packs of four dozen jars.
[C] Undisclosed
[D] By arrangement
See Also: Chutneys and Pickles

2

Moray Seafoods
9-13 Low Street, Buckie, Moray District, Grampian Region AB5 1UX
Tel: 0542 31296 Telx: 73287
Contact: Charles E Eckersley

Scampi Provencale

Range of ready to cook or microwave dishes including scampi a la Romana, scampi Provencale, and scampi in butter sauce, all in 300g cartons. Also frozen scampi tails, breaded scampi in natural or golden crumbs, king scallops and prawn schooners, all in 10lb cases or 1lb polybags. Local fish and shellfish supplied to order.
[C] Breaded scampi 1000 ton p.a, scallops 200 ton p.a, prawns 1000 ton p.a
[D] By arrangement
See Also: Fungi

9

Nannyma Foods Ltd
114-116 Springvale Estate, Cwmbran, Gwent NP44 5BG
Tel: 06333 69949
Contact: Talfryn Jenkins

Prawn curry

Range of prepared Indian seafood and shellfish dishes and savouries including prawn curry and samosas.
[C] Undisclosed
[W] King Frost 0472 359261, Capper and Co Ltd 0443 225500, Cardigan Frozen Foods 0239 613691
[D] By wholesaler
See Also: Meat: Pies and Prepared Dishes, Game: Pies and Prepared Dishes

1 ↔

Orkney Foods
Little Stonehall, Deerness, Orkney KW17 2QQ
Tel: 085674 333
Contact: Mrs Floris Couperwhite

Scallops mornay

Deep frozen Orkney seafood platter. Also scallops mornay supplied in 14g aluminium foil dish.
[C] Scallops mornay 800 p.wk
[D] By arrangement
See Also: Meat: Pâtés and Pastes, Fish: Pâtés and Pastes, Pies and Puddings

14

River Farm Smokery
Great Wilbraham Road, Bottisham, nr Newmarket, Cambridgeshire CB1 5J
Tel: 0223 811382
Contact: R F Enoch

Potted brown shrimps

Range of prepared seafood and shellfish including cooked oysters and langoustines, scampi and mussels in half shell, potted brown shrimps, cockles in garlic butter, salmon, and crab.
[C] Undisclosed
[D] By arrangement
See Also: Meat: Smoked, Game: Smoked, Fish Dealers, Shellfish Dealers, Fish: Pâtés and Pastes, Fish: Smoked, Sea Vegetables, Snacks and Savouries

1

Rousay Processors Ltd
Trumland Pier, Rousay, Orkney KW17 2PU
Tel: 085682 216 Telx: 75192
Contact: Pier Lees

Crabmeat

Hand picked crabmeat as 100% white claw meat or 50% brown meat packed in ½, 1lb packs in outers of two and four dozen. Also frozen scallops with low water content.
[C] Crab 200-300 ton p.a, scallops Jan-May
[D] By arrangement
See Also: Shellfish Dealers

12

Sea Farm (Shearwater) Ltd
Robinson House, Nuffield Way, Abingdon, Oxfordshire OX14 1RL
Tel: 0235 32030 Telx: 837822
Contact: Mr P W Stockdale

Moules mariniere

Range of mussel dishes including moules mariniere and moules bonne femme in single, double or multi portion packs with a seven day refrigerated life.
C Undisclosed
D By arrangement
See Also: Fish: Pâtés and Pastes

14

Starfish Ltd
Reker House, 17 Betts Avenue, Martlesham, Ipswich, Suffolk IPS 7RG
Tel: 0473 626662
Contact: Mrs Firman

Garlic mussels

Ready to cook mussels in a range of flavours including garlic, in retail pack of sixteen. Also cooked and peeled prawns, scampi and scallops.
C Undisclosed
D By arrangement

SMOKED

12 ↔

Alderley Trout Ltd
Alderley, Wotton-Under-Edge, Gloucestershire GL12 7QT
Tel: 0453 842540
Contact: J Costello

Smoked trout fillet

Hot smoked trout fillets and smoked trout pâté.
C Trout products 150 ton p.a
D By own transport within area
See Also: Fish Farmers

16

Andwell Mill Farms
Andwell Lane, Andwell, Basingstoke, Hampshire RG27 9PA
Tel: 025 672 4551 Telx: 858599
Contact: R E N Barder

Trout pâté

Own farmed smoked fillets of trout and salmon in ¼, ½, 1lb packs. 2lb sides of salmon also available.
C ½ ton trout p.wk, ½ ton smoked salmon p.wk
D By arrangement
See Also: Fish Farmers, Fish: Pâtés and Pastes

5

Annandale Trout Farm
Hallguards, Hoddom Bridge, Lockerbie, Dumfriesshire DG11 1AS
Tel: 05764 392, eves 251
Contact: Mr J Roberts

Trout

Scottish reared trout, fresh or smoked in a process combining cold and hot smoking, available vacuum packed and skinned on one side. Solway and Aberdeen salmon available as fresh or smoked fillets.
C Fresh trout 40-50 ton p.a, smoked trout 200 packs p.wk
D By arrangement

8

Arthur Bacon (Grimsby) Ltd
Wharncliffe Road, Fish Docks, Grimsby, South Humberside
Tel: 0472 43634
Contact: Mr Moore

Finnan haddock

Range of smoked fish including cod, haddock fillets, mackerel, finnan haddock, bloaters, and kippers, all supplied in 7lb boxes. Also full range of fresh fish in season available, twenty four hour delivery guaranteed.
C Undisclosed
D By arrangement

6 ↔

Ashdown Smokers
Skellerah Farm, Corney, nr Nootle, Cumberland LA19 5TW
Tel: 06578 324
Contact: E H Fellows

Prawns

Range of fish and shellfish cured and lightly smoked over oak, including whole sides and sliced salmon, whole and filleted trout, whole and filleted haddock, and kippers packed in pairs. Also Dublin Bay prawns boiled in sea water and dried in the smokehouse.
C Undisclosed
D By arrangement
See Also: Meat: Smoked, Game Dealers, Fish Dealers, Shellfish Dealers, Cheese

16 ↔

Atkinson Smoked Foods
Beacon Hill Farm, Exton, nr Corhampton, Southampton, Hampshire SO3 1NW
Tel: 0489 877899
Contact: Mr Atkinson

Trout

Range of smoked fish including smoked salmon, trout, eel, mackerel and kippers. Customers own fish smoked on request.
C Undisclosed
D By own transport
See Also: Game: Smoked

3

Band's of Perth
135 Glover Street, Perth, Perthshire PH2 0JB
Tel: 0738 24222 Telx: 76279 Fax: 0738 21892
Contact: Mr R H Critchell

Salmon

Hot and cold oak smoked salmon and trout in whole sides, sliced sides and 50-500g packs.
C Undisclosed
D By own transport within area
See Also: Game Dealers, Fish Dealers

1

Bannerman Seafood Ltd
The Burgage, Tain, Ross & Cromarty
Tel: 0862 2322 Fax: 0862 2812
Contact: R R Bannerman

Salmon

Scottish smoked salmon supplied in a range of pack sizes.
C Undisclosed
D By arrangement
See Also: Fish: Pies and Prepared Dishes

16

S Baron Ltd
Assembly Passage, Mile End Road, London E1 EUR
Tel: 01 790 2246 Telx: 887054 Fax: 01 790 8797
Contact: Mr G L Evans

Salmon — Range of smoked fish including Scottish and Canadian salmon, trout, and mackerel, prepared in the East End of London.
Ⓒ Undisclosed
Ⓓ By own transport nationally

1

Benesther Shellfish
Old Schoolhouse, Deerness, Orkney KW17 2QH
Tel: 0856 74267
Contact: Dennis Gowland

Oysters — Smoked Pacific oysters (Crasostrea Gigas) available in packs of six.
Ⓒ Undisclosed
Ⓓ By arrangement
See Also: Shellfish Dealers, Shellfish Farmers

10 ↔

Blackhurst of Shropshire
Drawwell, Clive, Shrewsbury, Shropshire SY4 3JN
Tel: 093928 329
Contact: Frances Blackhurst

Gravadlax — Scottish salmon cured in sea salt and smoked over oak supplied unsliced, sliced, interleaved, and laidback sides weighing 1½-2½lb, sliced packs weighing ¼-½lb. Also hot smoked Welsh trout weighing 5-7oz, smoked salmon pâté and gravadlax.
Ⓒ Undisclosed
Ⓓ By arrangement
See Also: Game: Smoked

12

Blaisdon Trout Farms & Isle Instant Ltd
Woodgreen, Blaisdon, Gloucestershire GL17 ORE
Tel: 0452 830936
Contact: R Wiggins

Salmon — Range of applewood and oak smoked fish including salmon unsliced, sliced in 4, 8oz, 1lb packs. Also fillets of trout and shellfish.
Ⓒ Smoked salmon 1 ton p.wk, smoked trout ½ ton p.wk
Ⓓ By own transport within area
See Also: Fish Farmers

15 ↔

Bridfish Ltd
Unit 1, Sea Road North, Bridport, Dorset DT6 3BD
Tel: 0308 56306
Contact: Patrick Gibb

Herring — Range of fish traditionally smoked over oak shavings including trout, salmon and herring packed in 7, 14lb boxes or to customers requirements.
Ⓒ 500kg p.a
Ⓓ By arrangement

12 ↔
Brown & Forrest
Thorney, Langport, Somerset TA10 0DR
Tel: 0458 251520
Contact: Michael Brown

Silver eel — Silver eel, hot smoked over beechwood available whole with an average weight 1½lb, 16oz fillets, or 8oz packs.
Ⓒ 2 ton p.a
Ⓓ By arrangement
See Also: Fish Dealers, Fish: Pâtés and Pastes

15 ↔
Burn Valley Trout Ponds
Burnhayes, Silverton, Exeter, Devon EX5 4BU
Tel: 08845 282
Contact: Chris Prentis

Smoked trout — Cold smoked own farmed rainbow trout available as sliced and interleaved whole sides, trimmed whole sides weighing up to 1½lb, or 4oz packs. Also hot smoked whole or filleted trout and smoked trout pâté.
Ⓒ Cold smoked trout 100lb p.wk, hot smoked trout 500 p.wk
Ⓦ Fish Farm Services, 0747 870791
Ⓓ By wholesaler, by arrangement
See Also: Fish Farmers

1 ↔
Caithness Salmon Smoking Co Ltd
Upper Smerral, Latheron, Caithness KW5 6DU
Tel: 05934 253
Contact: Archie Sinclair

Salmon — Scottish smoked salmon, farmed or wild, in ½-2lb sides unsliced or sliced. Also 4, 8, 1lb interleaved vacuum packs.
Ⓒ ½-¾ ton p.wk
Ⓓ By arrangement

9 ↔
Cenarth Smokery
Cenarth Smokeries, Newcastle Emlyn, Dyfed
Tel: 023987 579
Contact: Jane Kelsey

Sewin — Whole sides of smoked salmon weighing 1½-4lb. Also smoked sewin weighing 1-3lb.
Ⓒ Sewin Mar-Dec
Ⓓ By arrangement
See Also: Meat: Smoked

15
Channel Foods Ltd
Lower Quay, Newham Road, Newham, Truro, Cornwall TR1 2DT
Tel: 0872 71591 Telx: 45550 CHANNL G
Fax: 0872 73187
Contact: Simon Page

Kipper — Salmon, mackerel and kippers traditionally smoked over oak and mixed woods, supplied in bulk or vacuum bags.
Ⓒ Undisclosed
Ⓓ By own transport within area

15
Channel Fisheries
13 Penpethy Road, Brixham, Devon TQ5 8NN
Tel: 08045 51210
Contact: Mr Purnell

Salmon — Smoked wild salmon fished from the River Dart. Also Scottish farmed salmon available in 2-3lb sides.
Ⓒ Undisclosed
Ⓓ By own transport within area
See Also: Fish Dealers, Shellfish Dealers

14
Cley Smoke House
Cley, Holt, Norfolk NR25 7RF
Tel: 0263 740282
Contact: Mike Rhodes

Rollmop — Rollmops made from small Shetland herring pickled in spiced cider vinegar with onions and packed in ½lb, 1lb jars. Also supplied Lofoten Island kippers, bloaters and smoked salmon.
Ⓒ Rollmops 20st p.wk, kippers ½ ton p.wk
Ⓓ By arrangement

12 ↔
Coln Valley Fish & Game Co Ltd
Winson, Cirencester, Gloucestershire GL7 5ER
Tel: 028 572 400/593/614 Telx: 437269
Contact: M Henriques

Salmon — Range of fish including salmon, cod roe, and trout smoked over dry oak sawdust in a modern version of the old London Smokehole. Also prepared gravadlax with dill sauce, in 100g glass jars.
Ⓒ Salmon ¾ ton p.wk, trout 3000 p.wk
Ⓓ By own transport nationally
See also: Fish Dealers, Game Dealers

12
Combe Sydenham Fisheries
Combe Sydenham Country Park, Monksilver, Taunton, Somerset TA4 4JG
Tel: 0984 56284
Contact: Mr K C Y Jones

Trout — Own smoked trout available weighing 8oz-2lb. Also smoked trout pâté.
Ⓒ Undisclosed
Ⓓ By arrangement
See Also: Game Dealers, Fish Farmers

15
Cornish Smoked Fish Co Ltd
Charlestown, St Austell, Cornwall PL25 5NY
Tel: 0726 72356
Contact: Martin Pumphrey

Mackerel — Range of smoked fish including kippers, kipper fillets, cod roe, buckling and bloaters. Also available smoked salmon in

2-4lb sides, smoked trout in 1¼-1½lb sides, cold and hot smoked whole mackerel in plain or peppered fillets.
[C] Undisclosed
[D] By arrangement
See Also: Fish: Pâtés and Pastes

[1]

Cromack Ltd
Bath Street, Fraserburgh, Aberdeenshire AB4 4DX
Tel: 0346 27850
Contact: Peter Duthie

Mackerel — Fraserburgh and Ullapool mackerel smoked with a variety of garnishes including onion and capsicum, herbs and garlic, and mixed spices, all packed in 7lb boxes. Also rollmops and Bismarck herring in 6x2½lt tubs containing 4lb of fish, kippers, smoked sides of salmon or sliced in 200g packs.
[C] Smoked mackerel 5 ton p.wk, kippers 2 ton p.wk, smoked salmon 1 ton p.wk
[D] By arrangement

[9]

Cwm Trout Farm
Maes-y-Gwenith, Llanvair Discoed, Chepstow, Gwent NP6 6LN
Tel: 02917 719
Contact: Mr J B Margesson

Trout — Own farmed trout traditionally smoked over beechwood, in a range of sizes or packed to customers requirements.
[C] Undisclosed
[D] By own transport within area
See Also: Fish Farmers, Fish: Pâtés and Pastes

[15] [↔]

Devon Oak Smoked Foods Ltd
Unit 5, Townstal Trading Estate, Nelson Road, Dartmouth, Devon TQ6 9LA
Tel: 08043 4410
Contact: Mr A Watts

Mackerel — Range of smoked fish including mackerel fillets, wild Atlantic or Pacific salmon sides, prawns, eel, rainbow trout whole or sliced 4, 8oz packs, cod roe 3lb pack, undyed kipper fillets 5-6oz pack. Also salmon cocktail pieces 1lb pack or trays, and gravadlax. Will smoke to customers order.
[C] Undisclosed
[D] By arrangement
See Also: Meat: Smoked, Cheese

[12]

Donnington Fish Farm
Condicote Lane, nr Upper Swell, Stow-on-the-Wold, Gloucestershire GL54 1EP
Tel: 0451 30873
Contact: Mr P Murray

Trout — Own hot and cold smoked trout 8-14oz. Also available smoked eel and smoked trout pâté.
[C] Smoked trout 200 p.wk
[D] By arrangement
See Also: Fish Farmers

[3]

Dunbar Trout Farm
South Belton, Dunbar, East Lothian EH42 1RG
Tel: 0368 63244
Contact: David A Pate

Trout — Trout farmed in the clear limestone waters of the Biel Burn available hot smoked weighing 6-8oz. Sides of smoked salmon trout weighing ½kg also supplied.
[C] Trout 7 ton p.a, salmon trout unlimited
[D] By arrangement

[1]

Duncan Fraser (Game Dealer) Ltd
17 Queensgate, Inverness IVI 1DF
Tel: 0463 232744
Contact: Mr Duncan Fraser

Salmon — Range of smoked fish including salmon.
[C] Undisclosed
[D] By arrangement
See Also: Game Dealers

[16]

Fjordling Smokehouses
Heathlands Country Market, Honey Hill, Wokingham, Berkshire RG11 3PG
Tel: 0734 776688
Contact: Andrew Espir

Fjordling — Fjordling, a Norwegian-style trout smoked over oak, sold individually. Also available smoked trout, eel and fresh or frozen trout.
C Undisclosed
D By arrangement
See Also: Meat: Smoked, Game: Smoked

10 **Freshwater Trout Farm**
Macclesfield Road, Leek, Staffordshire
Tel: 053833 684
Contact: Mr R J Kimberley

Trout — Smoked trout available to order.
C Undisclosed
D By arrangement
See Also: Fish Farmers

3 **Fyne Craft Seafoods**
Otterferry, Argyll PA21 2DH
Tel: 070 082237
Contact: Michael Buchanan

Salmon — Traditionally smoked salmon weighing 1½-6lb. Also kippers, mackerel and gravadlax in packs of three.
C Undisclosed
D By arrangement
See Also: Game: Smoked

6 **Geo Devereau & Son Ltd**
38 Strand Street, Douglas, Isle of Man
Tel: 0624 73257
Contact: Miss Shirley Cain

Manx kipper — Manx kippers supplied in 1-6 pair packs or in 1 st boxes.
C Undisclosed May-Sep
D By arrangement

3 **George Armstrong**
80 Raeburn Place, Stockbridge, Edinburgh EH4 1HH
Tel: 031 3152 033
Contact: George Armstrong

Monkfish — Range of smoked fish including monkfish, herring and haddock. Fresh fish and shellfish also available.
C Undisclosed
D By arrangement

3 **George Campbell & Sons**
The Smokehouse, West Harbour Road, Granton, Edinburgh
Tel: 031 552 0376
Contact: Iain Campbell

Haddock — Range of smoked fish including haddock fillets, mackerel fillets, kippers, trout and cod roe.
C Undisclosed
D By arrangement
See Also: Game Dealers, Fish Dealers

3 **Glen App Fisheries Ltd/Finnarts Bay Smokers Ltd**
Glen App, Ballantrae, Ayrshire KA26 OPG
Tel: 05812 271
Contact: Mr Worsfold

Salmon — Scottish smoked salmon and trout, supplied whole, and in sides sliced and laid back.
C 15,000lb p.a
D By arrangement
See Also: Fish Farmers

15 **Goodiford Mill Trout Farm**
Kentisbeare, nr Cullompton, Devon EX15 2AS
Tel: 08846 233
Contact: Mrs L Kidd

Trout — Whole trout smoked from own farmed fish. Also smoked trout pâté with cream, lemon and parsley in ¼lb tubs.
C Undisclosed
D By arrangement

15 **Head Mill Trout Farm**
Head Mill, Umberleigh, North Devon EX37 9HA
Tel: 07698 80862
Contact: Mr R Boa

Trout — Hot smoked rainbow trout available whole or filleted and vacuum packed. Small quantities of potted trout with herbs packed in 3oz pots also available.
C 1,500 p.wk
D By own transport within area
See Also: Fish Farmers

3 ↔ **Inlaks Seafoods Ltd**
Unit 14, Prospect Business Centre, Dundee DD2 1TY
Tel: 0382 561549
Contact: Mr Foster Gault

Salmon — Scottish smoked salmon cured to a traditional recipe packed in whole sides, half sides and portion packs.
C Salmon 40 ton p.a
D By arrangement
See Also: Shellfish Dealers

3 **Inverawe Smokehouses**
Taynuilt, Argyll
Tel: 08662 446 Telx: 77841
Contact: R G Campbell-Preston

Salmon — Range of smoked fish including salmon, trout and eel, available fresh or frozen, whole or filleted. Also available Botargo (preserved trout eggs).
C Undisclosed
D By arrangement

1 ↔ **Inverness Salmon Co Ltd**
8 Riverside Field, Dingwall, Inverness IV15 9TN
Tel: 0349 61565 Telx: 75405 Fax: 0463 243234
Contact: Roy Stevens

Gravadlax — Oak and peat smoked salmon. Also gravadlax with ginger, mustard and dill sauce in 4oz jars, and coarse terrine of salmon.
C Gravadlax 100 sides p.wk
D By arrangement

12 ↔

Isis Fish Farm
Eynsham Mill, Oxford, Oxfordshire OX8 1EJ
Tel: 0865 881751
Contact: Derek Chapman

Salmon

Trout and salmon smoked on request.
C Undisclosed
D By arrangement
See Also: Eggs, Fish Dealers, Fish Farmers

16 ↔

John Nicholson
18 Bute Street, South Kensington, London SW7
Tel: 01 584 3275
Contact: John Nicholson

Haddock

Lightly oak smoked haddock. Also full range of fresh fish and shellfish available.
C Undisclosed
D By arrangement

16 ↔

Kennet Valley Fisheries
Lower Way Farm, Lower Way, Thatcham, Berkshire RG13 4TL
Tel: 0635 66699 Telx: 847860 ICELT
Contact: Martin Duggan

Trout

Smoked salmon and trout available.
C Salmon 12½ ton p.a, trout 4 ton p.a
D By arrangement
See Also: Game Dealers, Fish Farmers, Shellfish Dealers

16 ↔

Kileravagh Smoked Foods
Unit 7, Hedgend Industrial Estate, St Nicholas At Wade, Birchington, Kent CT7 ONB
Tel: 0843 47086 Fax: 0843 297861
Contact: Richard Davenport

Salmon

Traditionally cured Hebridean salmon smoked over applewood and oak in 4, 8, 16oz packs, whole sides vacuum packed or loose. Also available hot and cold smoked trout and mackerel, smoked salmon pâté and gravadlax.
C 5 ton salmon p.wk
D By arrangement

3 ↔

Loch Fyne Oysters Ltd
Ardkinglas, Cairndow, Argyll PA36 8BH
Tel: 04996 264/217
Contact: Mr Andrew Lane

Herring
Salmon

Range of cured and oak smoked fish and shellfish including salmon, gravadlax, trout, eel, herring and mussels. Salmon and gravadlax whole sides or sliced and laid back 2-5lb, smoked trout and eel 1-2lb, packs of five weighing 2½lb, kippers in ½, 1 st boxes, marinaded herrings in 5lb tubs, smoked mussels in 1lb vacuum packs.
C Smoked salmon 1 ton p.wk, gravadlax 7-10 ton p.a, kippers 20-25 ton p.a, smoked eel 1 ton p.a
D By arrangement
See Also: Fish Dealers, Shellfish Dealers, Shellfish Farmers

7 ↔

Lune Smoked Foods Ltd
Duke Street, St George's Quay, Lancaster LA1 1RB
Tel: 0524 69563
Contact: P A Flude

Prawn

Smoked Scotch salmon in 1½-5lb sides, vacuum packed and sliced in 4, 8oz packs. Also available smoked trout in 5lb boxes, smoked prawns in 1lb bags and a range of seafood pâtés and potted shrimps.
C Undisclosed
D By arrangement
See Also: Game: Smoked

15

Marine Cuisine
Germoe, Penzance, Cornwall TR20 9QU
Tel: 0736 762816 Telx: 934999 TXLINK G MBX 736722816
Contact: Mr David Bruce

Salmon

Traditionally oak smoked salmon and gravadlax in 100, 200g, 4, 8kg sliced packs.
C Undisclosed
D By arrangement
See Also: Game: Smoked

12 ↔

Minola Smoked Products
Kencot Hill Farmhouse, Filkins, Lechlade, Gloucestershire GL7 3QY
Tel: 036 786 391/556 Fax: 03678 6544
Contact: Hugh Forestier-Walker

Prawns

Smoked salmon whole sides weighing 1-6lbs, and ½, 1lb sliced packs. Also smoked haddock 2-5lb, and smoked prawns in 1, 10lb vacuum packs.
C Salmon 500-1000kg p.wk, haddock 300kg p.wk, prawns 100kg p.wk
D By arrangement
See Also: Meat: Smoked, Game: Smoked, Fish Dealers, Cheese

3 ↔

Mull Shellfish Ltd
Dunan, Ardtun, Bunessan, Isle of Mull, Argyll PA67 6DH
Tel: 06817 295
Contact: Ms Alice McKay

Mussels

Mussels smoked over hardwood and packed in sunflower oil. Any weight over 1lb available.
C 600lb p.wk
D By arrangement
See Also: Shellfish Farmers

6

New Mills Trout Farm
New Mills Trout Farm, Brampton, Cumbria CA8 2QS
Tel: 06977 2384
Contact: Mrs Jay Gray

Trout

Rainbow trout smoked over oak in 1lb packs or to customers requirements.
C Undisclosed
D By arrangement
See Also: Fish Farmers

10 ↔

Oak Smoked Products Ltd
Unit B/10, Hortonwood 10, Telford, Shropshire TF1 4ES
Tel: 0952 670180
Contact: Mr P Morgan-Jones

Salmon

Smoked salmon 1-2lb, 2-4lb unsliced or sliced sides, and 4, 8oz, 1lb sliced packs or gift packed with a bottle of champagne. Also available smoked salmon trout, mackerel and prawns.
[C] 1,500 sides p.wk
[D] By arrangement

14

Ogier Ltd
44 Bergen Way, Kings Lynn, Norfolk PE30 2JG
Tel: 0553 761876 Telx: 818464 OGIER G
Contact: Dan Ogier

Monkfish

Range of smoked fish including hot and cold Scottish salmon, whole and filleted trout, eel, mackerel, halibut, monkfish. Also mixed smokehouse dishes in retail and portion controlled catering packs.
[C] Salmon 4 ton p.wk, trout 5 ton p.wk, eel 2 ton p.wk
[D] By arrangement

9

The Old Mill
Llawhaden, nr Narbeth, Dyfed SA67 8EJ
Tel: 09914 256
Contact: Huw Jones

Trout

Own smoked rainbow trout available in packs of six. Also sides of salmon sliced and laid back, and smoked trout pâté in ¼, ½, 1lb foil tubs.
[C] 50-60lb p.wk
[D] By arrangement

10 ↔

The Old Mill Fisheries
Clifford Chambers, Stratford upon Avon, Warwickshire CV37 8HU
Tel: 0789 295389
Contact: Barrie Spratt

Trout

Trout hot smoked over hardwood sawdust packed in boxes of 12-24. Also cold smoked sliced trout in 4, 8oz packs and whole sides laid back, smoked trout pâté in 4, 6oz and 1lb tubs.
[C] Individual hot smoked 10 doz p.wk, cold smoked 6 sides p.wk, pâté 5lb p.wk
[D] By arrangement
See Also: Fish Farmers

1

Orkney Fish Farms
Cairston Road, Stromness, Orkney KW16 3JS
Tel: 0856 850514 Fax: 0856 850568
Contact: Kenneth Sutherland

Marinaded herring

Orkney herring marinaded to a traditional recipe in 500g, 2, 5kg packs. Range of smoked fish and shellfish products also available.
C Marinaded herring 40 ton p.a, smoked products and pâtés 15 ton p.a
D By arrangement
See Also: Fish Farmers

9

Pembrokeshire Fish Farms
Orielton Mill, Hundleton, Pembroke, Dyfed
Tel: 064681 393
Contact: Margot Bateman

Smoked trout pâté made with 80% trout flesh, supplied in 4, 8oz packs and 1½lb catering packs. Also available 6-8oz smoked trout.
C Undisclosed
D By arrangement
See Also: Fish Farmers

16

Phillips of Wight Farm
Wight Farm, Binstead, Isle of Wight PO33 4EH
Tel: 0983 65100 Telx: 86415 SALMON G
Contact: R V D Phillips

Sides of smoked salmon and smoked trout available.
C Undisclosed
D By arrangement
See Also: Fish: Pâtés and Pastes

3

Ritchie's of Rothesay
37 Watergate, Rothesay, Isle of Bute
Tel: 0700 3012/5414
Contact: Mr Neil Ritchie

Loch Fyne herrings traditionally kippered by splitting the fish down the back, lightly salting and smoking them for a mild cure. Smoked wild salmon also available.
C Kippered herrings Jul-Sep
D By arrangement

14

River Farm Smokery
Great Wilbraham Road, Bottisham, nr Newmarket, Cambridgeshire CB1 5J
Tel: 0223 811382
Contact: R F Enoch

Pike

Range of fish smoked over fenland peat, oak and hardwoods including pike, whole or in sides, salmon in 3-5lb sides or sliced in ½lb packs, whole mackerel or dry cured fillets, monkfish, eel, cockles, and oysters in shell. Also mussels in oil in 1, 5lb packs.
C ¼ ton p.wk
D By arrangement
See Also: Meat: Smoked, Game: Smoked, Fish Dealers, Shellfish Dealers, Fish: Pâtés and Pastes, Fish: Pies and Prepared Dishes, Sea Vegetables, Snacks and Savouries

6

L Robson & Sons (Fish Curers) Ltd
Craster, Alnwick, Northumberland NE66 3TR
Tel: 066 576 223
Contact: Mr Ken Robson

Kippers

Craster kippers smoked from herrings caught in Loch Fyne supplied loose or packed in 1, 2 and 4½lb boxes. Sides of smoked salmon also available.
C Kippers 1000st p.dy Jun-Sep, smoked salmon 40-100 sides p.wk Mar-Aug
D By arrangement

2 ↔

Rothiemurchus Estate
Fish Farm Shop, Rothiemurchus, Aviemore, Inverness-shire PH22 1QH
Tel: 0479 810703
Contact: Mrs Ballantine

Trout

Own farmed trout smoked over Speyside oak supplied whole 6-12oz, filleted 4-6oz, in vacuum packs.
C 50kg p.wk
D By arrangement

15 ↔

Salcombe Smokers
54 Fore Street, Kingsbridge, Devon TQ7 1NY
Tel: 0548 2006
Contact: J Barron

Salcombe smokies

Range of smoked products including Salcombe Smokies, hot smoked fillets of mackerel, available in 4-5 fillet vacuum packs weighing 1½lb or in 7lb boxes. Also North Atlantic salmon, trout, prawns in shell packed in 8oz, 1lb bags, pollock and haddock in 7lb boxes, and cod roe packed to customers requirements.
C Smokies 200kg p.wk, salmon 200kg p.wk, prawns 100kg p.wk, cod roe 100kg p.wk
D By arrangement

7

Scot Trout Ltd
The Motherwell Food Park, Bellshill Industrial Estate, Bellshill, Lanarkshire ML4 3JA
Tel: 0698 747272
Contact: Mr Philip A Marshall

Trout

Hot and cold smoked trout and smoked salmon available in 1-3lb packs. All products supplied in controlled atmosphere packs.
C Fresh and smoked trout 1,500 p.a, fresh and smoked salmon 300-400 ton p.a
D By arrangement
See Also: Fish Farmers

1

Scotts Fish Shop
3 Bridge Street, Kirkwall, Orkney
Tel: 0856 3170
Contact: Helen Watson

Salmon

Smoked farmed salmon from the Orkney Isles slow cured to a traditional recipe, available in sides, unsliced or sliced. Quantities of wild salmon on request.
C 100 sides p.wk Mar-May, Oct, 500 sides p.wk Nov-Dec
D By arrangement

16

Shaw Shellfish
Dell Quay Boatyard, Dell Quay,
Chichester, West Sussex
Tel: 0243 775626
Contact: Adam Shaw

Haddock

Traditionally oak smoked trout, eel, salmon, cod and haddock available, weighing minimum 4oz.
[C] Undisclosed
[D] By arrangement
See Also: Shellfish Dealers

11

Shellfish Seafoods Ltd
Watling Street, Hinckley, Leicestershire
Tel: 0455 619009 Telx: 34468 SHELFR G
Contact: Mr West

Trout

Eel, salmon and trout smoked over Warwickshire oak. Salmon supplied in whole sides or sliced weighing 1-1½, 1½-2lb.
[C] Salmon 100 sides p.wk, trout 1 cwt p.wk
[D] By own transport nationally
See Also: Game: Smoked, Fish Dealers, Shellfish Dealers

1

Shetland Smoked Salmon Ltd
Grantfield, Lerwick, Shetland 2EI 0NT
Tel: 0595 2727/2854 Telx: 75203 Fax: 0595 3794
Contact: Mr L A Williamson

Salmon

Scottish salmon farmed in Shetland waters, cured with salt, sugar or spirits and smoked over hardwood chips. Supplied chilled or frozen, as whole sides or sliced and interleaved and vacuum packed.
[C] 500 p.wk
[D] By arrangement

1 ↔

The Shetland Smokehouse
Skeld Industrial Estate, Skeld, Shetland ZE2 9NL
Tel: 0595 86 251 Telx: 937400 Onecom G
Fax: 0595 86 203
Contact: Mr David Hammond

Gravadlax

Farmed Shetland salmon smoked over oak and mahogany. Also salmon marinaded in cognac, spices and home grown herbs to produce a variety of gravadlax, in 5lb whole sides or 4, 8oz packs.
[C] Smoked salmon 2000kg p.wk, gravadlax 500kg p.wk
[D] By arrangement
See Also: Meat: Smoked

16

Silk Mill Fish Farm
Warren Mere, Portsmouth Road, Thursley, Surrey
Tel: 04868 21615
Contact: Mr R J Neale

Trout

Smoked trout and smoked trout pâté available. Also live trout weighing ½-5lb.
[C] 10 ton p.a
[D] By arrangement

2 ↔

Spey Valley Smokehouse
Cromdale, Grantown-on-Spey, Morayshire PH26 3LN
Tel: 0479 3078 Telx: 75467 SPEX G
Contact: Mr Coulson

Salmon

Farmed and wild Scottish salmon smoked in a traditional smokehouse, in 4, 8, 12oz packs, whole sides weighing 2¼lb. Also cold smoked trout whole side 1lb, sliced 12oz.
[C] Salmon 2000 sides p.wk
[D] By arrangement
See Also: Game: Smoked

3

R R Spink & Sons
35 Seagate, Arbroath, Angus
Tel: 0241 72023
Contact: R R Spink Jr

Arbroath smokies

Arbroath Smokies, a version of cured and smoked haddock from the east coast of Scotland, usually headed, gutted and left whole. Also smoked salmon marinaded in drambuie and a full range of fresh and frozen fish and shellfish.
[C] Undisclosed
[D] By arrangement

16

Springs Smoked Salmon
The Springs, Edburton, Henfield, West Sussex
Tel: 079156 338
Contact: Geoffrey Harris

Gravadlax

Gravadlax, Scottish smoked wild salmon as whole, ½ sides and 1lb packs. Also smoked trout and cod roe.
C 500 ton p.a
D By arrangement

15

Sylvesters Seafoods
Holt House, Richmond Road, Appledore, North Devon EX39 4LD
Tel: 02372 79101
Contact: Mrs Felicity Sylvester

Mackerel

Smoked salmon, mackerel and kippers supplied in season to customers requirements.
C Undisclosed
D By arrangement
See Also: Fish Dealers, Shellfish Dealers

3

Tarbert Fyne Foods Ltd
10 Scottish Food Centre, Motherwell Food Park, Bellshill, Strathclyde ML4 3JA
Tel: 0698 844654 Telx: 779899
Contact: Calum J Ross

Salmon

Scottish smoked salmon in 2, 4, 8, 14oz packs, or whole sides weighing on average 1kg.
C Undisclosed
D By arrangement
See Also: Fish: Pâtés and Pastes

16

Test Valley Game Produce Ltd
North Houghton, Stockbridge, Hampshire SO20 6LF
Tel: 0264 810526
Contact: D Dent

Salmon

Scottish smoked salmon.
C Undisclosed
D By arrangement
See Also: Game Dealers, Fish Farmers

16

Three oh Four
The Old Hall, Iden, Rye, East Sussex TN31 7XD
Tel: 07978 304
Contact: The Proprietor

Gravadlax

Smoked mackerel, gravadlax and smoked salmon in 2, 4, 8oz, 1lb packs or in whole sides.
C Undisclosed
D By arrangement
See Also: Fish: Pâtés and Pastes, Snacks and Savouries

3

Tobermory Fish Farm Ltd
Main Street, Tobermory, Isle of Mull PA75 6PX
Tel: 0688 2120 Fax: 0688 2140
Contact: Mrs Susie Carmichael

Trout

Scottish trout, hot and cold smoked in 10-17oz sides, sliced and unsliced or in 4, 8oz packs.
C Undisclosed
D By arrangement
See Also: Fish Farmers

16

The Weald Smokery
Mount Farm, Hawkhurst Road, Flimwell, East Sussex TN5 7QL
Tel: 058087 601
Contact: B P Nicholas

Freshwater eel

German-style smoked salmon, trout and freshwater eel, vacuum packed individually or in pairs. Also smoked mussels.
C 2 ton p.mth
D By own transport within area
See Also: Game: Smoked

6 ↔

Westmorland Smoked Foods
Cragg House, Casterton, Kirkby Londsdale, Cumbria LA6 2SD
Tel: 0468 41906
Contact: John Thompson

Gravadlax

Scottish smoked salmon and gravadlax in whole sides, or sliced and laid back, and 4, 8oz, 1lb vacuum packs or to customers requirements. Also hot smoked potted salmon.
C 1000 sides p.wk
D By arrangement
See Also: Cheese

1 ↔

William Jolly
Hatston Industrial Estate, Scott's Road, Kirkwall, Orkney
Tel: 0856 2417
Contact: Billy Jolly

Salmon

Variety of smoked salmon cures including traditional with salt, Scotch with salt, sugar and whisky, demerara with salt, sugar and rum, all supplied to customers requirements. Gravadlax also available.
C ½-1 ton p.wk
D By arrangement
See Also: Fish Dealers, Shellfish Dealers

SEA VEGETABLES

3 ↔

A Abrahams
The Strand, Colonsay, Argyll PA61 7TR
Tel: 09512 365
Contact: A Abrahams

Dulse

Locally grown dulse and laver.
C Undisclosed, winter season
D By own transport within area
See Also: Fish Farmers, Honey

[16]

Ark Fisheries
51-52 Cliffe High Street, Lewes, East Sussex BN7 2AN
Tel: 0273 476912
Contact: Mr B Wright

Samphire

Fresh samphire in season.
[C] Undisclosed
[D] By arrangement
See Also: Fish: Pies and Prepared Dishes

[16]

Botterell Seatrades Ltd
Harbour Road, Rye Harbour, Rye, East Sussex TN31 7TT
Tel: 0797 222875
Contact: Mr John Botterell

Samphire

Fresh samphire in season.
[C] 50-100lb p.wk mainly May-Jul
[D] By own transport
See Also: Fish Dealers, Shellfish Dealers

[9]

Mona Seafoods Ltd
The Oyster Hatchery, Brynsiencyn, Anglesey LL61 6TQ
Tel: 024873 411/412
Contact: D Lea-Wilson

Samphire

Fresh or tinned laverbread and small quantities of fresh samphire.
[C] Undisclosed
[D] By arrangement
See Also: Fish Dealers, Shellfish Farmers

[16]

C J Newnes & Partners
73 Billingsgate Market, London E14 8ST
Tel: 01 515 0793
Contact: C J Newnes

Samphire

Fresh samphire and laver, washed and trimmed, in season.
[C] Undisclosed
[D] By arrangement
See Also: Fish Dealers

[9]

Raymond Rees & Son
11 Market Precinct, Carmarthen, Dyfed
Tel: 0267 234144
Contact: Mr Raymond Rees

Laverbread

Fresh laverbread made from laver gathered from the coast of West Wales.
[C] 50lb p.wk
[D] By arrangement
See Also: Fish Dealers

[14]

River Farm Smokery
Great Wilbraham Road, Bottisham, nr Newmarket, Cambridgeshire CB1 5J
Tel: 0223 811382
Contact: R F Enoch

Samphire

Freshly picked samphire.
[C] Undisclosed
[D] By arrangement
See Also: Meat: Smoked, Game: Smoked, Fish Dealers, Shellfish Dealers, Fish: Pâtés and Pastes, Fish: Pies and Prepared Dishes, Fish: Smoked, Snacks and Savouries

[1] ↔

The Sea Vegetable Co Ltd
Pitkerrie, Balmuchy, Fearn, Ross & Cromarty IV20 1TN
Tel: 086287 272
Contact: Julian Clokie

Dulse

Dried sea vegetables from the northern reefs of Scotland, including sugar ware (sugar kombu) for salads or stews, finger ware (finger kombu) for soups and Japanese kebabs, dabberlocks (honey wakame) used in white meat dishes, grockle (herb kombu) used as a spicy flavouring, summer dulse, and autumn dulse with a stronger taste than grockle, and purple nori for tempura dishes, stuffing sushi rolls and making laver bread. All available in 15g packs, or in bulk.
[C] 3 tonne p.a
[W] Marigold, London 01 267 7368
[D] By wholesaler

[14]

J & J Shellfish Ltd
Alexandra Dock, King's Lynn, Norfolk
Tel: 0553 772520 Fax: 0553 691086
Contact: John Williamson

Samphire

Fresh samphire available in 1 ton lots.
[C] Jul-Sep
[D] By arrangement
See Also: Shellfish Dealers, Shellfish Farmers

[14] ↔

Suffolk Smock Company
Kyson Hill, Kyson Point, Woodbridge, Suffolk IP12 4DN
Tel: 03943 3429
Contact: Roger and Sarah Pinfold

Samphire

Suffolk marsh samphire picked daily during the season, trimmed and washed, sold in 6oz bunches or boxed in larger quantities.
[C] Undisclosed Jul-Sep
[D] By arrangement

[9]

Vin Sullivan of Abergavenny Ltd
Triley Mill, Abergavenny, Gwent NP7 8DE
Tel: 0873 2331
Contact: Mr John Sullivan

Samphire
Dulse

Welsh samphire, dulse slightly dried, and laverbread.
[C] Samphire and laverbread ½ ton p.wk, dulse summer season only
[D] By own transport nationally
See Also: Fish Dealers, Shellfish Dealers, Fresh Fruit

[9]

The Welsh Barrow
The Cawdor Arms Hotel, Llandeilo, Dyfed
Tel: 0558 823500 Telx: 48297 Fax: 0792 43651
Contact: Colin Pressdee

Laverbread

Laverbread rich in iodine, iron and trace elements, Porphyra Umbilicalis, washed, cooked, minced and packed in 210g cans.
[C] 25,000 cans p.a
[W] Robinski 01 969 9511, V.Benoist Ltd 01 743 0161
[D] By wholesaler

DAIRY

BUTTER

15

Friesian

Ashley Chase Estate
Higher Kingtston Russell Farm, Winterbourne Abbas, Dorchester, Dorset
Tel: 03083 292
Contact: Mr J Thacker

Farmhouse butter made from milk of own Friesian herd in clear wrapped ½lb curls.
C 2000kg p.mth Jan-Jul, Sep-Dec
D By arrangement
See Also: Cheese

16 ↔

Brandy butter

Mrs Beeton's Foods
Norwood Hill, Horley, Surrey RH6 OET
Tel: 0293 862087 Fax: 0293 862396
Contact: Clive Pick

Mrs Beeton's traditional additive free brandy butter in 3.8oz jars.
C Undisclosed
D By arrangement
See Also: Cakes, Biscuits and Pastries, Chutneys and Pickles, Hampers

9 ◯ ★

Jersey

Bryncerdin Farm Produce
Bryncerdin Farm, Ffostrosol, Llandysul, Dyfed
Tel: 023975 371
Contact: Mrs E J Wynne

Unpasteurised, organic, hand patted and slightly salted butter from pedigree Jersey herd in 250g round pots.
C Undisclosed
D By arrangement
See Also: Cream

7 ★

Friesian

T & J M Butler & Son
Lower Barker Farm, Inglewhite, Preston, Lancashire PR3 2LH
Tel: 0995 40334
Contact: Mrs T Butler

Farm butter available in 250, 500g packs.
C Undisclosed
D By arrangement
See Also: Cheese

3 ↔

Whey

Campbeltown Creamery Ltd
Campbeltown, Argyll PA28 6JU
Tel: 0586 52244 Telx: 777009
Contact: Ian Ireland

Whey butter from Friesian and Ayrshire herds in 25kg boxes.
C 200 ton p.a
W Express Foods Ltd
D By wholesaler
See Also: Cheese

12

Butter

Chewton Dairy Farms Ltd
Priory Farm, Chewton Mendip, Bath, Avon BA3 4NT
Tel: 076121 666
Contact: Mrs Marian Shaw

Hand patted butter in clear wrapped 250g packs.
C Undisclosed
D By arrangement
See Also: Cheese, Cream

14 ↔

Rum
Brandy

Coles Traditional Bakery Ltd
19 High Street, Saffron Walden, Essex
Tel: 0799 22126
Contact: Christopher J Cole

Brandy and rum butter packed in 900g packs in outers of twelve.
C Undisclosed
D By own transport nationally
See Also: Pies and Puddings, Jams and Preserves

12 ↔

Whey

Farmhouse Cheesemakers Ltd
Keward Farm, Glastonbury Road, Wells, Somerset BA5 1QD
Tel: 0749 78755 Telx: 94012342 Fax: 0749 77022
Contact: David Johnson

Butter traditionally prepared from whey cream in 250g packs.
C Undisclosed
D By arrangement
See Also: Cheese

10

Whey

Fowlers Forest Dairies Ltd
Forest Farm, Small Lane, Earlswood, Solihull, Warwickshire B94 5EL
Tel: 05646 2329
Contact: Mrs P Fowler

Lactic butter made with whey cream from Friesian herd in 250g packs.
C Undisclosed
D By own transport within area
See Also: Cheese

10 ★ ↔

Whey

V J Hares & Son
Millenheath, Higher Heath, Whitchurch, Shropshire
Tel: 0948 840288
Contact: The Proprietor

Farmhouse whey butter made with milk from own Friesian herd in 250, 500g packs.
C Undisclosed
D By own transport within area
See Also: Cheese

12 ↔

Flavoured butter

Holstius & Breet
Esperanza, Aust, Bristol, Avon BS12 3AX
Tel: 04545 3148 Telx: 449752
Contact: Robin D L Breet

Range of additive free flavoured butters including orange and parsley, Provencal herb, garlic, basil and tomato, and horseradish in 198g jars and 155g packs.
C Undisclosed
D By arrangement
See Also: Cheese, Mustards, Fudges and Toffee, Snacks and Savouries

7 ★

Whey

P J Huntbach
Hayfields Farm, Audlem, nr Crewe, Cheshire CW3 OEX
Tel: 0270 811394
Contact: Philip Huntbach

Salted whey butter in 500gm packs and 25kg boxes.
C 4 tons p.mth
W Mendip Foods
D By wholesaler, by own transport within area
See Also: Cheese

12 ★ **Hurstone Farmhouse**
Waterrow, Wiveliscombe, Somerset TA4 2AT
Tel: 0984 23441
Contact: John Bone

Farmhouse — Farmhouse butter made from unpasteurised milk of own Jersey herd in 8oz packs.
C Undisclosed
D By arrangement
See Also: Cheese, Cream, Milk

12 **D M Keen & Sons**
Moorehayes Farm, Cerrington Lane, Wincanton, Somerset DA9 8JR
Tel: 0963 32286
Contact: Stephen Keen

Whey — Whey butter in ½lb cartons. Also supplied double cream.
C Undisclosed
D By arrangement
See Also: Cheese

9 ● ★ ↔ **Rachel's Dairy**
Brynllys, Borth, Dyfed SY24 5LZ
Tel: 097081 489
Contact: Ms Rachel Rowlands

Guernsey — Organic farmhouse butter, from unpasteurised Guernsey cultured cream in 250g packs. Buttermilk also available.
C 120kg p.wk
D By own transport within area
See Also: Cheese, Yoghurt

10 ○ ★ **Rays Farm Products**
Rays Farm, Billingsley, Bridgnorth, Shropshire WV16 6PF
Tel: 029 924255
Contact: Mrs R Cartwright

Garlic — Range of additive free flavoured butters made from Channel Island milk including garlic, mint, rum.
C 35,000lt of milk equivalent (including cream) p.a
D By arrangement
See Also: Cream, Milk

15 **Streatfeild Hood & Co Ltd**
Denhay Farm, Broadoak, Bridport, Dorset BT6 5NP
Tel: 0308 22770/22717
Contact: Mrs A C Streatfeild

Whey — Hand curled farmhouse whey butter in 250g packs, 5kg boxes.
C 200kg p.wk May-Sep, 350kg p.wk Oct-Apr
D By arrangement
See Also: Cheese

9 ○ ★ **Teifi Cheese**
Glynhynod, Ffostrasol, Llandyssul, Dyfed SA44 5JY
Tel: 023 975 528
Contact: John Savage

Unsalted — Farmhouse butter, salted and unsalted, in ½, 1lb packs.
C 200lb p.mth
D By arrangement
See Also: Cheese, Milk

CHEESE

9 **Abergavenny Fine Foods Ltd**
Mamhilad, Gwent NP4 8RG
Tel: 0873 880844/880250
Contact: A J Craske

Pantysgawn — Pantysgawn Farm made from goat milk of own herd, with vegetarian rennet. Soft, mild cheese in a variety of flavours including plain, with herbs, black pepper, mixed sweet pepper, garlic and chives in 4oz rounds and 2lb logs.
C Undisclosed
D By own refrigerated transport within area, by arrangement
See Also: Milk

6 ★ **Alston Cheese**
Back Garth, The Butts, Alston, Cumbria CA9 3JU
Tel: 0498 81931
Contact: Kate Webb

High Pennine — High Pennine Goat Cheese, medium fat, natural rind, mild Caerphilly-type, with vegetarian rennet and matured 4-6 weeks. Tynedale and smoked Tynedale, fairly acid with characteristic buttery flavour, crumbly Dales-type texture, medium fat, natural rind, made from unpasteurised Ayrshire cow milk with vegetarian rennet, matured 6-10 weeks. Both in 1, 2, 6lb sizes.
C 500kg May-Dec
D By arrangement

10 ★ **Appleby of Hawkstone**
Abbey Farm, Hawkstone, Weston-under-Redcastle, Shropshire
Tel: 0948 840387
Contact: Mr Edward Appleby

Cheshire — Appleby's Hawkstone Cheshire, made from unpasteurised Friesian cow milk, hard pressed, with 48% fat content, traditional cloth bound cheese, matured 5-6 weeks with 9-12 month shelf life. Available in 4, 7, 17, 50lb cylindrical rounds. Double Gloucester, hard pressed, cloth bound cheese matured 3-12 months, handmade in traditional screw press and available in 4, 15, 30lb rounds. Also available goat cheese made from unpasteurised milk, cloth bound and rinded, in 7, 10lb rounds.
C Cheshire 7 ton p.mth, Double Gloucester 1½ ton p.mth, Goat 500lb p.mth
D By arrangement

6 ↔ **Ashdown Smokers**
Skellerah Farm, Corney, nr Nootle, Cumberland LA19 5TW
Tel: 06578 324
Contact: E H Fellows

Smoked — Range of cheeses smoked over oak and beech wood with cherry wood added to requirements including Alston Tynedale, 1, 2lb, Alston High Pennine, 2lb, Single

Gloucester, 3, 4lb, Hawkstone Cheshire coloured or white, 2½lb, Ribblesdale goat cheese, 5lb, and Cumberland smoked cheese.
C Undisclosed
D By arrangement
See Also: Meat: Smoked, Game Dealers, Fish Dealers

15 **Ashley Chase Estate**
Higher Kingston Russell Farm, Winterbourne Abbas, Dorchester, Dorset
Tel: 03083 292
Contact: Mr J Thacker

Cheddar — Mature farmhouse Cheddar made from milk of own Friesian herd with fat content of 50%, matured for nine months, in 4½kg vacuum sealed blocks for a two month shelf life.
C 46 ton p.mth
D By arrangement
See Also: Butter

16 ○ ★ **Dr C L Barran**
Woolhouse Farm, Stedham, Midhurst, West Sussex GU29 0QH
Tel: 042 876 387
Contact: Dr C L Barran

Madehurst — Madehurst, cheese made with unpasteurised whole milk from pedigree British White cows fed on herbal pastures, rennet free, round, pressed, with soft natural crust, matured 2-4 weeks, supplied in 1lb weights.
C Madehurst 200 cheeses p.a
D By arrangement

15 ○ ★ **Beenleigh & Harbourne Cheese**
Ticklemore Cheese Shop, 1 Ticklemore Street, Totnes, Devon TQ9 5EJ
Tel: 0803 865926
Contact: Sarie Cooper

Beenleigh Blue — Beenleigh Blue, full flavoured, natural crust cheese made from unpasteurised sheep milk, matured underground for seven months in 4lb drums. Harbourne Blue, an unpasteurised goat milk version of Beenleigh.
C Undisclosed
D By own transport within area

10 ↔ **Belton Farms Cheesemakers Ltd**
Belton, Whitchurch, Shropshire SY13 1JD
Tel: 0948 2125
Contact: Mr John H Beckett

Cheshire
Leicester — Cheshire, Cheddar, Leicester and Lancashire cheeses in 20, 5kg, 9lb wheels.
C 125 ton p.mth
D By arrangement

15 ● ↔ **T B Bersey & Son**
Sheviock Barton, Torpoint, Cornwall PL11 3EH
Tel: 0503 30909 Telx: 30909 Fax: 0503 30915
Contact: G Bersey

Sheviock — Pasteurised and unpasteurised sheep milk cheese with vegetarian rennet including Sheviock semi-hard, full fat, mild flavoured, marinaded in cider, matured for a minimum four weeks in 4½lb truckles, Ladywell, Camembert-type, with clean taste, matured 3-4 weeks, in 2lb weights, made to order.
C 500 p.mth
W Harvey & Brockless Odin(U.K), 01 622 3099
D By arrangement
See Also: Milk

15 ○ ★ **Blackdown Farm & Loddiswell Cheese**
Blackdown, Loddiswell, Kingsbridge, Devon TQ7 4EA
Tel: 054882 387
Contact: Mr and Mrs W L Martin

Goat — Goat cheese made from unpasteurised milk of own organically raised herd including Loddiswell Blackdown, medium fat, hard pressed, soaked in brine, matured for six weeks, with mild, clean flavour and good keeping qualities, in 3-5lb rounds. Loddiswell Banow, medium fat, unsalted, soft, mild, 2-3oz, sealed in plastic bags in a variety of flavours including plain, pickled in olive oil with herbs and mixed with organically grown herbs to order.
C 100lb p.mth
D By own transport within area
See Also: Fresh Meat, Milk

16

Bookers Vineyard
Foxhole Lane, Bolney, Sussex RH17 5NB
Tel: 044482 575
Contact: J M and R V Pratt

Goat — Range of cheeses made from own goat herd milk including Batting Hill, soft, uncrusted plain or with chives and garlic, in 7oz rounds. Also 7oz semi-hard cheese in wine with fennel and caraway in 1lb jar.
[C] Undisclosed
[D] By arrangement
See Also: Wine

7 ★

H S Bourne
The Bank, Malpas, Cheshire SY14 7AL
Tel: 094881 214
Contact: John Bourne

Cheshire — Cheshire cheese made on farm, white or coloured, hand-dipped in red wax, in 3½ 4, 10, 50lb cylinders.
[C] 10 ton p.mth
[D] By arrangement

7 ○ ↔

Bowling Alley Herb Farm
Commonside, Alvanley, nr Warrington, Cheshire
Tel: 09289 285
Contact: Mrs Felicity Elphick

Juniper — Soft cow milk cheese with vegetarian rennet, low fat, in a variety of five flavours including juniper, fennel, horseradish, and Eastern spice in 5oz, 4½lb tubs, suitable for freezing.
[C] Undisclosed
[D] By arrangement
See Also: Bacon and Hams, Fresh Herbs, Purees and Sauces

12 ★

Bredons Norton Dairy Goats
Brookfield Farm, Bredons Norton, Tewkesbury, Gloucestershire GL20 7E7
Tel: 0684 72209
Contact: Ms Jane Archer

Cheese crottin — Range of cheese made from unpasteurised goat milk including Bredon, soft, mild, matured for six weeks in a variety of flavours including plain, chives, peppers and garlic in 6oz, 1lb rounds with a shelf life of two weeks. Bredon Cheese Crottin, unpressed, semi-hard, strong flavour, yellow crust, matured for three months in 8oz truckles. Brensham hard pressed, crusted cheese, matured six weeks with a shelf life of 3-6 months, in 5, 8lb rounds.
[C] 100lb p.mth
[D] By arrangement
See Also: Milk

16 ★ ↔

British Sheep Dairy Products
Nepicar Farm, Wrotham Heath, Sevenoaks, Kent TN15 7SR
Tel: 0732 883040
Contact: Mr Harold Woolley

Carolina — Cheeses from 100% untreated sheep milk and vegetarian rennet including Carolina developed from Wensleydale recipe, hard, matured two months. Cecilia, hard, matured in Kentish hops.
Ⓒ Undisclosed
Ⓓ By arrangement
See Also: Milk, Yoghurt

9 ★

Brynonen Farm
Login, Whitland, Dyfed SA34 OUY
Tel: 09916 255
Contact: Lesley Bird

Senlac — Senlac, unpasteurised goat milk cheese, mild, creamy, Wensleydale-type with natural rind, matured for one month in 3, 5lb cylinders. Also soft goat milk curd cheese plain, mixed herbs in 4oz pots.
Ⓒ 300x5lb p.mth
Ⓓ By own transport within area

16 ★ ↔

Bunker Farm Produce
Bunker Farm, Basingstoke Road, Greenham Common South, Newbury, Berkshire RG15 8HH
Tel: 0635 45535
Contact: Ken Neale

Newbury goat — Newbury soft goat cheese from unpasteurised milk with vegetarian rennet in a variety of flavours including plain, garlic, and peppercorns in 8″ wheels weighing 3½lb. Unpasteurised curd cheese also supplied, in 1½lb tubs or in bulk.
Ⓒ Undisclosed
Ⓓ By own transport within area
See Also: Fresh Meat, Poultry Producers, Milk, Yoghurt, Purees and Sauces

7 ★

T & J M Butler & Son
Lower Barker Farm, Inglewhite, Preston, Lancashire PR3 2LH
Tel: 0995 40334
Contact: Mrs T Butler

Lancashire — Lancashire hard unpasteurised farmhouse cheese, made from milk of own Friesian herd, with buttery crumbly texture, matured one month for mild, six months for stronger flavour, in 3, 20, 40lb weights. Also available Lancashire sage with chopped fresh sage leaves.
Ⓒ 10 ton p.mth
Ⓓ By arrangement
See Also: Butter

15 ★

Butlers Farm
Butlers, Chittlehamholt, Umberleigh, North Devon
Tel: 07694 365
Contact: Sally Oatley

Goat — Butlers Farm Cheese, hard, made from unpasteurised goat milk, matured 2-4 months, in 2, 4lb sizes.
Ⓒ 12 cheeses p.mth Mar-Dec
Ⓓ By wholesaler

9 ○ ★ ↔

Caldey Island Estate Company
Caldey Island Dairy, Caldey Island Monastery, Caldey Island, off Tenby, Dyfed
Tel: 0834 2632
Contact: Brother Philippart

Caldey — Caldey made from unpasteurised milk of own herd, organic, strong, hard Cheshire-type cheese, in 40lb cylinders and 1lb pieces.
Ⓒ Undisclosed
Ⓓ By arrangement
See Also: Yoghurt

14 ● ★ ↔

Calluna Farm Products
Lodge Road, Hollesley, Woodbridge, Suffolk
Tel: 0394 411927
Contact: Mrs Helen Douglas

Cream — Soft pressed cream cheese from unpasteurised sheep milk with animal and vegetarian rennet, matured one week in a variety of flavours including plain, chives, garlic, and celery seed, ¾, 1½lb rounds with decorated top. Calluna ewes milk, full fat, hard cheese, matured three months in 4, 8lb sizes.
Ⓒ 200lb p.wk
Ⓓ By own transport within area
See Also: Eggs, Milk, Yoghurt, Fresh Salads

6

Calthwaite Dairy Products
Calthwaite, Penrith, Cumbria CA11 9QU
Tel: 076885 292
Contact: Clive Pattinson

Cottage cheese — Low fat cottage cheese made from Jersey separated milk with 3% fat content, in 175g cartons.
Ⓒ 1000kg p.mth
Ⓓ By own transport within area
See Also: Cream, Yoghurt, Prepared Salads, Jams and Preserves, Fudges and Toffee

3 ↔

Campbeltown Creamery Ltd
Campbeltown, Argyll PA28 6JU
Tel: 0586 52244 Telx: 777009
Contact: Ian Ireland

Mull of Kintyre — Scottish Cheddar cheese from milk of Friesian and Ayrshire herds with 34% fat content, nutty flavour, matured 4-12 months to give straw colour, in 2½, 5, 20kg rectangular blocks. Mull of Kintyre fully matured cheese in 567g black waxed truckles, and Highland extra matured cheese in 2½, 5, 20kg rectangular blocks.
Ⓒ 3000 ton p.a
Ⓦ Express Foods Ltd
Ⓓ By wholesaler
See Also: Butter

Rill Farm

Traditional Dairy Produce

Rill Farm is a family business producing a range of traditionally hand made cheeses, using the milk from our pedigree Friesian Cows and Goat herd. We have total control throughout all the stages of production from the milking parlours to the maturing room and are therefore able to produce a very high quality product.

CHEESES

Rill Farm cheeses are made in truckles of 3lb and 10lb in weight and have a natural, thin protective rind. The cheeses are all **UNPASTEURISED,** and made with **VEGETARIAN** rennet and purest salt, and contains no **ARTIFICIAL COLOUR, FLAVOUR OR PRESERVATIVE.**

COW MILK CHEESE

Rill Classic:
A plain cheese with no added flavouring

Rill with Wine:
Red Wine is added giving a fine pink marbling effect.

Rill with Rosemary:
Naturally grown rosemary is added

GOAT MILK CHEESE

Rill Classic:
A plain cheese with no added flavouring

Rill with Sage:
Naturally grown sage is added.

Rill with Rosemary:
Naturally grown rosemary is added

YOGHURTS

Our high quality yoghurt is free from all artificial additives (colourings, flavourings and preservatives) and is available in 16oz and 5oz containers. We make Natural and Fruit flavoured yoghurts in both cow and goat milk. The pure Fruit flavours available are Strawberry, Raspberry and Black Currant and two new flavours available are Hazlenut and Apricot. The goat milk yoghurt is particularly suitable for the bovine allergic, the elderly and the very young. Raw cane sugar is used throughout the yoghurt range.

Please contact Mrs Ruth Burrow for futher information
Mr & Mrs Burrow, Rill Farm, Ottery-St-Mary, Devon EX11 1QH
Telephone: Ottery-St-Mary (040481) 2899

10 ○ ↔

The Dairy House
Whitehill Park, Weobley, Herefordshire
HR4 8QE
Tel: 0544 318815
Contact: Miss Prudence M Lloyd

Soft curd

Curd cheese made either from whole milk with 12-15% fat or separated milk with less than 2% fat, in a variety of flavours including plain, chives and onion, garlic and herbs, supplied loose or in 4, 8oz pots.
C 1,200-1,500lb p.mth
D By own transport
See Also: Yoghurt, Cakes, Biscuits and Pastries

10 ★ ↔

J E & E R Dakin
Wackley Farm, Burlton, Shrewsbury, Shropshire SY4 5TD
Tel: 093922 660
Contact: Mr J E Dakin

Wackley

Wackley Farm, made from unpasteurised sheep milk, mild Coulommiers-type, in a range of flavours including plain, chives, garlic, and parsley in llb rounds. Available vacuum packed in ½, 1, 4lb sizes.
C 200lb p.mth
D By arrangements
See Also: Milk

15 ↔

Devon Oak Smoked Foods Ltd
Unit 5, Townstal Trading Estate, Nelson Road, Dartmouth, Devon TQ6 9LA
Tel: 08043 4410
Contact: Mr A Watts

Cheddar

Own blend of Cheddar and low fat cheese, smoked and re-shaped in traditional drum, covered with black pepper and chives.
C Undisclosed
D By arrangement
See Also: Meat: Smoked, Fish: Smoked

8

J & E Dickinson, Longley Farm
Longley Farm, Holmfirth, nr Huddersfield, Yorkshire HD7 1RS
Tel: 0484 684151 Telx: 51458 COMHUD G LONGL
Contact: J & E Dickinson

Yorkshire curd

Cottage cheese made with vegetarian rennet, plain or flavoured with pineapple or chives in 125, 250g, 2kg packs. Yorkshire Curd, with vegetarian rennet, supplied in cartons and 2st bags for baking.
C Undisclosed
D By arrangement
See Also: Cream, Yoghurt

16 ★

D & G Doble
Castle Hill Farm, Rotherfield, Crowborough, Sussex TN6 3RR
Tel: 089285 2207
Contact: D & G Doble

Castle Hill

Castle Hill Sussex Farmhouse, with vegetarian rennet, full fat, hard, in Caerphilly mould naturally crusted, matured 6-8 weeks. Castle Hill Curd, full fat, soft, available in a range of flavours including plain, garlic and chives, garlic and parsley, black pepper in 2, 4oz cartons, larger quantities available.
C Sussex Farmhouse 300x8-10lb p.mth, curd cheese 50lb p.mth
D By arrangement

15 ★ ↔

Dorset Blue Vinny
Shorts Green Farm, Motcombe, Shaftesbury, Dorset
Tel: 0747 2260
Contact: Ian Bailey

Dorset Blue Vinny

Reportedly sole producers of Dorset Blue Vinny, made from unpasteurised milk of own herd, medium fat, pressed blue cheese, matured 9-12 weeks, in 14-16lb truckles, 5lb size to order.
C 2-3 ton p.mth
D By arrangement

16 ● ★ ↔

Doves Farm Foods
Salisbury Road, Hungerford, Berkshire RG17 ORF
Tel: 0488 84880
Contact: Mrs Marriage

Full cream

Range of soft cheese made from unpasteurised milk of own goat herd, mild flavoured, smooth textured, full fat cream, in a range of flavours including plain, parsley and garlic, chives, and black pepper, in 75g tubs.
C Undisclosed
D By arrangement
See Also: Millers

3 ★

Drumturk Goats
Corb, Bridge of Cally, Blairgowrie, Perthshire PH10 7JX
Tel: 025086 267/223
Contact: Mrs Denise Ferguson

Drumturk White

Drumturk White, made from unpasteurised whole milk of Toggenburg and British Toggenburg goats, mild flavoured, soft white curd cheese, plain or salted in 4-6oz weights. Drumturk Pepper, made from double goat cream, mild flavoured, soft, coated in ground black peppercorns. Drumturk Herbed Oil, soft goat cheese, stronger, saltier than Drumturk White, immersed in a herbal blend of sunflower and olive oil, matured 2-4 weeks, packed in glass jars weighing 3oz.
C 40-200lb p.mth
D By arrangement

5 ○ ★

Easter Weens Enterprises
Easter Weens, Bonchester Bridge, nr Hawick, Roxburgh TD9 8JQ
Tel: 045086 635
Contact: Mr J Curtis

Bonchester

Bonchester, made from whole milk of pedigree Jersey herd, soft, full fat, lightly salted, strong flavour 10oz cheeses, with vegetarian rennet, in 3½oz cheeses. Teviotdale, full fat hard cheese covered in white penicillin mould, in 2½-3lb wheels.

[C] Bonchester 1,050lb p.mth Apr-Dec, Teviotdale 1,050lb p.mth Jun-Dec
[D] By Securicor

12 ● ★ ↔ **The Elms**
The Elms, Lower Westholme, Pilton, Shepton Mallet, Somerset BA4 4EL
Tel: 074989 371
Contact: C D Stone

Goat — Westholme, full fat, semi-hard goat cheese, Caerphilly-type matured for six weeks for mild flavour in 88g round truckles, or for three months for a mature cheese with firmer texture in 2kg round truckles.
[C] Undisclosed
[D] By wholesaler
See Also: Milk, Yoghurt, Fudges and Toffee

9 **Emlyn Creamery Ltd**
The Old Creamery, Newcastle Emlyn, Dyfed SA38 9DB
Tel: 0239 711054
Contact: Prof J Mann

Cwmard — Cwmard, hard goat milk, Caerphilly-type cheese matured for five days in 1, 9lb truckles and 4, 8oz portions. Classique, soft goat milk cheese, medium fat, in 125g containers. Emlyn, soft goat milk cheese, with 18% in excess of butter fat in 90, 500g containers.
[C] Undisclosed
[W] Western Cheese, Corsham Wiltshire
[D] By wholesaler, by arrangement

3 ★ **H J Errington & Co**
Ogscastle, Carnwath, Lanarkshire ML11 8NE
Tel: 089 981 257
Contact: H J Errington

Lanark Blue — Lanark Blue, made with unpasteurised sheep milk from own flock with 52% fat, hand made, Roquefort-type, mould ripened, hard cheese, matured three months in 3kg cylinders. Dunsyre Blue, made from unpasteurised Ayrshire cow milk, mould ripened semi-hard cheese in 3kg cylinders.
[C] 2 ton p.mth
[D] By own transport within area

6 ★

Eshott Farm
The Home Farm, Felton, Morpeth, Northumberland NE65 9EP
Tel: 067 087432
Contact: Mr T N H Sanderson

Eshott

Eshott, made from unpasteurised milk with vegetable or animal rennet, low and medium fat, soft cheese in a range of flavours including plain, herb, and pepper.
C Undisclosed
D By arrangement
See Also: Milk

12 ★

Exmoor Ewes Milk Cheese
Willett Farm, Lydeard St Lawrence, Taunton, Somerset TA4 3QB
Tel: 09847 328
Contact: Alan Duffield

Coleford Blue

Coleford Blue, made from unpasteurised sheep milk and vegetarian rennet, innoculated with penicillin Roquefortii, white mould crust, creamy texture showing some blueing, mild blue tang which strengthens with maturity in 2½kg truckles in packs of six, with twelve week shelf life.
C 500 p.mth
D By arrangement

7

Farm Maid Cheese/Singletons Dairies Ltd
Mill Farm, Preston Road, Longridge, nr Preston, Lancashire PR3 3AN
Tel: 077 478 2112/2113
Contact: Mr J F Vale

Bleasdale

Range of hard cheeses made with vegetarian rennet including Red and White Cheddar, Red and White Cheshire, Red Leicester, Double Gloucester, Wensleydale, Bleasdale made with red and white curd for mellow taste in 8, 20kg rounds or pre-packed into 200g sticks. Also hard cheeses mixed with herbs including Lancashire with chives, or sage, Cheddar with chives, Double Gloucester with chives, Red Leicester with peppers in 2½, 5kg rounds. Also available three day Lancashire curd with or without garlic.
C 200 ton p.mth
D By arrangement

12 ↔

Farmhouse Cheesemakers Ltd
Keward Farm, Glastonbury Road, Wells, Somerset BA5 1QD
Tel: 0749 78755 Telx: 94012342 Fax: 0749 77022
Contact: David Johnson

Caerphilly

Range of cheeses including traditional Farmhouse Cheddar made from pasteurised or unpasteurised milk with animal or vegetable rennet, Red Leicester with animal or vegetable rennet, Double Gloucester and Caerphilly made from unpasteurised milk.
C Undisclosed
D By arrangement
See Also: Butter

7 ★

Farmhouse Country Delicacies
The Homestead Farm, Pott Shrigley, Macclesfield, Cheshire SK10 5RU
Tel: 0625 72381
Contact: Joyce Dalton

Fruit liqueur

Range of unpasteurised soft goat milk cheese with no added rennet, flavours include plain, liqueur, herbs and spices, garnished with pressed flowers or spices. Also naturally soured hard cheese matured in calico cloth for three weeks.
C Undisclosed
D By arrangement
See Also: Fresh Meat, Milk

9 ◉ ★

Felin Gernos Dairy
Felin Gernos Dairy, Maesllyn, Llandysul, Dyfed SA44 5NB
Tel: 023 975 362
Contact: Mrs Gill Bond

Maesllyn Caerphilly

Maesllyn Caerphilly, made from mixed milk of Friesian and Ayrshire cows, with vegetarian rennet and very little salt, full fat, hard, brined for twenty four hours, matured for 7-10 days in 7lb wheels, best eaten within 3-4 weeks. Also smoked in 5lb wheels.
C 4000lb p.mth
D By arrangement

10

Fowlers Forest Dairies Ltd
Forest Farm, Small Lane, Earlswood, Solihull, Warwickshire B94 5EL
Tel: 05646 2329
Contact: Mrs P Fowler

Cheddar

Earlswood Farmhouse, firm, full bodied, full flavoured Cheddar, matured 3-12 months for mild to extra mature in 5kg wedges on the rind, 5kg rectangular packs.
C 1½ ton p.wk
D By own transport within area
See Also: Butter

14

Fullers Brickwall Farm Ltd
Brickwall Farm, Sible Hedingham, Halstead, Essex CO9 3RH
Tel: 0787 60329
Contact: Robert Fuller

Curd

Range of cheeses made from milk of own Jersey herd including skimmed cottage cheese in 4, 8oz, 1, 4lb tubs, low fat curd cheese set with rennet with chives in 3, 6oz, 1, 4lb tubs, whole milk soft cheese with creamy texture in a variety of flavours including plain, herbs and garlic, rolled in fresh herbs in 3oz tubs or 1lb containers.
C 100lb curd cheese p.mth, 150lb cottage cheese p.wk, 100lb whole milk cheese p.wk
D By arrangement
See Also: Cream, Milk, Yoghurt, Cakes, Biscuits and Pastries, Ice Creams and Sorbets

[4]

Glenshesk Dairies
67 Whitepark Road, Carnmoon, Ballycastle, Co Antrim BT54 6LP
Tel: 02657 62743
Contact: Mr John McKinley

Spring onion

Soft, handmade cow milk cheese with 13% fat content in a variety of flavours including plain, spring onion, garlic, pineapple, and raisin in 150g, 2kg tubs.
[C] 10,000 tubs p.mth
[D] By arrangement

[12] ★

H & E J Grant
Hamwood Farm, Trull, Taunton, Somerset TA3 7NX
Tel: 082342 248
Contact: Graham Grant

Cheddar

Farmhouse Cheddar, made from unpasteurised milk produced on farm, matured 7-12 months in 56lb cylinders.
[C] 10 ton p.mth
[D] By arrangement

[1] ★ ↔

Great Glen Foods Ltd
Old Ferry Road, North Ballachulish, Onich, Fort William, Inverness PH33 6RZ
Tel: 08553 277
Contact: Douglas Locke

Glencoe

Glencoe, made from Caledonian herd Anglo-Nubian goat milk, mild, full fat soft cheese available natural, with mixed herbs, chives, pepper, and garlic, fresh or frozen, in 225g rounds.
[C] Undisclosed
[W] Scottish Goat Products Ltd, 05403 692
[D] By wholesaler
See Also: Milk, Fudges and Toffee

[10] ★ ↔

V J Hares & Son
Millenheath, Higher Heath, Whitchurch, Shropshire
Tel: 0948 840288
Contact: The Proprietor

Farmhouse Cheshire

Farmhouse Cheshire, made exclusively from milk from own Friesian herd, soft textured, coloured and white in 40lb weights.
[C] 600-700 p.mth
[D] By own transport within area
See Also: Butter

7 ★

Henry Barnett & Sons
Overton Hall, Malpas, Cheshire SY14 7DG
Tel: 0948 860519
Contact: Mr Richard Barnett

Cheshire

Overton Hall Farmhouse Cheshire, traditionally waxed hard Cheese. Also Red Leicester and Double Gloucester made from whole unpasteurised milk and vegetarian rennet, clothbound, in 1, 20, 50lb sizes.
[C] 12 ton p.mth
[W] Mollington Farmhouse Cheese Co Ltd
[D] By wholesaler

2 ★

Highland Goat Products
Corglass Farm, Ballindalloch, Banffshire AB3 9BS
Tel: 08072 269
Contact: Mrs Jane Heape

Ballindalloch

Ballindalloch, made from unpasteurised goat milk of own herd, hard, with natural crust, matured for three months, wax covered in 4-5lb wheels. Strathspey, full fat goat cheese, mild with crumbly texture in 4-5lb wheels.
[C] 224lb p.mth
[D] By arrangement

1 ●

Highland Fine Cheese Ltd
Knockbreck, Tain, Ross & Cromarty
Tel: 0862 2034
Contact: Mrs E R Stone

Highland Crowdie

Range of naturally cultured soft Scottish cheese including Caboc, made to 15th century family recipe, rich double cream cheese rolled in toasted pinhead oatmeal in 4oz rolls. Highland Crowdie, semi-cooked low fat unpasteurised, with sharp citrus flavour, in 5oz, 5lb tubs. Garlic Crowdie, mixed with crushed wild garlic rolled in toasted hazelnuts in 4oz rolls. Gru Dhu, a Crowdie and cream cheese mixture rolled in crushed peppercorns in 4oz sizes.
[C] Undisclosed
[W] Messrs Crowson & Sons, East Kilbride
[D] By wholesaler

12 ↔

Holstius & Breet
Esperanza, Aust, Bristol, Avon BS12 3AX
Tel: 04545 3148 Telx: 449752
Contact: Robin D L Breet

Chilli and white wine

Potted spreading cheese in a variety of flavours including brandy and walnut, chilli and white wine, port and almond, horseradish, and hazelnut. Also available in 155g wrapped packs.
[C] Undisclosed
[D] By arrangement
See Also: Butter, Mustards, Fudges and Toffee, Snacks and Savouries

14 ⊙ ↔

A & K Hood
The Stables, Gresham, Norfolk NR11 8AD
Tel: 026377 468
Contact: Mr Hood

Jersey

Range of cheeses from organic Jersey herd including low fat soft cheese with no rennet, plain or with herbs, packed to customers requirements. Also full fat hard cheese, Wensleydale-type, low salt, matured for four weeks in 2-3lb weights.
[C] Undisclosed
[D] By arrangement
See Also: Fresh Meat, Poultry Producers, Milk, Fresh Vegetables, Jams and Preserves

15

D E Horrell Ltd
Lynher Valley Dairy, Netherton Farm, Upton Cross, Liskeard, Cornwall PL14 5BD
Tel: 0579 62244
Contact: Michael Horrell

Cornish Yarg

Cornish Yarg, full milk, Brie-type, wrapped in nettles, matured 2-3 weeks in 6lb wheels. Cornish Herb and Garlic, soft full fat mixed with six herbs and garlic. Cornish Pepper, soft full fat, coated in cracked peppercorns, both in 2lb lightly pressed truckles.
[C] Yarg 800 p.wk, soft cheeses 800 p.wk
[D] By arrangement
See Also: Yoghurt

Any Problems?

If you are looking for a particular product and it is not listed in the directory, please contact us on **01 727 9808.**

New Products?

Let us know on **01 727 9808** and we will follow it through for our next edition.

[3]

Howgate Dairy Products
Walltower, Howgate, Penicuik, Midlothian
Tel: 0968 72263
Contact: M T R Marwick

Crowdie

Range of Scottish cheeses made from pasteurised milk including Crowdie, low fat, lightly salted, plain or flavoured. Lothian, Camembert-type. Pentland, Brie-type, both mature soft cheeses. Langskaill, pressed Gouda-type with or without salt. Smallholder, Cheddar-type made from cow or goat milk, crumbly in texture with blue veining sometimes appearing at maturity. Also peat smoked soft cheese, cream cheese in oatmeal, goat cheese, yoghurt cheese and cottage cheese in 2, 5oz cartons, curd cheese, low and full fat, in 2kg boxes.
[C] 600lb p.mth
[D] By own transport within area
See Also: Cream, Milk, Yoghurt

[7] [★]

P J Huntbach
Hayfields Farm, Audlem, nr Crewe, Cheshire CW3 OEX
Tel: 0270 811394
Contact: Philip Huntbach

Cheshire

Cheshire cheese made from unpasteurised milk with vegetarian rennet, matured 3-4 weeks in 20kg cylinders and 18½kg blocks.
[C] 1 ton p.dy
[W] Mendip Foods, Wrenbury Dairy Products
[D] By wholesaler, by own transport within area
See Also: Butter

[12] [★]

Hurstone Farmhouse
Waterrow, Wiveliscombe, Somerset TA4 2AT
Tel: 0984 23441
Contact: John Bone

Hurstone

Hurstone, made from unpasteurised milk of own Jersey herd, full fat, hard, matured for 2-3 months in 2, 4, 8lb waxed truckles. Hurstone low fat also available.
[C] Undisclosed
[D] By arrangement
See Also: Butter, Cream, Milk

[10] [★]

Hutchinson Smith
Hinton Bank Farm, Whitchurch, Shropshire SY13 4HB
Tel: 2631
Contact: Mr Hutchinson Smith

Blue Cheshire

Blue Cheshire, traditional full fat cheese, blue veined with buttery texture, mild, nutty flavour in 20lb weights or smaller truckles to order.
[C] 1200-2000 cheeses p.mth
[W] Dairy Crest Foods
[D] By wholesaler

[10] [★] [↔]

Hyde Farm Cheese
The Hyde, Stokebliss, Tenbury Wells, Worcestershire WR15 8RS
Tel: 08854 324
Contact: Mrs Marris

Fromage Frais

Unpasteurised soft goat milk cheeses including Fromage Frais, whipped with 12% fat content in 100, 140g, 4lb tubs. St Fletcher, crust free roll with 16% fat content, flavoured with parsley, chives, garlic, coriander and nutmeg, rosemary and chives.
[C] Undisclosed
[D] By arrangement
See Also: Milk

[12] [↔]

Ilchester Cheese Co Ltd
Ilchester, Somerset BA22 8LZ
Tel: 840531 Telx: 46639 CHEECO G
Contact: Diana Fox

Romany

Range of cheeses including Applewood Smoked Cheddar, Glenphilly Whisky Chedder, Celebrity, Derby-type with celery in 2½kg wheels, 200, 400g waxed truckles, 170g wedges. County, alternate layers of Blue Stilton and Double Gloucester. Romany, combination of Caerphilly with onion and Double Gloucester in 140g wedges, 1¼kg half moons. Also Bouchettes, Ilchester cheese and potato in crumb coating and Toastmasters, Ilchester rarebits on french bread.
[C] Undisclosed
[D] By arrangement

[1]

Inchnavie Goats
Inchnavie Lower, Newbridge, Alness, Ross & Cromarty IV17 OXL
Tel: 0349 883585
Contact: Tim Dearman

Dalneich

Strath Averon, goat milk cheese made with vegetarian rennet, full fat, hard, matured for six weeks in 4lb rounds. Dalneich, soft goat cheese flavoured with seaweed.
[C] Undisclosed
[W] Scottish Goat Products Ltd 05403 692
[D] By wholesaler
See Also: Cream, Milk

[3] [★]

Ingle Smokehouse Ltd
Unit 8, Shore Road, Perth PH2 8BD
Tel: 0738 30121
Contact: Anne Brow

Gowrie

Gowrie, made from unpasteurised Friesian milk, full fat, hard pressed, cloth wrapped cheese. Madoch, made from unpasteurised goat milk, full fat, hard pressed, cloth wrapped or rolled in cinders. Liberton, made from unpasteurised ewe milk, full fat, hard pressed.
[C] Gowrie 1250lb p.wk, Madoch 50lb p.wk, Liberton 170lb p.wk
[D] By arrangement

3 ↔ **Islay Creamery Company Ltd**
Port Charlotte, Isle of Islay, Argyll PA48 7TY
Tel: 049685 229
Contact: Mr John Kissock

Islay Dunlop — Islay Dunlop hard cheese, Cheddar-type with no crust, matured up to six months for mild flavour, over six months for stronger flavour, in 40lb blocks.
[C] 300 ton p.a
[D] By own transport within area

9 ○ ★ **John & Jenny White Organic Smallholders**
Mount Pleasant, Pen y Bont, Carmarthen, Dyfed SA33 6PP
Tel: 09948 315
Contact: Jenny White

Pen y Bont — Pen y Bont, made from unpasteurised goat milk, Wensleydale-type, medium fat, mild flavoured, in a variety of flavours including plain, herbs, and garlic in 4-5lb flat rounds, waxed mini bonce weighing 12oz.
[C] 400lb p.mth
[D] By own transport within area
See Also: Milk, Yoghurt

15 ○ ★ ↔ **Kathryn Cornish**
Hedgemoor Farm, Bridford, Exeter, Devon EX6 7LW
Tel: 0647 52358
Contact: Kathryn Cornish

Goat — Full fat, soft cheese made from unpasteurised milk of mixed goat herd with vegetarian rennet, available fresh or frozen in 4oz tubs, or flavoured with herbs in 3oz tubs.
[C] Undisclosed
[D] By own transport within area
See Also: Milk, Yoghurt

12 ★ **D M Keen & Sons**
Moorehayes Farm, Verrington Lane, Wincanton, Somerset DA9 8JR
Tel: 0963 32286
Contact: Stephen Keen

Cheddar — Farmhouse Cheddar, made from unpasteurised whole milk, clothbound, matured 9-12 months to give nutty flavour in 60lb cylinders, 7lb truckles.
[C] 70 tonne p.a
[D] By arrangement
See Also: Butter

7 ★ **J J & R Kirkham**
Beesley Farm, Mill Lane, Goosnargh, Lancashire PR3 2SL
Tel: 0772 865335
Contact: Mr J J Kirkham

Lancashire — Lancashire, made from unpasteurised milk of Friesian herd, smooth flavour, matured from six weeks to twelve months, in wax coated cylinders.
[C] 85 cheeses p.mth
[D] By arrangement

9 **Knolton Farmhouse Cheese Ltd**
Overton on Dee, nr Wrexham, Clwyd LL13 0CG
Tel: 097873 221/0829 260485
Contact: Mr J Latham

Wensleydale — Range of farmhouse cheeses including Cheshire, white and coloured with open texture, rinded, waxed, matured 4-6 weeks in 9lb wheels. Wensleydale, white, clothbound, matured 2-4 weeks in 7kg truckles. Red Leicester, smooth, clothbound, matured 3-4 months in 10kg wheels. Sage Derby, hard, flavoured with rubbed sage, matured two months in 7kg, 9lb wheels. Also Lancashire, Double Gloucester and Chedder in 14kg black wax truckles.
[C] 30 ton p.mth
[D] By arrangement
See Also: Jams and Preserves

15 ★ ↔

Langage Farm Dairy Products
Langage Farm, Plympton, Plymouth, Devon PL7 5AW
Tel: 0752 337723
Contact: Peter Tremaine

Quarg

Range of soft cheeses made from milk of pedigree Jersey herd including cottage cheese with 4% butter fat, low fat with 7% butter fat, full fat with 27% butter fat, all in 4, 8oz, 4lb cartons, natural or flavoured to order. Also Quarg with under 0.5% butter fat.
C Low fat cheese 1000lb p.mth, full fat cheese 400lb p.mth, cottage cheese 2000lb p.mth
D By own transport within area
See Also: Cream, Milk, Cakes, Biscuits and Pastries, Ice Creams and Sorbets

10 ★

Leasowes Natural Dairy Produce
Stanton Long, Much Wenlock, Shropshire TF13 6LH
Tel: 074634 666
Contact: David Colley

Smythe Moor

Nature's Taste, made from unpasteurised goat milk with vegetarian rennet, full fat, soft cheese in 125g tubs. Smythe Moor hard goat cheese, full fat, vacuum packed in 3lb bags with a shelf life of two months.
C Undisclosed
D By arrangement
See Also: Yoghurt

9 ● ★ ↔

Little Acorn Products
Mesem Fach Farm, Bethania, nr Llanon, Dyfed SY23 5NL
Tel: 097 423348
Contact: Don and Karen Ross

Acorn Farmhouse

Acorn Farmhouse, made from unpasteurised sheep milk with vegetarian rennet, full fat, hard, washed rind, in 4½, 5lb truckles, or hamper size weighing approximately 1¼lb, with good keeping qualities, inclined to blue when cut.
C 400 cheeses p.mth
D By arrangement
See Also: Milk

9 ★

Llanboidy Farmhouse Cheeses
Cilowen Uchaf, Login, Whitland, Dyfed SA34 OTJ
Tel: 09946 303
Contact: Sue Jones

Llanboidy

Llanboidy, made from milk of rare breed Red Poll cattle grazed on Welsh pastures free from chemical sprays and herbicides, traditional, hard, full fat cheese, hard pressed, matured in own rind for two months, in 10lb wheels. Laverbread, full fat cheese flavoured with Welsh laverbread, hard pressed, matured in own rind for 10- 12 weeks, in 10lb wheels. Welsh Farmhouse, made from unpasteurised cow milk, full fat, hard pressed, matured in own rind 8-10 weeks, in 10lb wheels.
C 2400-3600lb p.mth
D By arrangement

9 ○ ★ ↔

Llangloffan Farmhouse Cheese
Llangloffan Farm, Castle Morris, Haverfordwest, Dyfed SA62 5ET
Tel: 034 85 241
Contact: Leon Downey

Llangloffan

Llangloffan, made from unpasteurised milk of own Jersey herd, hard, full fat naturally rinded cheese in 4, 9, 30lb sizes. Red Llangloffan, with chives and garlic.
C Llangloffan 1 ton p.mth, Red Llangloffan 1 ton p.mth Mar-Dec
D By arrangement

11

Long Clawson Dairy Ltd
Long Clawson, Melton Mowbray, Leicestershire LE14 4PJ
Tel: 0664 822332
Contact: Mr John Woodford

Blue Stilton

Blue Stilton, evenly veined, creamy texture, matured 9-12 weeks, in whole truckles weighing 8kg. Also halves, quarters, 1¼kg rings, wedges, 2¼kg mini Stiltons. White Stilton weighing 9-10kg. Also Blue Shropshire in similar sizes and weights.
C Undisclosed
D By arrangement

12

W H Longman & Sons (Farmhouse Cheesemakers Ltd)
North Leaze Farm, North Cadbury, Yeovil, Somerset BA22 7HD
Tel: 0963 40239
Contact: Mr M A Biggs

Cheddar

Somerset Cheddar, with or without vegetable colouring, matured to customers requirements, in 40lb blocks or 56lb cylinders on the rind. Also Double Gloucester and Leicester made with or without vegetable colouring, in 18lb flat cylinders on the rind.
C Undisclosed
D By arrangement

16 ★ ↔

Lodge Farm British Milk Sheep
Lodge Farm, Lower South Park Road, South Godstone, Surrey RM9 8LF
Tel: 0342 893191
Contact: E M and J A Pinard

Cream

Unpasteurised soft cheeses including curd cheese with 2-3 week shelf life, best eaten fairly fresh, rich cream cheese with very sharp flavour, suitable for cooking and freezing. Both available flavoured to customers requirements.
C 100lb p.mth
D By arrangement

12

Lubborn Cheese Ltd
North Street, Crewkerne, Somerset TA18 7AS
Tel: 0460 76102
Contact: Piers Feilden

Saanen goat	Somerset Brie, made from Friesian milk, full fat soft cheese, mould ripened, matured for six weeks, soft texture, in 5lb wheels. Capricorn goat, made from Saanen goat milk with vegetable rennet, full fat soft cheese, matured in 100g cylinders, 1kg square cutting blocks suitable for delicatessen counters. [C] Undisclosed [D] By arrangement

16 ● ↔

Malthouse Cottage Farm
Malthouse Lane, Ashington, Pulborough, West Sussex RH20 3BU
Tel: 0903 892456
Contact: Mrs J Ferris

Organic goat	Range of organic goat cheese, handmade with milk and herbs from own farm including soft, moulded, pressed and matured. [C] Undisclosed [D] By arrangement *See Also: Fresh Meat, Poultry Producers, Milk, Yoghurt*

12

Manor Farm (Castle Cary) Ltd
Manor Farm, Castle Cary, Somerset BA7 7PY
Tel: 0963 50286
Contact: Mr A J Churchhouse

Cheddar	Traditional Cheddar, rinded and matured for eight months, in 4, 5, 9lb truckles and 60lb weights. [C] Undisclosed [D] By arrangement

9 ○ ★

Marianglas
Maes Mawr, LLanllyfni, Caernarvon, Gwynedd LL54 6DG
Tel: 0286 881809
Contact: Mrs J Rickford

Marianglas	Marianglas, hard pressed, naturally crusted goat cheese, matured for one month in 1lb cylinders. Fullest flavour reached at two months. [C] 100lb p.mth [D] By own transport within area, by arrangement *See Also: Milk*

12 ○ ★

Martin Pitt
Levetts Farm, Marlborough, Wiltshire SN8 4DS
Tel: 0672 52035
Contact: Martin Pitt

Sheep milk

Range of unpasteurised soft goat milk cheese with vegetarian rennet, in natural, garlic and herbs, and black pepper. Also soft sheep milk cheese in natural, chives and smoked, packed in 115g wooden boxes.
[C] Undisclosed
[D] By own transport within area
See Also: Eggs, Purees and Sauces

1 ● ★

Meiklejohns Croft Organic Cheese
Meiklejohns Croft, Lamington, nr Invergordon, Ross & Cromarty IV18 OPE
Tel: 086 284 2358
Contact: Alasdair Hutchison

Strathrorie

Range of hard cheese made from unpasteurised milk, with vegetarian rennet, naturally rinded, including Strathrusdale goat cheese in 4-8lb rounds. Strathrorie, made with sheep milk, brine washed, in 4-8lb rounds. Caise na bo, Ayrshire herd milk, brine washed, in 4-8lb rounds. All with manchego print on rind. Also range of soft cheese made from cow, goat and sheep milk, lightly pressed, flavoured with garlic, rolled in oatmeal, sesame, thyme or seaweed.
[C] Strathrusdale 200kg p.mth, Strathrorie 200kg p.mth, Caise na bo 400kg p.mth
[D] By arrangement

12 ↔

Minola Smoked Products
Kencot Hill Farmhouse, Filkins, Lechlade, Gloucestershire GL7 3QY
Tel: 036 786 391/556 Fax: 036 786 544
Contact: Hugh Forestier Walker

Smoked cheddar

Range of English cheese smoked over whole oak logs including mild Cheddar, Cheddar smoked with paprika in 1, 2, 10lb packs. Chewton Mendip mature English Cheddar in 1, 7, 14lb packs, and 4lb Wedmore cheese.
[C] 50kg p.wk
[D] By arrangement
See Also: Meat: Smoked, Game: Smoked, Fish Dealers

12 ★

J A & E Montgomery Ltd
Manor Farm, North Cadbury, Yeovil, Somerset BA22 7DW
Tel: 0963 40243
Contact: Mr J A Montgomery

Cheddar

Farmhouse mature Cheddar made from unpasteurised milk of own Friesian herd in 53lb cylinders or 8lb truckles.
[C] 240-300 p.mth
[D] By arrangement

12 ★

Moorlands Goats Cheeses
Blackwood Hill, Rushton Spencer, nr Macclesfield, Cheshire SK11 ORU
Tel: 02606 336
Contact: Mary J D Gregory

Blackwood

Full fat soft goat cheese with mild, fresh flavour in 100, 200g, 1kg individual moulds, available plain, crushed garlic and herbs, mixed herbs, crushed black peppercorns or to customers requirements. Blackwood, blue mould ripened goat cheese with soft white creamy interior, matured 3-4 weeks, in 1kg wheels.
[C] 400kg p.mth
[W] Wilds of Mollington 0244 851 226, House of Callow 0533 541 637, Woods Cheese Factors 0625 25903
[D] By wholesaler

5 ★

Mr & Mrs M H Neilson
Windyknowe, Annan, Dumfries & Galloway DG12 5LN
Tel: 04612 4691
Contact: Mrs Carol Neilson

Barac

Barac, semi-hard whole sheep milk cheese, gentle flavour, matured three months, in waxed 3lb rounds, 1lb baby Barac available for Christmas. Corban, soft, Ricotta-type, available plain or with chives.
[C] 350lb p.mth, Corban May-Oct
[D] By arrangement
See Also: Milk

16 ★ ↔

Neal's Yard Creamery
Home Farm Cottage, Everlands Estate, Sevenoaks, Kent TN14 6HU
Tel: 0732 461020
Contact: Beatrice Garoche

Perroche logs

Range of cheese made from unpasteurised milk with vegetarian rennet including Perroche made from milk of mixed goat herd, in 4-8oz weights. Perroche logs, plain or coated with fresh herbs, in 1, 2lb weights. Fromage Blanc, made from cow milk, soft curd in 25cl, 2lb weights. Low fat cheese made from skimmed milk, salt free, soft, light and smooth, in 2lb weights. Wealden rounds, semi-soft, made from cow milk, Camembert-shape, with fresh herbs, in 9-10oz rounds.
[C] Perroche 200 p.mth, Perroche logs 100 p.mth, fromage blanc 100lb p.mth, low fat cheese 120lb p.mth, Wealden rounds 1000 p.mth
[D] By own transport within area
See Also: Cream, Yoghurt, Ice Creams and Sorbets

9 ○

Nevern Dairy Ltd
Glasdir Farm, Nevern, Pembrokeshire SA42 0NQ
Tel: 0239 820354 Telx: 48585 Fax: 0239 820044
Contact: Mr Andrew Threipland

Cheddar

Traditional farmhouse Cheddar, made from unpasteurised cow milk, handmade, cloth wrapped, matured for 6-9 months, in 56lb cylinders. Also Chedder made from both pasteurised and unpasteurised milk, with animal or vegetable rennet, in 4, 6lb truckles, 20kg blocks.
[C] 40 tonne p.mth
[D] By arrangement

10 ○ ★ ↔ **New House Farm**
New House Farm, Acton, Newcastle under Lyme, Staffordshire ST5 4EE
Tel: 0782 680 366
Contact: Mrs Deaville

Chives and garlic — Staffordshire Organic, made from unpasteurised cow milk of organically raised herd, hard pressed, clothbound, unwaxed, matured three months in 20, 40lb rounds, available plain, mixed herbs, chives and garlic.
C 4000 p.mth
D By arrangement
See Also: Milk, Ice Creams and Sorbets

16 **North Downs Dairy Co Ltd**
Grove Dairy Farm, Bobbing Hill, Sittingbourne, Kent ME9 8NY
Tel: 0795 844444 Telx: 966370 N DOWNS
Fax: 0795 844029
Contact: Mr P J Symes

Red Leicester — Pilgrims Choice, made from cow milk, hard, matured for a minimum of nine months, in 20kg, 25kg with rind. Red Leicester and Cheshire cheese, in 6½, 10, 25kg wheels.
C 7000 tonne p.a
D By arrangement

15 ○ ★ **Park Farm Cheeses**
Park Farm, Umberleigh, Devon
Tel: 07694 237
Contact: Hilary Charnley

Devon Garland — Range of hard, naturally crusted cheese made from milk of own Jersey herd with vegetarian rennet, including Devon Garland, lightly pressed, rich, flaky with high butter fat content and band of fresh herbs in 8lb wheels. Exmoor, rich, plain, flaky, in summer ripens to creamy, in 4-5lb wheels. Molland, rich, golden, Wensleydale-type, in 6-7lb truckles. Also Satterleigh, made with goat milk, hard, in 6-7lb truckles.
C Cow cheese 2000-3000lb p.mth, Goat cheese 400lb p.mth
D By arrangement

9 **Patchwork**
Faraway, Llandegla, Clwyd LL11 3BG
Tel: 097 888238
Contact: Margaret Carter

Feta — Spiced feta cheese in olive oil with Juniper berries, bayleaves, fennel, garlic and red pepper. Also available stilton and Guinness pâté.
C Undisclosed
D By arrangement
See Also: Game: Pâtés and Pastes, Vegetable Dishes, Cakes, Biscuits and Pastries

1 ○ ★ ↔ **Paupers Cheeses**
The Croft at Brubester, by Shebster, nr Thurso, Caithness
Contact: Ms Sue Kirby

Pauper's Spicy Herb — Pauper's Garlic and Herb, made from unpasteurised goat milk with vegetable rennet and fresh garlic, full fat, semi-soft, rolled in freeze dried herbs and matured for one week, with a 4-5 week shelf life. Also Pauper's Spicy Herb, rolled in black peppers, pimentos and marjoram, both in ½, 1½lb rounds.
C 200x1½lb p.mth
D By arrangement

9 ↔ **Pembroke Poultry**
Eastwood, Boulston, Haverfordwest, Dyfed
Tel: 0437 66372
Contact: Richard Llewellyn

Sheep — Camembert-type sheep milk cheese in 7, 14oz boxes.
C Undisclosed
D By arrangement
See Also: Poultry Producers

15 ★ **Pinhill Yoghurt**
Pinhill Farm, Sidbury, Sidmouth, Devon EX10 0QJ
Tel: 03957 211
Contact: Mrs Kitrina Bishop

Fromage Frais — Fromage Frais, made from unpasteurised sheep milk in a variety of flavours including natural, strawberry, apricot, and raspberry in 4oz pots.
C Undisclosed
D By own transport within area, by arrangement
See Also: Milk, Yoghurt

9 ○ **Plas Dairy Farm**
Llanfaelog, Ty Croes, Anglesey, Gwynedd LL63 5TU
Tel: 0407 810261
Contact: David Williams

Lactic curd — Range of cheese made with vegetarian rennet including lactic curd cow cheese, low fat with 6.5% fat content, in natural, garlic and herbs, chives, black pepper flavour. Lactic curd goat cheese, medium fat with 18% fat content, in natural, garlic and herb flavour, all in 120g tubs.
C 2000kg p.mth
D By arrangement

9 ★ **Pumpkin Produce**
Tyn Y Llwyn, Pontrhydygroes, Ystrad Meurig, Dyfed SY425 6DP
Tel: 097422 636
Contact: Gill Pateman

Smoked paprika cheese — Merlin Plain, made from unpasteurised milk of own goat herd with vegetable rennet, hard, sealed in wax, matured for 2-3 months weighing 2½lb, with a shelf life of six months when stored at 40F. Also available flavoured with olives, walnuts, smoked with paprika over oak for up to two days.
C 800lb p.mth
D By arrangement

9 ● ★ ↔ **Rachel's Dairy**
Brynllys, Borth, Dyfed SY24 5LZ
Tel: 097081 489
Contact: Ms Rachel Rowlands

Cottage cheese — Cottage cheese made from unpasteurised skimmed Guernsey milk with less than 1% fat. Also available, skimmed milk.
[C] Skimmed milk and cheese 500lb p.mth
[D] By own transport within area
See Also: Butter, Yoghurt

3 ★ **J & C I Reade**
Sgriob ruadh Farm Dairy, Tobermory, Mull
Tel: 0688 2235
Contact: Mrs Christine Reade

Isle of Mull — Isle of Mull, made from unpasteurised milk from own herd and vegetable rennet, traditional handmade hard cheese, Cheddar-type, matured for 6-12 months.
[C] Undisclosed
[D] By arrangement

6 ○ ★ **Redesdale Sheep Dairy**
Soppitt Farm, Otterburn, Newcastle upon Tyne NE19 1AF
Tel: 0830 20276
Contact: Mark Robertson

Wensleydale — Range of farmhouse cheese including Redesdale, made from cow milk, Gouda-type, brine salted, matured for two months, in 2½kg wheels. Real Wensleydale, made from mixed cow and sheep milk, hard, hand salted, clothbound, matured for six weeks in 3½kg cylinders. Coquetdale, made from cow milk, semi-soft, nutty flavour, brine salted, matured for one month in 1½kg rounds. Farmhouse Gouda, made from cow milk, matured for eight weeks in 2½kg wheels.
[C] Undisclosed
[W] A Porter, 0423 322323
[D] By wholesaler, by own transport within area
See Also: Cream, Milk, Yoghurt

15 ★ **Rill Farm**
Rill Farm, Ottery St Mary, Devon EX11 1QH
Tel: 040481 2899
Contact: Mrs Ruth Burrow

Goat — Rill Farm, made from unpasteurised milk of own Friesian herd, with vegetable rennet, full fat, hard with natural rind, in 3, 9lb truckles, available flavoured with wine or rosemary. Rill Farm Goat, a goat

milk version of Rill Farm. Also available soft goat cheese with chives or garlic.
Ⓒ Cow milk cheese 1½ ton p.mth, goat milk cheese 800lb p.mth
Ⓓ By arrangement
See Also: Yoghurt

7 ★

D S & A Rutter
Old Beachin, Churton, nr Chester, Cheshire CH3 6LU
Tel: 082 925 268/270
Contact: Mr D S Rutter

Cheshire

Farmhouse Cheshire, made from unpasteurised milk, coloured or white, crumbly hard, matured 2-3 weeks, in 1kg, 5, 10, 12lb sizes and 10, 20kg cylinders. Mild Cheshire, matured 10-14 days, in 10kg sizes. Wensleydale, made from unpasteurised milk, white, fairly crumbly, hard. Double Gloucester made from unpasteurised milk with vegetable colouring, traditional, hard, matured for three months, in 45lb weights.
Ⓒ 190 ton p.a
Ⓦ Mendip Foods
Ⓓ By wholesaler
See Also: Ice Creams and Sorbets

1 ★

Scottish Goat Products Ltd
Station Road, Newtonmore, Inverness-shire PH20 1AR
Tel: 05403 692
Contact: Douglas Locke

Glencoe

Ben Wyris, unpasteurised hard goat milk cheese flavoured with chives. Glencoe, unpasteurised soft goat milk cheese flavoured with mixed herbs, black pepper, chives and garlic.
Ⓒ Undisclosed
Ⓓ By arrangement
See Also: Fresh Meat, Milk, Yoghurt, Fudges and Toffee

15 ★ ↔

Sharpham Creamery
Ashprington, Totnes, Devon TQ9 7UT
Tel: 080423 600
Contact: Izabella Carroll

Elmhirst

Sharpham, made from unpasteurised Jersey milk with vegetarian rennet, farmhouse Coulommiers-type, surface mould ripened, soft with 55-60% fat content, matured for three weeks in 8″ wheels weighing 2½lb, 6″ wheels weighing 1lb. Ashprington, made from partially skimmed Jersey milk with vegetarian rennet, semi-soft, orange red to dusty brown in colour, smooth flavour and lingering bite which strengthens with maturity, matured 4-5 weeks, Elmhirst, triple cream cheese with added cream, white surface mould, ripened in 6″ wheels weighing 1½lb.
Ⓒ Sharpham 500 cheeses p.mth Mar-Dec, Ashprington 50 cheeses p.mth Mar-Dec, Elmhirst 60 p.mth Mar-Dec
Ⓓ By arrangement

11 ★

J Shelley
Fishpool Cottage, White Gritt, nr Minsterley, Shropshire SY5 0JN
Tel: 058 861 337
Contact: Mrs J Shelley

Goat

Range of soft cheese made from unpasteurised goat milk with vegetarian rennet and 2-3 week refrigerated shelf life, including Hyssington, mature Pont l'Evêque- type, strong and creamy with white mould, matured 5-10 days in 10-12oz squares. Plain Coulommiers-type, mild flavour, in 6-8oz 4″ diameter rounds. Soft curd cheese Neufchâtel-type, mild flavoured, available plain, garlic, chives, cucumber and mint, and mixed fresh herbs, or rolled in sesame seed, celery seed, and crushed peppercorns weighing 2oz.
Ⓒ 150lb p.mth
Ⓓ By arrangement, by own transport within area

12 ◯ ★ ↔

Sleight Farm
Timsbury, Bath, Avon BA3 1HN
Tel: 0761 70620
Contact: Mary Holbrook

Tymsboro

Range of unpasteurised sheep and goat milk cheese including Farmhouse Feta, made from sheep milk, preserved in sea salt brine, mild flavour strengthening with several months storage. Emlett, made from sheep milk, soft Brie-type, creamy, delicate flavour, matured 2-5 weeks in 7oz cylinders. Mendip, hard goat cheese made in basket mould to resemble Pecorino, moist, creamy when young, strengthening over 2-6 month maturing period. Tymsboro, soft goat cheese, mild when young, strengthening like chevre over 2-4 weeks maturing period, in 7-8oz, 1½-2lb sizes. Tyning, hard sheep milk cheese matured for up to one year. Also available small goat cheeses decorated with herbs, pepper, and rosemary.
Ⓒ Undisclosed, Feta, Emlett, Tymsboro Feb-Nov, Mendip Apr-Feb
Ⓓ By arrangement

9 ◯ ↔

Sterling Business Associates
The Creamery, Newcastle Emlyn, Dyfed SA38 9DH
Tel: 0239 711054
Contact: Mr Fred Park

Classique

Goat's Classique, soft, medium fat cheese processed by ultra-filtration, with twenty one day shelf life, plain, in 125g tubs. Classique, soft, medium fat cow cheese, in a range of flavours including plain, orange, pineapple, strawberry, raspberry, chives, mixed spice, garlic, and onion in 125g tubs.
Ⓒ Goat's Classique 4000kg p.mth, Cow's Classique 8000kg p.mth
Ⓓ By arrangement
See Also: Milk

15

Streatfeild Hood & Co Ltd
Denhay Farm, Broadoak, Bridport, Dorset BT6 5NP
Tel: 0308 22770/22717
Contact: Mrs A C Streatfeild

Cheddar

Farmhouse Cheddar, rinded, clothbound, mild or mature in 56lb cylinders and 4-5lb Dorset drums, boxed if required.
[C] 50 ton p.a
[D] By arrangement
See Also: Butter

[9] ★

Summergill Dairies
Grosmont, Abergavenny, Gwent NP7 8HN
Tel: 0981 240686
Contact: Robin and Jo Ransome

Skirrid

Skirrid, made from unpasteurised ewes milk, firm, 100% halal, mild, white cheese marinaded in mead, matured for three months in 4lb truckles.
[C] 120 p.mth
[D] By arrangement

[14] ★

Susan Moore Dairy Products
Cranes Watering Farm, Starston, Harleston, Norfolk IP20 9NE
Tel: 0379 852387
Contact: Susan Moore

Beckvale

Range of full fat soft cheese made from unpasteurised Channel Island milk with vegetarian rennet, handmade, slightly salted Coulommier-type including Depwade, with mixed herbs. Beckvale with bay leaves, both weighing 250g. Cream cheese, available plain, herb and garlic in 4oz pots. Also curd cheese, low fat cottage cheese made from skimmed Jersey and Guernsey milk, available plain, chives, and pineapple.
[C] 150lb p.mth winter season
[D] By own transport within area, by arrangement
See Also: Fresh Meat, Cream, Yoghurt, Ice Creams and Sorbets

[16] ○ ★ ↔

Sussex High Weald Dairy Sheep
Putlands Farm, Duddleswell, Uckfield, East Sussex TN22 3BJ
Tel: 082571 2647
Contact: Mr Mark Hardy

Halloumi

Halloumi, made from unpasteurised sheep milk, with salt, mint, full fat, Cyprus-type, individually vacuum packed in 200, 300g sizes. Ricotta, made from the unpasteurised whey of sheep milk, with vegetarian rennet, Italian-style cheese.
[C] 2000kg p.mth
[D] By wholesaler
See Also: Milk, Yoghurt

[7]

Sutton Dairy Goats
The Cottage, Eddisbury Lodge, Delamere, Northwich, Cheshire CW8 2JD
Tel: 0829 51264
Contact: Mrs E Sutton

Sutton Mild English

Sutton's Mild English, made from goat milk with vegetarian rennet, full fat, soft, available plain or flavoured with chives, garlic, and garlic and parsley, in 100g tubs.
[C] Undisclosed
[D] By arrangement
See Also: Milk, Ice Creams and Sorbets

[8] ○ ★

The Swaledale Cheese Company
Gallowfields, Richmond, North Yorkshire DL10 4SU
Tel: 0748 4044/4932
Contact: David Reed

Swaledale

Swaledale, made to a traditional Swaledale recipe with unpasteurised milk, semi-soft, full fat, with a natural rind, matured for 3-4 weeks in 1, 5½lb rounds.
[C] 2½ ton p.mth
[D] By arrangement

[6]

Teesdale Supply Stores
The Post Office, Main Street, Cotherstone, Barnard Castle, Co Durham, DL12 9PG
Tel: 0833 50255
Contact: Mrs D Christon

Cotherstone

Cotherstone, made from cow milk, hard, distinctive flavour, pale cream in colour with edible crust, in 2-6lb cylinders.
[C] 16lb p.wk
[D] By arrangement

[9] ○ ★ ↔

Teifi Cheese
Glynhynod, Ffostrasol, Llandyssul, Dyfed SA44 5JY
Tel: 023 975 528
Contact: John Savage

Caws Fferm Teifi

Caws Fferm Teifi, made from unpasteurised milk, with vegetarian rennet and low sodium salt, lightly pressed, naturally rinded curd farmhouse cheese, available in a variety of flavours including plain, garlic, celery and garlic, garlic and onion, cumin seed, sweet pepper, chives, and mustard seed.
[C] 1500kg p.mth
[D] By arrangement
See Also: Butter, Milk

[6] ○ ★ ↔

Thornby Moor Dairy
Thornby Moor Dairy, Aikton, Wigton, Cumbria CA7 OJZ
Tel: 0965 43160
Contact: Carolyn Fairburn

Cumberland Farmhouse

Cumberland Farmhouse, made from unpasteurised cow milk, hard, creamy textured, clothbound, matured 8-18 weeks in 1, 2, 5, 10, 20lb sizes, available plain, oak smoked, and flavoured with herbs. Allerdale, made from unpasteurised goat cheese, smooth, hard, with full sweet flavour, clothbound or waxed, matured 8-12 weeks in 1, 2, 5, 10lb weights. Bewcastle, made from ewe milk, hard, sweet, nutty flavour, rinded in 1, 2, 4lb rounds.
[C] Cumberland Farmhouse 2400lb p.mth, Allerdale 800lb p.mth, Bewcastle 120lb p.mth Jan-Sep
[D] By arrangement

[9] ↔

Tregaron Foods
Unit 1, Station Road, Tregaron, Dyfed SY25 6HX
Tel: 09744 8944 Telx: 35851 CYM EX Fax: 0239 711181
Contact: John Jones

Goat — Hard pressed goat milk cheese, plain and smoked, in 5-8lb rounds, 4oz packs suitable for vegetarians.
Ⓒ Undisclosed
Ⓓ By arrangement
See Also: Milk

9 ★

Treseli Cheese
Blaenffynon Farm, Blaenwaun, Whitland, Dyfed
Tel: 09946 420
Contact: Ms Marion Davies

Caerphilly — Cheddar cheese, made from unpasteurised milk with vegetable rennet, matured 6-8 months, in 1, 20lb truckles. Also Caerphilly, semi-hard, pressed, matured for twelve days, in 7-10lb truckles. Also hard and soft pressed goat cheese in 1-10lb rounds.
Ⓒ Undisclosed
Ⓓ By arrangement

9 ○ ★

Tyn Grug Farmhouse Cheese
Goetre Isaf, Betws Bledrws, Lampeter, Dyfed SA48 8NP
Tel: 0570 45237
Contact: Dougal Campbell

Tyn Grug — Tyn Grug, unpasteurised traditional full fat farmhouse Cheddar, naturally rinded, dry nutty flavour, milder in summer months, in 6, 18, 35lb rounds.
Ⓒ 1 ton p.mth
Ⓓ By arrangement

16 ★ ↔

Village Maid
282a Hyde End Road, Spencers Wood, Reading, Berkshire RG7 1DN
Tel: 0734 884564
Contact: Mrs A S Wigmore

Spenwood — Spenwood, made from unpasteurised sheep milk with vegetarian rennet, full fat, semi-hard, pressed, natural rind, matured for six months, in 5lb cylinders. Wellington, made from unpasteurised Guernsey milk, hard, pressed, fruity flavour, rich yellow colour, matured for six months, in 5, 10lb cylinders.
Ⓒ Undisclosed
Ⓦ James Aldridge, 01 650 1411
Ⓓ By wholesaler, by own transport within area

15 ○ ★

Vulscombe Cheese
Higher Vulscombe, Cruwys Morchard, Tiverton, Devon EX16 8NB
Tel: 0884 252505
Contact: G J Townsend

Vulscombe — Vulscombe, made from goat milk, full fat, mild flavoured, pressed, available in a range of flavours including plain, fresh herbs and garlic, and garlic and peppercorns, in 6¼oz cylinders.
Ⓒ 1700 cheeses p.mth
Ⓓ By arrangement

11

Webster Dairy
Websters Dairy, Saxelbye, Melton Mowbray, Leicestershire
Tel: 0664 812223
Contact: Margaret Callow

Stilton — Traditional Stilton with old fashioned creamy texture and colour and large uneven blue streaks, in 8lb drums. Traditional White Stilton in 16lb drums.
Ⓒ Blue Stilton 1700 p.mth, White Stilton 300 p.mth
Ⓦ House of Callow, Leicester, 0533 541 637 (John Plint)
Ⓓ By wholesaler, by own transport within radius of 150 miles

9 ● ↔

Welsh Organic Foods Ltd
Unit 20-21, Llambed Industrial Estate, Tregaron Road, Lampeter, Dyfed SA48 8LT
Tel: 0570 422 772
Contact: Mr Dougal Campbell

Pencarreg — Pencarreg, made from organic cow milk with vegetarian rennet, full fat, soft, white mould ripened crust, in 10″ rounds weighing 3½-4lb, or 10x5oz boxed portions. Cardigan, made from cow milk with vegetarian rennet, hard, Caerphilly-type, in 10″ rounds weighing 7½-8lb, or 20x4oz boxed portions.
Ⓒ Pencarreg 4 ton p.mth, Cardigan 6 ton p.mth
Ⓦ Abergavenny Fine Foods 0873 880844, Cambrian Traditional Foods 0654 710033, Caws Cymru 0239 75362, Rachel's Dairy 0970 871489
Ⓓ By wholesaler

4

West Ulster Farmers Ltd
Dromore Road, Irvinestown, Co Fermanagh, Northern Ireland
Tel: 03656 21219 Telx: 74611 WSTULS G
Fax: 03656 28222
Contact: Mr John Kennedy

Goat — Soft mild goat cheese from British Saanen herd, 11.5% fat content, available fresh or frozen in 4oz packs, 2kg containers.
Ⓒ 4 ton p.mth
Ⓓ By arrangement
See Also: Fish Dealers, Milk, Fungi

6 ↔

Westmorland Smoked Foods
Cragg House, Casterton, Kirkby Londsdale, Cumbria LA6 2SD
Tel: 0468 41906
Contact: John Thompson

Smoked Cheddar — Farmhouse Cheddar and Lancashire cut into 6lb wheels and kiln smoked for eighteen hours.
Ⓒ 2 ton p.mth
Ⓓ By arrangement
See Also: Fish: Smoked

15 ★ ↔

Wheatland Cheese
Wheatland Farm, Winkleigh, Devon EX19 8DJ
Tel: 0837 83361
Contact: Ann Dickman

Wheatland Moor

Range of cheese made with vegetarian rennet including Wheatland, full fat, soft cheese with white rind weighing 8oz. Wheatland Moor, semi-hard cheese with natural rind in 1, 4lb sizes. Smythyn, semi-hard cheese with washed rind in 1, 4lb sizes.
C Wheatland 2000 cheeses p.mth, Moor and Smythyn 2000lb p.mth
D By own transport within area

16 ★

Wield Wood Estate
nr Alresford, Hampshire SO24 9RU
Tel: 0420 63151
Contact: Mrs O Mills

Petit Friese

Range of cheese made from unpasteurised sheep milk including Petit Friese, Labna-type, soft cheese made from drained yoghurt curd, available plain or with fresh chives. Walda, Gouda-type, hard cheese, available plain or with green peppers and caraway seeds. Ricotta, made from sheep whey with no added milk.
C 200-300kg p.mth Jul-Mar
D By arrangement
See Also: Milk

16 ◯ ★ ↔

Willowdown
Humphreys Farm, Nutley, Uckfield, Sussex TN22 3LS
Tel: 082571 2432
Contact: Mrs Margaret Willcock

Sussex goat

Range of cheese made from unpasteurised milk of own organically grazed British Saanens with vegetarian rennet including medium fat, soft moulded cheese in 4oz cylinders, 8-10oz batons available plain or flavoured with herbs and garlic, or rolled in crushed peppercorns. Hard cheese, Caerphilly-type, matured 2 months in 2-3lb cylinders, available plain or flavoured with garlic and chives.
C Soft cheese 120lb p.mth, hard cheese 60lb p.mth
D By own transport within area
See Also: Milk, Yoghurt

10 ★

W J & T E Windsor & Sons
Lodge Farm, Black Park, Whitchurch, Shropshire SY13 4JP
Tel: 0948 2958
Contact: Mr W J Windsor

Cheshire

Unpasteurised farmhouse Cheshire, coloured or white, matured for one month, in 45-50lb cylinders, with smaller cheeses to order.
C 15-20 cheeses p.dy
D By arrangement

7

Wolfen Mill Dairy Co Ltd
Goose Lane, Chipping, nr Preston, Lancashire PR3 2QB
Tel: 09956 262
Contact: J Procter

Lancashire

Range of cheese made with vegetarian rennet including Lancashire, mild at two weeks or traditionally matured for six weeks to five months. Cheshire, coloured or white, matured for six weeks. Double Gloucester, matured 8-10 weeks. Red Leicester, matured 10-12 weeks, all in 5, 8, 13, 20kg sizes.
C 50 ton p.mth
D By arrangement

9 ★

T J A Young
Pantllyn, Blaenycoed, Carmarthen, Dyfed
Tel: 026787 478
Contact: Mr Young

Abernant

Pantyllyn, made from unpasteurised cow milk, mild, semi-soft, natural rind, matured for 3-6 weeks in 8-10lb rounds, available plain or flavoured with herb and garlic. Abernant, made from one part goat and two parts cow milk, mild, semi-soft, natural rind, in 8-10lb rounds.
C 150 p.mth
D By arrangement

CREAM

15

Bearah Farm
Bearah Farm, Buckland Brewer, Bideford, Devon EX39 5NA
Tel: 02375 314
Contact: Trevor Mills

Clotted

Farm produced cream including Devonshire clotted cream in 4, 8oz pots and double cream in 5, 10 oz pots, both also supplied in 2-6lb catering trays.
C Undisclosed
D By own transport within area and by Datapost

16 ★

J W Boyd & Son Ltd
Leacon Farm, Charing, Ashford, Kent TN27 0EN
Tel: 023371 2405/2788
Contact: D R Boyd

Whipping

Unpasteurised cream separated without artificial heat including double cream in 5oz tubs, double and whipping cream in 10oz tubs, 1pt cartons, 2pt plastic bottles and ½, 1 gal aluminium cans.
C Whipping cream 30 gal p.dy
D By arrangement

16 ↔

Bramble Farm Dairy
Bramble Farm, Shere Road, West Horsley, Surrey KT2A 6ER
Tel: 04865 3087
Contact: Mrs W Joy

Double cream

Pasteurised double cream from own herd in 130, 260g pots.
[C] Undisclosed
[D] By own transport within area
See Also: Yoghurt

9 ○ ★

Bryncerdin Farm Produce
Bryncerdin Farm, Ffostrosol, Llandysul, Dyfed
Tel: 023975 371
Contact: Mrs E J Wynne

Jersey

Unpasteurised organic Jersey cream in 8oz, 1pt cartons.
[C] Undisclosed
[D] By arrangement
See Also: Butter

16 ● ★

Busses Farm Organic Produce
Busses Farm, Harwood Lane, East Grinstead, West Sussex RH19 4NL
Tel: 0342 21749
Contact: Michael Duveen

Whipping

Unpasteurised single, double and whipping cream made from milk of own herd in ¼, ½ pt cartons and catering packs.
[C] Undisclosed
[D] By arrangement
See Also: Yoghurt

6

Calthwaite Dairy Products
Calthwaite, Penrith, Cumbria CA11 9QU
Tel: 076885 292
Contact: Clive Pattinson

Jersey

Cream from Calthwaite pedigree herd of Jersey cows including pasteurised double, whipping, and single cream in 500ml, 4.5lt quantities. Also vanilla and strawberry Jersey ice cream in 500ml, 1, 2, 4lt quantities.
[C] Cream 150 gal p.wk, ice cream 200 gal p.wk
[D] By own transport within area
See Also: Cheese, Yoghurt, Prepared Salads, Jams and Preserves, Fudges and Toffee

12

Chewton Dairy Farms Ltd
Priory Farm, Chewton Mendip, Bath, Avon BA3 4NT
Tel: 076121 666
Contact: Mrs Marian Shaw

Whey

Whey cream in ¼, ½, 1pt, 1 gal containers.
[C] Undisclosed
[D] By arrangement
See Also: Butter, Cheese

3

D & D Dairies
Broich Road, Crieff, Perthshire PH7 3BR
Tel: 0764 4271
Contact: Robert Simpson

Double cream

Fresh pasteurised single and double cream produced from own herd in a variety of sizes from 5fl oz-1 gal packs.
[C] 200 gal p.wk
[D] By own transport within area, by arrangement
See Also: Milk, Yoghurt

9 ★ ↔

David Roberts & Son
Tal-y-Bryn Farm, LLanefydd, Denbigh, Clwyd LL2 7AD
Tel: 074 579256
Contact: Gareth Roberts

Whipping

Double and whipping cream with sweet, nutty flavour resulting from herds grazed, on herbal meadows.
[C] Undisclosed
[D] By own transport within area
See Also: Milk, Yoghurt

16

Dentons Dairy Farm Shop
17 High Street, Lambourne, Berkshire
Tel: 0488 72484
Contact: Sarah Denton

Jersey

Double and single cream from pedigree Jersey herd, in 4, 8oz, 1pt cartons.
[C] 10 gal p.wk
[D] By own transport within area
See Also: Milk

8

J & E Dickinson, Longley Farm
Longley Farm, Holmfirth, nr Huddersfield, Yorkshire HD7 1RS
Tel: 0484 684151 Telx: 51458 COMHUD G LONGLEY
Contact: J & E Dickinson

Soured cream

Extra thick double cream, whipping cream, single and soured cream in cartons or bulk.
[C] Undisclosed
[D] By arrangement
See Also: Cheese, Yoghurt

15 ★ ↔

East Devon Dairies Ltd
Roebuck Farm, Heathpark, Honiton, Devon EX14 8SD
Tel: 0404 2705
Contact: D Underdown

Whipping

Devonshire cream available as double, single, and whipping in sizes from 5oz cartons to 2½lt polybottles.
[C] 2000lt p.wk
[D] By arrangement
See Also: Milk

15 ↔

Eveleigh Jersey Dairy Produce
Eveleighs, Cruwys Morchard, Tiverton, Devon EX16 8LB
Tel: 0884 257510
Contact: Miss Nora M Bishop

Clotted

Devonshire clotted cream from own herd of pedigree Jersey cows, in 4, 8oz, 2, 3, 4lb cartons. Unpasteurised cream also available.
[C] Clotted cream 300kg p.mth
[D] By own transport within area

14 ★

Fullers Brickwall Farm Ltd
Brickwall Farm, Sible Hedingham, Halstead, Essex CO9 3RH
Tel: 0787 60329
Contact: Robert Fuller

Jersey

Untreated cream from own Jersey herd, which needs careful refrigeration and should be used within 48 hours, in 5, 10oz, 1 gal containers. Sour cream and cultured buttermilk also available.
[C] Undisclosed
[D] By arrangement
See Also: Cheese, Milk, Yoghurt, Cakes, Biscuits and Pastries, Ice Creams and Sorbets

12 ● ★ ↔

Hardwick Estate
Path Hill Farm, Whitchurch, nr Reading, Oxfordshire RG8 7RE
Tel: 07357 2955
Contact: Sir Julian Rose Bt

Guernsey

Fresh, untreated organic Guernsey cream in 5, 8oz cartons, available May-Oct.
[C] Undisclosed
[D] By arrangement
See Also: Fresh Meat

12 ★

A R & S E Howe
Ivy Cross Farm, Oxlynch Lane, Standish, Stonehouse, Gloucestershire GL10 3DH
Tel: 045382 2505
Contact: Mrs S Howe

Clotted

Unpasteurised double cream with 48% butterfat from pedigree Channel Island Guernsey herd. Also clotted cream, with 55% butterfat, made by traditional methods, in 5, 10oz, ½, 1 gal containers.
[C] 80lt p.day
[D] By arrangement

3 ★

Howgate Dairy Products
Langskaill, Howgate, Penicuik, Midlothian
Tel: 0968 72263
Contact: M T R Marwick

Buttermilk

Double cream with 48% butterfat, whipping cream with 42% butterfat and single cream with 24% butterfat. Also available sour cream and buttermilk.
[C] Undisclosed
[D] By own transport within area
See Also: Cheese, Milk, Yoghurt

15

Hurstone Farm Dairy Products
Hurstone Farm, Chittlehamholt, Umberleigh, Devon EX37 9PG
Tel: 07694 514
Contact: Mrs A Sutton

Clotted

Pasteurised clotted cream from own Jersey and Guernsey herd, in 4, 8oz, 1-8lb containers. Also thick double cream from own Jersey herd in 5, 10fl oz, ½gal containers.
[C] Clotted cream 1 ton p.mth
[D] By own transport within area, by arrangement

12 ★

Hurstone Farmhouse
Waterrow, Wiveliscombe, Somerset TA4 2AT
Tel: 0984 23441
Contact: John Bone

Jersey

Somerset double cream made from unpasteurised milk of own Jersey herd, in 5, 10oz cartons. Also clotted cream made to order.
[C] Undisclosed
[D] By arrangement
See Also: Butter, Cheese, Milk

16 ★ ↔

Inchnavie Goats
Inchnavie Lower, Newbridge, Alness, Ross & Cromarty IV17 OXL
Tel: 0349 883585
Contact: Tim Dearman

Goat

Unpasteurised single cream made from goat milk, in 110ml tubs.
Ⓒ Undisclosed
Ⓓ By arrangement
See Also: Cheese, Milk

16 ↔

Knightsbridge Farm
Hellingly, Hailsham, East Sussex BN27 4HH
Tel: 04353 2574
Contact: G R S Steven

Jersey

Double cream from own Jersey herd in 5, 10oz cartons.
Ⓒ 50-75lt p.wk
Ⓓ By own transport within area
See Also: Ice Creams and Sorbets

16 ★

S E Lane
White House Farm, Biddenden, Ashford, Kent
Tel: 0580 291 374/289
Contact: M P Sargent

Clotted

Unpasteurised Jersey cream in 5, 10oz, 1lt, 2, 4 pt cartons. Also clotted cream in 5, 10oz, 1lt packs.
Ⓒ 600lt p.wk
Ⓓ By arrangement
See Also: Milk, Yoghurt, Ice Creams and Sorbets

15 ★ ↔

Langage Farm Dairy Products
Langage Farm, Plympton, Plymouth, Devon PL7 5AW
Tel: 0752 337723
Contact: Peter Tremaine

Clotted

Prize winning Devonshire clotted cream from Jersey herd, cooked by own special method, supplied fresh or blast frozen, in 2, 4, 8oz, 1, 2½lb quantities. Cultured sour cream also available.
Ⓒ Clotted cream 2 ton p.mth
Ⓓ By own transport within area
See Also: Cheese, Milk, Cakes, Biscuits and Pastries, Ice Creams and Sorbets

12 ★ ↔

J & P Langman
Perrotts Brook Farm, Cirencester, Gloucestershire GL7 7BS
Tel: 028 583283
Contact: Lady Langman

Jersey

Untreated Jersey cream from own antibiotic free herd, in 5, 10oz, 1pt cartons, 1 gal cans.
Ⓒ Undisclosed
Ⓓ By own transport within Oxford, London, Bristol, Worcester areas
See Also: Yoghurt

15 ↔

Leworthy Mill
Woolfardisworthy, nr Bideford, Devon EX39 5PY
Tel: 02373 445
Contact: D Price

Clotted

Devonshire clotted cream from milk of pedigree Jersey herd in ¼, ½, 2, 3lb cartons.
Ⓒ 2,500lb p.a
Ⓓ By arrangement
See Also: Ice Creams and Sorbets

16 ↔

Loseley Dairy Products Ltd
Estate Office, Guildford, Surrey GU3 1HS
Tel: 0483 571881 Telx: 859972 Fax: 0483 302056
Contact: Miss Ann Cleveland

Sour cream

Range of fresh Jersey cream including double, single, extra thick single, sour (cultured cream), and whipping.
Ⓒ Undisclosed
Ⓓ London, South and South East England, West Country and West Midlands
See Also: Yoghurt, Millers, Ice Creams and Sorbets

10 ↔

Madresfield Dairy Ltd
Home Farm, Madresfield, Malvern, Worcestershire WRI 5AJ
Tel: 06845 4379
Contact: Janet Lomas

Clotted

Clotted cream in 8oz pots.
Ⓒ Undisclosed
Ⓓ By arrangement
See Also: Yoghurt

11

Manor Farm Dairy Products
Manor Farm, Thrussington, Leicestershire
Tel: 0664 74245
Contact: Mr Peter Holmes

Whipping

Double, single and whipping cream from Rearsby herd of pedigree Friesian cows, in 5, 10oz, 1pt, 1 gal quantities.
Ⓒ Undisclosed
Ⓓ By arrangement
See Also: Yoghurt

12 ★

Mr & Mrs J K Morrish & Son
Ham Farm, Wellington, Somerset TA21 9JB
Tel: 082347 2796
Contact: Mr J K Morrish

Double

Unpasteurised double cream from own Jersey herd available in 4, 8oz cartons or in bulk.
Ⓒ Undisclosed
Ⓓ By arrangement
See Also: Milk

15 ★ ↔

S J & S A Munnings
Whippletree Farm, Bridford, nr Exeter, Devon EX6 7HU
Tel: 0647 52402
Contact: Sue Munnings

Clotted — Traditional Devonshire clotted cream from own Jersey herd, in ¼, ½lb cartons, 7lb bowls.
[C] 6 ton p.a
[D] By arrangement

16 ★ ↔

Neal's Yard Creamery
Home Farm Cottage, Everlands Estate, Sevenoaks, Kent TN14 6HU
Tel: 0732 461020
Contact: Beatrice Garoche

Crême fraîche — Crême fraîche, cultured, slightly sour double cream, in 25cl, 2lb tubs.
[C] Undisclosed
[D] By own transport within area
See Also: Cheese, Yoghurt, Ice Creams and Sorbets

10 ○ ★

Rays Farm Products
Rays Farm, Billingsley, Bridgnorth, Shropshire WV16 6PF
Tel: 029 924255
Contact: Mrs R Cartwright

Channel Island — Channel Island double cream, fresh or frozen, in 5, 10oz cartons.
[C] 35,000lt of milk equivalent including butter p.a
[D] By arrangement
See Also: Butter, Milk

6 ○ ★

Redesdale Sheep Dairy
Soppitt Farm, Otterburn, Newcastle upon Tyne NE19 1AF
Tel: 0830 20276
Contact: Mark Robertson

Ayrshire — Farmhouse cream from herd of Ayrshire cows.
[C] Undisclosed
[W] A Porter 0423 322323
[D] By wholesaler, by own transport within area
See Also: Cheese, Milk, Yoghurt

15 ↔

A E Rodda & Son
The Creamery, Scorrier, Redruth, Cornwall TR16 5BU
Tel: 0209 820526
Contact: Mr Philip Rodda

Clotted — Cornish clotted cream in ¼, ½, ¾, 1lb cartons.
[C] Undisclosed
[D] By arrangement

15 ○ ↔

Roskilly Cream
Tregellast Barton, St Keverne, Helston, Cornwall TR12 6NX
Tel: 0326 280479
Contact: Mrs R Roskilly

Clotted — Clotted and double cream with sweet, nutty flavour produced on farm from own Channel Island herd, in 4, 8oz cartons, 2lb catering tubs. Whipping cream also available in ½, 1 gal cans.
[C] 200lb p.wk, winter, 700lb p.wk Jul-Aug
[D] By own transport within area, by arrangement
See Also: Ice Creams and Sorbets

14 ★

Susan Moore - Dairy Products
Cranes Watering Farm, Starston, Harleston, Norfolk IP20 9NE
Tel: 0379 852387
Contact: Susan Moore

Whipping — Unpasteurised Channel Island cream, double, single and whipping, in ¼, ½, 2 pt cartons.
[C] Undisclosed
[D] By own transport within area, by arrangement
See Also: Fresh Meat, Cheese, Yoghurt, Ice Creams and Sorbets

10

A L & E M Thomas
Woonton Court Farm, Leysters, Leominster, Hereford & Worcester
Tel: 056887 232
Contact: Mr Thomas

Guernsey — Thick, untreated Guernsey cream with high fat content in ½, 1, 50 pt cartons.
[C] Undisclosed
[D] By arrangement

16 ★

J D & C Tucker
Oakhurst Farm, Burwash, Ethingham, East Sussex TN19 7DP
Tel: 0435 882328
Contact: Mrs C Tucker

Jersey

Unpasteurised or pasteurised double, single and whipping cream from own Jersey herd in 5, 10oz cartons.
C Undisclosed
D By wholesaler, by own transport within area
See Also: Milk, Yoghurt

15 ↔

West Dorset Farmhouse Dairy Products Ltd
Childhay Manor, Blackdown, Beaminster, Dorset
Tel: 0308 68555
Contact: Mr Tim Frost

Clotted

Double, single and whipping cream in 4, 8oz, 1pt, ½, 1 gal containers. Also clotted cream in 1-4lb cartons only.
C Undisclosed
D By arrangement
See Also: Ice Creams and Sorbets

MILK

9

Abergavenny Fine Foods Ltd
Mamhilad, Gwent NP4 8RG
Tel: 0873 880844/880250
Contact: A J Craske

Goat

Goat milk from own herd, fresh or frozen.
D By arrangement
See Also: Cheese

12 ● ★ ↔

Anne North
Stowaway, Daisybank Road, Charlton Kings Common, Cheltenham, Gloucestershire GL53 9QQ
Tel: 0242 522767
Contact: Mrs Anne North

Goat

Organic goat milk, fresh or frozen, in 1pt bags.
D By arrangement

15 ● ↔

T B Bersey & Son
Sheviock Barton, Torpoint, Cornwall PL11 3EH
Tel 0503 30909 Telx: 30909 Fax: 0503 30915
Contact: G Bersey

Sheep

Pasteurised or unpasteurised sheep milk from organically raised herd.
D By arrangement
See also: Cheese

16 ⊙

Blackburn and Haynes/Meadow Cottage
Meadow Cottage Farm, Churt Road, Headley, Bordon, Hampshire GU35 8SS
Tel: 0428 712155
Contact: Mrs Celia Haynes

Jersey

Milk from Jersey cows fed on organically fertilised grass and maize.
D By arrangement
See Also: Ice Creams and Sorbets

15 ⊙ ★

Blackdown Farm & Loddiswell Cheese
Blackdown, Loddiswell, Kingsbridge, Devon TQ7 4EA
Tel: 054882 387
Contact: Mr and Mrs W L Martin

Goat

Unpasteurised goat milk from own organically raised herd.
D By own transport within area
See Also: Fresh Meat, Cheese

3 ★

H C Blythe
Henryston Farm, Sorn, Mauchline, Ayrshire KA5 6NF
Tel: 0290 51422
Contact: Hugh Blythe

Sheep

Unpasteurised sheep milk, fresh or frozen.
D By arrangement

7

Bodfari Creamery
Rough Hill Farm, Marlston Cwm Lache, nr Chester, Cheshire CH4 9JS
Tel: 0244 671111
Contact: Cavan Molloy

Channel Island

Friesian and Jersey milk from Channel Island herd packed in bottles, cartons or catering packs.
D By arrangement
See Also: Bacon and Hams, Yoghurt

16 ⊙ ↔

Bowyers Court Farm
Wisborough Green, West Sussex RH14 0EP
Tel: 0403 700494
Contact: Mr K Watson

Goat

Pasteurised milk from goat herd, fresh or frozen, in 1pt cartons.
D By own transport within area
See Also: Fresh Meat, Yoghurt

12 ★

Bredons Norton Dairy Goats
Brookfield Farm, Bredons Norton, Tewkesbury, Gloucestershire GL20 7E7
Tel: 0684 72209
Contact: Ms Jane Archer

Goat

Unpasteurised goat milk available all year, supplied fresh or frozen.
W Cotswold Dairy, Bishop's Cleve Dairy
D By wholesaler, by arrangement
See Also: Cheese

16 ★ ↔ **British Sheep Dairy Products**
Nepicar Farm, Wrotham Heath, Sevenoaks, Kent TN15 7SR
Tel: 0732 883040
Contact: Mr Harold Woolley

Sheep — Unpasteurised and pasteurised sheep milk from own herd, fresh or frozen, in 1pt containers.
D By arrangement
See Also: Cheese, Yoghurt

16 ↔ **Bunker Farm Produce**
Bunker Farm, Basingstoke Road, Greenham Common South, Newbury, Berkshire RG15 8HH
Tel: 0635 45535
Contact: Ken Neale

Goat — Unpasteurised milk from Anglo-Nubian goat herd, fresh or frozen, in 1pt plastic bags.
D By own transport within area
See Also: Fresh Meat, Poultry Producers, Cheese, Yoghurt, Purees and Sauces

14 ● ★ ↔ **Calluna Farm Products**
Lodge Road, Hollesley, Woodbridge, Suffolk
Tel: 0394 411927
Contact: Mrs Helen Douglas

Sheep — Unpasteurised sheep milk from British milk flock, frozen.
D By own transport within area
See Also: Eggs, Cheese, Yoghurt, Fresh Salads

16 ★ **Cedaridge Dairy Products**
Milleys Cottage, Bramlands Lane, Woodmancote, nr Henfield, West Sussex
Tel: 0273 492121
Contact: John Wilkins

Sheep — Unpasteurised sheep milk supplied frozen.
D By own transport within area
See Also: Cheese, Yoghurt

16 ⦿ ★ ↔ **Clayton Dairy Goats**
Holt Valley Farm, Underhill Lane, Clayton, Sussex BN6 9PL
Tel: 07918 5158
Contact: Mrs W B Thomson

Goat — Unpasteurised goat milk from organically raised herd, frozen or fresh to order, in 1pt cartons.
D By own transport within area
See Also: Cheese

10 ★ ↔ **Court House Farm**
Atch Lench, Evesham, Hereford & Worcester WR11 5SP
Tel: 0386 870225
Contact: Lucy McFarlane

Saanen goat — Milk from herd of British Toggenburg and British Saanen goats, fresh or frozen.
D By arrangement
See Also: Cheese

3 **D & D Dairies**
Broich Road, Crieff, Perthshire PH7 3BR
Tel: 0764 4271
Contact: Robert Simpson

Low fat — Low fat or full cream milk from own herd.
D By own transport within area
See Also: Cream, Yoghurt

10 ★ ↔ **J E & E R Dakin**
Wackley Farm, Burlton, Shrewsbury, Shropshire SY4 5TD
Tel: 093922 660
Contact: Mr J E Dakin

Sheep — Unpasteurised sheep milk, fresh or frozen.
D By arrangement
See Also: Cheese

9 ★ ↔ **David Roberts & Son**
Tal-y-Bryn Farm, LLanefydd, Denbigh, Clwyd LL2 7AD
Tel: 074 579256
Contact: Gareth Roberts

Buttermilk — Unpasteurised and pasteurised milk from own Friesian herd grazed on herbal meadowland. Naturally cultured buttermilk also available in 10oz, ½gal quantities.
D By own transport within area, by arrangement
See Also: Cream, Yoghurt

16 **Dentons Dairy Farm Shop**
17 High Street, Lambourne, Berkshire
Tel: 0488 72484
Contact: Sarah Denton

Jersey — Pasteurised milk from pedigree Jersey herd, in 1, 2pt cartons.
D By arrangement
See Also: Cream

15 ↔ **East Devon Dairies Ltd**
Roebuck Farm, Heathpark, Honiton, Devon EX14 8SD
Tel: 0404 2705
Contact: D Underdown

Semi-skimmed — Milk from Devon herds, unpasteurised and pasteurised, semi-skimmed and skimmed.
D By arrangement
See Also: Cream

12 ● ★ ↔ **The Elms**
The Elms, Lower Westholme, Pilton, Shepton Mallet, Somerset BA4 4EL
Tel: 074989 371
Contact: C D Stone

Goat
Sheep — Goat or sheep milk from mixed herd grazed on chemical free pastures, fresh or frozen.
D By arrangement
See Also: Cheese, Yoghurt, Fudges and Toffee

6

Ayrshire

Eshott Farm
The Home Farm, Felton, Morpeth, Northumberland NE65 9EP
Tel: 067 087432
Contact: Mr T N H Sanderson

Several grades of milk from reportedly the oldest Ayrshire herd in England, including untreated, pasteurised, semi-skimmed and skimmed.
D By arrangement
See Also: Cheese

7 ★

Goat

Farmhouse Country Delicacies
The Homestead Farm, Pott Shrigley, Macclesfield, Cheshire SK10 5RU
Tel: 0625 72381
Contact: Joyce Dalton

Unpasteurised goat milk, frozen.
D By arrangement
See Also: Fresh Meat, Cheese

14 ★

Jersey

Fullers Brickwall Farm Ltd
Brickwall Farm, Sible Hedingham, Halstead, Essex CO9 3RH
Tel: 0787 60329
Contact: Robert Fuller

Skimmed and unpasteurised Gold Top milk produced from own Jersey herd.
D By arrangement
See Also: Cheese, Cream, Yoghurt, Cakes, Biscuits and Pastries, Ice Creams and Sorbets

1 ★ ↔

Goat

Great Glen Foods Ltd
Old Ferry Road, North Ballachulish, Onich, Fort William, Inverness PH33 6RZ
Tel: 08553 277
Contact: Douglas Locke

Unpasteurised goat milk from Caledonia or Anglo-Nubian goat herd, fresh or frozen.
W Scottish Goat Products Ltd 05403 692
D By wholesaler, by arrangement
See Also: Cheese, Fudges and Toffee

10 ★

Friesian

Hadley Park Farm
Hadley Park Farm, Leegomery, Telford, Shropshire
Tel: 0952 3677
Contact: Edward Dorrell

Unpasteurised milk from pedigree Friesian herd.
D By own transport within area
See Also: Ice Creams and Sorbets

16 ↔

Shrikand

Hall & Sons (Dairy Farmers) Ltd
Pinner Park Farm, Pinner, Middlesex HA5 45U
Tel: 01 863 1075
Contact: Mr James Hall

Milk and milk based products especially for Asian and Indian markets, including cream, concentrated milk made without heat by reverse osmosis. Also Indian desserts including Shrikand, a sweet milk dessert made from yoghurt, flavoured with cardamom, sattram and pistachio.and kosher dairy products including milk, ice cream and soft cheese.
D By arrangement

15 ★

Sheep

Hartslock Ewes Milk
Higher Wringworthy, Morval, nr Looe, Cornwall PL13 1PR
Tel: 05034 691
Contact: Julian George

Unpasteurised sheep milk supplied fresh or frozen.
D By arrangement
See Also: Poultry Producers

6 ★ ↔

Unpasteuris-ed

R Holmes & Sons
Whitburn Moors Farm, Sunderland Road, Cleadon, Tyne & Wear SR6 7UN
Tel: 091 5293127
Contact: Mr F Holmes

Unpasteurised milk from own farm herd.
D By own transport within area
See Also: Yoghurt

14 ◯ ★ ↔

Jersey

A & K Hood
The Stables, Gresham, Norfolk NR11 8AD
Tel: 026377 468
Contact: Mr Hood

Unpasteurised milk from organically fed Jersey herd.
D By arrangement
See Also: Fresh Meat, Poultry Producers, Cheese, Fresh Vegetables, Jams and Preserves

3 ★

Goat

Howgate Dairy Products
Langskaill, Howgate, Penicuik, Midlothian
Tel: 0968 72263
Contact: M T R Marwick

Unpasteurised frozen goat milk.
D By own transport within area, by arrangement
See Also: Cheese, Cream, Yoghurt

12 ★

Jersey

Hurstone Farmhouse
Waterrow, Wiveliscombe, Somerset TA4 2AT
Tel: 0984 23441
Contact: John Bone

Unpasteurised milk from own Jersey herd, supplied fresh only.
D By arrangement
See Also: Butter, Cheese, Cream

10 ◯

Goat

Hyde Farm Cheese
The Hyde, Stokebliss, Tenbury Wells, Worcestershire WR15 8RS
Tel: 08854 324
Contact: Mrs Marris

Pasteurised and unpasteurised goat milk supplied fresh or frozen.
D By arrangement
See Also: Cheese

[1]

Inchnavie Goats
Inchnavie Lower, Newbridge, Alness, Ross & Cromarty IV17 OXL
Tel: 0349 883585
Contact: Tim Dearman

Goat — Goat milk, fresh or frozen.
[D] By arrangement
See Also: Cheese, Cream

[16] ○ ★ ↔

Island Country Farms
Asheybrook, Ashey, Ryde, Isle of Wight PO33 4AT
Tel: 0983 65686
Contact: Mr J H Fisher

Goat — Unpasteurised goat milk, fresh or frozen.
[D] By arrangement
See Also: Fresh Meat, Poultry Producers, Yoghurt, Fresh Fruit

[9] ○ ★

John & Jenny White Organic Smallholders
Mount Pleasant, Pen y Bont, Carmarthen, Dyfed SA33 6PP
Tel: 09948 315
Contact: Jenny White

Goat — Goat milk from herd reared on wholefood, additive free diet, fresh or frozen.
[D] By own transport within area
See Also: Cheese, Yoghurt

[15] ○ ★ ↔

Kathryn Cornish
Hedgemoor Farm, Bridford, Exeter, Devon EX6 7LW
Tel: 0647 52358
Contact: Kathryn Cornish

Saanen goat — Unpasteurised milk from British Saanen goats, frozen.
[D] By own transport within area
See Also: Cheese, Yoghurt

[16] ★

S E Lane
White House Farm, Biddenden, Ashford, Kent
Tel: 0580 291 374/289
Contact: M P Sargent

Jersey — Unpasteurised milk from Jersey herd, supplied fresh.
[D] By arrangement
See Also: Cream, Yoghurt, Ice Creams and Sorbets

[15] ★ ↔

Langage Farm Dairy Products
Langage Farm, Plympton, Plymouth, Devon PL7 5AW
Tel: 0752 337723
Contact: Peter Tremaine

Jersey — Unpasteurised Channel Island milk from pedigree Jersey herd.
[D] By arrangement
See Also: Cheese, Cream, Cakes, Biscuits and Pastries, Ice Creams and Sorbets

[15] ○ ★ ↔

C D & J E Leach
Quither Down Farm, Hayedown, Milton Abbot, Tavistock, Devon PL19 0NN
Tel: 082286 309
Contact: C D Leach

Sheep — Milk from Friesland and Dorset sheep organically raised on farm, unpasteurised, frozen, in 4pt containers, packed in 3 gal quantities.
[D] By arrangement

[13] ★ ↔

G J Little
Priestley Farm, Church Road, Flitwick, Bedfordshire MK45 5AN
Tel: 0525 712978
Contact: Mrs A M Little

Jersey — Unpasteurised milk and cream from own Jersey herd, in 5, 10 fl oz, 1, 2, 4 pt cartons.
[D] By own transport within area

[9] ● ★ ↔

Little Acorn Products
Mesem Fach Farm, Bethania, nr Llanon, Dyfed SY23 5NL
Tel: 097 423348
Contact: Don and Karen Ross

Sheep — Unpasteurised sheep milk from pedigree Friesland flock raised on organic pastures, available frozen in 1pt sachets.
[D] By arrangement
See Also: Cheese

[16] ○ ★

Lympne Market Garden
Garden House, Lympne Place, Lympne, Kent CT21 4PA
Tel: 0303 66183
Contact: Mr Fairley

Goat — Unpasteurised Saanen goat milk, fresh or frozen.
[D] By arrangement
See Also: Fresh Fruit

[16] ● ↔

Malthouse Cottage Farm
Malthouse Lane, Ashington, Pulborough, West Sussex RH20 3BU
Tel: 0903 892456
Contact: Mrs J Ferris

Goat — Goat milk from free-range herd, non-intensively raised on farm, fresh or frozen.
[D] By arrangement
See Also: Fresh Meat, Poultry Producers, Cheese, Yoghurt

[9] ○ ★

Marianglas
Maes Mawr, LLanllyfni, Caernarvon, Gwynedd LL54 6DG
Tel: 0286 881809
Contact: Mrs J Rickford

Goat — Milk from British Alpine and Anglo-Nubian goats, fresh or frozen.
[D] By own transport within area
See Also: Cheese

16 ★

Middle Farm Shop/English Farm Cider Centre
Middle Farm, Firle, nr Lewes, East Sussex BN8 6LJ
Tel: 032183 411/303
Contact: Mr John Pile

Pookhill

Unpasteurised fresh milk from Pookhill pedigree herd with over 4% butter fat.
D By arrangement
See Also: Meat: Pies and Prepared Dishes, Cakes, Biscuits and Pastries

12 ★

Mr & Mrs J K Morrish & Son
Ham Farm, Wellington, Somerset TA21 9JB
Tel: 082347 2796
Contact: Mr J K Morrish

Jersey

Unpasteurised frozen milk from own Jersey herd, in 2 pint containers.
D By arrangement
See Also: Cream

5 ★

Mr & Mrs M H Neilson
Windyknowe, Annan, Dumfries & Galloway DG12 5LN
Tel: 04612 4691
Contact: Mrs Carol Neilson

Sheep

Sheep milk from farm flock, frozen.
D By arrangement
See Also: Cheese

16 ★ ↔

Nature's Gardens
62 Lavender Hill, London SW11 5RQ
Tel: 01 223 4618
Contact: Eva

Goat

Unpasteurised goat milk from Surrey Docks farm, frozen.
D By arrangement
See Also: Yoghurt

10 ○ ★ ↔

New House Farm
New House Farm, Acton, Newcastle under Lyme, Staffordshire ST5 4EE
Tel: 0782 680 366
Contact: Mrs Deaville

Cow

Unpasteurised milk from own herd.
D By arrangement
See Also: Cheese, Ice Creams and Sorbets

11 ★

North Abbey Dairy Sheep
50 North Road, Great Abington, Cambridgeshire CB1 6AS
Tel: 0223 892308
Contact: Philip Sutcliffe

Sheep

Unpasteurised sheep milk produced to British Sheep Dairying Association standards, from Friesland and Poll Dorset breeds, supplied frozen in 1pt bags.
D By arrangement

14 ○ ★ ↔

Ostler Products
Laurels Stables, Horringer, Bury St Edmunds, Suffolk IP29 5SN
Tel: 0284 3835
Contact: Mrs Ann James

Sheep

Untreated sheep milk from pedigree Friesland dairy herd fed on organic pastures, fresh or frozen, in 1pt sachets.
D By own transport within area

15 ★

Pinhill Yoghurt
Pinhill Farm Sidbury Sidmouth Devon EX10 0QJ
Tel: 03957 211
Contact: Mrs Kitrina Bishop

Sheep

Fresh and frozen unpasteurised sheep milk.
D By arrangement
See Also: Cheese, Yoghurt

10 ○ ★

Rays Farm Products
Rays Farm, Billingsley, Bridgnorth, Shropshire WV16 6PF
Tel: 029 924255
Contact: Mrs R Cartwright

Jersey

Milk from Jersey herd raised on own farm, in 2pt cartons.
D By arrangement
See Also: Butter, Cream

6 ○ ★

Redesdale Sheep Dairy
Soppitt Farm, Otterburn, Newcastle upon Tyne NE19 1AF
Tel: 0830 20276
Contact: Mark Robertson

Ayrshire

Unpasteurised cow milk from Ayrshire herd.
D By own transport within area
See Also: Cheese, Cream, Yoghurt

15 ○ ★

Roger C Jones
Lipton Farm, East Allington, nr Totnes, Devon TQ9 7RN
Tel: 054852 252
Contact: R Jones

Jersey

Unpasteurised, organically produced milk from Jersey herd.
D By arrangement

11 ↔

Rutland Goats
The Manor, Stoke Dry, nr Uppingham, Rutland LE15 9JG
Tel: 0572 823588
Contact: R J Salmon

Goat

Goat milk from Rutland herd, fresh or frozen, in 1pt cartons packed in cases of six.
D By arrangement

8 ○ ★

Ryehill Goat Herd
Ryehills, Marton Lane, Pickering, Yorkshire YO18 8LW
Tel: 0751 76158/73026
Contact: G A Todd

Goat

Goat milk from Toggenburg and Saanen herd, fresh or frozen in 1pt quantities.
D By arrangement
See Also: Yoghurt

1

Scottish Goat Products Ltd
Station Road, Newtonmore, Inverness-shire PH20 1AR
Tel: 05403 692
Contact: Douglas Locke

Goat

Long life UHT goat milk in 500ml tetra brik cartons or 1pt bags.
D By own transport within area
See Also: Fresh Meat, Cheese, Yoghurt, Fudges and Toffee

12 ★

Southleaze Sheep Shop
No 1 Southleaze Farm, Swindon, Wiltshire
Tel: 0793 523134
Contact: Stewart Bell

Sheep

Unpasteurised sheep milk from pedigree Friesland flock, slightly sweeter than cow milk with a high fat content, fresh or frozen. Cheese and ice cream also available.
D By own transport within area, by arrangement

8 ↔

St Helens Farm
Barmby-on-the-Marsh, Goole, North Humberside
Tel: 0757 630100
Contact: Angus Wielkopolski

Goat

Pasteurised goat milk, fresh or frozen.
D By arrangement
See Also: Yoghurt

9 ○ ★ ↔

Sterling Business Associates
The Creamery, Newcastle Emlyn, Dyfed SA38 9DH
Tel: 0239 711054
Contact: Mr Fred Park

Goat

Goat and cow milk, frozen only.
D By arrangement
See Also: Cheese

16 ○ ★ ↔

Sussex High Weald Dairy Sheep
Putlands Farm, Duddleswell, Uckfield, East Sussex TN22 3BJ
Tel: 082571 2647
Contact: Mr Mark Hardy

Sheep

Unpasteurised sheep milk from herd raised to organic standards, with rich slightly sweet taste, fresh or frozen, in 1pt, 5lt packs.
D By arrangement
See Also: Cheese, Yoghurt

7

Sutton Dairy Goats
The Cottage, Eddisbury Lodge, Delamere, Northwich, Cheshire CW8 2JD
Tel: 0829 51264
Contact: Mrs E Sutton

Goat

Pasteurised goat milk, fresh or frozen, in 1pt cartons.
D By arrangement
See Also: Cheese, Ice Creams and Sorbets

9 ○ ★ ↔

Teifi Cheese
Glynhynod, Ffostrasol, Llandyssul, Dyfed SA44 5JY
Tel: 023 975 528
Contact: John Savage

Organic

Unpasteurised milk organically raised from own herd.
D By arrangement
See Also: Butter, Cheese

9 ↔

Tregaron Foods
Unit 1, Station Road, Tregaron, Dyfed SY25 6HX
Tel: 09744 8944 Telx: 35851 CYM EX Fax: 0239 711181
Contact: John Jones

Goat

Spray dried powdered goat milk, with no additives, in 5x50g retail packs and 20kg manufacturing packs.
D By arrangement
See Also: Cheese

16

J D & C Tucker
Oakhurst Farm, Burwash, Ethingham, East Sussex TN19 7DP
Tel: 0435 882328
Contact: Mrs C Tucker

Jersey

Pasteurised whole and skimmed milk and untreated whole milk from Jersey herd, fresh in 2pt bottles.
D By arrangement
See Also: Cream, Yoghurt

15 ★ ↔

Waterloo Farm
Clayhidon, Cullompton, Devon EX15 3TN
Tel: 0823 680273
Contact: Cmdr A G Trotter

Sheep

Unpasteurised, homogenised sheep milk from the Foxfire flock of pedigree Friesland sheep.
D By own transport within area
See Also: Yoghurt

4

West Ulster Farmers Ltd
Dromore Road, Irvinestown, Co Fermanagh, Northern Ireland
Tel: 03656 21219 Telx: 74611 WSTULS G
Fax: 03656 28222
Contact: Mr John Kennedy

Goat
Sheep

Cow and goat milk, also available unpasteurised frozen sheep milk in 1pt containers.
W Herdgates Ltd, Victory Place, London SE17, 01 703 7980/01 701 8439
D By wholesaler
See Also: Fish Dealers, Cheese, Fungi

16 ★

Wield Wood Estate
nr Alresford, Hampshire SO24 9RU
Tel: 0420 63151
Contact: Mrs O Mills

Sheep

Unpasteurised sheep milk, high in protein, calcium, zinc and B group vitamins, frozen.
D By own transport within area
See Also: Cheese

16 ○ ★ ↔

Willowdown
Humphreys Farm, Nutley, Uckfield, Sussex TN22 3LS
Tel: 082571 2432
Contact: Mrs Margaret Willcock

Saanen goat

Organically produced unpasteurised goat milk from own British Saanens, fresh or frozen.
D By own transport within area
See Also: Cheese, Yoghurt

YOGHURT

7

Bodfari Creamery
Rough Hill Farm, Marlston Cwm Lache, nr Chester, Cheshire CH4 9JS
Tel: 0244 671111
Contact: Cavan Molloy

Low fat

Low fat, skimmed milk yoghurt from own Channel Island herd, plain or in a range of twenty flavours in 4, 5oz pots.
C Undisclosed
D By arrangement
See Also: Bacon and Hams, Milk

16 ↔

Bowyers Court Farm
Wisborough Green, West Sussex RH14 0EP
Tel: 0403 700494
Contact: Mr K Watson

Black cherry

Goat milk yoghurt in plain and a variety of whole fruit flavours including black cherry, strawberry, raspberry, apricot, and blackcurrant, sweetened with demerara sugar, in 5, 10, 19oz (natural only) cartons.
C 6000 cartons p.wk
D By own transport within area
See Also: Fresh Meat, Milk

16 ↔

Bramble Farm Dairy
Bramble Farm, Shere Rd, West Horsley, Surrey KT2A 6ER
Tel: 04865 3087
Contact: Mrs W Joy

Greek

Live, low fat yoghurt from own herd, plain and in a variety of ten flavours in 150, 500g (natural only) pots, 5lt buckets for catering trade. Also live Greek- style yoghurt with 9% fat content.
C 7000lt p.mth
D By arrangement
See Also: Cream

16 ↔

British Sheep Dairy Products
Nepicar Farm, Wrotham Heath, Sevenoaks, Kent TN15 7SR
Tel: 0732 883040
Contact: Mr Harold Woolley

Sheep

Sheep milk yoghurt with twenty one day shelf life in 5oz containers.
C Undisclosed
D By arrangement
See Also: Cheese, Milk

16 ↔

Bunker Farm Produce
Bunker Farm, Basingstoke Rd, Greenham Common South, Newbury, Berkshire RG15 8HH
Tel: 0635 45535
Contact: Ken Neale

Goat

Thick, rich goat yoghurt made from milk of Anglo-Nubian herd, plain or with honey in 5, 10, 20 fl oz tubs.
C Undisclosed
D By own transport within area
See Also: Fresh Meat, Poultry Producers, Cheese, Milk, Purees and Sauces

16 ●

Busses Farm Organic Produce
Busses Farm, Harwood Lane, East Grinstead, West Sussex RH19 4NL
Tel: 0342 21749
Contact: Michael Duveen

Blackberry

Range of full and low fat live yoghurt made with organically grown fruit and honey in four flavours, blackberry, apricot, raspberry, and strawberry in 150, 500g containers.
C Undisclosed
D By arrangement
See Also: Cream

9 ↔

Caldey Island Estate Company
Caldey Island Dairy, Caldey Island Monastery, Caldey Island, off Tenby, Dyfed
Tel: 0834 2632
Contact: Brother Philippart

Peach Melba

Range of skimmed and low fat yoghurt including natural, strawberry, raspberry, blackcurrant, and peach melba.
C Undisclosed
D By arrangement
See Also: Cheese

[14] ● ↔

Calluna Farm Products
Lodge Road, Hollesley, Woodbridge, Suffolk
Tel: 0394 411927
Contact: Mrs Helen Douglas

Sheep

Greek-style sheep yoghurt, thick and creamy with crust, set in 150, 500g pots.
[C] Undisclosed
[D] By own transport within area
See Also: Eggs, Cheese, Milk, Fresh Salads

[6]

Calthwaite Dairy Products
Calthwaite, Penrith, Cumbria CA11 9QU
Tel: 076885 292
Contact: Clive Pattinson

Low fat

Yoghurt from Calthwaite pedigree Jersey herd natural and fruit flavours in 500g, 5kg packs. Also low fat natural and fruit flavours in 150g, 500g, 5kg packs.
[C] Yoghurt 3000 gal p.wk
[D] By own transport within area
See Also: Cheese, Cream, Prepared Salads, Jams and Preserves, Fudges and Toffee

[16]

Cedaridge Dairy Products
Milleys Cottage, Bramlands Lane, Woodmancote, nr Henfield, West Sussex
Tel: 0273 492121
Contact: John Wilkins

Sheep

Two unpasteurised, firm set, plain yoghurts, one made from Lactobacillus Acidophilus, the other from Streptococcus Thermophilus and Lactobacillus Bulgaricus cultures in 10oz pots. Range of plain sundaes with fruit base and yoghurt topping also available in 8oz pots.
[C] Undisclosed
[D] By own tranport within area
See Also: Cheese, Milk

[3]

Cockburn & Skelton
Ledlewan Farm, Killearn, Glasgow G63 9LL
Tel: 0360 50344
Contact: Mr Ewen L Cockburn

Goat

Goat milk yoghurt.
[C] Undisclosed
[D] By own transport nationally
See Also: Cheese, Milk

[3]

D & D Dairies
Broich Road, Crieff, Perthshire PH7 3BR
Tel: 0764 4271
Contact: Robert Simpson

Fruit

Range of fruit yoghurt made from milk of own herd.
[C] 100 gal p.wk
[D] By own transport, by arrangement
See Also: Cream, Milk

[10] ○ ↔

The Dairy House
Whitehill Park, Weobley, Herefordshire HR4 8QE
Tel: 0544 318815
Contact: Miss Prudence M Lloyd

Greek

Low fat yoghurt plain or with added fruit. Also Greek-style yoghurt.
[C] 150-200 gal p.wk
[D] By own transport
See Also: Cheese, Cakes, Biscuits and Pastries

[9] ↔

David Roberts & Son
Tal-y-Bryn Farm, LLanefydd, Denbigh, Clwyd LL2 7AD
Tel: 074 579256
Contact: Gareth Roberts

Low fat

Low fat yoghurt from own herd grazed on herbal meadows, natural and in a range of eight flavours in 5, 10oz, ½ gal quantities.
[C] Undisclosed
[D] By own transport within area
See Also: Cream, Milk

[9]

DBS Products
Ddol Bach Farm, Llanelian, Colwyn Bay, Clwyd LL29 6AY
Tel: 0492 60339
Contact: Mr Andre Van Der Bijl

Sheep — Sheep milk sugar free yoghurt made from milk of own herd packed in 125ml pots.
[C] Undisclosed
[D] By arrangement

8

J & E Dickinson, Longley Farm
Longley Farm, Holmfirth, nr Huddersfield, Yorkshire HD7 1RS
Tel: 0484 684151 Telx: 51458 COMHUD G LONGLEY
Contact: J & E Dickinson

Kosher — Prize winning yoghurt, natural and in a range of fruit flavours in a variety of cartons and bulk packs. Kosher yoghurt also available.
[C] Undisclosed
[D] By arrangement
See Also: Cheese, Cream

15

P & C A Duncan
Stapleton Farm, Langtree, Torrington, Devon
Tel: 08055 414
Contact: Peter and Carol Duncan

Greek — Live, thick low fat yoghurt in 142, 454g pots, fruit yoghurt, with or without raw cane sugar, in 142g pots. Also Greek-style yoghurt with honey, or with lemon curd made from fresh eggs, lemon and butter, in 180g pots. Sour cream in 114g pots also available.
[C] 1 ton p.wk of each
[D] By arrangement
See Also: Cakes, Biscuits and Pastries, Jams and Preserves

12 ● ↔

The Elms
The Elms, Lower Westholme, Pilton, Shepton Mallet, Somerset BA4 4EL
Tel: 074989 371
Contact: C D Stone

Goat
Sheep — Yoghurt made from goat or sheep milk natural or flavoured with organically grown soft fruit and no added sugar, in 145, 450g cartons.
[C] 500 p.wk
[D] By arrangement
See Also: Cheese, Milk, Fudges and Toffee

15

D H J Foot Ltd
West Dibberford Farm, Beaminster, Dorset DT8 3HD
Tel: 0308 68229
Contact: David Foot

Low fat — Yoghurt with low fat and low sugar content flavoured with fresh fruits in 3, 4, 5oz pots and to customers requirements.
[C] 20,000 units p.wk
[D] By own transport, by arrangement

14

Fullers Brickwall Farm Ltd
Brickwall Farm, Sible Hedingham, Halstead, Essex CO9 3RH
Tel: 0787 60329
Contact: Robert Fuller

Gold Top yoghurt — Live, low fat yoghurt, natural with no sugar, flavoured with fruit and brown sugar. Also Gold Top yoghurt in 5oz, 1pt, 1 gal quantities.
[C] Undisclosed
[D] By arrangement
See Also: Cheese, Cream, Milk, Cakes, Biscuits and Pastries, Ice Creams and Sorbets

9

Healthfood Products (Wales) Ltd
Unit 1, Queensway Meadows Industrial Est, Newport, Gwent
Tel: 0633 282478
Contact: Dr Ara

Drinking yoghurt — Range of low fat fruit drinking yoghurt set with pectin, including peach, strawberry, and pina colada in 250ml pull ring cans.
[C] Undisclosed
[D] By arrangement

6 ↔

R Holmes & Sons
Whitburn Moors Farm, Sunderland Road, Cleadon, Tyne & Wear SR6 7UN
Tel: 091 5293127
Contact: Mr F Holmes

Fresh fruit — Whole milk yoghurt with fresh fruit in 150g pots.
[C] 6000 pots p.wk
[D] By own transport within area
See Also: Milk

15

D E Horrell Ltd
Lynher Valley Dairy, Netherton Farm, Upton Cross, Liskeard, Cornwall PL14 5BD
Tel: 0579 62244
Contact: Michael Horrell

Live — Live, whole milk plain yoghurt, in 11 fl oz cartons.
[C] Undisclosed
[D] By arrangement
See Also: Cheese

3

Howgate Dairy Products
Langskaill, Howgate, Penicuik, Midlothian
Tel: 0968 72263
Contact: M T R Marwick

Yoghurt — Natural and a range of twelve fruit flavoured yoghurts.
[C] Undisclosed
[D] By own transport within area
See Also: Cheese, Cream, Milk

16 ○ ↔

Island Country Farms
Asheybrook, Ashey, Ryde, Isle of Wight
PO33 4AT
Tel: 0983 65686
Contact: Mr J H Fisher

Goat

Goat milk yoghurt in individual tubs.
[C] Undisclosed
[D] By arrangement
See Also: Fresh Meat, Poultry Producers, Milk, Fresh Fruit

9 ○

John & Jenny White Organic Smallholders
Mount Pleasant, Pen y Bont, Carmarthen, Dyfed SA33 6PP
Tel: 09948 315
Contact: Jenny White

Goat

Thick set natural yoghurt from organically raised herd in 150, 500ml cartons.
[C] 288lt p.mth
[D] By arrangement
See Also: Cheese, Milk

15 ○ ↔

Kathryn Cornish
Hedgemoor Farm, Bridford, Exeter, Devon
EX6 7LW
Tel: 0647 52358
Contact: Kathryn Cornish

Goat

Goat milk yoghurt, sugar free in a variety of flavours in 5, 8 fl oz, 1pt tubs.
[C] 45 gal p.wk
[D] By own transport within area
See Also: Cheese, Milk

16

S E Lane
White House Farm, Biddenden, Ashford, Kent
Tel: 0580 291 374/289
Contact: M P Sargent

Low fat

Low fat yoghurt made from Jersey milk and whole fruit, with 0.05-0.1% fat content in 5, 10oz, 1, 10lt cartons.
[C] 40 gal p.wk
[D] By arrangement
See Also: Cream, Milk, Ice Creams and Sorbets

12 ↔

J & P Langman
Perrotts Brook Farm, Cirencester, Gloucestershire GL7 7BS
Tel: 028 583283
Contact: Lady Langman

Sheep

Yoghurt from milk of own Jersey herd, low or full fat, in natural or fruit flavours, in 5½oz, ½, 1pt quantities. Also supplied Greek-style yoghurt in a range of flavours including butterscotch, chocolate, lemon, rhubarb, and ginger. Sheep yoghurt, natural only in 5½oz, ½, 1pt quantities.
[C] Cow yoghurt 280 gal p.wk, sheep yoghurt 30 gal p.wk
[D] By own transport within area
See Also: Cream

10

Leasowes Natural Dairy Produce
Stanton Long, Much Wenlock, Shropshire
TF13 6LH
Tel: 074634 666
Contact: David Colley

Live

Range of live, low and full fat cow and goat milk yoghurt, plain and flavoured, sweetened with raw cane sugar, in 125, 150, 300, 600g tubs.
[C] Undisclosed
[D] By arrangement
See Also: Cheese

16 ↔

Loseley Dairy Products Ltd
Estate Office, Guildford, Surrey GU3 1HS
Tel: 0483 571881 Telx: 859972 Fax: 0483 302056
Contact: Miss Ann Cleveland

Live

Natural yoghurt made from low fat separated Jersey milk, set in carton. Range of whole fruit flavoured live yoghurt and Greek-style natural live yoghurt also available, with 9% fat content.
[C] Undisclosed
[D] By arrangement
See Also: Cream, Millers, Ice Creams and Sorbets

10 ↔

Madresfield Dairy Ltd
Home Farm, Madresfield, Malvern, Worcestershire WRI 5AJ
Tel: 06845 4379
Contact: Janet Lomas

Black cherry

Range of semi-skimmed whole fruit yoghurts in a variety of flavours including pineapple, black cherry, and peach melba in 125ml, 5oz tubs, 4lt containers. Also Greek-style strained yoghurt in 8oz pots.
[C] Undisclosed
[D] By arrangement
See Also: Cream

16 ● ↔

Malthouse Cottage Farm
Malthouse Lane, Ashington, Pulborough, West Sussex RH20 3BU
Tel: 0903 892456
Contact: Mrs J Ferris

Goat

Yoghurt made from own goat herd, available plain or fruit flavoured, in 5oz cartons.
[C] Undisclosed, produced to order
[D] By arrangement
See Also: Fresh Meat, Poultry Producers, Cheese, Milk

11

Manor Farm Dairy Products
Manor Farm, Thrussington, Leicestershire
Tel: 0664 74245
Contact: Mr Peter Holmes

Low fat

Low fat yoghurt made from milk of Rearsby Friesian herd within an hour of

milking, available natural, with or without sugar, in 5, 10oz tubs. Also range of ten flavours in 5oz tubs.
Ⓒ Undisclosed
Ⓓ By arrangement
See Also: Cream

16 ↔

Nature's Gardens
62 Lavender Hill, London SW11 5RQ
Tel: 01 223 4618
Contact: Eva

Skimmed milk

Live, thick, unstrained yoghurt made from equal parts cow milk and dried skimmed milk powder in 8oz, 1pt cartons.
Ⓒ 140pt p.wk
Ⓓ By arrangement
See Also: Milk

16 ↔

Neal's Yard Creamery
Home Farm Cottage, Everlands Estate, Sevenoaks, Kent TN14 6HU
Tel: 0732 461020
Contact: Perry James

Greek style

Greek-style live yoghurt containing double cream in 150ml, ½, 1lt cartons.
Ⓒ 800-1000lt p.mth
Ⓓ By own transport within area
See Also: Cheese, Cream, Ice Creams and Sorbets

15

Pinhill Yogurt
Pinhill Farm, Sidbury, Sidmouth, Devon EX10 0QJ
Tel: 03957 211
Contact: Mrs Kitrina Bishop

Sheep

Range of Greek-style sheep milk yoghurt including plain, strawberry, raspberry, apricot, blackcurrant, and fruits of the forest in 5, 10, 16oz pots.
Ⓒ 1000 p.day
Ⓓ By own transport within area
See Also: Cheese, Milk

9 ● ↔

Rachel's Dairy
Brynllys, Borth, Dyfed SY24 5LZ
Tel: 097081 489
Contact: Ms Rachel Rowlands

Live

Organic live yoghurt from Guernsey skimmed milk in 142g, ½lt pots.
Ⓒ 2000lt p.wk
Ⓓ By own transport within area
See Also: Butter, Cheese

6 ○

Redesdale Sheep Dairy
Soppitt Farm, Otterburn, Newcastle upon Tyne NE19 1AF
Tel: 0830 20276
Contact: Mark Robertson

Sheep

Farmhouse yoghurt from sheep milk set in 125g pots.
Ⓒ Undisclosed
Ⓓ By own transport within area
See Also: Cheese, Cream, Milk

15

Rill Farm
Rill Farm, Ottery-St-Mary, Devon EX11 1QH
Tel: 040481 2899
Contact: Mrs Ruth Burrow

Goat

Cow and goat milk yoghurt stirred by hand, flavoured with local fruit including raspberry, strawberry, blackcurrant, with raw cane sugar, packed in 5, 16oz cartons.
Ⓒ Undisclosed
Ⓓ By arrangement
See Also: Cheese

8 ○

Ryehill Goat Herd
Ryehills, Marton Lane, Pickering, Yorkshire YO18 8LW
Tel: 0751 76158/73026
Contact: G A Todd

Goat

Goat milk yoghurt, in a range of flavours including vanilla, muesli, raspberry, strawberry, and blackcurrant in 150, 500g pots.
Ⓒ 100 gal p.wk
Ⓓ By arrangement
See Also: Milk

1

Scottish Goat Products Ltd
Station Road, Newtonmore, Inverness-shire PH20 1AR
Tel: 05403 692
Contact: Douglas Locke

Goat

Whole and low fat goat milk yoghurt in a range of flavours including natural, cherry, peach melba, raspberry, and strawberry in 141g pots.
Ⓒ 96,000 pots p.mth
Ⓓ By own transport within area
See Also: Fresh Meat, Cheese, Milk, Fudges and Toffee

8 ↔

St Helens Farm
Barmby-on-the-Marsh, Goole, North Humberside
Tel: 0757 630100
Contact: Angus Wielkopolski

Goat

Goat milk yoghurt in natural, honey and fruit flavours in 125g pots.
Ⓒ 20,000 pots p.wk
Ⓓ By wholesaler
See Also: Milk

14

Susan Moore - Dairy Products
Cranes Watering Farm, Starston, Harleston, Norfolk IP20 9NE
Tel: 0379 852387
Contact: Susan Moore

Live

Whole Channel Island milk live yoghurt, natural or flavoured with local fruit in 150g cartons and catering packs.
Ⓒ Undisclosed
Ⓓ By own transport within area
See Also: Fresh Meat, Cheese, Cream, Ice Creams and Sorbets

16 ◯ ↔

Sussex High Weald Dairy Sheep
Putlands Farm, Duddleswell, Uckfield,
East Sussex TN22 3BJ
Tel: 082571 2647
Contact: Mr Mark Hardy

Sheep

Thick, creamy, Greek-style sheep yoghurt, plain or flavoured with natural fruit and a little raw demerara sugar, in 5, 8oz tubs, catering packs to order.
C Undisclosed
D By arrangement
See Also: Cheese, Milk

16

J D & C Tucker
Oakhurst Farm, Burwash, Ethingham,
East Sussex TN19 7DP
Tel: 0435 882328
Contact: Mrs C Tucker

Jersey

Range of low fat yoghurt made from separated Jersey milk, in a range of flavours including natural, blackcurrant, peach melba, black cherry, raspberry, and strawberry.
C Undisclosed
D By arrangement
See Also: Cream, Milk

15 ↔

Waterloo Farm
Clayhidon, Cullompton, Devon EX15 3TN
Tel: 0823 680273
Contact: Cmdr A G Trotter

Sheep

Thick sheep yoghurt from Foxfire flock of pedigree Friesland sheep with 5% fat content, in 142, 284ml tubs, 1pt pots.
C Undisclosed
D By own transport within area
See Also: Milk

16 ◯ ↔

Willowdown
Humphreys Farm, Nutley, Uckfield,
Sussex TN22 3LS
Tel: 082571 2432
Contact: Mrs Margaret Willcock

Goat

Live yoghurt from organically reared British Saanen goats.
C Undisclosed
D By own transport within area
See Also: Cheese, Milk

New Products?

Let us know on **01 727 9808** and we will follow it through for our next edition.

Whilst every effort has been made to ensure that the information is correct, **British Food Finds** cannot be held responsible for any errors or omissions.

5

HORTICULTURAL PRODUCE

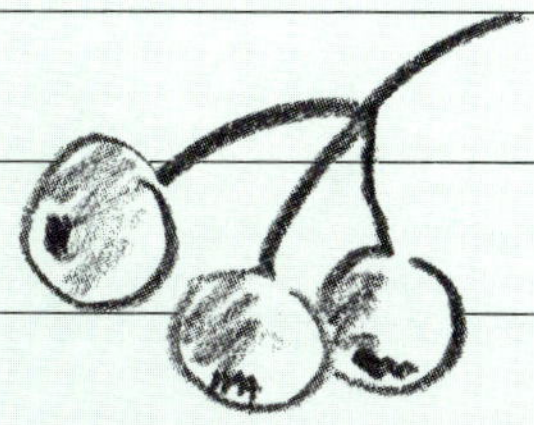

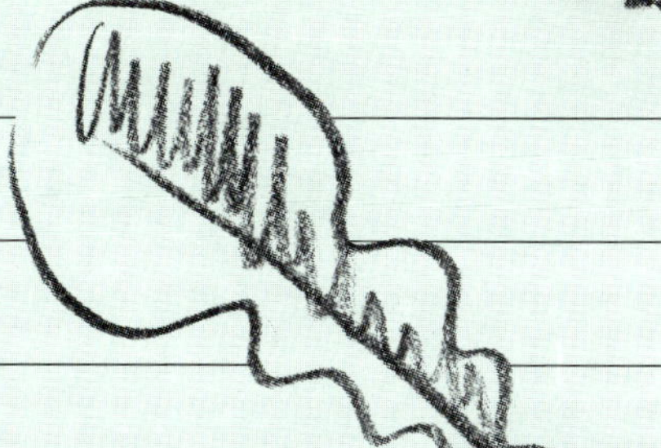

APPLES

Some of the choicest varieties of apples were developed during the Victorian and Edwardian eras. The merits of the season's Blenheim or Ribston were discussed with as much enthusiasm and in as much detail as the chateau and vintage of a claret. English apples were appreciated for their wide range of subtle flavours. Hundreds were grown by orchardists and in the walled gardens of country houses to provide greater diversity and interest, from the end of July right round to the following May.

Now rationalisation has radically reduced the number of varieties on sale. Farm shops, however, are providing an increasingly large selection. Buying locally also overcomes some of the problems leading to many varieties' disappearance from the commercial markets - the limited shelf life of the earliest, and easy bruising.

In the best varieties, sweetness and acidity are well balanced and, like the well-ripened Cox, further enhanced by complex aromatic flavours. The development of these aromatic components is particularly favoured by our climate, through the soil, and by the way the fruit is grown and stored. Above all, for an apple to taste its best, it must be properly ripened.

The following notes describe some of the more interesting and more recently introduced varieties available. The tasting notes are based on apples grown in the South East and, where appropriate, stored under natural-amateur conditions.

The farm shops have been selected because they sell a wide range of varieties and in particular some of the older, choicer ones. It has not been possible at this stage to make any evaluation of these apples. It should be noted that it is rare to find crab apples on sale but many fruit farms use crab apple trees as pollinators in the orchards and may well be willing to pick these if asked.

The apple harvest is divided into four: early season - apples ripening and ready for eating in August to early September; mid-season - apples ripening in September to October; late season - apples needing storing and ready for eating in October to December; extra-late season - apples needing storing and ready for eating December to March or later.

Written and compiled by Joan Morgan

EARLY SEASON - VARIETIES RIPENING EARLY AUGUST - EARLY SEPTEMBER

The flavours of the earlies are generally light and refreshing. Compared with the later Cox or Ribston they have few aromatic components. The earliest are best eaten straight from the tree; they rapidly go over and become mealy.

Beauty of Bath Once the first apple to appear in the markets, small-to-medium sized, round and yellow, mottled, flushed and striped with pink and red; flesh creamy white, often stained pink under the skin, juicy and sharp, it has a fairly acid taste, yet with plenty of sweetness in good ripe fruit. It keeps for only days and soon goes mealy. (Crimson Beauty is a more highly coloured form).

Discovery Main August apple, round and bright red; flesh creamy, sometimes stained pink and firmly textured, juicy and sweet, reminiscent of Worcester with a light strawberry flavour, it keeps for two weeks.

George Cave Ripening after Beauty of Bath, green-yellow, with orange red cheek and dark red striping; flesh creamy, strongly sweet and sharp, a more intense taste than, for example, a Discovery. It keeps for a week or so.

Grenadier Large green cooker, yellow and golden by September but usually picked early in August before maturity. Cooking to a sharp puree early in its season; later it keeps more of its form and the flavour is richer. Greater acidity, resulting in easier cooking, if grown in the North.

Miller's Seedlings Kentish apple, cream flushed with pink and red stripes; flesh crisp, glistening with juice, light sweet taste, with plenty of acidity, but needs to be ripe. It keeps for two weeks to a month under cool conditions but requires careful handling. (Red Miller's Seedling is a more highly-coloured form.)

MID-SEASON - VARIETIES RIPENING SEPTEMBER-OCTOBER

These apples also ripen on the tree, but keep several weeks or longer if stored in cool, dark conditions. Many of these varieties have rich and interesting flavours.

Ellison's Orange Ellison's Orange, because of its hardiness, has always been especially popular in the North of England. Greenish-yellow with an orange-red cheek; flesh perfumed, sweet and well-balanced with acidity, a rich aromatic taste which becomes distinctly aniseed-flavoured after picking. (Red Ellison's Orange is a more highly-coloured form.)

Greensleeves Modern variety, pale green becoming yellow with combined flavour of its parents: Golden Delicious and James Grieve. A hard apple with strong acidity eaten early when green (later flesh becomes softer and the taste sweet).

James Grieve Yellow with a pink flush stippling on the cheek; flesh crisp but melting, very juicy and sharp. Acidity can be too much early in season and is often picked green for cooking, but with keeping the acidity mellows to savoury quality.

Katy Recently introduced to English orchards. A bright red skin from its Worcester parent; the flesh white and juicy; lightly strawberry-flavoured, with plenty of acidity coming from its other parent, James Grieve.

Laxton's Epicure (Epicure) Raised by the Laxton brothers at the beginning of this century to provide the flavour of a Cox throughout the season. Greenish-yellow with red flush and red stripes; flesh creamy-white, juicy, sweet, light and delicate, a hint of strawberry from its other parent, Wealthy, an American variety.

Laxton's Fortune (Fortune) Red stripes and a pink flush; the flesh pale cream, sweet, juicy; lightly aromatic with a slight strawberry flavour. Needs to be well-ripened and coloured or tends to be flat and empty.

St Edmund's Pippin (St Edmund's Russet) Golden, almost completely covered in russet, sometimes with an orange cheek; flesh dense, richly flavoured and when well ripened has a taste of pears. (Golden Russet is a more golden form.)

Worcester Pearmain Famed for its brilliant red colour and heavy regular crops, regrettably now usually picked early, when green, with only a dull red flush; flesh white when fully ripe, firm, densely sweet, with a strong strawberry taste.

LATE SEASON - VARIETIES FOR EATING IN OCTOBER-DECEMBER

The period when some of the most distinguished varieties mature. Harvested from early to mid-October, the fruit develops its full flavour after a period of storage and remains in season for a couple of months.

Farm shops store and sell these when mature, or sell recently picked for customers to store themselves. The periods given here are a variety's natural season in good amateur conditions - dark, at a constant cold temperature. Commercial practice, using refrigerated stores and the more refined controlled atmosphere storage, can now often extend this. Controlled atmosphere storage is used to keep fruit for long periods of over 6 months.

Blenheim Orange Grown only to limited extent, but still much sought-after. Round, large to medium-sized, yellow with red cheek, some russetting; the flesh pale cream, crumbling, sweet with a plain yet addictive taste of fruit and nuts. Medium-sized have the best dessert flavour, larger ones used for cooking, to make a stiff puree, traditionally for Apple Charlotte. For cooking, best used early; later becomes sweeter and develops the characteristic taste and texture. Ripe for eating from end of October.

Bramley's Seedling Popular cooker, large, green with brownish-red flush and stripes on the cheek. On sale as early as August, but these are undeveloped, acidic and starchy with none of a Bramley's strong flavour. Cooks to a pale cream puree, sharp and fruity. With keeping becomes sweeter and in Spring serves as a sharp eating apple. Season: end Oct-Mar under natural conditions, longer under controlled atmosphere storage (does not mature in above way, but resembles fruit early in its season)

Cox's Orange Pippin Most widely grown dessert apple. Golden-yellow with orange cheek, red stripes, some russetting; flesh deep cream, juicy, sweet, perfectly balanced with acidity, intensely aromatic yet delicate. At its best when picked about the beginning to middle of October, eaten towards the end of month and into November. (Queen Cox is a more highly-coloured form.) Season: Oct-Jan under natural storage; Feb-Mar in cold stores and controlled atmosphere

Charles Ross Large, dual-purpose, yellow flushed with orange-red, but coarsely textured. Used early as a culinary apple, when cooked slices of fruit retain their shape, tasting sweet and light; later, as a dessert apple, sharp, aromatic, but coarsely textured and flavoured compared to its Cox parent. (Red Ross is a more highly-coloured form.) Season: Oct-Nov

Egremont Russet Golden, developing an orange cheek under the light brown russet; flesh dense, distinctly flavoured, early in season quite juicy with a fruity nutty taste, later russet flavour - nutty, or like dried leaves. Season: Oct-Nov; Jan-Feb, kept in cold storage

Gala New Zealand apple becoming popular with the smaller fruit growers. Yellow, flushed with orange and red stripes; flesh crisp, juicy, sweet with plenty of balancing acidity, lightly aromatic, with good, fresh, though not intense, flavour. (Royalty Red is a more highly-coloured form.) Season: Nov-Dec

Lord Derby Particularly popular in the Midlands and the North. A large green cooker, becoming yellow, tending to keep some of its form when cooked, with a sharp strong taste. More acidity grown in North, cooking more readily to a puree. In the South, best used early as the flavour tends to fade. Season: picked green mid-Sep, keeping Nov-Dec

Lord Lambourne Large-to-medium sized, orange and red cheek; flesh crisp, juicy, sweet, with strawberry flavour. Season: Oct-Nov

Orleans Reinette Old European variety grown for many years. Yellow with red cheek and a fine network of russetting; the flesh creamy-sweet, on the dry side with an intense aromatic and nutty flavour. Often referred to as a small Blenheim, but sweeter and richer. Season: Nov-Jan

Peasgood Nonesuch Very large cooker, pale green to yellow, flushed with orange and red; cooks to a cream puree, quite sweet and delicately flavoured, easily swamped by sugar. Season: late Sep-Dec

Ribston Pippin One of the most highly regarded Victorian and Edwardian dessert apples, probably the parent of Cox. Yellow with orange-red cheek, some russetting; flesh deep cream, juicy, sweet, well-balanced with acidity and strongly aromatic. Season: mid Oct-Dec

Sunset Yellow with orange-pink flush and some red stripes; flesh creamy, crisp, juicy and sweet, with plenty of balancing acidity and robust aromatic flavour - like its Cox parent but sharper, not so subtly flavoured. The tree tends to overcrop so fruit can be small but this does not affect flavour. Season: Oct-Dec, coming into season just before the Cox

EXTRA-LATE SEASON - VARIETIES FOR EATING IN DECEMBER-MARCH

Last varieties to be picked, from the middle to end of October, maturing in December, the New Year or later, to carry the apple season around to possibly the following May. The same storage requirements apply as in the previous section: some fruit farmers barn-store these varieties, others use cold stores.

Ashmead's Kernel Recently re-appreciated for its fine quality. Green-yellow with red-brown flush, stripes and fine russetting; flesh white, firm, juicy, sweet with plenty of acidity and intense aromatic flavour reminiscent of acid-drops. Season: Dec-Feb

D'Arcy Spice An East Anglian variety, where it has remained since it originated there over two hundred years ago. Green, becoming yellow, covered in a dingy russet; flesh firm, white, quite juicy, sharp and fruity with a hot spicey taste. It needs a wet climate, and should be left on the tree as long as possible. Season: Jan-Mar, longer with careful barn storage

Edward VII Thought to be a seedling of Blenheim Orange and Golden Noble. One of the choicest cooking apples, cooking to a translucent juicy puree. Not as sharp as a Bramley but similar when used early in its season, later it is milder. Season: Dec-Mar

Jupiter A very modern variety, a Cox Starking cross. Yellow with an orange-red cheek, some russetting; flesh cream, crisp, juicy and aromatic, with looser texture than the Cox. It can, however, be only lightly flavoured. Season: Nov-Feb

Laxton's Superb Green-yellow, covered with a deep rusty-red cheek, sweet and lightly aromatic, though in warm years the flavour is more intense and stronger. Season: Nov-Feb

Kidd's Orange Red A New Zealand variety, parent of Gala; in a good year one of the finest-flavoured apples. Conical-shaped with scarlet flush; sweet with some acidity and intense yet delicate aromatic taste reminiscent of flowers, like Parma violets. Requires lots of sun and should not be picked too early. Season: Nov-Feb

Suntan Modern variety raised to provide a late aromatic apple. Golden-yellow, with an orange-red cheek; flesh deep cream, firm, juicy, sweet, with plenty of acidity and intensely aromatic, stronger and sharper than a Cox, at its best in the New Year. Season: Jan-Feb

Spartan Canadian variety, dark mahogany-red; the white flesh of its McIntosh parent and late keeping properties of Newtown Pippin both old North American apples, sweet, fruity with a flavour perhaps of raspberries, often described as vinous. The skin is tough: if picked too early it will be sharp and woody. Season: Nov-Feb, longer in cold store

Tydeman's Late Orange Green, turning yellow, with a dull red flush, red stripes, specks of russet; flesh deep cream, firm, with plenty of acidity and strong aromatic flavour, like a Cox, but sharper. Fruit can be small, though still of good flavour. Season: Dec-Mar

8

Ampleforth College Orchards
Ampleforth College, Ampleforth, Yorkshire
YO6 4HA
Tel: 04393 485
Contact: S Murfitt

Early Season Beauty of Bath, Discovery, George Cave, Miller's Seedling, Grenadier
Mid-Season Greensleeves, James Grieve, Laxton's Epicure, St Edmund's Pippin

Late Season Blenheim Orange, Bramley's Seedling, Cox's Orange Pippin, Egremont Russet, Lord Derby, Lord Lambourne, Orleans Reinette, Sunset
Extra-late Season Jupiter

16 **Avalon Farm**
Old Barn Lane, Churt, Farnham, Surrey GU10 2NA
Tel: 042873 5161
Contact: Mr C N Rhodes

Early Season Discovery, Worcester Pearmain
Mid-Season James Grieve
Late Season Bramley's Seedling, Cox's Orange Pippin, Egremont Russet
Extra-late Season Spartan

9 **Berry Hill Farm**
Coedkernew, Newport, Gwent NP1 9UD
Tel: 0633 680938
Contact: Fiona Peel

Early Season Discovery
Mid-Season Katy, Greensleeves
Late Season Gala, Queen Cox, Cox's Orange Pippin, Bramley's seedling
Extra-late Season Spartan
See Also: Fresh Fruit

16 **Blackmoor Estate**
Blackmoor, Liss, Hampshire GU33 6BS
Tel: 04203 3576
Contact: Mrs Priddle

Early Season George Cave, Discovery, Grenadier
Mid-Season Greensleeves, James Grieve, Katy
Late Season Bramley's Seedling, Cox's Orange Pippin, Egremont Russet, Gala
Extra-late Season Jonogold, Jupiter, Spartan

10 **Brandon Lane Fruit Farm**
Brandon Lane, Tollbar End, Coventry, Warwickshire
Tel: 0203 305757
Contact: The Proprietor

Early Season George Cave, Discovery, Grenadier
Mid-Season James Grieve, Katy, Worcester Pearmain
Late Season Bramley's Seedling, Cox's Orange Pippin, Lord Lambourne
Extra-late Season Spartan

16 **W Brice & Son**
Mockbeggar Farm, Higham, Rochester, Kent ME3 8EU
Tel: 0634 717425
Contact: P Brice

Early Season Discovery
Mid-Season Greensleeves, Katy, Laxton's Fortune, St Edmund's Pippin, Worcester Pearmain
Late Season Bramley's Seedling, Cox's Orange Pippin, Egremont Russet
Extra-late Season Spartan

12 **Charlton Orchards**
Creech St Michael, Taunton, Somerset TA3 5PF
Tel: 0823 412979
Contact: R A Small

Early Season Discovery, Grenadier
Mid-Season Katy, Laxton's Fortune, Merton
Late Season Bramley's Seedling, Cox's Orange Pippin, Lord Lambourne, Orleans Reinette
Extra-late Season Spartan, Suntan, Jonagold, Gloster

16 **Costrong Fruit Farm**
Plaistow Road, Kirdford, Billinghurst, West Sussex
Tel: 040377 391
Contact: Mr Nash

Early Season Grenadier, Miller's Seedling
Late Season Bramley's Seedling, Cox's Orange Pippin
Extra-late Season Spartan

14 **Crapes Fruit Farm**
Aldham, Colchester, Essex CO6 3RR
Tel: 0206 210406
Contact: Andrew Tann

Mid-Season Ellison's Orange, St.Edmund's Russet, Lobo
Late Season Orleans Reinette, Peasgood Nonesuch, Sunset, Ribston Pippin
Extra-late Season D'Arcy Spice, Kidd's Orange Red, Suntan

14 **David G Mitchell**
Bradfield Fruit Farm, The Street, Bradfield, nr Manningtree, Essex CO11 2UU
Tel: 0255 870696
Contact: D G Mitchell

Early Season George Cave, Discovery, Grenadier, Jerseymac
Mid-Season James Grieve, St Edmund's Pippin, Worcester Pearmain, Tyderman's Early, Greensleeves
Late Season Bramley's Seedling, Cox's Orange Pippin, Egremont Russet
Extra-late Season Ashmead's Kernel, Spartan, Crispin, Ida Red

10 **Dinmore Fruit Farm**
Dinmore, Hereford HR4 8ED
Tel: 056884 361
Contact: Mrs Angela Morley

Late Season Sunset
Extra-Late Season Kidd's Orange, Red Ida, Tyderman's Late Orange

15 **Elwell Fruit Farm**
Netherbury, Bridport, Dorset DT6 5LF
Tel: 030888 283
Contact: Mr P H Jackson

Early Season George Cave, Discovery
Mid-Season Greensleeves, James Grieve, Katy, Laxton's Fortune, St Edmund's Russet, Worcester Pearmain
Late Season Bramley's Seedling, Cox's Orange Pippin, Egremont Russet, Gala, Lord Lambourne, Sunset
Extra-late Season Spartan, Suntan, Jonagold, Elstar, Fiesta

7 **Haworth's Fruit Farm**
Eddisbury Fruit Farm, Yeld Lane, Kelsall, Cheshire CW6 OTE
Tel: 0829 51300/51188
Contact: C G Haworth

Early Season Discovery, Grenadier
Mid-Season James Grieve, Katy, Howgate Wonder
Late Season Cox's Orange Pippin, Spartan, Bramley's Seedling, Gala, Sunset
Extra-late Season Kidd's Orange Red, Chiver's Delight, Crispin, Golden Delicious

12 **Hayles Fruit Farm**
Winchcombe, Cheltenham, Gloucestershire GL54 5PB
Tel: 0242 602123
Contact: D Harrell

Early Season Discovery
Mid-Season Worcester Pearmain
Late Season Blenheim Orange, Bramley's Seedling, Cox's Orange Pippin, Egremont Russet
Extra-late Season Spartan

13 **Hertfordshire College of Agriculture & Horticulture**
Oaklands, St Albans, Hertfordshire AL4 OJA
Tel: 0727 62214/53614/506
Contact: J G Beeby

Early Season Discovery
Mid-Season Katy, Greensleeves, Laxton's Fortune, Tydeman's Early, Worcester
Late Season Bramley's Seedling, Cox's Orange Pippin, Egremont Russet
Extra-late Season Spartan

16 **Hewitts Farm**
Chelsfield, Orpington, Kent BR6 7QR
Tel: 0959 34271/34666 Fax: 0959 39258
Contact: Mr Rolstone

Early Season George Cave, Discovery, Grenadier
Mid-Season Ellison's Orange, James Grieve, Katy, St Edmund's Russet
Late Season Bramley Seedless, Cox's Orange Pippin, Charles Ross, Egremont Russet, Gala, Lord Derby, Lord Lambourne, Sunset
Extra-late Season Spartan

16 ↔ **Hill Farm Orchards**
Droxford Road, Swanmore, Southampton SO3 2PY
Tel: 04897 8616
Contact: Helen Starkey

Early Season Discovery, Grenadier
Mid-Season Greensleeves, James Grieve, Katy, Laxton's Fortune, Worcester Pearmain
Late Season Bramley's Seedling, Cox's Orange Pippin, Egremont Russet, Gala, Lord Lambourne
Extra-late Season Ashmeads Kernel, Tydeman's Late Orange
See Also: Juices

13 **Home Cottage Farm**
Bangors Road South, Iver Heath, Buckinghamshire SLO OBB
Tel: 0753 653064
Contact: P Hinde

Early Season Grenadier
Mid-Season Laxton's Fortune
Late Season Blenheim Orange, Bramley's Seedling, Cox's Orange Pippin, Charles Ross, Egremont Russet, Lord Lambourne
Extra-late Season Laxton's Superb, Spartan
See Also: Fresh Fruit

16 **Hunt's Fruit**
Sharewoods Farm, New England Lane, Sedlescombe, Battle, Sussex
Tel: 042487 354
Contact: C J Hunt

Early Season Discovery, Grenadier
Mid-Season Greensleeves, James Grieve, Katy, Laxton's Fortune, Worcester Pearmain
Late Season Bramley, Cox's Orange Pippin, Egremont Russet, Gala, Lord Derby
Extra-late Season Ashmead's Kernel, Jupiter, Laxton's Superb, Kidd's Orange Red, Spartan, Suntan

10 **John Dowty**
Fruit & Vegetable Centre, Ombersley, Droitwich, Worcestershire WR9 OJH
Tel: 0905 620404
Contact: N Dowty

Early Season Discovery, Grenadier
Mid-Season James Grieve, Katy, Laxton's Fortune, Worcester Pearmain
Late Season Bramley's Seedling, Cox's Orange Pippin, Egremont Russet, Lord Derby, Lord Lambourne
Extra-late Season Laxton's Superb, Spartan

12 **Midwinter Fruit Farm**
Milton Hill, Abingdon, Oxfordshire OX14 4DP
Tel: 0235 831247
Contact: Philip Midwinter

Early Season Beauty of Bath, George Cave, Discovery, Grenadier, Tydeman's Early Worcester
Mid-Season Laxton's Fortune
Late Season Bramley's Seedling, Cox's Orange Pippin, Egremont Russet, Gala, Lord Lambourne
Extra-late Season Laxton's Superb, Spartan, Tydeman's Late Orange

12 **Millets Farm & Crabtree Pick Your Own**
Millets Farm, Garford, Abingdon, Oxfordshire OX13 5PD
Tel: 0865 391555
Contact: Mr J L Carter

Early Season Discovery, Williams
Mid-Season Laxton's Epicure, Worcester Pearmain, Cox's Orange Pippin
Late Season Bramley's Seedling, Lord Lambourne, Comice
Extra-late Season Laxton's Superb, Spartan
See Also: Fresh Vegetables,

12 **North Perrott Fruit Farm**
North Perrott, Crewkerne, Somerset TA18 7SU
Tel: 0460 72883
Contact: H W F Hoskyns

Early Season Discovery
Mid-Season Ellison's Orange, James Grieve, Katy, St Edmund's Pippin, Worcester Pearmain
Late Season Blenheim Orange, Bramley's Seedling, Cox's Orange Pippin, Egremont Russet, Lord Lambourne, Queen Cox, Sunset
Extra-late Season Ashmead's Kernel, Jupiter, Laxton Superb, Kidd's Orange Red, Spartan

14 **Olivers Orchard**
Olivers Lane, Colchester, Essex CO2 0HH
Tel: 0206 330208
Contact: Mr R M Knowles

Early Season Discovery, Grenadier
Mid-Season Greensleeves, Katy, Laxton's, Charles Ross Fortune, St Edmund's Russet
Late Season Bramley's Seedling, Cox's Orange Pippin, Egremont Russet
See Also: Fresh Fruit, Fresh Vegetables

16 **Ringdon Farm**
London Road, Hurst Green, Etchingham, East Sussex TN1 7QY
Tel: 058087 385
Contact: Mr Dench

Early Season George Cave, Discovery, Grenadier
Mid-Season Greensleeves, James Grieve, Worcester Pearmain, Jonagold
Late Season Bramley's Seedling, Cox's Orange Pippin, Egremont Russet, Lord Lambourne
Extra-late Season Suntan, Spartan, Ida Red, Melrose Crispin

10 **Snittersfield Fruit Farm**
Kings Lane, Stratford-upon-Avon, Warwickshire CV37 0QA
Tel: 0789 731 560/388/244
Contact: R A Corser

Early Season George Cave, Discovery, Grenadier
Mid-Season James Grieve, Katy, Worcester Pearmain
Late Season Blenheim Orange, Bramley's Seedling, Cox's Orange Pippin, Egremont Russet
Extra-late Season Laxton's Superb, Spartan

11 **Spring Hill Farm**
Moor Lane, Calverton, Nottingham, Nottinghamshire NG14 6FZ
Tel: 0602 652129
Contact: D R Smith

Early Season Discovery
Mid-Season James Grieve, Katy, St Edmund's Pippin
Late Season Bramley's Seedling, Cox's Orange Pippin, Egremont Russet

12 **Stawell Fruit Farm**
Stawell, Bridgewater, Somerset TA7 9AE
Tel: 0278 722732
Contact: Charles Graham

Early Season Discovery, Grenadier
Late Season Sunset, Cox's Orange Pippin, Bramley's seedling

12 **Tatworth Fruit Farm**
Tatworth, Chard, Somerset TA20 2SG
Tel: 0460 20272
Contact: A R Davies

Early Season George Cave, Discovery, Grenadier
Mid-Season Lord Lambourne, Katy, Worcester Pearmain
Late Season Bramley, Cox's Orange Pippin, Egremont Russet, Sunset, Spartan
Extra-late Season Kidd's Orange Red, Ida Red
See Also: Fresh Vegetables,

14 **Tower Fruit Farm**
Stretham Road, Wilburton, nr Ely, Cambridgeshire CB6 3RY
Tel: 035389 267
Contact: T W Ball

Early Season Discovery, Worcester Pearmain
Late Season Bramley's Seedling, Cox's Orange Pippin, Egremont Russet
Extra-late Season Spartan

14 **Tyler's**
The Cedars, Thorpe Market Road,
Roughton, Norwich, Norfolk NR11 8TB
Tel: 0267379 777
Contact: Mrs R Tyler

Early Season Discovery
Mid-Season Greensleeves, James Grieve, Laxton's Fortune, Worcester Pearmain
Late Season Bramley's Seedling, Cox's Orange Pippin, Egremont Russet, Lord Derby
Extra-late Season Spartan, Suntan, Jonogold
See Also: Fresh Fruit

12 **West Bradley Fruit Farm**
West Bradley House, West Bradley,
Glastonbury, Somerset BA6 8LT
Tel: 04585 0227
Contact: W T Allen

Early Season Discovery
Mid-Season James Grieve
Late Season Blenheim Orange, Bramley's Seedling, Chiver's Delight, Cox's Orange Pippin, Charles Ross, Egremont Russet, Gala, Lord Lambourne, Sunset
Extra-late Season Laxton's Superb, Spartan, Suntan

10 **Withers Fruit Farm**
Wellington Heath, Ledbury, Herefordshire
HR8 1NF
Tel: 0531 2017
Contact: F A Leeds

Early Season George Cave, Discovery, Grenadier
Mid-Season Katy, Laxton's Fortune
Late Season Bramley's Seedling, Cox's Orange Pippin, Egremont Russet, Lord Lambourne
Extra-late Season Spartan
See Also: Fresh Fruit

FRESH FRUIT

3 **C A & D B M Acheson**
Easter Ballindean Farm, Inchture,
Perthshire PH14 9QS
Tel: 0828 86256
Contact: C A Acheson

Tayberries — Tayberries, blackberries and raspberries supplied fresh or frozen. Fresh strawberries also available.
[C] Tayberries 5 ton Jul-Dec, blackberries 5 ton Aug-Dec, raspberries 20 ton Jul, strawberries 20 ton Jun-Aug
[D] By arrangement

16 **Avalon Farm**
Old Barn Lane, Churt, Farnham, Surrey
GU10 2NA
Tel: 042873 5161
Contact: Mr C N Rhodes

Blueberries — Fresh blueberries in season.
[C] Undisclosed
[D] By arrangement
See Also: Apples

9 **Berry Hill Farm**
Coedkernew, Newport, Gwent NP1 9UD
Tel: 0633 680938
Contact: Fiona Peel

Tayberries — Range of soft fruit including strawberrries and tayberries.
[C] Strawberries 5 ton p.wk Jun-Jul, tayberries 6000lb p.mth Jul
[D] By arrangement
See Also: Apples

14 ↔ **Charles & Shirley Trollope**
Clay Barn Orchards, Fingringhoe,
Colchester, Essex CO5 7AR
Tel: 020635 405
Contact: Charles Trollope

Quince — Vranja and pear-shaped quince. Also apples.
[C] Quince 8-12 ton Oct-Nov
[D] By arrangement

7 ● **Coopers Organic Growers**
Great Knowley, 139 Blackburn Road,
Chorley, Lancashire PR6 8TH
Tel: 02572 64458
Contact: Mr Cooper

Blackcurrant — Range of organic fresh fruit including blackcurrants supplied ripe and frozen on the stalk suitable as garnish.
[C] Undisclosed
[D] By arrangement
See Also: Fresh Herbs, Fresh Salads, Fresh Vegetables

3 **Gagie House Farm**
Gagie House, Gagie by Dundee, Tayside
DD4 0PR
Tel: 082621 207
Contact: France A Smoor

Blueberries — Range of soft fruit including Bogota and Korona strawberries, raspberries, tayberries, blueberries and brambles, all packed in 8oz punnets. Also gooseberries and red and white currants.
[C] Raspberries 15 ton Jul-Sep, strawberries 25 ton, tayberries 2 ton
[W] Kentish Garden
[D] By arrangement

15 ● ↔ **The Gardens**
Buckland-in-the-Moor, Ashburton, Devon
TQ13 7HN
Tel: 0364 53169
Contact: Charles Staniland

Strawberries — Organically grown strawberries.
[C] 600lb p.mth May-Aug
[D] By arrangement
See Also: Fresh Herbs, Fresh Salads, Fresh Vegetables

16 ●

Garlands Organic Farmshop
Garlands Farm, Gardeners Lane, Upper Basildon, nr Reading, Berkshire RG8 8LN
Tel: 0491 671556
Contact: Mr C Raymont

Sunberries

Range of organic soft fruit including sunberries, loganberries and raspberries.
C Undisclosed
D By arrangement
See Also: Fresh Salads, Fresh Vegetables

15 ●

Graeme Fisk
The Granary, Prinkle Farm, Bodle Street, Hailsham, East Sussex BN27 4UD
Tel: 0323 833541
Contact: Graeme Fisk

Blackcurrant

Organically grown blackcurrants.
C ¼ ton p.mth Jul-Aug
D By arrangement
See Also: Fresh Vegetables

8 ○ ↔

R Holmes & Sons
West House Farm, Birstwith, Harrogate, North Yorkshire HG3 3AW
Tel: 0423 770200
Contact: Mr I Holmes

Redcurrants

Strawberries, raspberries, blackcurrants, gooseberries and redcurrants.
C Undisclosed
D By arrangement
See Also: Fresh Meat, Fresh Vegetables

13

Home Cottage Farm
Bangors Road South, Iver Heath, Buckinghamshire SLO OBB
Tel: 0753 653064
Contact: P Hinde

Tayberries

Raspberries and tayberries.
C Undisclosed
D By arrangement
See Also: Apples

16 ○ ↔

Island Country Farms
Asheybrook, Ashey, Ryde, Isle of Wight PO33 4AT
Tel: 0983 65686
Contact: Mr J H Fisher

Strawberries

Organic strawberries.
C Undisclosed
D By arrangement
See Also: Fresh Meat, Poultry Producers, Milk, Fresh Herbs, Fresh Salads, Fresh Vegetables

15 ↔

Island Exotics
The Cottage, Houge Mague, Capelles, St Sampson, Guernsey
Tel: 0481 45853
Contact: Martin Langlois

Babaco

Babaco, a South American hybrid cross of the mountain pawpaw, with texture of melon and taste of lemon strawberry, can be used for sweet or savoury dishes, weighing 1-3lb in boxes of nine.
C 5000 p.wk May-Jul, 500 p.wk Aug-Apr
D By arrangement

15 ↔

John Lacey
Randabel, Grandes Rocques, Catel, Guernsey
Tel: 0481 55838
Contact: John Lacey

Kiwi fruit

Kiwi fruit, Hayward variety, in 3kg trays of about twenty five fruits per tray, in condition ready for ripening.
C 15-20 ton Nov-May
D By arrangement

16 ○

Lympne Market Garden
Garden House, Lympne Place, Lympne, Kent CT21 4PA
Tel: 0303 66183
Contact: Mr Fairley

Raspberries

Organically grown raspberries including Malling Delight.
C Undisclosed Jul-Aug
D By arrangement
See Also: Milk, Fresh Vegetables

10 ↔

R D McGuffie & Son
New Farm, Elmhursts, Lichfield, Staffordshire WS13 8EX
Tel: 0543 263756
Contact: S A McGuffie

Redcurrants

Strawberries, raspberries, gooseberries, blackcurrants and redcurrants, available fresh in season or frozen at on site freezing facilities.
C Strawberries 100 ton late Jun-early Aug, raspberries 30 ton early Jul-early Aug, gooseberries 30 ton mid Jun-Jul, blackcurrants and redcurrants 10 ton mid Jun-late Jul
D By arrangement
See Also: Fresh Vegetables

11 ●

Mangreen Gardens
Mangreen, Swardeston, Norwich, Norfolk NR14 8DP
Tel: 0508 70444
Contact: Mr William Duffield

Strawberries

Range of fresh organic fruit including early strawberries.
C Undisclosed
D By arrangement
See Also: Fresh Salads, Fresh Vegetables

15

F H Mann (Bushy Park) Products
Knowle Orchards, Budleigh Salterton, Devon EX9 7AL
Tel: 03954 2174
Contact: Joanna Hunt

Pears

Plums, pears and strawberries available in season.
C Undisclosed
D By arrangement
See Also: Cider

THE TASTE OF
EXOTIC CLIMATES
The
GUERNSEY
BABACO
A versatile fruit that can be used in sweet or savoury dishes, served cooked or chilled and is an excellent compliment to many main courses.
SOMETHING NEW
UNDER THE SUN
Grown under glass for quality and flavour.
MARKETED BY:
GUERNSEY
GROWERS
CO-OPERATIVE
LTD.
P.O. Box No. 35, Bulwer Avenue,
St. Sampsons, Guernsey, Channel Islands.
Telephone: 0481 46211

[12] ●

M Murray
Berwick Lodge, Station Road, Henbury, Bristol, Avon BS10 7TD
Tel: 0272 506742
Contact: Mr M Murray

Plums

Range of fresh organic fruit including redcurrants, blackcurrants, plums and gooseberries.
[C] Undisclosed
[D] By own transport within area
See Also: Fresh Vegetables

[7] ● ↔

Oakcroft Gardens
Oakcroft Gardens, Cross o' th' Hill, Malpas, Cheshire SY14 8DH
Tel: 0948 860213
Contact: Ms M S Fardonji

Blackcurrant

Range of organic fresh soft fruit including strawberries, raspberries and blackcurrants.
[C] Undisclosed May-Jul
[D] By arrangement
See Also: Fresh Herbs, Fresh Vegetables

[14]

Olivers Orchard
Olivers Lane, Colchester, Essex CO2 0HH
Tel: 0206 330208
Contact: Mr R M Knowles

Raspberry

Variety of top and soft fruit grown including William, Onward, Conference and Comice pears. Also strawberries, raspberries and blackcurrants. Due to geographic location crops tend to be three weeks early.
[C] Undisclosed Jun-Oct
[D] By arrangement
See Also: Apples, Fresh Vegetables

[9] ● ↔

Organic Farm Foods (Wales)
Unit 25, Lampeter Industrial Estate, Lampeter, Dyfed SA48 8LT
Tel: 0570 423099
Contact: Peter Segger

Strawberries

Range of organically grown soft fruits.
[C] Undisclosed
[D] By arrangement
See Also: Fresh Vegetables

[12]

Oxford Pick Your Own Farm
Hill Farm, Elsfield, Oxfordshire OX3 SW9
Tel: 086735 618 Fax: 086735 463
Contact: Peter Clarke

Blackberries

Range of pick your own fresh soft fruit including strawberries, raspberries, currants, tayberries, gooseberries and blackberries.
[C] Undisclosed Jun-Nov
[D] By arrangement
See Also: Fresh Vegetables

[16]

S D N & C M Preston
Badsell Park Farm, Matfield, Tonbridge, Kent TN12 7EW
Tel: 089283 2549
Contact: Mrs C M Preston

Strawberries

Variety of soft and top fruits including Ostara strawberries, tayberries, Cox, Discovery, Early Worcester apples and Conference and Comice pears, all available in season. Sweetcorn also supplied.
[C] Strawberries 15,000lb Aug-Oct, Cox apples 10,000lb Sep-Nov, sweetcorn 200lb Sep-Oct, Conference pears 20,000lb Sep-Nov, tayberries 150lb Aug-Sep
[D] By arrangement

[13] ● ↔

Stoneybridge Organic Nursery
Stoneybridge Organic Nursery, Tywardreath, Par, Cornwall PL27 2TY
Tel: 0726 813858
Contact: Mr D R Pascoe

Gooseberries

Range of fresh organic fruit, including strawberries, tayberries, blackcurrants and gooseberries.
[C] Undisclosed
[D] By arrangement
See Also: Fresh Salads, Fresh Vegetables

[15]

D G J Tanner
Sopley Farm, Sopley, Christchurch, Dorset
Tel: 0425 72451
Contact: Robin Reeks

Strawberries

Elvira, Hapil, Gorella, Elisanta and Rapella varieties of strawberry and five varieties of raspberry supplied fresh.
[C] Strawberries Jun-Sep, raspberries Jul-Aug
[D] By arrangement
See Also: Fresh Vegetables

[11] ●

S L & J D Tidy
The Anchorage, Salisbury Road, Broughton, nr Stockbridge, Hampshire
Tel: 0794 301234
Contact: Mr S L Tidy

Tayberries

Range of organic fresh fruit including tayberries.
[C] Undisclosed Jun-Dec
[D] By arrangement
See Also: Fresh Vegetables

[15] ●

Trehane Blueberries
Simons Ground, Stapehill, Wimborne, Dorset BH21 7ND
Tel: 0202 873642
Contact: Mr D J Y Trehane

Blueberries

Organically grown American high bush blueberries.
[C] 30 ton Jul-Aug
[D] By arrangement

FRESH HERBS

12 ↔

Arne Herbs
Limeburn Nurseries, Limeburn Hill, Chew Magna, Avon BS18 8QW
Tel: 0272 333399
Contact: Anthony Lyman-Dixon

Moroccan peppermint

Unusual garden herbs including Neapolitan and Opal basil, Moroccan peppermint, Greek oregano and many others. Oriental vegetables also available.
[C] Neapolitan and Opal basil 50kg p.mth Mar-Oct, Moroccan peppermint 100kg p.mth Mar-Oct, other herbs 200kg p.mth Mar-Oct, oriental vegetables 500kg p.mth
[D] By Datapost, by own transport within area
See Also: Dried Herbs and Flavourings, Teas and Infusions

10

Ashfield Herb Nursery
Hinstock, Market Drayton, Shropshire TF9 2NG
Tel: 095279 392
Contact: Mrs Beard

Marjoram

One hundred varieties of herbs including rosemary, marjoram, sage and mint supplied in 3″ pots.
[C] 500 plants p.mth Mar-Nov
[D] By arrangement

12

Bloxham Herb Garden
Firs Hill, Tadmarton Road, Bloxham, Banbury, Oxfordshire OX15 4HR
Tel: 0295 720434
Contact: R D Myburgh

Thyme

Twenty five varieties of culinary herbs cut to order on day required, packed in perforated polythene bags and sold by the gram.
[C] Undisclosed
[D] By arrangement

7 ○ ↔

Bowling Alley Herb Farm
Commonside, Alvanley, nr Warrington, Cheshire
Tel: 09289 285
Contact: Mrs Felicity Elphick

Chervil

Herbs fresh cut or dried according to season including chervil, dill, parsley, sorrel, tarragon, and thyme.
[C] Undisclosed chervil, parsley all year round
[D] By arrangement
See Also: Bacon and Hams, Cheese, Purées and Sauces

6 ○

Bradley Gardens Nursery
Bradley Gardens, Sled Lane, Wylam, Northumberland NE41 8J2
Tel: 0661 852176
Contact: Mrs Susan Hick

Basil
Hyssop

Range of over twenty varieties of fresh herbs including tarragon, hyssop, basil, dill, rosemary in 20, 100g packs.
[C] Undisclosed
[D] By arrangement

7 ●

Coopers Organic Growers
Great Knowley, 139 Blackburn Road, Chorley, Lancashire PR6 8TH
Tel: 02572 64458
Contact: Mr Cooper

French tarragon

Range of fresh organic herbs including French tarragon.
[C] Undisclosed
[D] By arrangement
See Also: Fresh Fruit, Fresh Salads, Fresh Vegetables

14 ○ ↔

Culpeper
Hadstock Rd, Linton, Cambridge CB1 6NJ
Tel: 0223 891196 Telx: 81698/81524
Contact: Ian Thomas

Angelica
Horseradish

Range of cut and potted medicinal and culinary herbs including angelica, caraway, cowslip and horseradish.
[C] Cut herbs undisclosed Apr-Oct, potted herbs 30,000 Mar-Oct
[D] By arrangement
See Also: Jams and Preserves, Teas and Infusions

14 ○ ↔

Denham End Farm
Denham, Bury St Edmunds, Suffolk IP29 5EE
Tel: 0284 810653
Contact: Caroline Holmes

Dill — One hundred and fifty varieties of herbs organically grown. Small quantities of unsprayed vegetables also available in summer.
Ⓒ Undisclosed
Ⓓ By arrangement

16 ↔ **Frenchland Herb Farm**
Ashington, Sussex RH20 3DF
Tel: 0903 892476
Contact: Rowena Green

Purple sage — Range of fresh, cut herbs including dill, chervil, rosemary, basil and chives, pre-packed or loose to customers requirements. Also herbs grown under contract including purple sage, garlic, chives and lemon balm.
Ⓒ Undisclosed
Ⓓ By arrangement

15 ↔ **Fresh Guernsey Herbs**
Lahuque, Les Abreuveurs, St Sampson, Guernsey
Tel: 0481 56176
Contact: Mr Ian Lloyd

Rocket — Herbs including applemint, chives, dill, lemon thyme, rocket, sage and sorrel. Salad herbs including salad burnet and purslane available throughout year. All supplied cut in clear plastic sleeves or boxed for catering trade. Also range of edible flowers, borage, chives, hyssop and marigold in season.
Ⓒ Undisclosed
Ⓦ Beantree Produce
Ⓓ By wholesaler

15 ● ↔ **The Gardens**
Buckland-in-the-Moor, Ashburton, Devon TQ13 7HN
Tel: 0364 53169
Contact: Charles Staniland

Sweet basil — Range of organically grown herbs including sweet basil.
Ⓒ Mixed herbs 1000 bunches p.mth May-Jul, sweet basil 40kg p.mth Jun-Sep
Ⓓ By arrangement
See Also: Fresh Fruit, Fresh Salads, Fresh Vegetables

15 ● **Haygrove Honey Farm**
Twyford, Shaftesbury, Dorset SP7 OJF
Tel: 0747 811855
Contact: John Davies

Coriander — Variety of organically grown herbs including parsley, dill, coriander and chives.
Ⓒ Bunches 50 p.mth
Ⓓ By own transport within area, by arrangement
See Also: Fresh Vegetables, Honey

14 ○ ↔ **The Herbary Prickwillow**
Ely, Cambridgeshire CB7 4SJ
Tel: 0353 88456 Telx: 265871 MONREF G
Contact: Peter Petts

Hyssop — Culinary herbs including basil, borage, chervil, hyssop, marjoram, oregano and camomile in 20g packs in boxes of twenty five or loose in -, ¼, ½, 1kg. Also thirty varieties of edible flowers. Any herb propagated to customers requirements.
Ⓒ 1000kg p.mth
Ⓓ By own transport nationally

10 ↔ **Hereford Herbs**
Ocle Pychard, Herefordshire HR1 3RB
Tel: 0432 820379 Telx: 35332 HSA G
Contact: Mr Geoffrey Loyd

Sweet cicely — Frozen culinary herbs for use in their frozen state including parsley, tarragon, marjoram, sweet cicely and lemon balm supplied in packs made up to customers requirements.
Ⓒ Undisclosed
Ⓦ Brake Bros.
Ⓓ By wholesaler, by own transport nationally

16 ↔ **Hollington Nurseries Ltd**
Woolton Hill, Newbury, Berkshire RG15 9XT
Tel: 0635 253908
Contact: J Hopkinson

Curry plant — A wide range of culinary herbs including bergamot, curry plant and lovage.
Ⓒ Undisclosed Mar-May, Sep-Nov
Ⓓ By arrangement

16 ↔ **Iden Croft Herb Farm**
Frittenden Road, Staplehurst, Kent TN12 0DH
Tel: 0580 891432
Contact: Rosemary Titterington

Primrose
Marigold — Range of over thirty fresh cut culinary herbs available in small and large volume by kilo weight or in catering packs. Edible flowers a speciality including primrose, elderflower, marigold, nasturtium, mallow and violet. Also available, trimmed and pre-chopped parsley and coriander.
Ⓒ Any quantity herbs with prior notice throughout year, flower packs Apr-Oct
Ⓦ Kenya Veg, Spitalfield 01 377 8813, Greenhill Mushrooms, Covent Garden 01 720 8681
Ⓓ By wholesaler, by Datapost, by Securicor
See Also: Fresh Salads

16 ○ ↔ **Island Country Farms**
Asheybrook, Ashey, Ryde, Isle of Wight PO33 4AT
Tel: 0983 65686
Contact: Mr J H Fisher

Herbs — Range of potted and cut herbs.
Ⓒ Undisclosed
Ⓓ By arrangement
See Also: Fresh Meat, Poultry Producers, Milk, Fresh Fruit, Fresh Salads, Fresh Vegetables

12 ●

Jekka's Herb Farm
Rose Cottage, Shellards Lane, Alveston, nr Bristol, Somerset BS12 2SY
Tel: 0454 418878
Contact: Jekka McVicar

Good King Henry

Over three hundred varieties of organically grown fresh herbs and edible leaves including good King Henry, dandelion, lemon, purple, sweet and bush basil, Chinese chives, bucklers leaf and French sorrel, nasturtium and heartsease in 3½, 4¼" pots packed in trays of twenty.
Ⓒ Undisclosed Mar-Sep
Ⓓ By arrangement

10 ↔

Lighthorne Associates
Moreton Morrell, Warwick, Warwickshire CV35 9DB
Tel: 0926 651426 Telx: 317356
Contact: Mrs Anne Turner

Chives

Range of fresh herbs including dill, mint, chives, sorrel, lovage and thyme supplied cold chained packed to customers requirements.
Ⓒ 500kg p.mth
Ⓓ By arrangement

8 ● ↔

Lowfield Organic Growers
Lowfield, Exelby, Bedale, North Yorkshire
Tel: 0677 23166
Contact: Chris Holbrey

Greek cress

Twenty varieties of organically grown fresh herbs including Greek cress and seven varieties of basil.
Ⓒ Undisclosed
Ⓓ By arrangement
See Also: Fresh Salads, Fresh Vegetables

10

Malvern View Herbs
Malvern View, Longdon Hill End, Upton-On-Severn, Worcester WR8 0RN
Tel: 06846 2581
Contact: S Lawley

Chervil

Range of fresh, hand cut herbs including dill, sweet and purple basil, French tarragon, chervil, coriander, Italian mint, sorrel and salad burnet.
Ⓒ Dill 80kg p.mth May-Oct, Basil 20kg p.mth Jun-Sep, French tarragon 40kg p.mth Mar-Sep
Ⓓ By arrangement

10 ↔

Meadowsweet Herbs
The Castle, Upton Bishop, Ross-on-Wye, Herefordshire
Tel: 0989 85215 Fax: 0989 64043
Contact: Mr James Lambe

Thyme

Range of organic herbs including parsley, mint, chives, dill, thyme and rosemary supplied washed, chopped and frozen in bulk.
[C] Undisclosed
[D] By arrangement

14 ● ↔

Netherfield Herbs
37 Nether Street, Rougham, nr Bury St Edmunds, Suffolk IP30 9LW
Tel: 0359 70452
Contact: Ms Lesley Bremness

Orach

Over one hundred varieties of herb plants, cut herbs or salad herbs including purple and gold orach, purslane, rocket, salad burnet and chervil.
[C] Undisclosed
[D] By arrangement

7 ● ↔

Oakcroft Gardens
Oakcroft Gardens, Cross o' th' Hill, Malpas, Cheshire SY14 8DH
Tel: 0948 860213
Contact: Ms M S Fardonji

Buckler leaf sorrel

Range of organic fresh herbs including basil, coriander, buckler leaf sorrel and chives.
[C] Undisclosed
[D] By arrangement
See Also: Fresh Fruit, Fresh Vegetables

16 ○ ↔

Park Hill Produce & Appledore Salads
Park Hill, Appledore, Ashford, Kent TN26 2BJ
Tel: 023 383201
Contact: Mr Smith

Coriander
Fennel

Organically grown chives, coriander, dill, fennel, mint and sorrel.
[C] Undisclosed Apr-Oct
[D] By arrangement
See Also: Game Farmers, Fresh Salads, Fresh Vegetables

10 ↔

Paul Taylor (Garden Supplies)
Woodstock, Cottage Lane, Whitacre Heath, Coleshill, Birmingham BH6 2EJ
Tel: 0675 62136/81578
Contact: Mr Paul Taylor

Chervil

Range of herbs including sorrel, lovage, purslane, coriander and summer savory. Also elderflower, calendula and nasturtium flowers supplied for garnish.
[C] Undisclosed, sorrel, lovage Apr-Nov, chervil Jun onwards
[D] By arrangement
See Also: Fresh Salads, Fresh Vegetables

10 ○ ↔

Pilgrims Herbs
Gate House Farm, Dinedor Cross, Herefordshire HR2 6PF
Tel: 0432 73382
Contact: Mr Neil Morris

Italian parsley

Range of fresh culinary herbs including basil, sorrel, bronze fennel, dill, Italian parsley, rosemary and tarragon.
[C] Undisclosed
[D] By arrangement

1 ○ ↔

Poyntzfield Herb Nursery
Black Isle, by Dingwall, Ross & Cromarty IV7 8LX
Tel: 03818 352
Contact: Duncan Ross

Lemon verbena

Over three hundred varieties of organically grown herbs including Greek oregano, French tarragon, lemon verbena, saffron, ginseng, liquorice, oyster plant, Scots oregano and Scots lovage.
[C] Undisclosed
[D] By arrangement

11 ● ↔

Pre Emma Herbs
The Loke, Ipswich Road, Newtown Flotman, Norwich, Norfolk NO15 1PN
Tel: 0508 470768
Contact: Mr Brinkman

Pineapple sage — Range of thirty organic fresh culinary herbs including basil, oregano, dill, fennel, bronze fennel and pineapple sage supplied cut in 1kg packs or trays.
[C] Undisclosed
[D] By arrangement

3 ○ ↔

Scotherbs
Waterybutts, Grange by Errol, Perth PH2 7SZ
Tel: 08212 228
Contact: Stanley Turner

Angelica — Over eighty varieties of herbs including chives, coriander, mint and thyme supplied by the gram. Also herb plants including angelica, fennel and sorrel.
[C] Undisclosed May-Oct
[D] By arrangement

7

Sellet Hall Herbs
Sellet Hall, Whittington, Carnforth, Lancashire LA6 2QF
Tel: 0468 71288
Contact: Mrs Judy Gray

Applemint — Wide variety of cut culinary herbs including applemint, garlic chives and sweet marjoram with an extended season due to heated greenhouse.
[C] Undisclosed Mar-Dec
[D] By arrangement

16 ↔

R & G Stevens
Lucas Green Nurseries, West End, Woking, Surrey GU24 9LY
Tel: 04867 4041/88011 Telx: 859818
Herbs G
Contact: Sales Office

Tarragon — Range of over twenty herbs including chives, basil, sorrel and tarragon in bunched or pre-packed form.
[C] Undisclosed
[W] Stand 2, Growers Pavilion, New Covent Garden Market 01 720 6990
[D] By wholesaler

9

Vin Sullivan of Abergavenny
Triley Mill, Abergavenny, Gwent NP7 8DE
Tel: 0873 2331
Contact: Mr John Sullivan

Herbs — Range of fresh local herbs.
[C] Undisclosed
[D] By own transport nationally
See Also: Fish Dealers, Fresh Fruit, Fresh Vegetables, Fungi

15 ↔

Welcombe Country Fayre
Darracott Farm, Welcombe, nr Bideford, Devon EX39 6HG
Tel: 028 883322
Contact: Sally Hollis

Sorrel

Range of fresh cut herbs including parsley, mint, chives, oregano, sage, rosemary, thyme and sorrel. Also supplied mixed herb packs containing three herbs to complement pasta, fish, poultry, salad or red meats, in overwrapped trays or in 4, 8oz packs for freezing. Dried herbs also available.
C 400 trays p.mth, seasonal herbs May-Sep
D By arrangement

14 ○ ↔

Westhall Herbs
Church Lane, Westhall, nr Halesworth, Suffolk IP19 8NU
Tel: 050279 646
Contact: Mildred Durne

Evening primrose

Variety of herbs including rocket, coriander, evening primrose and oregano, in 3½″ pots. Minimum order 100 pots.
C Each variety 100 pots p.mth Apr-Oct
D By arrangement

8 ↔

Yorkshire Herbs
The Herb Centre, Middleton Tyas, Richmond, North Yorkshire DL10 6RR
Tel: 0325 77 686
Contact: Mr Ron Elvidge

Sorrel

Range of fresh cut herbs including basil, chives, mint, rosemary, sorrel and thyme. All available in over-wrapped polystyrene trays or bunched to customers requirements.
C Undisclosed
D By arrangement

FRESH SALADS

15

C & L Barter (Golden Springs)
Waddock, Dorchester, Dorset DT2 8QX
Tel: 0305 852203 Fax: 0305 853880
Contact: Mr Charles Barter

Watercress

Watercress grown in spring water pumped from Dorset sub-strata, supplied fresh or packed with ice.
C Undisclosed
D By arrangement

10 ↔

Blackdown Growers
Bericote Road, Leamington Spa, Warwickshire CV32 6QP
Tel: 0926 20170
Contact: Simon Cox

Chinese cabbage

Chinese cabbage and range of lettuce including radicchio, oak leaf, little gem, endive and escarole packed in trays to customers requirements.
C Chinese cabbage Jun-Dec, lettuce Apr-Nov
D By own transport within area

7 ●

Blairs
Low Carr Nursery, Head Dyke Lane, Pilling, nr Preston, Lancashire PR3 6SJ
Tel: 0253 790471
Contact: Mrs P Blair

Florence fennel

Organically grown tomatoes, cucumber, lettuce, celery, yellow, white and green peppers, and Florence fennel.
C Undisclosed
D By own transport within area
See Also: Fresh Vegetables

14 ● ↔

Calluna Farm Products
Lodge Road, Hollesley, Woodbridge, Suffolk
Tel: 0394 411927
Contact: Mrs Helen Douglas

Tomato
Cucumber

Organically grown tomatoes and cucumber with small quantities of lettuce, radishes and spring onions.
C Tomatoes 400-500lb p.wk Jun-mid Oct, cucumber 400-500lb p.wk Jun-mid Oct
D By arrangement
See Also: Eggs, Cheese

11 ● ↔

Chevelswarde Organic Growers
Chevel House, The Belt, South Kilworth, nr Lutterworth, Leicestershire LE17 6DX
Tel: 085 881309
Contact: Mrs R Daltry

Wallop lettuce

Organically grown salad varieties including wallop lettuce, a cos and flat lettuce cross, and curly endive.
C Endive Apr-Oct
D By arrangement

7 ●

Coopers Organic Growers
Great Knowley, 139 Blackburn Road, Chorley, Lancashire PR6 8TH
Tel: 02572 64458
Contact: Mr Cooper

Lolla rossa

Range of fresh organic lettuce including lolla rossa, lolla bionda. Also Japanese salad leaves.
C Undisclosed
D By arrangement
See Also: Fresh Fruit, Fresh Herbs, Fresh Vegetables

12 ↔

M J Davison
Ploddy House, Newent, Gloucestershire GL18 1JX
Tel: 0531 820 240/488
Contact: M J Davison

Oak leaf lettuce

Variety of lettuce including oak leaf and red lettuce. Also endive and radicchio.
C Undisclosed, red lettuce Jun-Oct, endive May-Jan, radicchio Jun-Jan
D By arrangement

3 ○ ↔

East Wind Ltd
Unit 1/10 St Mary's Workshop, Henderson Street, Leith, Edinburgh
Tel: 031 553 6850
Contact: Ian Dunn

Alfalfa sprouts

Alfalfa sprouts supplied plain or in spicy mix with radish and celery seed.
[C] 1000lb p.wk
[W] Ambrosia Whole Foods 0224 648810
[D] By wholesaler, by arrangement

15 ● ↔

The Gardens
The Gardens, Buckland-in-the-Moor, Ashburton, Devon TQ13 7HN
Tel: 0364 53169
Contact: Charles Staniland

Butterhead lettuce

Range of organically grown fresh salads including red lettuce, butterhead, crisphead, endive, lolla rossa and rocket.
[C] 100 plants p.mth
[D] By arrangement
See Also: Fresh Fruit, Fresh Herbs, Fresh Vegetables

16 ●

Garlands Organic Farmshop
Garlands Farm, Gardeners Lane, Upper Basildon, nr Reading, Berkshire RG8 8LN
Tel: 0491 671556
Contact: Mr C Raymont

Red oak lettuce

Range of fresh organic lettuce including red oak, webbs, little gem and green oak.
[C] Undisclosed Jun-Oct
[D] By arrangement
See Also: Fresh Fruit, Fresh Vegetables

3

Gowrie Growers/Scot Herb Growery
Waterybutts Farm, Grange, Errol, Perthshire
Tel: 082 12228
Contact: Robbie Wilson

Quatro stagioni

Range of lettuce including oak leaf, lolla rossa, lolla bionda, quatro stagioni. Also curly endive.
[C] Undisclosed Jun-Oct
[D] By arrangement
See Also: Fresh Vegetables

16 ● ↔

Home Grown Salads
River House, Stour Street, Canterbury, Kent CT1 2PA
Tel: 0227 67989 Telx: 96201 APS
Contact: Graham Ward

Cherry tomatoes

Little gem lettuce and gardeners delight cherry tomatoes. Herbs also available.
[C] Little gem lettuce Apr-Dec, cherry tomatoes Jul-Oct
[D] By arrangement
See Also: Fresh Vegetables

16 ↔

Iden Croft Herb Farm
Frittenden Road, Staplehurst, Kent TN12 0DH
Tel: 0580 891432
Contact: Rosemary Titterington

Mixed leaf pack

Mixed salad leaf packs including red oak, claytonia, purslane and red orache, grown to demand with packs made up to customers requirements, with or without edible flowers.
[C] Undisclosed Apr-Oct
[W] Kenya Veg, Spitalfield 01 377 8813, Greenhill Mushrooms, Covent Garden 01 720 8681
[D] By wholesaler, by Datapost, by Securicor
See Also: Fresh Herbs

16 ○ ↔

Island Country Farms
Asheybrook, Ashey, Ryde, Isle of Wight PO33 4AT
Tel: 0983 65686
Contact: Mr J H Fisher

Salad produce

Organically grown salad produce.
[C] Undisclosed
[D] By arrangement
See Also: Fresh Meat, Poultry Producers, Milk, Fresh Fruit, Fresh Herbs, Fresh Vegetables

11 ↔

Jack Buck Growers
Oak House Coldstores, Holbeach Bank, Spalding, Lincolnshire PE12 8BL
Tel: 0406 22615
Contact: Tony Ringrok

Chicory

Varieties of chicory available all year. Also small quantities of shallots and celeriac.
[C] Chicory 20,000lb p.wk
[D] By arrangement

8 ● ↔

Lowfield Organic Growers
Lowfield, Exelby, Bedale, North Yorkshire
Tel: 0677 23166
Contact: Chris Holbrey

Misticanza

Range of organically grown fresh lettuce including red, red lotto, green lotto, oakleaf. Also batavian endive, rocket, purslane, radicchio, edible flowers and Misticanza, a blend of herbs, salads and flowers.
[C] Misticanza May-Oct, purslane Apr-Nov
[D] By arrangement
See Also: Fresh Herbs, Fresh Vegetables

11 ●

Mangreen Gardens
Mangreen, Swardeston, Norwich, Norfolk NR14 8DP
Tel: 0508 70444
Contact: Mr William Duffield

Radicchio

Fresh organic salads including spring and winter lettuce, rocket and a range of chicory including radicchio.
[C] Undisclosed chicory Nov-Mar
[D] By arrangement
See Also: Fresh Vegetables

16 ○ ↔

Manor Farm Pantry
Alresford Watercress Ltd, Manor Farm, Old Alresford, Hampshire SO24 9DH
Tel: 0962 734230
Contact: J R Bevan

Watercress

Watercress organically grown in spring water.
C Undisclosed
D By arrangement
See Also: Soups

15 ●

Meadows Farm Organic Produce
c/o 15 Victoria Grove, Bridport, Dorset DT6 3AD
Tel: 0308 24839
Contact: R F Williams

Fennel

Range of organically grown fresh salads including little gem, cos, round lettuce and fennel.
C Undisclosed Jun-Sep
D By arrangement
See Also: Fresh Vegetables

15 ●

Moorfoot Organic Garden
Woodland Road, Denbury, nr Newton Abbot, Devon
Tel: 0803 862499
Contact: Linda Phelps

Iceberg

Range of organic fresh lettuce including butterhead, iceberg, cos, lolla rossa and salad bowl. Also mizuna, chicory, endive, fennel and chickweed.
C Undisclosed
D By arrangement
See Also: Fresh Vegetables

16 ○ ↔

Park Hill Produce & Appledore Salads
Park Hill, Appledore, Ashford, Kent TN26 2BJ
Tel: 023 383201
Contact: Mr Smith

Mizuna

Organically grown mizuna, rocket, endives, shungiku and a range of cress and lettuce.
C Undisclosed
D By arrangement
See Also: Game Farmers, Fresh Herbs, Fresh Vegetables

10 ↔

Paul Taylor (Garden Supplies)
Woodstock, Cottage Lane, Whitacre Heath, Coleshill, Birmingham BH6 2EJ
Tel: 0675 62136/81578
Contact: Mr Paul Taylor

Lamb's lettuce

Range of continental lettuce including red leaf, endive, salad bowl and lambs lettuce.
C Undisclosed, red leaf lettuce, salad bowl Jun-Nov, endive Jun-Dec, lambs lettuce Oct-Feb
D By arrangement
See Also: Fresh Herbs, Fresh Vegetables

13 ●

Rosehaven
110 Cinques Road, Gamlingay, Sandy, Bedfordshire SG19 3NR
Tel: 0767 50142
Contact: Eleanor Hodges

Lettuce

Organically grown early lettuce.
C Undisclosed Mar-May
W Natural Foods Ltd, London
D By wholesaler, by arrangement
See Also: Poultry Producers, Fresh Vegetables

14 ↔

Samford Agriculture
The Bramleys, Burstall, Ipswich, Suffolk IP8 3DN
Tel: 047387 402
Contact: Mrs Seinet

Radicchio

Varieties of salad including radicchio, corn salad and red lettuce produced in relatively small quantities.
C Undisclosed, radicchio Jul-spring, corn salad autumn-winter
D By own transport within area
See Also: Fresh Vegetables

12 ● ↔

Somerset Organic Producers
Wyvern Farms, Seavington St Michael, Ilminster, Somerset TA19 OPZ
Tel: 0460 42149
Contact: Mr R Vernon-Dier

Endive

Organically grown salads including red lettuce, merveille, broad and curly endive.
C Flat lettuce 100 doz p.mth Jun-Sep, cos 100 doz p.mth Jun-Sep
D By arrangement
See Also: Fresh Vegetables

14 ↔

M D & S C Spindler
12 Ipswich Road, Newbourn, Woodbridge, Suffolk IP12 4NS
Tel: 047336 651
Contact: Mr M D Spindler

Lettuce

Glasshouse grown round lettuce in boxes of twelve. Also cucumber and tomatoes.
C Lettuce 6000 boxes Dec-Apr
D By arrangement
See Also: Fresh Vegetables

13 ● ↔

Stoneybridge Organic Nursery
Stoneybridge Organic Nursery, Tywardreath, Par, Cornwall PL27 2TY
Tel: 0726 813858
Contact: Mr D R Pascoe

Florence fennel

Range of fresh, organic salads including chicory, beef, yellow and cherry tomatoes and Florence fennel.
C Undisclosed
D By arrangement
See Also: Fresh Fruit, Fresh Vegetables

11

R J Watts
South Fen Farm, Bourne, Lincolnshire PE10 0DN
Tel: 077589 231
Contact: R J Watts

Celery — Fresh, self-blanched and trenched celery available chilled, washed or prepared as petioles.
[C] Self-blanched celery 25,000 doz Jul-Nov, trenched celery 30,000 doz Nov-Jan
[D] By arrangement
See Also: Fresh Vegetables

15 ●

Western House Organic Fruit Farm
Western House, Totnes, Devon
Tel: 0803 862066
Contact: Charles Riggs

Radicchio — Organically grown chillis and radicchio.
[C] Radicchio 200-250lb Aug-Dec
[D] By arrangement
See Also: Fresh Fruit, Fresh Vegetables

FRESH VEGETABLES

10 ↔

Aconbury Sprouts
Unit 4c, Gooses Foot Industrial Estate, Kingstone, Hereford & Worcester
Tel: 0981 251016
Contact: Mike Booth

Alfalfa sprouts — Range of fresh bean sprouts including alfalfa, mung, aduki beans, chick peas and lentils in 4, 8oz bags and 1-4lb catering packs.
[C] 2000 packs p.wk
[W] Mack & White, 021 622 4111 Peter Watson, 0272 773338
[D] By wholesaler

7 ●

Blairs
Low Carr Nursery, Head Dyke Lane, Pilling, nr Preston, Lancashire PR3 6SJ
Tel: 0253 790471
Contact: Mrs P Blair

Courgettes — Organically grown carrots, early potatoes, courgettes, leeks and onions.
[C] Undisclosed
[D] By own transport within area
See Also: Fresh Salads

16 ●

Boathouse Farm Organic Produce
Isfield, nr Uckfield, East Sussex TN22 5TY
Tel: 082575 302
Contact: Hamilton Hill

King Edward potato — Organically grown King Edward potatoes.
[C] 18 ton Oct-Mar
[D] By arrangement
See Also: Fresh Meat, Eggs, Millers

16 ↔

Breach Farm Courgettes
Breach Farm, Cranbrook, Kent TN17 2LJ
Tel: 0580 714124
Contact: G and B Robertson

Squashes — Winter and summer squash, and round courgettes with a nutty flavour. Also available courgette flowers in trays to order.
[C] Round courgettes 200 trays p.dy, summer squash 50 trays p.dy
[D] By arrangement

3 ● ↔

Cambo/Sir D Erskine & Ptrs
Cambo, Kingsbarns, St Andrews, Fife KY16 8QD
Tel: 0333 50313
Contact: Peter Erskine

Pentland Hawk potato — Organically grown pentland hawk potatoes.
[C] Undisclosed Oct-Nov
[D] By arrangement

7 ●

Coopers Organic Growers
Great Knowley, 139 Blackburn Road, Chorley, Lancashire PR6 8TH
Tel: 02572 64458
Contact: Mr Cooper

Jerusalem artichoke — Range of fresh organic vegetables including pink fir apple, red craig royal and golden wonder potatoes, courgette flowers and red Jerusalem artichokes.
[C] : Undisclosed
[D] : By arrangement
See Also: Fresh Fruit, Fresh Herbs, Fresh Salads

14

Eros Asparagus
Kenny Hill, Mildenhall, Suffolk IP28 8DS
Tel: 035 375 394
Contact: Mrs C A Sore

Asparagus

Asparagus.
C Undisclosed, asparagus May-Jun, asparagus crowns Oct-Apr
D By arrangement

2 ○ ↔

Fieldfare Organic Growers
Burnside Farm, Mosstowie, Elgin, Moray, Grampian
Tel: 034385 237
Contact: David Benson

Swiss chard

Organically grown range of vegetables including Swiss chard and curly kale.
C Undisclosed
D By arrangement

15 ● ↔

The Gardens
Buckland-in-the-Moor, Ashburton, Devon TQ13 7HN
Tel: 0364 53169
Contact: Charles Staniland

Courgettes

Organically grown courgettes and tomatoes.
C 40-50x12lb boxes p.mth Jun-Oct
D By arrangement
See Also: Fresh Fruit, Fresh Herbs, Fresh Salads

16 ●

Garlands Organic Farmshop
Garlands Farm, Gardeners Lane, Upper Basildon, nr Reading, Berkshire RG8 8LN
Tel: 0491 671556
Contact: Mr C Raymont

Chard

Range of organically grown fresh vegetables including carrots, beetroot and chard.
C Undisclosed Jul-Oct
D By arrangement
See Also: Fresh Fruit, Fresh Salads

16 ○

Garrard Organic Farm
Sky Farm, Swife Lane, Broadoak, nr Heathfield, Sussex BN21 8UR
Tel: 0435 882167
Contact: Mr R Garrard

French beans

Range of vegetables including early broad beans and late French beans.
C French beans undisclosed end Sep, broad beans 250lb end May
D By arrangement

3

Gowrie Growers/Scot Herb Growery
Waterybutts Farm, Grange, Errol, Perthshire
Tel: 082 12228
Contact: Robbie Wilson

Calabrese

Range of fresh vegetables including celeriac, kohlrabi, mange-tout, baby leeks, pak choi and calabrese.
C Leeks Jun-Oct, calabrese Sep-Oct
D By arrangement
See Also: Fresh Salads

15 ●

Graeme Fisk
The Granary, Prinkle Farm, Bodle Street, Hailsham, East Sussex BN27 4YD
Tel: 0323 833541
Contact: Graeme Fisk

Spinach

Organically grown cabbage, spinach, runner beans, parsley and swede.
C Cabbage 2000lb Jun-Aug, spinach 1000lb Jul-Nov, runner beans 2 ton Aug-Sep, parsley 200lb Jul-Dec, swede 1 ton Nov-Dec
D By arrangement
See Also: Fresh Fruit

10 ● ↔

Green Acres Organic Growers
Green Acres, Dinmore, Hereford HR4 8ED
Tel: 056884 7045
Contact: David Jenkins

.Sugar snap peas

Organically grown range of vegetables including celeriac, sugar snap peas, broad beans, calabrese, desiree potatoes, runner beans and sweet corn.
C Broad beans 30 cwt p.mth Jun-Aug, calabrese 600 p.mth Jul-Oct, runner beans 40 cwt p.mth Aug-Oct, potatoes 1 ton p.mth Jul-Mar, sweet corn 500 p.mth Sep-Oct
D By arrangement
See Also: Fresh Meat

12 ●

Hardwick Organic Gardens
Flat 2 The Ridgeway, Hardwick Estates, Whitchurch on Thames, Pangbourne, Oxfordshire RG 7RB
Tel: 07357 5224
Contact: Iain Tolhurst

Bunched carrots

Range of fresh organically grown vegetables including brassicas, bunched carrots, brussel sprouts,and cabbage. Also available strawberries.
C Potatoes Jul-Nov
D : By arrangement

14

Hassy
PO Box 11, Soham, Cambridgeshire CB7 5XO
Tel: 0353 720027 Telx: 81480 Fax: 0353 723112
Contact: Jane Garrod

Asparagus
Celery

Range of vegetables including mange-tout, beans, asparagus, courgettes, celery, leeks, baking potatoes, carrots, onions and red beet.
C Celery Jul-Dec, leeks Jul-May, asparagus May-Jun, carrots Jun-Apr
D By own transport nationally

15 ● **Haygrove Honey Farm**
Twyford, Shaftesbury, Dorset SP7 OJF
Tel: 0747 811855
Contact: John Davies

Courgettes
Sweetcorn

Variety of organically grown vegetables including broad beans, French beans, courgettes, sweetcorn, leeks, globe artichokes and cherry tomatoes.
Ⓒ Beans 25kg p.mth Jun-Sep, courgettes 50kg p.mth Jul-Sep, sweetcorn 100 p.mth Aug-Sep, leeks 25Kg p.mth Jun-Jan, globe artichokes 50 p.mth Aug
Ⓓ By own transport within area
See Also: Fresh Herbs, Honey

8 ○ ↔ **R Holmes & Sons**
West House Farm, Birstwith, Harrogate, North Yorkshire HG3 3AW
Tel: 0423 770200
Contact: Mr I Holmes

Broccoli

Organically grown broad beans, peas, broccoli, cauliflower, courgettes, potatoes.
Ⓒ Undisclosed
Ⓓ By arrangement
See Also: Fresh Meat, Fresh Fruit

16 ● ↔ **Home Grown Salads**
River House, Stour Street, Canterbury, Kent CT1 2PA
Tel: 0227 67989 Telx: 96201 APS
Contact: Graham Ward

Summer squash

Summer and winter squash.
Ⓒ Summer squash Jun-Oct, Winter squash Oct-Feb
Ⓓ By arrangement
See Also: Fresh Salads

14 ○ ↔ **A & K Hood**
The Stables, Gresham, Norfolk NR11 8AD
Tel: 026377 468
Contact: Mr Hood

Kohlrabi
Jerusalem artichoke

Organically grown vegetables including Jerusalem artichoke, globe artichoke, kohlrabi and calabrese. Also lettuce
Ⓒ 40-60lb p.mth of each in season, lettuce 20lb p.mth
Ⓓ By arrangement
See Also: Fresh Meat, Poultry Producers, Cheese, Jams and Preserves

16 ○ ↔ **Island Country Farms**
Asheybrook, Ashey, Ryde, Isle of Wight PO33 4AT
Tel: 0983 65686
Contact: Mr J H Fisher

Marrow

Organically grown vegetables including marrow, courgettes, aubergines and potatoes.
Ⓒ Undisclosed
Ⓓ By arrangement
See Also: Fresh Meat, Poultry Producers, Milk, Fresh Fruit, Fresh Herbs, Fresh Salads

16 ↔ **Kingcob Garlic**
Mersley Farms, Newchurch, Sandown, Isle of Wight PO36 ONR
Tel: 0983 865229 Telx: 86748
Contact: Colin Boswell

Garlic

Fresh peeled and unpeeled garlic, sweet corn, bunched carrots and asparagus.
Ⓒ Fresh peeled garlic 150 ton Aug-Dec
Ⓓ By arrangement

12 ↔ **The Kitchen Garden**
Old Down House, Tockington, Bristol BS12 4PG
Tel: 0454 413605
Contact: Robert Bernays

Sugar snap peas
Mange-tout

Sugar snap peas, mange-tout and sweet corn. Also range of salads, herbs, soft and top fruit.
Ⓒ Undisclosed
Ⓓ By own transport within area
See Also: Jams and Preserves, Ice Creams and Sorbets

16 ● **Laines Organic Farm**
Laines Farm, 47 Newberry Lane, Cuckfield, West Sussex
Tel: 0444 452663
Contact: Mr Farber

Squash

Range of over twenty five fresh organic vegetables including mange-tout, sugar snap peas, broad and French beans, broccoli, spinach, leeks, beetroot, onions and eight varieties of pumpkin and winter squash - red peni, green hoilraedo, butternut, green chestnut and ebony acorn.
Ⓒ Undisclosed squash Aug-Dec
Ⓓ By arrangement

8 ● ↔ **Lowfield Organic Growers**
Lowfield, Exelby, Bedale, North Yorkshire
Tel: 0677 23166
Contact: Chris Holbrey

Mitsuka
Pak choi

Range of organically grown fresh Japanese greens including mizuna, pak choi and mitsuka. Also available courgette flowers in season.
Ⓒ Undisclosed
Ⓓ By arrangement
See Also: Fresh Herbs, Fresh Salads

16 ○ **Lympne Market Garden**
Garden House, Lympne Place, Lympne, Kent CT21 4PA
Tel: 0303 66183
Contact: Mr Fairley

Runner beans

Organically grown moneymaker tomatoes, runner and climbing French beans, courgettes, and bambi and China rose radishes.
Ⓒ Undisclosed Mar-Feb
Ⓓ By arrangement
See Also: Milk, Fresh Fruit

3 ↔

Macfarlane Brothers
South Melville Farm, Lasswade, Midlothian
EH18 1AN
Tel: 031 663 8038
Contact: Mr Colin Macfarlane

Parsnips
Spinach

Range of vegetables including broccoli spears, green, red, white and savoy cabbage, cauliflower, carrots, parsnips, spinach, leeks, swede, sprouts and turnips. Also red, continental and iceberg lettuce.
C Undisclosed
D By own transport within area and by arrangement

11 ●

Mangreen Gardens
Mangreen, Swardeston, Norwich, Norfolk
NR14 8DP
Tel: 0508 70444
Contact: Mr William Duffield

Kale

Range of fresh organic vegetables including mange-tout, peas, early carrots and kale.
C Undisclosed
D By arrangement
See Also: Fresh Salads

10 ↔

R D McGuffie & Son
New Farm, Elmhursts, Lichfield,
Staffordshire WS13 8EX
Tel: 0543 263756
Contact: S A McGuffie

Asparagus

Limbras asparagus.
C 6 ton p.mth May-Jun
D By arrangement
See Also: Fresh Fruit

15 ●

Meadows Farm Organic Produce
c/o 15 Victoria Grove, Bridport, Dorset
DT6 3AD
Tel: 0308 24839
Contact: R F Williams

Courgettes

Range of organically grown fresh vegetables including peas, beans, courgettes and carrots.
C Undisclosed Jul-Sep
D By arrangement
See Also: Fresh Salads

12

Millets Farm & Crabtree Pick Your Own
Millets Farm, Garford, Abingdon,
Oxfordshire OX13 5PD
Tel: 0865 391555
Contact: Mr J L Carter

Pick your own

Pick your own fresh vegetables in season.
C Undisclosed
D By arrangement
See Also: Apples

15 ●

Moorfoot Organic Garden
Woodland Road, Denbury, nr Newton
Abbot, Devon
Tel: 0803 862499
Contact: Linda Phelps

Calabrese

Range of organic fresh vegetables including pepper, sweetcorn, courgettes, calabrese and garlic.
C Undisclosed
D By arrangement
See Also: Fresh Salads

15 ● ↔

J Morrish Farm Shop
East Acland, Landkey, Barnstaple, Devon
EX32 OLD
Tel: 0271 830216
Contact: Mrs J Morrish

Pentland dell potato

Organically grown potatoes including pentland dell, pentland ivories, majestic, desiree and maris piper.
C Undisclosed Sep-Jul
D By arrangement
See Also: Fresh Meat

12 ●

M Murray
Berwick Lodge, Station Road, Henbury,
Bristol, Avon BS10 7TD
Tel: 0272 506742
Contact: Mr M Murray

Onions

Range of fresh organic vegetables including carrots, onions and runner beans.
C Undisclosed
D By arrangement
See Also: Fresh Fruit

14 ↔

Norfolk Country
Roubham Farm, East Marling, Norwich
Norfolk NR2 6BT
Tel: 0953 718135
Contact: Mr J L Nelstrop

Asparagus

Range of vegetables including twelve varieties of asparagus, onions and potatoes.
C Asparagus 45,000lb Apr-Jun
D By arrangement

7 ● ↔

Oakcroft Gardens
Oakcroft Gardens, Cross o' th' Hill,
Malpas, Cheshire SY14 8DH
Tel: 0948 860213
Contact: Ms M S Fardonji

Mange-tout

Range of fresh organic vegetables including courgettes, French beans, mange-tout, peas and beetroot.
C Undisclosed
D By arrangement
See Also: Fresh Fruit, Fresh Herbs

14

Olivers Orchard
Olivers Lane, Colchester, Essex CO2 0HH
Tel: 0206 330208
Contact: Mr R M Knowles

Squash
Pumpkin

Squash and pumpkin available.
C Undisclosed
D By arrangement
See Also: Apples, Fresh Fruit

11 ●

T D Organ
East Farm, Normanby-by-Stow,
Gainsborough, Lincolnshire DN21 5LQ
Tel: 0427 788629
Contact: Dr T D Organ

Marrow
Beetroot

Organically grown vegetables including cabbages, carrots, runner beans, marrow and beetroot.
[C] Undisclosed
[D] By arrangement
See Also: Fresh Meat

9 ● ↔

Organic Farm Foods (Wales)
Unit 25, Lampeter Industrial Estate,
Lampeter, Dyfed SA48 8LT
Tel: 0570 423099
Contact: Peter Segger

Potatoes
Carrots

Range of organic vegetables including potatoes, carrots, spinach and courgettes.
[C] Potatoes 100 ton p.a, carrots 200 ton Oct-Mar
[D] By own transport within area
See Also: Fresh Fruit

12

Over Farm Market
Over, Gloucester GL2 8DB
Tel: 0452 21014
Contact: Rob Keene

Pumpkin
Squash

Varieties of squashes and pumpkins including scallopini, butternut and acorn. Also white sweetcorn, broad beans, courgettes, swedes and potatoes.
[C] Undisclosed broad beans Jun-Jul, white sweetcorn Aug-Oct
[D] By arrangement

12

Oxford Pick Your Own Farm
Hill Farm, Elsfield, Oxfordshire OX3 SW9
Tel: 086735 618 Fax: 086735 463
Contact: Peter Clarke

Shallot
Fennel

Range of pick your own fresh vegetables including mange-tout, baby carrots, fennel, sweetcorn, beetroot, shallots and swiss chard. Also pink fir apple potatoes available ready bagged.
[C] Undisclosed Jun-Nov
[D] By arrangement
See Also: Fresh Fruit

16 ◯ ↔

Park Hill Produce & Appledore Salads
Park Hill, Appledore, Ashford, Kent TN26 2BJ
Tel: 023 383201
Contact: Mr Smith

Baby turnips

Organically grown miniature carrots, leeks, beetroot and turnips especially for the restaurant trade.
Ⓒ Undisclosed
Ⓓ By arrangement
See Also: Game Farmers, Fresh Herbs, Fresh Salads

10 ↔

Paul Taylor (Garden Supplies)
Woodstock, Cottage Lane, Whitacre Heath, Coleshill, Birmingham BH6 2EJ
Tel: 0675 62136/81578
Contact: Mr Paul Taylor

Baby courgettes

Flowering baby courgettes, baby carrots and turnips and mange-tout.
Ⓒ Undisclosed, mange-tout Jul-Nov
Ⓓ By arrangement
See Also: Fresh Herbs, Fresh Salads

9

Pengelli Organic Growers
Pengelli, Hebron, Whitland, Dyfed SA34 OJX
Tel: 09947 481
Contact: Ms Chris Chaloner

Spinach

Range of organically grown fresh vegetables available all year, including courgettes, spinach, spring onions and beetroot.
Ⓒ Undisclosed
Ⓓ By arrangement

10 ● ↔

Pimhill
Lea Hall, Harmer Hill, Shrewsbury, Shropshire SY4 3DY
Tel: 0939 290342
Contact: Ginny Mayall

Swede
Carrots

Organically grown vegetables including potatoes, parsnips, beetroot, carrots and swedes.
Ⓒ Potatoes 20 ton p.mth, carrots 1 ton p.mth, swedes 1 ton p.mth Oct-Mar, parsnips and beetroot 1 ton p.mth
Ⓓ By own transport nationally for quantities of over 1 ton, by arrangement
See Also: Fresh Meat, Millers

14 ●

Poplar Farm Organic Vegetables
Poplar Farm, Silverleys Green, Cratfield, Halesworth, Suffolk
Tel: 037986 241
Contact: Anthony Gaze

Japanese pumpkin

Organically grown Japanese pumpkins including red kuri, buttercup and hokkaido, red Pyreneean garlic and spinach.
Ⓒ Undisclosed Pumpkins Sep-Nov, garlic Aug onwards, spinach Jun-Nov
Ⓓ By arrangement

10 ↔

A M Produce
Sandylane Nurseries, Baynhall, Kempsey, Worcestershire SR5 3PG
Tel: 0905 821473/840015
Contact: Mr Andrew McBride

Purple kohlrabi

Range of vegetables including white and purple kohlrabi and pumpkins.
Ⓒ White kohlrabi 600doz p.mth Jun-Oct, purple kohlrabi 400x12lb p.mth Jun-Oct, pumpkins 10-15 ton p.mth Sep-Oct
Ⓓ By arrangement

9

Puffin Marketing Services
Unit 2, Thornton Industrial Estate, Steynton, Milford Haven, Pembrokeshire
Tel: 06462 78861
Contact: Peter Cocks

Early potatoes

Range of early Pembrokeshire potatoes available fresh or chilled.
Ⓒ 5000 ton May-Aug
Ⓓ By arrangement

12 ↔

Rose Cottage Produce
Rose Cottage, Nottwood Lane, Stoke Row, Oxfordshire
Tel: 0491 681729
Contact: Mrs K Fotherby

French beans

Organically grown runner and French beans, courgettes and spinach. Also lettuce.
Ⓒ Undisclosed, runner and French beans Aug-Sep, courgettes Jul-Sep, lettuce Jun-Sep
Ⓓ By arrangement
See Also: Fresh Meat

13 ●

Rosehaven
110 Cinques Road, Gamlingay, Sandy, Bedfordshire SG19 3NR
Tel: 0767 50142
Contact: Eleanor Hodges

Squash

Organically grown squashes, garlic, sweetcorn and cherry tomatoes supplied fresh.
Ⓒ Squashes Sep-Jan, sweetcorn Sep-Oct, tomatoes Jul-Oct, garlic Aug-Dec
Ⓦ Natural Foods Ltd, London
Ⓓ By arrangement
See Also: Poultry Producers, Fresh Salads

14

Roudham Asparagus
Bridgham Manor Farm, East Harling, Norwich, Norfolk NR16 2RX
Tel: 0953 717294
Contact: Mr C Musker

Asparagus

Argenteuil variety of asparagus grown.
Ⓒ 4 ton p.mth May-Jun
Ⓓ By arrangement

12 ↔

Sambakes
Queenford Farm, Dorchester-on-Thames, Oxfordshire
Tel: 0865 340681
Contact: Mr Primett

Cara potato

Varieties of potatoes including cara and pentland squire available in 28, 55lb packs.
[C] Undisclosed
[D] By own transport locally

14 ↔

Samford Agriculture
The Bramleys, Burstall, Ipswich, Suffolk IP8 3DN
Tel: 047387 402
Contact: Mrs Seinet

Celeriac
Aubergine

Vegetables grown under glass, including celeriac, peppers, aubergines, courgettes and French beans.
[C] Undisclosed
[D] By own transport within area
See Also: Fresh Salads

3 ●

Simply Organic
Holding No 3, Walnut Grove, Kinfauns, nr Perth, Perthshire PH2 7JX
Tel: 0738 20390
Contact: Ken Paterson

Parsnip

Organically grown vegetables including parsnip, finger size early crop courgettes, broccoli, mavis bard and wilja potatoes.
[C] Courgettes 5x20lb boxes p.dy Jun-Oct, broccoli 5x20lb boxes p.dy Jan-Oct, potatoes 1 ton p.mth Jul-Apr
[D] By arrangement

12 ↔

P D Smales & Son
Lyburn Farm, Landford, Salisbury, Wiltshire SP5 2DN
Tel: 0794 390451
Contact: Mike Smales

Sweetcorn

Sweetcorn.
[C] 10,000 p.dy Jul-Nov
[D] By arrangement

8 ↔

M L & R C Snowden - Snowden Selected
Wharfedale Grange, Harewood, Leeds LS17 9LW
Tel: 0532 886320/886206
Contact: Mr Richard Snowden

Baby courgettes

Range of fifty vegetables including French turnips, early bunched carrots, flowering baby courgettes and baby leeks. Also continental salads and lettuces.
[C] French turnips, early bunched carrots Jun, flowering baby courgettes mid Aug-mid Sep, baby leeks Oct-Mar
[D] By arrangement

12 ● ↔

Somerset Organic Producers
Wyvern Farms, Seavington St Michael, Ilminster, Somerset TA19 OPZ
Tel: 0460 42149
Contact: Mr R Vernon-Dier

Spinach

Co-operative of vegetable growers producing broad breans, French beans, carrots, courgettes, celeriac, chard, leeks, onions, parsnips, potatoes, spinach, spring onions, cucumber and varieties of cabbage.
[C] Onions 4000lb p.mth Jun-Apr, potatoes 5-10 ton p.mth Jul-Apr, spinach 800lb p.mth Jun-Oct
[D] By arrangement
See Also: Fresh Salads

14 ↔

M D & S C Spindler
12 Ipswich Road, Newbourn, Woodbridge, Suffolk IP12 4NS
Tel: 047336 651
Contact: Mr M D Spindler

Celeriac

Range of vegetables including stringless runner beans, green peppers and arvi celeriac in 10lb boxes.
[C] Celeriac 100 boxes mid Oct-Dec
[D] By arrangement
See Also: Fresh Salads

13 ● ↔

Stoneybridge Organic Nursery
Stoneybridge Organic Nursery, Tywardreath, Par, Cornwall PL27 2TY
Tel: 0726 813858
Contact: Mr D R Pascoe

Swiss chard

Range of fresh organic vegetables including Swiss chard and maris bard potatoes grown under glass.
C Maris bard Apr onwards
D By arrangement
See Also: Fresh Fruit, Fresh Salads

15

D G J Tanner
Sopley Farm, Sopley, Christchurch, Dorset
Tel: 0425 72451
Contact: Robin Reeks

Courgettes

Ambassador courgettes, enorma runner beans, horizon, commanche, jubilee and October gold sweetcorn all supplied fresh.
C Courgettes mid Jun-Sep, runner beans late Jul-Sep, sweetcorn Aug-Oct
D By arrangement
See Also: Fresh Fruit

12

Tatworth Fruit Farm
Tatworth, Chard, Somerset TA20 2SG
Tel: 0460 20272
Contact: A R Davies

Sweetcorn

Range of vegetables including enorma runner beans, sugar peas, butter beans, onward peas and jubilee, beacon and early king sweetcorn .
C Undisclosed, runner beans Aug-first frost, butter beans Jun-Aug, peas Jun- Jul, sweetcorn Sep-Oct
D By arrangement
See Also: Apples

11 ●

S L & J D Tidy
The Anchorage, Salisbury Road, Broughton, nr Stockbridge, Hampshire
Tel: 0794 301234
Contact: Mr S L Tidy

Swiss chard

Range of organic vegetables, including late cropping Swiss chard and endive.
C Undisclosed endive Sep-Oct
D By arrangement
See Also: Fresh Fruit

14 ○ ↔

Tuddy's Garden Shop
Ware House, Stebbing, Essex
Tel: 037 186 274
Contact: Tuddy Holles

French beans
Beetroot

Organically grown vegetables, including beetroot, carrots, runner beans, French beans and sweetcorn.
C Sweetcorn 1000lb, beetroot and carrot 600lb, runner beans 200lb, French beans 150lb Jul-Oct
D By arrangement
See Also: Chutneys and Pickles

16

C R Upton
The Lodge, 4 Top Road, Slindon, Arundel, West Sussex BN18 0RP
Tel: 024365 219
Contact: C R Upton

Pumpkin
Squash

Compost grown vegetables including golden marrow, courgettes and pumpkins. Also various squashes including golden nugget, patty pan and gem.
C Undisclosed, pumpkin Aug-Oct, golden marrow and courgettes Jul-Sep, golden nugget squash Aug-Oct, patty pan squash Jul-Sep, gem squash Oct-Sep
D By arrangement

9

Vin Sullivan of Abergavenny
Triley Mill, Abergavenny, Gwent NP7 8DE
Tel: 0873 2331
Contact: Mr John Sullivan

Baby vegetables

Range of local fresh baby vegetables.
C Undisclosed
D By own transport nationally
See Also: Fish Dealers, Fresh Fruit, Fresh Herbs, Fungi

11

R J Watts
South Fen Farm, Bourne, Lincolnshire PE10 0DN
Tel: 077589 231
Contact: R J Watts

Pickling onion

Fresh and chilled pickling onions.
C Pickling onions 200 ton Aug-Feb
D By arrangement
See Also: Fresh Salads

15 ●

Western House Organic Fruit Farm
Western House, Totnes, Devon
Tel: 0803 862066
Contact: Charles Riggs

Capsicum

Organically grown vegetables including capsicums, chillies, carrots, mange-tout and several varieties of peas.
C Undisclosed
D By arrangement
See Also: Fresh Fruit, Fresh Salads

FUNGI

14 ○ ↔

Birds Farm Mushrooms
Birds Farm, Flordon, Norwich, Norfolk NR15 1RN
Tel: 0508 470200
Contact: Mr Howes

Mushroom

Organically grown mushrooms.
C Undisclosed
D By arrangement

11 ◯ ↔

T D Livesey
Old Parks House, Smisby Road, Ashby-de-la-Zouche, Leicestershire LE6 5UB
Tel: 0530 412616
Contact: T D Livesey

Oyster

Cultivated oyster mushrooms. Also available shiitake, stropharia and caprinus mushrooms.
C Oyster mushrooms 200lb p.dy
D By arrangement

2 ↔

Moray Seafoods
9-13 Low Street, Buckie, Morayshire AB5 1UX
Tel: 0542 31296 Telx: 73287
Contact: Charles E Eckersley

Chanterelle

Chanterelle mushrooms gathered in Scotland.
C Undisclosed Aug-Sep
D By arrangement
See Also: Fish: Pies and Prepared Dishes

10

Much Birch Mushrooms Hereford
Mushroom Farm, Much Birch, Hereford HR2 8HY
Tel: 0981 540248
Contact: Mr Parry Rosser

Oyster

Oyster and standard mushrooms grown in Wales.
C Undisclosed
W Sid Wright, Hereford
D By wholesaler, by arrangement

9

Vin Sullivan of Abergavenny Ltd
Triley Mill, Abergavenny, Gwent NP7 8DE
Tel: 0873 2331
Contact: Mr John Sullivan

Wild mushroom

Fresh and dried wild mushrooms.
C Undisclosed
D By own transport nationally
See Also: Fish Dealers, Fresh Fruit, Fresh Herbs, Fresh Vegetables

4

West Ulster Farmers Ltd
Dromore Road, Irvinestown, Co Fermanagh, Northern Ireland
Tel: 03656 21219 Telx: 74611 WSTULS G
Fax: 03656 28222
Contact: Mr John Kennedy

Mushroom

Fresh mushrooms packed in 3lb containers.
C Undisclosed
D By arrangement
See Also: Fish Dealers, Cheese

PREPARED SALADS

4

Avondale Foods Ltd
Chestnut Farm, Dukestown Lane, Lurgan, Craigavon, Co Down BT66 8TB
Tel: 0762 341619 Fax: 0762 43779
Contact: Mr D Geddes

Stir-fry

Range of salads and fresh vegetables including coleslaw, Florida and Bombay salads available all year. Also range of stir-fry vegetable mixtures with bean sprouts, carrots, peppers and leeks, all pillow packed.
C Undisclosed
W Kilmeaden Foods, Portadown
D By wholesaler, by own transport within area

6

Calthwaite Dairy Products
Calthwaite, Penrith, Cumbria CA11 9QU
Tel: 076885 292
Contact: Clive Pattinson

Coleslaw

Homemade coleslaw containing cabbage, carrots, celery, salad dressing and Jersey cream.
C 750kg p.mth
D By own transport within area
See Also: Cheese, Jams and Preserves, Fudges and Toffee

15

Delicate Essence
35 Castle Street, Tiverton, Devon E416 6RE
Tel: 0884 257641
Contact: Virginia Mills

Waldorf salad
Tabouleh

Twenty prepared salads made with home made mayonnaise, free-range eggs and rennet free cheese including lemon or orange and hazelnut rice, tabouleh, carrot and coconut, Waldorf salad, Spanish salad, and Russian potato salad, all in 2,4lb sizes, or to customers requirements.
C Undisclosed
D By arrangement
See Also: Vegetables: Pâtés and Pastes

VEGETABLE DISHES

15 ↔

Alder Foods
Unit 60, Webbers Way, Dartington, Totnes, Devon TQ9 6JE
Tel: 0803 864428
Contact: David Walden

Onion bhaji

Range of handmade pastries including courgette pasties, onion bhajis, 10-12″ quiches made with broccoli, stilton and mushroom, and celery with walnut. Also available Devon cider fruit cake made with dried fruits.
C Undisclosed
D By arrangement

15

The Alternative Kitchen
Ganton Farm House, Bere Alston, Yelverton, Devon PL20 7HW
Tel: 0822 840144
Contact: Mrs Rosario Henshall

Vegetarian moussaka

Range of handmade vegetarian pies, homity pies, vegetarian moussaka and

vegetarian scotch eggs, all made with fresh ingredients, sizes to customers requirements.
C Undisclosed
D By arrangement

12 ⦿ **Broad Street Bakery**
14 Broad Street, Bath, Avon BA1 5LJ
Tel: 0225 62631
Contact: Rachel Demuth

Vegan pasties

Range of cheese and tomato pizzas, savoury croissants, vegan pasties. Also ten varieties of quiches handmade with free-range eggs and organic wholewheat flour including courgette and pepper, spinach and stilton.
C Undisclosed
D By arrangement
See Also: Breads

10 ↔ **Country Cooks Ltd**
Unit 1, Great Western Court, Ashburton Industrial Estate, Ross-on-Wye, Herefordshire HR9 7BW
Tel: 0989 66868
Contact: Jenny Allday

Nut lasagne

Range of wholefood vegetarian dishes including black eye bean bake, bean casserole, mixed vegetable crumble and nut lasagne.
C 3000kg p.mth
D By arrangement
See Also: Meat: Pies and Prepared Dishes, Ice Creams and Sorbets

6 ↔ **Country Fresh Foods (Cumbria) Ltd**
Unit 1, Longtown Industrial Estate, Carlisle, Cumbria CA6 5TJ
Tel: 0228 791788
Contact: Mr H W Frizell

Quiche Lorraine

Range of quiches including Lorraine, cheese and onion, and broccoli. Also available Cumberland pies.
C Undisclosed
D By arrangement
See Also: Snacks and Savouries

16 **Mrs Gill's Indian Kitchen**
The Spice House, Hastingwood Trading Estate, Harbet Road, London N18 1HR
Tel: 01 886 0424
Contact: Christopher Gill

Brinjal Lucknow

Range of additive free handmade, vegetable dishes including Brinjal Lucknow, Mattar Paneer and a variety of dahl dishes. All made with ground spices and fresh vegetables and packed in 12oz transparent bags.
C Undisclosed
D By arrangement
See Also: Dried Herbs and Flavourings

14 ↔ **Norfolk Smokehouses Ltd**
Poplar Farm, Worlingworth, Woodbridge, Suffolk IP13 7LR
Tel: 072 876212
Contact: J D Hildreth

Vegetable terrine

Additive free vegetable terrine and pâté, made with frozen vegetables, cream, milk, butter, bread and spices in 1.36kg containers.
C Undisclosed
D By arrangement
See Also: Meat: Pâtés and Pastes, Game: Pâtés and Pastes, Fish: Pâtés and Pastes

9 **Patchwork**
Faraway, Llandegla, Clwyd LL11 3BG
Tel: 097 888238
Contact: Margaret Carter

Quiche

Range of homemade 12" quiches made with free-range eggs, wholemeal flour and goat milk including cheese and onion, mushroom and tarragon, asparagus and sweetcorn. Also range of vegan pâtés available.
C Undisclosed
D By arrangement
See Also: Game: Pâtés and Pastes, Cheese, Cakes, Biscuits and Pastries

16 ↔ **St Nicholas Court Farm Ltd**
St Nicholas-at-Wade, nr Birchington, Kent CT7 0PT
Tel: 0843 47442 Fax: 0843 45623
Contact: J R S Tapp

Leek cobbler
Samosa

Range of sweet and savoury frozen vegetarian meals with wholemeal flour including leek and lentil cobbler, vegetable samosas, nutty vegetable pie and honeyed apricot with orange pie in 12x400, 24x400g packs.
C 1,000,000 p.a
D By arrangement
See Also: Millers

8 **Verity Steele Wholefood Vegetarian Meals**
Dunwell Cottage, Broughton, Malton, North Yorkshire YO17 0QJ
Tel: 0653 694084
Contact: Verity Steele

Veggie Pie

Additive free vegetarian and vegan prepared dishes including Veggie Pie with groundnuts, breadcrumbs, lentils and vegetables weighing 14oz. Also savoury stuffed pancakes with or without cheese sauce in packs of three weighing 1lb 2oz and Shepherd's spicy lentil pie weighing 15oz.
C Undisclosed
W Smallholder Country Foods, 0751 73026
D By wholesaler

PATES AND PASTES

15

Delicate Essence
35 Castle Street, Tiverton, Devon E416 6RE
Tel: 0884 257641
Contact: Virginia Mills

Vegetable and nut

Six handmade vegetarian pâtés and pastes including curry butter bean loaf, vegetable and nut pâté, cheese and lentil, layered cashew and mushroom roast, Spanish vegetable loaf and almond and tomato toasted terrine. All in 2lb loaves.
Ⓒ Undisclosed
Ⓓ By arrangement
See Also: Prepared Salads

CEREALS AND GRAINS

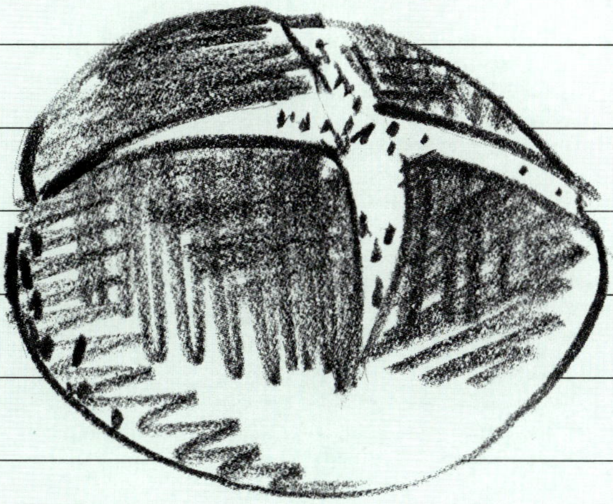

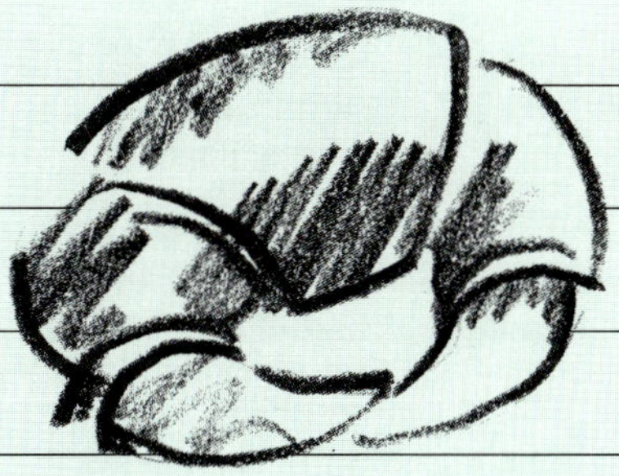

MILLERS

10

Avoncroft Museum of Buildings
Stoke Heath, Bromsgrove, Hereford & Worcester B60 4JR
Tel: 0527 31886/31363
Contact: Mr R M Sinclair

Wholemeal

Wholemeal flour produced from local wheat ground between French burr stones. In 500g, 1.5kg bags.
C Approx 20 ton p.a
D By arrangement

15

Beenleigh Enterprises/Manor Farm Foods
Beenleigh Manor, Harbertonford, Totnes, Devon
Tel: 080423 738
Contact: Mr A K Wilson-Gough

Organic rye

Range of flour including wholemeal, wheatmeal, organic rye and strong flour for bakers in 1½-32 kg bags. Semolina and bran also available.
C Flour 500 ton p.a
D By arrangement
See Also: Cider

16 ●

Boathouse Farm Organic Produce
Isfield, nr Uckfield, East Sussex TN22 5TY
Tel: 082575 302
Contact: Laurence Hill

Wholewheat

Stoneground organic wholewheat flour in 1½, 16, 32kg bags.
C Undisclosed
D By arrangement
See Also: Fresh Meat, Eggs, Fresh Vegetables

14 ● ↔

Boxford (Suffolk) Farms Ltd
Hill Farm, Boxford, Colchester, Essex CO6 5NY
Tel: 0787 210348/496 Telx: 94012299 COPLG
Contact: Tamara Unwin

Rye flour

Stoneground wholewheat and rye flours from organically grown grain in 1½, 32kg bags.
C Undisclosed
D By own transport within area

11 ↔

Caudwell's Mill Trust Ltd
Caudwell's Mill, Rowsley, Matlock, Derbyshire DE4 2EB
Tel: 0629 734374
Contact: M J Tilley

Strong wholemeal flour

Water powered mill producing strong wholemeal flour in 1½, 3, 6½, 32kg bags.
C 100 ton p.a
D By arrangement

10 ○

Charlecote Mill
Hampton Lucy, Warwick, Warwickshire
Tel: 0789 842072
Contact: Mr John Bedington

Stoneground wholemeal flour

Variety of stoneground wholemeal flours including fine for chapattis and pastry making, general purpose, strong containing some Canadian wheat, and organic. General purpose and organic flour in 1½kg bags, all in 12½, 25, 32kg bags.
C 89 ton p.a
D By own transport within area

11 ● ↔

Christy's
Grange Farm, Hockerton, Southwell, Nottinghamshire NG25 OPJ
Tel: 0636 812193
Contact: Mr S D Christy

Wholemeal flour

High protein organic wholemeal and wheatmeal flour for biscuits and pastry, stoneground to customers requirements in 1½, 32kg bags.
C 10 ton p.wk
D By own transport within area

15 ●

Crowdy Mill
Harbertonford, Totnes, Devon
Tel: 080423 340
Contact: Martin Watts

Wholemeal flour

Range of flours including wholemeal wheat, rye, brown, unbleached white, strong, standard plain, and organic stoneground. Also brown semolina and bran, all in 1½, 3, 6½, 12½, 25, 32kg bags.
C 2 ton p.wk
D By own transport within area

16 ● ↔

Doves Farm Foods
Salisbury Road, Hungerford, Berkshire RG17 ORF
Tel: 0488 84880
Contact: Mrs Marriage

Stoneground organic flour

Range of organic flours including stoneground white, self-raising, rye, rice, buckwheat, and barley in 1.5kg retail packs and 15, 25, 32kg sacks.
C 300 tonne p.wk
D By arrangement
See Also: Cheese, Cakes, Biscuits and Pastries

14 ● ↔

Downfield Windmill
Fordham Road, Soham, Cambridgeshire
Tel: 0533 707625
Contact: Mr Nigel Moon

Maizemeal

Range of organic stoneground flours including wholemeal, brown, oatmeal, maizemeal and ryemeal. Also stoneground wholemeal and brown flours in 1-32kg bags.
C 1-2 ton p.wk
D By own transport within area

16 ● **Eling Tide Mill**
The Toll Bridge, Eling, Totton, Hampshire SO4 4HF
Tel: 0703 869575
Contact: M L Mears

Wheatmeal flour
Wholemeal and wheatmeal flours stoneground from organically grown wheat, packed in 500g, 1½, 6, 12, 32kg bags.
C Undisclosed
D By arrangement

12 **Englands Mills**
Sea Mills, Berkeley, Gloucestershire GL13 9QR
Tel: 0453 811150
Contact: Richard England

Stoneground wholemeal flour
Range of speciality flour including stoneground wholemeal, wheatmeal in 1½, 32kg packs.
C 20 tonne p.wk
D By own transport nationally
See Also: Muesli

8 ↔ **J S R Farms Ltd**
Southburn Offices, Southburn, Driffield, East Yorkshire YO25 9ED
Tel: 0377 89264
Contact: Rosemary Kendall

Stoneground wholemeal
Stoneground wholemeal and wholemeal with nutty malted wheat flour made from untreated wheat grown on own farm, in 1½kg bags, 15kg sacks.
C 25 ton p.a
D By own transport within area

9 ↔ **Y Felin**
Mill House, St Dogmaels, Cardigan Dyfed SA43 3DY
Tel: 0239 613999
Contact: Michael Hall

Rye flour
Range of stoneground flour including wholemeal, wholewheat, unbleached white, 100% rye. Also available wholemeal flour with sunflower seeds, poppy seed, millet, sage and thyme.
C Approx 2 tonne p.wk
D By own transport within area, by arrangement

9 **Felin Crewi**
Penegoes, Machynlleth, Powys SY20 8NH
Tel: 0654 3113
Contact: Mrs Patti Partridge

Stoneground wholemeal flour
Stoneground wholemeal flour from water powered mill in 1½, 12, 32kg bags.
C Undisclosed
D By arrangement
See Also: Muesli

9 ↔ **Felin Geri Mill**
Cwm Cou, Newcastle Emlyn, Dyfed
Tel: 0239 710810
Contact: Michael Heycock

Stoneground wholemeal flour
Stoneground wholemeal, unbleached white flour, semolina and broad bran in 1½, 12, 32kg bags.
C 5 ton p.wk
D By arrangement

14 ● **Garboldisham Windmill**
nr Diss, Norfolk IP22 2RJ
Tel: 095 381 593
Contact: Adrian Colman

Brown rice flour
A range of stoneground organic flour including millet and buckwheat in 500g bags, wholewheat and brown rice flour in 1½, 3, 16kg bags.
C Undisclosed
D By own transport within area
See Also: Muesli

8 ● ↔ **Gillygate Wholefood Bakery Ltd**
Millers Yard, Gillygate, York YO3 7EB
Tel: 0904 610676
Contact: Blaise White

Rye
Stoneground wholemeal, granary and rye flour, in 500g, 1½, 3½, 25kg bags with bulk sizes to order.
C Undisclosed
W Suma Wholefoods of Halifax
D By wholesaler
See Also: Breads, Cakes, Biscuits and Pastries, Muesli

3 **Hamlyn Milling Ltd**
44 Glengate, Kirriemuir, Angus DD8 4HG
Tel: 0575 72121 Telx: 76594 Fax: 0575 73915
Contact: David Valentine

Stoneground oatmeal
Stoneground oatmeal in 500g, 1, 1½, 3, 25kg bags.
C Undisclosed
D By own transport and by arrangement
See Also: Muesli

15 ↔ **Hele Mill**
Ilfracombe, North Devon
Tel: 0271 63162
Contact: C L Lovell

Wholemeal stoneground
Five grades of stoneground wholemeal flour including fine, coarse and granary in 1½, 3.3, 32kg bags.
C 25 ton p.a
D By own transport within area
See Also: Muesli

12 ● **Herberts Flour Mill**
Crosshands Farm, Little Sodbury, Bristol BS17 GRJ
Tel: 0454 324729
Contact: Mr Trevor Herbert

Malted wheat flour
Stoneground organic wholemeal, wheatmeal, white and malted wheat flours all in 10, 32kg bags. Also available unbleached and untreated white flours

suitable for crusty breads.
Ⓒ Wholemeal and wheatmeal 40-50 tonne p.a, white flours 400 tonne p.a
Ⓓ By arrangement

10 ↔

Holgran Malt Products Ltd
Granary House, Wetmore Road, Burton-on-Trent, Staffordshire DE14 1TE
Tel: 0283 43221 Telx: 341929 GRANRY G
Contact: Alan Marson

Cereals

Miller using 100% extraction mill can supply blends of all types of cereals, in 10, 15, 16, 25, 50, 350kg bags, minimum order 1 ton.
Ⓒ Undisclosed
Ⓓ By arrangement
See Also: Muesli

3

John Ridley Projects Ltd
The Mill, Blair Atholl, Perthshire PH18 5SH
Tel: 079 681321
Contact: John Ridley

Wholemeal flour

Stoneground wholemeal and granary flour, coarse, medium and fine oatmeal in ½, 1½, 3, 12½, 25kg bags.
Ⓒ Soft wheat flour 100 ton p.a, hard wheat flour 60 ton p.a, oatmeal 80 ton p.a
Ⓓ By arrangement
See Also: Breads, Cakes, Biscuits and Pastries

13

W Jordan (Cereals) Ltd
Holme Mills, Biggleswade, Bedfordshire SG18 9JX
Tel: 0767 318222 Telx: 827525
Contact: Graham Lee

Strong wholemeal

Strong wholemeal, strong white plain, Country Cookbook plain, and Country Cookbook self-raising flours, using slow moving roller mill, in 1½kg, 28, 70lb bags.
Ⓒ Undisclosed
Ⓓ By arrangement
See Also: Cakes, Biscuits and Pastries, Muesli

14

Letheringsett Watermill
Letheringsett, Holt, Norfolk NR25 7YD
Tel: 0263 713153
Contact: Mike Thurlow

Wholewheat

100% wholewheat stoneground flour in a range of grades from fine to coarse ground, in 7, 14lb, 1½, 16, 32kg bags.
Ⓒ 4 ton p.wk
Ⓓ By arrangement
See Also: Breads

9

D & M Lickley & Sons
The Mill, Whitemill, Carmarthen, Dyfed SA32 7EL
Tel: 026788 209
Contact: D Lickley

Wholemeal stoneground

Felin Wen, 100% wholemeal stoneground flour made from 50% Canadian and 50% English wheat, Baragwenith Flour, white and wholemeal flour mixed, and wholemeal stoneground bran. All packed in 1½-32kg bags.
Ⓒ Minimum 3 ton p.wk
Ⓓ By arrangement

12

Lockyer & Son
Clapton Mill, Crewkerne, Somerset TA18 8PU
Tel: 0460 73124
Contact: C G Lockyer

Wholemeal white

Stoneground wholemeal and strong white bread flour milled since 1870 using traditional production methods with machinery driven by waterwheel, in 1½, 3, 6, 16, 32kg bags.
Ⓒ 100% wholemeal flour 2 ton p.wk, 80% wholemeal flour ½ ton p.wk
Ⓓ By arrangement

16 ↔

Loseley Dairy Products Ltd
Estate Office, Guildford, Surrey GU3 1HS
Tel: 0483 571881 Telx: 859972 Fax: 0483 302056
Contact: Miss Ann Cleveland

Wholemeal organic pastry

Stoneground wholemeal flour in 1½kg bags, 12½, 25, 32kg sacks. Frozen wholemeal organic pastry with no animal fats, suitable for sweet and savoury dishes, in 350g, 4kg packs. Also fresh quiches.
Ⓒ Undisclosed
Ⓓ By arrangement
See Also: Cream, Ice Creams and Sorbets

14 ●

W & H Marriage & Sons Ltd
Chelmer Mills, New Street, Chelmsford, Essex CM1 1PN
Tel: 0245 354455
Contact: Mr George Marriage

Wholemeal

Range of organic stoneground wholemeal flour in 1½, 15, 32kg bags.
Ⓒ Undisclosed
Ⓓ By arrangement

4

Marybrook Mills
Marybrook Mills, Raleagh Road, Crossfar, Downpatrick, Co Down BT30 93G
Tel: 0396 830 173/574
Contact: John Lewis-Crosby

Extra coarse wholewheat

Stoneground wholewheat flour, coarse, extra coarse, medium and fine or ground to customers requirements, in 1½, 32kg bags. White flour also available.
Ⓒ Undisclosed
Ⓓ By arrangement

11 ● ↔

Maud Foster Mill
Boston, Lincolnshire PE21 9EG
Tel: 0205 52188
Contact: Mr James Waterfield

Organic self-raising flour

Range of flour stoneground mainly by windmill power including wholemeal rye, wholewheat, untreated unbleached white,

organic self-raising, and semolina in 3½, 7, 14, 28, 56, 70lb bags.
[C] 5 ton p.wk, mainly wholemeal
[D] By own transport within area

9 ●

Melin Maesdulais
Porthyrhyd, Carmarthen, Dyfed SA32 8BT
Tel: 026786 472
Contact: Geoff Brace

Garlic and chive flour

Range of stoneground flour including organic wholemeal, malted wholemeal, 100% rye, high bran, and wheatgerm wholemeal. Also range of flavoured flours including garlic and chive, seed, seed and herb, and spice, in 1½, 10, 25kg bags. Broad and medium bran in 40kg sacks.
[C] 2 ton p.wk
[W] Huxleys Trading Co, 0222 692295
[D] By wholesaler, by own transport

16 ○

Michelham Priory
Hailsham, East Sussex BN27 3QS
Tel: 0323 844224
Contact: A C Gottlieb

Wholemeal flour

Wholemeal and brown flour stoneground from own grown wheat, using power from a restored water mill dating back to the Middle Ages.
[C] Undisclosed Mar-Oct
[D] By arrangement

16

Millers Damsel Enterprises Ltd
Lower Mill, Newbridge, Yarmouth, Isle of Wight PO41 0TZ
Tel: 0983 78228
Contact: John Pretty

Wholemeal flour

Stoneground wholemeal flour from Isle of Wight wheat in 500g, 1½, 32kg bags.
[C] 1 ton p.wk
[W] Forest Marketing Ltd of Wimbourne
[D] By wholesaler
See Also: Cakes, Biscuits and Pastries

16 ●

Neals Yard Flour Mill
266 Portobello Road, London W10
Tel: 01 960 1840
Contact: Julie Petrie

Rye flour

Stoneground wholewheat and rye flour, milled barley, rice and chick peas in 1½, 3, 6, 12, 32kg bags. Also millet and oatmeal available in 500g bags.
[C] Undisclosed
[D] By arrangement

2

North Eastern Farmers Ltd
Bannermill Beach Boulevard, Aberdeen
Tel: 0224 641255 Telx: 73488 Fax: 0224 637206
Contact: Uel Morton

Oatmeal

Oatmeal, oatflakes and oat-bran mix supplied in 500g, 1, 3kg bags.
[C] Undisclosed
[D] By arrangement
See Also: Muesli

11

North Leverton Windmill
West View, Sturton Road, North Leverton, Retford, Nottinghamshire DN22 0AB
Tel: 0427 880573
Contact: Mr Keith Barlow

Wheatmeal flour

Wholemeal and wheatmeal flour, stoneground using windpower from an early 19th century windmill, in 1½, 3½, 7, 14, 28lb, 4st bags and to customers requirements.
[C] Undisclosed
[D] By arrangement

15 ○ ↔

Otterton Mill
nr Budleigh Salterton, Devon
Tel: 0395 68521
Contact: Mrs Desna Greenhow

Wholewheat flour

Range of flour including wholewheat stoneground from English wheat, fine flour for cakes and pastries, bread flour in 1½kg bags or sacks to customers requirements from 28lb upwards.
[C] 4 ton p.wk
[D] By arrangement
See Also: Breads, Cakes, Biscuits and Pastries, Pies and Puddings, Chutneys and Pickles

10 ● ↔

Pimhill
Lea Hall, Harmer Hill, Shrewsbury, Shropshire SY4 3DY
Tel: 0939 290342
Contact: Ginny Mayall

Brown flour

Stoneground wholemeal plain and self-raising flour, and 85% extraction flour all ground to customers requirements, in 1½, 16, 32kg bags.
[C] Undisclosed
[D] By arrangement
See Also: Fresh Meat, Fresh Vegetables, Muesli

10 ↔

Rea Valley Mills
Claybury Mill, Cleobury Mortimer, Shropshire DY14 8QG
Tel: 0299 270034
Contact: Mr Jim Bartlett

Stoneground wholemeal

Water powered mill producing extra strong stoneground wholemeal and unbleached white flours suitable for bread, in 1½lb, 32kg bags.
[C] 40 ton p.wk
[D] By arrangement

12 ● ↔

Rushall Farms
Rushall Farms, The Manor, Upavon, Pewsey, Wiltshire SN9 6EB
Tel: 0980 630264
Contact: Mr C B Wookey

Wholemeal

Miller of stoneground wholemeal flour in 1½, 2½, 12½kg bags.
[C] Undisclosed
[D] By arrangement
See Also: Breads

11

Sidebottom's Flour
Black Firs Farm, Alderwasley, Derby, Derbyshire DE4 4GF
Tel: 062982 2447
Contact: Robin Sidebottom

Bran wheatgerm mix

Miller of stoneground wholemeal, wheatmeal and granary flour, rich bran and a mixture of bran and wheat germ. Flour available in 1½kg, rich bran in 20kg sacks.
[C] Undisclosed
[D] By arrangement

16 ↔

St Nicholas Court Farm Ltd
St Nicholas-at-Wade, nr Birchington, Kent CT7 0PT
Tel: 0843 47442 Fax: 0843 45623
Contact: J R S Tapp

Wholemeal

Stoneground wholemeal flour in 1½, 25, 32kg bags.
[C] 1000 ton p.a
[D] By own transport nationally
See Also: Vegetable Dishes

15 ● ↔

N R Stoate & Sons Ltd
Cann Mills, Shaftesbury, Dorset SP7 OBL
Tel: 0747 2475
Contact: N R Stoate

Maltstar

Range of flour including stoneground 81% plain, 81% and 100% self-raising, 100% wholemeal maltstar (a granary type flour containing coarse and fine rye flour and coarse and fine bran), 100% organic available to order. All packed in 1½, 8, 32kg bags. Coarse and fine bran packed in 30, 40lb bags.
[C] Undisclosed
[D] By arrangement

16 ○

Swanton Mill
Lower Mersham, Ashford, Kent
Tel: 023372 223
Contact: Mrs G Christiansen

Wholemeal

Water powered mill producing stoneground, hand sifted wholemeal flour from organically grown grain.
[C] Undisclosed
[D] By arrangement

14 ↔

Walsham Stoneground Flour Mill Ltd
Wattisfield Road, Walsham-le-Willows, Bury St Edmunds, Suffolk IP31 3BD
Tel: 03598 679/216 Telx: 817482
Contact: Mr Cooper

Wholewheat flour

Range of flour including stoneground wholewheat, strong white, plain and self-raising in 4lb, 1½, 32kg bags.
[C] 100 ton p.wk
[D] By arrangement
See Also: Muesli

6 ○ ↔

The Watermill
Little Salkeld, Penrith, Cumbria CA10 1NN
Tel: 076881 523
Contact: Nicolas Jones

Watermill Special Blend

Stoneground wholewheat flour in a range of grades including extra fine, medium fine and coarse. Watermill Special Blend, a mixture of wholewheat, wheatmeal, and soya flour, with sunflower and sesame seeds (ideal for vegetarians and vegans as it contains complete protein combinations). Also 100% rye flour, 85% barley flour, cracked wheat and self-raising flour also available. All supplied in 1½, 3, 6, 12½, 25, 32kg bags.
[C] Special Blend 60 ton p.a, 100% wholewheat 120 ton p.a, 85% wheatmeal 40 ton p.a, others undisclosed
[D] By arrangement
See Also: Muesli

14 ↔

G C & G Wilson
The Mill, Over, Cambridgeshire CB4 5PP
Tel: 0954 30742
Contact: Mr G C Wilson

Wholemeal flour

Wholemeal flour and flour of 75% extraction stoneground using a restored windmill in 3, 10, 70lb bags. Grain can be milled to customers requirements.
[C] Undisclosed
[D] By arrangement

12 ●

B M Young
Sturminster Newton Mill, Glebelands, Manston Road, Sturminster Newton, Dorset DT10 1AG
Tel: 0258 73151/72275
Contact: B M Young

Wholemeal flour

Wholemeal stoneground flour from locally grown grain in 1½, 32kg bags.
[C] 3 ton p.wk
[D] By own transport nationally

BREADS

7

Astley Training Bakery
116a Park Road, Chorley, Lancashire
Tel: 025 72 67442
Contact: Mr Howarth

Wholemeal

Range of white and wholemeal breads in 1lb loaves. Baps also available.
[C] Undisclosed
[D] By arrangement
See Also: Cakes, Biscuits and Pastries, Muesli

9

Berwyn Bakery
Industrial Estate, Bala, Gwynedd LL23 9XX
Tel: 0678 520126
Contact: David Williams

Brown wheatmeal

Brown wheatmeal, granary white, Hovis and mixed grain breads made to traditional family recipe in 400, 800g loaves.
[C] 40 ton p.mth
[D] By arrangement

10 ↔

The Bread Bin
72 Shropshire Street, Market Drayton, Shropshire
Tel: 0630 2795
Contact: Mr Tim Horcroft

Gingerbread

Range of bread including wholemeal granary, white with oats, cheese and onion in 400, 800g loaves.
[C] Undisclosed
[D] By arrangement
See Also: Cakes, Biscuits and Pastries

3 ●

Breadline Bakery Ltd
Unit 22, Mid Wynd, Dundee, Tayside DD1 4JG
Tel: 0382 24935
Contact: Mr Petale

Wholemeal — 100% wholemeal bread made with organic flour in 14oz loaves. Also wholefood cakes and buns.
[C] 500 loaves p.wk
[D] By arrangement
See Also: Pies and Puddings

12 ○

Broad Street Bakery
14 Broad Street, Bath, Avon BA1 5LJ
Tel: 0225 62631
Contact: Rachel Demuth

Walnut and linseed — Range of bread including organic wholewheat in 1, 2lb loaves, sunflower wholewheat in 1lb loaves, walnut and linseed in 1lb loaves. White 1, 2lb loaves also available.
[C] Undisclosed
[D] By arrangement
See Also: Vegetable Dishes, Cakes, Biscuits and Pastries

11 ↔

Catlin Bros Ltd
11 High Street, Grantham, Lincolnshire
Tel: 0476 65428
Contact: S P Hallam

Wheata — A range of wholemeal bread including Wheata (a steamed wholemeal loaf), organic, rye, and special breads made to order.
[C] Undisclosed
[D] By arrangement
See Also: Meat: Pies and Prepared Dishes, Game: Pies and Prepared Dishes, Cakes, Biscuits and Pastries

12 ↔

Cobbs Of Bath
11 Westgate Street, Bath, Avon BA1 1EQ
Tel: 0225 66158
Contact: Mr R N Cobb

Wholemeal — Soft, close textured wholemeal bread baked by traditional methods.
[C] 3000-4000 p.wk
[D] By own transport within area
See Also: Cakes, Biscuits and Pastries

16

Coleson & Co (Bakers) Ltd
91 Leather Lane, London EC1N 7TS
Tel: 01 405 2526
Contact: John Coleson

Harvester — A range of traditionally made bread including 100% wholemeal, harvester, brown wheat and rye, in 400g, 800g loaves. Rolls also baked.
[C] Undisclosed
[D] By arrangement
See Also: Cakes, Biscuits and Pastries

15 ↔

Country Bumpkins Bakery
105 Exeter Road, Exmouth, Devon
Tel: 03952 75004
Contact: Linda Joyce

Stoneground — 100% stoneground, fat free bread and rolls.
[C] Undisclosed
[D] By arrangement
See Also: Cakes, Biscuits and Pastries

11

A W Curtiss & Son Ltd
164 High Street, Lincoln, Lincolnshire LN5 7AF
Tel: 0522 30802
Contact: Mr L C Dickens

Lincolnshire plum — Plum bread, Lincolnshire speciality made with brown and white flour, dried fruit and cherries in 14oz loaves.
[C] 1500 p.wk
[D] By own transport nationally
See Also: Meat: Pies and Prepared Dishes, Pies and Puddings

12 ●

David Herbert's Bakery
12 York Road, Montpelier, Bristol BS6 5QE
Tel: 0272 47713
Contact: Anthony Herbert

Chollah — Range of wholemeal breads and rolls made with organic flour, including french baguettes, Jewish chollah bread, handmade croissants, sausage rolls and pasties.
[C] Undisclosed
[D] By arrangement

8 ● ↔

Gillygate Wholefood Bakery Ltd
Millers Yard, Gillygate, York YO3 7EB
Tel: 0904 610676
Contact: Blaise White

Cheese and fruit

Wholewheat bread, cheese and fruit loaves made from local wheat rolled on the premises in 1, 2lb loaves. Baps also produced.
Ⓒ 200-250 loaves p.dy
Ⓓ By arrangement
See Also: Millers, Cakes, Biscuits and Pastries, Muesli

3

John Ridley Projects Ltd
The Mill, Blair Atholl, Perthshire PH18 5SH
Tel: 079 681321
Contact: John Ridley

Clootie dumpling

Clootie dumplings, traditional Scottish dumpling in 2lb loaf tin size.
Ⓒ 200 p.dy Apr-Oct
Ⓓ By arrangement
See Also: Millers, Cakes, Biscuits and Pastries

4 ↔

Krusty Fayre
Unit 3, Dromore Road Trading Estate, Omagh, Co Tyrone
Tel: 0662 46850
Contact: Sean McGrath

Wholemeal porter

Range of traditional, handmade Irish breads including potato, griddle soda, wholemeal wheaten, and wholemeal porter made with Guinness.
Ⓒ Undisclosed
Ⓓ By arrangement, by Datapost

14

Letheringsett Watermill
Letheringsett, Holt, Norfolk NR25 7YD
Tel: 0263 713153
Contact: Mike Thurlow

Wholewheat

Small loaves made with 100% wholewheat stoneground flour.
Ⓒ 150 loaves p.wk
Ⓓ By arrangement
See Also: Millers

16 ● ↔

Natural Rise Foods
21 Bernard Road, London N15 4PE
Tel: 01 808 2007
Contact: Tony Donaghy

Sourdough

Sourdough breads baked by traditional methods using stoneground organic grain and unrefined yeast. Organic barley and rice loaves in 1½, 2lb sizes.
Ⓒ 1,300 p.wk
Ⓓ By own transport within area
See Also: Cakes, Biscuits and Pastries, Pies and Puddings

16 ●

Neals Yard Bakery Co-op
6 Neals Yard, London WC2
Tel: 01 836 5199
Contact: Janene Smith

Sunflower

Wholewheat bread made from 100% organic flour milled on the premises. Also available chive and garlic, fruit and malt, granary, sourdough, and sunflower breads.
Ⓒ 500-600 p.dy
Ⓓ By arrangement
See Also: Pies and Puddings

15 ○ ↔

Otterton Mill
nr Budleigh, Salterton, Devon
Tel: 0395 68521
Contact: Mrs Desna Greenhow

Rye

Wholewheat bread in 1lb loaves and 2lb bloomers. Also rye and granary loaves.
Ⓒ 350 loaves p.wk
Ⓓ By arrangement
See Also: Millers, Cakes, Biscuits and Pastries, Pies and Puddings, Chutneys and Pickles

15 ○ ↔

Robinson's of Charmouth
The Bakery, The Street, Charmouth, nr Bridport, Dorset
Tel: 0297 60213
Contact: Mr John C Robinson

Wholemeal

100% wholemeal bread with organic flour, 100% coarse wholemeal with extra bran added. Date and apricot slices, fruit slices and apple cakes also supplied.
Ⓒ Large loaves 1,200 p.wk, apple cakes 100-150 p.wk
Ⓓ By arrangement

12 ● ↔

Rushall Farms
Rushall Farms, The Manor, Upavon, Pewsey, Wiltshire SN9 6EB
Tel: 0980 630264
Contact: Mr C B Wookey

Wholemeal

Bread made from stoneground wholemeal flour.
Ⓒ Undisclosed
Ⓓ By arrangement
See Also: Millers

16 ●

South London Bakers Co-operative
639 Garratt Lane, Earlsfield, London SW18 4SX
Tel: 01 947 5264
Contact: Martin Shields

Fruit and nut

A range of breads including wholewheat, wheat and rye, fruit and nut, and malt loaf. All made using organic stoneground flour in 400, 800g loaves.
Ⓒ 1000 loaves p.dy
Ⓓ By own transport within area

12 ↔

Stoneground Ltd
78-82 Bedminster Parade, Bedminster, Bristol, Avon BS3 4HL
Tel: 0272 634666
Contact: Miles Kirke

Sourdough

Range of wholemeal breads and Northern European speciality breads including sourdough.
C Undisclosed
D By own transport within area
See Also: Cakes, Biscuits and Pastries, Pies and Puddings

6 ◯ ↔

The Village Bakery
Melmerby, Penrith, Cumbria CA10 1HE
Tel: 076881 515
Contact: A M Whitley

Sesame plait

Range of breads and rolls made with organic English wheat, stoneground by water power, baked in a wood fired oven including sesame plait, and homesteader.
C Undisclosed
D By arrangement
See Also: Cakes, Biscuits and Pastries, Pies and Puddings, Jams and Preserves

CAKES, BISCUITS AND PASTRIES

7

Antonelli Bros Ltd
Weymouth Road, Winton, Eccles, Manchester M30 8WW
Tel: 061 789 4485
Contact: Mr Roland Antonelli

Ice cream cone

Traditional rolled and moulded ice cream cone, wrapped in polythene inside a corrugated case, 12″x12″x24. Number of cones and weight vary according to variety.
C Undisclosed
D By arrangement

11

Appleby & Pemberton
Elmswell, Suffolk 1P30 9HD
Tel: 0359 41937
Contact: Almer Squires

Flapjack

Three varieties of flapjacks, date and hazelnut, coconut, apricot and cinnamon, all made with organic oatflakes, raw cane sugar, honey and whole fruit in 30, 35, 65g bars. Also available in 50g bar without added sugar.
C 5000 p.wk
D By arrangement
See Also: Snacks and Savouries

4

Arthur McCann Ltd
Victoria Bakery, Castle Street, Newry, Co Down BT34 2DA
Tel: 0693 62076 Fax: 0693 61316
Contact: Christopher McCann

Porter cake

Range of traditional handmade Irish biscuits and cakes including fruit cake, brack made with wholemeal flour, cherries, sultanas and raisins, and porter cake made with stout.
C Undisclosed
W Byrch Trent Ltd, London Atlantic Harvest Ltd, London
D By wholesaler, by own transport

7

Astley Training Bakery
116a Park Road, Chorley, Lancashire
Tel: 025 72 67442
Contact: Mr Howarth

Parkin

Range of loaf cakes weighing 1lb, traditional parkin also available.
C Undisclosed
D By arrangement
See Also: Breads, Muesli

4 ↔

Aunt Mollies Foods
9-11 Welland Street, Belfast BT4 1HU
Tel: 0232 456070
Contact: Mr Karl Devlin

Puff pastry

Additive free, ready rolled puff pastry in 13oz retail, 11lb catering packs, sweet and savoury short pastry in 13oz packs. Also available additive free, frozen cookie dough for customer to bake, in a variety of flavours including chocolate chip, cherry, coconut, and walnut in 12 biscuit retail, 50-100 biscuit catering packs.
C Undisclosed
D By arrangement

16 ↔

Mrs Beeton's Foods
Norwood Hill, Horley, Surrey RH6 OET
Tel: 0293 862087 Fax: 0293 862396
Contact: Clive Pick

Ginger biscuit

Range of additive free biscuits including wholewheat, ginger, and sultana, in 7oz packs.
C Undisclosed
D By arrangement
See Also: Butter, Pies and Puddings, Chutneys and Pickles, Hampers

8

E Botham & Sons Ltd
35-39 Skinner Street, Whitby, North Yorkshire YO21 3AH
Tel: 0947 602823
Contact: M Jarman

Gingerbread

Handmade traditional additive free Whitby gingerbread baked in 1lb loaves and packed in cartons of 18. Also a range of hand baked biscuits in 150, 200g packs in outers of 24.
C Undisclosed
W J Pinchbeck, 0529 60306 Mrs C Hynde, 0532 813440
D By wholesaler, by arrangement

9 ↔

Bowmont (Bakeries) Ltd
Burry Terrace, Machynys, Llanelli, Dyfed SA15 2DW
Tel: 0554 773063
Contact: Denzil Bowen

Welsh cake

Variety of cakes including pancakes, Scotch pancakes, Welsh cakes and jam splits, all pre-packed, customers own label if required.
[C] Undisclosed
[D] By own transport nationally

10 ↔

The Bread Bin
72 Shropshire Street, Market Drayton, Shropshire
Tel: 0630 2795
Contact: Mr Tim Horcroft

Gingerbread

Range of gingerbreads, cakes and bread pudding.
[C] Undisclosed
[D] By arrangement
See Also: Breads

12 ○

Broad Street Bakery
14 Broad Street, Bath, Avon BA1 5LJ
Tel: 0225 62631
Contact: Rachel Demuth

Bara brith

Handmade Bara brith, fruit and honey 12″ malt cakes made with free-range eggs, organic wholewheat flour and dried fruit.
[C] 60 p.wk
[D] By arrangement
See Also: Vegetable Dishes, Breads

15 ○ ↔

Carley & Co
34-36 St Austell Street, Truro, Cornwall TR1 1SE
Tel: 0872 77686
Contact: John and Shirley Carley

Fruit and nut

Biscuits made with organic flour and without added sugar, including fruit and nut in ten biscuit packs, and half coated carob in six biscuit packs.
[C] 200 packs p.wk
[D] By arrangement
See Also: Dried herbs and Flavourings

14 ↔

Cartwright & Butler Ltd
The Spice Mill, Wells-next-the Sea, Norfolk
Tel: 0328 710144 Telx: 817483 CANDB G
Contact: Marian Cartwright

Stoneground wholewheat biscuit

Biscuits made with butter and stoneground wholewheat flour including Savoury with rock salt, and sweet with raw cane sugar, available in Christmas packaging.
[C] Undisclosed
[D] By own transport nationally
See Also: Chutneys and Pickles, Teas and Infusions

11 ↔

Catlin Bros Ltd
11 High Street, Grantham, Lincolnshire
Tel: 0476 65428
Contact: S P Hallam

Grantham gingerbread

Grantham Gingerbread, a light, white biscuit, hollow like a macaroon, made to the orginal 1740 recipe. Also available a range of all butter Danish pastries, and Lincolnshire dough cake.
[C] Undisclosed
[D] By arrangement
See Also: Meat: Pies and Prepared Dishes, Game: Pies and Prepared Dishes, Breads

9

Cegin-Einon
Esgaireinon, Llanwenog, Llanbydder, Dyfed SA40 9XE
Tel: 0570 480599
Contact: Mrs Mary H Price

Bara brith

Handmade traditional fresh fruit pies and cakes including wedding and birthday cakes in a variety of sizes to order. Also Bara brith, a traditional Welsh fruit cake.
[C] 150 p.wk
[W] T & M Jones, Llanbydder Mrs Lewison, Mansfield, Llandyssal
[D] By wholesaler, by arrangement

9

Celtic Food Services
113 Marsh Road, Rhyl, Clwyd LL18 5UB
Tel: 0745 38679
Contact: Mr J Hebson

Fruit pie

Range of handmade fruit pastries and pies including apple crumble, in 12oz retail and 48oz catering sizes.
Ⓒ 25,000 p.mth
Ⓦ G T Owens Cash & Carry, Chester Hughes Meats, Bangor
Ⓓ By wholealer, by arrangement
See Also: Pies and Puddings

12 ↔

Cobbs Of Bath
11 Westgate Street, Bath Avon BA1 1EQ
Tel: 0225 66158
Contact: Mr R N Cobb

Bath buns

Bath buns based on a three hundred year old recipe.
Ⓒ 10,000 p.wk
Ⓓ By own transport within area
See Also: Breads

16

Coleson & Co (Bakers) Ltd
91 Leather Lane, London EC1N 7TS
Tel: 01 405 2526
Contact: John Coleson

Wedding cake

Celebration cakes in a variety of sizes, shapes and designs. Cake accessories also available.
Ⓒ Undisclosed
Ⓓ By arrangement
See Also: Breads

15 ↔

Country Bumpkins Bakery
105 Exeter Road, Exmouth, Devon
Tel: 03952 75004
Contact: Linda Joyce

Lardy cake

Lardy cake, rich in fruit, baked in the traditional oblong shape. Oat Crunch biscuits also available in 7oz packs.
Ⓒ Undisclosed
Ⓓ By arrangement
See Also: Breads

16

Crabtree & Evelyn (London) Ltd
55-57 South Edwardes Square, London W8
Tel: 01 603 1611 Telx: 837880 CEEC G
Contact: J Raven

Sultana crunch

Range of biscuits and cookies including sultana crunch, fruit Shrewsbury, and lemon cookies, in various size packs or country biscuit tins.
Ⓒ Undisclosed
Ⓓ By arrangement
See Also: Chutneys and Pickles

11

Mr Creaton's Food Products
Unit 2, Plant House, Royal Oak Way North, Daventry, Northamptonshire NN1 5PQ
Tel: 0327 702540
Contact: Mr Creaton

Crêpes

Range of crêpes made with flour, milk, oil, eggs and water including English, French, chocolate, and butter in retail packs of six, catering packs of one hundred.
Ⓒ Undisclosed
Ⓓ By arrangement

10 ○ ↔

The Dairy House
Whitehill Park, Weobley, Herefordshire HR4 8QE
Tel: 0544 318815
Contact: Miss Prudence M Lloyd

Cheesecake

Cheesecakes made with own soft cheese and double cream in 1, 2lb sizes.
Ⓒ 1lb size 200 p.wk, 2lb size 100 p.wk
Ⓓ By arrangement
See Also: Cheese

16 ● ↔

Doves Farm Foods
Salisbury Road, Hungerford, Berkshire RG17 ORF
Tel: 0488 84880
Contact: Mrs Marriage

Bourbon biscuits

Range of wholemeal biscuits baked with organic flour including standard digestives, carob coated digestives, Bourbons, and sugar free sweetened with fruit juices, honey and malt.
Ⓒ 4000 cases p.wk
Ⓓ By arrangement
See Also: Cheese, Millers

15

P & C A Duncan
Stapleton Farm, Langtree, Torrington, Devon
Tel: 08055 414
Contact: Peter & Carol Duncan

Wholewheat biscuit bar

Range of wholewheat biscuit bars weighing 35g including muesli, wheaty nut crunch, coconut crunch, and almond crunch. Muesli biscuits also available in 200g boxes.
Ⓒ Muesli bars 1000x36g bars p.wk, muesli biscuits 30,000x200g p.wk
Ⓓ By arrangement
See Also: Yoghurt, Pies and Puddings, Jams and Preserves

15 ↔

Durrans Confections Ltd
Poplar Drive, Kingsbridge, Devon 227 1QY
Tel: 0548 84 2806 Telx: 45139 DURCON G
Contact: Mr M Durrans

Sugar and spice

Range of traditional Devonshire hand baked biscuits including gingerbread,

sugar and spice, and fruit and nut in 200, 600, 800g packs.
Ⓒ Undisclosed
Ⓓ By arrangement
See Also: Fudges and Toffee

15

Forest Products
27b Dreadnought Trading Estate, Bridport, Dorset DT6 5BU
Tel: 0308 58111
Contact: Gavin Brooking

Banana biscuits

Range of handmade biscuits, including chocolate chip, banana and walnut packed to customers requirements.
Ⓒ Undisclosed
Ⓓ By arrangement
See Also: Chutneys and Pickles

14

Fullers Brickwall Farm Ltd
Brickwall Farm, Sible Hedingham, Halstead, Essex CO9 3RH
Tel: 0787 60329
Contact: Robert Fuller

Cheesecake

Five varieties of fresh cheesecake in a range of four sizes.
Ⓒ Undisclosed
Ⓓ By arrangement
See Also: Cheese, Ice Creams and Sorbets

8 ● ↔

Gillygate Wholefood Bakery Ltd
Millers Yard, Gillygate, York YO3 7EB
Tel: 0904 24045
Contact: Blaise White

Carrot cake

Range of cakes made from unrefined ingredients including apple and cider, and carrot and poppy seed in 1, 2lb sizes.
Ⓒ 24 cakes p.dy
Ⓓ By arrangement
See Also: Millers, Breads, Muesli

14 ○ ↔

Gobblin Wholefoods Ltd
Station Road Industrial Estate, Elmswell, Bury St Edmunds, Suffolk IP30 9PD
Tel: 0359 41841
Contact: Peter Dow

Banbury cake

Range of flapjacks including coconut, fruit and nut, apricot and cinnamon in 10″ rounds. Also available Banbury and Eccles cakes, shortbread, a variety of fruit slices and gâteaux, all made with organic stoneground wholewheat flour, free-range eggs, salt free margarine and goat's milk.
Ⓒ Undisclosed
Ⓓ By own refrigerated transport
See Also: Pies and Puddings

11

The Green Dragon Bakery Ltd
Blenheim Road, Airfield Industrial Estate, Ashbourne, Derbyshire DE6 1HA
Tel: 0335 42373 Fax: 0335 46394
Contact: Mr R L Johnson

Shortbread base biscuit

Hand baked speciality shortbread base biscuits.
C Undisclosed
D By arrangement

8

Hoo Ber Fayre
George & Dragon, Main Street, Wentworth, Rotherham, South Yorkshire SG2 7TN
Tel: 0226 742440
Contact: Margaret Dickinson

Ale and fruit cake

Range of cakes made with ale including fruit and chocolate fudge, individually boxed.
C Undisclosed
D By arrangement
See Also: Jams and Preserves

3

John Ridley Projects Ltd
The Mill, Blair Atholl, Perthshire PH18 5SH
Tel: 079 681321
Contact: John Ridley

Wholemeal scone

Biscuits and wholemeal scones made to traditional Scottish recipes.
C Wholemeal scones 600 p.dy, biscuits 1000 p.dy Apr-Oct
D By arrangement
See Also: Millers, Breads

13

W Jordan (Cereals) Ltd
Holme Mills, Biggleswade, Bedfordshire SG18 9JX
Tel: 0767 318222 Telx: 827525
Contact: Graham Lee

Original Crunchy Bars

Range of Original Crunchy Bars including coconut and honey, orange and carob, raisin and hazelnut, raspberry and apple, in single 33.3g bars and packs of six.
C Undisclosed
D By arrangement
See Also: Millers, Muesli

6

Lakeland Gateaux Ltd
Rayson Hall, Townhead, Ousby, Penrith, Cumbria CA10 1QB
Tel: 076881 686
Contact: Robert Mulliner

Chocolate cheesecake

Varieties of cheesecake including rum and raisin, pineapple, fudge and chocolate in eighteen portion sizes. Gâteaux include Black Forest, apricot with brandy, date and walnut, double chocolate, coffee, mandarin, and fruit cake, in sixteen portion sizes.
C Gâteaux 30,000 p.a, cheesecakes 15,000 p.a, fudge cakes 10,000 p.a
D By own transport within area

15 ↔

Langage Farm Dairy Products
Langage Farm, Plympton, Plymouth, Devon PL7 5AW
Tel: 0752 337723
Contact: Peter Tremaine

Cheesecake

Variety of cheesecakes made from farm cream and cheese including morello cherry, strawberry, blackcurrant, mandarin, and peach and pineapple and passion fruit in 7″ x2, 9″x3 rounds.
C Undisclosed
D By arrangement
See Also: Cheese, Ice Creams and Sorbets

7

B Lewis & Sons
Middlegate, White Lund Industrial Estate, Morecambe, Lancashire 0A3 3BN
Tel: 0524 61616
Contact: David Lewis

Liqueur gâteaux

Handmade fresh cream liqueur gâteaux and cream cakes in six portion 7″ rounds, twenty portion 12″ rounds. Also available cheesecakes in ten or sixteen portion sizes.
C Undisclosed
D By arrangement
See Also: Ice Creams and Sorbets

12

Marshfield Bakery
Westend Farm, Marshfield, Chippenham, Wiltshire
Tel: 0225 891709
Contact: Paul White

Marshfield Tiffin

Home made shortbreads, flapjacks and biscuits including Marshfield Tiffin, in re-sealable containers of ten with 4-6 week shelf life.
C Undisclosed
D By arrangement
See Also: Chutneys and Pickles

2

Mr McKenzie's Biscuits
41 Main Street, Turriff, Aberdeenshire AB5 5GB
Tel: 0888 62425/63737
Contact: Gerry McKenzie

Princess cake

Range of cakes, biscuits and pastries including bran and oat cookies, Viennese-type Princess cakes, and savoury Oval Alberts, all in 150g packs in outers of eighteen.
C Undisclosed
D By arrangement

10 ○ ↔

Meg Rivers Cakes
Main Street, Middle Tysoe, Warwickshire CU35 OSE
Tel: 0295 88799
Contact: Meg Dorman

Fruit cake

Sugar and fat free fruit cakes. Also cakes made with raw sugar, free-range eggs and untreated fruits. Traditional Christmas cake made with organic wholemeal flour and Granose margarine, supplied whole weighing 1, 2kg in gift packaging, in 50g slices and 500g wedges. Shortbread also available.
C Cakes 180 p.wk, cake slices 2000 p.wk
D By mail order
See Also: Pies and Puddings

15

Merrydale Celebration Cakes
Exeter Road, Newton Poppleford, Sidmouth, Devon EX10 0BJ
Tel: 0395 68470
Contact: Mrs R Wilson

Wedding cake

Range of traditional, rich fruit celebration cakes, including wedding and Christmas cakes in sizes from 6″ diameter boxed. Icing and cake decorating equipment also available.
C Wedding cakes 300 p.a, Christmas cakes 100 p.a, celebration cakes 150-200 p.a
D By arrangement

16 ○

Middle Farm Shop/English Farm Cider Centre
Middle Farm, Firle, nr Lewes, East Sussex BN8 6LJ
Tel: 032183 411/303
Contact: Mr John Pile

Rock cake

Range of cakes and pastries made with organic flour including cheese scones, rock cakes, mocha squares, Bakewell slice, butter shortbread, date and cherry squares, cider cake and Breton cookies. Also salmon and prawn, stilton and celery quiches and fresh pasta.
C Undisclosed
D By arrangement
See Also: Meat: Pies and Prepared Dishes, Milk

16

Millers Damsel Enterprises Ltd
Lower Mill, Newbridge, Yarmouth, Isle of Wight PO41 0TZ
Tel: 0983 78228
Contact: John Pretty

Wheat Wafer

Range of biscuits baked with stoneground Isle of Wight wheat including Wheat Wafers in a range of four flavours, original, sunflower oil and celery seed, sesame seed, and poppy seed. Cranbourne Crunchies in a range of five flavours, coconut, muesli, walnut, ginger parkin, and malt and bran, in 150g drum or cellophane refill packs. Also Ginger shorties in 200g drum or refill packs, and wheat savouries.
C Undisclosed
D By arrangement
See Also: Millers

2

Mitchell & Muil
Northfield Bakery, Granitehill Road, Aberdeen AB9 2AX
Tel: 0224 694058 Fax: 0224 693459
Contact: Mr Miller McLean

Shortbread

Pure butter Scottish shortbread made to a traditional recipe. Also oatcakes in 300, 450, 680, 900g cartons.
C Undisclosed
D By arrangement
See Also: Pies and Puddings

15

S Moores
The Biscuit Bakery, Morcombelake, Bridport, Dorset DT6 6ES
Tel: 0297 89243
Contact: Mr Keith Moores

Dorset Knob

Range of biscuit and cakes including Easter Cake, more of a biscuit than a cake, made with flour, sugar, currants and mixed spices. Dorset Knobs, a local speciality, a cross between a rusk and bread roll which after three bakings are crisp and dry. Also Dorset Shortbread, Walnut Crunch, and Chocolate Chip.
C Easter Cake 500,000 Dec-Mar, Dorset Knobs limited capacity Dec-Jan, others 1 ton p.wk
D By arrangement

1

Muir's
Graham Place, Stromness, Orkney
Tel: 0856 850213
Contact: Mr Muir

Butter puff biscuits

Range of traditional Scottish handmade biscuits including water, butter puff, rye, caraway seed, and Abernethy, in 150, 200, 300g packs.
C Undisclosed
D By arrangement

16 ↔

Natural Rise Foods
21 Bernard Road, London N15 4PE
Tel: 01 808 2007
Contact: Tony Donaghy

Oat bars

Oat bars made with currants, coconut, barley and apple juice, containing no sugar or dairy products.
C 50 doz p.wk
D By own transport within area
See Also: Breads, Pies and Puddings

11

The Old Original Bakewell Pudding Shop
The Square, Bakewell, Derbyshire DE4 1BT
Tel: 062981 2193
Contact: Graeme McBain

Bakewell pudding

Handmade Bakewell pudding in individual, three to four, and six to eight portion sizes.
C Undisclosed
D By arrangement

10

Orchard Apiaries
Castlemorton, Malvern, Worcestershire WR13 6BS
Tel: 068481 231 Telx: 312242 MIDTLX G
Contact: John H Heywood

Honey biscuits

Range of handmade biscuits with honey from own bees in 7oz, 200g tins in outers of twelve.
[C] 100 doz p.wk
[D] By arrangement
See Also: Mustards, Fudges and Toffee, Honey

15 ○ ↔

Otterton Mill
nr Budleigh, Salterton, Devon
Tel: 0395 68521
Contact: Mrs Desna Greenhow

Walnut and raisin cake

Range of organic wholewheat cakes including walnut and raisin, gingerbread, honey and oat. Also chocolate coconut biscuit in 6½″ squares.
[C] 300 p.wk
[D] By arrangement
See Also: Millers, Breads, Pies and Puddings, Chutneys and Pickles

15 ↔

Pan Fast Food Ltd
Unit 13 , Long Rock Industrial Estate, Penzance, Cornwall TR20 8HX
Tel: 0736 60656 Fax: 0736 4278
Contact: Mr Ron Inglis

Pancake

Frozen, 20cm crêpe-style pancakes made from wheatflour, eggs and skimmed milk. Organic vegan and buckwheat varieties also available. Packed twenty five to the bag in boxes of 100, 250, 400 or 500 bags.
[C] Undisclosed
[D] By arrangement

9

Patchwork
Faraway, Llandegla, Clwyd LL11 3BG
Tel: 097 888238
Contact: Margaret Carter

Cheesecake

Range of homemade 10″ cheesecakes made with free-range eggs and cream cheese including blackcurrant, banana, chocolate mint, and mandarin.
[C] Undisclosed
[D] By arrangement
See Also: Game: Pâtés and Pastes, Cheese, Vegetable Dishes

3

Paterson-Bronte Ltd
The Royal Burgh Bakery, Livingston, West Lothian EH54 5DN
Tel: 0506 31031 Fax: 0506 32800
Contact: Neil Thomas

Oatcakes

Biscuits and oatcakes baked to Scottish and Yorkshire recipes including giant oat, fruit, and chocolate-chip cookies. Also plain, girdle and bran oatcakes, all butter shortbread. Plain, half coated and assorted biscuits in 150, 200g mini-packs, oatcakes in 300g packs, shortbread in 100-500g packs.
C Plain biscuits 83,000 cases p.a, shortbread 52,000 cases p.a, oatcakes 89,000 cases p.a
D By arrangement

15

Peck and Strong
St Anne's Well, Lower North Street, Exeter, Devon EX4 3EX
Tel: 0392 216983
Contact: John Peck

Chocolate fudge cake

Chocolate fudge cake filled and iced with chocolate fudge. Blackcurrant cheesecake with a biscuit base, flapjack with fruit filling and Viennese flan.
C Undisclosed
D By own transport within area
See Also: Pies and Puddings

16

Pittas Pastries Ltd
25 Old Farm Avenue, Southgate, London N14 5QS
Tel: 01 886 6822
Contact: T Pittas

Kataifi pastry

Raw fillo-strudel pastry in 400g box and Kataifi, a very thin string like pastry in 500g bags. Also oriental pastries including baklava and kataifi packed in trays of 25 portions.
C Undisclosed
D By arrangement

14 ↔

Prospero Fine Foods Ltd
Wiveton, Norfolk NR25 7TF
Tel: 0263 711222
Contact: Carolyn Newman

Bavarois

Range of bavarois in a variety of flavours including chocolate and cointreau made with fresh double cream, eggs and fruit in 7″ cakes and individual portions. Also frozen pancakes.
C Undisclosed
W Hales Snails Ltd 01 231 0067
D By wholesaler
See Also: Ice Creams and Sorbets

16 ↔

Robert's Fudge Factory
Unit 2, West Hampstead Trading Centre, Blackburn Road, London NW6
Tel: 01 486 3821
Contact: Robert Habermann

Caramel slice biscuits

Chocolate fudge cake biscuits made with golden syrup, caramel slice biscuits. Also Rocky Road marshmallows packed in trays of 15 pieces.
C 5000 pieces p.wk
D By arrangement

11

Robin Hood Enterprises Ltd
12 Stonehill Close, Ranskill, Nottinghamshire DN22 8NG
Tel: 0777 818786
Contact: Michael Ward

Robin Hood cake

Range of cakes made to traditional family recipe including Robin Hood, soaked in brandy, Sherwood, soaked in sherry, and wholemeal vegetarian. All available plain, iced, covered with nuts and cherries weighing 2lb. Also 1lb edible greetings, 4½oz heart, 3½oz miniature cakes available.
C Undisclosed
D By arrangement

12 ↔

Sally Lunn's
Sally Lunn's House, 4 North Parade Passage, Bath, Avon BA1 1NX
Tel: 0225 61634
Contact: Mr Mike Overton

Buns

Sally Lunn buns, baked to an original 17th century recipe in Sally Lunn's own kitchens, individually boxed 6″x6″x2½″.
C 1000-2000 p.wk
D By arrangement

6 ↔

Sarah Nelson
Gingerbread Shop, Grasmere, Ambleside, Cumbria LA22
Tel: 09665 428
Contact: Mr Gerald Wilson

Grasmere gingerbread — Grasmere gingerbread baked on premises for over a hundred years, in packs of six weighing ½lb, packs of twelve weighing 1lb. Cumberland rum butter also available.
[C] Undisclosed
[D] By arrangement

3

Shortbread House of Edinburgh
14 New Broompark, Edinburgh EH5 1RS
Tel: 031 5520381
Contact: Mrs Anna M Wilson

Shortbread — Handmade shortbread available in cases of 6-12x500g tins. Also Dundee cake available.
[C] Shortbread 144kg p.dy, Dundee cake 12kg p.dy
[D] By arrangement

3 ↔

Simmers
Romano House, 43 Station Road, Corstophine, Edinburgh EH12 7AQ
Tel: 031 334 0852 Telx: 727369
Contact: Mr Alan Sillars

Liqueur cake — Variety of biscuits, shortbread, oatcakes and tinned liqueur cakes baked to traditional Scottish recipes. Biscuits available in 150g packs, oatcakes in 100-300g packs, shortbread in 100-630g packs and liqueur cakes in 1lb 12oz size.
[C] Undisclosed
[D] By arrangement
See Also: Marmalades

11

Spencer (Ashbourne Gingerbread) Ltd
26 St John Street, Ashbourne, Derbyshire DE6 1GH
Tel: 0335 43227
Contact: J R Pearson

Ashbourne gingerbread — Ashbourne gingerbread, a ginger shortbread biscuit in 330g speciality bag, 400g presentation box. Also a wide range of biscuits and cakes including Wakes cakes, oatcakes and brandy snaps.
[C] Ashbourne gingerbread ¼ ton p.wk
[D] By arrangement

12 ↔

Stoneground Ltd
78-82 Bedminster Parade, Bedminster, Bristol, Avon BS3 4HL
Tel: 0272 634666
Contact: Miles Kirke

Apple and carob cake

Carrot cake, apple and carob cake made from additive free, unrefined ingredients.
[C] Undisclosed
[D] By own transport within area
See Also: Breads, Pies and Puddings

15

Sweet Success
Hatchmoor Industrial Estate, Hatherleigh, nr Okehampton, Devon EX20 3LP
Tel: 0837 810016
Contact: Sarah Godfrey-Brown

Chocolate truffle cake

Range of cakes, gâteaux and pies including Black Forest, chocolate truffle cake, cherry cheesecake, Bakewell tart, and apple pies in various sizes from 4-16 portions. 8″ quiches and pies also available.
[C] Undisclosed
[D] By arrangement

9 ↔

Tregroes Waffle Bakery
Tregroes, Llandysul, Dyfed SA44 4NA
Tel: 055932 3468
Contact: Kees Huysmans

Waffle

Dutch waffles made to a traditional recipe sandwiched together with soft butter toffee filling, packed to customers requirements.
[C] Waffles 10,000 p.dy
[D] By arrangement

6 ↔

The Village Bakery
Melmerby, Penrith, Cumbria CA10 1HE
Tel: 076881 515
Contact: A M Whitley

Cumberland Rum Nicky

Range of traditional cakes and biscuits including Christmas and Dundee cake, Westmorland parkin and Cumberland Rum Nicky. All made with organically grown English wheat, free-range eggs and no animal fats and baked in wood fired brick oven. Christmas cakes in 1, 2, 3lb sizes.
[C] Christmas cake 2000 p.a, fruit cake 2000 p.a
[D] By arrangement
See Also: Bread, Pies and Puddings, Jams and Preserves

2 ↔

Walkers Shortbread Ltd
Aberlour on Spey, Scotland AB3 9PB
Tel: 03405 555 Telx: 739524 Fax: 03405 355
Contact: Mr J N Walker

Pure butter shortbread

Range of biscuits and cakes made to traditional recipes including pure butter shortbread and oatcakes Shortbread fingers and biscuits in 150g cartons, oatcakes in 300g cartons.
[C] Undisclosed
[D] By own transport within area

14

Wilson's Trading Co Ltd
Old Ryes, Stebbing Green, Dunmow, Essex CM6 3TE
Tel: 03718 6545 Telx: 818429
Contact: Mr and Mrs Wilson

Date and walnut biscuit

Range of biscuits and shortbreads in boxes and drums featured in the Design Council's Best of British Designs index. Biscuits include ginger, lemon, and walnut in 250g boxes, English spice, date and walnut, raisin, and fruit and nut in 250g drums. Also plain, ginger, and almond shortbread in 200g boxes, 250g drums.
[C] Undisclosed
[D] By arrangement
See Also: Jams and Preserves, Honey, Teas and Infusions

16

Woodnutts Ltd
97 Church Road, Hove, East Sussex BN3 2BA
Tel: 0273 205353
Contact: S MacGregor

Decorated cakes

Decorated cakes and handmade sugar novelties, in various sizes including 5kg packs.
[C] By post, Lynx Express Ltd
[D] By arrangement

8

York Patisseries Ltd
4 and 9 Roland Court, Huntington Road, Huntington, York
Tel: 0904 769727/761128
Contact: Barry Shillington

Pavlova cake — Range of handmade boxed gâteaux, pavlovas and liqueur fudge cakes available to order, fresh or frozen.
Ⓒ 2000 boxes p.wk
Ⓓ By own transport within area, by arrangement

MUESLI

12

Englands Mills
Sea Mills, Berkeley, Gloucestershire GL13 9QR
Tel: 0453 811150
Contact: Richard England

Muesli breadmix — Range of homemade muesli with no animal fats including breakfast muesli with or without sugar in 1kg packs. Also muesli breadmix in 1½, 32 kg packs and plain or chocolate covered muesli bars.
Ⓒ 2 ton p.wk
Ⓓ By own transport nationally
See Also: Millers

9

Felin Crewi
Penegoes, Machynlleth, Powys SY20 8NH
Tel: 0654 3113
Contact: Mrs Patti Partridge

Old Mill muesli — Homemade Old Mill muesli made from own stoneground wheatgerm and bran with over a third fruit and nuts and no added sugar in 750g, 2, 5, 20kg bags.
Ⓒ Undisclosed
Ⓓ By arrangement
See Also: Millers

14 ●

Garboldisham Windmill
nr Diss, Norfolk IP22 2RJ
Tel: 095 381 593
Contact: Adrian Colman

Oatmeal — Muesli and muesli based organic and non-organic cereal, in 750g, 2, 25kg bags.
Ⓒ Undisclosed
Ⓓ By own transport within area
See Also: Millers

8 ● ↔

Gillygate Wholefood Bakery Ltd
Millers Yard, Gillygate, York YO3 7EB
Tel: 0904 610676
Contact: Blaise White

Swiss — Four varieties of muesli, super, hazel, and brazil nut, Swiss, all made with organic flakes, unrefined ingredients and no added sugar. All available in 1, 2kg packs or bulk to order.
Ⓒ 50-100kg p.wk
Ⓓ By arrangement
See Also: Millers, Breads, Cakes, Biscuits and Pastries

3

Hamlyn Milling Ltd
44 Glengate, Kirriemuir, Angus DD8 4HG
Tel: 0575 72121 Telx: 76594 Fax: 0575 73915
Contact: David Valentine

Oatflakes — Oatflakes and jumbo oatflakes in 25kg sacks.
Ⓒ Undisclosed
Ⓓ By arrangement
See Also: Millers

15 ↔

Hele Mill
Ilfracombe, North Devon
Tel: 0271 63162
Contact: C L Lovell

Wheatflakes — Wheatflakes made with English wheat, no additives, in 1½, 3.3, 32kg bags.
Ⓒ 25 ton p.a
Ⓓ By own transport within area
See Also: Millers

10 ↔

Holgran Malt Products Ltd
Granary House, Wetmore Road, Burton-on-Trent, Staffordshire DE14 1TE
Tel: 0283 43221 Telx: 341929 GRANRY G
Contact: Alan Marson

Malted wheat flakes — Malted wheat flakes made by traditional malting method in 10-35kg sizes. Also cereal blends including 100% stone-free cooked grain and malt flour in 10-25kg bags.
Ⓒ Malted wheat flakes 9000 ton, cereal blends 3000 ton, malt flour 1000 ton p.a
Ⓓ By arrangement
See Also: Millers

13

W Jordan (Cereals) Ltd
Holme Mills, Biggleswade, Bedfordshire SG18 9JX
Tel: 0767 318222 Telx: 827525
Contact: Graham Lee

Apple and sultana — Additive free country muesli in 1.36kg packs, special recipe muesli in 500g packs. Original Crunchy, toasted oat cereal, in four varieties including natural, tropical fruit, apple and sultana, almond and raisin in 400g, 1.2kg sizes.
Ⓒ Undisclosed
Ⓓ By arrangement
See Also: Millers, Cakes, Biscuits and Pastries

2

North Eastern Farmers Ltd
Bannermill Beach Boulevard, Aberdeen
Tel: 0224 641255 Telx: 73488 Fax: 0224 637206
Contact: Uel Morton

Oatflakes — Muesli and oatflakes prepared with traditional Scottish steam cooking processes in 1, 3kg packs.
Ⓒ Undisclosed
Ⓓ By arrangement
See Also: Millers

10 ● ↔

Pimhill
Lea Hall, Harmer Hill, Shrewsbury, Shropshire SY4 3DY
Tel: 0939 290342
Contact: Ginny Mayall

Home grown muesli

Muesli containing own grown oatflakes and wheatflakes, hazelnuts, brazil nuts, peanuts, sultanas, raisins, currants and apple, with or without raw cane sugar in 500g, 3, 10, 25kg bags. Also available, bran, oatmeal, breakfast oats, jumbo oats, wheat flakes, and cracked wheat in 1, 10, 25kg bags. Wheat grain in 1½, 16, 25kg bags.
C Undisclosed
D By arrangement
See Also: Fresh Meat, Fresh Vegetables, Millers

1

E & M Shaw
Health Food Centre, 5 Princes Street, Thurso, Caithness KW14 7BQ
Tel: 0847 63561
Contact: E Shaw

Fruit and nut muesli

Producers of sugar free muesli containing fruit and nuts in 500g, 1kg packs. Other health food products available.
C Undisclosed
D By arrangement

15

Sun Cottage Wholefoods
Unit 8, Wyvern Buildings, Grove Trading Estate, Dorchester, Dorset
Tel: 0305 69966
Contact: T A Crabb

Dorset muesli

Range of cereals and muesli with no added sugar or salt including Super High Fibre Cereal with 55% fruit and nut, De-luxe Muesli with 40% fruit and nut, Fruit and Fibre Muesli with 35% fruit and nut, and Dorset Muesli with 45% fruit and nut, all in 500g, 1kg cartons.
C Undisclosed
D By own transport within area

14 ↔

Walsham Stoneground Flour Mill Ltd
Wattisfield Road, Walsham-le-Willows, Bury St Edmunds, Suffolk IP31 3BD
Tel: 03598 679/216 Telx: 817482
Contact: Mr Cooper

Wheat flakes

Range of muesli and flakes including nut muesli, natural bran, porridge, oats and wheat flakes in 500g to 32kg packs.
C Undisclosed
D By arrangement
See Also: Millers

6 ○ ↔

The Watermill
Little Salkeld, Penrith, Cumbria CA10 1NN
Tel: 076881 523
Contact: Nicolas Jones

Organic sugar free muesli

Two varieties of salt and sugar free muesli, standard and organic, and muesli base to which fruit and nuts can be added. Also toasted barley flakes, bran breakfast cereal, oatflakes, and oatmeal.
C Muesli 4 ton p.a
D By arrangement
See Also: Millers

PASTAS

16 ↔

The Delicatessen Shop
23 South End Green, London NW3 2PT
Tel: 01 435 7315
Contact: John Cavaciuti

Tortellini
Spirolini
Fusili

Range of fresh pasta made from Scottish durum wheat semolina including tortellini, made with ricotta, spinach and parmesan, spirolini, fusili, and red, green and white tagliatelle, all packed to customers requirements.
C 300lb p.wk
D By own transport within area
See Also: Purees and Sauces

9 ↔

Premier Pasta Ltd
Unit 34, Rassau Industrial Estate, Ebbw Vale, Gwent NP3 7RL
Tel: 0495 350255
Contact: Ms Kamma Andersen

Tortellini
Tagliatelle

Range of fresh pasta made from durum wheat including lasagne, tortellini, tagliatelle. Also spaghetti available in plain, tomato, green(verdi), and 100% stoneground wholewheat.
C 40-50 ton p.mth
D By own refrigerated transport nationally

PIES AND PUDDINGS

16 ↔

Mrs Beeton's Foods
Norwood Hill, Horley, Surrey RH6 OET
Tel: 0293 862087 Fax: 0293 862396
Contact: Clive Pick

Christmas plum pudding

Mrs Beeton's traditional Christmas plum pudding with cider, rum and brandy and real sixpenny pieces in ½, 1½lb puddings.
C Undisclosed
D By arrangement
See Also: Butter, Cakes, Biscuits and Pastries, Chutneys and Pickles, Hampers

3 ●

Breadline Bakery Ltd
Unit 22, Mid Wynd, Dundee, Tayside DD1 4JG
Tel: 0382 24935
Contact: Mr Petrie

Mexican chilli pasty

Range of homemade pies, pizzas and pasties made with organic wholemeal flour including bean and tomato pasty, Mexican chilli pasty, and curried vegetable pies.
C Undisclosed
D By arrangement
See Also: Breads

15

Budleigh Salterton Pâté & Otter Vale Products
Perriams Place, Budleigh Salterton, Devon EX9 6LY
Tel: 03954 3487
Contact: Mr and Mrs Worrall

Christmas pudding
Christmas pudding with rum, brandy, wrapped in muslin, in 1, 2½lb puddings.
[C] Undisclosed
[D] By own transport within Devon
See Also: Game: Pâtés and Pastes, Shellfish Dealers, Chutneys and Pickles

9

Celtic Food Services
113 Marsh Road, Rhyl, Clwyd LL18 5UB
Tel: 0745 38679
Contact: Mr J Hebson

Apple pie
Range of handmade meat and fruit pies including steak and kidney pie and Lancashire hotpot, in 12oz retail, 48oz catering sizes.
[C] 25,000 p.mth
[W] G T Owens cash & carry, Chester, Hughes Meats, Bangor
[D] By wholesaler
See Also: Cakes, Biscuits and Pastries

14 ↔

Coles Traditional Bakery Ltd
19 High Street, Saffron Walden, Essex
Tel: 0799 22126
Contact: Christopher J Cole

Christmas pudding
Traditionally made Christmas puddings made to one hundred year old family recipe with strong Suffolk Ale in 24x220g, 12x450g, 12x900g, 6x1350g, 6x1.8kg puddings.
[C] Undisclosed
[D] By own transport nationally
See Also: Butter, Jams and Preserves

11

A W Curtiss & Son Ltd
164 High Street, Lincoln, Lincolnshire LN5 7AF
Tel: 0522 30802
Contact: Mr L C Dickens

Mince pies
Mince pies made with homemade mincemeat. Also range of pastries including lemon, coconut and Swiss tarts.
[C] 6000 boxes of 6 pastries p.wk
[D] By own transport nationally
See Also: Meat: Pies and Prepared Dishes, Breads

15

P & C A Duncan
Stapleton Farm, Langtree, Torrington, Devon
Tel: 08055 414
Contact: Peter and Carol Duncan

Christmas pudding

Christmas puddings made to George IV's original recipe with rum, figs, brown sugar, brown breadcrumbs, spices and almonds.
Ⓒ Undisclosed
Ⓓ By mail order
See Also: Yoghurt, Cakes, Biscuits and Pastries, Jams and Preserves

14 ↔

Essex Larders
Pyes Farm, Barnston, Dunmow, Essex CM6 3PR
Tel: 0371 820272
Contact: Zinnia Campling

Figgy sly

Range of sweet pies including Bakewell, treacle tart, figgy sly, steamed sponge puddings, and Christmas pudding.
Ⓒ Undisclosed
Ⓓ By arrangement
See Also: Meat: Pies and Prepared Dishes

15

Foodies Pantry
28 Fore Street, Topsham, Devon EX3 OHD
Tel: 039287 5556
Contact: Martine Parker Brown

Pies and flans

Range of breads, biscuits, pies and flans including lamb and apricot pie, mushroom and gruyere cheese flan, and pork pie with sage and apple.
Ⓒ Undisclosed
Ⓓ By arrangement

14 ○ ↔

Gobblin Wholefoods Ltd
Station Road Industrial Estate, Elmswell, Bury St Edmunds, Suffolk IP30 9PD
Tel: 0359 41841
Contact: Peter Dow

Savoury slice

Savoury slice with cheese and onion, quiches, pizzas and pastries, all made with free-range eggs, goat milk and stoneground wholewheat flour.
Ⓒ Undisclosed
Ⓓ By arrangement
See Also: Cakes, Biscuits and Pastries

12 ○ ↔

Meg Rivers Cakes
Main Street, Middle Tysoe, Warwickshire CU35 OSE
Tel: 0295 88799
Contact: Meg Dorman

Christmas pudding

Fat free traditional Christmas puddings with organically grown wholemeal flour, Granose margarine, raw sugar, free-range eggs and untreated fruit in 400, 800g gift packed puddings.
Ⓒ Undisclosed
Ⓓ By mail order and by arrangement
See Also: Cakes, Biscuits and Pastries

2

Mitchell & Muil
Northfield Bakery, Granitehill Road, Aberdeen AB9 2AX
Tel: 0224 694058 Fax: 0224 693459
Contact: Mr Miller McLean

Christmas pudding

Christmas puddings made to a traditional recipe in 1, 2lb basins.
Ⓒ Undisclosed
Ⓓ By arrangement
See Also: Cakes, Biscuits and Pastries

16 ○ ↔

Natural Rise Foods
21 Bernard Road, London N15 4PE
Tel: 01 808 2007
Contact: Tony Donaghy

Seitan pie

Seitan (high protein wheat gluten) and mushroom pie.
Ⓒ Seitan pies 30 doz p.wk
Ⓓ By own transport within area
See Also: Breads, Cakes, Biscuits and Pastries

16 ●

Neals Yard Bakery Co-op
6 Neals Yard, London WC2
Tel: 01 836 5199
Contact: Janene Smith

Wholewheat croissants

Wholewheat savoury pasties, quiches, pizzas, croissants and filled pitta bread baked on the premises.
Ⓒ Pizza slices 80 p.dy
Ⓓ By arrangement
See Also: Breads

1 ↔

Orkney Foods
Little Stonehall, Deerness, Orkney KW17 2QQ
Tel: 085674 333
Contact: Mrs Floris Couperwhite

Orkney flan

Deep frozen Orkney savoury flans made to traditional recipes including bacon, egg and cheese, cheese and onion, broccoli, cheese and sausage, and bean weighing 142-170g in packs of two.
Ⓒ 750 p.wk
Ⓓ By own transport within area
See Also: Meat: Pâtés and Pastes, Fish: Pâtés and Pastes

15 ○ ↔

Otterton Mill
nr Budleigh, Salterton, Devon
Tel: 0395 68521
Contact: Mrs Desna Greenhow

Vegetarian pasty

Range of organic wholewheat puff pastry products including vegetarian and non-vegetarian savoury pasties made to traditional English recipes.
Ⓒ 400 savoury pasties p.wk
Ⓓ By arrangement
See Also: Millers, Breads, Cakes, Biscuits and Pastries, Chutneys and Pickles

15

Peck and Strong
St Anne's Well, Lower North Street,
Exeter, Devon EX4 3EX
Tel: 0392 216983
Contact: John Peck

Quiche

Quiches, pizzas and spiced vegetable pasties made with wholemeal flour, free-range eggs and vegetable margarine. Also frozen vegetable dishes.
[C] Undisclosed
[D] By own transport within area
See Also: Cakes, Biscuits and Pastries

15

Puddings Food Company
Welgoer Farmhouse, Poyntington, nr
Sherborne, Dorset
Tel: 096322 293
Contact: Mrs Wendy Horne

Sachertorte

Range of handmade, additive free pies and cakes made to own recipes including treacle tart, nut and raisin pie, chocolate caramel shortbread, Sachertorte and Harvest fruit cake packed in individual slices in trays of eighteen, fruit pies 2-4 portions.
[C] Undisclosed
[D] By arrangement
See Also: Meat: Pies and Prepared Dishes

11 ↔

Red Griffin Ltd/The Country Victuallers
Winkburn Hall, Newark, Nottinghamshire
NG22 8PQ
Tel: 0636 86465
Contact: Richard Craven-Smith-Milnes

Christmas pudding

Traditional Christmas puddings, prepared to Victorian recipe with rum, brandy, breadcrumbs, eggs, apples and lemon, wrapped in cling film and supplied in white pottery bowls in 2, 2lb 10oz, 3lb weights individually or boxes of four. Vegetarian Christmas puddings also available.
[C] 4000 p.a
[D] By arrangement
See Also: Bacon and Hams, Game: Pâtés and Pastes

8

Reginald P Bush
10 Vicarage Crescent, Grenoside, Sheffield,
South Yorkshire S30 3RE
Tel: 0742 460812
Contact: R P Bush

Ranmoor plum pudding

Mr Bush's original Ranmoor plum pudding, handmade to a family recipe with sultanas, raw cane sugar, fresh eggs, cognac and wine in 450, 900g, 1.35kg puddings. Also vegetarian pudding with vegetable fat and wholemeal flour.
[C] Undisclosed
[D] By arrangement

14

Ridleys Country Chandlers
Unit 4, Flitch Industrial Estate, Great
Dunmow, Essex CM6 1XJ
Tel: 0371 5744
Contact: Stephen Anderson

Christmas pudding

Ridley's Christmas pudding made with vine fruits, suet, sugar, oranges, lemons, almonds and Ridley's Bishop's Ale in 1, 2lb sizes.
[C] Undisclosed
[D] By arrangement
See Also: Chutneys and Pickles, Hampers

12 ○ ↔

Stoneground Ltd
78-82 Bedminster Parade, Bedminster,
Bristol, Avon BS3 4HL
Tel: 0272 634666
Contact: Miles Kirke

Pizza

Range of vegetarian savoury pasties, samosas, pizzas, quiches and rissoles, made with additive free, unrefined ingredients.
[C] Undisclosed
[D] By own transport within area
See Also: Breads, Cakes, Biscuits and Pastries

6 ○ ↔

The Village Bakery
Melmerby, Penrith, Cumbria CA10 1HE
Tel: 076881 515
Contact: A M Whitley

Christmas pudding

Sweet and savoury pies and puddings made with unrefined ingredients in wood fired oven, including spinach and nut pasty, vegetable and beef pasty, and Christmas pudding with fruit steeped in real ale, in 14, 24oz, 2lb sizes. Mince pies also available.
Ⓒ Undisclosed
Ⓦ Christmas puddings by Suma of Halifax
Ⓓ By wholesaler, by arrangement
See Also: Breads, Cakes, Biscuits and Pastries, Jams and Preserves

Any Problems?

If any suppliers listed in **British Food Finds 1989** let you down, do not deliver their goods, supply you with inferior produce, please let us know and we can follow it up for the next edition. Contact **Henrietta Green on 01-927-9808.**

7

PRESERVES, SAUCES AND SEASONINGS

CHUTNEYS AND PICKLES

15

Adam's Cottage
Adam's Cottage, Powerstock, nr Bridport, Dorset DT6 3TE
Tel: 030885 385
Contact: Deryn Warne

Peach

Range of chutney including apple, tomato, peach, and sliced lemon packed in 12oz glass jars with fabric tops.
C Undisclosed
D By arrangement
See Also: Jams and Preserves, Mustards

8 ↔

Apples Co-Operative Ltd
Valley Road, Hebden Bridge, West Yorkshire HX7 7BZ
Tel: 0422 844601
Contact: Ms Betty Fraser

Winter relish

Range of chutney and pickles made with fresh fruit and vegetables, unsulphured dried fruits and organic cider vinegar including apple and raisin, apple and marrow, mustard pickle, winter relish, and beet pickle in 12oz jars.
C 3000 doz p.mth
D By arrangement
See Also: Purees and Sauces

3 ↔

Arran Provisions Ltd
The Old Mill, Lamlash, Isle of Arran KA27 8JU
Tel: 07706 606 Telx: 779806
Contact: Iain A Russell

Curried fruit

Range of sweet and savoury chutney made with fruit and vegetables, wine or malt vinegar and spices in four flavours, rich fruit, curried fruit, cucumber, and tomato in 2, 4, 8, 12oz jars. Gift packs with customers own label if required.
C Undisclosed
D By own transport nationally
See Also: Jams and Preserves, Marmalades, Mustards

2 ↔

Baxters of Speyside Ltd
Fochabers, Morayshire IV32 7LD
Tel: 0343 820393 Telx: 73327 Fax: 0343 820286
Contact: Miss M E Foster

Spicy mixed fruit

Range of chutney including tomato, spicy mixed fruit, spicy plum and red pepper.
C Undisclosed
D By arrangement
See Also: Jams and Preserves, Marmalades, Soups

12

Beans & Things
15 High Street, Williton, Somerset
Tel: 0984 32711
Contact: J Rew

Fruit and vegetable

Mixed fruit and vegetable chutney made with cider vinegar in 230g jars, with customers own label if required.
C Undisclosed
D By arrangement
See Also: Mustards

16 ↔

Mrs Beeton's Foods
Norwood Hill, Horley, Surrey RH6 OET
Tel: 0293 862087 Fax: 0293 862396
Contact: Clive Pick

Gooseberry

Mrs Beeton's traditional gooseberry chutney and country chutney with plums in 7½oz jars.
C Undisclosed
D By arrangement
See Also: Butter, Cakes, Biscuits and Pastries, Jams and Preserves, Hampers

11

British Harvest Products
Unit 19, Bordon Trading Estate, Old Station Way, Bordon, Hampshire GU35 9HH
Tel: 04203 3244
Contact: Mr Hobson

Hot mango

Range of pickles and chutney including apricot, tomato, hot mango, mint and apple, and spiced fruit available in 200g jars.
C Undisclosed
D By arrangement
See Also: Dried Herbs and Flavourings, Jams and Preserves, Marmalades, Mustards, Purees and Sauces

15

Budleigh Salterton Pate & Otter Vale Products
Perriams Place, Budleigh Salterton, Devon EX9 6LY
Tel: 03954 3487
Contact: Mr and Mrs Worrall

Sweetcorn relish

Range of chutney and relishes including onion, pineapple, and sweetcorn relish with orange in 7oz jars.
C Undisclosed
D By own transport within area
See Also: Game: Pâtés and Pastes, Shellfish Dealers, Pies and Puddings, Jams and Preserves

14 ↔

Cartwright & Butler Ltd
The Spice Mill, Wells-next-the Sea, Norfolk
Tel: 0328 710144 Telx: 817483 CANDB G
Contact: Marian Cartwright

Chutney

Handmade chutney with raw cane sugar and cider vinegar in 12oz jars.
C Undisclosed
D By own transport nationally
See Also: Cakes, Biscuits and Pastries, Jams and Preserves, Marmalades, Teas and Infusions

16

Chanctonbury Herbs
104 High Street, Steyning, West Sussex BN4 3RD
Tel: 0903 815000
Contact: Rowena Green

Fruit

Range of handmade chutney and pickles made with fruit, fresh vegetables and herb vinegars in 12oz hexagonal jars.
C Undisclosed
D By arrangement
See Also: Marmalades, Mustards, Vinegars

16 ↔

Charles Gordon Associates Ltd
Hoe House, Peaslake, nr Guildford, Surrey GU5 9SR
Tel: 0306 730776 Telx: 859500 C/081
Contact: R A Stone

Apricot and walnut

Range of handmade chutney including apricot and walnut, apple and sultana, and apple in 170, 190g hexagonal jars, 30g miniature jars. Customers own label if required.
[C] Undisclosed
[D] By arrangement
See Also: Mustards, Purees and Sauces

12

Clare's Kitchen
Aycote Farm, Rendcomb, Cirencester, Gloucestershire GL7 7EP
Tel: 028583 555/463
Contact: Mrs Clare Benson

Chutney

Range of handmade chutney and pickles in 12oz, 2, 5, 6, 12lb jars. Also mustard, nut spread and humous.
[C] 8000 jars p.mth
[D] By arrangement
See Also: Jams and Preserves

16

Crabtree & Evelyn (London) Ltd
55/57 South Edwardes Square, London W8
Tel: 01 603 1611 Telx: 837880 CEEC G
Contact: J Raven

Apricot and gooseberry

Range of chutney cooked in open kettles for maximum flavour including apple, apricot and gooseberry in 10.6oz glass jars.
[C] Undisclosed
[D] By arrangement
See Also: Cakes, Biscuits and Pastries, Jams and Preserves, Marmalades, Mustards

7

Mrs Darlington's
Southlands, Newcastle Road, Nantwich, Cheshire CW5 7ET
Tel: 0270 67124
Contact: Mrs Darlington

Apple and tomato

Range of handmade chutney including apple, and tomato in 12oz jars.
[C] Undisclosed
[D] By arrangement
See Also: Jams and Preserves

13

Elsenham Quality Foods Ltd
Elsenham, Bishop Stortford, Hertfordshire CM22 6DT
Tel: 0279 812442 Telx: 81439 Egfood G
Contact: Mr Barry Franklin

Apricot and date

Range of English and Indian chutney including apricot and date, five fruit, sweet mango, and fruit and nut. Also range of gourmet relishes including courgette and sweetcorn, and tomato and chilli packed in 12oz jars and pots.
[C] Undisclosed
[D] By own transport
See Also: Jams and Preserves

15

Forest Products
27b Dreadnought Trading Estate, Bridport, Dorset DT6 5BU
Tel: 0308 58111
Contact: Gavin Brooking

Mango and real ale

Range of handmade chutney and pickles including mango and real ale in 8, 12oz jars.
[C] Undisclosed
[D] By arrangement
See Also: Cakes, Biscuits and Pastries, Jams and Preserves, Mustards

5 ↔

Galloway Lodge Preserves
24-28 High Street, Gatehouse-of-Fleet, Dumfries & Galloway DG7 2HP
Tel: 05574 357
Contact: Nigel Hesketh

Red tomato

Five chutneys including spiced orange and onion, spiced peach, red tomato, and apple and raisin in 7oz jars. Customers own label if required.
[C] Undisclosed
[D] By arrangement
See Also: Marmalades, Mustards

5 ↔

The Herb Pot
Dyemill, Sidmount Avenue, Moffat DG10 9B5
Tel: 0683 20681
Contact: Mrs Renate McMillan

Oriental

Variety of handmade chutney including lemon, apricot, Indian, apple and orange, cucumber, and oriental made with dried fruits and spices in 12oz glass jars.
C Undisclosed
D By arrangement
See Also: Dried Herbs and Flavourings, Mustards

3 ↔

Highland Products (Scotland) Ltd
Heather Hills Honey Farm, Bridge of Cally, Perthshire PH10 7JG
Tel: 025086 252
Contact: Norrie Lennox

Apple and raisin

Three chutneys, orange and onion, apple and raisin, and red tomato, all packed in beehive jar.
C 300 doz p.mth
D National carriers
See Also: Marmalades, Mustards, Honey

16 ↔

Kingsley Cavendish
The Manor House, Hurley, Berkshire SL16 5NB
Tel: 0628 824303 Telx: 849462
Contact: Mr S E White

Sweetcorn and apricot

Range of six chutneys blended with wine, spirit or liqueur including sweetcorn and apricot with sauterne, and courgette and rhubarb with chateauneuf du pape. Also five varieties of relish available. All packed in 12oz jars with customers own label if required.
C Undisclosed
D By own transport nationally
See Also: Jams and Preserves, Purees and Sauces

9

Leslie A Parsons and Sons (Burry Port) Ltd
Ashburnham Works, Burry Port, Dyfed SA16 0ET
Tel: 05546 3351/2 Telx: 48297 JOYTEL G
Contact: Rory Parsons

Beetroot pickle

Range of pickles including onion, beetroot, and egg in 270, 450ml, 2.27 litre jars in outers of twelve or catering packs of four dozen jars.
C Undisclosed
D By arrangement
See Also: Fish: Pies and Prepared Dishes

12

Marshfield Bakery
Westend Farm, Marshfield, Chippenham, Wiltshire
Tel: 0225 891709
Contact: Paul White

Hot gooseberry

Range of chutney including apricot, hot gooseberry, curried fruit, and banana and date.
C Undisclosed
D By own transport within area
See Also: Cakes, Biscuits and Pastries, Mustards

14

Melanie Knibbs
St Nicholas, Bevis Way, King's Lynn, Norfolk PE30 3AG
Tel: 0553 674703
Contact: Melanie Knibbs

Fenland chutney

Range of chutney handmade with locally grown ingredients including Norfolk, Fenland, lemon, and mustard seed in ½, 1lb jars.
C 100-200 jars p.wk
D By arrangement
See Also: Jams and Preserves, Marmalades

16 ↔

Oded Schwartz
24 Claverley Grove, London N3 2DH
Tel: 01 349 2242
Contact: Oded Schwartz

Onion confiture

Handmade pickles and chutney including carrot and almond chutney, onion confiture, piccalilli (sugar-free), red capsicum chilli sauce, and brandied clementines in 8, 12oz, 1lb jars.
C 50 doz of each line
D By arrangement
See Also: Game: Pies and Prepared Dishes

15 ○ ↔

Otterton Mill
nr Budleigh Salterton, Devon
Tel: 0395 68521
Contact: Mrs Desna Greenhow

Rhubarb

Chutney made with fruit in season including rhubarb, gooseberry, and apple in ½, 1lb jars.
C Undisclosed
D By arrangement
See Also: Millers, Jams and Preserves, Marmalades

5

J M Pettigrew
2 Oven Wynd, Kelso, Roxburghshire TD5 7HS
Tel: 0573 24234
Contact: Mr J Pettigrew

Orange

Range of chutney including apple, tomato, onion, hot gooseberry, beetroot, apricot, curry, orange, tropical fruit, and curried fruit in 8, 11oz jars.
C Undisclosed
D By arrangement
See Also: Marmalades, Mustards

16 ↔

Pickles And Sauces Unlimited
Etherington, 40 Collington Lane East, Bexhill, East Sussex
Tel: 0424 210537
Contact: Denis E H Dann

Apple and damson

Range of chutney and pickles including apple, apricot and fresh ginger, lemon and mustard seed, apple and damson, all available in 200g jars or to customers requirements.
C Undisclosed
D By arrangement
See Also: Purees and Sauces

14

Ridleys Country Chandlers
Unit 4, Flitch Industrial Estate, Great Dunmow, Essex CM6 1XJ
Tel: 0371 5744
Contact: Stephen Anderson

Apple and mint

Appletree Hill chutney handmade to old East Anglian recipe flavoured with plum, rhubarb, gooseberry, apple and mint, in 7oz jars.
C Undisclosed
D By arrangement
See Also: Pies and Puddings, Jams and Preserves, Mustards, Purees and Sauces, Hampers

3

Scone Palace
Scone Palace, Old Scone, Perth PH2 6BD
Tel: 0738 52300
Contact: Lt Cdr A R Robinson

Curried apple

Range of chutney including curried apple and sultana, peach and nut, rhubarb and gooseberry and crunchy fruit pickle in 198g hexagonal jars.
C 3000 p.a
D By arrangement
See Also: Marmalades

15

Shilstone Products
Unit 4, Exeter Road Industrial Estate, Okehampton, Devon EX20 1QA
Tel: 0837 3080 Telx: 42513 SHARET G
Contact: Richard Taylor-Young

Chutney

Traditional hot chutney packed in 14oz jars.
C Undisclosed
D By arrangement
See Also: Jams and Preserves, Mustards, Purees and Sauces, Chocolates

12

Taunton Foods Ltd
69 Staplegrove Road, Taunton, Somerset TA1 1DG
Tel: 0823 283801 Telx: 46529 TAUNT Fax: 0823 288622
Contact: Judie Kingston

Apricot and ginger

Range of chutney including apricot and ginger, cherry and apple, autumn fruit in 8oz jars.
C Undisclosed
D By arrangement
See Also: Jams and Preserves, Mustards

14 ○ ↔

Tuddy's Garden Shop
Ware House, Stebbing, Essex
Tel: 037 186 274
Contact: Tuddy Holles

Apple

Range of chutney and pickles including apple, tomato and beetroot.
C 2000lb p.a
D By arrangement
See Also: Fresh Vegetables, Jams and Preserves, Purees and Sauces

8

Village Green Preserves Ltd
Roth Hill Lane, Thorganby, York, Yorkshire YO4 6DJ
Tel: 0904 89761
Contact: M R Smith

Piccalilli

Range of chutney including green pepper, apricot, and piccalilli made with fresh vegetables in 10½oz jars.
C Undisclosed
D By own transport nationally
See Also: Jams and Preserves, Marmalades

16

Wendy Brandon
110 Stanford Avenue, Brighton, East Sussex BN1 6FE
Tel: 0273 506 868
Contact: Wendy Brandon

Ginger fig

Range of chutney made with no addded salt or sugar in a range of six flavours, mango, apricot, date, aubergine and sweet pepper, ginger fig, and Kashmiri apple. Available in 1½oz, ½lb jars.
C Undisclosed
D By own transport within area, by arrangement
See Also: Marmalades, Purees and Sauces

15

Wessex Fare Ltd
Station Road, Gillingham, Dorset SP8 4QA
Tel: 07476 2177/3153 Telx: 886089 Fax: 07476 4030
Contact: Rory Herbert

Mixed herb

Range of chutney including hot tomato, apple with mixed herbs, and rich fruit in 284g jars in outers of twelve.
C 15,000 doz p.mth
D By arrangement
See Also: Marmalades, Mustards, Soups

16

The Wooden Spoon Preserving Co Ltd
4 Scotton Street, Wye, nr Ashford, Kent TN25 5BZ
Tel: 0233 812251 Telx: 965267 Fax: 0795 28703
Contact: Peter & Ann Bolt

Handmade chutney

Range of six handmade chutney and four garnishes mixed with a wooden spoon in cartons of 72x1, 12x12oz jars. Customers own label if required.
C Undisclosed
W Scandinavian suppliers, 01 230 5341
D By wholesaler, by arrangement
See Also: Jams and Preserves, Marmalades, Purees and Sauces

DRIED HERBS AND FLAVOURINGS

12 ↔

Arne Herbs
Limeburn Nurseries, Limeburn Hill, Chew Magna, Avon BS18 8QW
Tel: 0272 333399
Contact: Anthony Lyman-Dixon

Tansy

Range of dried herbs including hyssop, tansy, pennyroyal and red sage.
[C] Undisclosed
[D] By Datapost, by own transport within area
See Also: Fresh Herbs, Teas and Infusions

11

British Harvest Products
Unit 19, Bordon Trading Estate, Old Station Way, Bordon, Hampshire GU35 9HH
Tel: 04203 3244
Contact: Mr Hobson

Barbecue herbs

Range of dried herbs for grilling and barbecueing including lemon grass and rosemary, thyme and rosemary. Also available herb mixture for cooking with game in 7oz hexagonal jar.
[C] Undisclosed
[D] By arrangement
See Also: Chutneys and Pickles, Jams and Preserves, Marmalades, Mustards, Purees and Sauces

15 ↔

Carley & Co
34/35/36 St Austell St, Truro, Cornwall TR1 1SE
Tel: 0872 77686
Contact: John and Shirley Carley

Gomasio

Sesame salt (Gomasio) made from roasted and flaked sesame seeds mixed with sea salt in 6oz, 1lb jars.
[C] 10-20 doz p.wk
[D] By arrangement
See Also: Cakes, Biscuits and Pastries, Mustards

10 ○

Fox's Spices Ltd
59 Aston Cantlow Road, Wilmcote, Stratford upon Avon, Warwickshire CV37 9XN
Tel: 0789 66420
Contact: Mr Pester

Indonesian Bumbus

Range of dried herbs and herb mixes, spices and spice mixes including Bumbus, an Indonesian cooking mixture, prepared mixes for kebabs and satays in 8oz retail packs, 10, 25kg wholesale packs.
[C] Undisclosed
[D] By own transport, by arrangement
See Also: Mustards

16

Mrs Gill's Indian Kitchen
The Spice House, Hastingwood Trading Estate, Harbet Road, London N18 1HR
Tel: 01 886 0424
Contact: Christopher Gill

Malay curry mix

Range of dried herbs and fifty blended spice mixes including Malay curry mix, chicken makhanualla and rogan josht, all in individual sachets.
[C] Undisclosed
[D] By arrangement
See Also: Vegetable Dishes

12 ●

Hambleden Herbs
Hambleden, Henley-on-Thames, Oxfordshire RG9 6SX
Tel: 0491 571598
Contact: Mike Brook

Caraway

Over one hundred varieties of organically grown dried herbs, including caraway, raspberry leaf and hyssop packed in 25, 50, 100g bags or larger quantities in cotton sacks.
[C] Undisclosed
[D] By arrangement

5 ↔

The Herb Pot
Dyemill, Sidmount Avenue, Moffat DG10 9B5
Tel: 0683 20681
Contact: Mrs Renate McMillan

Herb salt

Herb salt with sea salt and seven herbs in 6oz plastic bags. Also bouquet garni containing parsley, thyme, marjoram, basil and bay in 4oz plastic bags.
C Undisclosed
D By arrangement
See Also: Chutneys and Pickles, Mustards

16 ↔

The London Herb & Spice Company Ltd
Apothecary House, 18 Selsdon Road, South Croydon, Surrey CR2 6PA
Tel: 01 680 8337 Telx: 262984 LHS Fax: 01 760 0377
Contact: Brigitte Leveque

Bouquet garni

Cook Bags, a range of bouquet garni in perforated bags, in a variety of flavours for red meat, poultry, game and fish. Mint bags also available, all in packs of twenty bags.
C 300 cases p.mth
W United Carriers
D By wholesaler
See Also: Teas and Infusions

14

Maldon Crystal Salt Company Ltd
The Downs, Maldon, Essex CM9 7HR
Tel: 0621 53315
Contact: Mr Clive Osborne

Sea salt

100% natural sea salt free from bitter after taste available in 250, 500g cartons packed in outers of twelve.
C Undisclosed
D By arrangement

10 ↔

T O Williams of Wem
17 High Street, Wem, Shrewsbury, Shropshire SY4 5AA
Tel: 0939 32552
Contact: Mr A L Williams

Chestnut stuffing

Range of stuffing made with toasted breadcrumbs in a variety of flavours including sage and onion, chestnut, parsley and thyme, apple and sage, and spicey herb. All in 65g packs.
C Undisclosed
D By arrangement

JAMS AND PRESERVES

15

Adam's Cottage
Adam's Cottage, Powerstock, nr Bridport, Dorset DT6 3TE
Tel: 030885 385
Contact: Deryn Warne

Greengage

Range of handmade additive free jam and preserves including gooseberry and elderflower, plum, apricot, blackcurrant, quince and greengage packed in 12oz jars with fabric tops. Also orange and lemon marmalades.
C Undisclosed
D By arrangement
See Also: Chutneys and Pickles, Mustards

3 ↔

Arran Provisions Ltd
The Old Mill, Lamlash, Isle of Arran KA27 8JU
Tel: 07706 606 Telx: 779806
Contact: Iain A Russell

Wild rowan

Range of additive free preserves, jams and jellies made with fruit grown locally on the Isle of Arran including raspberry conserve and wild rowan jelly. Also range of preserves blended with liqueurs, all in 1, 2, 4, 8, 12oz jars. Gift packs available with customers own label if required.
C Undisclosed
D By own transport nationally
See Also: Chutneys and Pickles, Marmalades, Mustards

2 ↔

Baxters of Speyside Ltd
Fochabers, Morayshire IV32 7LD
Tel: 0343 820 393 Telx: 73327 Fax: 0343 820 286
Contact: Miss M E Foster

Wild bramble

Range of six handmade jams and preserves, strawberry, raspberry, blackcurrant, rhubarb and ginger, wild bramble, and apricot in 12oz jars, 1½oz mini pack size with customers own label if required.
C 1 million jars p.a
D By arrangement
See Also: Chutneys and Pickles, Marmalades, Soups

16 ↔

Mrs Beeton's Foods
Norwood Hill, Horley, Surrey RH6 OET
Tel: 0293 862087 Fax: 0293 862396
Contact: Clive Pick

Brandy mincemeat

Range of conserves made to Victorian recipes including strawberry, raspberry, and blackcurrant. Also luxury conserves with liqueur including strawberry with cointreau, breakfast marmalade with thin cut orange and whisky, and fine cut orange with ginger, all in 12oz jars. Also available, rich mincemeat with brandy in 12.3oz jars.
C Undisclosed
D By arrangement
See Also: Butter, Cakes, Biscuits and Pastries, Pies and Puddings, Chutneys and Pickles, Hampers

8

Bettys by Post
1 Parliament Street, Harrogate, Yorkshire HG1 2QU
Tel: 0423 526182
Contact: Sally Holme

Black cherry

Range of additive free whole fruit jam and preserves including strawberry, raspberry, apricot, and black cherry flavours, in octagonal jars.
C Undisclosed
D By arrangement
See Also: Marmalades, Chocolates, Teas and Infusions

12

Brendon Hill Crafts
3 Sminhays, Brendon Hill, Watchet, Somerset
Tel: 0984 40939
Contact: Elizabeth Jessup

Peach with brandy

Homemade preserves including Somerset strawberry jam made to traditional recipe, dark Exmoor marmalade with rum, and peach jam with brandy, all in ½, 1lb jars.
C Undisclosed
D By arrangement
See Also: Marmalades

11

British Harvest Products
Unit 19, Bordon Trading Estate, Old Station Way, Bordon, Hampshire GU35 9HH
Tel: 04203 3244
Contact: Mr Hobson

Lemon cheese

Additive free jams and jellies including lemon cheese, apple and mint, apple and sage, and red currant jelly, in 225g jars.
C Undisclosed
D By arrangement
See Also: Chutneys and Pickles, Dried Herbs and Flavourings, Marmalades, Mustards, Purees and Sauces

15

Budleigh Salterton Pâté & Otter Vale Products
Perriams Place, Budleigh Salterton, Devon EX9 6LY
Tel: 03954 3487
Contact: Mr and Mrs Worrall

Apple and mint jelly

Range of additive free jellies including apple and mint, redcurrant, quince and orange in 8oz sizes. Also available suet free mincemeat in 7½oz, 500g jars.
C Undisclosed
D By own transport within area
See Also: Game: Pâtés and Pastes, Shellfish Dealers, Pies and Puddings, Chutneys and Pickles

6

Calthwaite Dairy Products
Calthwaite, Penrith, Cumbria CA11 9QU
Tel: 076885 292
Contact: Clive Pattinson

Lemon cheese

Traditionally made preserves including lemon and orange cheese with fresh fruits, eggs, butter and oil of lemon in 200g jars. Also rum and brandy butter made to Cumberland recipe in 175g plastic cartons.
C Undisclosed
D By own transport within area
See Also: Cheese, Prepared Salads, Fudges and Toffee

14 ↔

Cartwright & Butler Ltd
The Spice Mill, Wells-next-the Sea, Norfolk
Tel: 0328 710144 Telx: 817483 CANDB G
Contact: Marian Cartwright

Plum with port wine

Handmade additive free preserves with raw cane sugar and high fruit content. Also range with liqueurs including plum with port wine, all in 12oz jars.
C Undisclosed
D By own transport nationally
See Also: Cakes, Biscuits and Pastries, Chutneys and Pickles, Marmalades, Teas and Infusions

7 ↔

Cheshire Fudge
107 Chestergate, Macclesfield, Cheshire SK11 6DP
Tel: 0625 29547
Contact: Sandra Hufton

Brandy and strawberry

Twelve varieties of fruit jams including brandy and strawberry, raspberry, and peach in 12oz jars.
C 600 jars p.dy
D By arrangement
See Also: Marmalades, Chocolates

12

Clare's Kitchen
Aycote Farm, Rendcomb, Cirencester, Gloucestershire GL7 7EP
Tel: 028583 555/463
Contact: Mrs Clare Benson

Jams and preserves

Range of additive free, handmade jams and preserves with 60% fruit content in 12oz, 2, 5, 6, 12lb jars.
C 8000 jars p.mth
D By arrangement
See Also: Chutneys and Pickles

14 ↔

Coles Traditional Bakery Ltd
19 High Street, Saffron Walden, Essex
Tel: 0799 22126
Contact: Christopher J Cole

Mincemeat

Variety of mincemeat with apricots substituted for the more traditional apple and blended with rum and sherry in 450g jars in outers of twelve.
C Undisclosed
D By own transport nationally
See Also: Butter, Pies and Puddings

15

W G & F S Cornick Ltd
24 Barrack Street, Bridport, Dorset DT6 3LY
Tel: 0308 22509
Contact: Mr F S Cornick

Morello cherry

Range of honey, jams and preserves including strawberry, raspberry, and morello cherry. Also available, range of fruit liqueurs made to order. Jams packed in 1½, 8, 12oz jars, 28lb pots.
C 20,000 jars p.dy
D By own transport
See Also: Marmalades

16

Crabtree & Evelyn (London) Ltd
55/57 South Edwardes Square, London W8
Tel: 01 603 1611 Telx: 837880 CEEC G
Contact: J Raven

Rhubarb and fig

Range of jams, preserves and jellies made in open copper kettles for maximum flavour including rhubarb and fig, melon and ginger, passion fruit curd, raspberry and kirsch, strawberry and curacao, and peach and amaretto. Also jellies including crab apple and quince, apple and mint herbal, in 56, 227, 340g glass jars.
C Undisclosed
D By arrangement
See Also: Cakes, Biscuits and Pastries, Chutneys and Pickles, Marmalades, Mustards

14 ○ ↔

Culpeper Ltd
Hadstock Rd, Linton, Cambridge CB1 6NJ
Tel: 0223 891196 Telx: 81698/81524
Contact: Ian Thomas

Herb jelly

Range of additive free herb jellies including tarragon, nettle, marigold, and sage. Also range of Indian chutneys and blended curry powders.
C Undisclosed
D By arrangement
See Also: Fresh Herbs, Teas and Infusions

7

Mrs Darlington's
Southlands, Newcastle Road, Nantwich, Cheshire CW5 7ET
Tel: 0270 67124
Contact: Mrs Darlington

Rhubarb and ginger

Range of seven handmade jams including rhubarb and ginger, strawberry, ginger, and apricot. Also marmalades and four fruit curds including lemon, lemon and wine, and orange in 12oz jars.
C Undisclosed
D By arrangement
See Also: Chutneys and Pickles

15

Dart Valley Foods
Cadleigh Close, Lee Mill, Ivybridge, Devon PL21 9PE
Tel: 0752 894795 Fax: 0752 690267
Contact: D C Hawkes

Handmade preserves

Range of additive free handmade preserves, some with no added sugar, in 1½, 4, 12oz, 1lb round jars or 8, 12oz hexagonal jars.
C 4 ton p.dy
D By arrangement
See Also: Marmalades

15 ↔

Dartington Foods Ltd
Lee Mill, Ivybridge, Devon PL21 9PE
Tel: 0752 896172 Telx: 42551 Fax: 0752 896172
Contact: James Waghorn

Kiwi in Kirsch

Range of fruit in kirsch including mango, kiwi, pineapple, and whole mandarins. Also available, fruit preserves with high fruit content , fruit marmalade with whisky or brandy.
C Fruits in alcohol 500,000 jars p.a, preserves 1 million jars p.a
D By arrangement
See Also: Purees and Sauces, Fudges and Toffee

16 ↔

Dorothy Carter Preserves
Iden, nr Rye, Sussex TN31 7NU
Tel: 07978 212
Contact: Mrs Dorian Campbell

Quince

Range of jam and preserves including loganberry, damson and quince. Also fruit jellies including quince, and medlar. All handmade with unrefined sugar and apple juice as setting agent in 12oz jars. Also available, strawberry, raspberry, blackberry, and apricot jam, in 1½oz jars.
C Undisclosed
D By arrangement
See Also: Marmalades

15

P & C A Duncan
Stapleton Farm, Langtree, Torrington, Devon
Tel: 08055 414
Contact: Peter and Carol Duncan

Mazard jam

Mazard jam, prepared from rare strain of wild cherry grown only in North Devon in 12oz jars.
C Undisclosed
D By arrangement
See Also: Yoghurt, Cakes, Biscuits and Pastries, Pies and Puddings

13

Elsenham Quality Foods Ltd
Elsenham, Bishop Stortford, Hertfordshire CM22 6DT
Tel: 0279 812442 Telx: 81439 Egfood G
Contact: Mr Barry Franklin

Lemon cheese

Range of liqueur preserves and jams made to traditional recipes in open copper pans including lemon cheese and strawberry preserve. Also range of marmalades, all in 12oz jars.
C Undisclosed
D By arrangement
See Also: Chutneys and Pickles

14

English Provender Company Ltd
Aldreth Farm, Aldreth, Cambridgeshire CB6 3PG
Tel: 0353 740069 Telx: 32496 KELOUK G
Fax: 0353 740151
Contact: Mrs Anne Parker

Strawberry and champagne

Range of jams and preserves made with raw cane sugar including strawberry and champagne, and plum with cognac. Also

available, range of dried herbs, chutneys and honey, all in 220, 225, 280, 340g jars, 42½g mini jars.
[C] Undisclosed
[D] By arrangement

[8] [↔] **Farmhouse Preserves**
Stumps Lane, Darley, Harrogate, North Yorkshire HG3 2RR
Tel: 0423 74578/780996
Contact: Mr Ian Dawson

Lemon curd — Lemon curd with eggs, sugar, lemon juice, butter and margarine. Handmade strawberry preserve with Yorkshire grown strawberries, cane sugar, lemon juice and powdered pectin. Also preserves with and without liqueurs or spirits all in 8oz jars, 1oz mini jars, with customers own label if required.
[C] Undisclosed
[D] By arrangement
See Also: Marmalades

[15] **Forest Products**
27b Dreadnought Trading Estate, Bridport, Dorset DT6 5BU
Tel: 0308 58111
Contact: Gavin Brooking

Gooseberry — Range of handmade jams including gooseberry, damson, plum, and cherry in 8, 12oz jars and gift packs of 1½, 2, 5oz jars.
[C] 200,000 jars p.mth
[D] By arrangement
See Also: Cakes, Biscuits and Pastries, Chutneys and Pickles, Mustards

[3] **Gremlin's**
Fanmore, Ulva Ferry, Isle of Mull, Argyll PA73 6LX
Tel: 06885 253/262
Contact: Gremlin Napier

Hip and haw — Range of additive free jams, jellies and preserves made from locally grown Isle of Mull fruits, including several wild varieties rowan, hip and haw, elderberry, bramble and sloe, in 8, 12oz jars.
[C] 100lb p.wk
[D] By own transport within area

[8] **Hoo Ber Fayre**
George & Dragon, Main Street, Wentworth, Rotherham, South Yorkshire SG2 7TN
Tel: 0226 742440
Contact: Margaret Dickinson

Lemon cheese

Handmade lemon cheese made with local farm eggs, butter and lemons in 227g hexagonal jars.
C Undisclosed
D By arrangement
See Also: Cakes, Biscuits and Pastries, Marmalades

14 ○ ↔

A & K Hood
The Stables, Gresham, Norfolk NR11 8AD
Tel: 026377 468
Contact: Mr Hood

Rowan and apple

Handmade wild fruit preserves with 1lb sugar to 1½lb fruit including rowan and apple, and elderberry in 1lb jars.
C Undisclosed
D By arrangement
See Also: Fresh Meat, Poultry Producers, Cheese, Fresh Vegetables

16 ↔

Kingsley Cavendish
The Manor House, Hurley, Berkshire SL16 5NB
Tel: 0628 824303 Telx: 849462
Contact: Mr S E White

Plum cognac walnut

Range of preserves blended with wine, spirits or liqueurs including dark plum with cognac and walnuts, and spiced Seville orange marmalade with grand marnier, packed in 1lb glass jars, with customers own label if required.
C Undisclosed
D By own transport nationally
See Also: Chutneys and Pickles, Purees and Sauces

12 ↔

The Kitchen Garden
Old Down House, Tockington, Bristol BS12 4PG
Tel: 0454 413605
Contact: Robert Bernays

Crab apple jelly

Jams and jellies made from own grown soft and mixed summer fruits including crab apple jelly, and redcurrant jelly in 8oz jars, with customers own label if required.
C Undisclosed
D By own transport within area, by arrangement
See Also: Fresh Vegetables, Ice Creams and Sorbets

9

Knolton Farmhouse Cheese Ltd
Overton-on-Dee, nr Wrexham, Clwyd LL13 0CG
Tel: 097873 221/0829 260485
Contact: Mr J Latham

Lemon curd

Handmade additive free lemon curd with fresh lemons, cane sugar, butter and eggs in 11oz jars, with customers own label if required.
C Undisclosed
D By arrangement
See Also: Cheese

16

Martlet Natural Foods
Horam Manor, Horam, Heathfield, East Sussex TN21 OJA
Tel: 04353 2254 Telx: 957266 APPLES G
Contact: Mr Andrew Howie

Apple jelly

Additive free spiced apple jelly, and redcurrant jelly in 225g jars.
C Undisclosed
D By arrangement
See Also: Mustards, Vinegars, Honey, Juices

12

McNeill's Fine Foods Ltd
Cross Lanes Farm, Rotherfield Greys, Henley-on-Thames, Oxfordshire RG9 4QA
Tel: 04917 513 Telx: 846424
Contact: Suzannah Webb

Handmade jam

Range of handmade jams, with or without added sugar, produced in small batches with pure fruit in 12oz jars. Customers own label if required.
C Undisclosed
D By arrangement
See Also: Marmalades, Purees and Sauces, Vinegars

14

Melanie Knibbs
St Nicholas, Bevis Way, King's Lynn, Norfolk PE30 3AG
Tel: 0553 674703
Contact: Melanie Knibbs

Lemon curd

Range of seasonal jams and jellies handmade with local ingredients including strawberry, raspberry, redcurrant, and lemon curd in ½, 1lb jars.
C 100-200 jars p.wk
D By arrangement
See Also: Chutneys and Pickles, Marmalades

9 ↔

Meridian Foods
Jedwells Foods Ltd, Corwen, Clwyd LL21 9RR
Tel: 0490 2024
Contact: Andrew Jedwell

Blueberry

Range of sugar free spreads including apricot, blueberry, blackcurrant, and morello cherry, 100% fruit sweetened with apple juice in 284g jars.
C Undisclosed
D By arrangement

14 ↔

Mister Bumbles Ltd
Highwaymans Vineyard, Risby, Suffolk
Tel: 0284 810969 Telx: 261376 LOFBND G
Contact: Hon Patrick Fisher

Apricot and almond

Range of hand bottled jams and preserves including lemon cheese, apricot with almonds, and strawberry with cointreau in 1½, 12oz jars.
C Undisclosed
D By arrangement
See Also: Wine

3 ↔

Nicoll's of Strathmore Ltd
Douglastown, Forfar, Angus DD8 1TL
Tel: 0307 63732
Contact: James Nicoll

Port wine

Range of jellies in four flavours including spiced apple, and Cockburn's port wine in 340g glass jars or patterned pottery jars.
C Undisclosed
D By own transport within area
See Also: Marmalades, Honey

15 ↔

Otterton Mill
nr Budleigh Salterton, Devon
Tel: 0395 68521
Contact: Mrs Desna Greenhow

Raspberry

Range of jams and preserves made from own garden fruits including raspberry in ½, 1lb jars.
C Undisclosed
D By arrangement
See Also: Millers, Chutneys and Pickles, Marmalades

11

Peak Farms Ltd
Yeaveley House Farm, Yeaveley, Ashbourne, Derbyshire DE6 2DT
Tel: 033523 254 Telx: 377106 CHACOM G HONE
Contact: John A Hill

Lemon Curd

Range of additive free traditional preserves, handmade in small batches including Sally's Lemon Curd with lemon juice, butter and lemon oil in ½oz, 1lb jars in outers of twenty. Also honey marmalade with hazelnuts or pineapple in 7oz hexagonal jars in outers of eight with gingham lids on request. Customers own label if required.
C 1 ton p.mth
D By arrangement
See Also: Hampers

14

Ridleys Country Chandlers
Unit 4, Flitch Industrial Estate, Great Dunmow, Essex CM6 1XJ
Tel: 0371 5744
Contact: Stephen Anderson

Bullace plum

Emily Ridley's range of sixteen jams and preserves including bullace plum preserve made with small, wild Essex plums. Honey also available in 8oz jars.
C Undisclosed
D By arrangement
See Also: Pies and Puddings, Chutneys and Pickles, Mustards, Purees and Sauces, Hampers

15

Shilstone Products
Unit 4, Exeter Road Industrial Estate, Okehampton, Devon EX20 1QA
Tel: 0837 3080 Telx: 42513 SHARET G
Contact: Richard Taylor-Young

Morello cherry

Range of handmade preserves, with or without liqueur, including strawberry with grand marnier, morello cherry with cherry brandy, apricot, and blackcurrant in 8, 12oz jars in outers of twelve.
C Undisclosed
D By arrangement
See Also: Chutneys and Pickles, Mustards, Purees and Sauces, Chocolates

12

Taunton Foods Ltd
69 Staplegrove Road, Taunton, Somerset TA1 1DG
Tel: 0823 283801 Telx: 46529 TAUNT Fax: 0823 288622
Contact: Judie Kingston

Quince

Range of additive free jams and jellies in fourteen varieties including whortleberry, quince, and lemon curd, in 8oz jars.
C Undisclosed
D By arrangement
See Also: Chutneys and Pickles, Mustards

14 ○ ↔

Tuddy's Garden Shop
Ware House, Stebbing, Essex
Tel: 037 186 274
Contact: Tuddy Holles

Rhubarb

Range of additive free homemade preserves including raspberry, rhubarb, cherry plum jam, and crab apple jelly.
C 2000lb p.a
D By arrangement
See Also: Fresh Vegetables, Chutneys and Pickles, Purees and Sauces

8

Village Green Preserves Ltd
Roth Hill Lane, Thorganby, York, Yorkshire YO4 6DJ
Tel: 0904 89761
Contact: M R Smith

Lemon curd

Range of jams and preserves, including strawberry, raspberry, black cherry, plum, and bramble with apple in 8, 12oz jars. Also lemon curd with sugar, fresh eggs, fresh lemons, butter and margarine in 8, 12oz jars. Also range of jellies including apple and mint, apple and sage, and redcurrant in 8oz jars.
C Undisclosed
D By own transport nationally
See Also: Chutneys and Pickles, Marmalades

6 ↔

The Village Bakery
Melmerby, Penrith, Cumbria CA10 1HE
Tel: 076881 515
Contact: A M Whitley

Apricot and almond

Range of conserves including damson, apricot and almond jam with brandy. Vegetarian mincemeat also available.
C Undisclosed
D By arrangement
See Also: Breads, Purees and Sauces

9 ↔

Welsh Lady Preserves
Bryn, Yffor, Pwllheli, Gwynedd LL53 6RL
Tel: 076681 0496
Contact: Dio Jones

Rhubarb and ginger

Sugar free spreads and preserves including rhubarb and ginger. Also lemon cheese, in 1½, 12oz jars.
[C] Undisclosed
[D] By own transport nationally

16

Whole Earth Foods Ltd
Cumberland Avenue, London NW10 7RG
Tel: 01 965 1355 Telx: 312242 MIDTLX G
Fax: 01 965 6742
Contact: James Edwards

Pure fruit spread

Range of fruit spreads sweetened with apple juice including black cherry, blueberry, apricot, Seville orange and peach. Also sugar free jams in same flavours, all in 10oz jars. Also available, smooth or crunchy peanut butter, with no salt, unsweetened or sweetened with apple juice, in 11oz jars. Also three nut butter made with peanuts, hazelnuts and almonds.
[C] Undisclosed
[D] By arrangement

14

Wilson's Trading Co Ltd
Old Ryes, Stebbing Green, Dunmow, Essex CM6 3TE
Tel: 03718 6545 Telx: 818429
Contact: Mr and Mrs Wilson

Cherry

Fruit preserves in capped jars with descriptive historical labels including apricot, raspberry, strawberry, cherry, blackcurrant and lemon curd, in 340g jars, with liqueurs in 227g jars. Miniature jars in wooden crates also available.
[C] Undisclosed
[D] By arrangement
See Also: Cakes, Biscuits and Pastries, Marmalades, Honey, Teas and Infusions

12 ↔

The Wiltshire Tracklement Company Ltd
High Street, Sherston, Wiltshire SN16 0LQ
Tel: 0666 840851 Fax: 0666 840022
Contact: Mr W M Tullberg

Apple and thyme

Range of jellies including apple and mint, sage, thyme, calvados and spiced apple in 250, 450g jars.
[C] 500 doz jars p.wk
[D] By arrangement
See Also: Mustards, Purees and Sauces

16

The Wooden Spoon Preserving Co Ltd
4 Scotton Street, Wye, nr Ashford, Kent TN25 5BZ
Tel: 0233 812251 Telx: 965267 Fax: 0795 28703
Contact: Peter and Ann Bolt

Mincemeat with brandy

Range of eighteen handmade jams. Also mincemeat with brandy, and fruit with liqueurs in cartons of 72x1, 12x12oz jars.
[C] 20,000 doz 12oz jars p.a, 250,000 doz 1oz jars p.a
[W] Scandinavian suppliers 01 230 5341
[D] By arrangement
See Also: Chutneys and Pickles, Marmalades, Purees and Sauces

MARMALADES

3 ↔

Arran Provisions Ltd
The Old Mill, Lamlash, Isle of Arran KA27 8JU
Tel: 07706 606 Telx: 779806
Contact: Iain A Russell

Orange and almond

Range of four marmalades, orange and almond, old fashioned honey and orange, demerara, and fine cut orange in 1lb jars.
[C] Undisclosed
[D] By own transport nationally
See Also: Chutneys and Pickles, Jams and Preserves, Mustards

12

Ashleigh Mill
25 Church Road, East Huntspill, Highbridge, Somerset
Tel: 0278 783466 Telx: 46661
Contact: Mrs R Young

Marmalade

Range of handmade marmalades, preserves and chutneys in 1lb jars and gift packs of 2x8oz jars.
C Undisclosed
D By arrangement

2 ↔

Baxters of Speyside Ltd
Fochabers, Morayshire IV32 7LD
Tel: 0343 820 393 Telx: 73327 Fax: 0343 820 286
Contact: Miss M E Foster

Scottish orange

Range of seven marmalades including three fruits, Scottish orange, and grapefruit with total sugar content of 64-67g per 100g, in 12oz jars, 1½oz mini-pack size. Customers own label if required.
C 1 million jars p.a
D By own transport within area
See Also: Chutneys and Pickles, Jams and Preserves, Soups

8

Bettys by Post
1 Parliament Street, Harrogate, Yorkshire HG1 2QU
Tel: 0423 526182
Contact: Sally Holme

Vintage blend

Three additive free marmalades, tangerine, three fruit, and vintage blend in octagonal jars. Also available tomato and mixed fruit chutneys.
C Undisclosed
D By arrangement
See Also: Jams and Preserves, Chocolates, Teas and Infusions

12

Brendon Hill Crafts
3 Sminhays, Brendon Hill, Watchet, Somerset
Tel: 0984 40939
Contact: Elizabeth Jessup

Exmoor

Dark Exmoor marmalade with rum in 1lb jars.
C Undisclosed
D By arrangement
See Also: Jams and Preserves

11

British Harvest Products
Unit 19, Bordon Trading Estate, Old Station Way, Bordon, Hampshire GU35 9HH
Tel: 04203 3244
Contact: Mr Hobson

Honey marmalade

Additive free Seville, Scottish honey and whisky marmalade in 225, 400g jars.
C Undisclosed
D By arrangement
See Also: Chutneys and Pickles, Dried Herbs and Flavourings, Jams and Preserves, Mustards, Purees and Sauces

14 ↔

Cartwright & Butler Ltd
The Spice Mill, Wells-next-the Sea, Norfolk
Tel: 0328 710144 Telx: 817483 CANDB G
Contact: Marian Cartwright

Whisky

Range of additive free marmalade made to traditional recipes with high fruit content including dark breakfast marmalade with whisky in 12oz jars.
C Undisclosed
D By own transport nationally
See Also: Cakes, Biscuits and Pastries, Chutneys and Pickles, Jams and Preserves, Teas and Infusions

16

Chanctonbury Herbs
104 High Street, Steyning, West Sussex BN4 3RD
Tel: 0903 815000
Contact: Rowena Green

Orange with tarragon

Range of additive free thick cut marmalade made with high fruit content including lemon, lime, and orange with tarragon, all in 12oz hexagonal jars.
C Undisclosed
D By arrangement
See Also: Chutneys and Pickles, Mustards, Vinegars

7 ↔

Cheshire Fudge
107 Chestergate, Macclesfield, Cheshire SK11 6DP
Tel: 0625 29547
Contact: Sandra Hufton

Honey and ginger

Range of marmalade including brandy, honey and ginger, in 12oz jars.
C 600 jars p.dy
D By arrangement
See Also: Jams and Preserves, Chocolates, Fudges and Toffee

15

W G & F S Cornick Ltd
24 Barrack Street, Bridport, Dorset DT6 3LY
Tel: 0308 22509
Contact: Mr F S Cornick

Brandy

Range of marmalades, medium and thin cut, with added brandy or whisky as required, in 1½, 8, 12oz jars.
C Undisclosed
D By own transport
See Also: Jams and Preserves

16

Crabtree & Evelyn (London) Ltd
55/57 South Edwardes Square, London W8
Tel: 01 603 1611 Telx: 837880 CEEC G
Contact: J Raven

Tangerine and lime

Range of additive free marmalades including ginger and orange, tangerine, and lime in 12oz glass jars.
C Undisclosed
D By arrangement
See Also: Cakes, Biscuits and Pastries, Chutneys and Pickles, Jams and Preserves, Mustards

15

Dart Valley Foods
Cadleigh Close, Lee Mill, Ivybridge, Devon PL21 9PE
Tel: 0752 894795 Fax: 0752 690267
Contact: D C Hawkes

No added sugar

Range of additive free handmade marmalades, with or without added sugar, packed in 1½, 4, 12oz, 1lb round jars or 8, 12oz hexagonal jars.
C 4 ton p.dy
D By arrangement
See Also: Jams and Preserves

16 ↔

Dorothy Carter Preserves
Iden, nr Rye, Sussex TN31 7NU
Tel: 07978 212
Contact: Mrs Dorian Campbell

Three fruits

Range of five additive free marmalades, handmade in small open pans with fruit and unrefined sugar, including fresh lime, orange, three fruits, bitter orange, and orange with madeira in 12oz jars, three fruits and orange with madeira also in 1½oz jars.
C Undisclosed
D By arrangement
See Also: Jams and Preserves

8 ↔

Farmhouse Preserves
Stumps Lane, Darley, Harrogate, North Yorkshire HG3 2RR
Tel: 0423 74578/780996
Contact: Mr Ian Dawson

Lemon and ginger

Range of ten additive free marmalades, handmade in small quantities, including bitter sweet Seville, orange, lemon, grapefruit, three fruits, Seville with stem ginger, lemon with stem ginger, and Seville with whisky in 8, 12oz jars and 1oz mini jars. Customers own label if required.
C 200 jars Seville orange marmalade p.wk
D By own transport nationally
See Also: Jams and Preserves

5 ↔

Galloway Lodge Preserves
24-28 High Street, Gatehouse-of-Fleet, Dumfries and Galloway DG7 2HP
Tel: 05574 357
Contact: Nigel Hesketh

Heather honey marmalade

Range of six marmalades including Heather Honey, Seville orange blended with Scottish heather honey in 12oz jars, with customers own label if required.
C 500 doz jars p.wk
D By arrangement
See Also: Chutneys and Pickles, Mustards

3 ↔

Highland Products (Scotland) Ltd
Heather Hills Honey Farm, Bridge of Cally, Perthshire PH10 7JG
Tel: 025086 252
Contact: Norrie Lennox

Orange and almond

Range of four marmalades, orange and almond, old fashioned honey and orange, demerara, and fine cut orange in beehive jar.
C 300 doz of each p.mth
D National carriers
See Also: Chutneys and Pickles, Mustards, Honey

8

Hoo Ber Fayre
George and Dragon, Main Street, Wentworth, Rotherham, South Yorkshire SG2 7TN
Tel: 0226 742440
Contact: Margaret Dickinson

Whisky

Handmade additive free marmalade including orange with whisky, and orange with honey in 227g hexagonal jars.
C Undisclosed
D By arrangement
See Also: Cakes, Biscuits and Pastries, Jams and Preserves

12

McNeill's Fine Foods Ltd
Cross Lanes Farm, Rotherfield Greys, Henley-on-Thames, Oxfordshire RG9 4QA
Tel: 04917 513 Telx: 846424
Contact: Suzannah Webb

Lemon marmalade

Range of orange and lemon marmalades,handmade in small batches in 12oz jars, with customers own label if required.
C Undisclosed
D By arrangement
See Also: Jams and Preserves, Purees and Sauces, Vinegars

14

Melanie Knibbs
St Nicholas, Bevis Way, King's Lynn, Norfolk PE30 3AG
Tel: 0553 674703
Contact: Melanie Knibbs

Seville orange

Handmade Seville orange, ginger and grapefruit marmalades made to a family recipe in ½, 1lb jars.
C 100-200 jars p.wk
D By arrangement
See Also: Chutneys and Pickles, Jams and Preserves

3 ↔

Nicoll's of Strathmore Ltd
Douglastown, Forfar, Angus DD8 1TL
Tel: 0307 63732
Contact: James Nicoll

Whisky

Range of marmalades in four flavours, orange, three fruit, whisky, and vintage in 340g glass jars or patterned pottery jars.
C Undisclosed
D By own transport within area
See Also: Jams and Preserves, Honey

15 ⦿ ↔

Otterton Mill
nr Budleigh Salterton, Devon
Tel: 0395 68521
Contact: Mrs Desna Greenhow

Lemon and lime

Range of marmalade including lemon, lemon and lime, orange, lemon and ginger all in ½, 1lb jars.
C Undisclosed
D By arrangement
See Also: Millers, Chutneys and Pickles, Jams and Preserves

5

J M Pettigrew
2 Oven Wynd, Kelso, Roxburghshire TD5 7HS
Tel: 0573 24234
Contact: Mr J Pettigrew

Grapefruit and rum

Range of additive free marmalade including orange, grapefruit and rum, grapefruit and whisky in 8oz jars, orange, grapefruit and whisky in 12oz jars.
C Undisclosed
D By arrangement
See Also: Chutneys and Pickles, Mustards

3

Scone Palace
Scone Palace, Old Scone, Perth PH2 6BD
Tel: 0738 52300
Contact: Lt Cdr A R Robinson

Three fruit

Range of three marmalades, whisky, three fruits, lemon and Seville orange, in 8oz jars.
C 1500 p.a
D By arrangement
See Also: Chutneys and Pickles

3 ↔

Simmers
Romano House, 43 Station Road, Corstophine, Edinburgh EH12 7AQ
Tel: 031 334 0852 Telx: 727369
Contact: Mr Alan Sillars

Carnoustie

Range of marmalade including Scottish and Carnoustie, in 8oz hexagonal jars.
C Undisclosed
D By arrangement
See Also: Cakes, Biscuits and Pastries

12

Thursday Cottage
Spaxton, Bridgwater, Somerset PA5 1DD
Tel: 027867 330
Contact: Mr K A Kunzli

Lemon marmalade

Handmade additive free marmalade including orange, grapefruit, lemon, ginger, and three fruit in 1lb jars. Also three fruit marmalade made with fructose in 14oz jars. Customers own label if required.
C 3000 doz jars p.mth
W Brewhursts, Surrey Nature Store, Bristol
D By arrangement

8

Village Green Preserves Ltd
Roth Hill Lane, Thorganby, York, Yorkshire YO4 6DJ
Tel: 0904 89761
Contact: M R Smith

Grapefruit

Three fruit marmalade made with sugar and natural pectin. Also thick cut, lemon, orange and grapefruit in 8, 12oz jars shrink wrapped in outers of six.
C Undisclosed
D By own transport nationally
See Also: Chutneys and Pickles, Jams and Preserves

16

Wendy Brandon
110 Stanford Avenue, Brighton, East Sussex BN1 6FE
Tel: 0273 506 868
Contact: Wendy Brandon

Orange and ginger

Range of marmalade including orange, orange and ginger, spiced lemon, and grapefruit in 1½, 12oz jars.
C Undisclosed
D By own transport within area, by arrangement
See Also: Chutneys and Pickles, Purees and Sauces

15

Wessex Fare Ltd
Station Road, Gillingham, Dorset SP8 4QA
Tel: 07476 2177/3153 Telx: 886089 Fax: 07476 4030
Contact: Rory Herbert

Seville

Range of six marmalades including three fruit, Seville, orange with cointreau in 227g jars in outers of twelve. Customers own label if required.
C 2000 doz p.mth
D By arrangement
See Also: Chutneys and Pickles, Mustards, Soups

14

Wilson's Trading Co Ltd
Old Ryes, Stebbing Green, Dunmow, Essex CM6 3TE
Tel: 03718 6545 Telx: 818429
Contact: Mr and Mrs Wilson

Tangerine

Marmalades in capped jars with descriptive historical labels including orange, tangerine, and grapefruit in 340g jars. Also with cognac or whisky liqueur in 227g jars.
C Undisclosed
D By arrangement
See Also: Cakes, Biscuits and Pastries, Jams and Preserves, Honey, Teas and Infusions

16

The Wooden Spoon Preserving Co Ltd
4 Scotton Street, Wye, nr Ashford, Kent TN25 5BZ
Tel: 0233 812251 Telx: 965267 Fax: 0795 28703
Contact: Peter and Ann Bolt

Marmalade — Range of eighteen marmalades in cartons of 72x1, 12x12oz jars.
Ⓒ 20,000 doz 12oz jars p.a, 250,000 doz 1oz jars p.a
Ⓦ Scandinavian suppliers, 01 230 5341
Ⓓ By wholesaler, by arrangement
See Also: Chutneys and Pickles, Jams and Preserves, Purees and Sauces

MUSTARDS

15

Adam's Cottage
Adam's Cottage, Powerstock, nr Bridport, Dorset DT6 3TE
Tel: 030885 385
Contact: Deryn Warne

Wholegrain — Handmade traditional wholegrain mustard with white wine and spices packed in hand thrown ceramic pots.
Ⓒ Undisclosed
Ⓓ By arrangement
See Also: Chutneys and Pickles, Jams and Preserves

11

Alison Horne
Glebe Cottage, Boley Road, White Colne, nr Colchester, Essex COD 2QD
Tel: 078 753097
Contact: Alison Horne

Honey and dill — Range of homemade mustard including horseradish, green peppercorn, honey and dill, garlic and chive, and red wine in 195g hexagonal jars. Also gift packs of three assorted 2oz hexagonal jars.
Ⓒ Undisclosed
Ⓓ By arrangement

3 ↔

Arran Provisions Ltd
The Old Mill, Lamlash, Isle of Arran KA27 8JU
Tel: 07706 606 Telx: 779806
Contact: Iain A Russell

Green peppercorn — Range of smooth and coarse grain mustard, with or without beer and spirits, including green peppercorn, and crunchy beer in 1, 2, 4, 8, 12oz jars and gift packs. Customers own label if required.
Ⓒ Undisclosed
Ⓓ By own transport nationally
See Also: Chutneys and Pickles, Jams and Preserves, Marmalades

12

Beans & Things
15 High Street, Williton, Somerset
Tel: 0984 32711
Contact: J Rew

Punjabi — Coarse mustard with wholegrain, cider vinegar and herbs and spices in five flavours including mint, and Punjabi in 170g jars, with customers own label if required.
Ⓒ Undisclosed
Ⓓ By arrangement
See Also: Chutneys and Pickles

11

British Harvest Products
Unit 19, Bordon Trading Estate, Old Station Way, Bordon, Hampshire GU35 9HH
Tel: 04203 3244
Contact: Mr Hobson

Tewkesbury — Range of additive free smooth and coarse Dijon-type mustard including honey with marjoram, black pepper, and Tewkesbury with juniper in 170g jars.
Ⓒ Undisclosed
Ⓓ By arrangement
See Also: Chutneys and Pickles, Dried Herbs and Flavourings, Jams and Preserves, Marmalades, Purees and Sauces

14 ↔

Burnham Mustard Company
1 The Quay, Burnham-on-Crouch, Essex CMO 8AS
Tel: 0621 783868
Contact: Anne Woolfson

Beer — Range of handmade mustard in eight flavours, horseradish, garlic, sherry, beer, chilli, honey, tomato and Burnham (Dijon-type) in 8oz glass jars, with customers own label if required. arrangement.
Ⓒ Undisclosed
Ⓓ By arrangement

15 ↔

Carley & Co
34/35/36 St Austell Street, Truro, Cornwall TR1 1SE
Tel: 0872 77686
Contact: John and Shirley

Honey — Mustard with freshly flaked seeds, cider vinegar, honey and spices in 11oz jars, with customers own label if required.
Ⓒ 10-20 doz p.wk
Ⓓ By arrangement
See Also: Cakes, Biscuits and Pastries, Dried Herbs and Flavourings

16

Chanctonbury Herbs
104 High Street, Steyning, West Sussex BN4 3RD
Tel: 0903 815000
Contact: Rowena Green

Thyme — Range of additive free mustard with fresh herbs including smooth with marjoram, and thyme in 8oz hexagonal jars.
Ⓒ Undisclosed
Ⓓ By arrangement
See Also: Chutneys and Pickles, Marmalades, Vinegars

16 ↔

Charles Gordon Associates Ltd
Hoe House, Peaslake, nr Guildford, Surrey GU5 9SR
Tel: 0306 730776 Telx: 859500 C/081
Contact: R A Stone

Real ale

Range of coarse grain mustard, preserved with vinegar and salt, in seven flavours, English vineyard, green peppercorn, English farmhouse, wholegrain, real ale, whisky, and Meaux-type in 170, 190g hexagonal jars, 30g miniature jars, with customers own label if required.
C Undisclosed
D By arrangement
See Also: Chutneys and Pickles, Purees and Sauces

16

Crabtree & Evelyn (London) Ltd
55/57 South Edwardes Square, London W8
Tel: 01 603 1611 Telx: 837880 CEEC G
Contact: J Raven

Honey

Blends of mustard including honey and tarragon in 9oz glass jars.
C Undisclosed
D By arrangement
See Also: Cakes, Biscuits and Pastries, Chutneys and Pickles, Jams and Preserves, Marmalades

6 ↔

Cumberland Mustard
Sharon Cottage, Slaggyford, Carlisle, Cumbria CA6 7NJ
Tel: 0498 81135
Contact: Marilyn Avens

Garlic

Range of mustard sweetened with honey in four flavours, original, horseradish, garlic, and green peppercorn in ½, 1lb jars.
C 500 jars p.wk
D By arrangement

9 ↔

Fieldfare
3 Maesgwynne Cottages, Cwmbrandy, Fishguard, Dyfed SA62 9PS
Tel: 0348 874032
Contact: Jane Hawkins

Spiced honey

Handmade mustard with wholegrain mustard seed flavoured with spiced honey, chives, and chilli with ginger in 6oz jars, 5lb buckets, 3x4oz jars in wooden spice rack.
C 60 doz jars p.wk
D By arrangement

15

Forest Products
27b Dreadnought Trading Estate, Bridport, Dorset DT6 5BU
Tel: 0308 58111
Contact: Gavin Brooking

Wholegrain

Range of additive free mustard, including English wholegrain, and mild honey in 8, 12oz jars and gift packs of 1½, 2, 5oz jars.
C Undisclosed
D By arrangement
See Also: Cakes, Biscuits and Pastries, Chutneys and Pickles, Jams and Preserves

10 ⦿

Fox's Spices Ltd
59 Aston Cantlow Road, Wilmcote, Stratford upon Avon, Warwickshire CV37 9XN
Tel: 0789 66420
Contact: Mr Pester

Horseradish and apple

Range of nine homemade wholegrain mustards including apple and mint, horseradish, and country apple, all made from organically grown produce.
C Undisclosed
D By arrangement
See Also: Dried Herbs and Flavourings

5 ↔

Galloway Lodge Preserves
24-28 High Street, Gatehouse-of-Fleet, Dumfries & Galloway DG7 2HP
Tel: 05574 357
Contact: Nigel Hesketh

Scotch crunchy

Range of five mustards with coarse grained medium mustard, brewed vinegar, herbs and spices, including honey and cinnamon, whisky, wholegrain, Scotch oatmeal, and Scotch crunchy in 6oz jars, with customers own label if required.
C Undisclosed
D By arrangement
See Also: Chutneys and Pickles, Marmalades

5 ↔

The Herb Pot
Dyemill, Sidmount Avenue, Moffat DG10 9B5
Tel: 0683 20681
Contact: Mrs Renate McMillan

Aromatic

Aromatic mustard with mustard seed and mustard powder, cider vinegar, apple juice, herbs and spices in 6oz glass jars.
C Undisclosed
D By arrangement
See Also: Chutneys and Pickles, Dried Herbs and Flavourings

3 ↔

Highland Products (Scotland) Ltd
Heather Hills Honey Farm, Bridge of Cally, Perthshire PH10 7JG
Tel: 025086 252
Contact: Norrie Lennox

Whisky

Range of wholegrain flavoured mustard including whisky, honey and cinnamon, and oatmeal in beehive jar.
C 300 doz of each p.mth
D National carriers
See Also: Chutneys and Pickles, Marmalades, Honey

12 ↔

Holstius & Breet
Esperanza, Aust, Bristol, Avon BS12 3AX
Tel: 04545 3148 Telx: 449752
Contact: Robin D L Breet

Guinness

Range of speciality mustards including brandy and black pepper, chilli, guinness and black treacle, horseradish, tarragon

and white wine, whisky and thyme in 65, 175g jars.
[C] Undisclosed
[D] By arrangement
See Also: Butter, Fudges and Toffee, Snacks and Savouries

12 **Marshfield Bakery**
Westend Farm, Marshfield, Chippenham, Wiltshire
Tel: 0225 891709
Contact: Paul White

Coarse grain — Range of mustard including Dijon with white wine and spices, and coarse grain with vinegar.
[C] Undisclosed
[D] By own transport within area
See Also: Cakes, Biscuits and Pastries, Chutneys and Pickles

16 **Martlet Natural Foods**
Horam Manor, Horam, Heathfield, East Sussex TN21 OJA
Tel: 04353 2254 Telx: 957266 APPLES G
Contact: Mr Andrew Howie

Coarse ground — Strong and mild coarse ground mustard in 170g jars.
[C] Undisclosed
[D] By arrangement
See Also: Jams and Preserves, Vinegars, Honey, Juices

10 **Orchard Apiaries**
Castlemorton, Malvern, Worcestershire WR13 6BS
Tel: 068481 231 Telx: 312242 MIDTLX G
Contact: John H Heywood

Welsh — Range of mustard made with honey produced on farm including mild English with honey and horseradish, Welsh with honey and leeks, all in 6oz hexagonal jars.
[C] Undisclosed
[D] By arrangement
See Also: Cakes, Biscuits and Pastries, Fudges and Toffee, Honey

5 **J M Pettigrew**
2 Oven Wynd, Kelso, Roxburghshire TD5 7HS
Tel: 0573 24234
Contact: Mr J Pettigrew

Dijon — Dijon, wholegrain and coarse grain honey mustard in 6½oz jars.
[C] Undisclosed
[D] By arrangement
See Also: Chutneys and Pickles, Marmalades

14 **Ridleys Country Chandlers**
Unit 4, Flitch Industrial Estate, Great Dunmow, Essex CM6 1XJ
Tel: 0371 5744
Contact: Stephen Anderson

Arcy Varly — Range of additive free mustard including Ridley's Arcy Varly Essex mustard with fresh horseradish, wholegrain and spices and Ridley's Essex Light Ale in 8oz jars.
[C] Undisclosed
[D] By arrangement
See Also: Pies and Puddings, Chutneys and Pickles, Jams and Preserves, Purees and Sauces, Hampers

15 **Shilstone Products**
Unit 4, Exeter Road Industrial Estate, Okehampton, Devon EX20 1QA
Tel: 0837 3080 Telx: 42513 SHARET G
Contact: Richard Taylor-Young

Dragon's Breath — Handmade Dragon's Breath mustard, in 5½oz jars.
[C] Undisclosed
[D] By arrangement
See Also: Chutneys and Pickles, Jams and Preserves, Purees and Sauces, Chocolates

12 **Taunton Foods Ltd**
69 Staplegrove Road, Taunton, Somerset TA1 1DG
Tel: 0823 283801 Telx: 46529 TAUNT Fax: 0823 288622
Contact: Judie Kingston

Wholegrain with honey

Range of three mustards, English wholegrain with honey and cider, English coarse with cider, and mustard and horseradish condiment in 8oz jars.
Ⓒ Undisclosed
Ⓓ By arrangement
See Also: Chutneys and Pickles, Jams and Preserves

12

Taylor & Lake
Park Farmhouse, Sandford St Marin, Oxford OX5 4AH
Tel: 060 883 366
Contact: Mark Lake

Dill

Dill mustard made with mild mustard grains, olive oil, dill and spices in 200g jars. Also dill sauce, made with spirit vinegar, dill and spices in 170g jars.
Ⓒ Undisclosed
Ⓓ By arrangement

15

Wessex Fare Ltd
Station Road, Gillingham, Dorset SP8 4QA
Tel: 07476 2177/3153 Telx: 886089 Fax: 07476 4030
Contact: Rory Herbert

Sesame

Range of four mustards including Hot Black, sesame, coarse ground, and dill in 85, 170g jars in outers of twelve. Customers own label if required.
Ⓒ 2000 doz p.mth
Ⓓ By arrangement
See Also: Chutneys and Pickles, Marmalades, Soups

15

West Country Sauce Company
1 Halsdon Close, 247 Exeter Road, Exmouth, Devon EX8 3NG
Tel: 0395 266677
Contact: Mrs P Kerley

Mustard sauce

Homemade additive free mustard sauce prepared with vinegar, sugar, mustard spices and mustard seed in 6oz bottles.
Ⓒ Undisclosed
Ⓦ Fine Foods of Europe, 036 782616
Cottage Delights, 0538 361011
Ⓓ By wholesaler

12 ↔

The Wiltshire Tracklement Company Ltd
High Street, Sherston, Wiltshire SN16 0LQ
Tel: 0666 840851 Fax: 0666 840022
Contact: Mr W M Tullberg

Tarragon

Range of additive free mustard with four coarse ground varieties, full strength, honey mild, tarragon, and black in 200, 340g jars. Also five fine ground varieties including Taunton cider, green peppercorn, and hot English in 200g jars. Two dry mustards, mild yellow and mild black in 75g jars. Customers own label if required.
Ⓒ 1200 doz p.wk
Ⓓ By arrangement
See Also: Jams and Preserves, Purees and Sauces

PUREES AND SAUCES

8 ↔

Apples Co-Operative Ltd
Valley Road, Hebden Bridge, West Yorkshire HX7 7BZ
Tel: 0422 844601
Contact: Ms Betty Fraser

Ketchup sauce

Three ketchup sauces with no added sugar or salt, fruity, spicy, and tomato in 340ml bottles.
Ⓒ 3000 doz p.mth
Ⓓ By arrangement
See Also: Chutneys and Pickles

7 ○ ↔

Bowling Alley Herb Farm
Commonside, Alvanley, nr Warrington, Cheshire
Tel: 09289 285
Contact: Mrs Felicity Elphick

Garlic mayonnaise

Range of mayonnaise including garlic, and dill in 5oz-4lb tubs. Also vinegars.
Ⓒ Undisclosed
Ⓓ By arrangement
See Also: Bacon and Hams, Cheese, Fresh Herbs

11

British Harvest Products
Unit 19, Bordon Trading Estate, Old Station Way, Bordon, Hampshire GU35 9HH
Tel: 04203 3244
Contact: Mr Hobson

Barbecue sauce

Additive free barbecue sauce made with vintage cider, onion, spices and sea salt.
Ⓒ Undisclosed
Ⓓ By arrangement
See Also: Chutneys and Pickles, Dried Herbs and Flavourings, Jams and Preserves, Marmalades, Mustards

16 ↔

Bunker Farm Produce
Bunker Farm, Basingstoke Rd, Greenham Common South, Newbury, Berkshire RG15 8HH
Tel: 0635 45535
Contact: Ken Neale

Mayonnaise

Homemade mayonnaise with free-range eggs, sunflower oil and lemon juice, and flavours added according to customers requirements, in 300ml jars or in bulk.
Ⓒ Undisclosed
Ⓓ By own transport within area, by arrangement
See Also: Fresh Meat, Poultry Producers, Cheese

16 ↔

Charles Gordon Associates Ltd
Hoe House, Peaslake, nr Guildford, Surrey GU5 9SR
Tel: 0306 730776 Telx: 859500 C/081
Contact: R A Stone

Mustard and horseradish — Horseradish sauce made with horseradish root blended with sunflower oil and wine vinegar in 170, 190g jars, 30g mini jars with customers own label if required.
[C] Undisclosed
[D] By own transport nationally
See Also: Chutneys and Pickles, Mustards

15 ↔ **Dartington Foods Ltd**
Lee Mill, Ivybridge, Devon PL21 9PE
Tel: 0752 896172 Telx: 42551 Fax: 0752 896172
Contact: James Waghorn

Fudge sauce — Additive free fudge and chocolate dessert sauces.
[C] 100,000 jars p.a
[D] By arrangement
See Also: Jams and Preserves, Fudges and Toffee

16 ↔ **The Delicatessen Shop**
23 South End Green, London NW3 2PT
Tel: 01 435 7315
Contact: John Cavaciuti

Walnut — Range of pasta sauces including hot clam sauce, pesto, walnut, tomato with wine and spices, mushroom and tomato, and bolognaise all in 1lb weights.
[C] 300x1lb p.wk
[D] By own transport within area
See Also: Pastas

16 **Gramma's Ltd**
PO Box 218, East Ham, London E6 4BG
Tel: 01 470 8751
Contact: Mrs D Moore

Pepper sauce — Range of nine handmade concentrated pepper sauces in four strengths, made from fresh Caribbean hot peppers, with over twenty five herbs and spices, vinegar, sunflower oil, sea salt and raw cane sugar, packed in 1½oz jars in outers of six. Tropical pepper chow also available.
[C] 5000 p.mth
[D] By arrangement

9 **Green Dragon Animal Free Foods**
Hafod Fadog, Aber Road, Llanfairfechan, Gwynedd
Tel: 0248 680267
Contact: Haydn Jones

Soya mayonnaise — Range of sugar free sauces made without animal products, including mayonnaise made with soya solids and oils, and vegan soya cheese in 150, 300g jars, 2½, 5lt catering tubs.
[C] Undisclosed
[D] By arrangement

16 ↔ **Kingsley Cavendish**
The Manor House, Hurley, Berkshire SL16 5NB
Tel: 0628 824303 Telx: 849462
Contact: Mr S E White

Passion fruit puree — Fruit puree sauces blended with wine, spirits or liqueur, in six flavours including strawberry puree with grand marnier, and passion fruit puree with white rum. Three varieties of ketchup also available in 50cl glass containers, with customers own label if required.
[C] Undisclosed
[D] By own transport nationally
See Also: Chutneys and Pickles, Jams and Preserves

7 ↔ **Kite Wholefoods**
The Old Mill, Galgate, Lancaster, Lancashire LA2 OPR
Tel: 0524 752100
Contact: Mark Walsh

Mayonnaise — Additive free mayonnaise in a range of flavours including plain, herb and black mustard, garlic, lemon, tomato and tamari in 325, 650g jars, 2.6kg catering packs.
[C] 300 doz p.mth
[W] Suma, Halifax, 0422 45513 Marigold, London, 01 267 7368
[D] By wholesaler

12

Martin Pitt
Levetts Farm, Marlborough, Wiltshire SN8 4DS
Tel: 0672 52035
Contact: Martin Pitt

Mayonnaise

Homemade additive free mayonnaise, made with free-range eggs, sunflower oil, honey, cider vinegar, lemon juice, sea salt, herbs and spices in 275g, 2kg jars, 5, 10kg plastic buckets.
[C] Undisclosed
[D] By arrangement
See Also: Eggs, Cheese

12

McNeill's Fine Foods Ltd
Cross Lanes Farm, Rotherfield Greys, Henley-on-Thames, Oxfordshire RG9 4QA
Tel: 04917 513 Telx: 846424
Contact: Suzannah Webb

Fudge sauce

Range of additive free fudge sauces made to traditional recipe flavoured with coffee, brandy, rose, almond, chocolate, butterscotch, violet and honey, in 7oz jars. Customers own label if required.
[C] Undisclosed
[D] By arrangement
See Also: Jams and Preserves, Marmalades, Vinegars

16 ↔

Pickles And Sauces Unlimited
Etherington, 40 Collington Lane East, Bexhill, East Sussex
Tel: 0424 210537
Contact: Denis E H Dann

Chocolate sauce

Chocolate sauce handmade to traditional recipe using bitter Swiss chocolate in 200g glass jars or to customers requirements.
[C] Undisclosed
[D] By arrangement
See Also: Chutneys and Pickles

14

Ridleys Country Chandlers
Unit 4, Flitch Industrial Estate, Great Dunmow, Essex CM6 1XJ
Tel: 0371 5744
Contact: Stephen Anderson

Cranberry sauce

Range of additive free purees and sauces including Emily Ridley's cranberry sauce made with port.
[C] Undisclosed
[D] By arrangement
See Also: Pies and Puddings, Chutneys and Pickles, Jams and Preserves, Mustards, Hampers

15

Shilstone Products
Unit 4, Exeter Road Industrial Estate, Okehampton, Devon EX20 1QA
Tel: 0837 3080 Telx: 42513 SHARET G
Contact: Richard Taylor-Young

Mayonnaise

Mayonnaise made with fresh cream and eggs in 6½oz jars.
[C] Undisclosed
[D] By arrangement
See Also: Chutneys and Pickles, Jams and Preserves, Mustards, Chocolates

6

Straker & Leatham
2 Market Street, Hexham, Northumberland NE46 3NU
Tel: 0434 602929/607011
Contact: Catherine Leatham

Amatriciana sauce

Range of additive free handmade pasta sauces including olive and tomato, aubergine, and Amatriciana with parma ham, onion, garlic, wine and herbs in 700g jars shrink wrapped in outers of six.
[C] Undisclosed
[W] Jeal Fine Foods
[D] By arrangement

14 ○ ↔

Tuddy's Garden Shop
Ware House, Stebbing, Essex
Tel: 037 186 274
Contact: Tuddy Holles

Horseradish

Range of additive free sauces, including horseradish.
[C] 2000lb p.a
[D] By arrangement
See Also: Fresh Vegetables, Chutneys and Pickles, Jams and Preserves

6 ↔

The Village Bakery
Melmerby, Penrith, Cumbria CA10 1HE
Tel: 076881 515
Contact: A M Whitley

Rum and brandy butter

Rum and brandy butter made with light Muscavado raw cane sugar in 150g plastic tubs and stoneware pots.
[C] Undisclosed
[D] By arrangement
See Also: Breads, Jams and Preserves

16

Wendy Brandon
110 Stanford Avenue, Brighton, East Sussex BN1 6FE
Tel: 0273 506 868
Contact: Wendy Brandon

Spiced apple

Handmade fruit sauces without added sugar in four flavours, cranberry, cranberry and orange, plum, and spiced apple in 1½oz, ½lb jars.
[C] 2-3000 jars p.mth
[D] By own transport within area
See Also: Chutneys and Pickles, Marmalades

12 ↔

The Wiltshire Tracklement Company Ltd
High Street, Sherston, Wiltshire SN16 0LQ
Tel: 0666 840851 Fax: 0666 840022
Contact: Mr W M Tullberg

Horseradish and dill

Hot and strong homemade horseradish made with grated fresh horseradish mixed with cream or mustard in 180ml jars. Customers own label if required.
[C] 200 doz jars p.wk
[D] By own transport within area
See Also: Jams and Preserves, Mustards

16

The Wooden Spoon Preserving Co Ltd
4 Scotton Street, Wye, nr Ashford, Kent TN25 5BZ
Tel: 0233 812251 Telx: 965267 Fax: 0795 28703
Contact: Peter and Ann Bolt

Fruit sauces

Range of six handmade fruit sauces in cartons of 72x1, 12x12oz jars.
[C] Undisclosed
[W] Scandinavian Suppliers 01 230 5341
[D] By wholesaler, by arrangement
See Also: Chutneys and Pickles, Jams and Preserves, Marmalades

9 ↔

Zest Foods
4 St Giles park, Pool Road, Newtown, Powys SY16 3AZ
Tel: 0686 622058
Contact: Tim Clarke

Pesto

Pesto, basil sauce made with fresh basil, nuts, parmesan cheese, garlic, cold pressed sunflower oil and spices, vegetarian version with vegetable rennet cheese, vegan version without cheese. Also parsley relish made with parsley, almonds, green chillies, and sesame oil, all in 163, 340g jars.
[C] Pesto 12,000 jars p.mth, parsley relish 8000 jars p.mth
[D] By arrangement

British Food Finds is here to help-

If you know of a producer of speciality food not listed in **British Food Finds 1989,** please let us know so that we can include them in our next edition.

For editorial entries contact **Henrietta Green on 01 727 9808.**

VINEGARS

14 ○ ↔ **Aspall Cyder**
Aspall Hall, nr Debenham, Stowmarket, Suffolk IP14 6PD
Tel: 0728 860510 Fax: 0728 861031
Contact: John Chevallier Guild

Cyder vinegar — Additive free Cyder vinegar made with organically grown apples from Suffolk, in ½, 1lt bottles, 5, 25lt packs. Red and white wine vinegars also available in 50cl wine bottles, 5lt packs.
[C] Undisclosed
[D] By own transport nationally
See Also: Juices

16 **Chanctonbury Herbs**
104 High Street, Steyning, West Sussex BN4 3RD
Tel: 0903 815000
Contact: Rowena Green

Thyme — Range of additive free flavoured vinegars made with fresh aromatic herbs including thyme, tarragon and basil in 16fl oz screw top bottles.
[C] Undisclosed
[D] By arrangement
See Also: Chutneys and Pickles, Marmalades, Mustards

16 **Martlet Natural Foods**
Horam Manor, Horam, Heathfield, East Sussex TN21 OJA
Tel: 04353 2254 Telx: 957266 APPLES G
Contact: Mr Andrew Howie

Honegar — Variety of vinegars including red wine, white wine, garlic, tarragon, raspberry, dill, cider, cider vinegar and honegar, a 50% blend of cider vinegar and pure honey in 500ml, 1lt bottles. Also available concentrated herb and citrus marinades in 500ml bottles.
[C] Undisclosed
[D] By arrangement
See Also: Jams and Preserves, Mustards, Honey, Juices

12

McNeill's Fine Foods Ltd
Cross Lanes Farm, Rotherfield Greys,
Henley-on-Thames, Oxfordshire RG9 4QA
Tel: 04917 513 Telx: 846424
Contact: Suzannah Webb

Flavoured vinegars

Range of flavoured vinegars including rose petal, orange and green pepper, honey and caper, honey and fennel in 225ml bottles.
Ⓒ Undisclosed
Ⓓ By arrangement
See Also: Jams and Preserves, Marmalades, Purees and Sauces

Any Problems?

If you are looking for a particular product and it is not listed in the directory, please contact us on **01 727 9808.**

British Food Finds is here to help-

If you know of a producer of speciality food not listed in **British Food Finds 1989,** please let us know so that we can include them in our next edition.

For editorial entries contact **Henrietta Green on 01 727 9808.**

SWEETS

BOILED SWEETS

16 ↔

Bentley's Confectionery Ltd
10 Rosslyn Mansions, Watling Avenue, Edgware, Middlesex HA8 0LL
Tel: 01 951 0366/1141 Telx: 267788 INSITE G Fax: 01 951 3649
Contact: Susan Wells

Travel sweets

Old Masters, travel sweets packed in 100, 200g tins decorated with old master paintings.
Ⓒ Undisclosed
Ⓓ By arrangement
See Also: Fudges and Toffee

5 ↔

Border Country Cousins
The Garden Factory, Lennel Road, Coldstream, Berwickshire TD12 4EP
Tel: 0890 2631
Contact: John C Balfour

Berwick cockles

Range of traditional sweets including Berwick cockles, fruit candies, and Edinburgh rock, in boxes, 113g tubs, 227g boutique jars. Also available butterscotch drops and mixed fruit drops.
Ⓒ Undisclosed
Ⓓ By arrangement
See Also: Fudges and Toffee

9

F W Bray & Sons
12b Pontmorlais, High Street, Merthyr Tydfil, Mid Glamorgan CF47 8UB
Tel: 0685 723135
Contact: Mr F F V Bray

Peardrops

Traditional boiled sweets in a range of flavours including blackberry, and raspberry. Also fruit fish, peardrops, nutty cluster, stick barley sugar, stick aniseed and Braymints available in 5lb glass jars.
Ⓒ Undisclosed
Ⓓ By arrangement

15 ↔

Bristow's Of Devon (MPG) Ltd
Marsh Lane, Crediton, Devon EX17 1ET
Tel: 03632 3421 Telx: 42746 Fax: 03632 2792
Contact: Mr K C Bristow

Mint humbugs

Range of boiled sweets including butterscotch, mint humbugs, fruit sweets and barley sugars. All available gift wrapped and packed in presentation boxes and tins from 75g-1kg.
Ⓒ Undisclosed
Ⓓ By arrangement
See Also: Fudges and Toffee

3

Cameo
15 West Telferton, Edinburgh EH7 6UL
Tel: 031 669 6123
Contact: Mr D N Spratt

Edinburgh Rock

Range of handmade boiled sweets including Edinburgh rock, and Berwick cockles, packed loose in jars and 100, 200g cartons, rock in 100g sticks. Also After Dinner Mints.
Ⓒ 10-15 ton p.mth
Ⓓ By arrangement

2

Dee Valley Confectioners
Station Square, Ballater, Aberdeenshire AB3 5QL
Tel: 033855 499
Contact: Mr Derek Skein

Boiled sweets

Handmade boiled sweets in 100g, 51b bags.
Ⓒ 2 tons p.wk
Ⓓ By arrangement
See Also: Fudges and Toffee

15 ↔

Ernest Jackson & Company Ltd
29 High Street, Crediton, Devon EX17 3AP
Tel: 036 32 2251 Telx: 42506 EJACKS G
Contact: Mr L C Walker

Devon violet cachoux

Range of sugar free pastilles suitable for diabetics available in five flavours, fruit, blackcurrant, mint, lemon menthol, and cherry menthol in 85g cartons. Also Devon violet and Devon floral cachoux packed in 28g cartons.
Ⓒ Undisclosed
Ⓓ By own transport nationally
See Also: Fudges and Toffee

3

Jenny's Home Made Sweets (Edinburgh) Ltd
3 Baronscourt Road, Edinburgh EH8 7ET
Tel: 031 661 4583
Contact: Mr Walter E Innes

Barley sugar

Range of boiled sweets made with cane sugar and liquid glucose including old fashioned, hard boiled mint, humbug, barley sugar, and kola cubes in 5lb glass jars.
Ⓒ 2 ton p.wk
Ⓓ By arrangement
See Also: Fudges and Toffee

1 ↔

Kyleburn Confectionery
Mid-Clyth, Lybster, Caithness KW3 6BA
Tel: 059 32353
Contact: Mr J M Donn

Humbugs

Range of handmade boiled sweets including barley sugar, butterscotch, humbugs and fruit drops in 5½lb jars. Also available lettered rock made to order in packs of twenty four and forty eight.
Ⓒ Undisclosed
Ⓓ By arrangement

16 ↔

Sandown Shanklin Confectionery
The Old Bakery, Apse Heath, Sandown, Isle of Wight PO36 0JR
Tel: 0983 863174
Contact: T Thurston

Yacht drops

Island Maid Yacht Drops, tiny boiled sweets in lemon, peppermint, and barley sugar flavours in 1½oz decorated tins. Also Wight Mints, similar to Edinburgh rock in 5, 7oz mini jars, range of unwrapped boiled sweets including humbugs, and handmade personalised rock to order.
Ⓒ Undisclosed
Ⓓ By arrangement

8

A L Simpkin & Company Ltd
Hunter Road, Sheffield, South Yorkshire
S6 4LD
Tel: 0742 348736
Contact: John Simpkin

Lozenges

Variety of fruit drops with added vitamin C in 200g tins or stick packs. Also medicated lozenges in four varieties, suitable for children and adults, in stick packs, and Extra Strong and Special Mild sucrose free mints wrapped in foil laminated packs.
C Undisclosed
D By arrangement

CHOCOLATES

16

Ackermans Chocolates Ltd
Unit 9, St Pancras Commercial Centre, 63 Pratt Street, London NW1 0DP
Tel: 01 482 3731
Contact: W Krattiger

Truffles

Range of handmade continental chocolates including After Dinner Thins, plain discs in mint, mocca, and orange. Also shaped chocolate novelties and fourteen flavours of truffles packed loose in 3kg packs or in boxed selections.
C Undisclosed
D By arrangement

3

Arran Sweetie Kitchens
Douglas Centre, Brodick, Isle of Arran
Tel: 0770 81207
Contact: Mrs Lyn Williams

Liqueur

Range of handmade chocolates made from traditional Arran recipes including truffles and liqueur chocolates in boxes weighing ¼lb upwards.
C Undisclosed
D By arrangement
See Also: Fudges and Toffee

16 ↔

Beaulieu Chocolate Parlour
Hidden Cottage, High Street, Beaulieu, Hampshire SO4 27YA
Tel: 0590 612279
Contact: Ruth Riversedge

Champagne truffles

Range of forty chocolates made with couverture with 50% cocoa solids including New Forest Bark, toasted almonds in plain chocolate, champagne truffles, and plain chocolate covered walnut dusted in cocoa powder. Also personalised chocolates with fruit centres and chocolate figurines in plain, white and milk chocolate.
C Undisclosed
D By own transport nationally
See Also: Fudges and Toffee

8

Bettys by Post
1 Parliament Street, Harrogate, Yorkshire
HG1 2QU
Tel: 0423 526182
Contact: Sally Holme

Armagnac truffles

Bettys milk, white and plain continental chocolate selection including chocolate coffee beans, champagne and armagnac truffles, in boxes weighing between 190-340g.
C Undisclosed
D By arrangement
See Also: Jams and Preserves, Teas and Infusions

7 ↔

Cheshire Fudge
107 Chestergate, Macclesfield, Cheshire
SK11 6DP
Tel: 0625 29547
Contact: Sandra Hufton

Belgian

Handmade Belgian couverture chocolates and truffles in dark, milk and white chocolate, available in boxes weighing ¼lb upwards or supplied loose.
C Undisclosed
D By arrangement
See Also: Jams and Preserves, Fudges and Toffee

7

The Chocolate House
1 Glenfield Park, Philips Road, Blackburn, Lancashire BB1 5PF
Tel: 0254 581019 Telx: 63540 CENTRIM G
Fax: 0254 680833
Contact: Ms Susie Bristow

Brandy logs

Range of handmade chocolates made with cream, Swiss chocolate and fresh or dried fruit including white chocolate rum truffles, cointreau and brandy logs, milk and dark chocolate brazils and marzipan pigs all in boxes weighing ¼-7lb.
C 6000 chocolates p.wk
D By arrangement

14

Confiserie Schweitzer
22a Magdalene Street, Cambridge CB3 0AF
Tel: 0233 312181
Contact: Mrs K Schweitzer

Passion fruit

Range of chocolates and truffles in dark, milk, and white chocolate including white champagne, dark raspberry and passion fruit in 3lb boxes or loose. Also available range of continental pastries and gâteaux including brioche and truffle cake.
C Undisclosed
D By arrangement

9

Country House Farms of Wales Ltd
Pennant House, Hamilton Terrace, Milford Haven, Dyfed
Tel: 0547 528347
Contact: Deidre Thomas

Whinberry

Range of chocolates handmade with couverture, with 55% cocoa solids including mousse centres in apple, apricot, whinberry, and crystallized ginger in 8oz boxes.
C Undisclosed
D By arrangement

10

Cromwells Chocolatiers
20 Church Street, Upton Upon Severn, Worcestershire WR8 0HT
Tel: 06846 4606 Fax: 06846 3042
Contact: Betty Philip

Champagne truffle

Handmade Belgian couverture chocolates and truffles in orange curacao, champagne, cointreau, vanilla, rum, and pernod flavours. Also enrobed fruit and fudge chocolates made with butter, cream and fruit purées in 2kg boxes or ballotins.
C Undisclosed
D By arrangement

9 ↔

Daisy's Chocolates
26 Ffrwdgrech Industrial Estate, Brecon, Powys LD3 1XX
Tel: 0874 5212
Contact: Mr Gary Francis

Mint wafers

Range of chocolates including truffles, noisettes, marzipans, creams, and nuts packed in outers weighing 5lb, with smaller acetate boxes available. Also handmade plain chocolate mint wafers packed in 4lb boxes, milk and plain chocolate nut discs topped with walnut half. Easter eggs made to order with customers name or message in white icing.
C Undisclosed
D By own transport within area

16 ↔

Dorchester Chocolates
11a Butts Road, Alton, Hampshire GU34 1E3
Tel: 0420 84181 Telx: 858487 Fax: 0420 84517
Contact: Mr Colin Neville

Cream of rose

Range of handmade, milk or plain chocolates made with traditional flavourings including oil of violet, attar of rose, and double cream, packed to requirements. Customers own label if required.
C Undisclosed
D By own transport

3 ↔

Fisher Donaldson
21 Crossgate, Cupar, Fife KY15 5HA
Tel: 0334 52551
Contact: Mr Milne

Fresh cream truffle

Fresh cream truffles in a variety of flavours including grand marnier, whisky, brandy, cointreau and peppermint. Also soft and hard centred chocolates, all packed in ¼, ½, 1lb boxes, with customers own label if required.
C Undisclosed
D By arrangement

11

B N Fowler & Co
Bath Street, Bakewell, Derbyshire DE4 1BX
Tel: 06981 3388
Contact: Mr B N Fowler

Maraschino

Range of handmade milk and plain chocolates and truffles made with fresh cream including rum, brandy, maraschino and cointreau in 120, 200, 350, 500g boxes.
C Undisclosed
D By own transport within area, by arrangement
See Also: Fudges and Toffee

11 ↔

Hansen's Choice
46 High Street, Billingborough, Lincolnshire NG34 OQR
Tel: 0529 240359
Contact: Mr Hansen

Whole fruit

Range of hand finished chocolates made with fresh cream, alcohol, butter, whole fruit and Belgian couverture in dark, milk and white varieties, all in ½-2lb tins and 2kg boxes.
C Undisclosed
D By own transport

8

Humphreys Exclusive Confectionery
16 Leeds Road, Ilkley, West Yorkshire LS29 8DJ
Tel: 0943 609477
Contact: David Humphreys

Fresh cream truffles

Forty eight varieties of chocolate including fresh cream truffles and liqueurs. Also range of moulded Christmas and Easter figures. Customers own label if required.
C Undisclosed
D By arrangement

14 ↔

Jennie's Confectionery
43 Owlstone Road, Cambridge CB3 9JH
Tel: 0223 327453
Contact: Mrs Jennie Spriggs

Champagne truffles

Range of handmade additive free chocolates and truffles made with cream and Swiss couverture including champagne and liqueur truffles, all made to order packed in 100, 200, 400g boxes, or loose in trays.
C Undisclosed
D By arrangement

14 ↔

Linden Lady Chocolates
Walnut Tree Farm, Birch Road, Copford, Colchester CO6 1DR
Tel: 0206 330240
Contact: Caroline King

Bittermint chocolates

Range of handmade truffles made with fresh cream, rum, whisky and brandy. Also bittermint chocolates made with dark chocolate, oil of peppermint and fondant made to order in containers for weigh-out sales. Customers own label if required.
C Undisclosed
D By arrangement
See Also: Fudges and Toffee

[5]

Lydia Wight
Main Street, Reston, Berwickshire TD14 5JS
Tel: 08907 61303
Contact: Brian Wight

Marzipan

Range of additive free handmade, plain and milk chocolates including caramel, fudge, creams, truffles and marzipan packed in 9oz boxes or packs, 6oz batons.
[C] Undisclosed
[D] By arrangement

[10] ↔

Maureen's of Brimfield Ltd
Amatuk, Brimfield, nr Ludlow, Shropshire SY8 4NX
Tel: 058 472 222
Contact: Kenneth M Foster

Ludlow Mints

Range of plain and milk chocolates made with couverture containing 44% cocoa solids including nut, truffle, and Turkish delight. Also Ludlow Mints, heart shaped, coated with plain chocolate couverture, all packed in 5lb loose weigh-out boxes, in 200, 400g boxes.
[C] 2 ton chocolates p.wk
[D] By own transport nationally
See Also: Fudges and Toffee

[1] ↔

Robertson (Orkney) Ltd
Cairston Road, Stromness, Orkney KW13 3BS
Tel: 0856 850640
Contact: Mr James Robertson

Ginger

Range of truffles with whisky, rum, and brandy in 200, 400g packs. Also Chocolate Gingers in 160g packs. Customers own label if required.
[C] Undisclosed
[D] By arrangement
See Also: Fudges and Toffee

[10]

Rowena's Fudge
The Viewlands, Longridge, Dunston, Staffordshire ST19 9AL
Tel: 078571 3137
Contact: Mrs Christine Bowyers

Peppermints

Chocolate dipped peppermints and handmade milk chocolate rum truffles in 125, 175g packs or cellophane bags.
[C] Undisclosed
[D] By arrangement
See Also: Fudges and Toffee

16 ↔

Sara Jayne
26 St John's Hill Grove, London SW11 2RG
Tel: 01 228 9068
Contact: Sara Jayne

Calvados truffles

Range of handmade, plain and liqueur truffles made with Dorset double cream and bitter couverture with 37% cocoa butter, in calvados, crême de menthe and armagnac, supplied loose.
Ⓒ 50lb p.wk
Ⓓ By arrangement
See Also: Fudges and Toffee

16 ↔

Scotts
Crockmead, Mark Cross, East Sussex TN6 3NH
Tel: 089285 2668
Contact: Mr Mike Scott

Gift boxed

Range of additive free chocolates packed in a range of gift boxes specialising in personalised presentation, decorated with ribbons and flowers and printed to customers requirements. Packed in boxes of 2, 4, 6, 12, 24 chocolates.
Ⓒ Undisclosed
Ⓓ By own transport nationally

15

Shilstone Products
Unit 4, Exeter Road Industrial Estate, Okehampton, Devon EX20 1QA
Tel: 0837 3080 Telx: 42513 SHARET G
Contact: Richard Taylor-Young

Pineapple

Range of chocolates and enrobed fruits including handmade truffles, ginger, fruits, orange, and pineapple in 4, 8oz packs, 225, 600, 1200g presentation boxes. Customers own label if required.
Ⓒ Undisclosed
Ⓓ By own transport, by arrangement
See Also: Chutneys and Pickles, Fudges and Toffee

14 ↔

Trustin Foods
Chase Road, Northern Way, Bury St Edmunds, Suffolk IP32 6NT
Tel: 0284 66265 Telx: 81117 G TRUSTIN
Contact: Mr Derek Wilson

Chocolate raisins

Handmade rum and coffee truffles, packed in acetate boxes with sixteen truffles per box. Also chocolate enrobed peanuts, almonds, and raisins, sugar coated almonds, and chocolate mint creams.
Ⓒ 6000 cases p.a
Ⓓ By own transport nationally
See Also: Juices

16 ↔

Village Fayre
369 Uxbridge Road, Hatch End, Pinner, Middlesex HA5 4JN
Tel: 01 428 6757/9090
Contact: Angela Jay

Praline

Range of handmade chocolates including champagne, Irish whiskey, rum and raisin liqueur, creams, and pralines. Also handmade dragées, pâté de fruit and marzipan fruits. Available in a variety of packs designed to customers requirements.
Ⓒ Undisclosed
Ⓓ By own transport nationally

7

Waterfield's (Leigh) Ltd
Crompton Fold Bakery, Manchester Road, Leigh, Lancashire WN7 2LS
Tel: 0942 608033
Contact: Richard Waterfield

Fresh cream

Range of over forty handmade chocolates made with Belgian couverture, fresh cream, salt free butter and fresh fruit pulp, in plain, milk, and white chocolate, in 1kg boxes or presentation boxes. Customers own label if required.
Ⓒ Undisclosed
Ⓓ By arrangement

FUDGES AND TOFFEE

15 ↔

Abbeydale Foods Ltd
12 Plymouth Road Industrial Estate, Tavistock, Devon PL19 9QN
Tel: 0822 614800
Contact: John Rowe

Liqueur fudge

Fudge made with raw cane sugar, milk solids, vegetable oils, butter and cream, in 100g bars, 200, 300g packs or to customers requirements.
Ⓒ 3-5 ton p.wk
Ⓓ By arrangement

16 ↔

Ann Barker's Fudge Ltd
Courtwick Lane, Littlehampton, Sussex BN16
Tel: 0903 717938
Contact: Bruce Barker

Cherry brandy fudge

Range of thirty flavours of fudge, homemade in copper pans, including cherry brandy, maple, walnut, coffee, and ginger in 142g packs. Also available pineapple and mint flavour coconut ice.
Ⓒ 4-5 ton p.dy
Ⓓ By own transport

3

Arran Sweetie Kitchens
Douglas Centre, Brodick, Isle of Arran
Tel: 0770 81207
Contact: Mrs Lyn Williams

Goat Fell Mint Cake

Thirty varieties of handmade fudge and sweets made from old Arran recipes including Arran Goat Fell Mint Cake. Also Crofter's Relish made with swedes, turnips, onions, vinegar and demerara sugar packed in 12oz jars.
Ⓒ Undisclosed
Ⓓ By arrangement
See Also: Chocolates

15 ↔

Barbara Townsend Ltd
The Warehouse, Lower Broad Oak Road, Ottery St Mary, Devon EX11 1UD
Tel: 040481 4700
Contact: Philip Saunders

Fudge

Range of traditional fudge and toffee made in gas fired copper pans with full cream sweetened condensed milk, in 120, 185, 400, 900g gift packs or loose.
Ⓒ 2 ton p.wk
Ⓓ By arrangement

15 ↔

Bay Tree Candies
Unit 1F, Barbican Rise, East Looe,
Cornwall PL13 1QQ
Tel: 05036 2413
Contact: Mrs L A Gibson

Cornish cream fudge

Thirty flavours of handmade fudge cooked in open copper pans with Cornish clotted cream and butter, in 105, 212, 425g boxes, 8lb boxes for weigh-out sales, 150g bars with customers own label if required.
Ⓒ 100-1000kg p.wk
Ⓓ By arrangement

16 ↔

Beaulieu Chocolate Parlour
Hidden Cottage, High Street, Beaulieu,
Hampshire SO4 27YA
Tel: 0590 612279
Contact: Ruth Riversedge

Cream fudge

Handmade fresh cream fudge, toffee and brittles.
Ⓒ Undisclosed
Ⓓ By arrangement
See Also: Chocolates

16 ↔

Bentley's Confectionery Ltd
10 Rosslyn Mansions, Watling Avenue,
Edgware, Middlesex HA8 0LL
Tel: 01 951 0366/1141 Telx: 267788 INSITE G Fax: 01 951 3649
Contact: Susan Wells

Chocolate caramels

Milk chocolate caramels individually wrapped in gold twist foil packed in 175g Heritage, 300g Souvenir tins. Also handmade bittermints, English toffee and fudge in 300g packs.
Ⓒ Undisclosed
Ⓓ By arrangement
See Also: Boiled Sweets

5 ↔

Border Country Cousins
The Garden Factory, Lennel Road,
Coldstream, Berwickshire TD12 4EP
Tel: 0890 2631
Contact: John C Balfour

Macaroon bars

Range of twelve flavours of fudge including vanilla, butterscotch, walnut, and whisky in 110g wrapped bars, 113g cellophane bags, 200, 227, 260g boxes and 8, 10lb boxes for weigh-out sales. Also available Scottish tablet (hard fudge) in 110g wrapped bars, toffee in 200g, 1lb boxes, macaroon bars made with fondant centres, coated in chocolate and rolled in coconut.
Ⓒ Undisclosed
Ⓓ By arrangement
See Also: Boiled Sweets

15 ↔

Bristow's Of Devon (MPG) Ltd
Marsh Lane, Crediton, Devon EX17 1ET
Tel: 03632 3421 Telx: 42746 Fax: 03632 2792
Contact: Mr K C Bristow

Clotted cream fudge

Range of fudge and toffee including clotted cream toffee and clotted cream fudge, packed in decorated presentation boxes and tins weighing 75g-1kg.
Ⓒ Undisclosed
Ⓓ By arrangement
See Also: Boiled Sweets

6

Calthwaite Dairy Products
Calthwaite, Penrith, Cumbria CA11 9QU
Tel: 076885 292
Contact: Clive Pattinson

Chocolate Mint Country Fudge

Golden Country and Chocolate Mint Country Fudge made with butter, Jersey cream and milk in 100g packs, 2kg boxes.
Ⓒ 200kg p.mth
Ⓓ By own transport within area
See Also: Cheese, Prepared Salads, Jams and Preserves

7 ↔

Cheshire Fudge
107 Chestergate, Macclesfield, Cheshire
SK11 6DP
Tel: 0625 29547
Contact: Sandra Hufton

Full cream fudge

Range of six flavours of fudge made with full cream milk. Also toffee made to traditional recipe in boxes weighing ¼lb upwards.
Ⓒ Undisclosed
Ⓓ By arrangement
See Also: Jams and Preserves, Chocolates

[15] ↔

Dartington Foods Ltd
Lee Mill, Ivybridge, Devon PL21 9PE
Tel: 0752 896172 Telx: 42551 Fax: 0752 896172
Contact: James Waghorn

Clotted cream fudge

Traditional West Country clotted cream fudge and toffee packed in boxes, bars, bags or loose.
[C] 3 ton p.wk
[D] By arrangement
See Also: Jams and Preserves

[2]

Dee Valley Confectioners
Station Square, Ballater, Aberdeenshire AB3 5QL
Tel: 033855 499
Contact: Mr Derek Skein

Tablet

Fudge and hard tablet fudge in 100g, 5lb bags.
[C] 2 ton p.wk
[D] By arrangement
See Also: Boiled Sweets

[15] ↔

Durrans Confections Ltd
Poplar Drive, Kingsbridge, Devon 227 1QY
Tel: 0548 7373 Telx: 45139 DURCON G
Contact: Mr M Durrans

Fudge

Real Devonshire cream fudge and toffee in 125, 200, 400g boxes.
[C] Undisclosed
[D] By arrangement
See Also: Cakes, Biscuits and Pastries

[12] ● ★ ↔

The Elms
The Elms, Lower Westholme, Pilton, Shepton Mallet, Somerset BA4 4EL
Tel: 074989 371
Contact: C D Stone

Goat milk fudge

Vanilla, carob, and chocolate flavoured fudge made with unpasteurised goat milk and raw cane sugar in 120g packs.
[C] Undisclosed
[D] By own transport
See Also: Cheese

[15] ↔

Ernest Jackson & Company Ltd
29 High Street, Crediton, Devon EX17 3AP
Tel: 036 32 2251 Telx: 42506 EJACKS G
Contact: Mr L C Walker

Liquorice

Only Natural, liquorice combined with aniseed made to traditional recipe, packed in 100g sachets or one dozen pack.
[C] Undisclosed
[D] By own transport nationally
See Also: Boiled Sweets

[11]

B N Fowler & Co
Bath Street, Bakewell, Derbyshire DE4 1BX
Tel: 06981 3388
Contact: Mr B N Fowler

Honey and almond

Handmade fudge in vanilla, rum and raisin, chocolate, honey and almond flavours in 20, 200, 350, 500g boxes.
[C] Undisclosed
[D] By own transport within area
See Also: Chocolates

[1] ↔

Great Glen Foods Ltd
Old Ferry Road, North Ballachulish, Onich, Fort William, Inverness PH33 6RZ
Tel: 08553 277
Contact: Douglas Locke

Islay Tablet

Islay Tablet, a handmade low fat traditional goat milk fudge in a range of eighteen flavours including 10 year old Islay malt whisky in ¼lb packs, 12oz bags, 1lb boxes.
[C] 20,000 units p.mth
[W] Scottish Goat Products Ltd, 05403 692
[D] By wholesaler, by Securicor, by own transport within area
See Also: Cheese, Ice Creams and Sorbets

[12] ↔

Holstius & Breet
Esperanza, Aust, Bristol, Avon BS12 3AX
Tel: 04545 3148 Telx: 449752
Contact: Robin D L Breet

Passion fruit fudge

Range of homemade fudge including Irish cream liqueur, passion fruit, honey and nut in 113g cellophane bags. Also fudge sauces including chocolate, coffee, and honey in 3x198g hexagonal jars.
[C] Undisclosed
[D] By arrangement
See Also: Butter, Mustards, Snacks and Savouries

[3]

Jenny's Home Made Sweets (Edinburgh) Ltd
3 Baronscourt Road, Edinburgh EH8 7ET
Tel: 031 661 4583
Contact: Mr Walter E Innes

Tablet

Plain tablet made with butter and condensed milk in 80g bars. Also macaroon bars.
[C] Tablet 7 cwt p.wk, macaroons ½ ton p.wk
[D] By arrangement
See Also: Boiled Sweets

[15]

Johnstons Confectionery
152 Wareham Road, Lytchett Matravers, Poole, Dorset BH16 6DT
Tel: 0202 623745
Contact: Mrs Anne Johnston

Petits Fours

Handmade marzipan petits fours rolled into a variety of shapes, including hearts and fruits, in boxes of 6-12, loose, or packed in baskets. Customers own label if required.
[C] Undisclosed
[D] By arrangement

[8] ↔

Jon's Confectionery Ltd
Victoria Road, Sowerby Bridge, Yorkshire HX6 3AQ
Tel: 0422 831515
Contact: David Whitehouse

Cream toffee

Handmade toffee and fudge made with butter, cream, brown sugar in a variety of flavours. Customers own label if required.
[C] Undisclosed
[D] By arrangement

15

Ken Stuart Confections Ltd
Lee Mill, Ivybridge, Devon PL21 9PE
Tel: 0752 896172 Telx: 42551 Fax: 0752 896172
Contact: James Waghorn

Turkish delight

Traditional handmade West Country fudge made with clotted cream. Also Turkish delight, customers own label if required.
Ⓒ Fudge 250 ton p.a, Turkish delight 300 ton p.a
Ⓓ By arrangement

14 ↔

Linden Lady Chocolates
Walnut Tree Farm, Birch Road, Copford, Colchester CO6 1DR
Tel: 0206 330240
Contact: Caroline King

Maple and walnut fudge

Handmade fudge in a range of five flavours, rum and raisin, coffee, chocolate, fresh cream, maple and walnut packed in containers for weigh-out sales.
Ⓒ Undisclosed
Ⓓ By arrangement
See Also: Chocolates

10 ↔

Maureen's of Brimfield Ltd
Amatuk, Brimfield, nr Ludlow, Shropshire SY8 4NX
Tel: 058 472 222
Contact: Kenneth M Foster

Rum and raisin fudge

Range of fudge in five flavours, vanilla, chocolate, coffee, walnut, rum and raisin in 85g boxes, with vanilla, chocolate, rum and raisin packed in 5lb boxes for weigh-out sales. Also available a range of flavours of toffee including treacle, liquorice, rum and butter in 100g bags.
Ⓒ Sugar confectionary 10 ton p.wk
Ⓓ By own transport nationally
See Also: Chocolates

10

Orchard Apiaries
Castlemorton, Malvern, Worcestershire WR13 6BS
Tel: 068481 231 Telx: 312242 MIDTLX G
Contact: John H Heywood

Nougat

Range of fudge, caramels and nougat made with own honey including honey and hazelnut fudge, and chocolate coated honey fudge.
Ⓒ Undisclosed
Ⓓ By arrangement
See Also: Cakes, Biscuits and Pastries, Mustards, Honey

1 ↔

Robertson (Orkney) Ltd
Cairston Road, Stromness, Orkney KW13 3BS
Tel: 0856 850640
Contact: Mr James Robertson

Treacle

Handmade fudge in twenty flavours including ginger, chocolate, coffee, and maple. Also range of toffee and caramels including butterscotch, treacle and chocolate in 200, 400g packs, with customers own label if required.
Ⓒ Undisclosed
Ⓓ By arrangement
See Also: Chocolates

16

Robinclay Ltd
Maple Walk, Bexhill-on-Sea, East Sussex TN39 4SN
Tel: 04243 5899 Telx: 957485 ROBINC G
Contact: Mrs E Clay

Petits fours

Range of handmade marzipan and crystallized fruit petits fours packed in 100, 150, 200g gift boxes, and loose by weight.
Ⓒ 50 kg p.mth
Ⓓ By arrangement

10

Rowena's Fudge
The Viewlands, Longridge, Dunston, Staffordshire ST19 9AL
Tel: 078571 3137
Contact: Mrs Christine Bowyers

Butterscotch fudge

Six flavours of handmade fudge, vanilla, butterscotch, cherry brandy, coffee, chocolate, rum and raisin in 1.25, 175g packs or cellophane bags.
Ⓒ Undisclosed
Ⓓ By arrangement
See Also: Chocolates

16 ↔

Sara Jayne
26 St John's Hill Grove, London SW11 2RG
Tel: 01 228 9068
Contact: Sara Jayne

Vanilla

Additive free handmade vanilla fudge made with sugar, single cream and flavoured with vanilla pods in 1″ squares packed loose.
Ⓒ 50lb p.wk
Ⓓ By arrangement
See Also: Chocolates

1

Scottish Goat Products Ltd
Station Road, Newtonmore, Inverness-shire PH20 1AR
Tel: 05403 692
Contact: Douglas Locke

Goat milk fudge

Range of additive free goat milk fudge.
Ⓒ Undisclosed
Ⓓ By arrangement
See Also: Fresh Meat, Cheese, Ice Creams and Sorbets

15

Shilstone Products
Unit 4, Exeter Road Industrial Estate, Okehampton, Devon EX20 1QA
Tel: 0837 3080 Telx: 42513 SHARET G
Contact: Richard Taylor-Young

Fudge

Handmade fudge packed in 115, 230g silver boxes. Customers own label if required.
Ⓒ Undisclosed
Ⓓ By arrangement
See Also: Chutneys and Pickles, Chocolates

8 ↔

Stanleys Toffee
Hornbeam Park, Hoomstone Road, Harrogate, North Yorkshire HG2 8QY
Tel: 0423 872778
Contact: K Bancroft

Clotted cream caramel

Handmade toffee and fudge. Also lettered rock, mint cake, Edinburgh rock, sugar novelties. All packed in a range of gift boxes and tins, customers own label if required.
Ⓒ Undisclosed
Ⓓ By arrangement

ICE CREAMS AND SORBETS

12 ↔

Barnard & Gooding
Keward Farm, River Road, Dawlet, Bridgewater, Somerset TA6 4SE
Tel: 0278 685173
Contact: Jim Barnard

Chocolate chip

Range of ice cream made with whole milk, fresh cream, fresh fruit, chocolate and liqueurs including chocolate chip, banana, ginger, cointreau and orange in 115ml individual tubs, 1, 4lt family and catering packs. Also available goat milk ice cream.
Ⓒ 50 ton p.a
Ⓓ By arrangement

16 ↔

Berrydale Special Ices
5 Lawn Road, London NW3 2XS
Tel: 01 722 2866 Telx:264671
Contact: Michelle Berriedale-Johnson

Tofu

Range of tofu based ice cream, lactose and cholesterol free and low calorie in four flavours, Canton sherbet made with orange, lemon and ginger, chocolate, mixed berries, maple and walnut in 100, 400g containers.
Ⓒ Undisclosed
Ⓓ By arrangement

16

Blackburn and Haynes/Meadow Cottage
Meadow Cottage Farm, Churt Road, Headley, Bordon, Hampshire GU35 8SS
Tel: 0428 712155
Contact: Mrs Celia Haynes

Skimline

Skimline, milk ice with 2½% butter fat made with semi-skimmed milk and unrefined cane sugar. Also additive free dairy ice cream with milk and double cream from own pedigree Weydown Jersey herd. All in 110ml tubs, 1, 2, 4lt containers.
Ⓒ 2,500lt of each variety p.wk
Ⓓ By own transport nationally
See Also: Milk

9 ↔

Clwyd Cream Ices Ltd
St Asaph Avenue, Kinmel Bay, Rhyl, Clwyd LL18 5HA
Tel: 0745 4039
Contact: Kevin Nesbitt

Soya ice cream

Range of ice cream, sorbets and filled cones made with real fruit. Also cholesterol free soya ice desserts, all packed in 2, 4, 10lt tubs or to customers requirements.
Ⓒ Undisclosed
Ⓓ By own transport and by arrangement

11

The Coach House
Lea, nr Matlock, Derbyshire DE4 5GJ
Tel: 062 984346
Contact: Mrs Shaw

Maple and walnut

Range of fifteen flavours of ice cream made from Jersey milk, cream and whole fruit including maple and walnut, honeycomb toffee, Hokey Pokey (white chocolate and mint) chocolate, and ginger in ½, 1, 2, 4lt tubs.
Ⓒ 960lt p.wk in summer
Ⓓ By own transport
See Also: Cheese

10 ↔

Country Cooks Ltd
Unit 1, Great Western Court, Ashburton Industrial Estate, Ross-on-Wye, Herefordshire HR9 7BW
Tel: 0989 66868
Contact: Jenny Allday

Blackcurrant sorbet

Range of ice cream made with fresh fruit and cream including marron layered with chestnut puree, coffee and walnut with maple syrup, chocolate with coffee fudge, loganberry, damson, and brown bread with raw cane sugar and wholemeal bread. Also sorbets including raspberry, blackcurrant, passion fruit, mango, and lemon all in ½lt packs.
Ⓒ 3,500lt p.mth
Ⓓ By own transport within area
See Also: Meat: Pies and Prepared Dishes, Vegetable Dishes

12 ↔

Cricket St Thomas Ice Cream
Cricket House, Cricket St Thomas, Chard, Somerset TA20 4DB
Tel: 046030 755
Contact: R Taylor

Blackberry ice cream

Dairy ice cream made from whole milk and double cream from own herd, and fruit in

thirteen flavours including crême caramel, blackberry, apricot and orange, mint chip and brandy in 110ml tubs, 1, 2, 4, 10lt containers. Also four sorbets made from fruit and spring water, orange, blackberry, lemon, and kiwi in 1, 2lt containers.
[C] 20,000 litres p.a
[D] By own transport nationally

9 ↔ **Denbigh Farmhouse Ices**
Gwaenynog, Denbigh, Clwyd LL16 5NU
Tel: 074 571 4053
Contact: Mr John Edwards

Apricot brandy and almond

Dairy ice cream made with whole milk and double cream from own herd in a range of twenty flavours including wild cherry, orange and brandy, apricot brandy and almond, grand marnier, and toffee chip. Also available flavoured yoghurt ice cream made with skimmed milk and a variety of fruit sorbets, all in ½, 1, 2, 4lt packs.
[C] Undisclosed
[D] By own transport within area

9 **Franks Ice Cream Ltd**
2 New School Road, Garnant, nr Ammanford, Dyfed SA8 1LL
Tel: 0269 822203
Contact: Mr Joe Dallavalle

Cherry

Range of twenty ice creams and sorbets made with whole milk, double cream and whole fruit including pineapple, cherry, and kiwi fruit in ½, ¾, 1lt tubs, 4lt catering packs.
[C] 600 gal p.dy
[D] By arrangement

14 **Fullers Brickwall Farm Ltd**
Brickwall Farm, Sible Hedingham, Halstead, Essex CO9 3RH
Tel: 0787 60329
Contact: Robert Fuller

Jersey ice cream

Range of additive free Jersey ice cream available in 750ml, 2, 4lt sizes.
[C] Undisclosed
[D] By arrangement
See Also: Cheese, Cakes, Biscuits and Pastries

1 ↔ **Great Glen Foods Ltd**
Old Ferry Road, North Ballachulish, Onich, Fort William, Inverness-shire PH33 6RZ
Tel: 08553 277
Contact: Douglas Locke

Drambuie

Ice cream made from Caledonian goat milk in four flavours, vanilla, chocolate, Islay malt whisky, and drambuie in 100, 500, 750 ml, 1, 2, 4½lt packs.
[C] Undisclosed
[W] Scottish Goat Products Ltd 054 03692
[D] By wholesaler
See Also: Cheese, Fudges and Toffee

10 **Hadley Park Farm**
Hadley Park Farm, Leegomery, Telford, Shropshire
Tel: 0952 3677
Contact: Edward Dorrell

Honey

Range of ice cream including Irish coffee, kiwi, and honey in 85ml, ½, 1, 2, 4lt containers.
[C] 60,000lt p.a
[D] By arrangement
See Also: Milk

12 ↔ **The Kitchen Garden**
Old Down House, Tockington, Bristol BS12 4PG
Tel: 0454 413605
Contact: Robert Bernays

Ginger and meringue

Ice cream, sherbets and sorbets with own grown fruits in a range of flavours including chocolate, ginger and meringue, brown bread, and toffee in ½, 1, 2lt containers.
[C] Undisclosed, fruits in season
[D] By own transport within area
See Also: Fresh Vegetables, Jams and Preserves

16 ↔

Knightsbridge Farm
Hellingly, Hailsham, East Sussex BN27 4HH
Tel: 04353 2574
Contact: G R S Steven

Liqueur ice cream

Ice cream made from Jersey cream and milk, in a range of flavours including liqueurs in 750ml, 2lt cartons.
C 120lt p.wk
D By own transport within area

16 ↔

La Maison des Sorbets Ltd
13a Park House, South Bank Business Centre, 140 Battersea Park Road, London SW11 4NB
Tel: 01 720 8983/4
Contact: Michael Cobb

Plum sorbet

Range of fresh fruit sorbets including peach, melon, plum, and damson, with exotic fruit and alcohol sorbets made to order in 5lt tubs. Also available nougatine, marmite des sorbets, iced soufflés, glacés, bombes and parfaits and a range of full milk dairy ice cream. Also available French patisseries, including fruit mousses, charlottes, chocolate truffle cake and fresh fruit flans.
C Undisclosed
D By arrangement

16

S E Lane
White House Farm, Biddenden, Ashford, Kent
Tel: 0580 291 374/289
Contact: M P Sargent

Yoghurt ice cream

Range of ice cream made from milk and cream of own Jersey herd, whole fruit and eggs including vanilla, coffee, kahlua, hazelnut and creme de cacao, whisky and ginger, and butterscotch. Also six fruit sorbets and a range of low fat yoghurt ices with 2% fat content in four flavours. All in ½, 1, 2lt packs.
C 600lt p.wk
D By arrangement
See Also: Cream

15 ↔

Langage Farm Dairy Products
Langage Farm, Plympton, Plymouth, Devon PL7 5AW
Tel: 0752 337723
Contact: Peter Tremaine

Banana Nut Crunch

Range of additive free dairy ice cream in thirty flavours including banana nut crunch, blackberry and apple crumble, strawberry cheesecake in ½, 2, 4, 10lt packs.
C Undisclosed
D By arrangement
See Also: Cheese, Cakes, Biscuits and Pastries

7

B Lewis & Sons
Middlegate, White Lund Industrial Estate, Morecambe, Lancashire 0A3 3BN
Tel: 0524 61616
Contact: David Lewis

Strega bombe

Fourteen varieties of dairy ice cream made from fresh cream including zabaglione, marsala wine, black cherry with kirsch, pistachio. Also mixed flavour strega bombe, cassata bombe and seasonal novelty ices.
C 15,000 gal p.mth in summer
D By arrangement
See Also: Cakes, Biscuits and Pastries

15 ↔

Leworthy Mill
Woolfardisworthy, nr Bideford, Devon EX39 5PY
Tel: 02373 445
Contact: D Price

Jersey ice cream

Devonshire additive free ice cream made from Jersey milk and full cream in 85ml, ½, 1, 2, 4lt tubs.
C 6000lt May-Oct
D By arrangement
See Also: Cream

16 ↔

Loseley Dairy Products Ltd
Estate Office, Guildford, Surrey GU3 1HS
Tel: 0483 571881 Telx: 859972 Fax: 0483 302056
Contact: Miss Ann Cleveland

Belgian chocolate sorbet

Ice cream made from 20% Jersey cream in a range including Old-fashioned Vanilla, Acacia Honey and Ginger, Montezuma Chocolate, Woodland Hazel, Sovereign Strawberry, Brazilian Mocha, Rum and Raisin. Also sorbets including lemon, pineapple and blackcurrant, dairy ice cream, and sorbet bombes in a range of flavours including rich Belgian chocolate in individual or six portion sizes. Ice cream in 110.9, 500, 750ml, 2, 4lt sizes, sorbets in 110.9, 750ml, 2lt sizes.
C Undisclosed
D By own transport nationally
See Also: Cream, Millers

16

Minghella Isle of Wight Ltd
The Minghella Centre, Woottonbridge, Isle of Wight PO33 4DL
Tel: 0983 883545
Contact: Mr Jeffrey

Fudge and almond

Fifty four flavours of dairy ice cream made with fresh milk, cream and fresh fruit including peach brandy, fudge and almond, grand marnier, praline, buttered pecan, and Swiss rum truffle. Also a range of sorbets including kiwi fruit, lime, champagne, passion fruit and grapefruit. Also yoghurt and diabetic ice cream in four flavours. All available in 10lt-500lt packs.
C Undisclosed
D By arrangment

16 ↔

Neal's Yard Creamery
Home Farm Cottage, Everlands Estate, Sevenoaks, Kent TN14 6HU
Tel: 0732 461020
Contact: Perry James

Mexican honey ice cream

Ice cream made from whole milk and double cream with vanilla and Mexican honey.
C Undisclosed
D By own transport within area
See Also: Cheese

10 ○ ↔

New House Farm/Betty's Homemade Ice Cream
New House Farm, Acton, Newcastle under Lyme, Staffordshire ST5 4EE
Tel: 0782 680 366
Contact: Mr M J Deaville

Apricot and ginger

Dairy additive free ice cream made from organic milk and cream, unrefined cane sugar, honey and eggs in a range of ten flavours including apricot and ginger, English toffee, chocolate and orange, chocolate, and peppermint.
C Undisclosed
D By arrangement
See Also: Cheese

9 ↔

Pembrokeshire Farmhouse Ice Cream
Upton Farm, Cosheston, Pembroke, Pembrokeshire SA72 4SE
Tel: 0646 682425
Contact: R M Francis

Christmas pudding ice cream

Range of dairy ice cream made with cream, milk, eggs and fresh fruit in a range of flavours including lemon, raspberry, gooseberry, Victoria plum, chocolate, stem ginger and Christmas Pudding, made with five star brandy and fruit in a 620ml pudding basin. Also available a range of sorbets including champagne, lychee, and redcurrant. All supplied in ½, 1, 2, 4lt containers.
C Undisclosed
D By own refrigerated transport, National carriers

11

Perfect Parfait
265 Wollaton Vale, Wollaton, Nottingham NG8 2PX
Tel: 0602 281613
Contact: Lynne Chapman

Grand Marnier and chocolate

Handmade frozen parfait ice cream desserts made with double cream, eggs, sugar and alcohol including peach liqueur, grand marnier with chocolate, Bailey's Irish coffee, and woodland fruit. All in ½lt tubs, 1lt loaf tins, 4lt plastic catering tubs. Customers own label if required.
C Undisclosed
D By arrangement

11

Prestons Ice Cream
Rafters, Top Street, North Wheatley, Retford, Nottinghamshire DN22 9DE
Tel: 0427880 642
Contact: Guiseppe Zaccaria

Vanilla

Handmade ice cream made with skimmed milk powder in a range of flavours including vanilla, chocolate, and strawberry in 1, 2, 4 fl oz tubs, 4lt containers.
C 400 gal p.wk
D By own transport within area

14 ↔

Prospero Fine Foods Ltd
Wiveton, Norfolk NR25 7TF
Tel: 0263 711222
Contact: Carolyn Newman

Chestnut and honey

Handmade additive free fruit sorbets made with raw cane sugar and liqueurs in a range of flavours including strawberry and passion fruit, blackcurrant and cassis, mango with grand marnier. Also a range of handmade dairy ice cream made with double cream, raw cane sugar, fruit and eggs including brown bread, peach and brandy, orange and cointreau, chestnut and honey. All in 500ml boxes, 2lt tubs.
C Undisclosed
W Hales Snails Ltd 01 231 0067
D By wholesaler
See Also: Cakes, Biscuits and Pastries

16 ↔

The Real Ice Company
Lodge Road, Staplehurst, Kent TN12 OQY
Tel: 0580 892200
Contact: David Alfille

Pink champagne sorbet

Range of twenty additive free real fruit sorbets made with egg white, fruit and sugar including passion fruit, mango, pink champagne, and lychee. Also dairy ice cream in a range of ten flavours including English toffee, orange and brandy, hazelnut and walnut in ½, 1, 2, 4lt containers, with customers own label if required.
C Undisclosed
D By own transport nationally

15 ○ ↔

Roskilly Cream
Tregellast Barton, St Keverne, Helston, Cornwall TR12 6NX
Tel: 0326 280479
Contact: Mrs R Roskilly

Honey and hazlenut

Ice cream made from milk and cream from own Channel Island herd, natural fruit purees in range of flavours including wild cherry, walnut and whisky, honey and hazlenut. Also fruit ices including bilberry, lime, and passion fruit.
C Undisclosed
D By own transport within area
See Also: Cream

7

D S & A Rutter
Old Beachin, Churton, nr Chester, Cheshire CH3 6LU
Tel: 082 925 268/270
Contact: Mr D S Rutter

Strawberry ice cream
Vanilla and strawberry ice cream in 1, 2, 4lt packs.
C 150lt p.wk
D By arrangement
See Also: Cheese

15 ↔
Salcombe Dairy Ltd
Shadycombe Road, Salcombe, Devon TQ8 8DX
Tel: 054 884 3228
Contact: Peter Howard

Christmas pudding ice cream
Christmas pudding ice cream made with double Devon cream, soft brown sugar, molasses and dried fruit marinaded in cognac and topped with cognac flavoured white ice cream, in packs of ten puddings. Also ice cream made with double Devon cream and butter, whole fruits and liqueurs in a range of flavours including blackcurrant, cherry brandy, and cassata in 2, 4, 10lt packs, 500ml tubs. Also eight flavours of sorbets including champagne, in 2, 4lt packs, 500ml tubs.
C Puddings 10,000 Oct-Dec, ice cream 600 gal p.mth, sorbet 300 gal p.mth
D By own transport within area

1
Scottish Goat Products Ltd
Station Road, Newtonmore, Inverness-shire PH20 1AR
Tel: 05403 692
Contact: Douglas Locke

Islay malt whisky ice cream
Ice cream made from Caledonian goat milk in four flavours, vanilla, chocolate, Islay malt whisky and drambuie available in 100, 500, 750 ml, 1, 2, 4½lt packs.
C Undisclosed
W Scottish Goat Products Ltd 054 03692
D By wholesaler, by arrangement
See Also: Fresh Meat, Cheese, Fudges and Toffee

10
September Dairy Products
New House Farm, Almeley, nr Kington, Hereford
Tel: 05446 561
Contact: Carey Glyn-Jones

Tayberry
Additive free ice cream made with whole milk, cream, honey and free-range eggs in a range of seven flavours including honey, tayberry, coffee, and muesli in 110ml individual tubs, 1, 4lt catering packs.
C 75lt p.wk
D By arrangment

10 ↔

Shepherds Ice Cream
Cwm Farm, Peterchurch, Hereford HR2 0TA
Tel: 0981 550716
Contact: Mr Martin Orbach

Ginger ice cream

Sheep milk ice cream with 6.5% fat content, made from milk of own flock, in vanilla, chocolate, strawberry, pistachio, lemon, and ginger flavours. All packed in 110ml individual tubs, ½, 2lt catering packs.
Ⓒ 10,000lt p.a
Ⓓ By arrangment

7 ↔

Snugbury Jersey Ice Cream
Park Farm, Hurleston, Nantwich, Cheshire CW5 6BU
Tel: 0270 624830
Contact: C Sadler

Strawberry ice cream

Range of ten flavoured additive free ice creams made from whole milk, double and clotted cream and whole fruit including cherry, strawberry, rum and raisin, crunchy hazelnut chips. All in 110ml tubs, ½, 1, 4lt scoop containers. Lemon sorbet also available.
Ⓒ 2000lt p.wk
Ⓓ By arrangement

9

B Sidoli & Sons Ltd
Market Square, Ebbw Vale, Gwent
Tel: 0495 303692
Contact: Mr Sidoli

Bilberry

Range of forty flavours of ice creams and sorbets made with whole milk, cream and whole fruit including mango, bilberry, blackcurrant, apple, passion fruit, and coconut in ½, 2, 4, 10lt tubs.
Ⓒ 5000 gal p.wk
Ⓓ By arrangement

14

Susan Moore - Dairy Products
Cranes Watering Farm, Starston, Harleston, Norfolk IP20 9NE
Tel: 0379 852387
Contact: Susan Moore

Channel Island ice cream

Dairy ice cream made from milk and cream from Jersey and Guernsey milk and fruit in 0.12, 0.481lt or catering packs.
Ⓒ Undisclosed
Ⓓ By own transport
See Also: Fresh Meat, Cheese

7

Sutton Dairy Goats
The Cottage, Eddisbury Lodge, Delamere, Northwich, Cheshire CW8 2JD
Tel: 0829 51264
Contact: Mrs E Sutton

Goat milk ice cream

Goat milk ice cream available in ½lt packs.
Ⓒ Undisclosed
Ⓓ By arrangement
See Also: Cheese

7

Tattenhall Dairy Products Ltd
Drumlan Hall, Newton Lane, Tattenhall, nr Chester, Cheshire CH3 9NE
Tel: 0829 70995
Contact: Tom Fell

Apricot yoghurt ice cream

Twenty two varieties of ice cream, traditionally made from dairy milk and double cream including coffee liqueur, Christmas pudding, cointreau, and ginger. Also range of fruit sorbets including kiwi, cherry kirsch, passion fruit, and low fat yoghurt ice made with skimmed milk. All in 105ml, ½, 1lt, 4lt retail and catering packs.
Ⓒ 1000lt p.dy
Ⓓ By arrangement

9

J Thayer & Sons Ltd
Dairy Ice Creamery, Wentloog Road, Rumney, Cardiff CF3 8ED
Tel: 0222 778808 Telx: 497992 THAYER G
Contact: Brian Gregory

Toffee almond

Range of dairy ice cream made with fresh double cream, milk, eggs and butter including strawberries and cream, toffee almond, and dessert mint chocolate in 100 ml, ½, 1, 2, 4lt tubs. Also available range of mousses, sorbets and real fruit lollies.
Ⓒ Undisclosed
Ⓓ By own transport nationally

15 ↔

Thorne Farm
Thorne Farm, Pancrasweek, Holsworthy, Devon EX22 7JD
Tel: 04909 253342
Contact: Mr Clarke

Kiwi

Dairy ice cream made with whole milk, 48% double cream, skimmed milk powder, glucose and cane sugar in a range of fifteen flavours including kiwi, Malaga rum and raisin, and pistachio in 100ml tubs, 1, 2, 4, 10lt packs.
Ⓒ 3000lt p.wk
Ⓓ By arrangement

15 ↔

West Dorset Farmhouse Dairy Products Ltd
Childhay Manor, Blackdown, Beaminster, Dorset
Tel: 0308 68555
Contact: Mr Tim Frost

Raspberry

Range of whole milk dairy ice cream including vanilla, chocolate, mint chocolate chip, blackcurrant, coffee, hazelnut, and raspberry in 15ml, 4, 10lt tubs.
Ⓒ Undisclosed
Ⓓ By arrangement

8

Yorkshire Dales Ice Cream
Aireside Mills, Cononley, Keighley, West Yorkshire BD20 8LW
Tel: 0535 36644
Contact: Tim Wilson

Chocolate

Additive free range of ice cream made with butter, sugar, cream, eggs and whole fruit in chocolate, coffee, orange and passion fruit, and hazelnut flavours. Also lemon and orange fruit sorbets, all in ½, 1, 4½lt tubs. Milk ice lolly also available.
Ⓒ Undisclosed
Ⓓ By arrangement

New Products?

Let us know on **01 727 9808** and we will follow it through for our next edition.

MISCELLANEOUS

HAMPERS

16 ↔

Mrs Beeton's Foods
Norwood Hill, Horley, Surrey RH6 OET
Tel: 0293 862087 Fax: 0293 862396
Contact: Mrs Di Brown

Custom made

Custom hamper packing services.
Ⓒ Undisclosed
Ⓓ By arrangement
See Also: Butter, Cakes, Biscuits and Pastries, Chutneys and Pickles, Honey

15

Devon Quail
Poole Farmhouse, Thorverton, Exeter, Devon EX5 5PN
Tel: 0392 860946
Contact: Tim Brooks

Devon hampers

Selection of hampers packed to order with local Devon produce.
Ⓒ Undisclosed
Ⓓ By arrangement
See Also: Game Farmers, Honey

15

Heal Farm
Kings Nympton, Umberleigh, Devon EX37 9TB
Tel: 07695 2077
Contact: Anne Petch

Oak smoked ham
Turkey

Wicker hampers containing wide range of food including selection of Heal Farm meat, smoked trout, cheese, turkey, Devon clotted cream and homemade Christmas pudding.
Ⓒ Undisclosed
Ⓓ By own transport within area, British Rail
See Also: Fresh Meat, Game Farmers

2

A I Massie
The Farmhouse, 11 Chapel Street, Aberdeen AB1 1SQ
Tel: 0224 640681
Contact: Alex Massie

Scottish produce

Range of gift hampers containing customers choice of Scottish goods from wide selection including smoked salmon, smoked trout, farmhouse cheese, jams, preserves, biscuits and confectionery.
Ⓒ Undisclosed
Ⓓ By arrangement

11

Peak Farms Ltd
Yeaveley House Farm, Yeaveley, Ashbourne, Derbyshire DE6 2DT
Tel: 033523 254 Telx: 377106 CHACOM G HONEY
Contact: John A Hill

Peak District produce

Range of wicker baskets filled with Peak District seasonal speciality products in small medium, large and extra large sizes.
Ⓒ Undisclosed
Ⓓ By arrangement
See Also: Jams and Preserves, Honey

14

Ridleys Country Chandlers
Unit 4, Flitch Industrial Estate, Great Dunmow, Essex CM6 1XJ
Tel: 0371 5744
Contact: Stephen Anderson

Traditional produce

Range of hampers packed to customers requirements including pickles, chutneys, jams, preserves, Christmas pudding, mincemeat, chocolates, mustards and honey.
Ⓒ Undisclosed
Ⓓ By arrangement
See Also: Pies and Puddings, Chutneys and Pickles

9

Roberts of Port Dinorwic Ltd
Griffiths Crossing Industrial Estate, Caernarfon, Gwynedd LL55 1TS
Tel: 0286 76111
Contact: Mr Roberts

Meat

Range of hampers containing a selection of fresh and cooked meats including Conway, with cooked hams and pies, and Caernarfon with a selection of prime cuts and joints, all delivered within twenty hours.
Ⓒ Undisclosed
Ⓓ By arrangement
See Also: Bacon and Hams

16

Trencherman Hampers
Hurst House, Hurst, Berkshire RG10 0SH
Tel: 0734 342116 Telx: 858893 FLETE LG
Contact: Miss Caroline Watt

Christmas produce

Gift hampers available at Christmas packed to customers requirements with traditional Christmas pudding, Belgian chocolates, Stilton and Cheddar cheese, Scottish smoked salmon, whisky and brandy.
Ⓒ 8-10,000 p.a
Ⓓ By arrangement

HONEY

3 ↔

A Abrahams
The Strand, Colonsay, Argyll PA61 7TR
Tel: 09512 365
Contact: A Abrahams

Sycamore

Sycamore, heather, and wild thyme honey supplied mainly on the comb weighing 12-13g.
Ⓒ 200-400lb p.a
Ⓓ By own transport within area
See Also: Shellfish Farmers

2

J & E Anderson
Luncarty Villa, Gladstone Terrace, Turriff, Aberdeenshire AB5 7AP
Tel: 0888 62705
Contact: John Anderson

Heather

Clover and heather honey from the Scottish Highlands in ½, 1lb jars.
Ⓒ Undisclosed
Ⓓ By arrangement

16 ↔

Mrs Beeton's Foods
Norwood Hill, Horley, Surrey RH6 OET
Tel: 0293 862087 Fax: 0293 862396
Contact: Clive Pick

Honey royale

Mrs Beeton's traditional additive free honey including honey with cream and honey royale in 12oz jars.
C Undisclosed
D By arrangement
See Also: Butter, Cakes, Biscuits and Pastries, Chutneys and Pickles, Hampers

1

Black Isle Apiaries
Dungrianach, Millbank Road, Munlochy, Rossshire IV8 8ND
Tel: 046381 309
Contact: Alastair Taylor

Blossom

Scottish blossom and heather honey in 1lb glass jars. Also honeycomb weighing 8-10oz.
C Undisclosed from June
D By own transport within area

15

Devon Quail
Poole Farmhouse, Thorverton, Exeter, Devon EX5 5PN
Tel: 0392 860946
Contact: Tim Brooks

Devon

Devon honey.
C Undisclosed
D By arrangement
See Also: Game Farmers, Hampers

15

Exeter Bee Supplies
64 Haven Road, Exeter, Devon EX2 8DJ
Tel: 0392 56725/36775 Telx: 42513
Contact: Mrs Pam Smith

Honeycomb

Set and clear Devon honey in 1½oz, ½, 1lb jars, ¼lb ceramic pots. Also honeycomb sections, customers own label if required.
C Undisclosed Sep-Dec
D By own transport

9 ↔

Gwent Vales Apiaries
Bryn-y-Pant Cottage, Upper Llanover, Abergavenny, Gwent NP7 9ES
Tel: 0873 880625
Contact: L Chirnside

Welsh honey

Welsh honey in ½, 1lb jars or assorted gift pots.
C Undisclosed
D By arrangement

15 ●

Haygrove Honey Farm
Twyford, Shaftesbury, Dorset SP7 OJF
Tel: 0747 811855
Contact: John Davies

Royal jelly

Set and clear honey in 1lb jars. Also honeycomb sections in ½lb plastic trays and royal jelly available to order.
C Honey 5 ton p.a, comb ¼ ton p.a during extraction Jun-Aug
D By own transport within area
See Also: Fresh Herbs

3 ↔

Highland Products (Scotland) Ltd
Heather Hills Honey Farm, Bridge of Cally, Perthshire PH10 7JG
Tel: 025086 252
Contact: Norrie Lennox

Heather

Scottish heather and blossom honey in 12oz, 1lb beehive jars, 12oz tubs, 1lb jars, 7lb tins. Customers own label if required.
C 10-40 ton p.a
D National Carriers
See Also: Chutneys and Pickles

16

Kingsley Honey Farms
Shortheath Common, Kingsley, Hampshire GU35 9JS
Tel: 04203 2293
Contact: Mrs D Reed

Set

Set and clear honey in 1lb jars and a range of glass and ceramic pots.
C 1000kg p.mth
D By arrangement

16

Martlet Natural Foods
Horam Manor, Horam, Heathfield, East Sussex TN21 OJA
Tel: 04353 2254 Telx: 957266 APPLES G
Contact: Mr Andrew Howie

Honey royale

Speciality honey in two blends, honey royale with honey, pollen and royal jelly, and honey royale extra with honey, pollen, ginseng and royal jelly in 454g jars.
C Undisclosed
D By arrangement
See Also: Jams and Preserves, Juices

3 ↔

Nicoll's of Strathmore Ltd
Douglastown, Forfar, Angus DD8 1TL
Tel: 0307 63732
Contact: James Nicoll

Heather

Range of three honeys, Scottish heather, Scottish flower, and blended with drambuie in 340g glass or patterned pottery jars.
C Undisclosed
D By own transport within area and by arrangement
See Also: Jams and Preserves

10

Orchard Apiaries
Castlemorton, Malvern, Hereford & Worcester WR13 6BS
Tel: 068481 231 Telx: 312242 MIDTLX G
Contact: John H Heywood

Heather

English and Welsh heather honey in 8, 12oz hexagonal jars.
C Undisclosed
D By arrangement
See Also: Cakes, Biscuits and Pastries, Mustards

10

J & E Orton Bee Farmers
Occupation Rd, Sibson, nr Nuneaton, Warwickshire
Tel: 0827 880471
Contact: J Orton

Comb honey

Runny or set English honey in 8oz, 1lb jars. Also comb honey in 8oz packs.
C 8-10 ton p.a
D By own transport within area, by arrangement

11

Peak Farms Ltd
Yeaveley House Farm, Yeaveley, Ashbourne, Derbyshire DE6 2DT
Tel: 033523 254 Telx: 377106 CHACOM G HONE
Contact: John A Hill

Lime

Range of flower honey including rape, clover, lime, and heather packed in 7oz hexagonal jars in outers of eight and English Beehive ceramic pots in outers of eighteen.
C Undisclosed
D By arrangement
See Also: Jams and Preserves, Hampers

5

J M Pettigrew
2 Oven Wynd, Kelso, Roxburghshire TD5 7HS
Tel: 0573 24234
Contact: Mr J Pettigrew

Honey

Range of honey in 8, 12oz jars.
C Undisclosed
D By arrangement
See Also: Chutneys and Pickles

9 ↔

Ridgeway Pottery and Honey Farm
Rock Cottage, Llawhaden, nr Narberth, Dyfed SA67 8D6
Tel: 09914 268
Contact: Mr John Baum

Welsh

Welsh honey in 4oz handmade stoneware pots.
C 700 units p.mth
D By arrangement

15

Vivian's Honey Farm
Hatherleigh, Devon
Tel: 0837 810437
Contact: George Tonkin

Wild flower

Wild flower and heather honey in ½, 1lb glass jars, or ¼, ½lb pottery jar made by local Devon potters.
C Undisclosed
D By arrangement

14

Wilson's Trading Co Ltd
Old Ryes, Stebbing Green, Dunmow, Essex CM6 3TE
Tel: 03718 6545 Telx: 818429
Contact: Mr and Mrs Wilson

Clear
Set

Set and clear honey in 454g jars, 114, 227g shaped pots, with customers own label if required.
C Undisclosed
D By arrangement
See Also: Cakes, Jams and Preserves, Teas and Infusions

SNACKS AND SAVOURIES

11

Appleby & Pemberton
Elmswell, Suffolk 1P30 9HD
Tel: 0359 41937
Contact: Almer Squires

Bombay mix

Range of snacks and savouries sweetened with honey and raw cane sugar including banana chips, yoghurt coated peanuts and raisins, roasted pistachios and Bombay mix. All in 20, 30, 35, 50g packs, 1.5, 2.2kg jars.
C 20,000 packs p.wk
D By arrangement
See Also: Cakes, Biscuits and Pastries

3

Argyll Frosted Foods
Unit 11, Sandbank Industrial Estate, High Road, Sandbank, Dunoon, Argyll PA23 8PB
Tel: 0369 3239
Contact: A C Johnston

Monarch of the Glen

Range of Scottish prepared savoury snacks and dishes including Beef Bonnie Prince Charlie, Crail's Catch with salmon, and Monarch of the Glen with venison in individual plastic dishes suitable for microwave and oven.
C Undisclosed
D By arrangement

8

Belvedere (Ferriby) Ltd
27 Low Street, North Ferriby, North Humberside HU14 3DD
Tel: 0482 633885
Contact: Conrad Hartley

Onion bhajis

Range of Indian savoury snacks including onion bhajis, samosas, lamb and vegetable snacks, spring rolls and pakoras in 7, 11oz packets.
C Undisclosed
W Ron Harker, Bradford
D By wholesaler

12

Ceres Wholesale Ltd
Unit 4, Watercombe Industrial Park, Yeovil, Somerset BA20 2EB
Tel: 0935 23208 Fax: 0935 29599
Contact: Mr P Jenkins

Japanese rice crackers

Range of snacks and savouries including pistachios, nuts, dates, red lentils, Japanese rice crackers and vegetarian sausage and burger mix, all packed in heat sealed clear cellophane packs of 125g. Customers own label if required.
C 10 ton p.wk
W Survival Foods, Hertfordshire, Community Foods, London
D By wholesaler

6 ↔

Country Fresh Foods (Cumbria) Ltd
Unit 1, Longtown Industrial Estate,
Carlisle, Cumbria CA6 5TJ
Tel: 0228 791788
Contact: Mr H W Frizell

Potato skins

Range of frozen baked potatoes including potato skins, topped halves and whole potatoes in plain, cheese and onion, smoky bacon and tomato,and prawn cocktail fillings weighing 5-12oz. Also varieties of frozen omelette including Spanish.
[C] Undisclosed
[D] By arrangement
See Also: Vegetable Dishes

6

Dale Country Foods Ltd
1 Cumbie Way, Newton Aycliffe, Co Durham DL5 7EN
Tel: 0325 300471
Contact: K M Parsons

Sesame and honey bar

Range of additive free cereal bars including sesame and honey, chocolate and hazelnut, and chocolate fruit and nut all made with raw cane sugar, butter, wheat flakes, honey, glucose and Afghan raisins in 30g packs in outers of three.
[C] Undisclosed
[D] By arrangment

12 ↔

Holstius & Breet
Esperanza, Aust, Bristol, Avon BS12 3AX
Tel: 04545 3148 Telx: 449752
Contact: Robin D L Breet

Coriander and thyme olives

Range of additive free speciality olives flavoured with cardamom and orange, coriander and thyme, lemon and garlic, chilli and anchovy in extra-virgin olive oil. Also spiced nuts.
[C] Undisclosed
[D] By arrangement
See Also: Butter, Mustards, Fudges and Toffee

16

Raj Foods
56b Minerva Road, Park Royal, London NW10 6HJ
Tel: 01 965 6533
Contact: Mr R Radia

Samosa

Traditional Indian meat and vegetable samosas, various bhajis, and a range of ready to eat curries including lamb, beef, chicken, prawn, tandoori in 8½oz without rice, 11½oz with rice sizes.
[C] Undisclosed
[D] By arrangement

14

River Farm Smokery
Great Wilbraham Road, Bottisham, nr Newmarket, Cambridgeshire CB1 5J
Tel: 0223 811382
Contact: R F Enoch

Smoked almonds

Smoked almonds and peanuts.
[C] Undisclosed
[D] By arrangement
See Also: Meat: Smoked, Game: Smoked, Fish Dealers

15

Selected Savouries
Hatchmoor Industrial Estate, Hatherleigh, nr Okehampton, Devon EX 20 3LP
Tel: 0837 810016
Contact: Derek Godfrey-Brown

Steak and kidney

Range of snacks and savouries including individual steak and kidney pot meals, vol au vents and sausage rolls boxed in freezer containers in various sizes. Also vegetarian range including Better Bangers, meat free sausages made with textured vegetable protein in 160g packs of eight.
[C] Each line 80 p.dy
[D] By arrangement

16

Three oh Four
The Old Hall, Iden, Rye, East Sussex TN31 7XD
Tel: 07978 304
Contact: M Garbett

Smoked nuts

Range of smoked nuts.
[C] Undisclosed
[D] By arrangment
See Also: Fish: Pâtés and Pastes

SNAILS

12

British Snail Farmer Association
Barrow Farm, Rode Hill, Rode, Somerset
Tel: 0373 830 300
Contact: Jacques Aubree

Live snail

Fresh or frozen free-range Helix Aspersa Major snails.
[C] Undisclosed fresh Sep-Mar
[D] By arrangement

11 ↔

Britsnail Ltd
6 Stoughton Avenue, Leicester LE2 2DR
Tel: 0533 706794 Telx: 94016494 OILS G
Contact: Charles Wells

Coquilles des escargots

British farmed frozen snails packed fifty to the bag. Also range of individual frozen prepared snail dishes including coquilles des escargots with smoked bacon and parmesan cheese, snail pâté with spinach and spring onions, and escargots Bourguignone, snails with garlic butter.
[C] 2000 frozen packs p.wk
[D] By arrangement

16 ↔

Densworth Snails
Densworth Farm, Funtington Road, East Ashling, nr Chichester, West Sussex PO18 9AP
Tel: 0243 575342
Contact: Mr S Jessop

Snails with cider

Farmed British snails live or cooked in a variety of dishes including with herbs sealed in shell with garlic butter, or with cider sealed with cheese and chives. All in 6, 12, 60 vacuum or blast frozen packs or to customers requirements.
[C] 500 doz p.wk
[D] By own transport within area

16

Hales Snails Ltd
25 Pages Walk, London SE1 4SB
Tel: 01 231 0067
Contact: Gordon McGerty

Herb and cheese snails

Frozen free-range British snails from the Mendips in herb and cheese sauce in catering pack of ten dozen.
[C] Undisclosed
[D] By arrangement

[7]

Pegasus Aquaculture And Mollusc Farms
17M Jackson Street, Westside Industrial Estate, St Helens, Merseyside WA9 3AT
Tel: 0744 451556
Contact: Mr C E Lancaster

Snails in herb broth — British farmed snails cooked in herb broth supplied in 9″x4″ vacuum packs with six to the pack.
[C] 200,000 (4 ton) p.a
[D] By arrangement

[9] [↔]

The Snail Centre
Plas Newydd, 90-92 Dinerth Rd, Colwyn Bay, Clwyd LL28 4YH
Tel: 0492 48253
Contact: Mr R E Groves

Garlic snails — Several species of snail available fresh or frozen and prepared in court bouillon and sealed with garlic butter ready for heating.
[C] Undisclosed
[D] By arrangement

[15] [↔]

South West Snails
Yeolands Farm, Ermington Road, Ivybridge, Devon PL21 0LF
Tel: 0752 897040
Contact: Mr D Calvert

Snail caviar — Snails supplied frozen or vacuum packed. Also available prepared snail including snails in garlic, cocktail snails and snail caviar.
[C] 1 ton p.mth all year
[D] By arrangement

SOUPS

[2] [↔]

Baxters of Speyside Ltd
Fochabers, Morayshire IV32 7LD
Tel: 0343 820 393 Telx: 73327 Fax: 0343 820286
Contact: Miss M E Foster

Lobster bisque — Range of soups including lobster bisque, cream of asparagus, and vegetarian beetroot.
[C] Undisclosed
[D] By arrangement
See Also: Chutneys and Pickles

[13]

Bender & Cassel Ltd
Blackhorse Road, Letchworth, Hertfordshire SG6 1HL
Tel: 0462 686971 Telx: 825265 SOUP Fax: 0642 670214
Contact: G J Pratt

Duck and cranberry — Range of vegetable, seafood, meat, game and speciality soups including cream of broccoli, cream of smoked salmon, smoked mackerel, duck and cranberry, real turtle, and tomato and garlic packed in trays of 12x410g or 6x795g tins.
[C] 14 ton p.wk
[D] By arrangement

16 ↔

Manor Farm Pantry
Alresford Watercress Ltd, Manor Farm, Old Alresford, Hampshire SO24 9DH
Tel: 0962 734230
Contact: J R Bevan

Cream of watercress — Cream of watercress soup from organically grown watercress. Supplied frozen in 2x5 retail packs.
[C] Undisclosed
[D] By arrangement
See Also: Fresh Salads

16

The New Covent Garden Soup Company Ltd
296 Wandsworth Bridge Road, London SW6 2UA
Tel: 01 731 2621 Telx: 266835 SUKLG Fax: 01 731 8259
Contact: Caroline Jacobs

Carrot and coriander — Range of homemade, additive free soups including vichyssoise, carrot and coriander, chicken lemon and tarragon and a soup of the month. All chilled with a shelf life of fourteen days, packed in 1pt cartons in outers of twelve.
[C] Undisclosed
[D] By arrangement

15

Wessex Fare Ltd
Station Road, Gillingham, Dorset SP8 4QA
Tel: 07476 2177/3153 Telx: 886089 Fax: 07476 64030
Contact: Rory Herbert

Mussel — Range of ten condensed and ready to serve soups including watercress, mussel, carrot, lentil and kidney in 15oz cans in outers of twelve.
[C] 3000 doz p.mth
[D] By arrangement
See Also: Chutneys and Pickles

Any Problems?

If any suppliers listed in **British Food Finds 1989** let you down, do not deliver their goods, supply you with inferior produce, please let us know and we can follow it up for the next edition. Contact **Henrietta Green on 01-927-9808.**

British Food Finds is here to help-

If you know of a producer of speciality food not listed in **British Food Finds 1989,** please let us know so that we can include them in our next edition.

For editorial entries contact **Henrietta Green on 01 727 9808.**

10

DRINKS

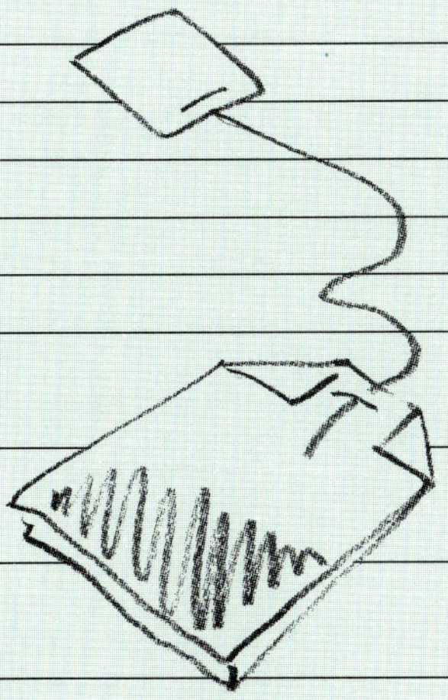

CIDER

The process of cider-making is simple and has changed little since our ancestors made the fortunate discovery of fermenting crab apples.
The apples are first crushed and the pulp pressed. Then nature is allowed to take its course, the yeasts in the fruit transform the sugars into alcohol.
The quality and range of ciders is due partly to the cider apple, of which there are over six hundred varieties with subtle differences in flavour, tannin and strength, and partly to the skill in blending and to the instinct to know when to stop fermentation.
There are at least one hundred quality farmhouse traditional draught ciders - from rough to smooth, sweet to dry, ciders to quaff and ciders to sip.

14 ◯

Aspall Cyder
Aspall Hall, nr Debenham, Stowmarket, Suffolk IP14 6PD
Tel: 0728 860510 Fax: 0728 861031
Contact: John Chevallier Guild

Clear, light orange coloured cider, consistency of a light wine, good apple and after taste, made from blend of cider and culinary apples grown with no chemicals or preservatives, still, medium sweet, still dry, still extra dry, in ¼, 1lt bottles.
C 100,000 gal p.a
D By arrangement
See Also: Vinegars, Juices

15

Beenleigh Enterprises/Manor Farm Foods
Beenleigh Manor, Harbertonford, Totnes, Devon
Tel: 080423 738
Contact: Mr A K Wilson-Gough

Cider made from local apples, mostly Sweet Alford and Foxs Whelp, fermented with apples own yeast, sweetness controlled by racking off, no filtration or additives, supplied by apple type or blend.
C 5000 gal p.a
D By arrangement
See Also: Millers, Juices

16

Biddenden Cider
Biddenden Vineyards, Little Whatmans, Biddenden, Ashford, Kent
Tel: 0580 291726
Contact: Mr R A Barnes

Clear light yellow coloured cider, made from blend of culinary and dessert apples, distinctive tangy flavour, in 1lt bottles, 5 gal polycasks. Also Monks Delight, cider blended with honey, spices and apple wine, Biddenden Special Reserve, cider matured in oak whisky casks.
C Undisclosed
W The English Farm Cider Centre 032183 303/411
D By wholesaler, by arrangement
See Also: Wine

10

Black Bull Cider
Norbury's, Crowcroft, Leigh Sinton, nr Malvern, Worcestershire
Tel: 0886 32206
Contact: Mr T P Norbury

Clear light orange coloured cider, good aroma and full body, made with a champagne yeast and filtered clear, in ½, 1, 5 gal containers, 5 gal polycasks, range of glass bottles, demijohns. Perry also available.
C Over 50,000 p.a
W The English Farm Cider Centre 032183 303411, Saffron Ciders 079987 427
D By wholesaler, by arrangement

12

Blands
Church Road, Oldbury-on-Severn, nr Bristol, Avon BS12 1QG
Tel: 0454 413124
Contact: Vernon Bland

Range of West country cider, dry and sweet, still and carbonated in 11 gal steel kegs with a two year shelf life.
C 2000 kegs p.mth
D By arrangement

12

Broad Oak Cider
Greyfield, High Littleton, Avon
Tel: 0761 72316
Contact: Mr Ralph McNalty

Draught farm cider made by traditional methods, dry, tangy, cloudy and strong, in 5 gal polycasks. Also Broad Oak perry in 5 gal polycasks.
C Up to 1½ million gal p.a
W Saffron Ciders 079987 427
D By wholesaler, by arrangement

15

Bromell's Devon Farm Cider
Lower Uppacott, Tedburn St Mary, nr Exeter, Devon
Tel: 06476 294
Contact: Mr E Bromell

Cloudy yellow cider, strong, full bodied consistency, made with local apples by traditional methods, dry, medium, medium sweet and sweet (with added sugar), in ½-50 gal sizes, 5 gal polypins.
C 40,000 p.a
D By arrangement

12

Burrow Hill Cider
Pass Vale Farm, Burrow Hill, Kingsbury Episcopy, Martock, Somerset PA12 5BU
Tel: 0460 40782
Contact: Mr Julian Temperley

Vintage farmhouse cider pressed from apples grown on farm, additive free, in 1pt-5 gal containers. Burrow Hill cider also used to make Somerset version of calvados.
C 80,000 gal p.a
W The English Farm Cider Centre 032183 303/411
D By wholesaler, by own transport within area

15 **Churchward's Cider**
Yalberton Farm, Paignton, South Devon
Tel: 0803 558157
Contact: Mr Vic Churchward

Made from mixed cider apples fermented in own yeast, with distinctive flavour and strength, in 1lt-5 gal containers, 1, 3lt bottles, 5 gal polycasks.
[C] Undisclosed
[W] The English Farm Cider Centre 032183 303/411
[D] By wholesaler and by arrangement

12 **Coates Farmhouse Cider**
Showerings Ltd, Kilver Street, Shepton Mallet, Somerset BA4 5ND
Tel: 0749 3333 Fax: 0749 44209
Contact: The Marketing Manager

Cloudy yellow, middle strength cider, with good aroma and subtle apple taste, in 5 gal polycasks. Also Addlestones, cask conditioned cider for serving through hand pump.
[C] Undisclosed
[D] By arrangement

15 **Cornish Scrumpy Co Ltd**
Callestock Cider Farm, Penhallow, Truro, Cornwall TR4 9LW
Tel: 0872 573355
Contact: David Healey

Strong vintage scrumpy, matured in oak vats, dry and medium sweet, made mainly from Yarlington Mill, Dabinett and Sweet Alford cider apples. Also weaker medium sweet, all available in 1, 2lt PET bottles, 2.4, 4.9lt stone jars and 23lt barrel. Also range of country wines including gooseberry, apple, and redcurrant.
[C] Cider 12,000 gal p.mth, wine 400 gal p.mth
[D] By arrangement

15 **Countryman Cider**
Felldownhead, Milton Abbot, Tavistock, Devon PL19 09R
Tel: 082 28226
Contact: N W Lawrence

Range of scrumpy, dry, medium and sweet made from bitter sweet apples in 70cl glass bottles, 1, 2lt PET bottles, 5 gal polybarrels, 2½, 5lt carrykegs, miniature and ½, 1, 2pt stone jars.
[C] Undisclosed
[W] St Austell Brewery Co 0726 74444, Dartmoor Leisure Ltd 082 287 412
[D] By wholesaler, by arrangement

10 **Dunkerton's Cider**
Hays Head, Luntley, Pembridge, Leominster, Herefordshire HR6 9ED
Tel: 05447 653
Contact: Mr Ivor Dunkerton

Cloudy orange coloured cider, good aroma and body, mature apple taste, made from mixed old and new varieties of local cider apples, varieties fermented individually, then blended. Also Kingston Black, Court Royal, Breakwells Seedling single apple ciders and traditional perry, all fruit unsprayed. All in 1lt, 1, 5 gal containers.
[C] Undisclosed
[W] The English Farm Cider Centre 032183 303/411, Saffron Ciders 079987 427
[D] By wholesaler, by own transport

16 **Godshill Farmhouse Cider**
The Cider Barn, Godshill, Isle of Wight
Tel: 0983 840680
Contact: Mr Peter Cramp

Cider made from cider apples including Yarlington Mill, Chisel Jersey and Dabinett, medium sweet (with added sugar) and dry, mainly unfiltered in 1, 2lt bottles, ¼, 1 gal plastic containers.
[C] Undisclosed
[D] By arrangement

15 **Gray's Farm Cider**
Halstow, Tedburn St Mary, Devon
Tel: 06476 236
Contact: Mr T Gray

Cider with good aroma, mellow mature flavour, made from old fashioned bitter sweet varieties of apples grown on farm and locally, additive free, in plastic containers and 5 gal polycasks.
[C] 20,000 gal p.a
[W] The English Farm Cider Centre 032183 303/411
[D] By wholesaler and by arrangement

15

Inch's Cider Company Ltd
Western Barn, Winkleigh, Devon EX19 8AP
Tel: 083783 560
Contact: David Martin

Dry, medium dry and medium sweet scrumpy matured in oak vats for three years in 0.275-2lt bottles and casks.
[C] Scrumpy 40,000lt p.mth, vintage scrumpy 5,000lt p.mth
[D] By own transport, by arrangement
See Also: Juices

10

Knights Cider
Crumpton Oaks Fruit Farm, Storridge, Malvern, Herefordshire
Tel: 06845 4594
Contact: Keith Knight

Traditionally made clear still cider, with good apple taste and aftertaste, overall champion 1987 Hereford Cider Museum.
[C] 100,000 gal
[W] Aston Manor Brewery, Birmingham
[D] By wholesaler, by arrangement

15

Nicholas Downs Ltd
Wiscombe Winery, Southleigh, Colyton, Devon EX13 6JF
Tel: 040487 360
Contact: Mr Nicholas Downs

Farmhouse cider, dry, medium and sweet, made from locally grown, unsprayed and untreated apples in 1lt bottles.
[C] 1500 gal p.a
[D] By arrangement
See Also: Wine

15

F H Mann (Bushy Park) Products
Knowle Orchards, Budleigh Salterton, Devon EX9 7AL
Tel: 03954 2174
Contact: Joanna Hunt

Devon cider made from a blend of culinary and dessert apples in 2lt bottles.
[C] 1,500 gal p.a
[D] By arrangement
See Also: Fresh Fruit, Juices

12

Rich's Farmhouse Cider
Mill Farm, Watchfield, nr Highbridge, Somerset TA9 4RD
Tel: 0278 783651
Contact: Mr Gordon Rich

Still cloudy cider made from West Country apples, distinctive taste, good aroma and full bodied, in 5 gal polycasks, ½, 1lt cans.

[C] Undisclosed
[W] The English Farm Cider Centre 032183 303/411
[D] By wholesaler, by arrangement

14 ↔

The Suffolk Cider Company Ltd
The Cider House, Friday Street,
Brandeston, Woodbridge, Suffolk IP13 7BP
Tel: 072882 537
Contact: Mr Michael Hall

Strong clear cider made from eating and cooking apples, fermented with champagne yeast, matured in oak vats, in 1, 2lt, 330ml bottles, 4½ gal polypins.
[C] Up to 50,000 gal p.a
[D] By arrangement
See Also: Juices

12

Thatcher's Farmhouse Cider
Myrtle Farm, Station Road, Sandford,
Avon BS19 5RA
Tel: 0934 822862
Contact: Mr John Thatcher

Cloudy strong tangy cider, unfiltered, made by traditional methods, dry, medium or sweet, in ½ gal containers, 5 gal polycasks. Also Sandford Superb, clear, still, in 1, 2lt bottles, 5 gal polycasks.
[C] 250,000 gal p.a
[W] The English Farm Cider Centre 032183 303/411, Saffron Ciders 079987 427
[D] By wholesaler, by arrangement

15

Yearlstone Cyder
Yearlstone Vineyard, Chilverton, Coldridge,
Crediton, Devon
Tel: 03635 302
Contact: Miss Gillian Pearkes

Cider made from locally grown chemical free cider apples, fermented with German wine yeast, matured in oak casks and gently filtered. Yearlstone Gold, dry and crisp vintage and Yearlstone Cyder Royale, fuller, medium dry both in 70cl bottles, ½, 1 gal plastic containers.
[C] 1000 gal p.a
[W] Dartington Farm Foodshop
[D] By wholesaler
See Also: Juices, Wine

JUICES

The trend towards healthier eating has stimulated growth in the fruit juice market. Freshly squeezed juice is gaining in popularity. It is made from only freshly squeezed fruit and contains 100% fresh natural juice with between 15% and 20% natural fruit cells. It has to be kept refrigerated which gives it a shelf life of 7 days. As it is untreated it retains its full nutritional value, unlike juices made from concentrates which are reconstructed with water (66% being the norm) and pasteurised. Orange is the most popular flavour, accounting for approximately 60% of all sales, with freshly pressed apple second. Seasonal juices are being introduced as the fresh fruit becomes available. The juice and the zest (for example of lemons) is also being used as ingredients to produce fresh yoghurt, sorbets, desserts and frozen gâteaux.

14 ○ ↔

Aspall Cyder
Aspall Hall, nr Debenham, Stowmarket,
Suffolk IP14 6PD
Tel: 0728 860510 Fax: 0728 861031
Contact: John Chevallier Guild

Apple

Additive free pasteurised apple juice made with organically grown Suffolk apples bottled in ¼, 1lt bottles, with customers own label if required. Also apple juice blends available.
[C] Undisclosed
[D] By own transport nationally
See Also: Vinegars, Cider

15

Beenleigh Enterprises/Manor Farm Foods
Beenleigh Manor, Harbertonford, Totnes,
Devon
Tel: 080423 738
Contact: Mr A K Wilson-Gough

Apple

Drew Orchards, additive free Devon pressed apple juice made from a mixture of dessert and cooking apples in 70cl glass bottles.
[C] 30,000 bottles p.a
[D] By own transport within area
See Also: Millers, Cider

11 ↔

Belvoir Fruit Farms Ltd
Grantham, Lincolnshire
Tel: 0476 870225
Contact: Lord John Manners

Elderflower cordial

Range of fruit cordials including Belvoir elderflower, raspberry made with 70% fruit juice, blackcurrant, lemon and bitter lemon cordials all in 50, 70cl glass bottles.
[C] Elderflower cordial 6,500 bottles p.a, raspberry cordial 1,500 bottles p.a, blackcurrant 6,000 bottles p.a
[D] By arrangement

14

Cavendish Manor Vineyards
Nether Hall, Cavendish, Sudbury, Suffolk CO10 8BX
Tel: 0787 280221
Contact: Basil Ambrose

Grape
Apple

Cox, Russet and Pippin apple juice. Also grape juice in 70cl glass bottles.
[C] Undisclosed
[D] By arrangement

11 ●

W G & M J Cherry
Sweetapples Orchards, Stowupland, Stowmarket, Suffolk
Tel: 0449 674791
Contact: Mrs Gavin Cherry

Organic apple

100% Cox or 100% Russet organic apple juice from apples grown on farm, bottled in 700ml glass bottles.
[C] 10-20,000 bottles p.a
[W] Odin, Covent Garden, Organic Farm Foods, Wales
[D] By wholesaler, by arrangement

7 ↔

Cooke Bros (Tattenhall) Ltd
Calypso Soft Drinks, Tattenhall, Chester, Cheshire CH3 9PX
Tel: 0829 70315
Contact: Mr S M Shepherd

Fruit

Varieties of fruit juice including orange, apple and pineapple. Also soft drinks in 185ml plastic cups with foil lids or 4-6 variety packs.
[C] Undisclosed
[D] By arrangement

14 ○ ↔

Copella Fruit Juices Ltd
Hill Farm, Boxford, Colchester, Essex CO6 5NY
Tel: 0787 210348 Telx: 94012299 COPLG
Contact: Mrs T Unwin

Blackcurrant and apple

Range of additive free, farm pressed fruit juice including apple, blackcurrant and apple, cherry and apple, carrot and apple. Also organic apple juice, all available in a range of bottles and cartons.
[C] Undisclosed
[W] Countrywide Network, 0787 210348
[D] By wholesaler

16

Cottage Farms Ltd
Crundalls, Matfield, Tonbridge, Kent TN12
Tel: 089 272 2702
Contact: Mr P Sutton

Apple

Cottage Farm, additive free clarified apple juice made with a Bramley base and a variety of apples in 1lt bottles.
[C] Undisclosed
[D] By own transport within area

16

Dounhurst Farm
Dounhurst Farm, Wisborough Green, Billinghurst, Sussex RH14 OAB
Tel: 0403 77 209
Contact: T Mursell

Apple

Pasteurised, unfiltered apple juice made from Cox and Bramley with no added sugar in 300ml cans.
[C] Undisclosed
[D] By own transport within area and by arrangement

15

Four Elms Fruit Farm
Harpford, Sidmouth, Devon EX10 ONJ
Tel: 0395 68286
Contact: Mr R J Smedley

Apple

Pressed pasteurised apple juice made from Cox and Bramley with vitamin C added as antioxidant in 70cl bottles.
[C] 10,000-20,000 bottles p.a
[D] By arrangement

11

Fresh Fruit Juice Manufacturing Ltd
Bell House, Fleming Road, Corby, Northamptonshire NN17 2SW
Tel: 0536 61599 Fax: 0536 68028
Contact: Mr R Harwood

Clementine

Range of fruit juices, 100% fresh, from whole fruit, untreated and additive free including orange, grapefruit, lemon, pineapple, clementine, mandarin and ruby blood orange. Also lemon and orange peel in vacuum packs. Juices in 500ml, 1lt, ½ gal packs, customers own label if required.
C Undisclosed
D By own refrigerated transport, by arrangement

4 ↔

Greengate Foods Ltd
110 Trewmount Road, Dundannon, Co Tyrone BT71 7EE
Tel: 08687 84606 Telx: 74656 GREENGATE
Contact: Mr I McMurray

Apple

Apple juice concentrate made from Bramley packed to customers requirements.
C Undisclosed
D By arrangement

15

Hancocks Cider & Mineral Waters
Mill House, Clapworthy Mill, South Molton, Devon EX36 4HU
Tel: 07695 2678
Contact: Mr Hancock

Ginger beer

Seven varieties of carbonated drinks including lemonade and ginger beer made to an old traditional recipe. Also cider.
C Undisclosed
D By own transport within area

16 ↔

Hill Farm Orchards
Droxford Road, Swanmore, Southampton SO3 2PY
Tel: 04897 8616
Contact: Helen Starkey

Apple

Homemade pure apple juice pressed on farm from Cox and Bramley apples with no added sugar.
C Undisclosed
D By arrangement
See Also: Apples

15

Inch's Cider Company Ltd
Western Barn, Winkleigh, Devon EX19 8AP
Tel: 083783 560
Contact: David Martin

Apple

Sparkling apple juice and apple liqueur in 1lt bottles.
C Undisclosed
D By arrangement
See Also: Cider

[15]

F H Mann (Bushy Park) Products
Knowle Orchards, Budleigh Salterton, Devon EX9 7AL
Tel: 03954 2174
Contact: Joanna Hunt

Apple — Pasteurised unfiltered Devon apple juice made from dessert and cooking apples in 250, 750ml rectangular tin foil sachets.
[C] 30,000lt p.a
[D] By own transport within area and by arrangement
See Also: Fresh Fruit, Cider

[16]

Martlet Natural Foods
Horam Manor, Horam, Heathfield, East Sussex TN21 OJA
Tel: 04353 2254 Telx: 957266 APPLES G
Contact: Mr Andrew Howie

Apple — Range of three apple juices including concentrate in 500ml pack, freshly pressed in 690ml pack and sparkling in llt pack.
[C] Undisclosed
[D] By arrangement
See Also: Jams and Preserves, Honey

[16]

Penshurst Vineyards
Grove Road, Penshurst, Kent TN1 18DU
Tel: 0892 870255
Contact: Mr D Westphal

Apple — Pasteurised, additive free apple juice from Bramley, Cox and Spartan in 1lt bottles.
[C] 4000-5000 bottles p.a
[D] By own transport within area and by arrangement
See Also: Wine

[10] ↔

Pullens Farm Fruit Juices
Ridgeway Cross, nr Malvern, Hereford and Worcester WR13 5JN
Tel: 088684 232/599 Telx: 333175 STOKES
Contact: Mr M Brigden

Apple — Range of apple juice including blend of Cox and Bramley with medium sweet flavour, Egremont, made from Russet with a nutty flavour and Discovery, with a sharp flavour, all in 70cl glass bottles.
[C] Blend of Cox and Bramley, unlimited, Egremont 2000 bottles p.mth, Discovery 2000 bottles p.mth
[D] By arrangement
See Also: Wine

[12]

Sherston Earl Vineyards Ltd
Sherston, nr Malmesbury, Wiltshire SN16 0PY
Tel: 0666 840716
Contact: Mr N Sellers

Apple — Medium sweet apple juice made from Cox and Bramley with added Vitamin C as preservative in 70cl bottles.
[C] 500 bottles p.mth
[D] By arrangement

14 ↔

The Suffolk Cider Company Ltd
The Cider House, Friday Street,
Brandeston, Woodbridge, Suffolk IP13 7BP
Tel: 072882 537
Contact: Mr Michael Hall

Apple

Additive free apple juice made from Cox and Russet in 330ml, 70cl bottles
Ⓒ Undisclosed
Ⓓ By arrangement
See Also: Cider

14 ↔

Trustin Foods
Chase Road, Northern Way, Bury St Edmunds, Suffolk IP32 6NT
Tel: 0284 66265 Telx: 81117 G TRUSTIN
Contact: Mr Derek Wilson

Dill

Vegetable juices, ideal for seasoning including dill, celery and garlic in 12x57ml shake and pour glass bottles. Also available fruit squashes including lemon and lime, orange, and pineapple in 12x700ml glass bottles.
Ⓒ Undisclosed
Ⓓ By arrangement
See Also: Chocolates, Teas and Infusions

10 ↔

Wye Valley Fruit Farms Ltd
Linton, Ross-on-Wye, Hereford HR9 7SD
Tel: 098982 626 Telx: 35382
Contact: Mr R Burton

Apple and blackberry

Pressed fruit juice including cloudy and clear apple, golden Russet, apple and blackberry, apple and blackcurrant, and apple and plum in 680ml glass bottles. Also clear apple juice in 3lt bag-in-box.
Ⓒ Undisclosed
Ⓓ By arrangement

15

Yearlstone Cyder
Yearlstone Vineyard, Chilverton, Coldridge, Crediton, Devon
Tel: 03635 302
Contact: Miss Gillian Pearkes

Apple

Additive free apple juice pressed from late picked apples in 70cl bottles.
Ⓒ Undisclosed
Ⓦ Dartington Farm Shop
Ⓓ By wholesaler, by arrangement
See Also: Cider, Wine

LIQUEURS

9

Brecon Brewery
15-16 Ffrwd Grech Industrial Estate,
Brecon, Powys LD3 8DR
Tel: 0874 2926 Fax: 08474 4905
Contact: Daffyd Gittings

Swyn Y Mor

Swyn Y Mor - 40%, herb flavoured mellowed whisky. Welsh Chwisgi, Merlyn Welsh Cream Liqueur - 17%, white, honey flavoured, fairly neutral creamy liqueur.
C 3000lt p.hr
D By arrangement
See Also: Malt Whisky

8

Bronte Liqueur Co Ltd
2 The Calls, Leeds LS2 7JU
Tel: 0532 439111 Telx: 557934
Contact: Mr Graham Howden

Bronte liqueur

Bronte Yorkshire Liqueur - 34%, fruity blend of honey, herbs, spices and brandy with delicate orange flavour bottled in ceramic jar.
C 200-300 cases p.mth
D By arrangement

15

Devonshire Meadows Ltd
Maristow Park, Broadly Park Road, nr
Plymouth, Devon LS2 7JU
Tel: 0752 784411 Telx: DEVMED G
Contact: Mr White

Devonshire Royal

Devonshire Royal Cream Liqueur - 17%, pale brown, blend of Devon cream, French brandy and Scotch whisky, rich and creamy, with flavour reminiscent of coffee and butterscotch.
C Undisclosed
D By arrangement

15

Dittisham Fruit Farm
Capton, nr Dartmouth, Devon TQ6 OJE
Tel: 080421 452
Contact: E B Kain

Fruit

Devon Fruit Liqueur - 25%, in raspberry, blackcurrant, and strawberry. Light, rustic, different from French equivalents with higher strength and less flavour, produced quarterly on small scale by pressing frozen fruit and adding grain spirit.
C Undisclosed
D By arrangement

3

Glenturret Distillery Ltd
Glenturret, Crieff, Perthshire PH7 4HA
Tel: 0764 2424 Fax: 0764 4366
Contact: P J M Fairlie

Malt

Malt liqueur.
C Undisclosed
D By arrangement
See Also: Malt Whisky

16

Goldwell Ltd
East Malling, Maidstone, Kent ME19 6BS
Tel: 0732 841356 Telx: 957030
Contact: The Sales Office

Country Satin

Range of cocktails produced with British wine, spirits, fresh cream and selected flavours including Country Satin - 14.5%, blend of malt whisky and Devon cream, light brown, soft chocolate bouquet and flavour. Calypso - 14.5%, blend of rum and cream, yellow, strong banana flavour. Beachcomber - 14.5%, blend of rum and cream, white with coconut flavour.
C Undisclosed
D By arrangement

16 ↔

Hallgarten Wines Ltd
53 Highgate Road, London NW5 1RR
Tel: 01 267 2041 Telx: 27715 HALLGA G
Contact: Peter Hallgarten

Glen Mist

Glen Mist Scotch Whisky Liqueur - 35%, rich, full flavoured, Scotch whisky, herb and spice flavoured liqueur. Can-y-Delyn Welsh Mist, whisky based liqueur similar to Glen Mist, bottled in Wales.
C Undisclosed
D By arrangement

1

Highland Wineries
Moniack Castle, Kirkhill, Inverness
Tel: 0463 83283
Contact: Mrs P M Fraser

Moniack

Moniack sloe liqueur in 70, 75cl bottles.
Ⓒ Undisclosed
Ⓓ By arrangement
See Also: Wine

5

Inver House Distillers Ltd
Moffat Distilleries, Towers Road, Airdrie, Lanarkshire ML6 8PL
Tel: 0236 69377 Telx: 778084
Contact: Alastair Douglas

Heather Cream

Heather Cream liqueur, a blend of fresh double Scottish cream and malt whisky.
Ⓒ Undisclosed
Ⓓ By arrangement

16

John Milroy Ltd
3 Greek Street, London W1V 5LA
Tel: 01 437 0893/2385 Telx: 268489
Contact: Sales Office

Bailey's

Range of liqueurs including Bailey's Irish Cream.
Ⓒ Undisclosed
Ⓓ By arrangement

3

John Murray and Co (Mull) Ltd
Calgary Bay, Isle of Mull
Tel: 041 952 9190
Contact: Roderick Bartholomew

Columba

Columba Cream Liqueur - 17%, pale beige with honey, cream and whisky flavour, the driest of British cream liqueurs.
Ⓒ Undisclosed
Ⓓ By arrangement

16

Lamberhurst Vineyards
Ridge Farm, Lamberhurst, Kent TN3 8ER
Tel: 0892 890286
Contact: Mr Absalom

Apricot

Range of Kent fruit liqueurs including Apricot, dark orange, strong kernel and apricot flavour. Blackcurrant, light, full fruity purple liqueur with elegant bouquet. Cherry, deep red liqueur with clean, ripe, cherry flavour. Raspberry, red, slightly smokey, raspberry flavour lighter than French variety.
Ⓒ Undisclosed
Ⓓ By arrangement
See Also: Wine

16

Merrydown Wine Plc
Horam Manor, Horam, Heathfield, Sussex TN21 OJA
Tel: 04353 2254 Telx: 957266 APPLES G
Contact: Mr Peter Oxford

Mead

Mead Liqueur - 17%, dark golden with light, full, elegant, lasting flavour on palate and honey bouquet bottled in stone jar.
Ⓒ 200 cases p.a
Ⓓ By arrangement

12

J R Phillips and Co Ltd
Avonmouth Way, Avonmouth, Bristol, Avon BS11 9HX
Tel: 0272 823651 Telx: 44367
Contact: Brands Manager

Pink Clove

Range of Phillips Old English Cordials including Aniseed - 5%, white, rich full aniseed bouquet, delicately balanced flavour. Grenadine - 3%, red, rich fruity nose, with mildly sweet full flavour. Lovage - 8%, golden, herby bouquet, light sweetish leafy taste. Peppermint White and Green - 5%, strong peppermint bouquet with equally strong taste. Pink Clove - 7.5%, bright red, strong clove bouquet with strong aggressive taste. Shrub - 6%, red, rich fruity bouquet, lightly sweet. Also Hawkes Sloe Gin - 25%, reddish brown with fine sloe flavour.
Ⓒ Undisclosed
Ⓓ By arrangement

3

Ronald Morrison & Co Ltd
Pentland Bottling Hall, Pentland Park, Salamander Place, Edinburgh U86 7JL
Tel: 031 554 4404 Telx: 727217
Contact: The Sales Manager

Glayva

Glayva Scotch Liqueur - 40%, dark golden, full herb and whisky bouquet, with strong whisky with flavours taste, rich but not too sweet.
Ⓒ Undisclosed
Ⓓ By arrangement

16

Seagram UK Ltd
Seagram Distillers House, Dacre Street, London SW1H ODR
Tel: 01 222 4343 Telx: 916251
Contact: Sales Office

Lochan Ora

Lochan Ora Whisky Liqueur - 40%, amber, strong whisky bouquet, light, dry with long whisky after taste.
Ⓒ 1000 cases p.a
Ⓓ By arrangement
See Also: Malt Whisky

4 ↔

St Brendan's Irish Cream Liqueur Co Ltd
19 Tamlaght Road, Omagh, Co Tyrone BT78 4QE
Tel: 0662 46146 Telx: 747630 LECOMA G
Fax: 0662 41434
Contact: Mr Brian Duncan

St. Brendan's

St. Brendan's Irish Cream - 17%, old Irish cream spirit liqueur supplied in 5, 70, 75cl satinised bottles. Poole's - 17%, pink fruity liqueur in 5, 75cl white flint bottles.
Ⓒ St. Brendan's 50,000 cases p.a, Poole's 20,000 cases p.a
Ⓦ Irish Bonding Group, Northern Ireland
Ⓓ By wholesaler

MALT WHISKY

3

Arthur Bell & Sons
Cherrybank, Perth PH2 ONG
Tel: 0738 2111 Telx: 76275
Contact: Sales Office

Bladnoch

Bladnoch Lowland - 40%, light and delicate nose, smooth and delicate but full taste. Blair Atholl Highland - 40%, light and fresh nose, clean aroma, medium hint of peat with nice round finish. Dufftown Highland - 40%, very distinctive nose with pleasant hint of sweetness, round and gentle medium bodied, with pleasant lingering taste.
C Undisclosed
D By arrangement

9

Brecon Brewery
15-16 Ffrwd Grech Industrial Estate, Brecon, Powys LD3 8DR
Tel: 0874 2926 Fax: 08474 4905
Contact: Daffyd Gittings

Swyn Y Mor

Swyn Y Mor - 40%, herb flavoured mellowed whisky. Prince of Wales, 10 year old single malt Welsh whisky.
C 3000lt p.hr
D By arrangement
See Also: Liqueurs

3

Wm Cadenhead Ltd
32 Union Street, Campbeltown, Argyll
Tel: 0586 54258 Telx: 779571 Whisky G
Contact: W Y Thomson

Rare malts

Rare malts - 46%.
C Undisclosed
D By arrangement

3

Glenturret Distillery Ltd
Glenturret, Crieff, Perthshire PH7 4HA
Tel: 0764 2424 Fax: 0764 4366
Contact: P J M Fairlie

Glenturret

Glenturret - 40%, pure single Highland malt, 8-21 year old, rich, full bodied. Malt liqueur also available.
C Undisclosed
D By arrangement
See Also: Liqueurs

2

Gordon and MacPhail
58-60 South Street, Elgin, Morayshire IV30 1JY
Tel: 0343 45111
Contact: Sales Office

Aged malt

Rare and aged malts.
C Undisclosed
D By arrangement

2

J & G Grant
Glenfarclas Distillery, Marypark, Ballindalloch, Banffshire AB3 9BD
Tel: 08072 245 Telx: 739804 Fax: 08072 234
Contact: Sales Office

Glenfarclas

Glenfarclas Highland - 40%, 10 year old. 43%, 21 year old. 45%, 15 year old. 60%, 8 year old, rich, delicious nose, full of character and flavour.
C Undisclosed
W Sichell & Sons Ltd, 01 930 9292
D By wholesaler

3

Wm Grant & Sons Ltd
206-208 West George Street, Glasgow G2 2PE
Tel: 041 248 3101 Telx: 778314
Contact: Sales Office

Glenfiddich

Balvenie Highland - 40%, excellent nose, well pronounced aroma, distinctive flavour with sweet aftertaste. Glenfiddich Highland - 40%, light delicate touch of peat with pleasing soft sweetness.
C Undisclosed
D By arrangement

3

Invergordon Distillers
9-21 Salamander Place, Leith, Edinburgh EH6 7JL
Tel: 031 554 4404 Telx: 72624
Contact: Sales Office

Glenallachie

Isle of Jura Highland - 40%, 10 year old, agreeable aroma, with charming full bodied flavour and round finish. Glenallachie Speyside - 40%, 12 year old, elegant with delightful bouquet, smooth bodied with light sweet finish, extremely well balanced.
C Undisclosed
D By arrangement

2

The MacAllan Distillers Ltd
Craigellachie, Banffshire AB3 9RX
Tel: 03405 471 Telx: 739556
Contact: Sales Office

The MacAllan

The MacAllan - 40%, 10 year old single Highland malt, smooth aroma with silky bouquet and full, delightful taste.
C Undisclosed
W Mathew Clark & Sons Ltd, 01 253 7646 (England and Wales), Peter Thomson (Perth) Ltd, 0738 29621/8(Scotland)
D By wholesaler

3

Macdonald & Muir Ltd
Macdonald House, 186 Commercial Street, Leith, Edinburgh EH6 6NN
Tel: 031 554 4477 Telx: 72406
Contact: Sales Office

Glenmoray

Glenmorangie Highland - 40%, 10 year old, fresh and sweet with subtle hint of peat, medium bodied with sweet fresh finish. Glenmoray Highland - 40%, 12 year old, fresh light aroma, light and pleasant with malty taste and clean finish.
C Undisclosed
W Dent & Reuss Ltd, 0432 276411
D By wholesaler

3

J & A Mitchell & Co Ltd
Springbank Distillery, Campbeltown, Argyll PA28 6ET
Tel: 0586 52085 Telx: 7795 71 WHISKY G
Contact: Sales Office

Campbeltown

Springbank Campbeltown - 46%, 12, 15, 21, 25, 30 year old, with excellent nose, full aroma and hint of peat, full bodied with lots of length on palate from the only Campbeltown distillery in production.
Ⓒ Undisclosed
Ⓓ By arrangement

3

Morrison Bowmore Distillers
Springburn Bond, Carlisle Street, Glasgow G21 1EQ
Tel: 041 558 9011 Telx: 778340 Fax: 041 558 9010
Contact: Sales Office

Glen Garioch

Auchentoshan Lowland - 40%, 5, 10, 12, 18 year old, delicate slightly sweet nose, light, with good aftertaste. Bowmore Islay - 40%, light peaty smokey nose, healthy, middle range Islay with medium weight and smooth finish. Glen Garioch Highland - 40%, 10 year old, light aroma, medium flavour, finishes roundly.
Ⓒ Undisclosed
Ⓓ By arrangement

4

Old Bushmills Distillery Co Ltd
Bushmills, Co Antrim BT57 8XH
Tel: 02657 31521 Telx: 747355 BUSH G
Fax: 02657 31339
Contact: Mr William J McCourt

Old Bushmills

Single Malt - 40%, 10 year old, light distinctive nose with hint of peat, smooth, well rounded flavour with a nice malt finish.
Ⓒ Undisclosed
Ⓦ Mathew Clark & Sons Ltd, 01 253 7646 (England and Wales), D Rintoul & Co Ltd, 041 332 8085/6/7 (Scotland)
Ⓓ By wholesaler

3

Robertson & Baxter Ltd
106 West Nile Street, Glasgow G1 2QX
Tel: 041 332 6361 Telx: 778076
Contact: Sales Office

Glengoyne

Glengoyne Highland - 40%, 10 year old, light fresh aroma, pleasant all round malt taste. Glengoyne - 43%, 17 year old, similar but more mature.
Ⓒ Undisclosed
Ⓦ Moreland Agencies, 01 253 7646
Ⓓ By wholesaler

3

The Scotch Malt Whisky Society
87 Giles Street, Edinburgh EH6 6BZ
Tel: 031 554 3452
Contact: Anne Dana

Cask strength

Cask strength malt about 60%, up to 21 year old.
Ⓒ Undisclosed
Ⓓ By arrangement

16

Seagram UK Ltd
Seagram Distillers House, Dacre Street, London SW1H ODR
Tel: 01 222 4343 Telx: 916251
Contact: Sales Office

The Glenlivet

The Glenlivet Highland - 40%, 12 year old, light, delicate nose with lots of fruit, medium light with trace of sweetness and quite full on palate.
Ⓒ Undisclosed
Ⓓ By arrangement
See Also: Liqueurs

3

United Distillers
99 Borron Street, Glasgow G4 9XF
Tel: 041 332 9900
Contact: Sales Office

Glendullan

Glendullan Highland - 43%, 12 year old, attractive fruity bouquet, firm mellow taste with delightful finish and smooth lingering aftertaste.
Ⓒ Undisclosed
Ⓓ By arrangement

3

William Teacher & Sons Ltd
St Enoch Square, Glasgow G1 4BZ
Tel: 041 204 2633 Telx: 778138 Fax: 041 204 1256
Contact: Sales Office

Glendronach

The Glendronach, 12 year old, original and matured in sherry casks. Teacher's 60 - guaranteed 60%.
Ⓒ Undisclosed
Ⓓ By arrangement

REAL ALE

12

Bunce's Brewery
The Old Mill, Netheravon, Salisbury, Wiltshire SP4 9QB
Tel: 0980 70631
Contact: J A Bunce

Benchmark

Unfiltered and cask conditioned beer brewed with English malted barley and two varieties of hops used whole. Best Bitter - 1042, Paler Benchmark - 1035, both on draught and in 10, 20lt containers and 4, 8pt plastic bottles.
Ⓒ 1,500 gal p.mth
Ⓓ By arrangement

16

Fuller, Smith & Turner
Griffin Brewery, Chiswick, London W4
Tel: 01 994 3691
Contact: The Sales Manager

Chiswick Bitter

One of London's two long standing independent brewers. Chiswick Bitter - 1035.5, pleasant, hoppy. London Pride - 1041.5, fruity, rounded.
ESB - 1055.75. Extra Special Bitter. All on draught.
Ⓒ Undisclosed
Ⓓ By arrangement

10

Marston
PO Box 26, Shobnall Road, Burton on Trent, Staffordshire
Tel: 0283 31131
Contact: Mr John Stoton

Owd Rodger

The only brewery still using the Burton Union system for brewing their stronger ale. Capital - 1030, light, mild. Mercian Mild - 1032, dark, fruity. Burton Bitter - 1037, well balanced. Pedigree - 1043, smooth, full bodied. Merrie Monk - 1043, powerful, dark. Owd Rodger - 1080, heavy, rich. All on draught.
C Undisclosed
D By arrangement

16

Pitfield Brewery/The Beer Shop
8 Pitfield Street, London N1 6HA
Tel: 01 739 3701
Contact: Terry Jennings

Dark Star

Pitfield bitter - 1038. Hoxton Best Bitter - 1048. Dark Star - 1050, voted Supreme Champion Beer of Britain 1987 by CAMRA. All on draught in 36pt polypins, 72pt firkins. Dark Star also supplied in ½pt bottles in outers of twelve.
C 4,320 gal p.mth
D By arrangement

14

T D Ridley & Sons Ltd
88 Broomfield Road, Chelmsford, Essex CM1 155
Tel: 0245 353513 Fax: 0245 490114
Contact: Mr John Smith

Essex Light Ale

Ridley's Pale Ale - 1034. Mild Ale - 1034. Old Bob Premium Bitter - 1038/42. Rustic Bitter - 1031/34. All on draught in 9, 18 gal casks, 11 gal kegs. Bottled beers include Essex Light Ale, Pale Ale and Old Bob Strong Pale Ale.
C Old Bob Strong Ale 25,000 gal p.mth, Ridley Pale Ale 20,000 gal p.mth, Essex Light Ale 7000 gal p.mth
D By arrangement

16

Shepherd Neame
17 Court Street, Faversham, Kent
Tel: 0795 532206
Contact: Mr D Townsend

Stock Ale

Kent's last surviving independent brewery. Master Brew - 1036, fine, hoppy. Stock Ale - 1036, full, dark. Best Bitter - 1039, premium bitter. All on draught.
C Undisclosed
D By arrangement

5

Traquair House
Innerleithen, Peeblesshire, Borders
Tel: 0896 830323
Contact: Peter Maxwell-Stuart

Bear Ale

Brewery in the oldest occupied house in Scotland, famous for its widely exported strong bottled ale. Bear Ale - 1050, strong, draught. House Ale - 1075, usually bottled but occasionally draught.
C Undisclosed
D By arrangement

TEAS AND INFUSIONS

14 ↔

Accord Services
Infusion House, Rougham Industrial Estate, Bury St Edmunds, Suffolk IP30 9ND
Tel: 0359 70679
Contact: Mr Ian Lay

China

Importers of thirty varieties of tea including China and traditional tea made with new method of putting larger leaves into teabags. Also herbal tea blended to customers requirements, all supplied from 2½kg upwards.
C Undisclosed
D By arrangement

12 ↔

Arne Herbs
Limeburn Nurseries, Limeburn Hill, Chew Magna, Avon BS18 8QW
Tel: 0272 333399
Contact: Anthony Lyman-Dixon

Peppermint

Range of thirty five herbs suitable for tisanes and infusions including peppermint.
C Undisclosed
D By Datapost, by own transport within area
See Also: Fresh Herbs, Dried Herbs and Flavourings

8

Bettys by Post
1 Parliament Street, Harrogate, Yorkshire HG1 2QU
Tel: 0423 526182
Contact: Sally Holme

Formosa Peach Blossom

Range of thirty one teas including ten scented varieties with cinnamon, orange, lemon, bitter almond and passion fruit. Also Formosa Peach Blossom, Chinese green tea and vintage darjeeling, all in 1lb boxes or packs of three gift caddies.
C Undisclosed
D By arrangement
See Also: Jams and Preserves, Chocolates

16

Brash of London
Hayes House, 142 Greenwich High Road, London SE10 8PT
Tel: 01 858 6946
Contact: Mrs Pomerance

Darjeeling

Range of traditional tea and malted drinks including darjeeling and earl grey in 50, 100, 200, 750g packs.
C Undisclosed
D By arrangement

14 ↔

Cartwright & Butler Ltd
The Spice Mill, Wells-next-the Sea, Norfolk
Tel: 0328 710144 Telx: 817483 CANDB G
Contact: Marian Cartwright

Tea

Specially blended tea in 125g scarlet bags.
C Undisclosed
D By own transport nationally
See Also: Cakes, Biscuits and Pastries, Chutneys and Pickles

14 ◯ ↔

Culpeper Ltd
Hadstock Rd, Linton, Cambridge CB1 6NJ
Tel: 0223 891196 Telx: 81698/81524
Contact: Ian Thomas

Cowslip

Tisanes including camomile, lime blossom and cowslip flowers supplied in re-sealable envelopes.
C Undisclosed
D By arrangement
See Also: Fresh Herbs, Jams and Preserves

16 ↔

The London Herb & Spice Company Ltd
Apothecary House, 18 Selsdon Road, South Croydon, Surrey CR2 6PA
Tel: 01 680 8337 Telx: 262984 LHS Fax: 01 760 0377
Contact: Brigitte Leveque

Rosehip

Range of flavoured herb tea in string and tag bags with envelopes including rosehip, limeflower and mint, lemon verbena, and elderflower all in packs of twenty five.
C 300 cases p.mth
W United Carriers
D By wholesaler
See Also: Dried Herbs and Flavourings

12

D J Miles & Co, Tea and Coffee Merchants
Porlock, nr Minehead, Somerset TA24 8TU
Tel: 0643 862585
Contact: Mr D J Miles

Earl grey

Traditional tea in 125g-4kg packs, teabags in boxes of 80, 240g, and speciality tea in 125g cartons and 2kg bags.
C Tea 150 chests p.wk
D By arrangement

12 ↔

New English Teas Ltd
Brookland Farm, Stone Allerton, Axbridge, Somerset BS26 2NU
Tel: 0934 712874 Telx: 444550 TMSRMA
Contact: Mr A R Brown

Apple

Flavoured tea including apple. Also traditional tea including assam and java in boxes of ten and presentation packs of five.
C Undisclosed
D By arrangement

14 ↔

Trustin Foods
Chase Road, Northern Way, Bury St Edmunds, Suffolk IP32 6NT
Tel: 0284 66265 Telx: 81117 G TRUSTIN
Contact: Mr Derek Wilson

Rosehip

Herbal tea including camomile, mint, orange, and rosehip in teabags and 12x25 sachets. Also special blend of tea in 12x500g wooden chest.
C Undisclosed
D By arrangement
See Also: Chocolates, Juices

16 ↔

R Twining & Co Ltd
South Way, Andover, Hampshire SP10 5AQ
Tel: 0264 62161 Telx: 47218
Contact: Mr D Dancy

Fruit tea

Fifty varieties of tea including herbal, fruit and traditional supplied loose in 50g cartons, 125, 250g metal caddies, packs of 25, 50, 100 teabags.
C Undisclosed
D By carrier, by arrangement

14

Wilson's Trading Co Ltd
Old Ryes, Stebbing Green, Dunmow, Essex CM6 3TE
Tel: 03718 6545 Telx: 818429
Contact: Mr and Mrs Wilson

English breakfast

Range of tea including English breakfast and earl grey in 125g containers, tea bags in 50g containers, or in various presentation boxes.
C Undisclosed
D By arrangement
See Also: Cakes, Biscuits and Pastries, Jams and Preserves, Honey

WATER

6

Abbey Well Ltd
Abbey Well, Morpeth, Northumberland NE61 6JF
Tel: 0670 513113 Fax: 0670 515821
Contact: A C Robson

Mineral

Sparkling or still mineral water filtered through white Northumberland sandstone, in 50cl, 250ml, 1lt green glass bottles. Also available still water in 2lt plastic bottles.
C Undisclosed
D By own transport within area, by arrangement

6 ↔

Aqua Trading Ltd
Tees House, Trenchard Avenue, Thornaby, Stockton On Tees, Cleveland TS17 OEQ
Tel: 0642 750284 Fax: 0642 760216
Contact: Mr Andrew Moffat

Northumbrian Spring

Sparkling or still Northumbrian Spring, packed in 250ml, 1lt bottles. Also 18.9lt plastic containers for use with chilled water dispensers in still form.
C 1 million lt p.a
D By arrangement

12 ↔

Blackdown Ltd
Higher Whatley, Otterford, Chard, Somerset TA20 3QL
Tel: 046 034477
Contact: Mr G Wakley

Blackdown Hills

Sparkling or still Blackdown Hills, low in sodium natural spring water in 1½lt, 500ml plastic containers. Also in 33ml, 1 lt PET, 25, 70cl, 1 lt glass bottles.
C Undisclosed
D By arrangement

16 ↔

Brecon Beacons Natural Waters Ltd
9th Floor, C P House, Uxbridge Road,
London W5 5PL
Tel: 01 840 6175 Telx: 263318 COMIDL G
Fax: 01 840 7061
Contact: Mr J A Dickinson

Mineral — Mineral water bottled on site at Brecon Beacons National Park. Brecon St David's, still in 2lt PVC, 1lt clear glass bottles. Brecon Carreg, sparkling in 1lt, 33cl green glass bottles.
Ⓒ 80,000 gal p.mth
Ⓓ By arrangement

16

Buxton Mineral Water Company Ltd
6 Lygon Place, London SW1 WO3R
Tel: 01 730 0784 Telx: 917550 Fax: 01 824 8201
Contact: Mr Richard Hancock

Mineral — Still or sparkling Buxton, natural mineral water. Also available with a hint of orange, lemon or lime flavour from organic fruit extracts. Still in 1lt glass, 2, 5lt plastic bottles, sparkling in 200ml, 1lt glass, 2lt plastic bottles.
Ⓒ Undisclosed
Ⓓ By arrangement

1 ↔

Caithness Spring Water
Berriedale, Caithness KW7 6HD
Tel: 05935 262237
Contact: W Thompson

Sutherland Spring — Sutherland Spring, a peat flavoured lightly coloured spring water from the Scottish Highlands in 1lt bottles. Still or sparkling Caithness Spring, filtered low mineral spring water in various size bottles.
Ⓒ 25 million lt p.a
Ⓓ By arrangement

9 ↔

Carmarthen Water Ltd
Prysg, Maesycrugiau Pencader, Dyfed
Tel: 055935 627
Contact: Mrs Beryl Davies

Prysg Spring — Still or sparkling water from Prysg spring in the Teifi valley, still in 1lt glass bottles in cases of twelve, sparkling in 1lt, 250ml glass bottles in cases of twenty four.
Ⓒ Undisclosed
Ⓓ By arrangement

11 ↔

Catley Abbey Natural Seltzer Water Co
Chapel Farm, Martin Dales, Woodhall Spa,
Lincolnshire LN10 6XT
Tel: 0526 52931
Contact: Mr D Tonge

Catley Abbey seltzer
Catley Abbey, Britain's only natural seltzer water, effervescent with high mineral content, especially lithium, in 1/3, 1lt glass bottles.
[C] Undisclosed
[D] By arrangement

[13] ↔
Chiltern Hills Pure Mineral Water Ltd
Bourne End Mills, Hemel Hempstead, Hertfordshire HP1 2RW
Tel: 04427 5522 Telx: 825075 WARDCO G
Contact: P E Rogers

Mineral
Still or sparkling mineral water, low in sodium and nitrates, extracted from source through chalk of Chiltern hills. Sparkling in 250ml, 1lt, 2lt PET bottles, still in 2lt OPVC, 250ml, 1lt PET bottles.
[C] Undisclosed
[D] By arrangement

[12] ↔
A & D R Friend
Lower Brimley Coombe Farm, Stoke Abbott, Beaminster, Dorset DT8 3JZ
Tel: 0308 68792
Contact: Mr A Friend

Spring
Medium hard spring water in 1½lt plastic bottle and 5lt plastic can with handle.
[C] 12,000lt p.mth
[D] By arrangement

[16] ↔
Highland Spring Ltd
35 Headford Place, London SW1X 7DE
Tel: 01 235 0954 Telx: 76573 WATERS G
Contact: Mr John Biggs

Highland Spring
Still or sparkling Highland Spring, soft mineral water, low in sodium chloride and nitrate, still in 3cl, ½, 1lt PVC bottles, sparkling in various sizes.
[C] Undisclosed
[D] By arrangement

[12] ↔
Minerva Spa Water Co Ltd
Hayeswood Farm, Timsbury, Bath, Avon BA3 1HQ
Tel: 0761 70523 Telx: 449249
Contact: Miss Mary Young

Saxon Spring
Still or sparkling Saxon Spring, Somerset spring water in 85, 500ml, 1½lt PVC bottles. Also in 200, 330ml, 1lt glass bottles.
[C] Undisclosed
[D] By arrangement

[16]
The Nestle Co Ltd
St George's House, Croydon, Surrey CR9 1NR
Tel: 01 686 3333 Telx: 23117 STGCRO G
Fax: 01 686 6072
Contact: Mr Adrian F Pratt

Ashbourne
Still or sparkling Ashbourne, spring water from the Derbyshire Peak District in 250ml, 1/3, 1lt glass bottles.
[C] Undisclosed
[D] By arrangement

[13]
Schweppes Ltd
Grosvenor Road, St Albans, Hertfordshire AL1 3AD
Tel: 0895 31313 Telx: 338011 STALB G
Contact: Mr J Coles

Malvern water
Still or sparkling Malvern Water, spring water from Worcestershire, in 1lt glass and 1½lt plastic bottles.
[C] Undisclosed
[D] By arrangement

[12] ↔
Somerset Spring Water Company
The Firs, Biscombe, Churchstanton, Taunton, Somerset TA3 7PZ
Tel: 0823 60385
Contact: Mr D J Gupwell

Somerset Spring
Still or sparkling Somerset Spring Water from the Blackdown Hills in 1/3, 1½, 5lt PVC bottles.
[C] Undisclosed
[D] By own transport within area, by arrangement

3

Strathmore Mineral Water Company
126 West High Street, Forfar, Angus DD8 1BP
Tel: 0307 66147 Telx: 779968 Fax: 0307 66072
Contact: D Critchley-Salmonson

Mineral water with lime

Still or sparkling natural mineral water available in 220ml, ½, 1lt glass bottles and 1, 1½, 2lt PET bottles. Also mineral water flavoured with lime, lemon and orange.
C ½-1 million litres p.mth
D By arrangement

15 ↔

Torpeek Farm Products
Torpeek Farm, Ivybridge, Devon PL21 0DS
Tel: 0752 892334
Contact: Mr D Veale

Devon Dew

Still or sparkling Devon Dew, soft spring water in 1/3, ½, 1½lt PVC bottles, still also in 1 gal containers.
C 8000lt p.mth
D By arrangement

9 ↔

Trofarth Industries Ltd
Trofarth, Abergele, Clwyd LL22 9PF
Tel: 074576 340/688
Contact: Mrs A Hosking

Decantae spring

Decantae Spring Water, bottled at source in the Snowdonia foothills, low in heavy metals and salts in 250ml, 1lt glass bottles, 1½, 2 lt PVC and PET bottles.
C Undisclosed
D By arrangement

WINE

16

Adgestone Vineyard
Upper Road, Adgestone, Sandown, Isle of Wight
Tel: 0983 402503
Contact: Mr K C Barlow

Adgestone

Muller Thurgau, Reichensteiner and Seyval from 9 acres first planted late 1960s. Winner of Gore Browne Trophy.
C 5000 cases p.a
W Deinhard & Co
D By wholesaler

16

Berwick Glebe Vineyard
Frensham Cottage, Berwick, nr Polegate, East Sussex BN26 6SP
Tel: 0323 870361
Contact: Miss J Broster

Berwick Glebe

Berwick Glebe, produced from Muller Thurgau, Reichensteiner grapes grown on own 2 acre vineyard first planted 1979. Alfriston Glebe from Sussex grown Muller Thurgau grapes, medium dry.
C Undisclosed
D By arrangement

16

Biddenden Cider
Biddenden Vineyards, Little Whatmans, Biddenden, Ashford, Kent
Tel: 0580 291726
Contact: Mr R A Barnes

Ortega

Muller Thurgau, dry with steely fruitiness. Ortega, deeper in colour with unusual and rich fruity flavour, both from 18 acres first planted 1969.
C Undisclosed
D By arrangement
See Also: Cider

16

Bookers Vineyard
Foxhole Lane, Bolney, Sussex RH17 5NB
Tel: 044482 575
Contact: J M & R V Pratt

Muller Thurgau

Muller Thurgau producing dry and medium dry wines.
C 20,000 bottles p.a
D By arrangement
See Also: Cheese

10

Broadfield Court Estate
Bodenham, Herefordshire
Tel: 056884 483
Contact: Keith James

Huxelrebe

Dry Huxelrebe, Reichensteiner, medium dry Seyval in 75cl bottles.
C 15,000 bottles p.a
W Victoria Wine, Justinian & Brooks, St James St, W1
D By wholesaler

14

Bruisyard St Peter Vineyard
The Winery, Church Road, Bruisyard, Saxmundham, Suffolk IP17 2EF
Tel: 072 875281
Contact: Mr I H Berwick

Muller Thurgau

Muller Thurgau, full flavoured, medium dry estate bottled from 10 acres, first planted 1974. English Vineyards Association Seal of Quality 1986.
C Undisclosed
D By arrangement

16

Carr Taylor Vineyards
Westfield, Hastings, East Sussex TN35 4SG
Tel: 0424 752501
Contact: Mr D Carr Taylor

Méthode champenoise

Schonburger, Kerner-Huxel, Gutenborner and Reichensteiner, dry to medium dry. Also a crisp sparkling wine fermented in the traditional méthode champenoise, from 21 acres first planted 1972.
C Undisclosed
D By arrangement

12

Castle Cary Vineyards
Honeywick, Castle Cary, Somerset BA7 7LP
Tel: 0963 50323
Contact: P C Woosnam Mills

Madeleine Angevine

Muller Thurgau blended with Seyval grapes for medium dry white, with Madeleine Angevine for a dry wine. Both from 5½ acres, first planted 1979.
C Undisclosed
D By arrangement

12

Chalkhill Vineyard
Knowle Farm, Bowerchalke, Salisbury, Wiltshire
Tel: 0722 780041
Contact: Mark Thompson

Kerner

Muller Thurgau, Bacchus and Kerner grapes blended to produce dry, medium and medium dry white wines in the French style, from 6 acres first planted 1980. Customers own label if required.
C 2000 cases p.a
D By arrangement

16

Chiddingstone Vineyards Ltd
Vexour Farm, Chiddingstone, Edenbridge, Kent TN8 7BB
Tel: 0892 870277 Fax: 0892 515868
Contact: Mr D Quirk

Gutedel

Pinot Noir, Gutedel blended to produce dry table wine. Also Kerner, Seyval Blanc and Chasselas, all from 14 acres first planted 1978.
C Undisclosed
D By arrangement

14

Chilford Hundred Wine Co Ltd
Chilford Hall, Linton, Cambridge CB1 6LE
Tel: 0223 892641 Telx: 817574 EDSUP MARK
Contact: Simon Alper

Siegerrebe

Muller Thurgau, Huxelrebe, Ortega, Schonburger and Siegerrebe blended to produce dry and medium dry wines.
C Undisclosed
D By arrangement

16

Chilsdown Vineyard
The Old Station House, Singleton, nr Chichester, Sussex PO18 ORX
Tel: 0243 63398
Contact: Mr I Paget

Reichensteiner

Muller Thurgau and Reichensteiner blend, crisp, fruity, dry, best drunk fairly young, from 13 acres first planted 1972.
C Undisclosed
D By arrangement

15

Cornish Mead Co Ltd
The Meadery, Newlyn, Penzance, Cornwall TR18 5QF
Tel: 0736 63942
Contact: Mr J Moore

Strawberry

Traditionally fermented mead wine, honey liqueurs and full strength wines in blackberry, strawberry and elderberry in decanters, gift packs, 75cl, 8½cl bottles.
C 1000 gal p.mth
D By arrangement

9

Croffta Vineyard
Groes-Faen, Pontyclun, Glamorgan CF7 8NE
Tel: 0443 223876
Contact: Mr J Bevan

Seyval

Muller Thurgau, Seyval Blanc, Madelaine Angevine, dry, crisp wines, from 3 acres first planted 1975.
C Undisclosed
D By arrangement

16

Ditchling Vineyards
Claycroft, Beacon Road, Ditchling, Hassocks, Sussex
Tel: 079 182634
Contact: Mr D Mills

Reichensteiner

Muller Thurgau, Ortega, Reichensteiner, dry wines with fresh acidity, from 5 acres first planted 1979.
C Undisclosed
D By arrangement

16

Downer Vineyard
Clappers Lane, Fulking, Henfield, Sussex BN5 9NH
Tel: 079 156484
Contact: Cmdr E Downer

Muller Thurgau

Muller Thurgau, a refreshing wine with a fruity bouquet.
C Undisclosed
D By arrangement

14

Elmham Park Vineyard
Elmham House, Dereham, Norfolk
Tel: 036 281571
Contact: Mr R Don, MW

Apple

Muller Thurgau and Madeleine Angevine blend, dry, fruity wine with good crisp acidity, from 7 acres, first planted 1966. Also Norfolk apple wine, medium dry, 8% by volume.
C Undisclosed
D By arrangement

12

Fonthill Vineyard
The Old Rectory, Fonthill Gifford, Tisbury, Wiltshire SP3 6QH
Tel: 0747 870231/871230
Contact: C P M Craig-McFeely

Rosé

Muller Thurgau, Reichensteiner and Seyval blended to produce medium dry, medium and dry white table wines. Also rosé blended by addition of Dunkelfelder, Seibel, Leon Millot.
C 3000-30,000 bottles p.a
D By own transport, by arrangement

16

Hambledon English Wines Ltd
Hambledon Vineyard, Hambledon,
Hampshire PO7 6RY
Tel: 070132 475
Contact: John Patterson

Pinot Meunier

English table wine from a blend of Seyval, Pinot Meunier and Chardonnay grapes.
[C] 1000 p.a
[D] By arrangement

1

Highland Wineries
Moniack Castle, Kirkhill, Inverness
Tel: 0463 83283
Contact: Mrs P M Fraser

Silver Birch

Range of country wines including silver birch wine made from sap of birch trees, meadowsweet and dark red blueberry wines. Mead also available.
[C] 8000 cases p.a
[D] By arrangement
See Also: Liqueurs

16

Ightham Vineyards Ltd
Ightham Vineyards, Ivy Hatch, nr
Sevenoaks, Kent TN15 OPG
Tel: 0732 810348
Contact: James Corfe

Schonburger

Muller Thurgau - 90% with Reichensteiner - 10%. Huxelrebe and Schonburger blended to produce light, dry wine with fruity bouquet from 3 acres first planted 1972.
[C] 10,000 bottles p.a
[D] By arrangement

16

Lamberhurst Vineyards
Ridge Farm, Lamberhurst, Kent TN3 8ER
Tel: 0892 890286
Contact: Mr Absalom

Rosé

Muller Thurgau, delicate Muscat bouquet, crisp, dry finish. Seyval Blanc, well balanced, fruity medium dry. Reichensteiner, light medium dry, with soft bouquet. Schonburger, medium dry with spicy full bodied rich flavour and smooth finish, all from 48 acres first planted 1972. Also available medium dry Rosé.
[C] Undisclosed
[D] By arrangement
See Also: Liqueurs

15

Loddiswell Vineyard
Lilwell, Loddiswell, Kingsbridge, Devon
TQ7 4EF
Tel: 0548 550221
Contact: Reg and Betty Sampson

Siegerrebe

Muller Thurgau, Reichensteiner and Siegerrebe blended for medium dry and sweet white Emglish table wines, from 7 acres first planted 1977.
[C] 18-20,000 bottles p.a
[W] Peter Dominic, Kingsbridge; Fergusons, Plymouth; St.Austell Breweries, Wickham and Bideford
[D] By arrangement

16

Lurgashall Winery
Windfallwood, Lurgashall, nr Petworth,
West Sussex GU28 9HA
Tel: 042878 292 Telx: 94012825 KTYPG
Fax: 073081 4917
Contact: Lindsey Bampton

Banquet mead

Range of country wines including elderflower, fragrant, medium dry, made from fresh flowers in 75cl bottles. Banquet Mead made from pure honey in 5 gal containers. Cassis, 17% alcohol in 37½cl stoppered glass bottles.
[C] 700 gal p.mth
[D] By arrangement

16

Meon Valley Vineyard
Hill Grove, Swanmore, Southampton,
Hampshire SO3 2PZ
Tel: 0489 877435
Contact: C J Hartley

Zweigeltrebe

Muller Thurgau and Seyval Blanc blended to produce medium dry fruity wine. Rosé from Pinot Meunier and Zweigeltrebe blend. Red from Triomphe d'Alsace. Country fruit wines and cider also available.
[C] Undisclosed
[D] By arrangement

14 ↔

Mister Bumbles Ltd
Highwaymans Vineyard, Risby, Suffolk
Tel: 0284 810969 Telx: 261376 LOFBND G
Contact: The Hon Patrick Fisher

Abbey Knight

Abbey Knight English wine, estate grown and bottled.
[C] Undisclosed
[D] By arrangement
See Also: Jams and Preserves

15

Nicholas Downs Ltd
Wiscombe Winery, Southleigh, Colyton,
Devon EX13 6JF
Tel: 040487 360
Contact: Mr Nicholas Downs

Apple

Range of Devonshire country wines including apple, apple and blackberry, apple and blackcurrant all fermented with untreated local apples and wild fruits, sweet through to dry, in 70cl, 1lt bottles.
[C] 2000 gal p.a
[D] By arrangement
See Also: Cider

16

Penshurst Vineyards
Grove Road, Penshurst, Kent TN1 18DU
Tel: 0892 870255
Contact: Mr D Westphal

Reichenstei-ner

Muller Thurgau, Reichensteiner and Seyval Blanc, light, fruity wines, from 12 acres first planted 1972.
[C] Undisclosed
[D] By own transport within area
See Also: Juices

10 ↔

Pullens Farm Fruit Juices
Ridgeway Cross, nr Malvern, Hereford and Worcester WR13 5JN
Tel: 088684 232/599 Telx: 333175 STOKES
Contact: Mr M Brigden

Apple

Dry and medium dry apple wine, 11%, made from English apples in 70cl bottles.
Ⓒ Undisclosed
Ⓓ By arrangement
See Also: Juices

16

Rock Lodge Vineyards
Scaynes Hill, West Sussex RH17 7NG
Tel: 044486 224 Telx: 878189 Fax: 044486 541
Contact: Norman Cowderoy

Muller Thurgau

Muller Thurgau first planted in 1965, yielding dry through to medium sweet white English table wines. Cider also available.
Ⓒ 40,000 bottles p.a
Ⓓ By arrangement

16

Seymours Vineyards
Forest Road, Horsham, Sussex RH12 4HL
Tel: 0403 52397
Contact: H C McMullen

Schonburger

Seyval Blanc and Kerner Schonburger grown on double guyot system, first planted 1981.
Ⓒ 6000 bottles p.a
Ⓓ By own transport within area

8

St Marys Country Wines
3a The Parkside Centre, Terry Avenue, York YO2 1JP
Tel: 0904 611074
Contact: Brian Reid

Blackberry

Range of country fruit wines made with locally grown ingredients including elderberry, plum, cherry, blackberry and orange in 75cl bottles.
Ⓒ 160 gal p.mth
Ⓓ By arrangement

16

Staple Vineyard
Church Farm, Staple, Canterbury, Kent
Tel: 0304 812571
Contact: Mr W Ash

Huxelrebe

Muller Thurgau, Huxelrebe and Reichensteiner, dry, fruity English wines, from 7 acres first planted 1974.
Ⓒ Undisclosed
Ⓓ By arrangement

16

Steyning Vineyard
Nash, Horsham Road, Steyning, West Sussex BN4 3AA
Tel: 0903 814988
Contact: Joyce Elsden

Medium dry

Medium dry white wine in 75cl bottles with metal caps.
Ⓒ Undisclosed
Ⓓ By arrangement

16

Tenterden Vineyards
Spots Farm, Small Hythe, Tenterden, Kent TN30 7NG
Tel: 05806 3033
Contact: Nicole Turner

Special Reserve

Tenterden medium white, medium dry rosé, oak matured Special Reserve and Muller Thurgau dry white wines.
Ⓒ Undisclosed
Ⓓ By arrangement

16

The Thames Valley Vineyard
North Lodge, Stanlake Park, Twyford, Reading, Berkshire RE10 OBN
Tel: 0734 340176
Contact: Mr J E Leighton

Schonburger

Reichensteiner single sweet white wine and dry white, oak matured. Also sweet wine from Schonburger grape.
Ⓒ Dry white 200 bottles p.mth, Reichensteiner 400 bottles p.mth, Schonburger 300 bottles p.mth
Ⓓ By arrangement

12

Three Choirs Vineyard Ltd
Rhyle House, Welsh House Lane, Newent, Gloucestershire GL18 ILR
Tel: 053 185223
Contact: Mr T Day

Huxelrebe

Muller Thurgau, Huxelrebe, Reichensteiner and a blend of all three, from 20 acres first planted 1973.
Ⓒ Undisclosed
Ⓓ By arrangement

16

Three Corners Vineyard
Beacon Lane, Woodnesborough, Kent CT13 0PA
Tel: 0304 812025
Contact: Lt Col C Galbraith

Tricorn Trocken

Tricorn Siegerrebe, dry with strong grapey flavour. Tricorn Trocken, fresh, fruity and dry blend of Reichensteiner and Siegerrebe grapes. Melange, medium dry blend with delicate bouquet and fruity flavour.
Ⓒ 4000 bottles p.a
Ⓓ By arrangement

11

Wickham Vineyard
Wickham Vineyard, Botley Road, Shedfield, Hampshire SO3 2HL
Tel: 0329 834042
Contact: Mr J Charnley

Bacchus

Schonburger, Reichensteiner and Bacchus, from 7 acres first planted 1984.
Ⓒ Undisclosed
Ⓓ By own transport within area

12

Wootton Vineyard
North Wootton, Shepton Mallet, Somerset BA4 4AG
Tel: 074 989359
Contact: Major C Gillespie

Seyval

Seyval, fragrant, delicate with good nose and fresh acidity. Schonburger and Muller Thurgau, refreshing dry finish, all from 6 acres first planted 1971.
Ⓒ 1,500 cases p.a
Ⓓ By arrangement

15

Yearlstone Cyder
Yearlstone Vineyard, Chilverton, Coldridge, Crediton, Devon
Tel: 03635 302
Contact: Miss Gillian Pearkes

Chardonnay

Dry Madeleine Angevine, medium dry Siegerrebe and crisp, white wine from Chardonnay grape. Also oak matured red wine, all in 75cl bottles.
Ⓒ 8000-10,000 bottles p.a
Ⓦ Dartington Farm Shop
Ⓓ By wholesaler, by arrangment
See Also: Cider, Juices

D

N

O

P

A

B

C

D

E

T

U

V

W

Y

Z

1

Highlands and Islands (Map ref. 1)

2

Grampian Region (Map ref. 2)

3

Central Lowlands (Map ref. 3)

4

Northern Ireland (Map ref. 4)

5

Border Region (Map ref. 5)

6

North England and the Isle of Man (Map ref. 6)

7

North West England (Map ref. 7)

8

Yorkshire and Humberside (Map ref. 8)

9

Wales (Map ref. 9)

13

Northern Home Counties (Map ref. 13)

14

East Anglia and Essex (Map ref. 14)

15

South West and the Channel Islands (Map ref. 15)

Product Information Literature Service - PILS

TO ENSURE THAT YOU RECEIVE THE FREE BROCHURES YOU REQUIRE WITHOUT DELAY, FILL IN THE COUPON BELOW, CIRCLING THE NUMBERS OF THE BROCHURES NEEDED AND RETURN THE COUPON TO BRITISH FOOD FINDS. WE WILL DO THE REST.

use the power of a circle

TABLEWARE - This impressive brochure from French Kitchen & Tableware Supply Co, illustrates and gives sizes and capacities of their wide range of equipment.
CIRCLE NO. F1

TROUT AND SALMON - Andwells, Hampshire, is one of the few trout farms both growing and processing its own trout. This leaflet describes the various products available.
CIRCLE NO. F2

CREPES - Now in a new, moister form, and incredibly easy to use Mr Creatons ready made Crepes come in English style, French style, Buckwheat, Chocolate and Butter.
CIRCLE - NO. F3

FRUIT JUICE - A range of delicious fruit juices available from Fresh Fruit Juice Mfg Ltd. Contact them for further details.
CIRCLE NO. F4

OYSTERS - This leaflet from Colchester Oyster Fishery explains a little of the history surrounding farming of oysters in the Colchester area, and highlights two products available form this progressive company.
CIRCLE NO. F5

WELSH LAMB - Shown in clear illustrations are the steps necessary to prepare various cuts of lamb. Details are also given about the standards of the Welsh Lamb Enterprise.
CIRCLE NO. F6

CHRISTMAS PUDDINGS - The ingredients in this 100 year old recipe include a strong Suffolk Ale (brewed by Greene King), sugar, suet, flour, almonds, bread, fresh oranges and lemons with a fine selection of vine fruits. All combined to produce a mouthwatering delicacy.
CIRCLE NO. F7

WELSH LAMB - This leaflet from Welsh Lamb Enterprise explains the reasons why the organisation was formed, and what its marks on carcasses mean.
CIRCLE NO. F8

WINE - The English Wine Centre stocks wines from over 30 different English vineyards and is the focal point for general information about the industry. Sponsors of the annual English Wine & Regional Food Festival, Alfriston, East Sussex.
CIRCLE NO. F9

BANKING/FINANCE - Barclays has produced a free, informative guide to the ins and outs of farm finance, with useful reference sections covering everything from management accountancy to grants and taxation. You're better off talking to Barclays.
CIRCLE NO. F10

PILS Reader Card

PLEASE PRINT IN BOLD CAPITAL LETTERS

Return to: **British Food Finds, MPI Ltd, 4 Hubbard Road, Houndmills, Basingstoke RG21 2UH, Hampshire, England.**

Company ____________________

Address ____________________

____________________ Country ____________________

Attention of ____________________ Position ____________________

Telephone ____________________ Telex ____________________

My profession is: *(please tick)*

❑ Chef ❑ Restaurateur ❑ Hotelier ❑ Retailer ❑ Private use ❑ Other, please specify ____________________

CIRCLE NUMBERS REQUIRED

1	2	3	4	5	6	7	8	9	10	11	12	13
14	15	16	17	18	19	20	21	22	23	24	25	26

OYSTERS - This very well produced brochure describes the Loch Fyne Oyster Co, and the fine oysters, langoustines, kippers, trout and herring they have available.
CIRCLE NO. F11

MEATS - Rare breeds. No antibiotics. Non-intensive farming. Beef, pork, lamb, venison. Traditionally cured, smoked, Bacon. Hams. Nine varieties robust, coarse cut meaty sausages. Hampers. Delivery nationwide.
CIRCLE NO. F13

WICKER BASKETS - This colourful brochure from Pullman Pans illustrates the many different types of baskets on offer.
CIRCLE NO. F15

HAMPERS - Illustrated are some of the attractive hampers and gift packs available in Mrs Beeton's gift range.
CIRCLE NO. F17

UNPASTEURISED CHEESE - Rill Farm produces traditionally handmade unpasteurised cheeses in both cow and goat milk from our own pedigree herds. The naturally rinded truckles are available in 3lb or 10lb sizes, with vegetarian rennet used throughout. Rill Farm cow and goat milk yoghurt is additive free and flavoured with pure fruit and raw cane sugar.
CIRLCE NO F19

SOFT CHEESE - Like all things natural Glenshesk quality soft cheese is an individual. As versatile as your imagination whether used as a dip, in a salad or simply on biscuits, Glenshesk makes it special.
CIRCLE NO. F21

FOOD ROUTES GUIDE - Written by Henrietta Green, who is also the author of British Food Finds, this guide is the ideal companion for travellers who are not only anxious to sample the delights of British food, but also wish to see, and possibly participate in, how it is produced.
CIRCLE NO. F23

SCOTTISH SALMON - A variety of speciality and rather different styles of smoked salmon products is offered by The Inverness Salmon Co, including oak smoked salmon and an exciting ginger cured Gravadlax.
CIRCLE NO. F25

CATERING EQUIPMENT - TSE-BROWNSON, manufacturers of high quality catering equipment and specialists in hygienic 18/8 stainless steel, include within their catalogue a range of food trolleys, electrically heated or chilled.
CIRCLE NO. F12

BABACO FRUIT - Guernsey Babaco is one of the most versatile and exotic fruits to appear in recent years with simple to prepare inspirational dishes to tempt the palate.
CIRCLE NO. F14

TAYSIDE FOODS - This superb brochure clearly illustrates many of the individual delicacies available from the Tayside area. Suppliers are highlighted and indexed.
CIRCLE NO. F16

CHEESE - North Downs Dairy Company, specialist factors of traditional farmhouse cheese, and the products they offer, are described in their brochure.
CIRCLE NO. F18

MEAT/LIVESTOCK COMMISSION - A useful little 7 day guide to healthy eating containing several interesting recipes.
CIRCLE NO. F20

HAMPERS - Wickers hampers filled with a variety of fresh produce, standard Christmas edition feeds eight. We can design exclusive hampers for company gifts at Christmas or anytime.
CIRCLE NO. F22

BRITISH FOOD FINDS 1990 - Did you miss out in not advertising in the 1989 edition of this award winning directory? If so enquire now for details of next year's advertising rates.
CIRCLE NO. F24

ABERDEEN ANGUS BEEF - Frank Godfrey Ltd is a certified supplier of Aberdeen Angus Beef and also supplies free range organic pork, Wild Highland venison, Gressingham duck and prize winning country style pork sausage.
CIRCLE NO. F26

Typeset by Compuprint Ltd.

Artwork by Typematter Graphics, Basingstoke,
Hampshire

Printed and Bound in Great Britain by Drogher Press,
Christchurch, Dorset